ADMIRAL
SIMS *and the*
Modern American Navy

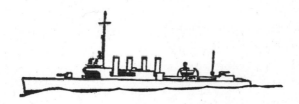

WITH ILLUSTRATIONS

ELTING E. MORISON

The Riverside Press Cambridge
HOUGHTON MIFFLIN COMPANY · BOSTON

The Riverside Press
CAMBRIDGE . MASSACHUSETTS
PRINTED IN THE U.S.A.

To

THE INSURGENT SPIRIT

and to

THOSE OFFICERS

WHO HAVE MAINTAINED IT

WITHIN THE UNITED STATES NAVY

IN TIME OF PEACE

PREFACE

G. F. R. HENDERSON, disturbed by his lack of preparation, accused himself of 'something worse than presumption' in presenting his life of Stonewall Jackson to the public. As a Colonel, Henderson had commanded troops under fire; as an instructor at Sandhurst, he had taught military tactics; as a professor at the Staff College, he had lectured on military science and history. Secure in his professional experience and knowledge he could enjoy an honest humility without suffering from a sense of inadequacy.

No such confidence is permitted to me. If it were something worse than presumptuous for a Colonel to write the life of a General, it must appear no better than arrogance for a civilian to attempt the biography of an Admiral. It is clear that a few years of reading can serve only to provide a superficial knowledge of a subject to which men devote whole lifetimes. And it is equally plain that a man who has never worn the uniform cannot hope to recognize and understand the professional spirit in all its manifestations.

In extenuation for proceeding in the face of such obvious disqualifications, three things can be put forward. I can, in the first place, avail myself of Colonel Henderson's excuse that to wait for someone qualified to write the lives of great captains is to wait for long in ignorance of their achievements. Military men, especially in America, have demonstrated their traditional distrust of new weapons by their reluctance to exchange the sword for the pen, while historians, an equally careful brotherhood, understand that to produce the life of a soldier is to lose a professional reputation.

In the second place, the career of Admiral Sims does not confront the biographer with all the conventional military complexities. Tactics, strategy, and the intricacies of naval engagements occupy but a small part of the pages that follow. For twenty months Sims was in command of the largest fighting force this country had ever assembled in time of war, but for forty years he devoted himself to the development of his profession in time of peace. His problems during these years were of a nature more simple for the civilian to understand than those confronting a Commander in the field. And it is of the first importance that the civilian have an understanding of these problems of a military establishment in time of peace. If Sims and men like him are to achieve their purpose, progress in a conservative profession, they must have the support of an educated citizenry. It is the hope that this book will assist in providing for future naval reformers the kind of intelligent encouragement from the public which Sims and his colleagues did not always enjoy in their lifetimes.

Finally, an attempt has been made to dispel my ignorance of the profession in which Sims lived. With what success this has been done the reader can best judge, but with what pleasure I alone can know. That it has been done at all is due to the encouragement and guidance given me by more than a hundred officers, active and retired, of the United States Navy. During the past four years these men have opened their houses, their correspondence, their ships, their minds and their memories with a generosity and patience for which no adequate thanks can be given. Through them I have obtained a respect and affection for their calling and from them I have gained whatever understanding of their profession may be discovered on the following pages.

It is impossible to enumerate all the varied acts of kindness, but to several men and women I should like to express my gratitude.

Commodore Albert L. Key from the beginning gave me valuable advice, encouragement, and criticism. Captain Dudley W. Knox, Director of the Office of Naval Records and Library, assisted me greatly in the investigation of the papers under his care. In many other ways he sought to increase my knowledge of the man on whose staff he twice served. Rear Admiral R. R. Belknap has been a constant source of information and inspiration. All three officers have saved me from embarrassing errors by the care with which they read the manuscript.

Captain H. A. Baldridge kindly prepared photostats of some letters in the Museum at Annapolis and gave me much useful information about Admiral Sims' work as Inspector of Target Practice.

Captain E. S. Kellogg, the Curator of the Naval Historical Foundation, assisted me in examining the collections there and recalled for my benefit many of his experiences when he served with Admiral Sims.

Admiral Joseph Strauss, Rear Admiral Hutchinson I. Cone, who died while the work was in progress, Rear Admiral W. B. Fletcher, Rear Admiral John R. Beardall, Captain R. D. White, Captain J. V. Babcock, Captain B. B. Wygant, Captain R. R. Emmett, and Commander Homer C. Poundstone generously assisted me in ways too numerous to mention.

President J. P. Baxter III of Williams and Professor Frederick Merk of Harvard kindly read large sections of the manuscript. To both I am indebted for suggestions and criticism. To Mr. Merk particularly I owe a personal debt of long standing for his constant encouragement and advice over a period of years, and for whatever indications of historical training may be remarked in this book.

To the family of Admiral Sims, his brothers, sisters, and children, I am grateful for many acts of kindness, and especially to Mrs. Sims, who permitted me complete freedom of investigation among her husband's papers.

My own family at all times gave me necessary encouragement and frank criticism.

The pleasant work of giving credit where credit is due could go on almost indefinitely. Yet this list must end and it should properly end with her to whom no adequate return can ever be made. As one of the few who read introductions to books on history, I long ago came to believe that such books, for some reason, could rarely be written by single men. Why this is so I now understand. But with more assurance than most I can say that without my wife I would not have written the pages that follow.

E. E. M

Upland Farm
Peterborough, New Hampshire
May, 1942

CONTENTS

ILLUSTRATIONS

Between pages 64 *and* 65

*(With the exception of the U.S.S. Nevada, all reproductions of ships
are through the courtesy of the Office of Naval Records and Library.
Dates refer to the time of laying down the keels.)*

PART ONE

The Years of Preparation

It lies with you to determine whether, when you become old, you will have to regret the wasted years of your youth; whether at that period of life you will find yourselves simply 'practical men' — 'beefeaters' — or really educated military naval officers. It will depend largely upon self-instruction and self-discipline.

WILLIAM S. SIMS *in an Address before the Naval War College, 1920*

I

***

1858 - 1876 *Early Youth*

***

Lord John Fisher is supposed to have said that he would be
God damned if he would risk the fate of the British Empire because it was Buggins' turn to take the Fleet. Buggins, the symbol
of mediocrity in high place, lived only in the imagination of the
great Englishman. Yet he is not exclusively British; his name is
written on the Navy lists of every nation.

Special circumstances conspire to ensure his survival. A military establishment is a society organized for a purpose that is, in
time of peace, neither immediate nor real. It is likewise an
isolated world for which regulations and traditions provide a
kind of artificial natural law. Within this framework Buggins
can achieve the appearance of competence. His personality is
invested with the power of recognized authority, while his inefficiency is neutralized by the effectiveness of the routines which he
performs. Thus buttressed by the sanctions of his profession, he
can rise from grade to grade untouched by the process of natural
selection that would eliminate him from leadership in civil life.
All this can happen because it is difficult for men to sustain the
fiction of war throughout long periods of peace, and for military
men war is the one reality.

The framework by which Buggins is supported may serve as a
cage for more talented men. So much was apparent to Mr. H. G.
Wells when he condemned a whole profession. It was his opinion
that 'The professional military mind is by necessity an inferior,
unimaginative mind; no man of high intellectual quality would
willingly imprison his gifts in such a calling.'

3

It was in such a calling that William Sowden Sims began his career in 1880. At that time our Navy, as its officials admitted, was badly equipped, badly administered, and badly maintained. For the next forty-two years Sims labored to improve the condition of our first line of defense. In the course of that time he explored most of the regions of naval thought: ship design, gunnery, tactics, education, promotion, and military administration. On everything he touched he left his own distinctive mark.

The years of his active service embraced a period of extraordinary change. The first four ships on which he served were sailing vessels built of wood. His last command was a dreadnought that is still an effective unit in our battle line. When Sims first went to sea, our Fleet reminded David Dixon Porter, the Admiral of the Navy, of the Chinese forts on which dragons were painted to frighten away the enemy. When he died, there was the modern American Navy, and at his death, in September, 1936, the *New York Herald Tribune* believed that he had 'influenced our naval course more than any man who ever wore the uniform.'

The career of Admiral Sims is a refutation of the theory that the military profession is a prison for gifted men. Yet it demonstrates that if officers are to lead valuable lives within their profession, they must possess some special gift. Doctors, lawyers, scientists, have to deal with the actual present; they can sharpen their learning against the whetstone of reality. But between an officer and the practice of his profession lies a void that can be closed only by an act of imagination. Officers, incapable of such an act, must fall back upon the ritual of their calling, or the lessons of old wars. Admiral Sims could imagine reality. It was this that gave him his distinction and driving power. He remembered Pearl Harbor before it happened.

There is a rule of thumb in the Sowden family that runs, 'Grandfather had sixteen children; fourteen lived; twelve married and averaged nine children apiece.' Grandfather was William Sowden, born an Englishman in the city of Leeds. In the second decade of the last century he came to Canada with his young wife and took up a thousand acres near the village of Port Hope, halfway between Toronto and Kingston on the lovely rolling shores of Lake Ontario. His is a frontier story, not unfamiliar to many

Americans, which begins with years of hardship, sacrifice, and unending labor. From this rich land his growing family were fed, clothed, and trained in an occupation which was at that time still a way of life. The cash crop was wheat, which William Sowden took each year in rowboats sixty miles along the shore to the mills at Kingston, old Fort Frontenac, the first bastion of the French imperial wilderness.

He was patient; he was thrifty; he was tireless; and so he prospered. In the course of time he became a figure of some eminence in the little community, where he, with one other, was entitled to call himself 'gentleman.' For twelve years he served as police magistrate. In the discussion of town affairs he always spoke as one having authority. Nor was he, a large, handsome man who appeared to one observer both 'solid and determined,' ill-equipped for his position. Somehow in England before he came to Canada, he had acquired a 'considerable education,' which he supplemented throughout his life with occasional reading in English and French. Fearless and just he was, but also tolerant and gentle as only a man with over one hundred grandchildren must be. In the end this tenderness of spirit proved his undoing, for he lost much of his money because he 'just couldn't avoid' endorsing other people's notes.

As he grew older, the burden of the thousand acres became too great to carry alone, so he divided the land up into three parts and built three houses of brick, manufactured from the clay pits on the place. One of these houses he kept for himself; the others he gave to two sons who remained to help him in the farming. It was upon this farm, under the kind eye of his grandfather, the patriarch, that William Sowden Sims, born October 15, 1858, lived until he was ten years old.

Alfred Sims, the boy's father, had come to Port Hope in 1854 to build a harbor, but the best day's work he ever put in in the village was on June 2, 1856, when he married Adelaide Sowden. Before they ever met, it is said, they were in love with each other. It was a romance at first rather reluctantly fostered by the local photographer who sold a little tintype of Miss Sowden only under the threat of force. Young Mr. Sims, attracted by the dark serene beauty of the picture in the window, had stepped in to learn the young girl's name and to buy the tintype. But the

5

photographer, out of regard for professional ethics, had refused to sell, although he unwisely revealed his subject's name. The firm young man said that unless he could have the picture he would be obliged to tell the young girl's brother, Sanford, whom he had just met, that her picture was being used for 'commercial purposes,' and that in all probability Sanford would respond with an offer to 'beat up the photographer.' Negotiations of sale were resumed and Mr. Sims departed shortly after in possession of the tintype. The perfection of a nineteenth-century idyll or the imagination of a later more wistful age supplies the information that the young lady on her part saw a picture of Alfred Sims at the home of a friend and reached the immediate decision that it was the likeness of the man she must marry.

Her choice, made with the precipitance of innocence or intuition, was nevertheless a good one. Alfred W. Sims had been born twenty-nine years before at Mount Holly, New Jersey. His grandfather, John Simm, had come from Scotland to Pennsylvania in 1793. Most of the descendants of this man had remained in that state. When the time had come for him to choose a career, Alfred at first determined to be a lawyer and attended Dickinson College for a few years to equip himself for the profession. But he soon discovered that he had no liking for the law and turned instead to engineering, where his natural abilities could be put to better advantage.

The greatest opportunities in the field at that period lay with the railroads which were reaching out into the West. Accordingly young Sims sought and obtained employment with the Pennsylvania Railroad. For nine years, after turning twenty-one, he worked as a roadman with the engineering corps, surveying the course which the 'Main Line' was to follow to the West, and on various smaller subsidiaries. In 1854 he undertook independently the task of a new harbor for Port Hope, Canada, where he met Adelaide Sowden and began the more important work of rearing a large family.

After their marriage, the Alfred Simses settled on the Sowden place. When work on the harbor was finished, the young husband had difficulty in obtaining another position and accepted his father-in-law's invitation to live and work on the farm. Unfortunately, despite his mechanical turn, he was 'one of the most helpless men who ever lived' when confronted with a task requiring the use of his hands.

If he was incapable in the world of material things, his wife was not. For all her feminine beauty she was a practical, efficient person who could wield a plane as well as a knitting needle. Her grandchildren still serve tea on massive carved trays which she constructed in her leisure hours, and many of them have inherited from her the ability to use their hands effectively. Inherited characteristics are revealed in inanimate objects as well as in the body or the mind, and William Sowden Sims was nowhere more the son of his mother than in his carpentry work. There is no subtlety in the trays or bookshelves these two have left to their descendants, but there is utility and precision and above all durability. If one can find the delicate eighteenth-century artistry of Duncan Phyfe in a chair, so may one conclude, from their substantial creations, that people with Sowden blood are prepared for the rough and-tumble of the world.

For almost twelve years, with a few interruptions, the Simses lived on the Sowden farm. To the second son, William, the locale of his birth was a permanent irritation because it raised doubts of his nationality in the minds of the citizens of the country he later served, and it put a weapon in the hands of those enemies who maintained that he loved England better than the United States. But there is no doubt that he was legally born an American,[1] while the nature of his patriotism can safely be left until the time in his life when he was called upon to prove it. To those doubting his right to citizenship in the United States, he himself perhaps supplied the best answer in his question, 'Had I been born in a stable would I have been a horse?' Though his birth in Port Hope was to trouble him in the future, it was the rare good fortune of his youth.

---

[1] In later years the question of Sims' citizenship was so frequently debated that the following is worth quoting: 'All children born out of the limits and jurisdiction of the United States, whose fathers may be at the time of their birth citizens of the United States, are declared to be citizens of the United States; but the rights of citizenship shall not descend to children whose fathers never resided in the United States.' (U.S.C.A., title 8, chap. 6.) Of the several cases bearing upon this issue that might be cited: Doyle vs. Town of Diana, 1922 (196 N.Y.S. 864, 203 Appellate Division 239), deals with a situation closely resembling that of Sims. It clearly establishes, as does the law above, Sims' right to American citizenship despite his Canadian mother and the locale of his birth.

7

No school, probably, is as good as a farm for growing boys. The disciplines of rhetoric and the amusements of recess are artificial beside the regimen imposed or the joys provided by agrarian life. With his brother young William at an early age was set to work at the countless tasks of farming — pulling weeds, thinning mangles, tending gap, tasks for which he received a modest compensation.

It was a normal, comfortable childhood with enough work to keep him busy — but not out of mischief, which an uncle said 'he was always going into or coming out of.' The diversions were the usual pleasures of farm life, brightened with attendance at the camp meeting held every five weeks by the circuit rider and by the weekly conducted tours of the place which were given for the benefit of the cousins from the 'city' when they came to Sunday lunch. Of all the anecdotes of his youth which have come down, only one presages a future characteristic of the man. Reporters who always found him good copy in later years would have been delighted to know that his grandfather one day, hearing an enormous commotion in the yard, rushed out to find Will 'on his hunkers' biting the nose of a small dog.

When he was seven, the carefree years were over and Will started out every morning to walk the two miles to the schoolhouse at Bletchers' Corner. It was an institution which, in later years, was recalled frequently to his mind. He remembered, with a kind of Dickensian horror, the little wooden building, the rude wooden benches, the ignorant tyrannical master, and the readers filled with colorless parables of the good deeds of 'hateful and impossible children.' In the fall, at the beginning of the term, the question of discipline was settled by a series of hand-to-hand encounters between the large farm boys and the teacher. On one occasion, when two small children loitered in getting the water, they were birched until the blood came through their cotton shirts. 'We were,' he remembered, 'not so much encouraged to learn as punished for not succeeding.'

The educational opportunities offered by the little red school were conscientiously avoided by young William. He was the laggard schoolboy creeping like snail unwillingly to school, ever anxious for the four o'clock release when he could return to his ponies, his bows and arrows, and his barefooted expeditions of discovery. Such merit as he may have acquired in his teacher's eye can be attributed less to his own ability than to his almost complete dependence upon his older brother. Hal, an able student and a good teacher, was always anxious to explain the mysteries of grammar or arithmetic to his more high-spirited brother, but Will was content to obtain the answer without waiting for the explanation.

The Simses stayed at Port Hope until Mr. Sims was granted a contract to build a small railroad near Woodstock, Vermont. It was a sad day for William when he, with his brothers and sisters, packed to leave Canada for the last time. There were now five of them, Harry, William, Louisa, Mary, and Alfred Varley.

Woodstock proved to be only an unsatisfactory interval in their lives. After a month's work on the railroad, hardpan was struck in a cut through a hillside, and the venture, never securely organized financially, failed. The Simses lived at a hotel, and in these surroundings were unable to establish the settled family life which had made existence so pleasant in the spacious days at Port Hope. At times it must have seemed to the young and competent mother that her husband never would settle down in a good and secure position. From Woodstock, he carried his family into New York for a year while he worked with a tiny railroad in the Walkville Valley. From there, the trail led to Canada, where he attempted to survey a line for a company that was projecting a railroad loosely but perhaps not inaccurately described as running from Toronto into the Canadian wilderness. Here too, another year was spent before word was received that a company in Pennsylvania was seeking the services of an engineer. In September, 1872, Alfred Sims started out again upon his journeys, but this was to be his last remove.

He went to Orbisonia, Pennsylvania, to survey the line of the East Broad Top Railroad. East Broad Top Mountain, sprawled over three counties, contained eighty square miles of coal within its rugged sides. The thirty-three-mile narrow-gauge railroad, surveyed by Alfred Sims and his two sons, Harry and William, in the fall and winter of 1872, was constructed to carry the coal from the mountain to the main line of the Pennsylvania at Mount Union. When the first ten-mile section of track was completed, Mr. Sims was offered the position of Chief Engineer of the road at a salary of twenty-five hundred dollars. He accepted at once and sent word to his wife and the other children to join him immediately.

When the family arrived, they took up quarters in Orbisonia. There they lived until 1885, when they moved across the river to Rockhill Furnace into a home built for them by the railroad. In the course of time the company expanded, and with it Alfred Sims grew in the eyes of his employers and fellow citizens. The coal from the mountain proved to be reducible to 'bright open tenacious and strong coke,' which could be used for smelting iron ore. The East Broad Top Company therefore joined with the Rockhill Furnace Coal and Iron Company to form a corporation capitalized at about three million dollars, which built at Rockhill two of the biggest furnaces east of the Mississippi. With elaborate ceremony on January 1, 1876, these were opened for business with Mr. Sims in charge as superintendent.

In truth he had become a man of substance in the towns of Orbisonia and Rockhill Furnace. There is a story that at one time the advance agent for a travelling circus came to town to make arrangements before the performers arrived. He stopped in at the Orbisonia station to see the superintendent, Mr. Sims, about transportation facilities. When he was finished with his business he said, 'And now where will I find a school director to see if I can use the playground?' Mr. Sims told him he was a school director, and would take care of the matter. 'And where can I find the superintendent of the furnace to see about buying some coal?' Mr. Sims said he could take care of that too. 'And where can I find the burgess to get a permit?' And Mr. Sims replied that he would see about the permit as well since he was the burgess.

After years of delay, uncertainty, and disappointment, his little bark came in. The citizens of Orbisonia who read the *Huntingdon Globe* on April 18, 1895, could provide a hundred anecdotes to prove the rather general observations made by the editor upon the death of their first citizen. 'Mr. Sims was a close student, a man of great intelligence, and it was a pleasure to mingle with him in social confab.' 'Mr. Sims' domestic relations were very sweet and endearing. He doted on his children and they reciprocated in kind.'

10

Most of all, doubtless his neighbors approved of the description of the 'domestic relations.' What a happy family it was! When the youngest child, Adelaide, was born in 1874, there were six of them. Together they made excursions on the railroad — when the whole crowd rode on flatcars draped with flags — to the coal mines at Robertsdale and the furnaces across the river at Rockhill. There were charades and trips into the Tuscaroras and dances into which the whole family and their guests entered with breathless excitement. And behind it and guiding it all Mrs. Sims went placidly on at her work, cooking, sewing, observing with a quiet pride.

In such an atmosphere William lived until he was seventeen years old. Nor was he the quietest member of the family group. The high spirits of his early youth grew more pronounced as he grew older. It was always he who was the first to suggest a lark with the boys or to plan complicated little jokes on the long-suffering mother and father. He was considered 'a great hand at teasing,' especially the girls. Unfortunately in school he did no better than before, and Hal, as previously, was chiefly responsible for whatever favorable reports he obtained. The schools in Orbisonia were, on the word of the superintendent himself, unsatisfactory, so the two boys went off to the Port Royal Academy, not far from Orbisonia. After two years here it was time to think of a college for them, but the question of finances rather limited their choice. The problem appeared at first to be solved when Congressman Stenger asked Alfred Sims if he would care to have either of his boys take the examination for the Naval Academy. Only one other boy from the district was applying. The chances seemed good that one of the Simses would beat him out, so the three young men took the examination together.

From no one's point of view were the results of this examination satisfactory. The third applicant had not been able to meet the physical requirements; Harry Sims was discovered to be too old for admittance; but the worst candidate of all had been William.

The Professor of Mathematics at Annapolis reported that judging 'by the general character of Sims' examination and from my previous experience in such cases I should say that there was

11

little probability of Mr. Sims finally succeeding at the Academy, although with good teaching he may succeed at the (next) candidate's examination.'[2] Worse still were the findings of the Head of the Department of English Studies, the famous Professor Soley, who found William deficient in spelling, grammar, and geography. Gross carelessness led in part to the candidate's downfall, but sheer ignorance too was apparent. The final verdict of the Head of the Department was rendered in the following highly qualified recommendation: 'From the simple character of the branches in which he failed I am of the opinion that he might prepare himself for the next examination in June.' Less sanguine was the Superintendent of the Academy, who wrote to the Secretary of the Navy after reading these comments, 'Judging from these letters it would seem to me better if a more promising candidate should be presented.' The opinion was forwarded to Congressman Stenger.

Both the politician and the boy proved undeterred by these unflattering reflections. Why the Congressman told Mr. Sims the appointment was still his if his son cared to try again is not entirely clear. Testifying fifty years later before a Senate committee, William himself said it was because his father had some political influence and the other possible candidate had 'no politics in him at all.' In other versions no other aspirant appears, and it is not improbable that the Admiral was indulging in the tolerant amusement he reserved for politicians of all kinds. The truth seems to be that there was no other candidate, so the boy had the field to himself if he cared to compete. He was moved to try again because his failure was a challenge to his ability. He had neglected, as he said, to take Hal into the examination with him and therefore he discovered for the first time the depths of his ignorance. From January to June he tutored under 'the best teacher I ever had,' one Doctor Kidder at Shirleysburg. At home he worked unceasingly. His family remembers how he would hide away in his room for hours until suddenly he would burst downstairs, catch up his mother, waltz her around the parlor vigorously for ten minutes, only to return again to his work.

[2] This letter and those that follow are in the Superintendent's Office, United States Naval Academy.

In June, 1876, he and his father went together to Annapolis, where the young man again took his entrance examinations. On the way they stopped at Baltimore and 'went to a variety theatre,' where Mr. Sims 'laughed harder' than his son had ever seen him before.

It was four months before his eighteenth birthday when he left the pleasant home in Orbisonia. Despite the unsatisfactory results of his first entrance examinations, he was not ill-equipped for his task. Intellectual discipline he had not yet learned, and his knowledge save of the most elementary aspects of the three R's was confined to unacademic subjects. But for his failings he could supply reasonable excuses. His schooling had been haphazard and occasional; it had been obtained chiefly from teachers who were as ignorant of their duties as they were of the hearts of boys. To offset these intellectual handicaps he had proved, during the six months he worked with Doctor Kidder, that he could apply himself continuously and successfully to his lessons when his interest or his desire to prove himself was aroused.

One source of his potential strength had been discovered by one of his teachers in Canada, who remarked to Mrs. Sims with a grammatical ineptitude which may explain in part her pupil's later difficulty with rhetoric, 'Willie is the baddest boy in the class, but I like him best.' Like his father, he was a pleasure to meet 'in social confab,' but there was more than his father's quiet forcefulness in him. For the moment, however, this lay concealed from most observers and probably from the boy himself. Only later did he recognize and occasionally wonder at the power of his own determination. Probably his will lay dormant in the early years because, in the happy family, there was little occasion to exert it. Always he remained well adjusted within himself and his environment.

Another asset with which he started his journey to the Academy was the astonishing good looks inherited from both his father and mother. He had the former's heavy-lidded eyes and large frame, while from his mother he obtained a generous mouth and nose and a complexion that was the envy of all women. But in truth he was more handsome than either, for both were good-looking only in a well-proportioned, large-featured, open way: the father genial and honest; the mother competent and sensible. In the son, these things had been somehow fused and refined; he possessed a grace and a certain elegance which the parents lacked.

Within as well as without, he had improved upon his inheritance. To the competence and manual dexterity of his mother he had added the patient efficiency of his father's mind, without including the unassuming quality in that man which prevented him from rising higher than he did. Somewhere, probably from his maternal grandfather, he had picked up a mental clarity and doggedness which lay long hidden behind his youthful indolence and carelessness. There was, too, some *tertium quid* in his personality, that untroubled harmony of the voices of the spirit, which Pythagoras called the greatest good. It was from this that he derived that proud and unassailable security which gave him force and direction beyond that of his ancestors and immediate family.[3]

[3] Complete documentation has been dispensed with in this first section, which deals chiefly with Sims' personal development. At the end of each chapter a list of principal sources is given. The basic material for these first five chapters is drawn from the extensive Sims papers. Unless otherwise stated all personal letters are taken from this collection. Occasional footnote citation will be made where the source of information is not clearly indicated in the text. The information in the above chapter was drawn largely from a dictated memorandum of W. S. Sims; a privately printed genealogy of the Sims family; town histories; and recollections of friends and relatives of the Sims family. To the brothers and sisters of Admiral Sims; to Joseph V. Sims, a cousin; to W. B. Burnham of Port Hope; and especially to J. William Wetter, President of the East Broad Top Railroad and Coal Company, I am greatly indebted.

2

1876 - 1882   *The United States Naval Academy*

O<small>N</small> J<small>UNE</small> 22, 1876, the Medical Board of the Naval Academy found 'William Sowden Sims free from deformity and disease and imperfections of the senses and otherwise physically qualified, according to the Regulations, to enter the Academy.' Three days later he could write to his mother that 'I have at last received the reward for my long studying and I am now a cadet midshipman, and by the time you get this letter I will be on board the *Santee* where I will have to remain until September to form a class with the candidates coming in then.' The reward had once again almost eluded his grasp, for he failed arithmetic on the first day and was forced to take another examination, which he barely passed. He was not far from the truth when, in later years, he frequently announced, 'I just scraped in by the skin of my teeth.'

During those first few days there were more painful experiences than examinations to trouble his spirit. 'The cadets have lots of fun with candidates and ask all sorts of ridiculous questions and you say "sir" after each answer.' But he walked, throughout the early weeks, with a circumspection he soon outgrew. 'You don't have to answer, but it is policy to do so and very respectfully at that, because if we are impudent or "gally" as they call it, they will put our names down and haze you after you get in.'

Analyzed through the distorting lenses of fifty years his 'whole time at the Academy' was 'an unhappy one,' but this harsh conclusion was probably a more faithful reflection of his later opinion of Annapolis as an educational institution than of his undergraduate experiences while there. It is true that his 'career was a struggle to get a passing grade of 2.5 on a basis of 4,' and that he found the rigid discipline of military life irritating after the carefree independence of his youth. But he appears also to have discovered a variety of methods to mitigate the trials of hard work and unquestioning obedience.

The routine of life at Annapolis has varied little in the last sixty years. In 1876 there was the early reveille, sounded in the winter before the last stars had died in the sky, and likewise the early taps at ten o'clock. In between there was classwork and study — chiefly on technical or professional subjects, a good deal of formation drill with setting-up exercises for the fourth classmen, and an hour or two of freedom. More than in most institutions, perhaps because of its peculiar purposes, education at Annapolis was cast in a rigid form. Boys learned by rote the pages from 173 to 194 and recited parrot-like when called upon. In the French class every part of a sailing ship was learned in French, though sail was disappearing and the boys were to live on American vessels. Students were required in mathematics to memorize one hundred and seventy-five empirical formulae which they could not deduce since the formulae depended upon experimental data that were withheld. It was an unimaginative, wholly uncompromising system of education, and its defects lingered in Sims' mind for half a century. Certainly it was all of these things, but obedience, thoroughness, and hard work are lessons as valuable for youth as initiative and excitement. If the Naval Academy in 1876 was only half an educational system, certain progressive schools of the present day are merely the other half.

The Class of 1880 was, at its beginning, very large, with ninety-four members in all, including cadet engineers. At the end of the scholastic year each boy was rated within the class on the basis of his intellectual accomplishments as measured by his classroom marks; at the end of undergraduate life his final position in the class was arrived at by an average of all his marks for all the years. The final position has a far greater importance to graduates of Annapolis than to young men leaving civilian colleges because it regulates their position on the Navy list. Promotion is, or was from the time Sims graduated until 1899, determined solely by seniority, and a man advanced up the list from his first place after graduation only as vacancies appeared ahead of him.

For the first two years at the Academy, Sims remained a firmly entrenched inhabitant of the 'wooden section.' In fact for a time it was a question in the minds of the authorities whether he should be retained. Gradually, however, he improved his position, and when the records of his six years' study and training were finally tallied, he received his permanent position in the exact middle of his class.

It was not a class of unusual distinction; only a handful of men will be remembered even by naval historians. Four became Admirals and served during the World War — Edward Simpson in the Philippines, Albert Niblack at Gibraltar, Hugh Rodman in command of the battle force that operated with the British Grand Fleet in the North Sea, and Sims at London. Of those who retired with lesser rank, Homer Poundstone has deserved more recognition than he has obtained for his early designs of the all big-gun ship, the precursor of Lord Fisher's *Dreadnought*. Beyond these, only one merits special attention — Philip Rounseville Alger, who led his class. In varying lights and shadows this handsome, brilliant man will appear on the following pages.

With only two of his classmates did the young man have any close personal relationship. His roommate for part of the four years was the gay and clever Albert P. Niblack of Indiana. Between the two there grew up an affectionate intimacy. Later, time, geography, and professional differences of opinion placed barriers between them, but for twenty years they remained the closest of friends. With them Homer Poundstone, 'bilged' from the class ahead for unauthorized activity in the hazing of candidates, formed a waggish triumvirate. Throughout the four years, they were 'thick as thieves.'

Beyond these two Sims appears to have known no one well, but he had the faculty of getting along with all. His high spirits led him frequently to take part in the countless projects by which the boredom of strict discipline was relieved. Upon one occasion all the boys in his dormitory carried coal, piece by piece in their pockets, up to a room on the top floor all winter long until by spring over a ton was stored in the lofty bin. The joke seems to have consisted simply in the problem presented to the administration of how to get rid of so large a quantity of coal. Another time they all carried up gravel and poured it down the stair wells after lights, to the confusion of the officer in charge.

Occasionally Sims practiced more occult humors. In the class ahead was a plain and literal young man who was approached one day by Sims with the good-natured query, 'What are you going to do now?' The young man outlined his plans for the immediate future in such precise detail that Sims' fancy was tickled and he shortly after accosted his friend with the same question, only to have it answered in the same manner. Over a period of a week the whole process was repeated frequently, to the immense delight of Sims and the increasing wonder of the older boy. Finally doubts of the interrogator's sanity entered his mind and he observed to friends that 'Sims might be touched in the head.' In the years to come many, many people, the majority of them English, were to offer opportunities for somewhat similar pleasantries.

Even the sombre problems of the classroom could be turned to good account. A professor asked whether a rocket would go up in a vacuum and debate over the question was prolonged over two days. Arguments grew heated and sides were taken. A procession was formed by one group who marched up and down with signs announcing that 'It won't go up,' while a more accurate and fortunately longer line shouted along the streets of Annapolis that 'It will go up.' In all these typical and timeless undergraduate pranks Sims entered with whole-hearted enthusiasm, and if he knew few well, he was liked by all.

For some of his high spirits he suffered. Throughout his four years he was always near the top of his class, if not in marks, at least in demerits; and it is necessary to record that he grew worse rather than better. True, his sins were usually minor. He threw chalk, he forgot 'his book and caused confusion in the ranks thereby,' he allowed his dressing-gown to 'be adrift at 10.00 A.M.,' and once he left 'an unauthorized cushion on a chair.' As a firstclassman he enjoyed the questionable distinction of being reported by Alfred Thayer Mahan as disorderly upon the quarterdeck and disrespectful to the officer of the deck.

Serious offenses he did not commit, but serious he could not be. At drill he would 'skylark with the hose nozzle,' in class he would skylark with his pencil and paper, and in his room he would simply skylark. The pages of the great book in which demerits were entered seemed to attest the truth of the fact that his greatest difficulty was in applying himself continuously to the task at hand. Even when he endeavored to correct this fault he erred on the other side. Once as a first-classman he was reported for busily answering a signal flag four times after the flag had been hauled down.

During the summers, the class took the usual practice cruises on the *Constellation*. This too, in retrospect, was 'not a pleasant experience,' for the quarters were cramped; he had to sleep in a hammock and live 'like a common sailor.' The objection here is based almost entirely on the grounds of physical comfort. Hot water, a comfortable bed, privacy, and a bathtub; with these he was as happy as in a castle, but they comprised an irreducible minimum. In justification of his criticism, it should be said that as a tall young man he suffered greatly from the lack of headroom on the old ship. Years later when the *Constellation* lay at Newport he would point out to his children the low beams on the gundeck and remark, 'You will find some of my bloody hairs up there.'

In June, 1880, the four years at the Academy were over, but a two-year cruise lay ahead of the young men before they could receive their commissions. For this period Sims, together with several classmates, served on the flagship of the North Atlantic Squadron, the *Tennessee*. She was a wooden full-rigged ship of almost five thousand tons. In June at Portland, Maine, where the young men joined her, Sims began the professional career that was to last for forty-two years.

It was a strange navy he entered. To a young lady who complained a few years later that America had no ruins and no curiosities, Oscar Wilde's Canterville Ghost replied, 'No ruins! No curiosities! You have your Navy and your manners!' Concerning the former, at least, the apparition appears to have been correct. No less caustic were the officials, civilian and professional, who dwelt upon the inadequacies of the Navy with a candor that would have horrified many of their successors in office. In the year 1881, Secretary Hunt began his annual report with the ominous words: 'The condition of the Navy imperatively demands the prompt and earnest attention of Congress. Unless some action be taken in its behalf it must soon dwindle into insignificance.' 'These things,' he concluded sadly, 'ought not to be.'

Point was given to the Secretary's remarks by the report in the same year of a board of officers. In this it was stated that only twenty-six of the sixty wooden vessels on the Navy list were ready for duty, and the Admiral of the Navy, David Dixon Porter, observed that of these only eighteen 'had the speed to pursue or the power to escape from a swift cruiser.' In theory there were thirteen first-rate men-of-war, but actually the only one capable of active service was the *Tennessee*, judged by the Board an 'expensive and unsatisfactory type.' The whole fleet reminded Porter 'of the ancient Chinese forts on which dragons are painted to frighten away the enemy.'

No more satisfactory were the navy yards. 'Not one [of seven] has the appliances for building a first-class ship of war.' One of the largest was at Boston, where 'there has been more waste (to use the mildest term) — for the past twelve years, than in any other; and the Department has had a great deal of trouble with the political factions who claim to control the establishment.' Other yards were little better.

If ships and yards were inadequate, the armament was worse. The Advisory Board, appointed by the Secretary, found that 'At the present time there are no guns in the service that will compare in power or efficiency with corresponding calibres of foreign artillery.' Most of the ordnance consisted of smoothbores 'entirely obsolete,' though a few of these had been converted into rifles that were 'greatly deficient in power.'

The unsatisfactory condition of the material of the Navy was matched by that of the personnel. The enlisted force was considerably smaller than the seventy-five hundred permitted by law, and many were foreigners 'who might or might not prove faithful to the flag in time of war.' On the other hand, too many officers were coming from Annapolis and the various grades were so choked with men that promotion, determined purely by seniority, was very slow. The lowest midshipman on the list could not expect to reach the grade of Ensign for nine years, and he would be eligible for retirement by the time he could be commissioned a Commander. 'Boys,' said the Admiral of the Navy, 'should be taught to understand this matter in its true light' and then there 'might not exist such insane competition to enter naval service.'

In addition to the defects of material and personnel, there were weaknesses of the administrative system that governed the operations of the naval establishment. In 1842, three Naval Commissioners, who served as the military advisers of the Secretary, had been eliminated when the bureau system of administration had been created. Forty years' experience had seemed to prove that the bureau chiefs, concerned with tasks essentially civil in character, such as building guns, designing ships, and supplying provisions, had been unable to act, in addition, as responsible military advisers of the Secretary. From year to year it was increasingly plain 'how little the Secretary of the Navy could rely upon the bureaus for favorable results.'

In review the Admiral admitted that it was 'a very poor exhibit,' but he believed it better 'to present the whole truth at once in order that a remedy may be applied.' He was too trusting of the power of the whole truth alone. Solutions for most of the problems so clearly stated in 1881 were long deferred. Few men then could have dreamed how long and bitter would be the struggle for reform in the United States Navy. Certainly the cadet midshipman who in the summer of that year was cruising in West Indian waters never dreamed of it. His mind, filled with the 'new sounds, new sights, new air' of strange ports, was little concerned with the Navy's future. The major interests of his young life were not poor guns, bad ships, slow promotion, and inadequate administration, but dances and parties and girls, and most of all himself. Yet in the annual reports on the state of the Navy in 1881, almost the full bill of particulars for his professional career had been drawn up. It was twenty years before he even read the bill.

But in a modest way he gave early promise of his future. Shortly after he joined the *Tennessee*, he realized that the steerage, the quarters for the junior officers, was 'wholly inadequate.' Twenty-five young men were packed into one small room which was ventilated by only two airports. All of the gear of these twenty-five was stowed in two compartments eleven feet by seven.

The equipment of the steerage itself was deplorable. Chairs were broken, the table was stained and decrepit, the linen was soiled with ink, alcohol, and tallow. Upon surveying these premises, tolerated by so many generations of midshipmen, Sims rebelled, thus beginning a course of independent action against the inefficiencies of constituted authority that ended with his death.

With the aid of a carefully drawn diagram Sims explained to the head of the mess, Lieutenant Lyman Arms, that the quarters were too small to accommodate the twenty-five junior officers. Somewhere in a book on prison reform he had found statistics about the amount of air required to keep one man in good health. These he used to prove that the two airports were not sufficient to keep the steerage properly ventilated. Arms, convinced by this evidence, wrote a letter to the Bureau of Navigation requesting the enlargement of the steerage. This letter received the official approval of Captain Harmony of the *Tennessee*, who took the trouble to explain in his endorsement how the alterations could be made. The Navy Department acted quickly upon receiving this information. Within a week the twenty-five junior officers were given adequate locker room for their dunnage and the young men slept at night with the comforting knowledge that they were breathing an adequate amount of fresh air.

Substantially this is the story as Sims himself used to tell it in the days of his retirement, but there were variations on the central theme. He recalled that he first went to the Captain of the vessel with his tale of woe and received a cold reception. Then he wrote a letter to the Secretary of the Navy of which Captain Harmony disapproved. The Navy Department, however, replied to this letter with a telegram ordering the steerage enlarged. Thus, Sims recalled, he single-handed accomplished his purpose.

Memory is a curious thing; it appears to possess, in addition to its central property, the faculties of originality and selectivity. For this reason the differences in the two versions of the same story told above are worth mentioning at all. There were times in his career when, on more important issues than the space of a small room, Sims was to go his way alone to fight for what appeared to him to be the truth against the opposition of superior officers, bureaus, and the Department itself. The experiences of these years, some exhilaratingly successful, some bitterly disappointing, wore channels in his mind, and in recalling them his memory slipped along the grooves of habit. Thus he remembered his neatly lettered diagram, now gathering dust in the archives of the Department along with Lyman Arms' letter, but he forgot Lyman Arms entirely and he remembered Captain Harmony, not as a friend, but as an opponent.

There is a pleasant sequel to the story. The Bureau of Navigation would enlarge the space, but it would not improve the equipment. So Sims got the ship's carpenter to build a small locker which he stocked with stamps, cigars, pencils, paper, and so forth. From his brother officers he obtained their agreement to patronize his little shop on the understanding that all profits were to go to replacing the inadequate furnishings of the steerage. He was a sharp trader and the enterprise prospered. Three-cent stamps were sold for five. Two kinds of cigars were purchased, five- and ten-cent, with the balance heavily weighted for the former. If the boys were 'flush,' they paid ten cents for any kind of cigar, and if they were 'broke,' they paid five. Whenever a purchase was left lying around, 'it disappeared,' for the sharp-eyed proprietor threw overboard pencils, papers, or anything he found, to increase his business. Under such unhealthy monopolistic conditions, it was impossible not to make money, and soon the steerage was the richer by two settees, two table covers, new curtains, and several fine oil lamps.

Life for the passed midshipmen was not arduous in those days. At sea and in port, five of the young men were on watch with almost nothing to do but keep awake. There was no responsibility and little hard physical labor. The most difficult thing was to mitigate the tedium. For two years, cruising in the West Indies and along the east coast of the United States, Sims carried out his simple duties efficiently but without real interest.

Two years of cruising, visiting, occasional skylarking, passed quickly and pleasantly. In no time he found himself back in Annapolis in June, 1882, to take his final examinations. Now he was ready to begin the life for which he had been preparing during the past six years. If he gave no promise of unusual talents for his chosen field, he at least was as well equipped as most of

the young men in his class. 'He was always full of life and fun —
but was not particularly noted for brilliancy. He was always
ready, willing and anxious to do his whole duty and do it well.
He could tell more jokes than anyone I ever knew — and never
repeat. He was a good shipmate.' So remembered one of his
classmates who was with him on the *Tennessee*. Thus equipped
he began his service on a ship which bore the lovely name of a
river not far from Orbisonia.[1]

[1] The material for this chapter was obtained chiefly from the following sources:
Sims papers; letters to the writer from members of the Class of 1880, United States
Naval Academy; *Regulations of the United States Naval Academy*, 1876; *Conduct Rolls of
Cadets*, 1876–1880; *Annual Registers of the United States Naval Academy*, 1876–1882;
Report of the Secretary of the Navy, 1881; Navy Department Archives.

3

1883 - 1895 *A Liberal Education*

On January 10, 1883, Sims reported on board the *Swatara*, a ship-rigged sloop-of-war of nineteen hundred tons displacement. For the next six years he remained continuously at sea. During this period he found little enough in his profession to keep him busy or interested. Professional responsibilities were few for the junior officers who served on our little sailing ships. Sims, like his classmates, stood his watches, repeated the gun drills, and learned how to repel boarders with a pike. The vessels cruised independently, and no attempt was made to bring the fleet together for manoeuvres of any kind. Every winter during these years Sims visited the ports of the West Indies and Central America. The calls were occasionally enlivened by the revolutions which broke out sporadically in the lands below the Tropic of Cancer. Once indeed, while he was on the *Swatara*, Sims was placed in command of a small force sent to restore order in Panama while a rebellion was in progress. On a gondola car fitted with a howitzer and Gatling gun he ensured the safe passage of trains along the railroad that lay across the Isthmus.

In the summer the ships on which he served ran up along the Canadian coast. For all of these six years, first on the *Swatara* and, after 1886, on the *Yantic*, Sims followed this familiar round. Twice he broke the dull routine of his work with reports to the Bureau of Navigation. From Panama he sent seventy-five pages on the 'unbelievable mismanagement of the deLesseps' which could only result in the failure of the Panama Company 'to

25

complete the canal.' One summer in Canada he added thirty-five pages to the literature of the interminable dispute which revolved around fishery rights. Both these reports were received with the thanks and generous approval of the Bureau of Navigation.

In other ways Sims filled in his time. Occasionally he sent off to Chicago or New York newspapers long and detailed accounts of his trips to the towns that dotted the coastline of Central America. Readers were treated to extended observations about the causes of revolutions in Port au Prince or Aspinwall, while the author's family were informed of his irritation at the slack and erratic lives of the 'semi-barbarous' natives of the West Indies.

At all these ports of call the young man made friends. Wherever he visited he found fathers who were glad to talk with him and daughters who willingly took him about to see the points of interest. In Port au Prince there was a young woman whose 'hair was glossy as any silk,' in Portsmouth there was a 'Daisy girl' who could do 'the real American forty-foot slide,' and in Halifax there was a lovely English girl who could play tennis and even 'jump the net.' Most constant in his affections remained the Chamberlaines of Norfolk. Frequently during his cruises on the *Swatara* and *Yantic* he enjoyed the comfortable hospitality of their home. Not always was it unalloyed pleasure that awaited him in the living-room of the house on Bute Street. 'Did you ever notice,' he wrote off to a friend, 'the annoying peculiarity of the young men of a small town? A comparative stranger, a bird of passage, you call on some girls, when in come some young fellows, who, having known the girls since they were children, are naturally very familiar. That is all right, but it is very trying to the stranger who, by the way, is totally ignored by the young fellows. You can understand that this makes a disagreeable interruption. And while I feel savage over it, let me remark that to my, perhaps, rather seriously inclined mind, the society conversation of the average young man is imbecile.'

On his own ground, unhampered by alien interference, he acted with greater pleasure. He organized breakfast parties on board ship, presided over dances in the sail lofts of many navy yards on the Atlantic coast, and mixed a treacherous punch for impromptu receptions he planned in celebration of such things as Cleveland's victory over Blaine. It was all very light-hearted and pleasant; still he was left curiously unsatisfied by the rewards of good-fellowship. 'I sometimes wish,' he wrote his mother, 'I were not so unsociable with men in general, I mean officers I meet in different places, but their tastes as a general thing are so different from mine that I don't care for their society. It has been this way ever since I can remember, and I have to smile at myself playing my little game and making myself agreeable.' He was, he decided, a 'cranky' man.

The same reticence he noticed in his relations with the many young girls he saw on his cruises. As he examined the steady beating of his pulse, he was surprised he had not fallen in love. Apparently, the bachelor in his crankiness did not know what little girls are made of. 'A man is impressed,' he wrote a friend, 'by their absolute purity and womanliness, and to enjoy their society is to be a better man. . . . It is to our mothers, then our sisters, then our girl *friends* that we owe for any good that is in us wretched men. . . . There is one thing I do believe with all my heart and intellect, and that is that the hearts of gold in the breasts of these pure women are the vital and moving forces in our civilization. You know what men alone descend to. It is the desire of all men for the good opinion of such women that keeps us all from ruin.'

Near the end of his life, when he knew more of women and the impulses that drive men on to ruin, he suggested a firmer basis for morality. One day at tea his wife and children were investigating the subject of sin in its ecclesiastical, philosophical, and psychological aspects. The disputation tired him. 'Nonsense,' he broke in, 'every man has an innate sense of right and wrong!'

The sober-minded youth, bored with naval routines and finding only occasional satisfaction in the lighter pleasures of society, turned to the task of educating himself. At first he attacked the literature of the world in haphazard fashion, reading at random from Thackeray, Hugo, or Dickens. For a time the works of Shakespeare claimed his attention, though he viewed with an alarmed eye the character and habits of the author of 'this wonderful book.' 'If Donnelly can't prove that Bacon wrote it, all right. I will never believe that a drunken, uneducated lout like Shakespeare wrote it. I don't think blood can be squeezed from a turnip.'

He was distressed to find the inadequacies of his own education. In his haste to repair the damages of his untutored youth he became a 'sad bookworm.' A chance copy of the *Origin of Species* he found on board the *Yantic* and from that time forth he devoted himself to a study of evolution. Night after night the light in his cabin fell upon the pages wherein was revealed to him the miracle of the nineteenth century. With the aid of Smith and Buckle, Darwin and Huxley and Herbert Spencer, he fitted together his universe. Laissez faire was not a law of trade alone, but a necessary condition for man himself. Life was strife, perhaps, but the fit survived. If competition was brutal or ruthless, it was also a law of Nature. Let it be free and it would be fair. More than fair, it was necessary; for man, possessed of sympathy and intellect, could be kindled by its heat into an infinite development. The new enlightenment held forth the distant promise even of perfection in a world through which there ran one great increasing purpose.

One man above the others struck off in the earnest young officer a responsive chord. To his father he wrote: 'I have just finished reading a truly wonderful book, and I must confess that it powerfully influenced my mind. I can see no escape from the conclusions arrived at. The object of the book is to explain how, in this age of enlightenment, in the most promising country in the world, where material progress is every day advancing, there should be such an increase in poverty and misery, so many laborers only able to earn enough to keep their little children's bodies and souls together, and so many laborers unable to find employment at all. The book explains how all this can be remedied, and points to a future that surpasses all imagination. All this is demonstrated in the simplest possible manner and by the clearest logic. I believe the book thoroughly and I don't think any unprejudiced man can read it carefully without being convinced of its truth. The book is called *Progress and Poverty* by Henry George.'

Thus in these early years he prepared himself for the tasks that lay ahead. But he was, after all, a naval officer, and there were studies that could be turned to more immediate practical ad-

vantage. For a year on the *Yantic* he taught himself French with
the aid of a kindly Frenchman who was serving on board.
Progress was slower than he desired; he therefore decided to
apply for a year's leave to go to France to 'nail the thing down.'
The Navy Department, after some deliberation, granted his
request.

In January, 1889, after six years at sea, Sims set out for Paris.
Before sailing he had dinner in New York with Mr. Henry George
and his 'charming' family. On the way to France he stopped in
England long enough to receive an unfavorable impression of
that country. The weather was unpleasant, the armor in the
Tower of London was very badly constructed, and the living
conditions of the poorer people unbearable. 'Ye Gods,' he wrote
home, 'if I had the brains I would quit this business and give
them to the single tax. I see things here that make my blood boil.'

The year he spent in Paris was one of the most pleasant of his
life. In a little pension presided over by Madame Glatz he established the rigorous routine that always aided him in the accomplishment of whatever purpose he set himself. The study of
the language which he carried on throughout the day was
broken only by his fencing lessons, which, in turn, provided the
exercise he found indispensable to good health. At tea-time he
and Madame Glatz would converse in French or read over a
play before going to see it in the evening. The theatre was, in
fact, his great diversion. Bernhardt was in the capital that winter
and he saw her in *Renée Despard* and *Camille*. On other nights
there was the great Coquelin or that never-failing source of
pleasure the Opéra Comique.

All of the sights and sounds of Paris were carefully investigated.
In the pension were two American artists who introduced him to
the dark bohemian life of Montmartre. He was glad to find it
'quite different from what I had been led to expect from my
reading of the artist's life.' He even worked up a premature
optimism about the possibility of arriving at an appreciation of
art itself. Parshall, one of his friends, took him to the Luxem-
bourg and 'told us all about the great painters, and gave us an
idea of what art means. I am beginning to catch on a little bit.'
He never did catch on, and, as he grew older, he developed a
satisfactory complaisance about his aesthetic ignorance.

In time he came to know and respect the sensitivity of the French temperament, the precision of the French mind. In time too he came to love that beautiful city which was the centre of French civilization. Only one thing in that civilization disturbed him greatly. He had met with it first when he was an Ensign on the *Swatara*. At Devil's Island one day he had gone ashore to sketch. There he had seen 'ill-clothed, starved-looking men kicked and beaten like animals and chained like dogs at night.' As he was walking back to his ship, he fell in with a young Arab boy. 'I, of course, could not imagine that he could have been guilty of a great crime, for he was so young and frank looking. I gave him some cigarettes and asked him where his home was. Finally, I asked him when he was going back, then the whole expression of his face changed, and I will never forget the look of unutterable longing that came over his face as he stretched his hands to the east and with tears in his eyes said, "I will never see Arabia again." ' The guillotine, he had written his family, was more merciful than this method of punishment 'pursued by the most civilized people in the world.'

In Paris, 'the most beautiful city in the world,' he found it all again. 'It is all very grand to look at from the top of the Eiffel Tower a thousand feet in the air, provided you don't reckon the cost or listen to the voice of the great majority who are living in brutish misery when they can live at all. Most of the people die alone in their misery. Below this city, which is the pride of France, there is an immense net stretched across the Seine River to catch the bodies of those who can bear their misery no longer. This is the boasted civilization of France and our own country is not much better.'

Though the young man might wish that he were 'more sociable with men in general,' he did not lack a nobler compassion for humanity. This sense of justice, of social consciousness lay at the very roots of his character. It was the wellspring from whence flowed the tireless energies of the reformer he later became.

For one year he remained in France. At the end of that time he could speak with fluency the language he had labored so assiduously to learn. An ear for languages, as he admitted, he did not have, but throughout his life persistence served where special gifts were lacking.

As he left Paris in 1889, he could look back with satisfaction on the years he had spent since he left the Academy. Less willing than most of his friends and classmates to accept the limitations of his professional life, he had applied himself to broader fields of learning with eagerness and understanding. By the time he was thirty-one years old, in 1889, he was ready to graduate from his rigorous course of self-instruction.

Fortunately for him, he was given the opportunity to try his hand at educating others. While he was still in Paris the Captain of the *Yantic* wrote to ask if Sims would like to serve with him on the *Saratoga*. This vessel had been obtained by the city of Philadelphia as a training ship for the purpose of teaching boys the elements of seamanship and navigation before they entered the merchant marine. The officers of the *Saratoga* were all members of the commissioned personnel of the Navy. They were expected, in addition to their other duties, to discipline and instruct the boys in their nautical studies.

Sims was delighted to accept this offer from his old commanding officer. He looked forward to work which would provide some diversion from the ordinary simple duties of a Watch Officer, and he looked forward especially to teaching boys. Upon his return from France he spent a few weeks' leave with his family in Pennsylvania before reporting on January 1, 1890, on board the *Saratoga*.

For the first few months he found himself very busy organizing his course in Navigation. More than the usual handicaps of the apprentice teacher were his because he inherited no textbooks or methods from a predecessor, and his pupils, in general, had had very little educational training. With customary seriousness of purpose, he set about his task. 'I am putting in my time,' he wrote his father in February, 'plugging away with my navigation classes, and am as busy as ever. I also have much to do in getting my house in order for the fellow who comes after me (three years hence) making copies of everything — notebooks, all problems, and a complete explanation of my system. Of course, I don't know who will succeed me and consequently care nothing about him, but I want to set a pace and standard that he will have no excuse for not following, as well as to identify the system with my name — which of course will do me no harm.'

The system which he developed was as old as Socrates, though fortunately for the students it avoided Socratic casuistry and was not designed to score points against some unsuspecting questioner. He began with an assumption of the pupils' complete ignorance of the subject, together with a fixed belief in their ability to learn it. From such fundamental questions as 'Where does the sun rise?' 'Where does the sun set?' and, 'Does the sun always set directly in the west?' he proceeded to the greater mysteries of navigation.

'There were,' he found, 'a thousand tricks about teaching boys.' He would arrive on deck after dinner with a pie offered as a reward to the boy who 'made the nearest purely mental estimate of the bearing of the sun under certain conditions of latitude.' In class each pupil was given a different problem. Those who solved theirs correctly were excused; those who did not were told to correct their mistakes and were in addition given another problem. He soon found that the ordinary textbooks were much too advanced for the boys' slender knowledge, so he wrote one himself which was designed solely for their use. Each member of the graduating class had to copy it before he left the ship. The work had a wider and more continuous use than its author had expected. In 1916, one of his old students who had become a master in the merchant marine wrote to Sims for a copy after his own had been burned with his vessel. Three months later, Sims replied that he had been trying to find the book. 'It has hardly ever been in my possession during the twenty-odd years since I left the *Saratoga*, but has been circulated among young officers who were preparing for their examinations from one grade to another.' Though the work was never printed, it has been copied a thousand times in longhand and is doubtless still in use on a few ships of our merchant marine.

Sims was an unusually happy and successful teacher. He was gratified at the end of his first year on the *Saratoga* to find that ninety per cent of his boys got over eighty on the four-day examination, which consisted entirely of working out positions under given conditions. But he was much more gratified by the continuing use to which his training was put. Throughout his life he was to have constant reminders of the value of his instruction. Pupils who became masters or officers in the merchant marine seldom failed to let him know of their success. When he was in London during the war, one wrote him that 'The 1916 Almanac correction for Polaris is given for the hour angle, the same as I used to do in Table IV on board the *Saratoga*. This year, 1917, I notice it is given for local sidereal time.' The question was how should the correction be made. This is the kind of testimonial few teachers ever get.

Life on the *Saratoga*, aside from the teaching, was not very exciting, though the ship was pleasant to serve upon, for she was steady and very fast. On one trip to Guadeloupe, she ran down the nineteen hundred nautical miles in ten days, which was 'almost steamer time,' but lacking an auxiliary the ship was completely at the mercy of the elements. Once on the way to Europe, Sims saw something which no man will ever see again. A thousand miles from land the ship was becalmed for fourteen days in the company of twenty sailing vessels — one, ninety-eight days out of Concepcion, Chile. It was, in some ways, a trying experience. 'Two weeks — that's fourteen days! Becalmed while the world — which is very big — turned round fourteen times on his axis. Becalmed while the sun rises fourteen times over a glassy sea, and sets fourteen times over the same. Stuck and waiting in mid ocean while all the mighty wheels of modern civilization are whizzing around us usual. Railroads, theatres, churches and electric lights all booming. Fast steamers passing you, ocean cables underneath you, and no news of the prospect of home rule in Ireland.' There were, however, compensations, for 'The planets keep me company every mid-watch. Jupiter shines with the calm white dignified light that seems in keeping — while Venus, as might be expected, gives out the soft warm homelike light-in-the-window-for-me kind of rays that the anxiously looked-for lighthouse gives out when you first sight it from seaward.' The Captain had brought his little son to bear him company and several other guests as well. It was pleasant to discover that the Captain's steward, in laying in provisions for them, had not counted upon fourteen days of calm. The guests were put on rations, while the wardroom continued to eat heartily.

In February, 1893, after three years on the *Saratoga*, Sims went to Washington for his examination for promotion to the grade of Lieutenant. Shortly after he was detached and sent home. While at Orbisonia, he learned that he was ordered to the cruiser *Philadelphia*, to which he reported in June.

The *Philadelphia* was the first ship of the new Navy upon which Sims served. Built by Cramp and Sons in 1888, she, together with the *San Francisco*, was the first vessel for which a premium had been offered for speed. She was a much bigger ship than any in which Sims had gone to sea, measuring 327 feet and displacing 4324 tons. In the Navy list she was rated as a protected cruiser, though her armor by present-day standards was most inadequate.

Sims found that the *Philadelphia* had many advantages. To begin with, she was as steady 'as a church,' rolling only five degrees when crossing the 'trades.' It was very pleasant never to 'think of putting racks on the tables or of securing anything in our rooms.' Electric lights were a special convenience, for they did not smell up the staterooms in the way the old oil lamps did, and they supplied a steady light for the inevitable reading. But the greatest advantage of all lay in the triple-expansion engines. 'Gales of wind are like armies that commence their attacks in due form with skirmishes and all the fuss and feathers of large bodies, but the squalls lie in ambush behind a peaceful horizon and discharge their blunderbusses point blank at the unlucky ship. A squall "raised cain" on the *Saratoga*, and required all hands to reduce sail in time to meet it. If it hit her with all sail on, it would burst every sail and perhaps dismast her. Many's the squall I have watched on the old ship during the mid watches. I was never caught by one but all the same they are responsible for some of my grey hairs.'

On the *Philadelphia* 'it is all different. She hasn't a square inch of sail — consequently the most vindictive squalls affect her about as much as a dog barking at the *Chicago Limited*. The officer of the deck has no anxiety concerning them except to get his raincoat on and the Captain's skylight closed before the squall strikes. It makes a difference in the wear and tear of standing night watches.'

The *Philadelphia* when Sims joined her at New York was on her way out to Hawaii. On the trip round the Horn he re-read

Darwin's account of the voyage of the *Beagle* in preparation for a seventy-page letter he wrote for the family describing the trip. At Callao the ship put in briefly to coal, a six-day process. Beside her in the harbor lay the homeward-bound British cruiser *Melpomene*. One night the *Philadelphia* mess gave a dinner for the English officers, and next morning the cruiser set out on the long voyage home. 'As they left the harbor, they steamed slowly past our ship — passing very close to the stern. We had a band and all the officers up on the poop, and as we said good-bye the band played "Home, Sweet Home" — which never I venture to say touches your landsmen's hearts as it does the sailor's under these circumstances. We could look right down on her decks. She was moving very slowly and the air was perfectly still, and as the band softly played the familiar air they uncovered their heads, and I saw many the brawny sailor gouge a tear out of the corner of his eye with a tarry thumb. Perhaps some foreign ship will play the tune for us when we start home in the summer of 1895.'

Through beautiful, quiet waters the *Philadelphia* made her way to Honolulu. The ship was a continual delight to him, especially her 'splendid engines.' He never tired of watching the 'six immense cylinders doing their work noiselessly and smoothly.' For others the transition was not so easy. One night the Chief Engineer, an 'old man used to old-fashioned engines and not up to managing high-powered triple-expansion machines,' locked himself in his room and cut his own throat.

For eleven months the *Philadelphia* remained in Hawaii while the islands lay under the blight of the revolution the sugar planters had directed against the rule of the native Queen Liliuokalani. There was little for the officers of the ship to do beyond arguing about the merits of the revolutionary government and playing tennis at a near-by court. Sims studied the political situation under the guidance of two Americans who had been serving the native Queen. Under the same expert direction he investigated life in the native society. During the rainy season he lightened the boredom by arranging an elaborate bachelors' dinner on board the ship. The occasion was noteworthy principally for Sims' emergence as a man of rhyme. Perhaps his most successful verse was composed for the ship's doctor. Leaning heavily upon *The Mikado* he addressed the medical man thus:

> The sun of gladness
> Has left the sky;
> In silent madness I long to die.
>
> The hopes I cherished
> When in shore clover
> At sea have perished;
> I'm sick all over.
>
> Oh, dear vicinity
> Of my divinity,
> Why linger yet
> When all is wet?
> May not a wretched landsman die?

The party was a distinct success and he received many compliments on his powers as a host and as a poet. In fact, he became the mess's laureate, enjoying a fame that excited him to a continuous production of not very metrical and sometimes incoherent verse. As he said good night to the departing guests, he was amused to have a lady tell him that the Executive Officer had told her he was a very able young officer, but too 'high-strung' and that he drank too much tea. He was, in fact, quite conscious and perhaps not a little proud of the impression he made upon his shipmates. 'I go ashore now so seldom I pass for a freak or a crank.'

The year wore on with no prospect of a settlement in Honolulu, but the *Philadelphia* could not wait. Early in August, 1894, when word was received that she was to proceed to San Francisco, she departed from Hawaii after a visit of almost eleven months. It was as well that she did not remain until the difficulties of the island were finally settled, for the solution of annexation was not arrived at until the era of flamboyant American imperialism set in during the Spanish-American War.[1]

[1] The chief source of material for this chapter was the Sims papers.

4

THE *Philadelphia* had been at San Francisco only two days when Sims received word that he was to be transferred to the *Charleston*, which was just leaving for the China Station. The mess was 'broken up' when he left, and he 'was about in the same condition.' The Executive Officer said, 'I have nothing to say, good-bye,' but his eyes 'were swimming.' The Japanese servant, with tears running down his face, could only murmur, 'I belly sorry.' Sims reflected, as he sadly departed for the *Charleston*, that ships would be happier and more efficient if their companies remained 'solid' throughout a cruise.

But he took comfort in his new ship. 'She is,' he wrote to his parents, 'very handsomely and comfortably fitted up inside — one of the handsomest if not the handsomest in the Navy and she is in perfect condition and clean as a pin.' The beauty and comfort were misleading. The *Charleston* was, in fact, a sorry object lesson for a country whose naval building program had never been intelligently planned. After the Civil War, virtually all naval construction ceased in the United States for a period of years while the existing Fleet was permitted to slide disgracefully into disrepair and obsolescence. In the eighties, under the continual prodding of successive secretaries and a few far-sighted naval officers, Congress roused itself to the construction of the new Navy. The modernization of the Fleet presented many complex problems for which it was difficult to find immediate solution. Since the period of our decline had coincided with great changes in the design and construction of warships abroad, the building of the new Navy was not accomplished without many painful errors and a good deal of foreign assistance. The history of the *Charleston* is a case in point.

It was commonly believed at the time of her construction that she was an exact copy of the Japanese cruiser *Naniwa-Kan*. Such was not the case, but the actual facts were hardly more creditable to our country. An American officer in England was directed to look around the British shipyards for any plans which would meet the *Charleston's* general specifications. His search resulted in the purchase of the blueprints of the *Naniwa-Kan* from Sir William Armstrong's firm at Newcastle-on-Tyne. The machinery for the proposed hull, however, was the product of a more painstaking eclecticism. It was discovered by our engineers that the designs combined various features of engines from no less than four vessels previously built by Sir William Armstrong. The general specifications were those of the Italian cruiser *Etna*, while refinements were added from the plans of *Naniwa-Kan*, *Giovanni Bausan*, and the Chilean cruiser *Esmeralda*.

Innumerable complications developed as the work on the vessel progressed. Separate parts of the engines failed 'to agree with each other as to proportion and location,' and many expensive changes had to be made by the shipyards. These changes were the result chiefly of a difference of opinion between the Secretary of the Navy and the Bureau of Steam Engineering which had been settled by the Secretary's ruling in his own favor. His faith in the source of the designs had been so great that he refused to allow the Bureau to make alterations in the specifications before the contracts were let.

Despite all the disadvantages under which she was constructed, the *Charleston* remained a reasonably efficient ship and led a not inactive or undramatic life. When Sims joined her she had already enjoyed a brief fame for her chase of the steamer *Itata* during the Chilean war, in the course of which she almost fought an engagement with one of her foster mothers, the *Esmeralda*. Much later, in the Spanish-American War, she provided an enduring subject for high-school debaters when she captured Guam from the Spanish.[1]

The *Charleston* proceeded to the China Station by way of Honolulu without untoward incident. On the way Sims dis-

[1] F. M. Bennett, *The Steam Navy of the United States*, Pittsburg, 1896, pp. 789–793.

covered a companion who was through many years to provide an ample compensation for the loss of his friends on the *Philadelphia*. 'He is Dr. Arnold and is already well known in the medical profession, having made a number of discoveries in microscopy, and invented a number of appliances for making microscopic examinations. Besides his attainments he is exceedingly well read, and one of the most whimsically witty men I know.' Somewhat to Sims' concern, he found that his new friend was always carrying on some controversy with the Navy Department. 'He knows such controversy does him no good, but he says his pot boils that way.'

The pot of this rugged, homely Southerner continued to boil that way, though he, more than others, always felt the scorch of its steam. In truth he was something of a mountebank. Will (Pilgarlic) Arnold he signed himself. On his watch chain hung a curious metal slug which had been formed when a Japanese and a Chinese bullet collided in midair. Arnold dug it out of the body of a Chinese soldier where it had lodged, and found it sufficiently interesting to make it the subject of a monograph. There was a loose flamboyance in his nature, a dark touch of the conspirator, a gift for too florid phrase that frequently irritated those who knew him.

Something in this strange man appealed to Sims. It may have been his honesty or his eager, not unexciting mind, or the furious zeal with which he pursued the trail of error. Undoubtedly, too, the Doctor had what is now called color. This always aroused Sims' interest wherever he discovered it, whether in his bootblack or in Lady Astor. On the *Charleston*, Arnold was only the best and wittiest of companions, but five years later he proved himself a reliable comrade-at-arms in the fight for better gunnery.

The *Charleston* arrived on the China Station at the moment when Japan for the first time was giving an impressive demonstration of its ability to upset the calculations of Western Europe. The Heavenly Kingdom, feeling the need to expand beyond its island borders in the autumn of 1894, was surprisingly defeating China in a war which had begun over a question of rights in Korea. The hostilities naturally imperilled the property and lives of foreign residents in Korea and China, and the *Charleston* was assigned to the task of protecting American nationals in disturbed areas. Such an area was Chemulpo, the port of Seoul in Korea, and there the *Charleston* arrived on November 10 to take up its patient watch. The city was quiet and the crew of the ship settled down for a month of inactivity and dull routine, but for Sims there began some of the most industrious weeks of his career.

On the trip from San Francisco the Captain had appointed him Intelligence Officer of the *Charleston*. Sims at first protested that he knew nothing of such work, to which his commanding officer replied, 'Neither do any of us.' Ignorant as he was of his new duties, he set about educating himself in the requirements of his position. In Washington there was, and still is, an Office of Naval Intelligence to which the Intelligence Officers of each ship were supposed to send reports on harbors, fortifications, or foreign vessels. The information thus assembled was collected, tabulated, and printed in little books which were distributed by the Office to each ship in the Navy.

Sims soon discovered that he had settled upon a very bad moment to begin his new service. The struggle for Korea had drawn an unusually large number of neutral warships to the disturbed area and time had to be taken from his other duties to report on each one of these. In addition, and far more important, the war was contributing significant lessons on the nature of naval warfare with modern weapons. Since the last great naval engagements, significant advances had been made in ship design, ordnance, and armor. The Sino-Japanese War provided, for the first time, an opportunity to test the value of many of these new departures.

From the moment the *Charleston* entered Chemulpo, Sims found himself busily engaged. 'This port has not been reported on since 1884, and I must verify or correct the old reports. There are six foreign vessels in the harbor. Our records contain certain information on five of them — save for certain items I have collected. The sixth is a fine new cruiser just out from England on which we have no information. I have collected it all — about forty pages.'

This matter of mere bulk was always a major preoccupation with him; he never ceased to be amazed at the massive results of his own enterprise. Once, in one of his not infrequent observations upon the inadequacy of his family's correspondence, he reminded them that he had produced 1543 pages for their edification while he was on the *Philadelphia*. The unnecessary length of most of his reports derived largely from the exigencies of a luxuriant prose style developed, perhaps, from an uncritical reading of Herbert Spencer's unpruned sentences. His good friend, Gherardi, delivered perhaps the most just evaluation of his method of reporting a few years later. 'There is so damn much hard common sense in it.... It's bully, it's ripping, fine.... It's windy too, but we expect that of you.'

The 'fine new English cruiser' was the seventy-five-hundred-ton *Crescent*. Of particular interest to Sims were her six-inch guns. At a recent target practice the best gun captain of the ship had established a record of twenty-four shots and eighteen hits in three minutes. Other gun captains had done nearly as well. Inasmuch as these results were really remarkable for the period, Sims paid especial attention to the rapid-fire battery of the *Crescent*.

There were two chief reasons for the unusual accomplishments. In the first place, pointers took up a position well forward of the breech of the gun and paid no attention to the process of loading. Each captain 'presses the electric button *each time* he has the aim, the mechanism of the breech being so arranged that the charge cannot be ignited until the plug *is locked*, when electric contact is made.' In the second place, the British were using a very effective sight which Sims fully explained with the aid of a diagram.

A short time later, while Sims was investigating the English ship *Daphne*, one of her officers showed him the manuscript copy of a report on the Yalu River battle. From this copy Sims obtained information for his own report of the battle. This engagement was very significant, for modern guns and armor had been used virtually for the first time.

It has been revealed in the fighting at Yalu River that modern shells, especially from the secondary battery, could set woodwork afire very easily. This was an important discovery because most of the ships constructed at this time contained a great deal of interior woodwork of all kinds. Another surprising result was the ability which the Chinese ironclads, or battleships, had displayed to withstand the withering fire of the Japanese cruisers. After four hours the twelve- and thirteen-inch guns of the Japanese had failed to inflict damage sufficient to put the Chinese ships out of action.

Naval theorists had another shock when the battle was terminated at sundown for lack of ammunition. Prior to Yalu River the almost universal belief had been that naval battles would be very short. The unexpected resistance of ironclads had prolonged the engagement, however, to such an extent that both sides ran out of shells before any decisive result had been achieved. These were lessons which were soon learned by naval men, and their influence upon future naval construction and design was far-reaching.

Sims found little to inspire him as he investigated the sordid motives that lay behind this adventure in Japanese imperialism. It was plain that the country was simply taking advantage of Chinese corruption and inefficiency to acquire new territory for her own expanding economy. He sympathized with the country's attempt to 'advance in civilization,' and he greatly admired the way in which the fleet was handled, 'but I am not wid 'em in this war.' They were better than their enemies because they were cleaner and more efficient, but they were a bloodthirsty and unscrupulous lot all the same. Whatever could be said for Japan, nothing could be put forward in extenuation of the activities of the other powers. Russia wanted a short cut from the Siberian Railroad to Vladivostok; France hoped to augment her winnings in the Tonquin conquest; England apparently wanted the whole world and seemed likely to get it. 'All bear the same relation to morality as robbing a drunken sailor — but moral codes and histories are written in different books.'

From his experience as an Intelligence Officer, Sims knew what part his own country must of necessity play in all this. 'The Americans want to mind their own business and I hope they will. It would be a real misfortune for us to acquire any territory in this direction, for we could not possibly hold it unless our fleet were as strong as the first power that wanted to take it away from us.' In actual fact we could not expect to protect any territory we might obtain, for 'as a military force the Navy is not counted. . . . I make numerous reports on vessels of the *Charleston's* tonnage that could "lick" us while we were spitting on our hands.'

He was clear on the reasons for our unpreparedness. 'To be sure there is extreme improbability of our getting into a row with anybody and that is the reason we are always behind and probably will remain so. We can't get an appropriation until it can be shown how much better other nations are in that respect, then by the time we get money and commence to build we are left behind again. I am aware that this is not the opinion of the American public, which is immensely impressed by the speed of the *Columbia* and the *Minneapolis*, but it is the truth all the same. I have just completed reports on twenty foreign vessels and I know whereof I speak.'

A few days after he had spoken, Port Arthur surrendered; a little later Wei Hai Wei fell into the hands of the Japanese. Sims sent home a description of this battle which dealt chiefly with the unexpectedly destructive effect of the big shells used by the Japanese and with the very successful and skilful Japanese torpedo attack on the Chinese ships which lay in the harbor. This attack, ably conceived and well carried out, was perhaps the decisive factor in the defeat of the Chinese fleet and the fall of Wei Hai Wei. His ultimate conclusions were that the Chinese had had very fine equipment and ordnance which they failed to use at all intelligently. Battleships had proved themselves superior to cruisers, but in this particular case the Chinese had been so incapable of manoeuvring properly that they had been defeated by inferior forces. All this indicated 'a boom in battleships' and he was sure 'that the jingoists would tear their hair and demand a dozen.'

This report on Port Arthur and Wei Hai Wei was to be his last. He had written so much, four hundred pages, that he had developed writer's cramp. When he asked to be relieved of his work, the ship's doctor supported his demands. It was, in truth, a very severe case, for his right hand became so swollen that he could not use it to write for some weeks. The malady was to pursue him for life; ever after he avoided longhand when he could.

But this was not the most disagreeable aspect of the work, he liked to believe. 'With my disinclination to meet strangers it was a severe trial to me to go on board a foreign ship in search of information,' and 'the work destroys for me all sense of leisure as it is never done — a new ship may come in sight at any minute.'

The fact that the work was disagreeable did not prevent him from doing it thoroughly. In the course of his first three months, he had sent in 'more work than the press copy book shows since she [the *Charleston*] has been in commission nearly seven years ago.' His predecessor had contributed only one page of information. This industry 'both astonished and delighted' the 'fool captain' of the ship. He was 'a time-server himself and couldn't quite comprehend a man's sending in work when an excuse would do as well. In the reports I have freely expressed my opinions, with my usual timidity, about various nautical matters, and the skipper by the force of explaining these opinions to others has come to regard them as his own in a measure and for fear they will be wasted he has written to various officials calling their attention to the [reports]. The reports go through the Admiral and he has written to the Secretary asking him to read the documents to the Admiral (who is by the way a puddin' head).'

Fortunately for Sims, the reaction of his superiors to these labors was of a more charitable nature. The Chief Intelligence Officer remarked that 'another mail is in from the Asiatic station and as usual the *Charleston* is ahead of everything else in Intelligence Reports.' It was possible that his report on the Yalu River action would change the method of electric wiring in warships. The Assistant Secretary and the Secretary himself noticed with pleasure and commendation 'the high character' of his efforts.

Early in April, Sims went to Newchang with some supplies for the *Petrel*, which had been stationed there for the protection of the one hundred and fifty foreigners in the city. While there he visited Doctor Arnold, who had been transferred to the *Petrel*. Arnold had had a busy winter, for there had been heavy fighting around Newchang and the city was filled with wounded Chinese soldiers. Since the armies of China had no medical corps to take care of these men, Arnold and an English surgeon had converted an old inn into a hospital. The Doctor took Sims to inspect his clinic, which was simply a mud structure built around a patio. The rooms were filled with the smoke of fires used to cook rice, the principal food of the patients. There were no beds 'or facilities to take care of the wounded which are laid in intervals of four or five feet from one end of these rooms to the other. . . . The wounded men have no bedding but lie in loose baggy clothing that is filthy beyond anything you could possibly imagine. . . . These dens of suffering would break your heart.'

The reverence the patients had for Doctor Arnold was very touching. 'As he came in sight through the smoke, those who were able would sit up and perform the Kow Tow, those who could not move would place their hands alongside their heads — and these were the desperately wounded indeed. It amounts to veneration. . . . On the doors and walls of these horrible wards the patients had fastened bits of paper on which were written Chinese characters signifying Heavenly Rest, Paradise on Earth, Complete Happiness, etc., etc. This to me is infinitely pathetic — the simple absence of cold, hunger, harsh treatment, and gunshot wounds, make a heaven on earth.'

Sorrow and pain he had watched in many places, but when he returned from Newchang he found them for the first time waiting for him aboard the *Charleston*. A letter from home brought word that his father was dying. The news, he wrote to a sister, came as 'a bullet in the breast.' Fortune, for thirty-six years, had spared him the sorrows of intimate personal tragedy and he had no practice in fortifying himself against the artillery of grief. So the knowledge of his father's condition 'came to him with a bitterness that I hope and believe none of you will feel as keenly as I do.' He would 'give everything he owned and his life besides to be at his father's bedside.' Hardest of all to bear was the fact that he was five thousand miles away. 'We travellers live with a picture of the homecoming constantly in our minds and we keep track of just how long our cruise will last. . . . The little scheme that was almost constantly in my mind was that I would take up smoking again before I returned so as to be able to smoke the *bonne pipe* with Dad in the little room.'

None on board could console him when he learned his father had died. His messmates, he wrote home, did not 'understand his real character.' To them he was a 'cheerful and mildly witty companion, critically inclined, and with rather too biting a tongue.' He withdrew, therefore, into his room and wrote to his mother that 'It can never be the same again.'

Fifteen years he had been to sea. During that time the actual family relationship had been supplanted by thoughts of home. The void of separation had been filled with those pictures which travellers must have constantly in their minds — pictures of a proud father, laughing sisters, and the voyager's return. 'The bullet' that lodged in the breast had shattered some familiar portraits in its course.

Consolation he did ultimately find in the thought that he could be of material assistance to his family. The father had never had the instinct for financial success, and Mrs. Sims was left in a precarious position after his death. He thanked the Lord that 'the glamour of a woman's face had never come between me and our family and that my entire heart does now and always has belonged to you.'

It was twelve months before he saw his family again. During this time there was very little for Sims to do but stand his watches, and train his division. When he had taken it over, most of the men had been 'time-servers,' performing their duties in a 'very listless manner.' 'So I set about establishing the same relations that existed between me and my boys on the *Saratoga*. They are a smart set of young fellows and I had no trouble. I worked for them, and pretty soon they began to work for me.' His experience on the school ship had taught him many things which stood him in good stead with his less willing pupils. 'I made them sectional views of all the guns, ammunition, etc., a complete catechism of all the things they were required to know in gunnery. Whenever I visited a foreign vessel to make a report to the Intelligence Office, I always told them about all the new points I found, explained the significance of the Yalu River Naval Fight, etc.'

When he was not at work on board ship, Sims went into the city to the English Club. There were a good many Englishmen and Americans who met there to play poker, which was too expensive, or to have a game of tennis, which he loved. Three or four times a week through these months he managed to make an enthusiastic if unscientific fourth in a game of doubles. One night there was a big party at the club and the industrious laureate got out his pencil and manufactured over one hundred pages of verse for the occasion. Next day the ship departed for Chemulpo, where she remained a month before returning home. On the way, there was a target practice which 'took a good deal of time since there was a year's supply of ammunition to use up.' His division made a handsome record.

All hands were very glad to set out for San Francisco in early June. After the excitement of the Sino-Japanese War had ended, the days at Nagasaki had seemed very long. One officer, finding them unbearable, had appealed to the President and the Secretary of the Navy to have his cruise shortened, after the Bureau of Navigation had refused to do so. Sims could only feel that the two dignitaries were 'very just' when they supported the Bureau, 'for when an officer can go to the President and override the Secretary and Chief of the Bureau of Navigation, there is no longer any proper discipline.' [2]

[2] The chief source of material for this chapter was the Sims papers.

5

1897 - 1900 *Eleven Thousand Pages*

I was impressed,' wrote Sims to his old friend Fullam in 1918, 'by your correspondence with Mr. [F. D.] Roosevelt. The point he makes that this business of military distinction is largely a matter of luck is a very just one. It certainly is. If I had not asked old John G. Walker to give me a year's leave in 1888 to study French in France, I would never have been Attaché there, and the rest of the duty I have had would probably not have followed.'

This philosophic reflection on the accident of military distinction is entirely justified, but Sims was unduly modest in assigning the cause of his appointment as Naval Attaché to Paris to the single fact that he could speak French. The industry with which he performed his Intelligence duties on the *Charleston* had not gone unremarked in Washington. In 1896, he was asked to teach a gunnery and ordnance course at Annapolis, and a short time afterward the Bureau of Ordnance offered him a desk in the Department. Both these positions he refused. More inviting was the proposal of the Chief Intelligence Officer, who asked Sims if he would like to go to Paris as Naval Attaché.

The bait was attractive, for 'the duty would be most congenial,' but Sims delayed giving a definite answer because he feared 'the expenses... would be more than a chap without private means could stand.' When he arrived home in Pennsylvania in August, 1896, he still had not made up his mind. Several other attractive offers he considered, among them the Executive's position on the *Saratoga*. In August he received word that he had been appointed 'Naval Attaché, U.S. Embassy at

Paris and U.S. Legations at Madrid and St. Petersburg.' Without further delay he accepted the attractive post.

After a few months spent in visiting naval stations and shipyards to acquaint himself with problems of ship construction, he set off for France. Paris, when he arrived there in early March, 1897, he found 'more beautiful than ever,' but he was not permitted to linger in the city. With his predecessor he made a long trip to Russia and an extended tour of the principal naval bases in Europe. The strenuous activity of these first months quite took the bloom off the work he had believed 'congenial.' 'I am in excellent health,' he wrote his family. 'I don't like the job so far. Your work is *never* done, and never will be, consequently you have no sense of leisure and no possibility of reading a book with a clear conscience. I will be very busy for at least a year, and after that just *busy.*'

Busy he was for a year and more. It was a life of constant travelling, constant attendance at official functions, and constant investigation into the naval enterprise of the countries to which he was attached. Back and forth across Europe, up and down the seacoast of France moved the indefatigable young Lieutenant, filling the pages of his notebook in his neat, flowing hand.

The letters and reports that went flying home as a result of these trips caught the eye of the new Assistant Secretary of the Navy, a young man named Theodore Roosevelt. On August 19, the Department took 'the opportunity for expressing its appreciation of the quality and quantity of the information furnished by' the young Lieutenant. To this formal announcement was added: 'Not perfunctory. I wish to add my personal appreciation of it. T. R.' Again in December the Department expressed its approval of 'the energy, zeal, and intelligence that you have displayed in the collection of so much valuable material in so short a time.' The inimitable touch of the Assistant Secretary was once more added: 'I am very much pleased; you have done *well;* your report and enclosures were as interesting as anything I have recently read.'

This interesting reading matter dealt chiefly with methods of European ship construction and target practice. In his trips to naval bases Sims had in six months seen enough to convince him that American gunnery was far less effective than that of the great foreign navies. No time was lost before his superiors were informed of this melancholy fact. To the Chief of the Office of Naval Intelligence he wrote in January, 1898, that European gun-pointers were 'far better trained than our own.' 'If we build ships of equal power and number, we should still be powerless to resist [the enemy] for the simple reason that they fire more rapidly and more accurately.' To another he wrote at the same time that too little attention was paid in America to 'the man behind the gun.' Pointers 'should be experts in the sense that Buffalo Bill and Colonel Carter are experts with small arms. We would now,' he concluded, 'be thrashed hands down by an English, French, German, and possibly Russian ship.'

Observations of this sort were always calculated to rouse the bounding spirits of Theodore Roosevelt. He wrote off to the Attaché requesting information on British methods of gunnery. Sims replied that his report on the cruiser *Crescent*, written in 1895 from the *Charleston*, gave full particulars. The Assistant Secretary replied that the report had been mislaid; no one seemed to know where it was. Only after a considerable search was it unearthed in the files of the Department. The burden of all the information that Sims was sending over was that the foreign navies were spending a great deal of time training gun-pointers to fire at actual targets, while Americans had no systematic methods of practice and were content to shoot up the yearly supply of ammunition without regard to the accuracy of the firing.

French and Russian training systems were fully reported upon. All the regulations, filling a hundred and fifty pages, governing the Russian practice were obtained in some subterranean way, translated, and forwarded to Washington.

That the collection of such information was not easy Sims impressed upon his family. 'My Russian reports are *very* interesting and important, and you can imagine the satisfaction it was to put them all safely in the bag last Friday. But I had to pay the fiddler a bit for them, for immediately they were disposed of, I collapsed and had to go home, and for two days could do nothing. . . . The information was collected in the face of considerable opposition, and I had to untangle countless lies to get at the truth. You can hardly imagine the worry and anxiety, which, of course, it would have been fatal to show. And the mental strain of sizing up each of the hundreds of officials I had to deal with, and getting on his right side, was considerable, specially when we both spoke a language [French] foreign to us.'

Spectacular results followed such effort. 'I am sure you can't easily imagine the strain of all this, and how absent-minded it makes you about small things. I have had extra keys to my apartment and office made, as I lock myself out frequently. It is with great difficulty that I can remember to post a letter to my home or to the office — I usually get someone else to do it. I made myself a cup of tea the other day and poured every drop of it in the sugar bowl before I noticed it — I was thinking about the reports.'

After such dreadful tidings it is unlikely that the anxious mother in Haverford was much comforted by the cheery assurance that 'I am very strong.'

Though the work was never-ending, there were yet diversions. Sims bought a bicycle on which he toured the Bois in the cool of the evening. The vehicle accompanied him on all of his trips. At Cherbourg once he fell in with a young French count. 'He had to walk his machine up many of the hills, while I rode alongside of him. However, he is a splendid fellow, and one of the few Frenchmen I have ever admired. He actually has a clear idea of virtue.'

Of social life he perforce saw something. 'Mrs. Porter [the Ambassador's wife] has a reception every Monday in their splendid house. I go, of course, but all these idle people bore me right smart.' Perhaps this was because he had to be on his very best behavior. 'When foreign officers criticize our vessels, I go 'em one better, and tell 'em we are only beginning to learn how to build them. It goes against the grain, for many times I could knock 'em clean over the ropes. Imagine my playing the rôle of the submissive, and the agreeable; but it must be done. I smile at the vapid gush of ignorant women and make them think I am a very appreciative and intelligent young (?) man. (Hair's growing thin in front.)'

One unexpected pleasure Sims had in November of his first year in Paris. The new Minister to Russia, Ethan Allen Hitchcock of St. Louis, stopped in the city on his way to St. Petersburg. The visit was made primarily to permit his wife and daughters to equip themselves properly for their pilgrimage into Russia. Sims called upon Mr. Hitchcock to introduce himself as the Naval Attaché. Apparently the men liked each other immediately. One night Sims went round for dinner to the hotel where the Hitchcocks were staying. Rather casually he reported afterward to his family that 'The new Minister to St. Petersburg is here with his family — wife and two growed daughters — rather good-looking girls.' The visit of the naval officer was more fully described by one of the 'growed' daughters in a letter to her sister in America. Anne Hitchcock wrote: 'Mr. Sims came for dinner and we all like him very much. He is a good deal older man than I had thought; he cannot be far from forty. He is splendidly tall and broad chested and has superb teeth, but he wears a very ugly square beard. He is tremendously clever and up on all sorts of subjects, and you may know that he is a good talker when I tell you that he entertained us from 7.30 to 12.15. I thought he never would go home, and yet I did not mind myself because I was interested in what we were talking about, but poor little Mother! She retired into her room early in the evening and indulged in forty winks, but they proved ineffectual, for her dear eyes would close in spite of the most heroic efforts. I do not know how Mr. S. escaped seeing her. I think John [John Shepley was married to the sister, Sarah Hitchcock] would like [him] and I am sure he would be interested in talking China and Japan with him. He wrote up most of the war out there.'

This last was a compliment to Sims' Intelligence reports from the *Charleston* that not even Mr. Roosevelt could have equalled. While Mrs. Hitchcock was drowsing quietly in her chair, the rest of the family had been treated to a rather breath-taking display of verbal fireworks on the part of their guest. The girls were advised to read *À Quoi Tient la Supériorité de l'Anglo-Saxon*; the Minister was startled by revelations of the inadequacy of the American Navy, and all three were informed of the military intricacies of the Sino-Japanese War. Occasionally throughout the next two years, until Mr. Hitchcock was called home to take a place in the Cabinet, the Naval Attaché saw the family, but how much of them he was to see in the remaining years of his life he did not then guess.

Miss Anne Hitchcock was an acute observer. The guest who exhausted the physical powers of her mother but not his own welcome, was superbly handsome. Tall, erect, beautifully proportioned, and, as he frequently pointed out, 'in perfect health,' Sims was an arresting figure. Whether or not the well-trimmed black beard marred the otherwise immaculate appearance was a matter of opinion. Some found it striking and others, like Miss Hitchcock, believed that it was downright ugly. She had guessed his age almost to the year; when he dined with them, he had just turned thirty-nine. Outwardly, perhaps, he seemed his age; but in many respects, he remained a boy grown tall. The surging, irrepressible, high spirits were those of an undergraduate; the bubbling, rather simple humor belonged to an irreverent schoolboy. Russians of high degree were referred to as 'Prince Wipeoffyourchinsky,' while the alert observer of the passing scene professed himself as 'right smart bored' with every official function he attended. Yet he reported each one with great care and in amazing detail. 'The Ambassador of a great power has gold lace and embroidery every place but on the seat of his "pants," and he would doubtless have it there but for the fact that the reverse side of embroidery is not smooth, and an Ambassador is only human after all.'

As time passed, it became apparent that Sims was making a dent in the unyielding substance of the Navy Department. In January, 1898, he heard from his Chief that 'Your report . . . has evidently not received the attention it should have received, or the English system of aiming and practice would have been better known here. I find that the English practice of constantly making contact [pressing the firing key so the gun would fire whenever the breech block was closed] when the sights are on, regardless of loading, is scarcely known at the Department, and it furnishes the very point we were seeking — the reason why they were able to fire so rapidly. This whole matter will go before Mr. Roosevelt next week. He is very much interested in the subject.'

A short time after this letter was received, both Mr. Roosevelt and his indefatigable Lieutenant were diverted by more enlivening matters. In April, 1898, the United States went to war with Spain. Immediately demands were made upon the Attaché at Paris for information about the movements of Spanish vessels. Sims, whose appointment to Madrid had been cancelled before he arrived in Paris, was informed by the Department that he could get all the necessary information from American consuls and agents in Spain. That was 'of course, a fool idea,' since some of our consuls were actually Spaniards. He therefore asked to be supplied with the necessary funds to establish his own agents. John D. Long, whose concern for universal peace antedated by many years his more modest enthusiasm for the United States Navy, opposed the idea until Alfred Thayer Mahan of the Strategy Board convinced him of its value. Money was sent and Sims set about building up his spy system. Strange men of many nationalities and from every walk of life made the acquaintance of the handsome American officer. An impoverished French baron got on the payroll as 'Special Agent in Madrid.' A doctor who practiced among the aristocracy in the Spanish capital came highly recommended, but proved in time to rely for most of his information upon a ready imagination. The most success- ful agent possessed a career that threw light upon the nature of French domestic politics. He arrived on the doorstep with a letter from a man named Clemenceau. Sims went to see the agent's sponsor and learned that Clemenceau employed the man whenever he needed more information on the motives of French politicians than could be gleaned from the pages of the journal of the Chamber of Deputies. The agent was in the Tiger's eyes 'a man of the world,' and loyal to his employers. In his spare time, indeed, he was an eminently respectable mayor of a French city not far from Paris. Others, less colorful, joined the ring un- til Sims had a representative in most of the large Spanish cities.

Back to Washington went reports on the defenses of Carta- gena, on the new Krupp guns at Podadero, on the political tem- perature of the Canaries, where there were two hundred thou- sand tons of coal and only a few guns without adequate ammuni- tion. To the Navy Department in early June it was explained that the *Cristobal Colon* had arrived in Santiago in bad condition. Her boilers needed repair and her speed had been reduced to one-third normal. The *Pelayo* was in no condition to fight at all,

for the Spanish had never spent sufficient money upon maintenance.

A few days later news of greater importance reached the
Naval Attaché. The Spaniards were planning to send a force
under Admiral Camara to threaten Admiral Dewey at Manila.
On the sixteenth of June, the ships set out from Spain. At Port
Said came the news of Cervera's defeat and Camara was brought
hastily back to protect the Iberian Peninsula. The Strategy
Board in America, when informed of this, expressed, through
Captain Mahan, its 'obligations . . . for the full and satisfactory
data' and told Sims that a fleet under Commodore Watson
would probably be sent to deal with Camara's fleet. Because
of this, Sims was to keep the Navy Department fully informed
of every movement of the Spaniards. 'I incline, myself,' wrote
Mahan, 'to think that it would be a good plan to allow it to
transpire that, if not molested at all by torpedo boats, our
squadron [Watson's] would probably abstain from bombarding
and confine its operations to the molestation of commerce and
to blockade in order to convince the enemy of their really exposed position under the most merciful pressure. . . .'

Exerting the influence of sea power upon history was apparently not nearly as amusing as writing about it. The great man
added: 'Will you make my respects to the Ambassador . . .? I
hope that the conduct of affairs will soon get into the peaceful
hands of his corps, and let me get back to my books and papers.'

Mahan's wish was granted, and the little war that meant so
much to Theodore Roosevelt was soon over. Again Sims returned to the pursuits of peace, enlivened at first as they were by
the blackmailing activities of many of his agents. The doctor in
Madrid with the aristocratic practice showed up at the Embassy
— which had moved to the Avenue Kléber — to demand compensation on a grand scale. 'I quite enjoyed the interview,' his
host reported afterward.

More pressing were the demands of the letter-press books.
Sims was anxious to beat his predecessor's record of fifteen full
books. Slowly the pages were covered with the information
gleaned on his endless travels. Characteristics of new vessels
launched in France and Russia, the location and extent of new
bases, changes in regulations, summaries of articles appearing in

the professional magazines, memoranda he acquired from official desks in strange ways, flowed onto the flimsy paper. There was a new naphtha factory in Russia; twenty-one of the cast-steel supports of the battleship *Bouvet* had cracked on a Mediterranean cruise; the cruiser *Duchalaya* had broken a cylinder head on her trials. More important was a complete study of the French method of naval administration in which particular attention was paid to the system by which new ships were designed. Its importance for the Navy Department lay in the fact that most of the principles upon which the French operated were disregarded or violated in America as they had been disregarded or violated in France until the deficiencies of the Navy had caused a cabinet to fall. Lighter matters did intrude. To the Bureau of Navigation Sims wrote that 'A party in Marseilles makes a proposition to build a submarine boat with four workmen in one month and expects it to make from 50 to 80 knots per hour under water, without consuming coal or other combustibles, and with a crew of two men.' For the benefit of some of the slower minds in the Bureau he added, 'It is unnecessary to say that it has never been tried, being entirely impracticable, and it is only forwarded as a sample of the contrivances that receive patents in France.' Another time he reported the French method of training carrier pigeons. When a gay subordinate added to the report a suggestion that the United States cross the pigeons with parrots so the birds could vocalize their messages, Sims was reproved by the Department.

In two years' time, with such varied information he filled his pages and broke all records. Twenty-two letter-press books containing eleven thousand pages stood on the shelves as evidence of his industry. When this work was done, he was on April 5, 1900, ordered home for three months' leave before going again on sea duty. Ten days later his orders were changed. At the request of the sponsors he was ordered by the Department to remain in Paris to judge a contest of life-saving devices. The work lasted all summer and Sims never did get home. A short holiday in France was all he had before joining the new battleship *Kentucky* at Gibraltar.

The *Kentucky* was on her way out to the China Station, so Sims would not see his family again for another three years. He was considerably disgruntled by this turn of events and believed that it had developed because the Department was unwilling to bear the cost of his transportation home. Whatever the reason, Sims in November, 1900, found himself aboard the newest ship in the Fleet, bound for China.

Whether Sims was sent to Paris because he could speak French or because of his fine work on the *Charleston*, he was not wrong in considering his service in France as a 'turning point in his career.' The foundations of the future were laid in the three years he spent in the only city that ever affected him by its personality. Twenty-five years later, he explained to a group of Senators what those years had meant to him. 'When I first went [to Paris] with the idea that the American officer had then, which he acquired from headlines in the press, that the American Navy was the hottest stuff that ever came down the pike, that every ship that we built was the last expression of naval architecture, and that our personnel was the best in the world — when I went over to the other side, I got acquainted with the French Navy, and the British Navy, and, God Help our Souls, the Russian Navy, too, I found that we were not in it at all, either in design or in marksmanship, and I made report after report.'

The noise of these reports was muffled in the long corridors of the Department after 1898, for Theodore Roosevelt was no longer there to amplify the sound. He was resting as patiently as possible in the lonely seclusion that surrounds an American Vice-President-elect as Sims stepped on the deck of the *Kentucky* at Gibraltar. One year later, almost to the day, the two were once again in correspondence. The knowledge Sims had acquired as a Naval Attaché was then combined with the power Mr. Roosevelt had assumed through a strange destiny, and the shock of the combination shattered the tranquillity of the United States Navy.[1]

[1] The material on Sims' personal life in this chapter is taken from the Sims papers and from letters written by men who knew him at the time. The correspondence with Theodore Roosevelt and Mahan is also in the Sims papers. Some of Sims' reports and a little material on his activities during the Spanish-American War can be found in the Navy Department Archives. Two volumes of his official letters for this period are in the files of the Secretary of the Navy in the National Archives.

PART TWO

The Years of Achievement

Above all things, let us not regard loyalty as a personal matter. It is due to our organization and our country under all circumstances and under all possible conditions. No faults on the part of superiors can excuse any failure in loyalty upon our part. This is easy to say but sometimes very difficult to live up to.

WILLIAM S. SIMS *in lecture on Military Character, 1916*

6

The United States Navy in 1900

THE United States Navy is the sum of diverse parts. There is the vast accumulation of material: ships, dockyards, bases, distributed over the face of the earth. There is the personnel, a large body of men skilled in particular techniques and controlled by the disciplines of a profession. There is finally the Navy Department, an elaborate organ of administration designed to direct the activities of the personnel and to ensure the continued maintenance of the physical property. These three elements in combination are the naval establishment of the United States, which exists for the purpose of waging successful war. Its final form, as an organization, is conditioned by this end; to understand its peculiar characteristics, it is necessary first to comprehend the eccentric nature of war itself.

Unlike most human endeavors, war is purely destructive. Its tools are weapons intended to annihilate, but equally subject to annihilation. In time of peace a naval establishment must maintain its material, but it must also be prepared to replace the sudden losses of the day of battle. At all times, in peace as in war, it is confronted by a kind of obsolescence more swift than time alone can bring. A new invention can shorten the effective life of an old weapon. A gun that is outranged by a newer gun loses much of its decisive striking power. Armor impervious to fifteen-inch shell is perfection while there are only fifteen-inch guns in the world; let there be more powerful guns and such armor might fail to prevent serious damage. A naval establishment must be organized in recognition of these necessities of rapid replacement and continued improvement of its material.

War is likewise an abnormal phenomenon; its occasions are infrequent; its duration uncertain; its demands are never constant or easily calculated. Therefore, a navy must be designed for needs which are real but which in normal times can only be assumed. The personnel must be trained in a profession the final object of which they seldom pursue. The officers of administration must forever nourish an initiative and resolution never required by the simple maintenance of existing equipment. Throughout a period of peace, the naval establishment must strive to create by artificial means the actual conditions of war.

Finally, war is not an end in itself, but in the famous phrase of Clausewitz, 'a continuation of policy by other means.' No naval establishment, therefore, should be an independent organism, but an instrument of the state subject to the desires of the national will. As a natural consequence, since both naval and political interests can claim a voice in the control of the Navy, the field of administration is divided into areas of professional and lay authority. The outlying regions of control are clearly defined but there is a middle ground common to both where the separate jurisdictions join, influence, and sometimes oppose each other. Some means must be discovered, in the successful naval establishment, to dispel confusion and provide coherence within this region of contact and doubt.

The central task imposed upon our naval organization by the nature of war is that of reconciling conflicting opposites. While existing material must be jealously watched over, it must also at times be recklessly destroyed and immediately replaced. The security of peace can be employed only for continuous preparation for the hazards of war. The profession especially instructed to understand the Navy's complicated machinery must share ultimate control with a group that ordinarily penetrates few of the mysteries of that profession. All these opposites must be embraced, all differences, whether of interest or opinion, must be reconciled, and yet that singularity of purpose and rapidity of action without which the life of the country would be endangered must be maintained. It will be well to bear in mind the complex nature of this task throughout the ensuing discussion of the United States Navy in 1900.[1]

MATERIAL

There were in the regular United States Navy in 1900 two hundred and fifty-four ships built, building, and authorized.[2] Eighteen were battleships, of which seven were in commission. Carrying in most cases four twelve- or thirteen-inch guns and eight eight-inch guns upon a displacement of about eleven thousand tons, these vessels were described in the official phrase as 'seagoing coastline battleships.' This confusing definition is a reflection of the confusion of American naval thought on questions of tactics and strategy at the end of the nineteenth century. The capital-ship theory of Mahan, with its emphasis upon the command of the sea, had not yet been completely accepted. Trust was still placed in 'passive defense' operations carried out close to our own shores.[3] As a consequence, our battleships were well gunned and heavily armored, but they were slow and incapable of extended cruises away from their bases. Likewise, they lacked sufficient freeboard to permit them to fight in heavy weather on the open sea.

Behind the biggest ships came the cruisers, armored, sheathed, and protected. Of all types there was a total of thirty-five, twenty of which were in actual existence. Smaller by three or four thousand tons than the battleships, they mounted main batteries of eight- and six-inch guns, supported by a secondary battery of rapid-fire guns. These numerous vessels cruised independently in time of peace and were expected, in the days of war, to harass and destroy enemy commerce on their solitary raiding activities. In a sense, in 1900 they were the main body

[1] For an illuminating discussion of naval administration see A. T. Mahan, 'The Principles of Naval Administration, Historically Considered,' *The National Review*, June, 1903. This essay also appears in the same author's *Naval Administration and Warfare*, Boston, 1908. A reading will reveal how greatly I am indebted to Mahan for both information and conclusions upon matters relating to this subject.

[2] All of the statistics for the United States Navy which follow were taken from *Annual Reports of the Navy Department for the Year 1900*, Washington, 1900.

[3] An interesting discussion of the changing theories of naval strategy from 1885 to 1900 can be found in Harold and Margaret Sprout's, *The Rise of American Naval Power*, Princeton, New Jersey, 1939, pp. 190–213.

of the Fleet, for the Civil War had apparently proved that the easiest way to defeat a nation was to bleed it to death by cutting the arteries of commerce.

It was understood that while these cruising raiders pursued their object it would be necessary to defend the home coast. To provide such defense ten monitors (four building) were available to supplement the work of the battleships. These monitors, small-tonnage, low-freeboard vessels mounting two to four ten- to twelve-inch guns, were expected in time of war to lie in the harbors and blast away at an invading force. They represent a vestigial remain of the body of the Civil War Fleet already rendered obsolete by the demands of modern strategy.

Lesser ships of great number were divided into several classes: forty-four gunboats (one building), thirty-five torpedo boats (fourteen building), sixteen torpedo-boat destroyers (all building), eight submarines (seven building). Of the remaining eighty-eight vessels, thirty-seven were unfit for modern warfare, and thirty-nine were tugs. There was one dynamite vessel, the *Vesuvius*, which had proved to be a costly, unsatisfactory experiment during her service in the Spanish-American War; one training ship for enlisted men; one dispatch vessel, the *Dolphin*, of the new Navy of the eighties; eight Civil War monitors; and one armored ram. The grand total of all these naval units was two hundred and fifty-four. Ninety-eight ships were in condition to wage a modern war, thirty-two were unfit for such purpose, while one hundred and twenty-four were either authorized by Congress or already in the course of construction.

This great armada was divided, for purposes of administration, among five stations: the Asiatic, North Atlantic, South Atlantic, Pacific, and European. On these stations ships were technically based, but the vessels did not operate together. Cruises were taken singly and fleet manoeuvres were almost unknown. In Rear Admiral Henry Clay Taylor's phrase of 1902, 'We have been a Navy of single ships and will not be strong until we learn to think in squadrons.'

There were eight yards and dry docks in the United States to build and maintain these ships. Seven were placed along the Atlantic coast from Maine to Florida, the eighth was on the Pacific at Mare Island, California. At each of these there was a

U.S.S. Constellation, 1794. One of the first six frigates of the United States Navy. The ship on which Sims took his summer cruise while at Annapolis

U.S.S. Tennessee, 1863. Displacement: 4105 tons; length: 335 feet; speed: 11 knots. 'She had a short life, but, as a consumer of money, a brilliant one.'

U.S.S. Swatara, 1872. Third-rate, ship-rigged sloop-of-war. Displacement: 1900 tons; length: 245 feet; speed: 10.5 knots. Main Battery: six nine-inch muzzle-loading smoothbores, one eight-inch pivot rifle

U.S.S. Philadelphia, 1888. Protected cruiser. Displacement: 4342 tons; length: 327 feet; speed: 19.6 knots. Main Battery: twelve six-inch guns

U.S.S Monterey, 1889. Coast defense barbette monitor. Displacement: 4084 tons; length: 256 feet; speed: 14 knots. Main Battery: two twelve-inch and two ten-inch guns. 'The *U.S.S. Terror-of-the-Far-East.* She is a double-elliptical, high-uffen-buffen, double-turreted, back-acting, submarine War junk.'

U.S.S. Brooklyn, 1893. Protected cruiser. Displacement: 9215 tons; length: 400 feet; speed: 21 knots. Main Battery: eight eight-inch guns

U.S.S. Kentucky, 1896. Battleship. Displacement: 11,500 tons; length: 368 feet; speed: 16 knots. Main Battery: four thirteen-inch and four eight-inch guns

U.S.S. Minnesota, 1903. Battleship. Displacement: 16,000 tons; length: 450 feet; speed: 18 knots. Main Battery: four twelve-inch and eight eight-inch guns

U.S.S. Nevada, 1912. Battleship. Displacement: 27,500 tons; length: 575 feet; speed: 20.5 knots. Main Battery: ten fourteen-inch guns

The United States Naval War College, Newport, Rhode Island

U.S.S. Parker, 1912. Destroyer. Displacement: 1036 tons; length: 300 feet; speed: 30 knots. Armament: four four-inch guns and eight eighteen-inch torpedo tubes

U.S.S. Sims, 1937. Destroyer. Displacement: 1570 tons; speed: 36.5 knots. Armament: five five-inch guns and twelve twenty-one-inch torpedo tubes. Sunk by enemy action in the Battle of the Coral Sea, May, 1942

In Command of the Flotilla

On the *Minnesota*

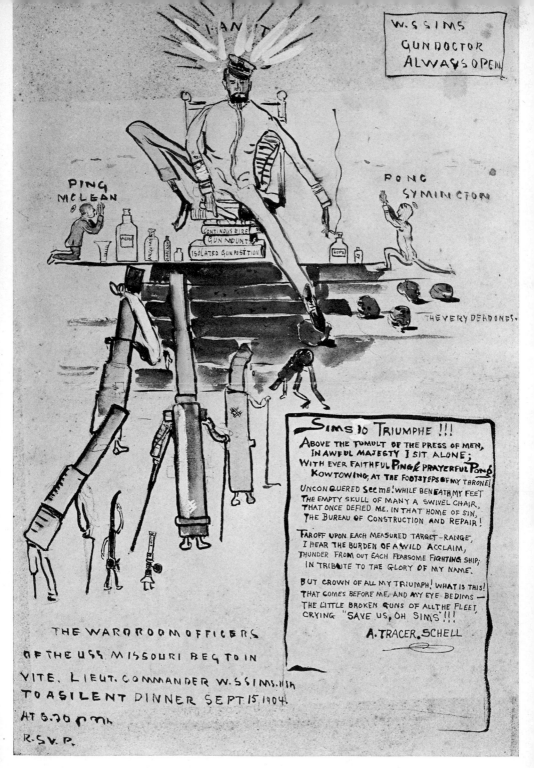

An Invitation for the Inspector of Target Practice, 1904

regular force of officers and men to perform the necessary work under the supervision of an Admiral who was in charge of the naval district.

In addition to these eight major yards, there were about twenty minor pay, coaling, and training stations scattered along our coastline or planted on our island possessions. But there were also other shore establishments of some magnitude: the Academy at Annapolis, the Observatory in Washington, the Gun Factory and the Proving Grounds at Indian Head, the Torpedo Station at Newport, and the Naval Home at Philadelphia. Added to these were the recruiting offices, hospitals, and dispensaries. There were too inspectors at shipyards, steelworks, and powder factories. In physical terms alone, the Navy of 1900 was a vast enterprise costing the American people some sixty-seven million dollars annually to maintain. In fact, it was so large that it could not be operated efficiently with the available man-power.

PERSONNEL

In his report for the year 1900, the Chief of the Bureau of Navigation was reluctantly forced to admit that 'Were the fleet to be manned with full complements as it would necessarily be if called upon to fight a first-class European power, the present personnel would form barely one-fourth of the total establishment.'

This serious lack of man-power was and continued to be for many years a source of inefficiency within the Navy and of grave danger to our national defense, but some small comfort could always be drawn from the quality of the men themselves. As late as the eighties of the past century, many of our enlisted force had been foreign-born or alien. But with the establishment of the new Navy and with the disappearance of sail, more and more native-born Americans entered the ranks. By 1900, 68 per cent of the 16,832 enlisted men had been born in this country, while only about 7 per cent retained their foreign citizenship. On the whole, the sailors were an efficient force fulfilling with skill the technical requirements of a craft that had changed greatly from the days of sail. But there were disturbing indications that their morale was not as high as it should have been. The Bureau of Navigation was forced to report that in 1899 there had been 2202 desertions, and this must suggest a considerable degree of dissatisfaction with the sailor's lot. Some undoubtedly deserted because they discovered after a few weeks that they were not fitted for life in the Navy, but many others departed illegally because of the severe disciplinary system then in use. Though the older, rigorous methods of punishment had largely disappeared with the disappearance of sail, still the regulations under which men worked were confining and observance of them was strictly enforced. The Navy did little to soften the hard demands of routine or lighten the hours of boredom on ship; there were no moving pictures in 1900 as there are every night now; the food was bad compared with the present day; and liberty was granted less frequently.

The enlisted force was under the command of 1683 commissioned officers, a body of men organized, trained, and skilled in a separate profession, but presenting no close analogy to the military castes of Europe.[4] In the old world, officers were almost a class of society, distinct from the rest of the world in their beliefs, manners, and habits of thought. From father to son the patrimony of militarism was bequeathed and maintained in its classic form through generations. The result was inevitable — the profession became in fact a caste, self-conscious and highly articulate, observing those beyond its confines with contempt and suspicion, while jealously guarding its own conventions and traditions. So well organized and disciplined was this group, and possessed of such vitality, that it became in time an influential factor in the life of a nation — a force in society and in government.

In navies it is more difficult, for a variety of reasons, to create such an élite corps than it is in armies, but it is almost impossible to conceive of one in the United States Navy. Our officers in 1900, as at present, were gathered together from all parts of the country and from every social class. Inclination, poverty, and the haphazard selective methods of congressional appointment all combined to recruit a heterogeneous collection of young men.

[4] Notice that the ratio of officers to men was almost exactly one to ten. In 1939, there were 10,597 officers and 110,187 enlisted men.

Certain factors united to bind them together — common under-graduate memories, naval traditions, similar training, the problems, techniques, and standards of a profession, the apathy and occasional suspicion of the nation which they served. But their diverse origins and temperaments and their allegiance, as a group, to the democratic process prevented them, and there is every reason to believe always will prevent them, from devel-oping that peculiar professional attitude and philosophy of which they are often accused.

Still they possessed, and fortunately, a professional morale, founded upon a sense of duty, nourished in the camaraderies of the wardroom, and, in 1900, invigorated by the recent victory over Spain. But during the period under review there did exist one serious cause of dissatisfaction within the commissioned ranks, the source of which was the system of promotion by senior-ity then in use. A law of 1899 had been passed to improve con-ditions, but it did little to alter the basic principle of seniority as the main criterion of advancement. To understand this prin-ciple one must first understand the way in which the corps of officers was organized.

The regular grades of the Navy arranged in the descending order of their importance are as follows: Rear Admiral, Captain, Commander, Lieutenant Commander, Lieutenant, Lieutenant junior grade, and Ensign.[5] Each of these seven ranks is limited in number by law. The same law specified the period in years during which an officer must remain in a particular grade before becoming eligible for promotion. The length of tenure in each grade is the same — seven years in 1900 — but the number of officers in each grade is quite different. There are naturally few men at the top — that is, Admirals — and many officers at the bottom — Ensigns and Lieutenants. The defect in this structure is discovered in the fact that all officers, before 1899, who did not retire voluntarily or were forced to resign because of physical disability, became in the fullness of time Admirals.

The method by which this highest rank in the Navy was reached was called promotion by seniority, which operated in

---

[5] In 1900 there were no regular grades of Admiral and Vice Admiral, though George Dewey held the specially created rank of Admiral of the Navy for his life-time. The grade of Commodore was discontinued in 1912.

the following fashion. When a midshipman graduated from Annapolis he was given a certain position in his class determined solely by his record at the Academy for the four preceding years. Throughout his career he maintained this same relative place in his class, but advanced up the Navy List as a whole and from grade to grade only as vacancies were created ahead of him through death or retirement. An officer could voluntarily retire after thirty years' service or he could be compelled to retire for reasons of physical disability. In any case an officer was automatically retired by law at the age of sixty-two.[6]

There were many grave disadvantages in this system, some accidental and temporary, others inherent and permanent. Of the former almost all were the result of the Civil War, during which young officers were rapidly advanced. After the conflict these officers continued to live into a tranquil old age in their abnormally high positions, thus blocking off the promotion of the men below who were forced to wait for the death of those above. So badly had the system jammed that in 1896 there were still in the service Lieutenants who had entered it in the Civil War. Even in normal times it was inevitable that advancement would be exasperatingly slow, for the Admirals at the top created a bottleneck through which it was difficult for each man in the progressively larger grades below to pass. Some idea of how effective this bottleneck was can be gained from the fact that frequently men arrived at the highest grade in the Navy only on the day of their retirement.

Distressing results were everywhere apparent. When a man could have the comfortable assurance of becoming an Admiral if, in the favorite phrase, he avoided crime, refrained from hitting an officer, and lived long enough, he would naturally confine his energies to the pursuance of these three negative ends. If mediocrity and occasional incompetence were treated with the same respect as was manifest ability, it was inevitable that initiative and independent activity would be considered almost as a positive danger. Finally, by this system of promotion, men were brought to responsible commands only after years in subordinate

[6] A fuller discussion of the method of promotion will be found in C. O. Paullin, 'Naval Administration in America, 1861–1911,' *The United States Naval Institute Proceedings*, vol. 40, May–June, 1914. *The United States Naval Institute Proceedings* is hereafter referred to as *N.I.P.*

grades at an age when they were ill-equipped to assume the great burdens of their positions.

The Personnel Act of 1899, framed upon the recommendations of a board under the chairmanship of Theodore Roosevelt, sought to improve these unhealthy conditions.[7] By its terms, the Secretary was authorized to keep a list of applications for voluntary retirement and 'in case the number of vacancies for each year in specified grades did not equal certain specified numbers, the President was authorized to select from the list of applicants the requisite number of officers and retire them.' If, however, the desired number of vacancies was not created in this way, a board was convened to select the required number of officers for retirement. To soften the blow, those leaving the service either voluntarily or under compulsion were given a pension of three-quarters of the total pay of the next higher rank. The board thus established remained in existence for eighteen years, until the whole system of promotion was altered in 1916.

It will be realized that this law of 1899 eradicated one of the evils of the existing method of promotion, for in cutting out the deadwood of the service it relieved the Navy of the most undesirable officers and also increased the rapidity of advancement. Still, promotion was a very gradual process during the next twenty years, for while 'the plucking board,' as it was called, was reducing the number passing through the bottleneck at the top, the larger classes yearly graduated from Annapolis were broadening the base at the bottom. But there was a more fundamental defect in the law of 1899: it eliminated the most incapable, but it did not provide for the selection and rapid advance of the most efficient. In accomplishing its negative purpose it disgraced the unfortunate without inspiring the able. In so doing, it encouraged the rule of the mediocre.

ADMINISTRATION

Two factors determine the characteristics of the system of

---

[7] An analysis of the bill and its effects is contained in Lieutenant E. L. Beach, 'Results of the Navy Personnel Law of March 3, 1899,' *N.I.P.*, vol. 28, June, 1902. Likewise see C. O. Paullin, *op. cit.*, p. 673 f.; John D. Long, *The New American Navy*, New York, 1903, pp. 81–88. The bill itself can be found in Sen. Doc. 418, 65th Congress, 3d Session.

naval administration in use in the United States.[8] The first is the dual nature of its objective and the second is the presence within the system of three distinct elements of control. Of the first factor Alfred Thayer Mahan many years ago provided a most illuminating description. With the aid of a Napoleonic aphorism, he suggested that a naval administration directs a force which must concentrate in order to fight and disperse in order to subsist. Since war is a military function while the method of subsistence is civil in character, the problem, he concluded, is one of 'embracing opposites.' Any successful system of administration must contain within itself the machinery to reconcile these two opposing forces. In addition, it must bring into combination the three elements which can claim an interest in the Navy — that is, the professional who fights the ships, the civilian who superintends the maintenance of the establishment, and the politician who represents the people for whom the Navy exists. The total organization is constructed upon considerations of equilibrium. Always the separate identity of the ends — of fighting and of mere existence — must be distinguished, the demands of both must be fulfilled, and the pursuit of the one must never prevent the attainment of the other. Within the Department itself the presence of the three interests, professional, civil, and political, must be recognized, the influence of each must be permitted to operate, and the predominance of any one avoided. Here, in the region of authority, it is imperative to establish a balance between the parts that will result not in a dead centre, but in the frictionless operation of the administrative machinery.

After several attempts to provide our Navy with an adequate administration, the Department was reorganized for the last time in 1842. In that year, a system was devised which existed until 1915, altered occasionally in form but unchanged in fundamental principle. The discussion that follows limits itself to the conditions of 1900, but it can be considered in general as applying to the conditions which have prevailed throughout the last century.

[8] Students especially interested in the problems of naval administration in the United States at this time are referred to John D. Long, *op. cit.*, vol. 1, chapters 3 and 4; C. O. Paullin's series of articles, 'Naval Administration in America,' *N.I.P.*, vols. 38, 39, and 40; A. T. Mahan, 'The United States Navy Department,' *Naval Administration and Warfare*, Boston, 1908.

The chief officer of administration in 1900 was the Secretary of the Navy, a member of the Cabinet appointed by the President of the United States. Professionally, his personality was split into many fractions. As a member of the Administration, he was the symbol of the National Government's control of the armed forces; by his existence alone he demonstrated the truth of the fact that the Navy was the servant of the people. As the responsible director of a military establishment, he superintended the operations of the Fleet — a professional activity carried out in his name by the officers afloat; and as the executive head, he also directed the maintenance of the Navy — a civil occupation, conditioned as Mahan has suggested by a military end. This work of maintenance covered a broad field of endeavor — too large for any single man to control — and so the civil duties of the Secretary, which in theory were concentrated in his person, were in practice divided among bureaus under the supervision of naval officers responsible to the Secretary.

It was this division of labor which was the great contribution of the law of 1842. By its terms, all of the goods and services required to keep the Navy in being were supplied by the activities of the separate bureaus, each charged with the responsibility for some particular contribution. Thus was recognized the principle of dispersion in order to subsist. In 1900, there were eight bureaus: Yards and Docks, Construction and Repair, Steam Engineering, Ordnance, Equipment, Supplies and Accounts, Medicine and Surgery, and the powerful Bureau of Navigation, in charge of personnel and the movements of ships. In the performance of his duty, each bureau chief acted with the authority of the Secretary, and each, except the Chief of the Bureau of Navigation, was engaged in a pursuit essentially civil in character.

The system had many advantages. The several specialized goods and services which contribute to the maintenance of a navy were distributed among the departments best equipped by experience and training to produce them. The chief executive officer, the Secretary, was relieved of the burden of superintending a multitude of particular operations and enabled to concentrate upon his general administrative duties. The areas of civilian and professional control were so clearly defined by law

71

that it appeared impossible for confusion or conflict to result. But there was also one defect which, always inherent in the structure, had been clearly revealed in the Civil War and again in the Spanish-American War.

Individually, the bureaus performed their duties admirably, but it proved difficult for several reasons to coordinate their activities properly. Each bureau chief, while responsible to the Secretary, was independent of his colleagues. Likewise each, though a naval officer, was also a human being, and thus, though theoretically concerned primarily with fulfilling the needs of the Navy, he sometimes in practice was more impressed by the immediate demands of his own division. Furthermore, while the official charged with the responsibility of bringing the work of the bureaus into combination — that is, the Secretary — was provided with the necessary authority, he frequently, as a layman, lacked the knowledge to do so. Proper coordination of the Department depended in large part upon the Secretary's understanding of the military necessities of the naval establishment, but no proper arrangement was made within the system for providing him with such information. By law, his only advisers were the bureau chiefs, and also by law these men were charged, not with the military requirements of the Navy, but with the civil operation of their own bureaus. Thus, as Mahan suggested, they were more advocates for the parts than advisers on the condition of the whole. The failure of the system lay in the fact that while it provided adequately, even very successfully, for dispersion in order to subsist, it failed to make provision for that concentration which is necessary to fight. The result was a tendency to maintain the Navy, not through the operation of subordinate bodies subject to the requirements of a military end, but through the activities of several independent and unregulated organizations concerned chiefly with their lay purposes.

Naturally this defect became most apparent in time of war. During the struggle with Spain it had been found necessary to appoint a Policy Board to plan the strategy and coordinate the work of the bureaus. With the termination of hostilities this board ceased to exist, though a desire for its continuance was expressed in some quarters. A few far-sighted men recognized that the Navy, if it was to operate effectively in time of war, needed some instrument capable of producing a military policy which would govern its actions in the days of peace. This instrument, a Policy Board or a Navy Council or a General Staff, in the opinion of these men, could alone divert the energies of the naval establishment from the methods of maintenance to the grand end of battle.

Most prominent among those who struggled for the establishment of such a permanently constituted body was Rear Admiral Henry Clay Taylor, a man whose services are still too little recognized and valued by his country. In 1899, he presented to Secretary Long a memorandum embodying his plan for such a board. It was, in his mind, to be a body of professional sailors enjoying a legal and perpetual existence, entrusted with all the duties of a General Staff. In part, his suggestions were heeded — to the extent that a General Board composed of naval officers was created in 1900, but it was not granted the wide powers Taylor had desired nor was it given existence independent of the Secretary. It was appointed by the Secretary to 'insure the efficient preparation of the fleet in case of war and in defense of the coast,' and it was expected to make battle plans and draw up specifications for the designs of our ships. There was, however, a fatal weakness in its powers; for it could only advise the Secretary and the bureau chiefs; its military recommendations could be disregarded with impunity.

The reason why this limitation of power was prescribed is not without interest. Lay opinion held in that time, as it does today, that such a professional body would dominate the Navy Department, enfeeble the Secretary, and establish a group of war lords that would inevitably undermine civilian control of the military arm. It was better, in the popular opinion, to possess a navy with no real military direction than to establish one beyond the reach of lay authority. Had this been the choice, popular opinion would certainly have been correct, but the alternatives as thus presented suggest a conscious or unconscious confusion. The General Board proposed by Admiral Taylor was subordinate to the Secretary, who could refuse to accept the advice it offered if he so desired. Taylor was anxious primarily to give it a permanent existence by law instead of by secretarial appointment; to make it responsible for its advice; and to make the

Secretary and the bureaus equally responsible for refusing to accept the Board's recommendations. Such responsibility the then Secretary was unwilling to extend.

One final administrative body remains to be investigated — the committees of Congress which supplied money to maintain the establishment. These committees represented the people's interest in the Navy. They received the budget of the Secretary, considered it, and voted for it if they found it good. They investigated the condition of the Navy, looked into its organization, framed legislation affecting it. Because they held the purse-strings and because they possessed the ultimate power to alter the Navy's structure by legislation, they were a determining factor in its existence. And because they were politicians and also laymen, they expressed in general the popular attitude toward the Navy, occasionally misunderstanding its needs and intentions.

The President of the United States, who by the Constitution was the Commander-in-Chief; the Secretary, who by law was his representative; the bureau chiefs, the General Board, the committees of Congress, together ruled the Navy. By conference, argument, and investigation they acquired a common knowledge and purpose which enabled them to pool their separate interests for the maintenance of the naval establishment. Occasionally, of course, the prejudices or desires of the civilian Secretary, the professional sailor, and the political committeeman would conflict. At such times unity could be restored only by compromise. This is the essence of our democratic system by which agreement is obtained through the concessions of sovereign interests; it was natural that the administration of the Navy should take its form from the government of our country. But because knowledge and power were unevenly distributed between the three great elements which united in control, the policies produced were sometimes shaped less in accordance with naval requirements than as a compromise upon which all could agree.

In terms of ships and men and organization, such was our Navy in 1900, but statistics or analyses which are limited to any one year do not reveal its most significant characteristic. It must be remembered that from 1898 until the World War the Navy was rapidly expanding. The long interval after 1865, during which our deteriorating forces were neglected by a nation weary of war, had no counterpart in the years following 1898. Our easy victory over Spain obtained for us far-flung imperial possessions and produced in the people an exalted mood. At Manila and Santiago the guns had ripped apart the veil behind which our manifest destiny lay hidden. Light-heartedly we accepted the new responsibilities that were revealed. We knew little of the nature of imperial problems, but we knew enough to understand that the security of empire rests upon a battle line of ships. Inevitably, therefore, the Navy began to grow.

Throughout its long existence the Navy has been subject to similar moments of sudden expansion, followed in the course of time by equally sudden but more prolonged intervals of contraction. It has waxed as the national tide rose to enthusiasm and waned when the same tide ebbed to apathy. Theoretically, of course, such spasms should be impossible. The size and nature of our Navy should be conditioned by the character of the foreign policy it is designed to implement — by threat or actual force. But in practice such has not been the case because rarely have we, as a nation, possessed a coherent and well-defined foreign policy. Catch phrases have served as the basis for our building programs: the Navy will be second to none, or it will be big enough for both oceans — but it will not have a base in Guam because that would antagonize Japan. Even in 1900 the white man's burden was more a moral obligation than a problem of diplomacy.

Much that follows in this book can only be explained in terms of this sudden, almost unpremeditated growth. Our little Navy, before the Spanish-American War, had pursued, almost forgotten, the tranquil rounds of peace. Many of the ships were old, while the new ones reflected in their design the uncertainties produced by the transition from sail to steam. The officers and men who operated the vessels were too few in number even for the existing Fleet. Two wars had proved the inadequacies of the system of administration. Upon this unsubstantial foundation the country sought to erect a Navy adequate to defend the interests of a world power. With what measure of success this effort was attended was revealed in 1918. But in the process of construction errors were committed, mistaken policies pursued, and unexpected weaknesses in the organization appeared. The burden of many of the following pages must consist of a discussion of these errors, policies, and weaknesses; for with the improvement of the Navy, Sims was primarily concerned, in all that part of his naval career which is still to be recorded.

7

1900 - 1901 *The China Station*

IF ALL books were biographies perhaps Calvinism would be the true religion, for the lives of great men often appear to remind us only that sublimity is predestined. The heroes, on paper, perform expected tasks, repeat familiar phrases, pursue only the appointed rounds. Watching these dead men caught fast in a web of accomplished fact, one is tempted to believe the Greeks were wrong; that in history, not in character, can destiny be read. Artificial though this determinism may be, it is yet extraordinarily convincing. There would be something horrifying in a biography of Theodore Roosevelt which permitted him to retire to private life in 1905 after four successful but quiet years as the Vice-President of the United States.

Biographers must weave the pattern of a man's life from the established facts. In our concern not to depart from this pattern, we come to assume that the man himself could not do so. We are even willing to go farther: to allow the end of a career to condition all the means by which it was attained. When some fortuitous circumstance has modified the course of events, it ceases to be accidental and acquires definite purpose. Logic can be discovered even in the bullet that killed McKinley. It is a fatal illusion. In every life, there must be hazard and uncertainty and the awful freedom of choice. In the affairs of men, there are chance tides rising in confusion to swell the casual eddy to the whirlpool.

Such a tide was running on the China Station in 1900 and, with that sense of timing which is the essential secret of most success, Sims was ready to take it when it reached the flood. Twenty years of patient, if unconscious, preparation for the task at hand lay behind him. Upon leaving the Academy he had been impressed with his own cultural and intellectual limitations. Only after these personal requirements were satisfied in the years of study and travel, could he turn with any interest to the demands of the service. On the *Charleston* and in Paris the nature of his work and the amazing industry with which he performed his labors enabled him to acquire an unusually thorough knowledge of naval affairs. Both personally and professionally he had approached maturity slowly, but he had possessed the wisdom to go his own gait. When in 1900 the schooling was over, he could feel sure that his education was sound. But at forty-two, an unmarried Lieutenant, the possibilities of private life and of rank temporarily exhausted, his continuous energies were forced to seek release beyond the narrow confines of routine. When fortune on the China Station placed new materials in his hands, he gladly went to work.

Sims joined the *Kentucky* at Gibraltar in November. She was a new ship commissioned only the preceding May, and with her sister, the *Kearsarge*, the pride of the Navy and the country. Displacing 11,450 tons, she measured 368 feet between perpendiculars. At her trials she had attained a speed of almost seventeen knots. Around the waterline there was an armor belt of a maximum thickness of sixteen and a half inches, while the turrets were protected by steel seventeen inches thick in some places. The armament was impressive. Her main battery was composed of four thirteen-inch, four eight-inch, and fourteen rapid-fire five-inch guns. Thirty-two guns of various calibre were contained in the secondary battery.[1] The position of the eight-inch turrets, which were placed directly upon and rigidly attached to the thirteen-inch turrets, was an innovation the value of which some observers questioned. But the Chief of the Bureau of Ordnance in 1900 stated that after firing trials no unfavorable reports had been received and he felt it safe to conclude that the vessel was 'an unqualified success.'[2] Popular opinion concurred in this professional estimate. There had been little dissent from

[1] *Annual Reports of the Navy Department for the Year 1900*, Washington, 1900, p. 736.
[2] *Ibid.*, p. 572.

the judgment of an author in *Munsey's Magazine* that the *Kentucky* and *Kearsarge* were 'the greatest fighting machines afloat.'

Since Sims had not seen an American warship in three years he was naturally much interested in this newest member of the Fleet. As the *Kentucky* moved through the Mediterranean toward Suez, he investigated her thoroughly and arrived at the conclusion that the ship was greatly inferior to European battleships of the period. One night in the wardroom he ventured to put forth several of his criticisms. 'The executive and the other officers became pale with rage in denouncing them — and me.' His remarks they thought were not only unjust and unjustifiable, but they revealed an attitude of mind which had been warped through exposure to European atmospheres. One's sympathy goes out to these officers, newly attached to the newest ship in the Navy, and the responses which followed Sims' observations are not at all surprising. But the facts were against the wardroom and in the end, 'after much discussion they were sadly obliged to acknowledge the justice of my criticisms.' [3]

During the ensuing weeks at sea, on the way to the China Station, Sims composed a report on the specific infirmities of the man-of-war. On February 2, 1901, when the *Kentucky* was in the Philippines, his work was finished and the result was forwarded through the Commanding Officer to the Navy Department.[4] In this report, Sims first attacked the machinery which was used to supply ammunition to the five-inch guns. It was, he said, so inefficient that, for want of ammunition, the guns could not be fired at their maximum rapidity as shown at the proving grounds, nor even as rapidly as 'foreign six-inch guns mounted on board ship.' Equally inadequate was the ammunition supply for the five-inch guns, and a serious defect, by foreign standards, lay in the extremely weak 'end-on fire' of the vessel. His most severe criticisms were reserved for the turrets which housed the great guns of the main battery. So large were the gunports that the probability of shells entering the turrets was very great. Since 'the loading, training, and elevating gear, the

---

[3] Undated memorandum on the *Kentucky* by W. S. S. Hereafter unless otherwise stated the documents cited will be found in the Sims papers.

[4] 'Arrangement of Magazines, Ammunition Supply and Installation of Battery, *U.S.S. Kentucky*, February 2, 1901.'

recoil system, and the ammunition hoists' were entirely unprotected, they were exposed to almost certain destruction. In addition, an open shaft for the shell and powder hoists ran straight down from the gun positions to the handling rooms below. Any spark which dropped from a gun breech would therefore fall directly into the handling room, which was adjacent to the powder magazines. As a proof of the danger inherent in this arrangement, Sims alluded to an accident on the Russian *Sissoi Veliki* that occurred during target practice. Flame from a gun which had been fired with the breech plug unlocked had singed the hair of men far below in the handling room. Only the fact that there was no powder in this room at the time prevented a catastrophe which could never have been avoided had the vessel been in action.

The report was couched in a quiet expository style; its conclusions were buttressed by frequent references to foreign battleships and the reports Sims had already made while a Naval Attaché. The mildness of tone was dictated by the necessities of official language and did not fully reflect the contempt Sims felt for the ship. Informally he gave release to feelings, never very gracefully restrained, in the observation that the '*Kentucky* is not a battleship at all. She is the worst crime in naval construction ever perpetrated by the white race.' [5]

[5] In 1925, Sims gave an investigating committee a delightful digest of this entire report.

'After I finished my tour as Naval Attaché in Paris, 1897 to 1900, they would not let me come home. They always have it in for a Naval Attaché, anyway. They think he is a sort of a pink-tea individual. Anyway, they sent me to join the *Kentucky* on the way out. I had never seen one of our battleships before. They were built while I was abroad. I was acquainted with the foreign ones. When I saw that battleship I was absolutely astounded. It is almost incredible that white men who have reached the present stage of civilization could have built a ship like that.

'Our Navy Department was so organized that the people who built the turrets were not the same people who built the guns. And the man that built the carriage the gun sat on was not coordinated with the man that built the turret, and he had a pyramidal mount that sat back so far from the front face of the turret that in order that the gun might be elevated and depressed they had to cut a hole in the front face of the turret that was big enough for four 12-inch shells to come into her without touching anything. You could stand on the quarter deck and look into that turret, and you could spit right down into the powder magazine. Now, that is a fact. You could stand in the bottom of the powder magazine, or rather, in the chamber out of the powder magazine, and looking up see a man smoking a cigarette right up on the bridge.   .   .   .   .

'A little girl was being shown about the ship. She was eleven years old, and she

In March, Sims received word that he was detached from the *Kentucky*, then at Cavite, and was ordered to report to the monitor *Monterey*, at Canton. It may be remarked parenthetically that such transfers of duty were not at all unusual in the service at this period, though such a practice was obviously detrimental to the efficiency of a ship. More than two hundred officers are reported to have passed through the cruiser *Brooklyn* in two years, about four and one-half times her normal complement of forty-six.[6] On the way to Canton, Sims broke his passage at Hong Kong, where most of the ships of the British Asiatic Fleet were stationed. While there, he met for the first time Captain, later Admiral, Sir Percy Scott.

This remarkable man had already begun his bitter journey to fame.[7] Equipped with a restless mind, he sought out many inventions, presenting his Admiralty with plans for an electric range-transmitter, a respirator for use on ships afire, and an improved signalling lamp. At the defense of Ladysmith it was his design for the mountings of 4.7-inch naval guns which ensured the relief of that beleaguered city. More permanently significant was the fact that the target-practice records of two ships under his command, the *Scylla* in 1898 and the *Terrible* in 1900, were the manifestoes of a revolution in naval gunnery; Scott with his development of the methods of continuous-aim firing was the father of that revolution.

If not a genius, as some have suggested, he at least possessed extraordinary ingenuity. His originality and initiative were the more surprising because they continued to operate in a navy where customs of the past are not infrequently mistaken for prophecies of the future. Ships, by the end of the nineteenth century, had become very delicate pieces of machinery, and he was one of the first to understand the implications of this transformation. But his greatest contributions were made in the field

walked over this gun deck where one gaping port after another was located, and she said, "I thought you told me these guns were protected by armor?" She said, "The armor is where the guns ain't." '

(*Hearing before the Select Committee of Inquiry into Operations of the United States Air Services*, House of Representatives, 68th Congress, Part 4, Washington, 1925, pp. 2977, 2978.)

[6] Philip R. Alger, 'Gunnery in Our Navy,' *N.I.P.*, Prize Essay, 1903, p. 27 n.

[7] For a fascinating account of Scott's career see his *Fifty Years in the Royal Navy*, New York, 1919. It is a full though rather intemperate story of his efforts at reform.

of gunnery, where what had been an art was changed, by the force of his theories, into a science. Yet always the path of success was made painful for him by the fact that his intelligence outran the collective wit of the Admiralty, which appears, if his memoirs are correct, to have made almost a career of opposing his suggestions. Even when his proposals were belatedly accepted, as they usually were, he derived only a kind of sour satisfaction from this tardy recognition, for his irascible brilliance enabled him to achieve success without enjoying it.

Whatever the cause — some said it was 'rum and bad manners' — his later life had something of the pathos of frustration in it. His King made him a baronet, but the suggestions he sent to the Admiralty were never received with the respect he believed they deserved. In 1909 there was a quarrel with that ambitious officer, Lord Charles Beresford, and though the cause was slight, the attending publicity reached 'even to the Dominions.' Hardly had the echoes of this altercation died away before Scott's name was again notoriously in the papers when his wife brought suit for divorce. When the case was settled, he retired from the Navy before his time was up, though he returned to serve during the World War. At Jutland the cup was filled when his sixteen-year-old son went down with a cruiser which Scott felt, quite correctly, was inadequately prepared to take up battle, in part because she lacked the system of director firing that he had recommended. For the great services he rendered he might have been dealt with more kindly, but perhaps, save on the Jutland Bank, he was only made to pay the penalties of his personality. In the pictures of his round, well-proportioned face, with its neat Van Dyke and large clear eyes, he seems a powerful, proud, almost disdainful man. From the embittered pages of his book one can guess he was a lonely one. 'Ubi saeva indignatio ulterius cor lacerare nequit,' reads the epitaph of Jonathan Swift; and now Sir Percy Scott has joined the Dean 'where savage indignation no longer tears the heart.'

The world's records of the *Scylla* and the *Terrible* were the result of Scott's development of the method of continuous-aim firing by which the most important error of gunfire at sea was eliminated. Before 1898 gunners had simply set their sights and waited for the roll of the ship to bring the gun on the target.

The source of inaccuracy in this procedure lay chiefly in what is known as the firing interval of the gunner; that is, the period during which the impulse or will to fire is translated into the act of firing. To ensure an aim that was true, the gunner had to estimate his own firing interval and then compensate for it by willing to fire an equivalent period before the rolling ship brought the sights on the target. Scott eliminated all the uncertainties of this system by devising a method of maintaining the sights on the target throughout the roll.

His discovery that such a thing was possible was almost accidental. On the *Scylla* in 1898 he had greatly improved the marksmanship of the gunners by replacing the old open sights with telescope sights.[8] Thus equipped, the 4.7-inch guns had proved to be very accurate in smooth water, but one day when practice was held in a rough sea the shooting was very poor. Only one man seemed to be able to fire anywhere near the target. Scott 'watched this one man . . . very carefully and saw that he could work his elevating wheel with such dexterity and speed as to keep his sight steady on the target notwithstanding the roll of the ship.' What one man did unconsciously, thought Scott, all men could be taught to do, and he devised a method by which his gunners could be instructed in continuous-aim firing.[9]

At Hong Kong, Sims learned from Scott and other British officers all he could about the special methods and mechanisms used in training gunners to fire throughout the roll of a ship. The information thus obtained he incorporated in his second report.[10] In the opening paragraph of this report on the *Terrible's* target practice, the significance of her record was emphasized by the statement that the *Terrible* was twenty per cent better

[8] Scott himself was not responsible for the introduction of telescope sights. As early as 1891, Bradley A. Fiske of the United States Navy had designed such a sight which in 1892 was given a trial on the *Yorktown*. At this time the instrument failed to impress the Commanding Officer, Robley D. Evans, the famous 'Fighting Bob,' who reported that 'In its present shape it is of no value on board ship.' The telescope sight of the United States Navy remained, until 1904, experimental and unsatisfactory; Fiske's part in its development has never been adequately recognized. The story is well told in his *From Midshipman to Rear Admiral*, New York, 1919, pp. 127, 171, 177, 213. Those anxious to obtain more detailed information about the value and development of the telescope sight in our Navy should consult Lieutenant Joseph Strauss, 'Telescope Sights for Guns,' *N.I.P.*, vol. 22, 1896.

[9] Admiral Sir Percy Scott, *op. cit.*, p. 96.

[10] 'The Remarkable Record Target Practice, *H.M.S. Terrible*,' March 15, 1901.

than the average of six other English ships in the matter of total number of hits out of the rounds fired at target practice. One hundred and four shots had been fired, of which eighty had found the target. This record was the more remarkable when the conditions of the practice were considered. The *Terrible*, moving at a speed of twelve knots, had fired at a target sixteen feet high by twenty feet long at ranges varying from 1130 to 1600 yards, roughly from three-quarters of a mile to a mile. Each gun fired two minutes — one minute for each of the two gun captains. The results had been verified by umpires selected from the Fleet. The six best gun captains had performed in spectacular fashion, making thirty-two hits out of thirty-four shots for an average of 5.33 hits per minute. For the period this was an incredible record for six-inch guns.

The secret of this success lay partly in the extremely efficient elevating gear of the British ships which 'allowed the pointer to keep his line of sight constantly on the target throughout the roll.' Sims described this gear at some length, for he believed that our own elevating mechanism was not designed to permit continuous-aim firing. The accuracy of the *Terrible's* guns was explained partly, too, by the telescope sights used. They were more powerful than their American equivalents, but their chief superiority was in the way they were mounted on the gun. The British pointer could hold his eye constantly against the eyepiece of the telescope throughout the recoil of the gun, since the eyepiece was protected by a heavy rubber cushion, while the American gunner, during the recoil, had to withdraw his eye or run the risk of severe injury.

From the machinery, Sims turned to the man behind the gun who 'required long and continuous practice [in keeping] the telescope constantly on the target.' This practice was obtained through the use of a contrivance called a 'dotter,' invented by Scott, which enabled gun captains to simulate firing their guns while the ship was in port under conditions not unlike those attending shooting in rough water.[11] At sea, motion was sup-

---

[11] 'Invented' is perhaps too strong a word. Dotters, or their very crude equivalent, had been in use for over fifty years in both the English and French navies, as Alger points out in his *Gunnery in Our Navy*, p. 43. These early devices, however, were designed only to train a man to estimate his 'firing interval,' and could not be used to teach continuous-aim firing, which was then, of course, unknown.

plied by the rolling of the vessel, but in port this condition was artificially produced by a moving target in the following fashion. Directly in front of the muzzle of a gun a small paper target was rigged which moved up and down when a crank was turned. On the muzzle of the gun itself there was a pencil which 'dotted' the target when pulled forward by a small electro-magnet. This magnet was, in turn, excited by an electric impulse set off when the firing key of the gun was pressed. In operation, one man turned the crank which moved the target vertically. Another, the gun captain, tried to follow the motion of the target by elevating and depressing his gun. When the sights were on the target, he pressed the firing button, which excited the magnet that drew the pencil forward. After dotting the target, the pencil, actuated by an escapement not unlike that on a typewriter, sprang back and to the right. When the gun was fired again, therefore, the pencil dotted a little to the right of its previous position. Each gunner fired for one minute and at the rate of about seven shots a minute. If all seven shots were hits, the target would be marked with seven dots in a line — like seven typewritten periods, for example. The men on the *Terrible* practiced on the 'dotter' every day except Sunday and the various records were posted for all to see.

The report ended with a comparison between American and British regulations for record target practice, which in no way was favorable to the former.

Our ships under General Order Number 9, issued in September, 1900, were allowed to select their own range, to give no credit for rapidity of fire, and to determine efficiency solely by the percentage of hits made. Quite naturally each ship tried, therefore, to fire at short range, at reduced speed, and very deliberately. Furthermore, our gunners did not have to hit the target. Hits were computed by plotting the course of a shot and estimating whether the shell would have hit a warship located in the position of the target. In considering all the defects of our regulations, Sims came to the conclusion that we were unable to determine, in any target practice conducted under them, the two most important factors in gunnery efficiency. It was impossible to learn the average number of shots and hits per minute for each calibre, nor could we discover the relative efficiency of each gunner. The point he was at particular pains to emphasize was that, with the advent of continuous-aim fire, speed had become a vital consideration. The criterion of effective gunnery had to be expressed in terms of hits per gun per minute. A pointer who fired eight times and made six hits in one minute was more desirable than one who fired four times and made four hits. Nothing in our regulations showed our recognition of this essential factor of speed.[12]

After dispatching this report, Sims remained at Hong Kong for some weeks while awaiting definite information on the movements of the *Monterey*, which had left Canton. He improved his time by visiting several British ships and discussing questions of gunnery and ship design with the English officers in the city. The defects of the *Kentucky* were still large in his mind. He was anxious to supplement his first report on her with a more comprehensive condemnation. He was the more encouraged to do this because of the gratifying reception which had been granted his first two papers, which had, he wrote his mother, 'made quite a sensation in the Fleet, but no one has attempted to refute my statements.' The work had proved 'very interesting' and he was not without 'hopes that it would do some good,' and to this end he expected 'to keep belting away at them — and perhaps it will have effect. I have made ten copies of my reports and passed them around, and some of them have already been sent to the United States to prominent officers who will ask about their contents, and everyone will be glad of the criticisms except the ones directly affected, that is the chiefs of the Bureaus of Construction, Navigation, and Ordnance.' He had not read his own reports in vain. Thus early he had laid his sights upon

[12] The unsatisfactory state of our gunnery at this period is perhaps best revealed in Philip R. Alger's 'Errors of Gunfire at Sea,' *N.I.P.*, vol. 24, December, 1900. He states in this article that of 9500 projectiles of all calibres fired at Santiago, only 123, or 1.3 per cent, hit Spanish ships. The same author's *Gunnery in Our Navy*, referred to previously, makes a much more thorough study of our gunnery after the introduction of continuous-aim fire than has been possible here. Some of his information he obtained from Sims' reports written from the China Station, but he goes far more deeply into the theoretical problems than Sims did. Those interested in pursuing the theoretical aspects further are referred to the excellent articles in the *Encyclopaedia Britannica* (13th ed.) on Ordnance and Sights, while more extended treatment of gunnery at sea can be found in the two textbooks used at Annapolis at this period: R. R. Ingersoll, *Text Book of Ordnance and Gunnery*, Annapolis, 1899, revised 4th ed., and W. F. Fullam and T. C. Hart, *Text Book of Ordnance and Gunnery*, Annapolis, 1903.

the target and he stood prepared to fire with continuous aim.

By May the report on the *Kentucky* and her sister ship, the *Kearsarge*, was ready.[13] The essential thesis of the thirty-five type-written pages is that the two newest American battleships afloat were much more vulnerable to the gunfire of any possible enemy than were comparable ships of foreign navies. Sims attacked the superimposed turrets especially vigorously. Upon a scale tracing of the after turrets he superimposed a scale drawing of the target used in the *Terrible's* record practice. Of the eighty hits made by the *Terrible* in that practice, seventy-nine, when plotted against the *Kentucky's* turrets, were likewise hits. Twenty-one of these were made upon the eight-inch turret that was placed above the thirteen-inch turret, and from this Sims concluded that the eight-inch turret was simply a 'save all.' To prove his point further, he projected the same target against the single great gun turret of the *Canopus* and showed that only thirty-six shells hit it.

When the comparison between the *Kentucky* class and the British *Canopus* was completed, the following defects in the former stood revealed. The guns of medium calibre, the five-inch guns, were mounted in violation of the essential principle of isolation of gun positions; the protection afforded by the turrets of the great guns was inadequate because the gunports were unnecessarily large; the superimposed turrets provided only an extra hazard which might be avoided by separating the two; the direct passage from turret to handling room left the ship when in action in the constant danger of total destruction. Reviewing these things, Sims felt it safe to decide that 'An impartial consideration of the facts above stated will, I believe, render it apparent that a battleship built on the same general plan as the *Kentucky* and *Kearsarge* would, even if armed with six-inch guns instead of five-inch guns, go into action with all the chances very heavily against her inflicting serious damage on a modern battleship of her weight before all of her own guns were put out of action, not to mention the slaughter of her men and the grave danger of her magazines being exploded.' As a final and derisive ges-

[13] 'Protection of Gun Positions *H.M.S. Canopus* Class Compared with That of the *Kentucky* and *Kearsarge*,' May 19, 1901.

ture he added a tracing of a photograph of the *Kentucky's* turrets with the large gunports outlined heavily in black. This photograph, as he was careful to point out, illustrated an article in *Munsey's Magazine* describing the *Kentucky* and entitled 'The Greatest Fighting Machines Afloat.'

The report was forwarded through the Captain of the *Monterey*, to whom Sims sent an explanatory letter in which he said, 'It may seem ungracious to attack one's last ship, but I am sure you will understand my motives in making what appears to me to be justifiable criticisms.' A week later, on May 27, 1901, Captain Stockton replied with a phrase which Sims never forgot and which he frequently quoted to less enlightened observers of his actions. 'We ought,' said Stockton, 'to stand in the light and be not afraid of the truth no matter how unsatisfactory.' But he added sadly, 'The pathway of the reformer... is hard and my experience at the War College leads me to sympathize with you in your efforts and rebuffs.'

Captain Stockton was apparently meditating more on his own past than on Sims', for at this time at least the latter had received far more praise for his reports than blame. Only a week after reading the above letter, he wrote to his brother Hal: 'I have circulated a good many copies of these reports (for I don't want them to be buried), and I have yet to find an officer who has read them who has not *accepted my views*, and acknowledged all my criticisms! This is a pretty state of affairs I don't think. The attitude toward me is one of approval, and of resentment toward the "Dept.," where the responsible parties reside. It remains to be seen what will be the attitude of these parties.'

He knew that he had some friends in Washington and that his three reports had created a favorable impression upon at least some of the mighty. Frances de Krafft, a very capable woman who had been employed in the Department in one capacity and another for twenty-five years, was in 1901 employed in the Bureau of Navigation. She, at about this time, wrote Sims a very encouraging letter. Captain Chester of the *Kentucky* had returned to Washington and had 'been blowing the Sims horn' in the corridors of the Department. The sounds had drifted into the office of the Admiral of the Navy and caught the attentive ear of Dewey himself, who, Miss de Krafft wrote, was reported to want

the young man on the General Board. There were implications
here which Sims thoroughly understood. 'If,' he wrote his
brother Hal, 'Admiral Dewey accepts them [the criticisms],
which he can readily do, as he is not at all responsible for the
plans of the vessels, he can force the whole "push" to change the
plans of the vessels about to be built. ... They [the General
Board] discuss all such matters and advise the Secretary. They
are consequently disliked by the great Bureau of Navigation,
which now plays second fiddle in those matters.'

There was a new incentive for Sims in this work during the
summer of 1901. His first papers on the *Kentucky* and on Scott's
system of gunnery had been the result, as he himself said, chiefly
of habit. He had learned to write daily reports from Paris and it
was natural for him to fill up his leisure with composition. But
the response to his third paper — the comparison of the *Ken-
tuckies* with the *Canopus* class — made him realize that his activity
could be directed toward a larger purpose. His correspondence
and his conversations brought out the fact that many men were
dissatisfied with the conditions of our Navy, and he ceased to
concern himself only with specific defects and turned to general
causes. Gradually it dawned upon him that he was attracting
the attention of men who could be mobilized for action and that
he had in his hands the instruments of a revolution. Nor is
revolution too dramatic a word to use in this connection. Sims
believed that the mechanical failures of our Navy — the poor
gun sights, our obsolete gun gear, our improperly designed warships — were not so much the result of mechanical incompetence
as of defects in the system of our naval administration. He began
during the months on the *Monterey* to devise methods by which
the manipulation of power in naval administration might be
transferred to different hands. It was his recognition of this
necessity that made him in the eyes of his brother officers a
revolutionary.

The sudden consciousness of his new position altered Sims
considerably, though, to the casual observer, he probably seemed
unchanged. He still kept to his room more than most of his
brother officers; he still, with that passion for exercise which
never left him, 'wet his shirt' once a day. On the China Station
he gave up, temporarily, playing tennis, and rowed in a sampan,

sometimes with a companion. 'I get ashore about 6 A.M. and paddle for a couple of hours through the endless canals that intersect the country on both sides of the river. The other fellows go with me occasionally, but they are hard to get up in the morning.' In the wardroom too he still argued as spiritedly and with as little respect for the opposition's point of view as of old, but these externals were the result of personal habit so strong that nothing could overcome it. Within, there was a change of which he himself was aware.

The energies that in his youth had flowed tranquilly through the several branches of a delta were now concentrated in force along the channel of a central interest. His letters to the family, which in earlier years had been so full of himself, his reading, his travels, were now largely devoted to the problems of his professional investigations. Only rarely did he go ashore, preferring during his hours of leisure to visit some man-of-war in the hope of discovering new material for the work in hand. Men who knew him then remember that the light in his room burned until two or three on many nights, but it did not fall upon the pages of Shakespeare and Thackeray as of old. 'I can't help feeling a bit guilty when I spend a few hours reading some useless but interesting "trash." Under this head my habits have classed all writings that don't tell you something useful. It is an awful thing to have no appreciation of pure literature but I haven't. Wit and stories about children are about all I care for. Habit is a curious thing. I feel more busy and much better satisfied when I have written something — no matter what — than when I have been reading a most instructive book.'

It would be unfair to many men to assume that he worked alone. Cooperation he obtained from several sources and the material for the reports was not infrequently supplied by many hands. This was the more true because in his criticisms he often merely articulated and clarified the unrest of certain elements — composed chiefly of the younger officers — within the service.

One of these young officers was Joseph Wright Graeme, who had graduated from the Academy three years before Sims met him on the *Monterey*, in 1901. This tall, serene young man looked out upon the world from behind his pince-nez with clear, untroubled eyes. He was what the generation that understood the phrase would have called a Christian gentleman; for his were the chivalric virtues. Sims came to know his gentleness, his tolerance, and his courage well, and for no man's character did he have a greater respect. At the time of Graeme's tragic and unnecessary death in the turret explosion on the *Kearsarge* in 1906, Sims wrote to his young widow, 'I have never loved any man more except my own brothers.' On the *Monterey* Graeme with youthful enthusiasm accepted the justice of Sims' criticisms and worked tirelessly to obtain material for the long reports, but his most valuable and permanent contribution to Sims' career was the undeviating loyalty of his friendship.

Homer Poundstone, a classmate, referred to by Sims frequently as 'Lbspierre,' was also on the *Monterey*. An enlisted man remembers that the two used to 'burn the midnight oil' together on the old monitor in 1901. Poundstone was at work upon the plan for a ship with a single-calibre main battery, which Sims called the 'SkeerdoNuthin.' The vessel was in fact an earlier version of Lord John Fisher's famous *Dreadnought*. Proper recognition has never really been given Poundstone for the originality of his design, disregarded as it was by the Department. He was an ideal companion for these late hours, honest, humorous, loyal. When Sims left to go to the *Brooklyn*, his classmate continued to send him material for the critical reports.

Ridley McLean first brought himself to Sims' attention through an argument the two had over superimposed turrets. He had stood ninth in the large class of 1894 — three ahead of Winston Churchill, the novelist, who later was connected with Sims through marriage. McLean's eager mind lay concealed behind a rather commonplace face. An observer who was fond of him remembers that 'he was of medium height and neutral coloring with a low forehead, straight unmanageable hair, a flat nose and rather too small eyes.' These rather alarming disadvantages were compensated for by an easy mobility and merriment in his countenance. Men liked him instinctively, and so did the many women with whom he was forever falling gracefully in and out of love. Born in Tennessee, he had the Southerner's love of gaiety and would dance all night if the occasion offered. His vitality was amazing. After an evening of revelry he would appear on duty as fresh and competent as if he had slept for twelve hours. At work he was tireless and he was one of the few men who could stay at his desk longer than Sims. They worked together happily and successfully for several years in the Target Practice Office at Washington after 1903. By the time the partnership was dissolved in the ordinary course of duty they left behind them a Navy that knew how to shoot. For this achievement Sims always gave the larger share of praise to his younger colleague. But there is credit enough for all in their accomplishments and it is not necessary here to seek an exact division. McLean himself was glad enough to know that his superior believed him to be 'the most brilliant mind I have ever had anything to do with.'

An officer who knew all this group has written that Poundstone and W. F. Arnold were the cheering section. Certainly that was part of their function, as it was part of the function of any man closely associated with Sims, but Arnold may deserve a better epitaph. Years later, when the Doctor was dead and almost forgotten, Sims wrote that he 'was one of the first to understand the method of gunnery training and his help in popularizing the system was very valuable. He was an efficient collector of information and a bitter critic of our inefficiency.' While the others went about their business quietly and efficiently as men interested only in the performance of their duty, Arnold illuminated his activity with the flares of a lively imagination. Where there were only naval officers intent upon acquainting their superiors with the advances made in gunnery, he found instead a Society for the Repression of Ignorant Assumption. And in the hands of its members he saw the great weapons of truth, before which the rotten defenses of the bureaus in Washington would crumble away. He recognized in himself a captain in the resolute forces of a crusade. Unfortunately, the captain was unpopular. One of the ablest of Sims' assistants thought that Arnold was 'red-eyed and argumentative, violent rather than strong,' and an officer wrote from Washington, 'You are getting somewhere, but for heaven's sake call off your friend Arnold.'

Behind the ornate façade of Arnold's personality Sims discovered a character in some ways not unlike his own, which he could admire and by which he may have been subtly influenced. For the Doctor the act of opposition was a necessity of life, and from him the naval officer may have discovered that opposition is sometimes a necessary part of the fulfilment of duty.

None can present a greater contrast to Doctor Arnold than Albert Lenoir Key, the Naval Attaché in 1901 at Tokyo. This fearless man came early into the vineyard of reform and with his superior attainments bore more than his share of the burden and the heat of the day. Only two years younger than Sims, he probably was, at this time, better known in the service. Certainly he knew more of the world beyond it. As recorder for the Personnel Board of 1899, he had had something to do with the change of the system of promotion and, more important, he had become a close friend of the Board's president, Theodore Roosevelt. Key, in 1898, had married a daughter of General Condit Smith, whose other daughter had married a young man named Leonard Wood. Thus through fortune and through marriage Key came to know well some of the influential people of his time, but the source of his own strength lay not so much in his friends as in his ability. His solid and thorough intelligence, accepting nothing supported simply by faith or a majority, worked independently through to its conclusions. Once the logic of his position was established, he defended himself with unruffled courage. Without the vindictiveness of so many reformers, he had the persistence upon which the success of so many reforms depends. Something of his spirit, it is hoped, can be understood after reading further in this book, for his own actions are more descriptive of his character than illustrative phrases.

These men — Graeme, Poundstone, McLean, Arnold, Key, joined later by R. R. Belknap — were the most active and able of the many who worked with Sims. They formed no such close association as Arnold's Society for the Repression of Ignorant Assumption would lead the observer to believe — some in fact barely knew each other — nor was Sims necessarily their acknowledged leader. They assisted him in collecting material; they advised him on his course of action; not infrequently they pleaded with him to moderate his harsh words or judgments; but they did these things individually and he himself always acted independently.

For four months after the second report on the *Kentucky*, forwarded to the Department on May 19, 1901, Sims sent no more official criticisms to Washington. Throughout the summer he remained on the *Monterey* at Hong Kong, but he was far from idle. His growing correspondence testified to the interest which the service was taking in his efforts. From an officer in the Bureau of Navigation he learned that his reports had made a great impression, and A. P. Niblack wrote him from Washington revealing the official dissatisfaction with conditions.[14] With the letter a clipping from the *New York Sun* was enclosed, which charged that systematic, progressive target practice did not exist and that we would 'get a good licking in our next war.' Niblack said that the Chief of the Bureau of Navigation had discussed this clipping with him and had said that the Bureau was 'worried over the target practice and that things were in a chaotic state. He told me in confidence that the reason the North Atlantic Squadron had been sent to the southern drill grounds was because their last target practice was so rotten it was a scandal. Five ships, five minutes, at a hulk. All five made two hits. Against orders they sunk the wreck. There has been lots of correspondence, and every one is "mum." The upshot of it was that he told me he wanted to create the billet of Inspector of Target Practice ashore and afloat and turn it over to me.'[15]

In the course of the summer, Sims kept his hand in by presenting to the Commanding Officer of the *Monterey* a criticism of the mounts of the ten-inch guns. There were more things than gun mounts wrong with the *Monterey* in his opinion, but he refrained from giving his criticism officially and contented himself with a description of the vessel he wrote to his friends in the wardroom of the *Kentucky*.

> I will proceed [he wrote to them] to give you a few points concerning the *U.S.S. Terror-of-the-Far-East*. She is a double-elliptical, high-uffen-buffen, double-turreted, back-acting, submarine War junk. She carries two twelve- and two ten-inch guns in round boxes on each end. You put the shell in, close the plugs, get outside, batten down, send the mail and list of probable changes ashore, and touch her off. The following day when she has cooled off they try it again if enough of the men have come to. She is about the shape of a sweet potato that has burst in the boiling.

[14] Albert P. Niblack to W. S. S., June 10, 1901.
[15] Albert P. Niblack to W. S. S., June 20, 1901.

She draws fourteen feet of mud forward, and 16' 6" of slime aft, and has three feet of discolored water over the main deck in fair weather. She has no anchors or chains — her only ground tackle being a large sucker under the forefoot. You run her nose up to the bank, put on the suction, and, barring an earthquake, the entire British Fleet couldn't yank her off.

She has two engines, both in double bottoms, and you ought to hear 'em tryin' to get out!! She is fitted with four double-ended, inverted, non-return blue mud tubular Irish boilers, with fire boxes on top so that gravity assists the draft. The engines are of the non-condensing type, and she puffs like a locomotive climbing a stiff grade with a couple of miles of coal cars.

All the clinker, ashes, buckets, shovels, etc. and an occasional sleepy coal passer are sucked up the flue and blown thousands of miles in the air. There are consequently no ash hoists.

She has warped since she was built, and don't go straight. The compass is set with the lubber's point fifty-two degrees on the starboard bow, for that is the direction in which she goes.

All hands are mighty proud of the ship and jealous of the *Ky*. They allowed as how the latter could lick any two foreign ships in the 'wourld!' I made 'em a short speech, gave 'em my reports to read, and they fell down dead. You get down below through several hatches or elevator shafts. Standing at the bottom of one of these you can look up and see the stars at high noon. The air they built into the ship is there yet, and at the present writing has a gentle odor of mild decay. In this atmosphere 80 volts will only drive an electric fan 40 revolutions, and the slip is 50 per cent.

Life on board is not wildly exciting. On the contrary I should say that, compared to the disorder caused on the *Ky*. by the demonstrations necessary to convince the wrong-headed, the atmosphere for miles around this vessel is decidedly and soporifically somniferous.

In March, 1901, Congress had appropriated money for two new battleships to be designed by the Board on Construction. This board, composed of the Chiefs of the Bureaus of Construction and Repair, Ordnance, Steam Engineering, Equipment, and Navigation, after deliberating for some little time found itself unable to come to any unanimous conclusion upon the type of ship required. On two major questions the various members were divided — the calibre and distribution of the secondary battery and the merits of the superimposed turret. When a majority and a minority report were issued by the Board clearly revealing the division of opinion, the matter was referred to the Secretary for decision.[16] The Secretary quite rightly believed himself incapable of rendering a wise decision in a technical question of this sort where even experts had disagreed. He therefore decided to consult various naval officers before making up his mind. Copies of the two reports were printed and sent to a number of high-ranking officers with a request for their comments. Sims was not one of the officers selected by the Secretary, but the Chief Constructor, Rear Admiral F. T. Bowles, who had read the report of the *Terrible's* target practice with interest, sent him the majority and minority reports. Here was an opportunity not to be lost, so Sims set to work on an unsolicited report for the Secretary.

By September 24, the task was finished, the paper was sent to the Secretary, and a copy was forwarded to Admiral Bowles. In general terms no better résumé of Sims' comments on the reports can be given than that contained in a letter he wrote to his friend Poundstone five days later:

> As you have seen by the papers, the board on construction came to a deadlock on the design of the new battleships and after they passed the deliberative stage and got personal the secretary of the navy decided to submit the question to a number of officers for their opinion. You have also, doubtless, seen that my various reports got to Washington in time for the row. Each side took parts of them to club the other side with. The supplementary reports and those extracts were published in part in the *Army and Navy Journal*. The whole controversy was printed in a confidential pamphlet accompanied by plans. . . . A copy was sent to me from the chief constructor's office. There was no letter with it — that is, I was not asked to express my opinion, but as you may surmise, I would not mind a little thing like that so I spat on my hands and went to work and durned hard work it has been. . . . The result is 'Comments on the Report of the Majority and Minority of the Board on Construction on the Design of a Seagoing Battleship,' a copy of which I enclose you. I have an idea that the secretary of the navy has not been urged to read my re-

[16] *Report of the Board on Construction on a Seagoing Battleship to the Secretary of the Navy,* July 12, 1901.

ports and knows little about them so I practically reviewed the whole ground and submitted the paper to him. There is considerable new matter ... and I think it will interest you. It has the usual aggressive and cock-sure style which I recognize as a fault but I cannot say a thing as if I didn't care whether anyone believed it or not. ... I have called a spade a spade and I have called a hole a hole and not a gun port. The whole controversy turns on the question of turrets. The majority doesn't like them and the battleship to equal the foreigner's can't be built without them except at the sacrifice of too many valuable qualities. The minority is in favor of turrets of all kinds, even the *Kentucky's* 'save all' towers, so there you are. Neither ship could stand up against those building abroad as I have tried to show and consequently I have criticised both impartially. The trouble is that they are planning their ships on opinions and not on a careful analysis of the fighting qualities of the ships we may be up against some day. All comparisons have been made with our turrets that are soap boxes compared to the new foreign turrets and in discussing the rapidity of fire in target practice they have drawn conclusions from the Spanish War. ...

If I am wrong I want to know it and I would really be very much obliged to you or any of the B'hoys if they would put it down on paper and give me a chance to come back at them.

That sounds a little like the Scotchman who said, 'I am open to conviction but I am damned if I wouldn't like to see the man who could do it.' [17]

Turrets were the main bone of contention, but the calibre of the secondary battery was almost equally important. The Board had disagreed over the relative merits of seven- and eight-inch guns,[18] and Sims came out strongly for the former, which could pierce any light armor as well as the larger calibre and which could be fired almost twice as fast. And he was at pains to point out that whichever guns were used it was of vital importance to isolate the various guns of a battery as much as possible. Not to do so was to 'take chances and that is not war.' The cocksure style he referred to in his letter was revealed at its best in the heavy sarcasm with which he treated the defense of the superimposed turret. If one gun on top of another is good, he asked why it is not sound construction to mount all of the

[17] W. S. S. to Homer Poundstone, September 29, 1901.
[18] *Report of the Board on Construction*, p. 2.

guns in a ship in a column extending skyward in a lofty tower.

It was not long before Sims received reactions from this report. On October 19 his friend McLean wrote him expressing disagreement with some of his contentions. The stronger light armor of the new ships seemed to McLean to justify the use of an eight-inch secondary battery and he strongly defended the superimposed turrets. Sims had, as in his report on the *Kentucky*, placed a target of the *Terrible's* record practice on a silhouette of the superimposed turret to prove that the eight-inch turret was simply a 'save all,' as he called it. McLean pointed out quite properly that 'You thus create a false impression. You compare total hits (on both 8 and 12 turrets) as against a single 12-inch turret not as against isolated 12- and 8-inch turrets as you should.' And with a heat not infrequently generated by Sims in those who opposed him he observed that 'the fact that you consider some of the advantages "claimed" as fallacious is not an argument at all.'

More pleasing was the letter from Admiral Bowles himself. 'Your comments are of great value and I shall make good use of them. If you are agreeable I may send you some recent turret plans for criticism. . . . One great difficulty of our designs has been that they have never been taken up for consideration until the appropriation has been made and have been pushed through and contracted for in a very incomplete state, not to mention the other difficulties which would be unveiling the family affairs of the Department.' [19]

At the end of October, Sims left the *Monterey* and joined the *Brooklyn*, flagship of the Asiatic Fleet. Admiral Remey, the Commander-in-Chief, through whose hands all of Sims' reports had passed on their way to Washington, had from the first been favorably impressed by the young man's energy, courage, and intelligence. He had arranged that Sims join his own staff as an aide 'with special Intelligence duties,' and he had made arrangements — against the desires and advice of some members of his own staff — for Sims to be left free to act as he pleased. [20]

[19] F. T. Bowles to W. S. S., November 3, 1901.

[20] Transcript of W. S. S.'s official record in the Bureau of Navigation, Washington. Letter from R. R. Belknap to the author, February 26, 1940. Belknap was on Remey's staff at the time.

The Admiral was one of the officers to whom the Secretary had referred the reports of the Board on Construction, and upon Sims' arrival on the *Brooklyn* he immediately asked the younger man's opinion in the matter. 'My reception on board here,' Sims wrote to Poundstone, 'was all I could have wished from all hands. He [Remey] called in the whole push [the staff] and asked me to state my ideas on the new ships, which I did all the way to the end, with sketches to beat the band. Finally he said he would recommend the same ship I had, and a couple of days later he called us all in to hear the reading of his rough report to see if it was o. k. In a very flattering paragraph he called special attention to the report of Willie Sims. . . . '

In fact, the Admiral was willing to hit as hard as his subordinate. To the Secretary he wrote that 'the *Kentucky*'s defects are glaring,' and that 'he was deeply impressed with the weak points of the ships in which we place such confidence.' He could conceive, he went on, 'of no graver question [than the design of new battleships] for naval officers to consider,' and he 'begged leave to add the wish that no plans would be accepted without the approval of the best informed men in the line of the Navy.' [21]

So encouraged with this support in high place was Sims that within the week he had completed a new paper on the shooting of *H.M.S. Terrible*.[22] There was an altered tone in the report, a savagery of attack that is a testament to the value Sims placed on Admiral Remey's encouragement. Again he attacked the size and shape of our target, our method of plotting imaginary hits, and our lack of intensive dotter training. With considerable irritation he pointed out that his previous reports had been 'gratifyingly acknowledged,' but 'unfortunately overlooked.' And in conclusion he bitterly observed that 'the success or failure of a ship must depend on the qualities of her *design* and of her *marksmanship*. We have sinned against all the military principles of the former and have carelessly neglected the latter to such an extent that we have placed ourselves beyond the possibility of success against an equal force of any one of our possible enemies including the Japanese. The American people, however, are none the wiser; on the contrary the Navy has been inordinately

[21] George C. Remey to the Secretary of the Navy. Undated copy in Sims papers
[22] 'Record Target Practice *H.M.S. Terrible* for 1901,' November 6, 1901.

flattered by a boastful press, which with the most patriotic intentions imaginable is too ignorant of such matters to criticize even our most glaring faults — Foreign Admiralties however are aware of them. . . . And,' he glumly added, 'democracy tends toward war and militates against proper preparation for it.'

To this report Admiral Remey appended the following endorsement.[23] 'I deem this paper worthy of the most serious attention, recommending that it be considered by the General Board, and also in connection with the plans of the ships to be built and building. No well-informed man can deny that our situation is extremely dangerous and it behooves us to spare no effort to attain that state of efficiency which the public and the *majority of the Navy* believe we have already reached.' ' "*The curse of the Navy,*" ' he quoted grimly, ' "*is the word improvise.*" '

The tide was rising. In early November, a few days after the above report had been sent to Washington, Sims wrote elatedly to Doctor Arnold announcing the recent progress of the Society for the Repression of Ignorant Assumption. 'Key,' he said, 'is sold and Mac is almost certainly one of us.' 'I have cautioned the *Montereys* not to talk too much or too triumphantly and I invite you to take a look at the wreck of the *Brooklyn* when I get through with her.' In a mood of buoyant optimism he wrote to Poundstone a day or two later after a conversation with Admiral Remey: 'I really believe that we have rendered it impossible for them to build any more fool ships, though they may build some bad ones. I even hope they will turn out a sure enough "fighting machine" this time. I have worked very hard over all this and have been getting madder and madder with each paper until I have finally arrived at a determination not to let it bring me with gray hairs in sorrow to the grave. I mean both as regards ships and target practice. I was going to play the game fair until I saw it was hopeless and then go into the press. I showed up target practice once before (in Paris) and they stowed the paper away — as soon as Teddy was out of the way. I could not have stood it again. However, things seem to be coming our way at last.'

But he treasured no illusions about the men who could place obstacles in the path of the things that might come his way.

[23] Endorsement of George C. Remey, November 6, 1901.

He knew where they lived and he thought he knew the only way to deal with them. To his old roommate, Niblack, he wrote on November 16: 'I don't envy you the job [of Inspector of Target Practice]. I would take it if they offered it to me but I would not expect to hold it long. I would want scalps or nothing, and if I couldn't have 'em I wouldn't play. I would probably insult some time-serving P[rincipal] D[ignitary] inside of a week and be sent to the South Pole, and I would rather go than give in.'

In March, 1901, he had 'invited the attention' of the Bureau of Navigation to the remarkable target practice of *H.M.S. Terrible*. In May he had believed that 'an impartial consideration of the facts ... would render it apparent ... that the *Ky.* would go into action with all the chances very heavily against her inflicting serious damage on a modern warship.' In September he called 'a hole a hole and not a gunport.' By November he was out for scalps. Nine months before, he had been a junior officer desiring to acquaint his superiors with the facts, and content to disturb the complacent notions of a wardroom mess, but in November he possessed a following, enjoyed a reputation, and was fighting for a cause. The times and his own temper counselled action. Reports and fair words of praise were well enough at the beginning, but after nine months he looked for results. 'I was going to play fair until it was hopeless and then go to the press,' but the bullet that killed McKinley changed his plan of attack. Teddy was no longer 'out of the way,' and on the day he wrote Niblack he also wrote a letter to the new President of the United States.

This letter sprang from no easy impulse of the moment, for there were many risks in writing it which Sims carefully considered. It was, in reality, an act of insubordination condemned alike by naval custom and the Navy Regulations. As a friend later wrote, 'It amounts in effect to reporting everyone in Washington for neglect of duty.' That he ran the risk of being subjected to formal court-martial proceedings Sims was well aware. Equally clearly he realized that whatever the official result, he would, by such a letter, inevitably antagonize some powerful superior officers who held his future in their hands. It is not too much to say that in addressing the President of the United States directly Sims was putting his professional career to the hazard. How did he come to take such a chance?

In September, 1901, Albert Lenoir Key met Sims at some port on the China Station, probably Manila. Here the two debated the merits of writing to the President as Key suggested. Key recognized the dangers of his proposal as well as Sims, but he knew Roosevelt well enough to suspect that the President's reaction would be favorable. For his own part Sims, though he had never met Mr. Roosevelt, remembered how greatly interested the latter had been in the reports he had sent from Paris in 1897. To both men also it seemed clear that no favorable action would ever be taken by the Navy Department upon the matters contained in Sims' reports.[24]

For a month after their conversation Sims still hesitated. On November 16, Key wrote to him: 'With reference to the personal letter you propose to write I have only one suggestion to offer; make it brief and do not make criticisms in it that would give anyone ground for saying that it was insubordinate or subversive of good discipline. Mention your reports by name only and say you are doing it because they may prove valuable to him in his reorganization policy we read about in the press.' Key's wise advice arrived too late, for on the same day he mailed it Sims had cast the die and written the following letter to the President:

Dear Sir: —

I beg that I may be pardoned for the liberty I take in addressing you a personal letter; and my only excuse for so doing is the vital importance of the subject that I wish to bring to your attention,

[24] Albert Lenoir Key to the writer, November 10, 1938, and in conversation April, 1940. Key is not certain where the meeting took place, although he is inclined to believe it was Manila. The exact date of the talk also is impossible to discover, though a comparison of the official orders of each leads both of us to believe it was early September. Key's own account of the meeting is as follows: 'He [Sims] showed me some exceedingly unsatisfactory replies he had received from one of the bureaus in Washington ... to certain recommendations he had made, which if adopted, he was sure would be effective in greatly increasing the accuracy and rapidity of the ship's gunfire. His recommendations had been flatly turned down, and the prospect of getting anything done appeared hopeless. I said to him that I had seen enough of the President, Theodore Roosevelt, to know that he was keenly interested in all matters relating to the efficiency of the Navy and that he was not strong for red tape, and I advised him to write a personal letter to the President and lay the whole situation squarely before him for consideration and such action as he might deem advisable. The result was just what I thought and hoped it would be.'

namely, the extreme danger of the present very inefficient condition of the Navy, considered as a fighting force.

You will doubtless recall that in 1897 when you were Assistant Secretary of the Navy, you initiated certain reforms in naval target practice as a result of information obtained from the Naval Attachés abroad concerning the progress in marksmanship in foreign navies. The Spanish War interrupted these reforms, and no progress whatever has been made since.

I have within the past few months submitted to the Navy Department a number of reports on foreign target practice, and on other matters in connection with the fighting efficiency of our vessels; and, after as exhaustive a study of these subjects as my opportunities would afford, I have, in the last of these reports, been forced to the very serious conclusion that the protection and armament of even our most recent battleships are so glaringly inferior in principle as well as in details, to those of our possible enemies, including the Japanese, and that our marksmanship is so crushingly inferior to theirs, that one or more of our ships would, in their present condition, inevitably suffer humiliating defeat at the hands of an equal number of an enemy's vessels of the same class and displacement.

I fully realize the extreme gravity of this statement; but it is the result of a long and conscientious study of the subject, and I am convinced that it is the plain truth; and this opinion is held by all the naval officers of my acquaintance who have seriously considered the subjects treated in the reports above indicated.

The Commander-in-Chief of the Naval Force on the Asiatic Station, Rear-Admiral Remey, in forwarding my last report to the Secretary of the Navy, states that he fully agrees with the conclusions therein given, and that he considers our present situation extremely critical.

In this report I have set forth as clearly as possible the reasons in support of the above statement — which reasons are principally based on information acquired during a period of three years as Naval Attaché to our Embassies at Paris and St. Petersburg, and one year on this station, where I have had opportunities of becoming familiar with the details of a number of the most recent foreign vessels.

It would have been my duty to have made these comparisons between our vessels and those of other nations, while I was occupying the position of Attaché, but I was unable to do so at that time as I was not then acquainted with the details of the construction of our latest vessels.

That my criticisms are, however, not exaggerated is unfortunately but too completely demonstrated by a recent special target practice in the North Atlantic Squadron which shows much greater inefficiency in marksmanship than I have reported, or than I could have imagined possible. Five ships each fired during five minutes at a hulk at a range of about 2800 yards and made a *total of two hits.* The hulk was afterwards sunk at close range.

I am aware of the irregularity of thus addressing you personally; but the danger of the false impression, that is universal throughout the United States concerning the efficiency of the Navy, appears to me so great, and the need of prompt and radical reform therefore so extremely urgent, that I hope I may not be considered as overstepping the bounds of propriety in inviting your personal attention to the papers indicated in the enclosed memorandum — particularly the last report which, with Admiral Remey's letter of transmittal, is now on file in the office of the Hon. Secretary of the Navy.[25]

It has frequently been reported that this letter set off in the President a series of pyrotechnical explosions. He is supposed to have ordered a target practice for the North Atlantic Squadron the results of which so appalled him that he cried: 'Telegraph to China for that young man. Give him entire charge of target practice for eighteen months. Do exactly what he says. If he doesn't accomplish something in that time cut off his head and try someone else.'[26] Certainly Mr. Roosevelt was capable of doing this, but, like so many things he could have done, he did not do it.

Instead he wrote the following letter:

My dear Lieutenant Sims:

I value your letter. I think you unduly pessimistic, as you certainly were at the outset of the Spanish-American War, when, as you may remember, you took a very gloomy view of our vessels even as compared with those of Spain. Nevertheless, I would a hundred-fold over that you erred upon the side of thinking us

[25] W. S. S. to Theodore Roosevelt, November 16, 1901.

[26] The *New York Times,* September 29, 1936, and Burton J. Hendrick's 'Sims' in *World's Work,* August, 1919. Sims himself may be responsible for the story. Cf. his testimony before the Select Committee of Inquiry, 1925, Part 4, p. 2977, of the *Hearing.*

not good enough than of thinking us too good; and many of the suggestions that you have made in the past, both upon the need of improving our gun practice and of doing away with or removing faulty construction in our battleships, have been genuinely fruitful.

I thank you for writing me; I shall always be pleased to hear from you, in criticism, or suggestion.

Sincerely yours,

THEODORE ROOSEVELT [27]

He also ordered that all of the reports which Sims had written from the China Station should be printed and distributed to every officer in the service. Niblack was put to work immediately to condense the many pages, a necessary task, and prepare them for publication.[28] The results of the letter were not as spectacular as newspaper men, or even Sims himself, remembered them. They were nevertheless substantial. The President had not been irritated nor had he betrayed him to his fellow officers. He had even asked Sims to write him again; one positive step he had taken to gain Sims a wider audience in the service, and an audience the more alert because it recognized the President's influence in what had happened.

Perhaps the most important result was a psychological one. From the President's response Sims knew he had his ear, and he guessed he had his interest. A way was open to the great source of power which alone could compel the bureaus into action. For the moment, on November 16, the success of his venture had hung in the balance, but now he could set forth again with confidence. Key five years later was not wrong in writing: 'And I advised you to write the President and bring the whole matter to his attention. You agreed with me that it seemed about the only thing left to be done. That was the turning point.'

[27] Theodore Roosevelt to W. S. S., December 12, 1901.
[28] Niblack to W. S. S., January 10, 1902.

8

I 9 0 I - I 9 0 2 *Gunfire at Sea*

To Sims,' a loyal friend explains, 'there were only two kinds
of paint — pitch-tar black laid on with a broad brush, filling every
crack and corner; and whitewash, which he abhorred. That
not using either might serve better in some cases, he would not
even consider.' Some of this pitch-tar black in which his reports
were written may have spread over the pages of the preceding
chapter, concealing from view the true nature of the forces
opposed to Sims. Against him, as he assumed, there were
naturally arrayed some blind, some stupid, some selfish men;
but there were also many intelligent, honest officers who did not
lack arguments to support their dissenting opinions.

In the Fleet, it is fair to say, most of the older men did not
believe in his criticisms. 'In a word,' says one observer, 'the
old Navy was tory. All through thirty stagnant years their hopes
for better things persisted. When at last they seemed to be coming true, to have their hopes completely dashed and apparently
incontrovertibly was too much to take lying down.' [1] For these
officers, proud of their way of life and loyal to it, rejection of the
Sims reports was the instinctive and immediate response. They
were the men of good will who in every walk of life, disliking
sudden change, swell the ranks of the majority.

Less sentimental, and more formidable, was the opposition of
those in the Navy Department who were responsible for the conditions which Sims criticized. Against the facts and figures he
accumulated to substantiate his case, they could marshal the

[1] Rear Admiral Reginald R. Belknap to the writer, February 26, 1940.

conflicting evidence of other facts and figures. Sims cast up accounts by adding the column of debit entries. There was, too, in the books of the Department a page for credits.

In the first place, some of the authorities were not as complacent about the state of our gunnery as their severest critic assumed. On July 1, 1899, the Chief of the Bureau of Navigation had issued a memorandum on naval marksmanship.

> It will be apparent [he had said] that all first-class powers have for years devoted more energy, time, and money to training their gun-pointers than we have. In the last few years the training of our gun-pointers has received more attention than formerly, and good results are manifest; but foreigners were doing years ago what we are now, while at present they are redoubling their efforts to keep in the lead.
>
> In this practice [foreign practice] only actual hits count in most countries, while with us the marking of the fall of the shot is very largely a matter of guess, though generally dignified by being called an estimate.

It was true that the Bureau of Navigation had not immediately tried to improve this situation by the adoption of continuous-aim gunfire. But, two full years after the remarkable record of *H.M.S. Terrible* in 1900, the British Admiralty itself had not yet fully accepted the methods of Percy Scott. Perhaps this was only a reflection of the conservatism of the English, but it could also mean that the greatest navy in the world had reason to distrust the value of Scott's notions of gunnery. Moreover, until some foreign admiralty adopted continuous-aim fire, the United States Navy could not be placed in the position of hopeless inferiority that Sims already claimed for it.

In his discussions of our modern battleships Sims ordinarily settled upon the *Kentucky* class, our newest men-of-war, as examples of our inadequacy. Yet the *Kentucky* herself could be used in defense of those who designed our vessels. She was a battleship of which the service as a whole was very proud. At the time of her launching she was the only man-of-war in the world with a ventilating system; her armament was equal to that of any possible foreign adversary's; the quarters for the officers and crew were larger and more comfortable than those of any ship of her class. The *Kentucky* was handsome, seaworthy, and comfortable; apparently a credit to the Navy and the country.

Sims, it will be recalled, had objected to the large gunports. In this he was not entirely alone. When the vessel visited Germany on a cruise, black canvas had been stretched across the ports to conceal the true extent of their great area. But this defect was not the result of miscalculation. Electric power had been used on the *Kentucky* to operate the training and elevating gear of the guns. This was a distinct improvement over the old hydraulic machinery, which failed whenever a leak occurred in the pipe line and upon which it was difficult to make rapid repairs. In addition, the designers had made it possible to rotate the turrets and to elevate or depress the guns by hand. To accomplish this it had been necessary to balance the guns on the mounts. This threw the trunnion point farther back, thus making imperative a larger gunport. The 'sacrifice of increased exposure,' as one officer connected with the Bureau of Ordnance at the time puts it, 'was deemed warranted by the assurance of the continued working of the guns in battle.'[2] From the point of view of the men in the Bureau of Ordnance this conclusion was sound. Their particular task was to design machinery which would keep the guns in action as long as possible, an obligation the Bureau had ingeniously discharged.

Furthermore, the protection of the guns could be defended by the logic of comparison. The *Majestic* class, British battleships of the nineties, had only 'thin-plate hoods' over the guns instead of the eleven-inch turrets of our ships.

It should be unnecessary to recapitulate Sims' arguments against the superimposed turrets. But it must be noticed that he had not reported on their most serious defect: the eight- and thirteen-inch guns had to be trained alike, since both turrets were turned by the same rotating gear. Furthermore, his most frequent criticism, that the upper turret was simply a 'catch-all,' while in substance correct, was improperly presented. He compared only the number of hits made upon the great gun turret of an English ship with the number of hits on both the twelve- and eight-inch turrets of the *Kentucky*, when he should have compared the latter with the number of hits made against the

[2] Admiral Joseph Strauss to the author in conversation, April, 1940.

separated twelve- and eight-inch turrets of the English ship.

Despite Sims' objections to these turrets there were many arguments in favor of them. The placing of the upper turret off-centre compensated the projecting weight of the guns, thus centring the total weight at the axis of rotation. By concentrating the guns, thus dispensing with separate rotating gear, it had been possible to save a great deal of weight. The principal batteries had been reduced 'to two impregnable gun emplacements' instead of distributing them over the ship behind lighter protection. 'End-on' fire had been increased and some of the saved weight had been used to shield the previously unprotected eight-inch ammunition supply. All these advantages combined to form the primary virtue. The tonnage of the *Kentucky* was limited by Congress. Upon this ship of restricted size it was necessary to include batteries and armor plates equal to those of possible foreign adversaries. Only by saving weight somewhere could this problem of construction be solved. These superimposed turrets were the ingenious solution of the Bureau of Ordnance.[3]

The shaft for the powder hoist was open and direct, which, Sims believed, greatly increased the danger of explosions from sparks falling from the gun position into the handling rooms. To this argument it was replied by the opposition that direct powder hoists were faster and simpler to operate than interrupted hoists, and that the danger from flarebacks was greatly overestimated.

A favorite target for Sims was the telescope sight, which in his eyes was not suitable for continuous-aim firing. This sight was still in the experimental stage in every navy of the world. After a good deal of research the Bureau of Ordnance had introduced such sights in the last years of the nineteenth century, before continuous-aim firing was much understood. They were probably no better and no worse than the ordinary service sights supplied to foreign vessels. The response of the service was immediate and critical. Many conservative officers, believing that the new device was a nuisance, declared that the old open

---

[3] In an article by Lieutenant Joseph Strauss, 'The Turrets of the New Battleships,' *N.I.P.*, vol. 21, 1896, p. 771, a clear description of these turrets together with a consideration of their many advantages is given.

sights were preferable. So great had the clamor become in 1901 that the Chief of the Bureau of Ordnance considered removing all sights from the guns.[4] It was difficult to take the word of a lieutenant that improved telescopes were needed when many of his colleagues were arguing that all telescopes ought to be eliminated.

Obviously there were two sides to the issues raised in Sims' reports. As a sailor, he was interested in how well a ship could fight. Most of his ablest opponents were concerned with building or equipping a ship, or more exactly, with constructing separate parts or providing special equipment. The ultimate test of a man-of-war is its ability to give and take punishment. Sims, as a line officer whose experience had provided him with an unusually well-educated professional mind, could recognize this. On the other hand, the position of the men in the Bureaus of Construction and of Ordnance prevented them from obtaining as clear a view of the final objective, concentrating, as they were, on particular ordnance or construction problems. They did their jobs, on the whole, well. Unfortunately, from the military point of view, they occasionally did the wrong jobs; not because they were ill-intentioned or incompetent, but because they were serving minor ends, reasonable in themselves, but in conflict with the major purpose — the creation of a fighting machine.[5] Thus the explanations by which these officers proved they were doing their duty could not disprove the fact that four twelve-inch shells could enter the large gunports, or that *H.M.S. Terrible* could fire its guns more rapidly, and accurately, than any of our ships.

There was here an inevitable conflict between men pursuing different objectives. It was comparatively easy for Sims, as a line officer who lived every day of his life on a ship, to recognize that the total military effectiveness of a man-of-war was more important than the mechanical perfection of its individual parts.

[4] Admiral Joseph Strauss to the author in conversation, April, 1940.

[5] Too much credit, however, must not be given the line officers, nor too severe blame laid upon the constructors. On February 25, 1905, Bradley A. Fiske wrote to Sims that 'What you say is true, but what about the line? It never gave a thought to problems of construction and design until recently. Bowles sent constructors abroad [while] the line fought the War College. Did the line show as much enthusiasm for their branch of the New Navy as the constructors did in their branch? Not much! As you say, demands from designers for individual opinions of line officers found them unprepared.'

With great insight, he grasped the true nature of the conflict between himself and those who disagreed with him. He understood that the organization of the Navy Department made it difficult if not impossible for the separate bureaus to subordinate their interests to the greater interest of the whole Navy. But it cannot be recorded that he was entirely just to the officers who opposed him. In his mind, they were too closely identified with their achievements, of which he disapproved, to deserve respect or even mercy. 'With a reformer's zeal,' a colleague in his early struggle wrote, 'he would close every loophole by which anyone subject to criticism might escape with some dignity, then to become as strong and useful an advocate as he had been a hindrance.' Much of the opposition, much of the bitterness, much of even the hatred that was raised against him, can be explained in that sentence. Much too of his success.

In October, 1901, Sims had joined the *Brooklyn*. Within the month he had taken advantage of the unusual freedom granted him by Admiral Remey to compose the previously discussed report on the target practice of *H.M.S. Terrible* for 1901 and the letter to President Roosevelt. At the same time he did not neglect his Intelligence duties. In November, just before he wrote his letter to Roosevelt, he sent two more papers to the Department.

The *Brooklyn* called at Vladivostok, and while there Sims inspected the Russian ship *Gromoboi*. He was impressed by the unusually heavy armament possessed by the cruiser, but he noticed that it was provided only 'at the expense of a greatly diminished protection to the guns and especially the ammunition supply.' 'It seems to me,' he reported, 'that, eliminating chance and assuming equal accuracy, the *Gromoboi* would be defeated by a cruiser of the *Iwate* class on the relative merits of the protection of the ammunition supply alone.' [6] Three years later at the battle of the Sea of Japan, the *Gromoboi* engaged the Japanese cruiser *Iwate*, and was put out of action in a very few minutes. Eighty men were killed because of her inadequate protection, which was, as Sims pointed out, superior to that of American cruisers of her time and class. Rarely were his predictions accorded a more dramatic fulfilment.

[6] Report on the Russian cruiser *Gromoboi*, November 7, 1901.

In the same harbor, Vladivostok, he wrote a report on the defenses of the city, which had remained theretofore a carefully guarded secret. His method of acquiring information for this, and all his other papers, is perhaps best described in his own words from a letter to Homer Poundstone.

Nothing was known about the place to amount to anything and Russians lied like troopers and said they were doing nothing. You could not go a mile from the town without being stopped by a sentry, for the place is a stronghold and nothing else. I got orders issued for a number of officers to keep their eyes peeled toujours for certain specified points, and picked out two remarkably wide-awake young ensigns, gave them each one side of the harbor, and told them to see what they could do. They were on their mettle and I'm damned if they didn't surprise me, old campaigner that I am. Each was accompanied by a youngster, just as if they were out for a tramp. One party eluded all the stupid sentries on his side and came in o.k. — calibre and date of guns, arcs of trains, etc., etc. There were sentries in all the batteries, but they got in all the same — keeping behind the guns, etc., as he passed on his beat. The other gang did even better work, but were unfortunately run in as they were on their way back to town but while still on forbidden territory. They had been walking since early morning and it was nearing sunset, and they were hungry enough to eat about a square foot of black bread each that the soldier gave them. They were marched into town by the Jimmies [Russians] armed to the usual teeth. They arrived about ten p.m. As they were entering town they met one of our marine corporals who was on liberty. He had a little vodki up his snoot and wanted to attempt a rescue. Sez he, 'Each of ye pick a man and I'll take the other one, and when I count three we'll break their faces.' Of course the youngsters would not consent. The Jimmies objected to his talking to the prisoners and turned him over to three others who detained him while the other party went on. There were mutual expostulations, but the languages would not mix, so the Corporal tapped them all on the points of the jaw and they probably never will find out what was the matter. The Corporal fled for the high seas and came off and reported the circumstances of the arrest of the young gentlemen. There was a council of war in my room, and the majority were for blowing the syreen or something like that, but I wouldn't have the Ad. informed or anything done about it — which would only give us away. I considered it 'up to the Russians' for the present — and sure enough it came out all right and the boys turned up smiling and smelling of vodki. They had been taken to Headquarters and questioned by the o. o. d. Of course they said they were out for a walk and got lost and all that.

The Roosky pretended to believe them and apologized. Then he sent out and ordered dinner sent in from a restaurant and gave them plenty of vodki — which they were wise enough not to drink much of. Then he showed them a military map and asked them to point out the road they had taken. They studied the map attentively — and remembered most of it — and pointed out as innocent a route as they could to account for their being in the middle of the most important reservation near a large mortar battery. Then he made more apologies and politely accompanied them to the landing and bade them tata. I haven't the least idea in the world that he reported to his commanding officer that he found two officers in the middle of a reservation guarded by his own sentries.

If you're thinking of attacking Vladivostok sometime in the future, just mind your eye!! and look out for shell coming down onto your head out of a clear sky, for they have modern rifled mortars to beat the band.

The life of an efficient Intelligence Officer had its lighter moments, which Sims enjoyed, as he did everything, to the full, but he returned, before the Vladivostok report was finished, to his sterner, self-imposed duties. During the two months he had been on the flagship, Sims had discussed the subjects of his reports with several young men attached to the ship — notably with R. R. Belknap, W. H. McGrann, and Edward C. Woods. Occasionally these matters had been talked over in the presence of the Admiral himself, who displayed a continuing interest in the work. In the course of time the thoughts of all these officers were led beyond the specific defects of our gunnery and ship design into the underlying causes for those defects. Admiral Remey became increasingly concerned with this problem and finally asked Sims to prepare a paper for him in answer to the question, 'How is it possible that the cleverest nation in the world in designing mechanical appliances could make such glaring mistakes in principles of the construction of its naval vessels?' [7]

[7] Quoted in an unpublished account of Sims' career by T. B. Kittredge. Sims papers.

It was the kind of lead which Sims was only too anxious to follow. By the eighth of December, he had his answer ready. In many respects this paper is the ablest attack on the administrative system of our Navy that he ever wrote.[8] In his first five reports he had striven simply to obtain technical improvements in our instruments of war, but now he was out for bigger game.

Our existing methods of determining plans for naval vessels were, according to Sims, 'a distinct failure.' For this there were several causes. In the first place, we had never taken full advantage of the inventive genius of our own people. We 'had assumed that we could select from the service officers with only Academy knowledge of gunnery and ask them to be gunnery experts.' We failed to realize 'that it is utterly impossible for the Chief of a technical Bureau, with his assistants, to compete successfully with the inventive genius of the world — which is practically what they have been doing.' In foreign navies the Bureaus of Ordnance and of Construction were largely bureaus of direction and administration — they did not attempt the impossible task of inventing all the necessary appliances and methods. 'Almost all the mechanical improvements have, and always must, come from the outside; and this is so thoroughly accepted abroad that... little attempt is made to go beyond giving direction to the inventive faculty of the technical staffs of the great private industries which, under government patronage, have developed a body of mechanical experts. . . .' The most serious cause of our failure to design good ships lay in the absence of a board of 'well-informed, high-ranking officers of experience' who would specify the nautical, tactical, and military qualities of the vessel for whose success in battle they were solely responsible.

From the work of criticism, Sims turned to his suggestions for improving the conditions he felt were responsible for our naval difficulties. In general he constructed his plan upon the principles of naval administration he had learned in France and which he had previously reported. At the head of the French Navy were the President and the Cabinet, who decided maritime policy. These policies were laid before a Supreme Council of the Navy, who recommended the classes, characteristics, and num-

[8] 'The Board on Construction and the Design of Battleships,' December 8, 1901.

bers of vessels necessary to implement the desires of the political heads of the country. The Supreme Council was composed wholly of high-ranking naval officers.

After 'considering all the available material from every source, the Supreme Council then recommended the displacement, battery, disposition of the guns, speed, and so forth of the various new gunboats, destroyers, or cruisers required.' These recommendations were sent to the various chiefs of the technical bureaus, who concerned themselves only with the mathematical and structural possibilities of carrying out the specified requirements. Invariably, as Bertin, a French constructor, observed, the Admirals wanted more than was possible, so the Supreme Council and the technical bureaus resolved their disagreements by discussion. But the technical men could never force the naval men to accept a solution to their problems which would weaken the military strength of a vessel.

The advantages of this system which appealed to Sims were threefold. The character of the naval building program — the number of ships and the various types of vessel to be built — was determined by the nature of the foreign policy the Fleet was intended to implement. The military qualities of all the ships were prescribed by a board of line officers, who would have to fight the ships. Questions of structural detail were worked out by the naval constructors. What was needed in America was a Chief of Staff and a Supreme Council, if good ships were to be built. France had only obtained them after a political scandal of the most unsavory sort, and Sims was careful to point out that 'if a speech in Congress exposed us, we couldn't defend ourselves.'

For almost three months after this report was finished, no others were sent to the Department. The *Brooklyn* was cruising for much of this time and Sims, removed from sources of information, was reduced to correspondence. January brought him welcome news from Washington. The Chief Intelligence Officer, Captain Sigsbee, sent him a letter expressing his great approval of the work Sims was doing. In the same mail, Niblack explained fully the situation in the Department. 'The President,' he wrote, 'has taken action on the memorandum I submitted to him of your reports — a sort of brief — and has ordered that it be issued to the service confidentially.' In addition, Niblack held out the promise that some dotters would soon be sent to the Asiatic Station and assured his friend that 'You have quite won out in this business but I don't mind saying that your language has unnecessarily hurt people. I have been able to smooth things over here by being on the spot.' This warning, which Niblack had sent before, was underscored by a letter of January 14 from Chief Constructor Bowles. 'I do not always agree in the matter,' he said, 'nor approve wholly of the manner of making them. It injures your usefulness in the service and you deal in a carping spirit with matters on which you may not have the best information.'

Far from heeding this warning, Sims cheerfully accepted it as an indication that at last he was getting somewhere. The favorable remarks he had received from Washington had never been accompanied by immediate action, and he hoped that criticism of him and his harsh tones might be the harbinger of reform. He wrote gaily to McLean to report progress and to explain that his next report would deal with marksmanship and gun-pointing. It was to be based largely on material that Arnold, Graeme and he himself had picked up in the last few months.

The new report, to which he referred, was finished on February 15, 1902, and bore the ominous title, 'The Crushing Superiority of British Naval Marksmanship over Ours, as Shown by Comparisons of Recent Record Practice.' [9] The history of this paper will be considered from the time it was written until the turmoil which it caused died away six months later, though this treatment does violence to the chronological structure of the whole narrative. Only by withdrawing the single thread of this report from the rather tangled skein of events that occurred in the year 1902 can its full significance be understood; and only thus can the real nature of the opposition that was directed against Sims be recognized.

To begin with, the paper was long — the longest so far — and it reviewed much of the ground covered in earlier communications. Again he asked that our elevating and training gear be altered to permit continuous-aim firing; again he emphasized the necessity of equipping our ships with dotters immediately,

[9] The original is in the files of the Secretary of the Navy, National Archives. A copy is also in the Sims papers.

and again he attacked our telescope sights. On these instruments
his hardest blows fell. 'As a matter of fact, our latest telescope is,
as an aiming device, a practically complete failure.' No provision had been made for cushioning the eye of the gun-pointer
against the jump of the telescope when the gun recoiled. The
cross-wires of the lens were so coarse that they obscured a
battleship at four thousand yards. It was impossible to correct
for the effect of 'speed and wind.' Lateral compensation had,
therefore, to be made by pointing the sight off the target. As
Sims brooded upon the utter inadequacy of our sights, he arrived
at an exasperated conclusion which he could not keep to himself.
'It is with anything but patience that one can refer to the self-
satisfied "opinions" of those officers who, in the pride of their
intellect, deliberately condemn the principle [of the telescope
sight] without further knowledge of the subject than that afforded
by the practically worthless instruments with which we have
been supplied.' 'Apparently,' he concluded, 'there are but too
many [officers] who have little conception of the manliness and
dignity of saying, in such case, "I don't know."'

The gist of the whole report is the great significance of continuous-aim firing, which he established by comparing British
target-practice figures with our own. Figures can prove much,
but Sims feared complacent minds might not read them.
Throughout the pages of this long report, he planted bombs to
startle his audience into attention. 'It is but another example of
the insufferable conceit which has paralyzed our Navy, and
which causes us boastfully and with boisterous satisfaction to
compare our appliances with those of our immediate past, while
foreigners are ahead of us in almost every particular.' 'We have
blithely and boastfully built ship after ship, and sprinkled champagne over them; when we should have wept tears over their
absurd military defects but for our complacently blissful ignorance of them.' 'Our present turrets ... are practically the
same shape and dimensions as Ericsson made them for us in the
conning tower of the first *Monitor*.' When these had detonated in
a reader's ears he probably was deaf to the following appeal for
understanding: 'My task of pointing out during the past year
the gross defects and deficiencies of our service has been bitterly
disagreeable and has cost me no little abuse from those who

cannot or will not see that not to have done so [being in possession of necessary information on foreign vessels] would have been
worse than indolent and cowardly.'

On February 22, Admiral George Remey forwarded the paper
on 'The Crushing Superiority of British Naval Marksmanship'
to the Navy Department with a favorable and tart endorsement,
in which he recommended that the paper be referred to the
General Board for consideration. 'I am not an alarmist,' he said,
'but I am satisfied beyond the slightest doubt that we are inferior
to foreign navies in gun mounts, sights, protection, and marksmanship to a perilous degree.' Then, after listing the specific
defects that occurred to him, he respectfully urged 'that the
officers of the service at large should be impressively informed of
our inferiority. Their present cheerful disbelief in the fact should
not be allowed to continue; and if they once understand how far
behind we actually are, we may confidently count on their zeal
and persistence to do their part to regain a position at least of
equality.' [10] In considering this endorsement, it must again be
emphasized that Admiral Remey was one of the most respected
officers in the service and that, as Commander-in-Chief of the
Asiatic Fleet, he was one of the most powerful and responsible
officers afloat.

In Washington the report made the rounds of the Department.
Secretary Long, without further comment, simply referred it to
Navigation,[11] the most powerful bureau of the Navy, in which
were performed, among others, the duties now delegated to the
Chief of Naval Operations. In his endorsement, the Chief of
the Bureau 'recognized fully the report's value as regards material' (with which Navigation had nothing to do) and expressed
himself as 'satisfied that the Bureau of Ordnance is taking the
necessary steps to keep up with modern requirements.' 'With
regard to personnel,' the Chief of the Bureau recognized 'that
a more systematic and progressive scheme of training officers
and men is needed, and Gunnery Instructions No. 1 is the first
step in this scheme.' [12]

[10] Endorsement of George C. Remey, files of the Secretary of the Navy, National
Archives.
[11] Endorsement of the Secretary of the Navy, National Archives.
[12] Endorsement of the Chief of the Bureau of Navigation, National Archives.

By the middle of April, the report had made its way to the Bureau of Ordnance, and on the twenty-second of the month the Chief of the Bureau had completed his elaborate endorsement.[13] The points raised by Sims and by Remey were considered one by one and at considerable length. In the first place, the Chief of the Bureau could see no reason for sending the report to the General Board as Admiral Remey had suggested, since the Bureau of Navigation had the responsibility for training pointers, and the Bureau of Ordnance the responsibility for material. Remey's statement about our inferiority might be true, but the Bureau took 'a more hopeful view' and did not share 'in such grave apprehensions.' From the *Naval and Military Record*'s editorial about the 'wretched state of [British] gunnery' it seemed possible to draw much consolation. Admiral Remey's remarks were based upon his experience with such ships as the *Kentucky* and the *Brooklyn*, which were six years old; our new ones would be much better. (Here it should be noticed that the *Brooklyn* and the *Terrible* were launched in the same year.) And, continued the Chief of the Bureau, if our ships were in some ways unsatisfactory, the British Navy was 'a veritable museum of antiquities.'

Admiral O'Neil's chief argument in criticism of Sims was his uncertainty about the possibility of continuous aim. 'If it had been stated that the continuous-aim method as practiced with Captain Scott's dotter was a useful exercise for training gun-pointers in manual dexterity, and in correcting the eye and judgment, no exception would be taken to such an assertion; but it is quite evident that actual target practice firing is not conducted on this principle and a practical test for a few minutes with a six-inch gun when the ship was rolling five degrees each way would show how impracticable such a method is.' He then proceeded to demonstrate mathematically that it would require five men at the elevating gear to produce the power necessary to follow a roll of five degrees in ten seconds with our six-inch guns. This demonstration was based upon figures obtained from experiments with a six-inch gun at the Washington Navy Yard, and it seemed to prove beyond reasonable doubt that the friction

[13] Endorsement of the Chief of the Bureau of Ordnance, Admiral O'Neil, National Archives.

generated in the trunnions of a six-inch gun could not be over-come by a single man. Hence it was safe to conclude that con-tinuous aim was impossible.

In conclusion Admiral O'Neil conceded that the 'service was indebted to Lieutenant Sims for his highly commendable zeal' and that 'intelligent criticisms should always be invited rather than shunned,' but 'the critic should realize that his opinions' merited only the same consideration 'as those from any other competent source in the service, even though such opinion be styled [in Sims' report] as "self-satisfied" and the product of "in-sufferable conceit." It should not be forgotten,' he added, 'that people may differ from us . . . and yet be as sincere as we are and may be quite as nearly correct as we are.'

It took some months for this endorsement to reach Sims and some months more for him to prepare a response to it, but by August 1 he had composed a paper in answer that was almost as long as his original report. It will be unnecessary to go into all of his rebuttal exhaustively, but some of his arguments must be considered.[14] He began by explaining that some of Admiral O'Neil's errors were the results of insufficient information. Had the Admiral read his previous six reports, he would have dis-covered that the *Terrible* did use continuous-aim firing in target practice. He then charged Admiral O'Neil with simply maintain-ing that our gun gear was as good as the British, when, throughout seven long reports, Sims had produced facts to prove exactly the contrary. From here Sims went on to a long and complicated mathematical refutation of O'Neil's mathematical demonstration that continuous-aim fire was impossible. The essence of Sims' argument was that O'Neil, taking his figures from a gun mounted on land at the Washington Navy Yard, had not taken into consid-eration Newton's first law of motion, which operated to assist the gunner in elevating or depressing a gun mounted on a moving ship. On land, the gunner had to overcome the force of the fric-tion in the trunnions by his own labor alone, while at sea the motion of the vessel assisted him in his work. But beyond this proof, Sims had the more convincing argument that continuous-aim firing was possible because it was done.

[14] Reply by W. S. S. to the endorsement of the Chief of the Bureau of Ordnance, August 1, 1902, National Archives. A copy is also in the Sims papers.

He had written the Gunnery Officer of the *Terrible*, Lieutenant Ogilvy, that 'some smart aleck at home doubts the possibility of C.A.F.,' to which Ogilvy pertly responded that 'I can knock your smart aleck out at once. . . . He seems to forget that you are not moving the gun and bringing it to rest, but that the energy you expend is only necessary to overcome the friction which prevents the gun from remaining horizontal. The energy required is small — it is no harder,' he said, with a rather sanguine hyperbole, 'for a man to do than it was for my old nurse to turn her sewing machine wheel for hours together.'

Sims inserted in his report a qualified apology for his methods. 'If I have been guilty of impropriety in the matter of impatience or intolerance I beg to be excused.' He granted that it was unpleasant for him and everyone else to tackle the question of the conceit of our service in such brusque terms — but since it was our biggest enemy it had to be done. For example, 'the *Brooklyn's* starboard gangway gun has been seen . . . during the past several years by practically every officer in the Navy; but I will venture to say that the veil of self-sufficiency, or whatever is the mysterious influence that paralyzes the critical faculty, has prevented everyone of them from fully realizing that all the vitals of the gun and every member of the crew would be exposed to certain destruction in action.'

Sims was not willing to let the matter rest with this reply to the Chief of the Bureau of Ordnance. On August 18, he wrote a personal letter to the officer who had only recently been placed in charge of the Bureau of Navigation — the extraordinarily able Rear Admiral Henry C. Taylor, who has been mentioned before in connection with his efforts to obtain a General Staff.[15] In this letter Sims invited the attention of Taylor to his reply to O'Neil's endorsement. His excuse for this unusual action was simply that 'the endorsement of the Bureau of Ordnance is not only a virtual denial of all of the evidence and information that has been submitted from this station within the past eighteen months on the subject of naval marksmanship, but the service has been informed through the Bulletin of Information [a confidential paper issued by the Office of Naval Intelligence once a month to all officers] on authority of the Bureau of Ordnance that

[15] W. S. S. to H. C. Taylor.

"continuous-aim firing with six-inch guns is mathematically impossible, except at insignificantly small angles of roll."'

The long sequence of these reports, endorsements, and letters was brought to a close in early September by a letter from Homer Poundstone, then in Washington, to Sims.[16] 'Your last paper and the letter to Admiral Taylor,' he began, 'have stirred up a most hell of a hornet's nest. . . . The Bureau [of Ordnance] in its endorsement was playing for time to save its face for they started as far back as last January to change existing mounts and de-signed the new ones, all looking to the adoption and use of the continuous-aim principle. When I asked Nibs why he hadn't informed you of this particularly — he said there was no time. They are trying to get things around your way, for they've put one eye guard of flexible rubber on the telescopes.'

But Poundstone pointed out that while most of 'the sensible people' were in accord with Sims, the changes had to be 'gradual, not sweeping.' There was not enough money to do the things inside of three or four years.

Again he voiced the fear that was in everyone's mind when they considered the recklessness of Sims' attack — 'The President had better be left alone; you've got them moving in the Depart-ment; and that's enough for now.' And he closed with the cheerful assertion that 'You can't possibly get yourself worse dis-liked than you are now, so keep it up. You have sent the entire gang to cover.'

About a week after the paper on 'The Crushing Superiority of British Naval Marksmanship' was finished, Sims was transferred, February 24, 1902, from the *Brooklyn*, homeward-bound, to the *New York*, the flagship of the Southern Squadron of the Asiatic Fleet. At the same time he assumed the twin duties of Fleet Intelligence Officer and Inspector of Target Practice, on the China Station. Though this was in the nature of a promotion and could be accepted as tangible recognition of his contribu-tions to the Navy, it is safe to say that Sims was sorry to leave the *Brooklyn*. Admiral Remey had proved a loyal and valuable friend, for whom he could have both respect and affection; per-haps to him more than any other naval officer Sims owed his early success. On the *Brooklyn*, too, there were three younger

[16] Homer Poundstone to W. S. S., September 6, 1902.

officers with whom he was especially congenial. McGrann,
Woods, and R. R. Belknap had worked tirelessly in his behalf,
and two of them were, in the future, to play important parts in
his career. The four used to gather in Sims' room to discuss and
argue about the reports that were in preparation. Not infrequently the major task of the three friends was to persuade the
older man to modify his language. One night, Woods and
Belknap were at work with Sims while McGrann in the next room
attempted to sleep before his morning watch. For some time the
two attempted to persuade Sims to describe an action of the
Navy Department in some gentler adjective than 'hopeless.'
Their intention was to find a word which meant the same thing,
but sounded as though it did not. In the course of their vain
search for the *mot juste*, the minutes passed and voices rose.
Sims rejected every suggestion until the problem was at last
settled by McGrann, who shouted through the bulkhead, 'Oh,
call it hopeless!' It was not all dull work nor solitary work, collecting material to explode the structure of the Navy Department.

So Sims left the *Brooklyn* with personal regrets, but these did
not interfere with his continued labors. On March 5, he finally
completed the paper which he had assured Arnold would make
a wreck of the *Brooklyn* — and he almost justified his boast.[17]
Once again with the aid of comparative figures, he proved the
startling ineffectiveness of our cruisers' gunnery.

By the time this report reached Washington, Sims had received another letter from Niblack telling him of the progress
made in gunnery since he (Niblack) had taken the office of Inspector of Target Practice.[18] He told of the new regulations
about to be released to the service and he pointed out that ten
Scott dotters had just been purchased. Most important of all,
the Department was aware of the unsatisfactory condition of our
marksmanship. 'You have done more than any one man in the
service to bring this question home very thoroughly. There is
not the slightest tendency in the Bureau of Navigation to blink

[17] 'The Fighting Efficiency of the *Brooklyn*,' March 5, 1902.

[18] A. P. Niblack to W. S. S., March 10, 1902. In a previous letter of December 29,
1901, Niblack had told his friend that after Sims' first letter of November 16 to
Theodore Roosevelt, 'the President sent for O'Neil [Chief of the Bureau of Ordnance]
and Taylor [Chief of the Bureau of Navigation] and asked their opinions. Cowles
got me to summarize your report. Meanwhile we have kept the fact secret that you
wrote him.'

at the truth or to dodge responsibility; but the best way to accomplish results is not to issue pronunciamentos. There is a terrific financial side to all this and when we get to asking for larger estimates we want to avoid the scandal in Congress and the press of airing all this thing in public.'

Sims was not as convinced as his friend that the Bureau of Navigation would not blink and he feared that the 'financial side' would provide the Department with a reason for permanent silence. He, therefore, decided to issue another pronunciamento and to direct it again to the source of power which the Department most feared. Early in March he wrote his second letter to President Roosevelt.[19] It is a long, detailed, and very clear statement of his case, which includes a review of all his activities from the time he joined the *Kentucky* in November, 1900. He had, Sims began, been called a pessimist, a paper man, a theorist, but he was none of these. He was, in fact, sanguine in tempera-, ment, in uniformly good health, and possessed of facts, not opinions. He had no personal ends to serve, no ambitions to gratify, but he was concerned to do his duty. Of the correctness of his views there could be little doubt; the facts sustained him, and of all the officers he had talked with, 'save those who had lost the power of consecutive thought, *not a single one* had failed to see the truth.' Of the nature of the opposition he would only say that 'I understand that it would be very difficult for any officer in the service to admit the justice of my criticisms, without having first carefully considered the information concerning foreign naval progress on which they were founded. It would in fact be impossible for anyone to do so, for the information does not exist in print; very few have a chance to acquire it, and almost none have even suspected our shortcomings. The consequence is that these bare conclusions come as a severe shock to officers who have believed, all their lives, as I had done until recently, that we were second to none. To accept them involves a deep humiliation that we should have fallen so far behind; and it is natural that this should, at first, be resented with more or less violent indignation — frequently misdirected against me.'

He then reviewed each of his reports and established as best he could the distinct inferiority of our own Navy. He was careful

[19] W. S. S. to Theodore Roosevelt, March 11, 1902.

to point out the names and dates of his papers so that the President would know where to find them if he so desired, and did not fail to underscore the significance of his position. 'I suppose there are many historical parallels — since men have always been the same; but I am intimately acquainted with only one. Many Frenchmen have described to me in bitterness, the absolute faith of the French people in their army, before the war of 1870, and the equally absolute faith of the army in itself. The parallel may be carried further. The French military attaché at Berlin at that time, finally realizing the situation, stated it in unmistakable terms. He warned his government of the inferiority of the French artillery — that was afterwards so crushingly demonstrated at Sedan. Here the parallel ends — for the present. His reports failed utterly to penetrate the inordinate conceit of the French, and were filed away without consideration; and he suffered in the esteem of his superiors for his supposed weakness in allowing his judgment to be warped by the glittering pageants of a military capital — and he did not escape the imputation of insincerity.'

With this second letter to President Roosevelt, to which Sims never received an answer, the major part of his work on the China Station was finished. Several more reports he did send to the Department before returning to Washington in December, but in the main they simply repeated or supplemented his earlier work. One perhaps deserves notice, a description of the Morris Tube Target.[20] This was a device for practicing continuous aim, superior to the dotter, since it used a sub-calibre rifle instead of a pencil to mark the target.

Besides his study and research Sims was kept busy with his own work as Inspector of Target Practice for the Southern Squadron. Here he made real progress. Dotter training was begun on all the ships and some of the Captains were persuaded to use the British target, counting only real hits, instead of our target upon which the hits were plotted. Through the summer of 1902 he watched delightedly while the ships under his supervision applied the new theories, and he had the pleasure of finding his vindication in the improved gunnery of the squadron. Gratifying also were the letters he received from older officers who had begun to hear

[20] 'The Morris Tube Target,' September 12, 1902.

more of his work. McCalla, a hero of the Boxer Rebellion and a friend of Jellicoe's, wrote approvingly to him, as did Richard Wainwright, who later was to become Aide for Operations. Philip Alger, his classmate, wrote applauding his ideas, but regretting his methods. Most pleasant of all were the letters from officers he did not know. To one such man he wrote: 'After a fellow has been cussed out for a couple of years and called a pessimist, a theorist, a paper man, a gallicized American, etc., etc., he finds no difficulty in making friends at once with even a total stranger that agrees with his pessimistic ideas too. I accordingly welcome you as a member of the S[ociety]. R[epression]. I[gnorant]. A[ssumption].' There were many new members who joined that summer.

In August, it will be recalled, Sims sent to Admiral O'Neil his reply to the latter's endorsement of the report on 'The Crushing Superiority of British Naval Marksmanship,' and in the same month he wrote the personal letter to Admiral Taylor which has been considered heretofore. Together the two communications had stirred up, in Poundstone's words, 'a most hell of a hornet's nest in the Department,' and they were Sims' last gesture from the China Station. On September 28, while the *New York* was on her way from Vladivostok to Japan, he received a telegram ordering him to report to the Chief of the Bureau of Navigation in Washington immediately. No reason was given for this sudden detachment from the China Station one year before his cruise was up, and Sims was left to speculate, on his long journey home, as to whether he was returning with honor or in disgrace. His buoyant optimism and the knowledge that his case was sound kept him from worrying too greatly about the future, but he could not guess that he had been appointed the new Inspector of Target Practice.[21]

There are several published explanations of how Sims obtained this appointment, differing in detail, but uniting on the essential conclusion that the man chiefly responsible for the choice was the President of the United States. An examination

[21] In later years Sims made much of the fact that he was left to worry about his fate all the way home. That he did not suffer greatly on the trip is suggested by Yates Stirling in his book *Sea Duty*, New York, 1939, p. 96. Stirling met Sims at the Palace Hotel in San Francisco. 'He [Sims] was on his way to Washington. He was full of his subject. "Come on back and help me fight them," he said.'

of the available evidence does not entirely bear out this opinion, for although Mr. Roosevelt's influence cannot be discounted, the credit seems to lie principally with another man. It is a complicated story, confused by an interplay of opinion, prejudice, and personality.

Early in 1902, Rear Admiral Henry C. Taylor had become Chief of the Bureau of Navigation. This man possessed a wisdom, courage, and vision that were unusual in the service of that time. Almost single-handed he had saved the War College at Newport from the attacks of duller officers who considered it a hothouse for 'paper men.' Virtually alone he had fought for the establishment of a General Staff, in which effort he was thwarted by the interference of an honest but unperceptive Secretary. One of his first actions as Chief of the Bureau of Navigation was to order the widely scattered individual units of the Fleet to come together for yearly manoeuvres, an indispensable practice, the value of which had been recognized previously almost alone by Admiral Luce. More important than these specific actions, Admiral Taylor had brought to his new duties an enlightened attitude, expressed in his own words, that 'We must admit the truth, take our licking from the press, and set our house in order.'

So greatly had Taylor been impressed by the reports Sims sent in from China that he wanted to appoint the junior officer Inspector of Target Practice. Powerful opposition to his choice developed within Taylor's own bureau. Captain W. S. Cowles, a hard-headed, fair-minded officer, held that Sims exaggerated the importance of continuous-aim firing. Cowles' word carried weight, for he was the brother-in-law and Naval Aide of the President. Captain Reginald Nicholson, in charge of personnel, joined Cowles in disapproval of Sims. These two officers reflected the attitude of the majority of the senior officers in the service. Their active opposition to Taylor's desire was supported by the silence of Rear Admiral Robley D. Evans. 'Fighting Bob' had gone to China in 1902 in command of a squadron. He was Taylor's brother-in-law. For reasons that will be made clear later, Evans made no mention of Sims' work either in his official reports or in his private letters to Admiral Taylor.[22]

[22] Material for this paragraph was obtained from R. R. Belknap in a letter to the writer, February 26, 1940. Belknap was in the Bureau of Navigation at the time.

On the other hand, several younger men urged the choice of Sims upon the Chief of the Bureau of Navigation. The brilliant Philip Alger, an ordnance expert, argued for his classmate. Another classmate, Homer Poundstone, and R. R. Belknap, recently returned from China, pressed their friend's claims to the position. One day Belknap was called into Taylor's office, to find him in conversation with Cowles and Nicholson. 'How about it,' asked the Chief of the Bureau, 'is Sims the real thing?' Belknap replied that he was. The younger men won out when Taylor made his courageous decision to bring back the stormy lieutenant who was opposed by most of the older officers.[23]

There was one unhappy aspect of Sims' return. He took the place of A. P. Niblack, who had retired as Inspector of Target Practice for reasons of ill-health. While active, Niblack had made some changes in our system of gunnery which failed to bring about any great improvement in our shooting. The criticism sent in by Sims naturally fell with severity upon Niblack, and Sims supplemented his official reports by caustic private letters to his friend. Furthermore, Sims had received word on several occasions that Niblack had not supported him as wholeheartedly as he might have done. Both Sims and his informants may have exaggerated the 'disloyalty' of Niblack, but the reports successfully broke the real intimacy that had existed between the two since the days at the Academy.[24] This was a personal sorrow. 'Nibs' and Homer Poundstone were the only men in the service who ever called him 'Billy.' The three had been 'thick as thieves' at the Academy. After graduation Sims always had reported to his family the occasions when he and the charming, witty Niblack dined or celebrated together in various parts of the world. After 1902 all that was over. As time passed, Sims came definitely to feel that his oldest friend had let him down upon various occasions. Yet it is a curious fact that he never in his life displayed toward Niblack the rather savage intolerance which he reserved for those men of whom he was fond but who he believed had deserted his cause.

[23] R. R. Belknap to the writer, March 6, 1940.
[24] That this break in the friendship of the two men was well known in the service is clear. Yates Stirling speaks of it (*op. cit.*, p. 95). A brief description of Sims and his work in the reform of target practice is given in this interesting book.

On September 28, Sims received his telegram. To the reader who has come thus far it is hoped that no apology must be made for the extended and at times severely technical treatment of his tour of duty in Asia. It was during this time that the whole direction of his life changed; that he laid the foundations of his future career; that he came, as the saying goes, into his own. The last word on these wonderful years belongs quite properly to him.

Here begins [he wrote Niblack on March 14, 1902] the sad story of my life. I knew nothing about ordnance to speak of when I came out here, and I don't know much now, but when the enormity of the ghastly *Ky.* failure once dawned on me, I made up my mind to accept nothing on faith, as I had always done, but to get to the bottom of everything. You cannot imagine the amount of work this has entailed. It is easy to write out things you know but not easy to reason out how things should be. I have given my entire energies to this work, to the exclusion of every personal consideration. I never go ashore except for exercise and the remainder of my time I stay in my room usually until 2 A.M.

I long ago decided that it would not be the same with my criticisms as it was six years ago. I wanted them refuted or accepted and I was perfectly willing that either should be done in peace; but in case of any underhand work — which was speedily forthcoming — I was perfectly prepared to go to any extent, and I still am. . . .

They were furious over my first paper and successfully stowed it away. . . . I therefore made up my mind that I would give my papers such a form that they would be dangerous documents to leave neglected on the files; that I would labor over them until I got them into such shape that the veriest landsman would understand them. . . . I was called a deliberate falsifier of facts and denounced in Ordnance, but in respectful and pitying terms of derision. But I was prepared, as I have said, to go to any lengths. I came to this conclusion last fall.

The citadel to be attacked was 'insufferable conceit' — and you want to call me off because I hold up to ridicule the foolish and dangerous vanities of these miserable failures. You object because I say things that hurt their feelings, because I indulge in personalities forsooth. Eh bien, mon vieux — the case is altogether too serious to consider little things like that even for a moment. Where it is a case of scalps we can afford to disregard such trifles as feelings.

I am playing this game to win or lose all. If I win (and success is assured), I will only claim as my reward the privilege of being left alone. I am not looking for anything; and I will not get in anybody's way. I admit a fondness for the Repression of Ignorant Assumption, especially in a good cause. On the whole it is perhaps fortunate that some men are that way. I am not a crank except in one sense of the word, the flesh pots mean nothing to me and the Department has no billet that I covet. I would not touch my cap for the softest snap going — much less accept it. This is not a virtue, it is a fact. Of course I am not insensible to the distinction of being selected for a responsible billet. . . .

I am perfectly willing that those honestly holding views differing from mine should continue to live; but with every fibre of my corpse I loathe indirection and shiftiness, and where it occurs in high places, and is used to save a face at the expense of the vital interests of our great service (in which silly people place such a childlike trust), I want that man's blood and I will have it, no matter what it costs me personally.

9

The great task of logistics, the art of military provision, is the maintenance of lines of communication. If men are to live and soldiers fight in time of war, there must be an uninterrupted flow of material from the permanent bases of supply to the ever-shifting army in the field. Sound tactics can win many victories, but, as Napoleon realized, in unsound logistics may be discovered the cause of countless defeats. Careers are not very different from campaigns; men as well as armies must solve this problem of provision. They must learn to accumulate along the way supplies of wisdom, judgment, knowledge. Especially they must take care never to overextend their lines of communication; never to lose contact with their past experience. Almost unconsciously Sims understood these human logistics. In every sector of his career he found resources. As he advanced to new positions, the past remained occupied territory, furnishing him with vital materials of information and experience.

Upon his return to Washington in October, 1902, Sims assumed the position of Inspector of Target Practice in the Bureau of Navigation. Several things claimed his immediate attention. First, he had to convince the service at large of the value of continuous-aim firing. Despite the fact that his reports had been circulated through the Navy in 1902, few officers had had the opportunity to see the new method of gunnery in actual practice. In Asia, under the auspices of Sims and Robley D. Evans, Scott's system had been introduced, but little was known about it in the Atlantic Fleet. The British had guarded their secret jealously;

131

so jealously in fact that they had kept it from a large part of their own service. Even in China the officers of the *Terrible* and the *Ocean* had refused to tell French and German officers anything about the new system. Sims, by virtue of his personality and because he was an American, had been given information vouchsafed to no other foreign officer. As he began work, therefore, his greatest immediate problem was the education of those who were unacquainted with the real principles of continuous-aim firing.

Part of this education was undertaken by his brilliant classmate Philip Alger, who, in 1903, wrote an able review of the whole subject.[1] This article was based, in part, upon Sims' reports from the China Station, though at his own request no mention was made of Sims. Alger clearly explained the virtues of Scott's methods, but failed adequately to explain that our own ordnance equipment could not be used with entire success for continuous-aim firing. This was probably because Alger had been connected with the Bureau of Ordnance.

The greater part of the work of education Sims had to undertake himself. His school was the Fleet, assembled under the command of Admiral Dewey at Culebra Sound, east of Puerto Rico. For several weeks in the early winter of 1902 he passed from ship to ship preaching his new gospel. The first fears that he would be received with hostility by the older officers were not borne out. 'I visited,' he wrote to Niblack, 'every ship in the squadron officially and asked to be given the opportunity to talk with all the line officers including the gunners. . . . Then I went over the whole business, illustrating by sketches. . . . It usually took me from three to four hours, and sometimes I visited three ships in the same day, which comes pretty near being work. Steady talking from 8 A.M. to 5 P.M. It is the truth I am telling you, that I cannot exaggerate the satisfaction with which all hands received this information. . . . Not a single false note.' He then went on to show why he believed his friend had failed to improve target practice. 'I don't think you gave it the attention you should have and you were handicapped by your friendship for the Bureau of Ordnance, but at all events you did not catch on to the true inwardness of the new principles of gunnery,

[1] Philip R. Alger, 'Gunnery in Our Navy,' *N.I.P.*, Prize Essay, 1903.

and you attempted a compromise which did not succeed —
they never do.'[2]

After several weeks in the Fleet, Sims returned to Washington.
He had done his work well. Most of the officers to whom he had
talked had been convinced by his persuasiveness, his arguments,
and his passionate interest in the subject. As a result of this first
visit, the crews of the ships began practicing daily with dotters
and Morris Tube Targets. For three months this training continued until enough progress had been made to justify a preliminary practice. During this period Sims returned again to
the Fleet, to assist officers in improvising sights and developing
training routines. He was everywhere at once, encouraging the
downhearted, persuading the unconvinced, firing all with his
own enthusiasm. Just before the practice began, Ridley McLean,
recently returned from China, joined Sims as his assistant.
The two began their long partnership in the Target Practice Office as the new system received its first trial off Pensacola.

The records of this practice were astonishingly good when one
considers the brief preparation that preceded the shooting.
On March 30 the Inspector of Target Practice described the
progress in a letter to Admiral Taylor. 'The *Indiana* beat the
record of the China Station today with her six-inch guns — with
an average of 40.6 per cent hits. Many of the men have hardly
ever fired her guns before.'

Other ships followed the *Indiana*'s example. The best record
was established by the *Alabama* which, with all her guns, made a
general average of sixty per cent hits. Thirty-three individual
gunners in the Fleet made perfect scores.[3] Such records convinced many of those who still doubted. Yet there remained
much work to be done, for the practice was rather the promise
than the achievement of success. All ships had fired at short
ranges, in smooth water, at slow speeds. Rapidity of fire had
not counted at all. The Pensacola trial simply proved that
properly trained gunners, even with improvised equipment,

[2] W. S. S. to A. P. Niblack. This letter, undated, is quoted in an unpublished account of Sims' career from 1900 to 1911 by T. B. Kittredge. This account, written
with Sims' assistance, is in the Sims papers.
[3] W. S. S. to R. S. Griffin. Quoted in the above account by Kittredge.

could shoot accurately, but the result gave Sims the necessary encouragement for his next step.

The greatest immediate need for our target practice was to establish a set of regulations that would be uniform throughout the service. To provide this, Sims and McLean in the spring of 1903 prepared a Drill Book, which was issued to the service in June.[4] Each ship was to be equipped with training devices, dotters, Morris Tubes, and loading trays. Each gun crew was to practice for at least two strings — about fifty dots — every day. Thus, by constant training, the pointers, sight-setters, and men who loaded the guns were to acquire an almost automatic proficiency. Their skill was to be tested twice yearly: once in a preliminary practice in which accuracy alone was considered, and once at a record practice in which speed as well as accuracy counted. The ultimate test of a gunner was to be the number of hits he made a minute. These practices were to be carried out at the conventional range of sixteen hundred yards.

The importance of gunnery was impressed upon the men by the increased wages paid to the pointers and gun captains. Cash prizes were awarded to the most effective, and a trophy was given to the best ship in each class. 'The spirit of competition ... is necessary to the development of the highest possible skill in gun-pointers, without which nothing is possible,' says the Drill Book. That this competition would be absolutely fair, a system of handicapping was worked out, whereby older vessels might shoot with newer ones on equal terms.

Competition was inspired even among the gunnery officers. 'Each officer ... was free to devise his own drill, number of men, and their duties, and all fired at target practice with guns of the same kind. Drills producing the best record were published for the Service, but all hands were still left free to improve them.'[5]

It should be noticed that the whole aim of these regulations was to train expert pointers and gun crews, to develop them to such a degree of skill as to enable them to make a large number of hits per minute. No practice was set to determine the 'battle

---

[4] *Instructions Governing the Training and the Target Practice Required for the Development of Expert Gun Pointers and Gun Crews*, June, 1903. This confidential booklet has formed the basis for the discussion of target practice that follows.

[5] W. S. S. to L. McC. Nulton, October 20, 1903.

efficiency' of each ship or of the Fleet. Until the men were trained in speed and accuracy, Sims saw no point in wasting ammunition at a practice that simulated conditions of actual warfare. He specifically refused to permit shooting at long range or in rough weather until he was sure that his men could hit the target under ideal conditions.[6]

McLean, as Sims was careful to point out, drew up the technical part of the Drill Book, but for the general spirit which pervaded all the regulations Sims himself was responsible. It may appear sententious to suggest that in his system he reproduced as faithfully as possible the conditions of life as he understood it. He possessed what professional baseball players call 'the old college try'; he was a competitor who believed that competition was the primary driving force in men's lives. Thus, in drawing up his rules for target practice, he established a game in which men could beat each other and in which they were rewarded for victory.

In the first eight months of his new duty, Sims had convinced many officers of the value of his new system, and he had devised training methods that would develop the accuracy of gunpointers. But if gunners were to attain the necessary degree of efficiency, the tools with which they worked had to be improved. The most important tool was the telescope sight. In Philip Alger's opinion 'the successful application of the telescope sight to naval guns is perhaps the most important improvement tending to accuracy of gunfire at sea since the introduction of rifled canon.' Sims' first trip to the Fleet at Culebra had reinforced his conviction that the service sights then in use were not adequate for the demands made upon them by the system of continuous-aim firing. In February, 1903, he so informed the Department. In April, Sims and McLean sent to the Department the design for a new sight which would eliminate, they believed, all the defects.[7] Little attention was paid to this contribution,

[6] Graphic descriptions of target practice can be found in the *Report of the Secretary of the Navy*, 1903; Philip R. Alger, *op. cit.*; and many magazines of the period. The *Scientific American* for these years had several articles on the subject, illustrated with very interesting pictures. The most informative discussion is by Albert Gleaves, 'Training Gunners in the United States Navy,' *World's Work*, June, 1904.

[7] This design was contained in a paper entitled 'Criticism of the New Sight for 7-Inch Gun Described in Bulletin of Information,' April 21, 1903.

which was soon followed with another report that severely criticized existing ordnance material.[8] For twenty-three pages Sims described the failures of gunnery devices that had been revealed in the first preliminary practice at Pensacola. Using the reports of gunnery officers, he explained how sights had jarred out of adjustment, primers had failed, friction disks had jammed, elevating gears had broken down, and so on. When the last page had been reached, the author had gone far to prove his contention that, until proper equipment was provided, a large part of the training which pointers received would be wasted.

The Bureau of Ordnance was in a difficult position. It was far easier for Sims to work out a training system to improve the human factor in gunnery than it was for the Bureau to prepare designs that would immediately eliminate the errors in the material factor. The new demands of continuous-aim firing had been thrust upon the Ordnance men unexpectedly, and it was impossible for them to make an answer that was at once immediate and satisfactory. The Chief of the Bureau put his case thus in 1904:[9] 'The awakening of a lively interest throughout the Fleet personnel in the target practice and in training of gun-pointers has led generally to very intelligent, though sometimes unreasonable, criticism of the Ordnance material. Such criticism must always, in the sum of its influence, be the most effective inspiration to improvement, and perhaps it is only natural to expect that occasionally such criticism should be unreasonable or unjust.'

Far less philosophic was Sims' own reaction to the situation. Part of his irritation was attributable to the fact that the Bureau did not move as fast as Sims wished it to, or indeed as it could have. After the preliminary practice of 1904, one year after Sims had presented his design for a new sight, it was clear that the sights still in use were unsatisfactory. He accordingly prepared a new report on the subject and saw that it reached the hands of the President. Upon reading this paper, Mr. Roosevelt sprang into action. By the Department he was informed that it would take seven years to replace the old sights. 'So he called

[8] 'The Defects in Gun Gear, Gun Sights, etc., at Pensacola,' May, 1903.
[9] Report of the Chief of the Bureau of Ordnance, in the *Report of the Secretary of the Navy*, 1904, p. 492.

in the young insurgents to state their side of the matter.' The insurgents, led by Sims, explained that 'designs for sight mounts could be prepared and that industrial firms could manufacture the appliances.' This would take, in the insurgents' opinion, about a year. The response from the Chief Executive was characteristic: 'I shall give the Bureaus an alternative: either they must find the money to resight the Navy with the best possible design of instruments or I shall take the matter up with Congress and tell them that the Navy's sighting devices are obsolete and inefficient.'[10] That Mr. Roosevelt did something of the sort is obvious. Within two years the Fleet was completely equipped with new sights.[11]

Though Sims could trace much of his success to the support of Mr. Roosevelt, the two never met until the first month of 1904. The naval officer had not called at the White House upon his return from China because he did not wish to create the impression that he was trading upon the relationship. Furthermore, he did not wish to embarrass the President before the new system of gunnery had proved a success. The first meeting between the two took place through the intercession of a third party. While Sims was in England in the late fall of 1903, discussing with Scott various gunnery problems, Captain (later Rear Admiral) Richard Wainwright proposed to Roosevelt that Sims be rewarded in some suitable fashion for his services. Wainwright was willing to see the young officer promoted over his head to the rank of Rear Admiral. This did not seem possible, since Sims had just been commissioned a Lieutenant Commander, but Admiral Taylor proposed giving him a cruiser. This Sims refused on his return from England on the ground that his system was not thoroughly proved. Nevertheless, the President was anxious to show his appreciation, and on the suggestion of the Secretary of the Navy invited the Inspector of Target Practice for lunch at the White House. Then began the long and fruitful personal friendship that lasted until the day of Mr. Roosevelt's death.

In 1904 the success of Sims' methods did indeed seem assured.

[10] W. S. S., 'Roosevelt and the Navy,' *McClure's Magazine*, November, 1922, p. 37.
[11] Report of the Chief of the Bureau of Ordnance, in the *Report of the Secretary of the Navy*, 1907, p. 484.

The records established in the record practice of 1903 and the preliminary practice of 1904 appeared to justify his greatest claims. Most pleasing to the Inspector was the spirit that prevailed among the gun crews. In the fall of 1903 he reported that one of the *Indiana's* eight-inch turrets made a percentage of '87.5 and the firing was much faster than any of our eight-inch guns have ever done before. The last string of four shots was very sensational, as the pointer did something that has probably never been done before. . . . He put all four through the bull's-eye, which is only fifty inches square, at a range of about 1600 yards. The enthusiasm following the fourth bull's-eye was something worth seeing. As soon as the pointer came out of the turret, he was seized by as many men as could get ahold of him. In spite of his struggles, in which his clothes were pretty well torn off him, he was taken to the pilot house and presented to the Captain; then all the officers of the ship and the umpires shook hands and he was carried down again.' Three years before, this ship would have fired by herself at an imaginary target. Her men would have been anxious to get a dirty job over with as soon as possible. Very few people outside the Bureau of Navigation would have known or cared how she compared with other vessels in the Fleet. Competition had won its point.

Less effusive but equally pleasing was the approval of the authorities. The Chief of the Bureau of Navigation remarked that 'The system of training for the development of gun-pointers and gun crews that is now in force has proved satisfactory, and was fully illustrated by the firing tests for accuracy by the new pointers of the Battleship Squadron. . . .' [12]

Following hard upon these words of praise came an incident that placed the entire system of gunnery in jeopardy. On April 13, 1904, there was an explosion in the turret of the *Missouri* while the ship was carrying out her spring practice. A 'flareback' from the gun had ignited a powder charge lying on the loading tray. Sparks and powder grains drifted down the hoist into the handling room and there set fire to other powder charges. Five officers and twenty-nine men were killed in this terrible accident.

[12] Report of the Chief of the Bureau of Navigation, in the *Report of the Secretary of the Navy*, 1903, p. 484.

There was a great stir in the press and men began to seek a cause for the explosion. It was suggested by some that the emphasis upon speed in target practice made it impossible to take adequate precautions against flarebacks and fires in the turrets. Two days after the accident the Washington *Post* observed that speed and efficiency could not go hand in hand. It added that the Bureau of Construction had been working on the problem 'of designing a turret which will prevent the communication of flame from the top of the turret, where the gun crews stand, to the handling room. . . . So far no satisfactory solution has been reached.' [13] This view that rapid firing was a dangerous hazard was taken up by several of the older men in the Department.[14] Unfortunately for Sims there was a grain of truth in the assertion. Before gunnery efficiency had been computed in hits per gun per minute, there had been no serious turret accidents, 'for the reason that,' as Lieutenant Commander Vogelgesang explained, 'we were so well content with the target practice we used to have in those days [before 1903], the interval of time between fires was so very long, and the time of loading was so protracted that there was no possibility of anything happening.' [15] Because of the kernel of truth in the argument, opposition to Sims' training methods grew rapidly. It became apparent that steps had to be taken immediately to head off the attack before it assumed formidable proportions. Admiral Taylor, who had so frequently come to Sims' rescue in the past, asked him to prepare a paper on the subject of turret accidents. Within a few weeks Sims had his answer ready.[16]

He began by explaining the necessity for speed in gunnery at sea. The major weapons of the Fleet were the heavy turret guns of the battleships. No one would send four ships against eight enemy vessels with much hope of success. By the same token it would be foolhardy to send four ships against an equal number, if the enemy could fire twice as fast. During the last two years,

[13] W. S. S., 'Roosevelt and the Navy,' *McClure's Magazine*, December, 1922, p. 57.

[14] For a complete explanation of this point of view see the testimony of Rear Admiral N. E. Mason, Rear Admiral W. L. Capps, and Rear Admiral G. A. Converse in *Hearings Before the Committee on Naval Affairs, United States Senate, on the Bill S. 3335*, Washington, 1908.

[15] *Ibid*, p. 129.

[16] 'The Danger of Exposed Handling Rooms and Turrets,' May 28, 1904.

Sims stated, the rapidity of fire of our great guns had increased from three to six thousand per cent, but we were still inferior to England in this respect. Speed, therefore, was an indispensable factor. Furthermore, it was not the cause of explosions.

Flarebacks — the flame that occasionally darted from the gun when the breech was opened — occurred no matter how slowly a gun was fired. Some device to eject the gas from the gun barrel was necessary, but such a device we did not possess. A far more fruitful source of accident could be found in the construction of the turrets. This was no new criticism. Four years before, on the *Kentucky*, Sims had pointed out that any sparks from the gun could drop perpendicularly down the open hoist into the handling room at the bottom of the ship. The handling room abutted on the magazine. In the *Missouri*, sparks had dropped down the hoist, just as Sims had predicted four years before. 'There is not,' he said, 'a modern vessel in any other navy in the world that has her handling rooms and magazines similarly exposed. . . . Since the time that powder was first used on fighting ships, the scuttles or holes through which the powder is passed up from the magazine passages to the guns have never before been placed vertically over each other, much less left entirely open.' To remedy this unhappy situation, he recommended a broken hoist that would prevent sparks from finding their way to the powder charges in the vitals of the ships. That these criticisms and suggested remedies were not new, he emphasized by pointing out that at least seventeen reports had been written on the subject by himself and others in the last three years. No action had been forthcoming.

This was another sombre passage in the strange counterpoint that went on between Sims and the bureaus during these years. To a friend he sent an illuminating explanation of the meaning of this antagonism:

> You will see at once that this paper [on exposed handling rooms] shows up a condition of affairs that makes the strongest kind of argument in favor of some scheme that will insure a more complete study of such important things as the design of a turret or a battleship. The men that use these appliances and who must ultimately be responsible for disaster in battle due to mechanical defects, should determine the requirements of the weapons they are to fight

with. The technical men should work out the details on the lines laid down. We will never be on a sure basis until the man who uses the weapons is the legal critic of them. At present the technical men build them, approve them, and resist all criticism that is disrespectful. This is human nature; but we must have a system that will neutralize the evil impulses of our nature — for all men are scamps to a certain extent; or, to put it more mildly, self-preservation is a law of nature.

Convincing though this report may have been to objective observers, it did not smother the fires of hostility that still burned in the Department. One day Sims found on his desk a memorandum advocating the computation of target-practice records on the percentage of hits rather than on the number of hits per minute. He heard that this paper was being sent around the Department in the hope that enough of the high authorities would sign it to convince the doubting that speed was a dangerous factor. In it he read the 'death warrant' of good gunnery. Once more he repaired to the great source of his strength in the White House. The meaning of the memorandum was explained to Mr. Roosevelt, and the eyes of the Chief Executive snapped fire as he replied, 'Leave this to me.' The order went out to the Navy that target practice would be conducted on a basis of hits per gun per minute.[17]

Thus was saved the system of gunnery that Sims had introduced. Unfortunately, steps were not taken at this time to alter the designs of the turrets in our battleships. Though the rapidity of our firing continued, the danger of exposed handling rooms likewise remained. Within four years there were two turret accidents, followed by a revealing Senate investigation in 1908. However fine the mills of the Department ground, they ground exceeding slow.

Shortly after Sims' successful defense of his system he suffered, together with the whole Navy, the loss of a courageous and intelligent advocate. Admiral Taylor died suddenly on a trip to Canada. Though his death was a personal blow to the Inspector of Target Practice, it likewise robbed Sims of support at the very moment he needed it most. In the summer of 1904 he withstood one more assault upon his training methods. Attack had been

[17] 'Roosevelt and the Navy,' *McClure's Magazine*, December, 1922, p. 58.

made on the grounds that it was 'trick shooting,' taking place at short ranges, in smooth water. The records were all very well, but they had nothing to do with fighting. One of the last requests which Admiral Taylor made of Sims was to ask him to write an answer to this criticism that was frequently made to the Chief of the Bureau of Navigation by senior officers.

In September, 1904, Sims made public his reply in the *Naval Institute Proceedings*.[18] Rifled guns of high velocity, he began, had increased the range so greatly that no pointer could estimate the range with any accuracy. 'The gunner of today must be trained simply to point his gun as directed and his sight will be set by direction of skilled range officers, advantageously placed for observing' the fall of the shot. From these two premises he advanced to his conclusion. 'When pointers have been trained to such a degree of skill that they can make a very large percentage of hits at the training range, under the favorable conditions prescribed for record practice, they have demonstrated their fitness for further training under less favorable conditions. To exercise them at the latter before they have achieved reasonable expertness at the former would be as unjustifiable a waste of ammunition as to exercise green riflemen at long ranges before they could hit the standard small arm target at 200 yards.'

Because there was much confusion about the question of training, he explained his regulations at great length. He admitted that the prescribed range was short — fourteen hundred to sixteen hundred yards — but he pointed out that the target used — seventeen feet by twenty-one feet — bore a definite relationship to that range. It was just big enough to compensate for all normal errors of the gun and just small enough to test a man's accuracy. If the range should be extended, as the critics demanded, to battle ranges — six thousand yards — the target would also have to be increased proportionately, if hits against it were to give any definite indication of a pointer's accuracy. This was something which few men — even naval officers — understood. He emphasized it especially because Percy Scott had just written to him that England had increased the range without increasing the size of the target and therefore destroyed all the value of Scott's training regulations.

[18] 'Training Rangers and Long Range Firing,' *N.I.P.*, vol. 30, September, 1904.

The article was not written in a gently persuasive style. Sims had, after three years, become tired of leading men up to justice when they proved obstinate. Upon the stupid or the unwilling he poured his vitriol, for he had learned that progress was largely a matter of strife. The criticisms of his system were not made, he believed, 'in the winsome spirit of seekers after truth, but with the slightly raised eyebrow and curled lip of the unthinking,' and he would answer them with an equal — if at times heavier — sarcasm. As he strode along the corridors of the Department, secure in his own rectitude, he found many objects for his continual attacks, but if he swung a big stick, he never learned to speak softly.

A gentler spirit, who had suffered perhaps more from the superior disregard of the Department, wrote him at about this time: 'I do think that you mistake for enemies men who are only opponents. I think it is right to tell you that you are very highly regarded in the service and that you have done useful work of the highest order. But I have heard your most cordial admirers deplore the fact that you often offend people, especially your seniors, by language and a manner that are unnecessarily harsh. They say you are your own worst enemy.' This admonition came from Bradley Fiske, whose range-finder ten years before had been brushed aside; whose telescope sight, the first ever constructed, had been condemned by his commanding officer, Robley D. Evans; who had even at this time envisioned the possibility of the director firing used on all warships today; and who in 1915 led the great fight of his life for a powerful Chief of Naval Operations. In every one of his efforts at reform he was right and in every one he was thwarted, sometimes temporarily and sometimes permanently, by the law of higher powers. Sims was aware of much of this when he replied to the above letter. 'It is not lack of comprehension or "conservatism" that has prevented progress, but downright and deliberate dishonesty. You know this as well as I do, and more than anyone you have suffered therefrom — you have thought best not to state it in your paper. Under the circumstances you may be right, but' — and it is Doctor Arnold's phrase — 'my pot does not boil that way.'

If the pot boiled, it likewise sang. Away from the Department and the irritations of the opposition, Sims was a different man.

Half the success of his system of target practice lay in his own hold over the men who worked under him. A good deal of his time was spent with the Fleet, watching the training, discussing problems with gunnery officers, talking with the men. In this personal give and take he was at his best, cracking the interminable jokes, turning the right word of praise, simply spreading the infection of his joy in living. 'He was so goddamn good-looking,' sighed a man who disliked him, and it was half his power. The commanding height, the immaculate uniform, the trim spade beard, the face bursting with confidence and health — there were few younger men who could resist this elegant figure. 'Fascinating,' recalls one, and fascinating he was.

In some electric way he made gunnery the passion of the men who worked for him. For three and a half hours a solitary engineer officer sat at his place at the wardroom table, listening in gathering gloom to talk of dotters, lateral compensations, and Morris Tubes. At last he rose and cried out in despair, 'Judas Priest, can't you talk about anything but gunnery?'

After a day on the ranges, Sims would join the wardroom, anxious to forget the tribulations of his job. Once, and not improbably many times, the wardroom of a ship at target practice sat 'in awed silence' while they listened to the 'great man' expound his theories throughout a meal. Toward dessert he broke off in the middle of a discussion and said, with a questionable simile: 'For heaven's sake, let's jolly it up. I feel as though I were having supper with the Twelve Apostles.'

Some genius in the wardroom of the *Missouri*, signing himself 'A. Tracer Schell,' caught the prevailing attitude of the younger men toward their mentor. On September 15, Sims was invited to 'a silent dinner' on the ship. The invitation was in the form of a picture of the Inspector of Target Practice. In a swivel chair mounted on blocks, labelled 'continuous fire,' 'isolated gun positions,' and 'gun mounts,' sits Sims, his head haloed in the words, 'I am it.' Surrounding his throne are bottles of 'dope,' 'abuse,' 'argument,' and 'sarcasm,' while in the distance kneel his two assistants, Ping McLean and Pong Symington. (The Morris Tube was called the Ping Pong Machine.) At the feet of the central figure roll the skulls of 'the very dead ones,' while

wounded, limping, and bandaged guns climb the steps leading
to the throne. A poem completes the invitation:

SIMS IO TRIUMPHE

Above the tumult of the press of men
In awful majesty I sit alone,
With ever faithful Ping and prayerful Pong
Kowtowing at the footsteps of my throne.

Unconquered see me! While beneath my feet
The empty skull of many a swivel chair
That once defied me in that home of sin,
The Bureau of Construction and Repair.

Far off upon each measured target range
I hear the burden of a wild acclaim
Thunder from out each fearsome fighting ship
In tribute to the glory of my name.

But crown of all my triumph! What is this
That comes before me and my eye bedims?
The little broken guns of all the Fleet,
Crying, 'Save us, O Sims!'

By 1905, the annual records of ships firing at short ranges
had appeared to justify the wisdom of Sims' short-range target
practice. Sims himself estimated that the speed and accuracy —
that is, the hits per gun per minute — of the great guns had increased in the three years over three thousand per cent. It
should be noticed here that this improvement took place under
the restricted conditions of record target practice and not at
battle ranges. By 1905, in view of the pointers' splendid records
and the promise of new sights, Sims was ready to advance to
the next step — the perfection of fire control.

Occasional references have been made to fire control in the
previous pages, but it has been unnecessary to explain it fully
until now. Repeatedly it has been observed that, until the end
of the nineteenth century, gun-pointers estimated their own range
and fired their own guns without reference to others. The introduction of high-velocity guns extended the ranges to such lengths
that a single gunner, from his position near the waterline, could
no longer estimate his range accurately or follow the flight of his
projectile throughout its course. Continuous-aim firing enabled

the pointer simply to keep his sight on the target, while all compensations were made for him by a gunnery officer. These two factors made men realize that it was possible to fire guns together — three or four at a time — under the control of one officer perched in the tops of a vessel. This officer from his elevated position could follow with a telescope the flight of a salvo and communicate to the sight-setters of all guns firing the changes of range that were necessary. In practice, fire control worked as follows: The officer in the tops — called a spotter and located in a fire-control station — estimated the range at which a battery would open — that is, with the aid of a range-finder he estimated how far away the target was. This range he communicated to all sight-setters, who set their sights accordingly. When this had been done, a 'ranging salvo' was fired. If it fell short of the target, the spotter estimated how far short, and communicated with the sight-setters below, telling them to advance their range — let us say fifty yards — calling out, 'Up fifty.'

Fire control depended, as can be seen, on accurate pointers and on sights which were set alike. By 1904, Sims was sure enough of his pointers to make a trial fire control with the ship *Alabama*, which had been fitted with special sights such as he and McLean had designed in 1903.[19] The results of this experiment convinced Sims and McLean that fire control was not only a possibility but a real necessity for ships in battle. Despite the usual disappointments attendant upon experiments, it was discovered that a spotter could follow the flight of a shell up to thirty-five hundred yards and could control the fire of the guns with considerable accuracy. At six thousand yards, battle ranges for the period, the spotter could not follow the flight of the shell throughout its course, but he could tell by the splashes what compensation was necessary.

It must not be assumed that Sims invented fire control. Bradley Fiske, as early as 1890, conceived of it as a possibility; the French and the Germans in 1900 recognized it as a probability; Scott had tried it in 1903. But Sims had understood the value of the idea and he had had the courage and patience to

---

[19] This experiment was the first step toward fire control. The results were explained to the service in the confidential *Experimental Spotting, Long-Range Firing, etc., held on the Alabama*, Washington, 1904.

wait until he was ready to put it into effect. Here lay the secret of his success as an administrator. Though he had not the kind of imagination which readily creates ideas of its own, he was not unimaginative. He could envisage the application of new ideas, and he had a clear, analytical mind that enabled him to select the sound theory from a jumble of impractical notions.

The experiment of 1904 was a beginning. In the fall of 1905, Sims was the moving spirit on a board which drew up, after the autumn target practice, the general principles upon which fire control rests even to the present day.[20]

The report explained fully the methods of range-finding, spotting, and controlling fire. Particular attention was paid to means of communication between the fire-control tower and the guns on deck. An intricate system of manual signals and telephonic communication was worked out which was not unlike, in principle, the system that is in use today. Refinements of all kinds have, of course, been added.

By 1905, Sims had successfully withstood all attacks upon his system of gunnery. He had produced results that were gratifying. He had trained his gunners to the highest point of efficiency and accuracy. He had fought for the improvement of the instruments with which these men worked. He had laid the foundations for spotting and fire control that are the basis for our modern gunfire at sea. It was an imposing record for three years of work. But there was still much to do. Those three years had been a period of education and training. What lay ahead of him was the application of that training and of the improved ordnance instruments to the conditions of actual battle. Only when battle efficiency practice at great ranges were held could he be positive that he had succeeded beyond all doubt or possibility of attack from without.

[20] 'Report of Board on Fire Control,' contained in the confidential *Report of Autumn Target Practice, 1905,* Washington, 1906.

10

1905 *Marriage*

IT WILL be recalled that in 1898 Sims had met the new Minister to Russia, Ethan Allen Hitchcock, when the latter stopped in Paris on his way to St. Petersburg. At dinner with the family he had startled the Minister with his revelations of the defects of our new battleships, and had recommended to the two Misses Hitchcock a book entitled *À Quoi Tient la Supériorité de l'Anglo-Saxon?* Thereafter whenever Mrs. Hitchcock was in Paris with her daughters, Sims called or was invited to a meal with all of them at their hotel.

In 1899, Mr. Hitchcock went back to America to serve as Secretary of the Interior in McKinley's Cabinet. A few months later, Sims went off to the China Station, so he saw no more of the family. Upon his return to Washington in 1902 the business of the Target Practice Office consumed so much of his time and interest that he went rarely into society and made no effort to re-establish his former friendship with the Hitchcock family.

One night at a reception at the White House he met Miss Margaret Hitchcock, the younger of the two daughters, who chided him jokingly on his failure to pay his respects to her family. He exonerated himself with the masculine excuse of his work, but he took the hint and went round to the house on K Street. There he found such a warm welcome awaiting him from all the family that he was moved to continue his calls until they became a matter of habit. On Mrs. Hitchcock's reception days, he made it his custom to arrive late and stay for dinner. After-

148

ward he would remain for a time talking business and politics with the Secretary while the two girls listened with interest.

Between the two men there grew up a mutual respect and affection, during these hours of talk. The Secretary had led a varied life before he achieved the eminence of a cabinet position. There had been some distinguished names in his family. His uncle had been one of Lincoln's military advisers, and Ethan Allen Hitchcock could trace his ancestry back to the great soldier whose name he bore. Born in Alabama, his early years had been spent in St. Louis. From there he had gone to the Orient with Olyphant and Company, where he acquired an adequate fortune at an early age. Returning at thirty-four to St. Louis, he opened the first plate glass factory in the Middle West, and in 1890 helped McKinley write the glass schedule for the tariff of that year. When McKinley ran for President, Mr. Hitchcock, because of his great respect for the man, contributed to his campaign fund. After the election he was appointed the Minister to Russia. In his position as Secretary of the Interior he fearlessly did much to eliminate fraud from the administration of public lands and instituted the first modest reclamation policy. His reform work met with the approval of McKinley and his successor Roosevelt. By 1904 he was considered one of the strong men in the latter's Cabinet.

Sometimes during Sims' calls the two daughters and he would adjourn to the parlor, where they would talk together. Margaret, the younger, was the more vivacious of the two, but Anne had a demure charm that did not escape the eye of the naval officer. Likewise she listened to his explanations of his work with more attention and apparent understanding than did most other women, and he found increasing pleasure in these conversations. For their part the girls thoroughly enjoyed this middle-aged handsome friend of their father.

In the spring of 1904, Sims went off to the target ranges for the *Alabama* experiment that was the first battle practice test of his new system. From there he wrote a letter to Anne Hitchcock in which he confessed that, after the firing of the great guns had proved him right, he stole away from the cheering men to a secluded place, and there he 'wept a little weep.' Had she known her correspondent as well then as she later did, Miss Hitchcock would have understood the implications of this unusual revelation, but at the moment they eluded her. In learned if feminine terms she replied to Mr. Sims that 'Kropotkin, that delightful Russian anarchist, says in his book that he feels sorry for a person who does not know the joy of making a scientific discovery on paper and then taking it to nature and proving it true.'

This was hardly encouraging but it was kindly, and the calls continued upon his return. It was almost a year more before Sims fully realized what had happened to him, and even then he had difficulty in making up his mind to tell Anne Hitchcock that he loved her. But his sister Adelaide urged him to do so and her sister Margaret, when consulted, was equally encouraging. So one night when Sims was talking as usual with the two girls in the parlor, Margaret slipped away as she had told him she would. Then he was left alone with the girl of his choice for the first time in his life. With characteristic simplicity he expressed his love. She, quite naturally, could only reply with feminine uncertainty to this unexpected news.

A few weeks later he sailed for England on one of his gunnery trips, with the matter still unsettled. On the way he slipped on a wet deck, to the vast amusement of his professional friends, and broke his collar bone, an accident of consuming interest to him, as was anything to do with his body. Anne cabled her regret and a flood of letters from England followed. Sometimes he wrote thirty pages a day, containing long accounts of his talks with Percy Scott, of his discussions with John Jellicoe, of dinner with Lord John Fisher and his lively daughters. He was delighted to find that the gunnery of the United States was superior to that of England, but to these heavy professional matters he added moving passages about his love and himself.

When he returned, Anne was almost willing. In the summer of that year he paid a visit to her family in Dublin, New Hampshire. There they took long walks beneath the shadow of Monadnock and on one bright summer morning they became engaged. The event was announced at a party to a group of friends, who frankly expressed their surprise.

Surprising in fact the engagement was. Sims at the time was forty-seven and could be looked upon, as one paper expressed it, as 'hopelessly a bachelor.' In his youth he had known several

girls rather intimately, but with none had he ever been in love.
Rather tranquilly too, if with becoming modesty, he had assumed
erroneously that none had ever been in love with him. With his
youth behind him, girls had been set aside as he devoted all his
energies to his profession, and as the years went on he became a
confirmed, complacent bachelor. It was a condition not without
interest to the wardrooms in which he was wont to explain himself.
He was quoted as being willing to 'give one hundred thousand
wives for one sure perfect plan of fire control,' and the wags on
the *Missouri* swore awful oaths to remain single until 'Sims himself should play the traitor's part.' In verse the talented Chaplain
Gleason celebrated the formation of the Bachelor's Protective
Association as follows:

> And so we're bondsmen of the higher life
> Where nought domestic our horizon dims.
> Our motto is: The Navy and the flag
> Our mistress; Glory until black Death trims
> Our spreading sails for us. Our epitaph:
> They loved their country and they followed Sims.

To the man himself and to his associates it seemed reasonable
to expect that he would continue to go his way alone; fires that
have been banked so long rarely rise in flames. There was something, therefore, unaccountable in the way he tumbled headlong
into love.

Equally surprising to herself and her friends was the capitula-
tion of Miss Hitchcock. Her rather wistful charm had impressed
many men, but she had planned to turn her hand to teaching
children. Much of her time in the years immediately preceding
her marriage had been given to really valuable work for the
blind. Though for one year she had lived at one of the most
sophisticated courts of Europe, and for five more had moved in
the self-conscious society of Washington, she had remained
strangely untouched by these experiences, retaining the simplicity
of her sheltered youth.

It was probably this more than anything which caught the
fancy and the admiration of the man who fell in love with her.
She seemed with her intelligence and appealing air of innocence
to fit the dream of fair women he had had on the *Swatara*. To
him, in fact, the whole thing seemed like some unique, perfect,

and unbelievable idyll, while to her this man who appeared 'different' from others was the only man she could have loved. Though they were different, far more different than either understood in 1905, and looked for different things in this world and the next, they wanted much the same things in each other. These they found for thirty years of extraordinary happiness. Where they could not supplement they wisely complemented. His simple force gave to her more complicated personality clearer purpose and direction, while she was a minister of grace seeking to defend not so much her husband as others from the consequences of his amazing power.

As they stood at the altar in St. John's Church on November 21, 1905, before the brilliant gathering of officers and cabinet members headed by the President, they were, in the conventional phrase, a handsome couple. But they both had something more than the conventional good looks. There was a fresh, unconscious quality about her that was most beguiling, while the well-molded masculinity of his features was softened by a kind of patrician elegance. If there was something unstudied in her attitude toward the appearance she presented to the world, her husband was more aware of his attributes.

Most men have gone over the brow of the hill, physically, at forty-seven, but Sims was in superb physical condition. With Thoreau he believed that every man is the builder of a temple called his body. This belief was tied in with his whole conception of himself. 'I have,' he once wrote his wife, 'just passed a brilliant physical examination.' Yet the thing was deeper than mere physical condition. It was as important for him to have well-kept fingernails as normal blood pressure or proper morals. Cleanliness, whether of mind or body or linens, was a passion with him. Much as he admired Theodore Roosevelt, he could not excuse him for appearing at lunch at the White House in a shirt he had worn while riding. Nor was he less severe upon a rising young poet who arrived at a tea given to him in Boston in what Sims probably unfairly called 'a dirty shirt.' All this had nothing to do with dandyism. His carriage was erect not because he was a sailor, but because he was a human being. He was immaculate because the sloven was indecent. The essence of his splendid security derived from his conviction that the mind and

body were as one and that over both, as permanent trustee, he
had an absolute control.

After the wedding there was a short honeymoon in Tennessee
before the couple returned to an apartment in Stoneleigh Court
on Connecticut Avenue. In this first apartment and in the small
house on Seventeenth Street to which they moved in October,
1906, the two established the daily routine which persisted
throughout their life together. Sims had a sense of the fitness of
things. He loved an established order in a room, a toolbox, his
own life. A sailor's career, broken into three-year fragments and
distributed over the face of the earth, lacks continuity, and Sims
therefore found unusual comfort and stability in his rigidly
established schedule. The timetable which governed their activities was largely of his devising, for he had been a bachelor too long
to understand the necessity of much compromise, and his wife
made most of the adjustments.

This schedule in turn was determined by his hard work, his
dislike of society, and his love of tea. Most of the day he was at
his office in the old Army and Navy Building. About five in the
afternoon he would return to his home, sometimes with a friend
like Commander Whittlesey (Uncle Whit to the children when
they arrived), to have a cup of tea. He had got in the habit of
breaking his afternoon in this way during his years at sea, and
tea became a kind of rite, with which nothing was allowed to
interfere. In those first years in the house on Seventeenth Street
there was always a frosted layer-cake on the curate's delight, and
Sims would inevitably climax the hour with the observation that
'It's astonishing how differently you feel when you have a cup
of tea and a slice of cake inside you.' He had a way of using such
remarks to set off an occasion, and at times both Mrs. Sims and
her guests would find the repetition tiring. If perchance Sims
forgot to observe how differently he felt, Commander Whittlesey
would remark with a smile, 'Why don't you say it and get it
off your mind?'

After tea Sims would take a walk and then after a bath he
would stretch out on a sofa, made especially long for this purpose.
For dinner he changed his clothes, even when, as happened most
frequently, the two were dining alone. After the meal he and
Mrs. Sims would read aloud to each other until ten o'clock each

evening. The nature of their reading was determined chiefly by his tastes — articles in *McClure's*, *Harper's*, or *Everybody's*; novels with action such as *Quo Vadis* or with some definite message like *The Honorable Peter Stirling*. Since he read more than most men for the purpose of learning something that could be applied immediately to his daily life, he looked for specific remedies rather than philosophical or theoretical concepts.

In a formal way they went out and entertained little. Society bored him. Especially he was irritated 'by the host who took one man off on a sofa and you have to sit in a chair with another man you don't want to talk to and who doesn't want to talk to you.' He preferred, if there must be dinners, to have what he called a 'general conversation.' This probably meant that he was not averse to a large audience for his endless stock of stories. At general conversation, in fact, that is, playing with an idea and throwing it back and forth among the guests, he never was particularly adept, though he could hold a gathering spellbound with anecdotes of his past. He could also be a very good listener if some other guest were recalling a colorful career or setting forth an interesting idea.

It was a quiet, comfortable, simple life upon which the two embarked, enriched by their mutual admiration and love for each other and by their sense of dependence and participation. In certain things, to be sure, they could not share. He, particularly, found difficulty in joining his wife in her special interests. Probably he never tried very hard, for long since he had found the futility of forcing his talents into unfamiliar channels.

The children, who were not long in coming, were almost his greatest joy and constant delight. Like so many military men and men of action, like Stonewall Jackson or Robert E. Lee, for example, his heart went out to little children. It was their innocence, their helplessness, their utter freshness that appealed to him. In the dark days of 1917 he wrote his wife for a doll to give to a little girl who lived in a livery stable not far from the Admiralty. With feelings such as this he could not get over the reality of children of his own after forty-seven years of waiting. In all there were five, Margaret, Adelaide, William, Anne, and Ethan. How well the Navy came to know those five through the ecstatic reports of their father! As with everything he had anything to do with, he was proud of them and reasonably certain of their superiority to others.

Sims in his lifetime was to have a few, and when all things are considered, a very few professional disappointments and bitternesses, but in his personal and private affairs he knew only the ways of tranquillity and happiness. For this he himself was partly responsible. He had a way of making up his mind, and his own conclusions became the ultimate realities. Likewise by his life at sea he was spared many of the minor irritations of home life: the babies not fresh and innocent, but tired, quarrelsome, and bawling; the decisions, disciplines, compromises, and all the rest of it. Thus spared, his symbols of blessed domesticity remained untarnished. Even in reality he was blessed, and for thirty years of married life he could rejoice, as few men can, that the lines had fallen in pleasant places.

II

Sims vs. Mahan

Sims' wide interests and great energies prevented him from concentrating exclusively upon his duties as Inspector of Target Practice even in his first years in Washington. One of the most important problems claiming his attention was the question of the proper design of our warships. Almost as soon as he returned to this country, he became involved in a discussion over two new battleships, the *Idaho* and *Mississippi*. These were two of five ships authorized by Congress on March 4, 1903, but they differed in size from the other three. The *Kansas*, *Vermont*, and *Minnesota* were to displace sixteen thousand tons, while the *Idaho* and *Mississippi*, though intended by the bill to contain the same armament, were specifically limited to thirteen thousand tons. Why this smaller tonnage was stipulated is not entirely clear. Some Congressmen distrusted the value of sheer size in a warship; some regretted the expense of great vessels. A few observers believed that the thirteen-thousand-tonners were authorized through the influence of a politician in whose state was a shipyard unable to build or service larger battleships. Whatever the reasons, Congress had its way and specified ships that were smaller, less efficient, and slower than the units of our existing battle line.

When the members of the Board on Construction considered plans for the *Idaho* and *Mississippi*, they found themselves in disagreement with each other. Unable to resolve their differences, the members of the Board referred the problem to the Secretary, who in turn asked the opinions of nine officers, among whom was Sims.

156

In August his reply was sent to the Secretary.[1] His remarks
were prefaced by a reiteration of his position taken earlier on the
China Station, that the method of designing ships by asking the
opinions of line officers was inefficient and dangerous. 'Any
service,' he said, 'must at all times be distinctly behind both the
latest information and the most advanced thought in any particular branch of the profession.'

Then he attacked the *Idahoes* on the following grounds: freeboard was so low that it would be impossible to fight in any
great seaway; the secondary battery was placed in open gun
positions without adequate protection; the superimposed turrets
were an invitation to concentrated attack from the enemy.
Finally, these ships were an unwise economy. 'It is said to be a
tradition of the American Navy that our vessels shall carry a
heavier battery on the same displacement than those of any
other nation. This tradition, which like all traditions is necessarily opposed to progress, can readily be fulfilled; but only at the
expense of other qualities — height of gun platform, speed, etc.
We of the richest nation in the world put more nominal gunpower
afloat for the same amount of money than many tax-ridden
countries, but it seems to me we do so at the distinct risk of a
disaster, depending on the weather; and, as the speed of our
fleets is apparently to be that of the slowest (*Idaho*) units, we will
not be able to choose our weather for battle.' His philosophical
observations concerning the effects of tradition on progress might
be wrong, but his objections to the *Idahoes* were not, though they
were disregarded. Indeed they had to be, since the Board on
Construction was bound to execute the will of Congress. The
ships, built at a cost of twelve million dollars, were sold, after a
few years of disappointing experience, to Greece. The people
of this country have frequently distrusted the motives and intentions of our naval men, but there have been a good many occasions when they have suffered more directly from the wilful
blindness of their own representatives and of themselves.

Of more permanent significance was Sims' part in the development of the all-big-gun ship. Before 1905, ships of the battleship
class mounted guns of mixed calibre in the main batteries. The
Kentucky, for example, had four thirteen- and four eight-inch

[1] W. S. S. to the Secretary of the Navy, August 7, 1903.

guns in its superimposed turrets. In the last months of 1906, however, a battleship was launched in England which rendered all previous vessels obsolete. This ship, the *Dreadnought*, contained a main battery of ten twelve-inch guns. In other ways she departed from the traditional principles of battleship design. She was faster, twenty-one knots; she was bigger, 17,900 tons; and she was heavily armored, eleven inches in her main belt. Lord John Fisher, the great English First Lord of the Admiralty, was the moving spirit behind the construction of the *Dreadnought*, but the origins of her design lie farther back in naval history.[2]

Almost forty years earlier, various countries had experimented with the type. In 1879, the French had built the *Amiral Duperre* with a main battery of four thirteen-inch guns and this was followed four years later by the *Amiral Baudin*, the first seagoing battleship without sail, which mounted four 14.6-inch guns. The British with the *Magentas*, the Germans with the *Brandenburgs*, and the Russian with the *Sinope* had all tried out battleships with single-calibre main batteries before the turn of the century, but all these vessels were before their time. Gunnery had not progressed to the point where it was possible to use this powerful armament with efficiency. Since the ships 'did not conform to the tactical ideas' of the period, the class was given up.[3]

The acceptance of steam, the improvement of long-range rifles, and the development of fire control revived interest in the design after 1900. Cuniberti, an Italian, in 1903 published an article in *Jane's Fighting Ships* advocating the principle of the all-big-gun ship. In the next year Lord John Fisher was, with the aid of others, engaged in preparing the 'fundamental ideas of the *Dreadnought*.'[4] Certain men in our Navy were busy on a similar project. The most advanced of these thinkers, at this time, appears to have been Homer Poundstone, Sims' old friend and classmate. He had first begun his researches into the problem while Sims was on the China Station in 1901. As early as 1903, Poundstone published in March and June two articles ad-

[2] An excellent discussion of the development of the all-big-gun ship idea is contained in Arthur J. Marder, *The Anatomy of British Sea Power*, New York, 1940, Chapter XXVII.

[3] William Hovgaard, *Modern History of Warships*, New York, 1920, pp. 56–57.

[4] Marder, *op. cit.*, pp. 527–528.

vocating battleships with main batteries of large, though mixed, calibre guns. He proposed four twelve-inch and four ten-inch guns, which would enable a ship to throw considerably more metal than the prevailing thirteen- and eight-inch main batteries. The ships he suggested in these two articles, christened by their designer the *Feasible* and the *Probable*, were concessions to the conservatives, who could not yet envision a single-calibre battleship. But Poundstone had prepared plans for a third and more daring vessel which he called the *Possible*. When considered in the light of the *Dreadnought*, laid down more than two years later, the characteristics of the *Possible* are interesting. She was five hundred feet long, displaced nineteen thousand tons, and had a speed of eighteen knots. Her main armament of twelve eleven-inch guns was contained in six turrets, two of which were on the centre line. In addition she had twenty-four three-inch rapid-fire guns for defense against torpedo craft. The main armor belt was at a maximum eleven inches thick. Compared with the *Dreadnought*, the *Possible* had a slightly larger displacement, was more heavily armed, was equally well — perhaps a shade better — protected, and was three knots slower.[5]

The *Possible* was too far in advance of its time to receive adequate consideration, though the subject of an all-big-gun battleship was under consideration in America as early as 1903. In the summer of that year the question was debated at a conference at the War College in Newport. Shortly thereafter the idea was taken up by the General Board. In October, 1903, the General Board asked the Bureau of Construction to 'prepare a tentative design for a battleship with a battery of 12 heavy turret guns, none of which shall be less than ten inches, and at least four of which shall be 12 inches.' Again in February of the following year the request for a design was repeated, but no plans were immediately forthcoming by the Bureau in return.[6]

It can be seen that by 1904 the subject of the all-big-gun battleship was receiving considerable attention in the Navy Department. Poundstone wrote Sims of his intention to capitalize on this interest by submitting his plans to the Bureau of Naviga-

[5] Details of the *Possible* were taken from a blueprint presented to the writer by Homer Poundstone.

[6] Marder, *op. cit.*, pp. 540–541; H. S. Knapp to W. S. S., July 9, 1908.

tion. On July 15, Sims replied advising him on the procedure necessary to get the designs before the General Board. He added that 'Jencks of the *Army and Navy Journal* told me a few minutes ago that Converse told him that they (the Board on Construction, I suppose) had decided that the next battleship to be designed would have nothing but 12-inch and 10-inch guns in the main battery, and principally 3-inch in the secondary. *The credit of this belongs largely to you, and you will get most all of it,* if you get your papers in in time.' 'Haste,' he concluded, 'is necessary because the "subject is booming." ' [7]

Poundstone planned to send in all three designs, but Sims preferred the *Possible*. From the gunnery point of view this was certainly the best ship. As Sims pointed out to his friend, a single-calibre ship had an enormous advantage 'in the matter of fire control over a vessel having guns of different calibres — also the great advantage of uniformity in the battery when it comes to replacing disabled men in battle.' [8] Ten days later he wrote again to Poundstone, who throughout this time was ill in the Naval Hospital. 'Yours of yesterday received this morning with your letter of transmittal and the blueprints of the *Feasible* and *Probable*. They are immensely more powerful than anything afloat, but I am so stuck on the all-eleven-inch ship that I can't think about any other one. Everything is drifting that way, so it is the sketch of the *Possible* that you want to get in.' [9] He assured his friend that he would see that the letter of transmittal 'and the blueprints are sent to the G. B. on Monday. Captain Whiskers is liable to forget all about it while mulling over the proper disposition of our fleet when we have sixty battleships.'

For some months the subject hung fire, although the General Board did consider the plans submitted by Poundstone. Nothing, however, was done until early October, when Theodore Roosevelt, who for some time had been an interested observer of de-

[7] This letter, together with those that follow, is not in the Sims papers. It is taken from a collection of letters bearing upon the all-big-gun battleship given to the Museum of the United States Naval Academy by H. C. Poundstone. Through the great kindness of Captain H. A. Baldridge (Retired) the writer has been given photostats of this correspondence.

[8] W. S. S. to H. C. Poundstone, July 15, 1904. From the Museum collection.

[9] W. S. S. to H. C. Poundstone, July 24, 1904. From the Museum collection. Sims, however, warned his friend that the 'Bureau of Construction and Despair' would 'TRY' to call the ship the 'IMPOSSIBLE.'

velopments, took a hand in the business.[10] On October 5 he
wrote to Sims asking for his opinion on the all-big-gun ship.
Sims replied next day that he believed 'that the great majority
of our naval officers who interest themselves in such matters
have long since been convinced that this is the only logical battery for a fighting vessel.' The two objections most frequently
raised against such a ship were: first, that it could not be built
upon a practicable displacement; and second, that 'the larger
the gun, the poorer its shooting qualities.' In answer to these
objections, Sims pointed out that Poundstone's *Possible* had a
designed displacement of nineteen thousand tons and that the
May, 1904, target practice had proved beyond all doubt that
big guns were more accurate than smaller ones.[11]

The President had sought Sims' opinion because he was concerned about the proposed armament of the *New Hampshire*, a
battleship that was soon to be built. With good cause Mr.
Roosevelt was alarmed, for a more bizarre armament could
hardly have been devised. Four twelve-inch, eight eight-inch,
twelve seven-inch, twenty three-pounders made up the several
batteries of the *New Hampshire*. As Sims pointed out to the
President, it would be impossible to control such guns properly,
while the seven-inch guns were so near the waterline that it
was difficult to believe that they could be used in any kind of
seaway.

Two days after receiving Sims' reply, the President on October
8 sent a memorandum to the Board on Construction suggesting
only eleven- or twelve-inch guns for the main battery of the *New
Hampshire* and an adequate number of three-inch guns for protection against torpedo boats. In this suggestion was contained
the essence of the all-big-gun ship, almost a year before the *Dreadnought* was laid down in England.[12] Sims was sanguine about the

[10] As early as 1902, Mr. Roosevelt knew of Poundstone's work. On December 27,
1902, the President wrote, 'It [Poundstone's paper on the big-gun ship] is excellent;
though I am not sure that I can get Congress to take the view I should like it to take
on the subject.' From the Museum collection.

[11] W. S. S. to Theodore Roosevelt, October 6, 1904. Secretary's files, National
Archives.

[12] Memorandum to the Board on Construction by Assistant Secretary C. H.
Darling, October 8, 1904. Secretary's files, National Archives. For a similar view
from Mr. Roosevelt see his letter to Secretary Morton October 6, 1904, quoted in
George T. Davis, *A Navy Second to None*, New York, 1940, p. 186 n.

chances of success at this time. Again, on October 6, he wrote to Poundstone that the 'subject is booming, and the fact that the "Old Man" is looking into it understandingly has set the whole gang at work.' Reassuringly he added, 'As far as I can make out, all hands are after the big ship.'

In fact, he was too sanguine. On October 17, 1904, the Board on Construction replied to Roosevelt's memorandum.[13] 'From time to time,' they said, 'suggestions have been made as to the desirability of eliminating all intermediate calibres of guns on battleships, reducing the armament to heavy guns and a light battery not exceeding three inches in calibre.' Nearly three years before, the Board admitted, they had rejected a skeleton design of such a ship drawn up by the Bureau of Construction. To strengthen their resistance, the Board pointed out that Admiral O'Neil (the Chief of the Bureau of Ordnance) had recently returned from abroad with the information that our *Connecticut* class was as powerful as anything built or building in Europe. Its final conclusion was 'that nothing has transpired during the past year which would justify extensive changes in the main battery of vessels building or recently designed.' Time must be given before radical changes could be made, and, for the moment, the Board remained satisfied that 'prolonged and mature consideration' had made the *Connecticuts* the most powerful in the world.

The Bureau of Navigation confirmed these findings.[14] The *New Hampshire*, limited by Congress to sixteen thousand tons, was too small for an all-big-gun ship. 'Seaway' was a loose phrase and there were some seaways in which the seven-inch guns could be fought. But the Bureau was not without hope that, when our designers had thought more about the subject and after more data had been accumulated, we might have an all-big-gun battleship.

The General Board, Sims, Bradley Fiske, Richard Wainwright, and others supported Roosevelt, but against them were ranged the Bureau of Construction, the Board on Construction,

[13] Memorandum of the Board on Construction, October 17, 1904. Secretary's files, National Archives.

[14] Memorandum of the Bureau of Navigation, October 15, 1904. Secretary's files, National Archives.

the Bureau of Navigation, and Sir William White, who wrote a special memorandum for the Secretary, disapproving the all-big-gun ship. Sir William's name at that time was one to conjure with, for he had designed most of the contemporary warships of the British Admiralty, and Roosevelt could do nothing but yield to the combined pressure of the authorities. So the matter was, for the moment, dropped.

In 1905, the sponsors of the all-big-gun ship gained a point when the *South Carolina* and the *Michigan* were authorized, with main batteries of eight twelve-inch guns. Several investigators have discovered, in this, reason to believe that the United States was first in the field with the *Dreadnought* type. Marder has done much to dispel this notion, but it must be emphasized that these two ships, laid down a few weeks before the *Dreadnought* had her first sea trials, were not comparable to the great English ship.[15] It is true that the *Michigans* had broadsides equal in weight of metal to the *Dreadnoughts* and that their heaviest armor was as thick as that of the English vessel, but they had been built on our classic displacement of sixteen thousand tons, were two and a half knots slower, and contained defects in design which made them incapable of standing up to such an opponent as the *Dreadnought*.

One year later, in 1906, another battleship, the *Delaware*, was authorized. For the first time in modern naval history, Congress did not stipulate the tonnage on which a ship was to be built. The *Delaware*, laid down in 1907, has been called the first 'true' dreadnought built by the United States. Though she contained certain defects in design that were later the subject of much discussion at a special conference called by President Roosevelt, her general characteristics of armament, heavy armor, and speed were certainly those of the dreadnought type. It is therefore clear that, by the time plans for this ship were prepared, a majority of both officers and politicians were reconciled to the introduction of the all-big-gun ship. But there was still in 1906, the year in which the *Delaware* was authorized, a minority, both in the Navy and Congress, who opposed the type.

In Congress this minority was led by the powerful Senator Hale of Maine, who was Chairman of the Senate Committee on

[15] Marder, *op. cit.*, p. 542.

Naval Affairs. The leadership of those in the Navy who advo
cated small, slow, mixed-calibre battleships was assumed by
Alfred Thayer Mahan. Ever since the Spanish-American War
he had been convinced that this traditional type of vessel was the
most suitable for our naval requirements. The war in Asia between the Russians and the Japanese confirmed him in his belief.
Thus, in 1906, those who wanted dreadnoughts found themselves
opposed, not only by a minority, but by a minority under the
dual leadership of one of the ablest men in the Senate and the
outstanding naval authority in the world.[16]

Probably at this distance it cannot be understood how potent
was the name Mahan; it alone was worth more in the public's
eyes than all the papers and memoranda ever composed by the
Bureau of Construction and Repair. In 1906 he was at the very
height of his fame. But he brought more than reputation to this
discussion, for within the strict confines of his intellectual boundaries, few men reasoned more incisively and clearly than did
Mahan. Here, too, it is not improper to remark upon another,
more subtle force that was always at his command. It is the
fashion now either to disparage or to disregard the quaintly
archaic style in which he made his observations; but even ears
accustomed to modern syncopations can discover a stately music
in his sentences. If his contemporary audience was convinced by
what he said, it was not less persuaded by the way in which he
said it. All his talents and his authority this gifted man placed
at the disposal of those who attacked the principle of the *Dreadnought*. The classic defense of his position he put forward in an
article published in June, 1906, in the *Naval Institute Proceedings*.
It was entitled 'Reflections, Historic and other, suggested by the
Battle of the Japan Sea.'

The information on the battle of the Japan Sea, upon which
Mahan's reflections were based, he had obtained from official
reports and an article in *Blackwood's Magazine*. From these data
he arrived at specific conclusions about the course of the battle
and at general conclusions about the value of small mixed-calibre
ships as opposed to all-big-gun ships. After reviewing the events
of the engagement as he understood them, he decided that

[16] A good, brief summary of the opposing views on the dreadnought type may be
found in George T. Davis, *op. cit.*, pp. 179–181.

'Togo, by good scouting and choice of position, secured beyond
reasonable hazard his strategic object of bringing the Russian
Fleet to battle, irrespective of speeds.' From here he proceeded
to a more general assumption. 'What is contended here is that
speed at its best is a less valuable factor in a battleship than fighting power, and that it is subject to more serious deductions, un-
avoidable and accidental, than fighting power is; and for these
reasons — original inferiority of value and greater uncertainty
of maintenance — it must be kept severely in its proper place of
subordination in the design of battleships.'

The actual situation in the Japan Sea, as he understood it,
led Mahan inevitably to this conclusion, but he went on to consider three other aspects of this question of speed. In battle the
unprotected funnels of ships were fine targets for secondary
batteries. When these funnels were perforated, the draft of the
fires and therefore the speed of the vessels was impaired. It was
not the part of wisdom, consequently, to build fast ships whose
initial advantage could be so soon destroyed. In addition,
Mahan pointed out that the speed of a fleet was determined by
its slowest unit, not its fastest, and dreadnoughts would therefore
be compelled to accept the tactics imposed by the rate of older
vessels. There was a corollary to this proposition that did not
escape him. 'In a fleet today, [a dreadnought's] speed will be
that of her slower sisters; more *Dreadnoughts* must be built to keep
up with her; and upon them in turn, according to the prevalent
law of progress, she will be a drag, for her successors will excel
her.' Mahan could only feel that 'this wilful premature antiquat-
ing of good vessels is a growing and wanton evil.' He wanted to
stabilize the battleship type where it was; to adopt some permanent standard beyond 'the crude one that each ship must be
bigger (and faster) than the last.'

From speed he turned to the question of the proper armament.
The Japanese had seventeen guns in the primary battery
(twelve- or ten-inch guns) and a hundred and ten in the secondary (six- and eight-inch guns). In Togo's division alone 'the
lighter pieces were to the heavy in the proportion of $2\frac{1}{2}$ to 1,
and we may be justified in assuming that calibre for calibre there
were at least four discharges of the secondary to one of the
heavier, with the consequent probability of a proportionate num-

ber of hits.' From this assumption Mahan went on to others — notably that most of the Russian vessels must have been sunk by the secondary batteries of the Japanese. He believed that the bottoms of the warships must have been exposed to enemy gunfire as the vessels rolled in the seaway and that against such targets 'penetrable to all guns, volume of fire is of the utmost importance; for while the aiming may be all of the best, the opportune moment of the shot's arrival when the bottom is exposed is beyond the control of the aptest gunner.' Because of their greater rapidity, quite obviously the secondary batteries could produce the greatest volume of fire; in fact, the Russians admitted that they had been blinded by the hail of shells from the Japanese guns. This argument alone was enough to justify Mahan's own faith in secondary batteries, but he produced another of the theoretical kind so dear to his heart.

Great guns meant actions at long ranges and 'the fleet which has thus placed its dependence on long-range fire has with it assumed the moral tone and temperament associated with the indisposition to close.' Closing was to Mahan the essence of successful action. 'I do not wish to lay undue stress on moral forces, undeniable as is the effect of habitual action, or prepossession upon moral strength; but I think appeal can be made confidently to history that the navy which, for any reason, habitually seeks to keep its enemy at a distance, in order to secure a preliminary advantage, usually fails to achieve more than a defensive success for the occasion, and in the long run finds itself brought to battle at an unexpected moment, under conditions unfavorable to it, both materially and morally.' Great guns and long ranges destroyed 'the mental attitude which keeps offensive power in the foreground; a steadfast prepossession in favor of its immortal superiority.'

All these things added up to a forceful argument against the all-big-gun ship of high speed. We would do far better, as a nation with wide naval responsibilities, to put the same amount of money and an equal trust in a fleet of smaller, more numerous ships than in a fleet of larger, less numerous vessels. The loss of one unit would be financially, materially, and morally less damaging. One ship in dry dock or coaling or destroyed would weaken the Fleet less seriously in numerical proportion to the whole. Speed might enable us to evade an enemy, but the offensive power of a mixed-calibre Fleet would ensure our crushing him.

Mahan's article produced the results expected from any contribution of his mind and pen. The press commented at length and favorably upon his findings; the small-ship men, both in the Navy and in Congress, found in his reflections the ultimate confirmation of their views; for a time even the President was shaken in his beliefs. On August 30, 1906, the President's Secretary, Mr. Loeb, wrote Sims informing him that Roosevelt would be interested in the naval officer's views on Mahan's article. Sims at the time was in Dublin, New Hampshire, taking a well-earned vacation. Early in the summer Mrs. Sims, who was expecting her first baby, had gone to Dublin to stay with her mother and father. Her husband had remained in Washington until late in August. Thus, for the first time, the two were separated for an extended period, and it had not been pleasant for either of them. Sims had even thought of resigning from the service, so he wrote his wife, to be with her and his children always. 'But no matter what may be, I know I can always turn to the little home and the dear little wife for sympathy and comfort, and in her sweet companionship forget all my relatively unimportant troubles. What a wonderful thing this is — the eternal phenomenon of love. But a little while ago and all thoughts of ever being a factor in the great circle of love had been banished from my mind for all time. Ah, ah! the wonder of it all that this should have come to me, a grisseled old bachelor from a young and accomplished woman with a loving heart and a clear head and the sweet maternal instincts of a true woman. I am exceedingly impatient for the day when our anxiety will be over in the joy of hearing the first cry of the wee one.' During the hot summer he wrote frequently to her of his anxiety about her health and suggested books for her to read and exercises for her to take. Now and again his mind leaped into the future and he 'saw the great cycle of love completed as we grow old together and live again love's young dream in our children.'

Considerations of his own health brought him back to the present. One night he had milk, bread, and just a little ham — simple food that he liked to the exclusion of all messy dishes with high seasoning. But the most important thing for health was to keep 'your lungs and heart in good condition with exercise in the open air.' So he prescribed for what was to be a permanently recalcitrant audience that 'all of us be outdoor people, you and me and the wee one shunning the stupid vanities and leading the simple life.'

Mr. Loeb's letter arrived two weeks before Sims rejoined his family a few days before a daughter, Margaret, was born to Mrs. Sims. Immediately Sims set to work on a letter to the President containing his views on Mahan's article. Composition proved difficult and the communication was not finished until September 24, 1906.

This letter was an admirable reply to the assertions of Captain Mahan.[17] At the very beginning Sims explained, as politely as he could, that the older man's conclusions were based 'upon information which is not entirely correct and upon inferences of his own from those facts that are contrary to the truth.' In the same issue of the *Proceedings* in which Mahan's reflections had appeared, there was also printed an account of the battle of Tsushima Strait by Richard Drace White, at one time Sims' assistant in the Target Practice Office. The material for this account had been obtained by White from a Russian observer; every attempt to check its accuracy had substantiated its veracity. The description of the engagement put forward by Commander White was quite different from that given by Captain Mahan. A significant error of the latter was his assumption that the Japanese Fleet had only a three-knot advantage over its Russian adversary and that Admiral Togo had not made use of this superiority in establishing his strategical position. Actually, the Japanese had enjoyed a six- or seven-knot advantage, which the Commander-in-Chief had used to maintain a predetermined and fairly constant range. Thus he had been able to concentrate the fire of his many ships upon a few of the Russians at any given moment. By this superiority alone Togo had been able to dictate the terms of battle and possessed 'an advantage so enormous that no conceivable strategical or tactical skill, and no possible

[17] This letter, variously revised and condensed, enjoyed a wide popularity. It appeared under the title, 'The Inherent Tactical Qualities of All-Big-Gun, One Calibre Battleships,' in the *N.I.P.*, December, 1906; in *Brassey's Annual*, 1907; and in Sen. Doc. 213, 59th Congress, 2d Session.

augmentation of gunfire (without increasing displacement) on the part of the Russians, could have prevented their defeat. . . .'

Before leaving this question, Sims pointed out that had the speeds of the two fleets been reversed, the Russians could have fled to Vladivostok and no action would have taken place. He also explained that no modern ship would lose much speed because of a perforated funnel. Forced drafts, used in any action, were almost hindered rather than helped by our 'present absurdly high funnels.' The British *Edgar* lost both its smokepipes in a gale and suffered no 'material diminution in her speed.'

The letter next took up the question of armament. One of Captain Mahan's assumptions, it will be remembered, was that 'volume of fire' of smaller calibres is important. Sims argued that 'volume of hitting' was much more significant in time of battle, presenting evidence to prove that, at the ranges at which the battle of the Japan Sea was fought, the great guns were much more accurate than the smaller guns. This conformed to the lessons he had learned in target practice. 'The bigger the gun, the greater its accuracy' was an axiom proved not only by mathematics but by actual experience. After a good many pages of figures he arrived at this essential conclusion. If the Japanese vessels had been all-big-gun ships, their fleet would have developed a greater rapidity of hitting with heavy guns (875 hits) than it actually did develop with twelve-, eight-, and six-inch guns (700 hits) — and this for the simple reason that, at long ranges, the hitting capacity of their heavy guns was 19.6 per cent while that of the small guns was only 2.1 per cent. (These percentages were clearly established and recognized as correct.)

Mahan also had failed to recognize that turrets were then being built which were practically invulnerable to all but the biggest shells; that heavy armor belt extending eight feet above the waterline was then being fastened to all big ships; and that conning towers and barbettes were likewise heavily armored. Since no secondary battery could pierce this armor, it was unwise to include the medium calibres on battleships.

Finally, Mahan had failed to realize that fire control had been developed to a high point during the past few years. Sims referred to the report of the Fire Control Board of 1905, which had explicitly stated that mixed calibres on a battleship made the control of fire difficult if not impossible. At battle ranges the splash of eight-, ten-, and twelve-inch shells looked so much alike that spotters could not easily tell the difference. Mixed calibres 'interfered' with each other and reduced the effectiveness of a ship's battery.[18]

In reply to Mahan's suggestion that the building of a *Dreadnought* would subject all older vessels to 'wilful premature' obsolescence, Sims observed that, while this might be true, nevertheless there was already the *Dreadnought* in England. 'It would undoubtedly be desirable if we could procure an international agreement that no nation would adopt for its armies a rifle superior to that now used. Similarly it would be desirable if the men-of-war could be limited, say, to twenty thousand tons. But in the absence of such an agreement we must keep pace with the increased efficiency in battleships as well as in small arms, otherwise we cannot reasonably expect to win battles. We have indeed no choice in the matter if we are to remain a world power.'

In conclusion, Sims asserted that the introduction of high-power guns and our knowledge of how to control them had done away with the necessity for 'closing.' Battles of the future would be fought at great ranges and 'the commander-in-chief of a fleet that is skilful in fire control and who has an undiscriminating disposition to close seems to me to be out of place as a commander of modern vessels.'

The President, greatly impressed with Sims' letter, wrote to him on September 27 that he 'regarded' his 'article as convincing and modelled the recommendation in my message accordingly.' He also had sent a copy of it to Captain Mahan. If Mr. Roosevelt needed further assurance, he received it in early October from Lee, the late Civil Lord of the British Admiralty, who took 'from knowledge acquired by the British Representatives with the Japanese Fleet exactly the ground you [Sims] took in your paper as to the imperative necessity of having twenty-thousand-ton ships, with turbines making twenty-five knots and heavily armored.'[19]

[18] It is interesting to notice that it is now possible to differentiate between the splash of different-sized shells through the use of distinctively colored powder charges for each calibre.

[19] Roosevelt to W. S. S., October 13, 1906.

Other men than the President remained to be convinced. Mahan's article created so much interest that Sims was anxious to obtain a hearing for his own case. The President gave him permission to publish his letter, which later appeared in the December issue of the *Naval Institute Proceedings*. Immediately Sims received confirmation of his views from a great number of officers who wrote their congratulations. A few believed, quite correctly, that he had overestimated and overemphasized the value of speed in a battleship, but all were unanimous in applauding his central position — that the all-big-gun ship was a necessity. Mixed with the approval of Sims, in almost all the letters, was a note of pleasure that his adversary had been defeated. The paper was the 'best of your many,' but 'Mahan ought to stick to the past or mingle with the line and learn about what he's trying to write about.' 'Really, William, you were cruel to him.' 'As for Captain Mahan — it would be an excellent thing for the service if he should confine his undoubtedly great literary ability to historical and literary questions.' 'A number of people say that your article makes a back number of Mahan. Hope it has that effect — he's dangerous.' 'It is unfortunate that Captain Mahan should have fallen into the practice of making loose generalizations from insufficient and obsolete data or both.' Aristides had been called the just too long.

It was, of course, a triumph for the Lieutenant Commander. Mahan had fought, almost alone in his profession, with something more mighty than the sword. Now Sims had cut the great man down with his own weapon. But Mahan was generous in defeat. He acknowledged that his information on the battle of Tsushima Straits was incorrect and he admitted that he did not know enough about the development of modern gunfire. Rather sadly he wrote that he could no longer take time from his other work to attend to the issues of the present. It was more than time he needed, for his historian's mind had drawn his evidence largely from the past. It was significant that he compared a perforated funnel to a lower mast that had been carried away — he was thinking in terms of 'the old seventy-four-gun ships, raking broadsides, and grappling irons.' Whatever his argument, he could not win, for the times were against him.

But the times, especially in a democracy, move slowly. Sims could not for the moment feel sure that he had done more than convince a President and defeat Mahan. More evidence had to be presented before other men could be persuaded. Fortunately, Sims was able to produce such evidence as a result of a trip he made to England in December, 1906.

The purpose of this visit was primarily to discuss fire-control methods with Percy Scott and Jellicoe, but he took with him the proofs of his article on the all-big-gun ship which appeared in the December issue of the *Proceedings*. This was to prove an invaluable part of his baggage. At the time of Sims' arrival in London the *Dreadnought* had just been commissioned. This remarkable vessel had been the answer of an equally remarkable man, Lord John Fisher, to the growing naval challenge of Germany. Built in an unprecedentedly short time — eighteen months (it required four years to build a battleship in America) — under conditions of complete secrecy, the *Dreadnought* was one of Mahan's 'wanton evils' which made every other existing vessel obsolete. During the months of construction, everyone had speculated on her specifications, but until December, 1906, no foreign officer had been able to obtain any information about her and only those British officers assigned to duty on the ship had seen her. It was a brilliant coup for the new First Lord, that gave England a jump of almost four years on all her rivals. But English public opinion at the time that Sims arrived in England was not convinced of the necessity for the ship. Especially after Mahan's article had been widely circulated in the country, much doubt had arisen concerning Fisher's experiment.

One of the first things Sims did upon arriving in London was to call on Lord John Fisher with his article. When the Englishman had read the galley proofs, he sought and gained the author's permission to publish Sims' paper in *Blackwood's Magazine*. In return the American asked if he could see the *Dreadnought*. Fisher told him it was impossible, but then advised him to talk with Jellicoe about it. After some discussion an elaborate subterfuge was devised. On December 17, Sims visited the Portsmouth Navy Yard, where the *Dreadnought* lay, and told the Admiral commanding that he had been refused permission to see the ship. A week later, the day before Christmas, he returned to Portsmouth in civilian clothes. At that time he was taken secretly over the whole ship.

The results of this visit to the *Dreadnought* he set down in a long report, which he sent, upon his return in January, to the Secretary, the Chief of the Bureau of Navigation, the Chief Naval Constructor, and the President. Over the contents and conclusions of this report it is unnecessary to linger. Suffice it to say that he explained fully the complicated precautions the British took to get the *Dreadnought* built before other nations knew of its existence as an all-big-gun ship. He showed that the big guns were a wise economy — each pound of metal thrown costing less in dollars or pounds than the metal thrown by mixed-calibre vessels. He described the ship's protection and went into considerable detail about her fire-control system. It was an able review of the whole case for vessels of the *Dreadnought* type.

When Sims returned from England, he found the President bent upon subduing the last remnants of opposition to the all-big-gun ship. This opposition existed largely in Congress, where it was combined with hostility to the Administration's constant efforts to increase the size of the Navy. To the Chairmen of the House and Senate Naval Committees, Mr. Roosevelt, early in January, sent a letter based almost wholly upon a summary Sims had prepared of his first article on the dreadnought type. An introductory paragraph written by the President stated that our justification to uphold the Monroe Doctrine and to dig the Panama Canal 'must rest primarily upon our willingness to build and maintain a first-class fighting fleet.' Mr. Roosevelt then expressed the hope that two big ships would be shortly authorized.[20]

The Congress then in session was 'nearly unique in its failure to make appropriations for the extension of the fleet.' When the letter failed to galvanize the Chairmen into immediate action, the President took the unprecedented step of releasing it to the press. Thus the big-navy policy and the controversy over the dreadnought type were thrown together before the public. In the discussions which followed, sufficient strength was ranged on the side of Roosevelt and Sims to secure the authorization of

[20] *New York Herald*, January 19, 1907.

one dreadnought early in February. From that time forward, though the naval policies of the President continued to be a subject of debate both in and out of Congress, the acceptance of the all-big-gun ship was almost universally admitted.

Park Benjamin, a well-known writer on naval affairs who refused to be reconciled to what he called 'The Shout for Big Ships,' reviewed the events leading up to the introduction of the type in the following acid terms:

> Let's build another Big Ship. We can just as easily settle plans for two as one.
>
> Let's build another Big Ship every year, and meanwhile let's talk about four of them.
>
> Let's get rid of all the battleships we have, quick, by applying to them a law which sends them into the dump if they need repairs costing more than ten per cent of the original price. (Thunders of applause from the William Cramp and Sons Ship Building Company.)
>
> That man Mahan has put in his oar, and must be choked off. Set Sims to making him into what the late John B. Gough used to call 'a horrible example.'
>
> Tell Sims to talk about more Big Ships: not four. TEN! [21]

Mr. Benjamin in his amusing summary implies an accusation against Sims and his supporters that has been repeated frequently since. He leaves the impression that Sims, by asking for ten ships, was taking a hand in the naval policy of the country. Such was not the case. Never in all his arguments did Sims express any opinion on the number of ships that should be built. Nor was his advocacy of the type tied in with his belief in any particular naval policy. He thought, purely in military terms, the all-big-gun ship was the most destructive weapon that could be devised. To build anything less would be militarily foolhardy. Inevitably his arguments were confused with the desires of the Roosevelt Administration for a big navy. This was natural, since Roosevelt asked for a big navy of dreadnoughts, using Sims' views to support his own.

Unfortunately, the distinction between the shaping of naval policy, which lies with Congress, and the constructing of weapons to implement that policy, which lies with the Navy, is a fine

[21] Park Benjamin, 'The Shout for Big Ships,' *The Independent*, January 31, 1909.

one. In defending the big ship Sims apparently defended a big
navy. On the other hand, when Congress tried to hinder the big-
navy policy by authorizing the thirteen-thousand-ton *Idahoes*,
it achieved only an unwarranted and unsuccessful invasion of the
field of naval design. If, as has been charged, the *Dreadnought*,
built by the will of Lord John Fisher, rendered all earlier battleships obsolete, no less were the *Idahoes*, built by the will of Congress, obsolete when launched. This confusion between the ends
and means of naval policy is one of the most fruitful sources of
error in the administration of armed forces in a democracy.

12

THE stature of Theodore Roosevelt, a recent critic has remarked, diminishes year by year. While this observation seems
justified, it unfortunately reveals nothing about the actual height
of the Bull Moose. Apparently such knowledge, now that he has
died, must forever be denied us. A man is supposed to be tried
at the bar of history. Actually he is summoned each generation
before a new court of appeals regulated by the particular standards and customs of the age. This is the rough justice of history
by which the real meaning of a man in his own time is not infrequently lost to sight. Especially will this be true of Theodore
Roosevelt. Personalities, even the most vigorous, lose their
effervescence in the open spaces of history and he was, essentially,
a personality. Then, too, his virtues, spectacular though they
were, are now strangely dated. They seem to belong specifically
to his own era, while his defects are hardy perennials
It therefore seems highly improbable that any historian or biographer will ever recapture the glamourous Teddy, who, if he
did not determine or even guide the main currents of his time,
yet floated upon them with a splendor all his own.

If the stature of the man diminishes on the main stage of our
national life, he remains an imposing figure against the narrower
settings of the United States Navy. He held office during some
of the most critical years of the Navy's history, before the problems of the transition from sail to steam were completely solved
and while the Navy was rapidly expanding to meet the demands
of an imperial obligation. That this period of change introduced

176

difficulties with which the Navy, as then established, was ill-equipped to deal he well recognized. He was better prepared with naval knowledge and understanding than any of his predecessors or, for that matter, than any of his successors in office. In seeking, as he did, to improve the system of promotion, the methods of designing our warships, and the organization of our naval administration, he was confronted by the traditional obstacles that hamper any man who attempts to alter existing conditions. For the most part he pursued his course with intelligence and courage. Only when his necessarily limited knowledge prevented him from making a decision on a purely technical matter, or when some proposed action involved too great political dangers, did his resolution waver. Roosevelt was never quite as righteous as he believed himself to be, but he was probably as righteous as any man who is a 'political animal' can be. He did not do everything he could have done for the Navy, but in laying the secure foundations of our modern first line of defense he did more than any President before or after him. Rear Admiral Stephen B. Luce, who well knew the powers a politician could wield for good or evil, believed that 'a blast upon his bugle trumpet is worth a thousand men.' More than once the President blew his horn before the walls of complaisance and tradition that sheltered the naval establishment from the attacks of the reformers.

In a way the groundwork of reform had been laid before Roosevelt took office. A good many officers had described the unsatisfactory conditions in the Navy, while a few of them had made suggestions for improvement. But in terms of accomplishment progress had been slow, because these men lacked the power to force their ideas upon a service that was temperamentally willing to stand pat. What the reformers had long needed was a friend at court with both the knowledge and the power to compel the Department to accept the necessary changes. In 1901 they were delighted to find that the court itself was their friend.

There were really two groups who were interested in improving conditions. In the first were such older officers as Henry C. Taylor, George C. Remey, Stephen B. Luce, Charles E. Clarke, Caspar Goodrich, and, with qualifications, Alfred Thayer Mahan. Most of them, like Taylor, in the Bureau of Navigation, used their elevated positions to bring about gradual changes from above. Others, like Mahan, whose tempered articles appeared occasionally in the magazines, tried to work from outside the immediate professional circles. All performed valuable services in educating the public and their brother officers in the needs of the new Navy, but they lacked the turbulence and enthusiasm so necessary to lead an open revolt against existing conditions. When that revolt took place, it was engineered chiefly by younger officers, with many of whom the reader is already acquainted.

G. B. Bradshaw, R. D. White, and C. R. Plunkett, all of whom served with Sims in the Target Practice Office, had a hand in the fight, as did C. T. Vogelgesang, Cameron Winslow, and Frank Hill. Bradley Fiske, more articulate and thoughtful than any of the others, but likewise more sensitive and retiring, contributed valuable assistance chiefly through his clear and balanced articles. There were, of course, others, but these men were especially active in the struggle which culminated in the Investigation of 1908. They were not a closely knit, self-conscious organization of crusaders, but they all worked, sometimes independently, sometimes cooperatively, toward the improvement of their Navy. Of this loose confederation of men there were no acknowledged leaders, but the two most effective and persistent were Albert Lenoir Key and Sims himself. These men had had greater experience than most of their supporters; they possessed wider professional knowledge and were equipped with unflagging determination. They also had superb self-confidence. Neither feared the power or influence of any man or group of men. Each one, too, had a special advantage. From 1905 to 1907 Key was the Naval Aide to Theodore Roosevelt. Sims followed him in the same position until 1909.

This intimate relationship with the President was of incalculable importance to the progress of reform. Especially for Sims it was an enormous psychological advantage. In the back of his mind there was always the thought that it was Roosevelt who had rescued him from obscurity. It was Roosevelt who had obtained the new telescope sights, who had encouraged the new system of gunnery, who had forced the *Dreadnought* on the temporizing constructors and an unwilling Congress. Sims, knowing by heart the winding paths that led through the bureaus of the

Navy Department, realized that Roosevelt possessed the power to make straight the way for the reformers.

Yet he could not be the blind idolater. 'I have also about finished *The Strenuous Life*,' he wrote his wife, 'which is really a series of essays setting forth Mr. R.'s discovery of the Ten Commandments. With few exceptions it is a dreary succession of platitudes from the morals that have come down thru the ages. It is a reliable guide for purity of action in public life, tho to accord with practice he should have added after many paragraphs, "This don't apply to personal friends.... If you apply this strictly (to the question of pensions for example), you will be excluded from public affairs." ' Yet Sims well knew that to the President he owed the greatest debt of his whole career. When the strenuous life came at last to a close in the early months of 1919, Sims was in London at the very height of his popularity, activity, and fame. 'Theodore Roosevelt is dead,' he wrote to his friend, Admiral Dunn; 'I have been able to think of nothing else for days.'

The first years of the twentieth century were filled with the clamor of reform. 'We waked up every morning,' said one who lived in Washington at the time, 'eager to know what new crusade we were off upon.' It was the day of the insurgent in politics and of the muckraker in social thought. Liberalism was a question of particulars — it concerned itself with a beef trust, an oil company, the shame of the cities; while, for the most part, it accepted the prevailing concepts of American government and society. Sims was a child of this age. He too worked with particulars, with all-big-gun battleships, systems of promotion, straight shooting. After Mahan had defined the place of the Navy in our national life, Sims rarely, if ever, questioned the definition. Philosophical generalities had no appeal for him; he would have been incapable of developing a theory about the influence of sea power upon history. Insurgency, with its emphasis upon the limited objective and the concentrated attack, was the mood that was most congenial to his temperament.

If he was an insurgent in attitude, he was a muckraker in method. Men like David Graham Phillips, Lincoln Steffens, Upton Sinclair, had devised a technique of exposure that was producing spectacular results. They were experts in synthesis,

179

adept at simplification, and skilled in the uses of the dramatic fact and the colorful phrase. Sometimes they were not above selecting their evidence to fit their own particular purposes, but their purposes were usually sound. Sims mastered this technique; indeed, he had used it successfully on the China Station several years before it achieved wider popularity. But there was an even stronger bond between him and the muckrakers, for both believed in the compelling force of an aroused public opinion. The point of those nineteenth-century philosophers, whom Sims had studied long before on the *Swatara*, had been that man was a reasonable being. If the facts were put before him, he could understand them; he could be trusted to arrive at sensible conclusions from his study of the evidence. Sims was not whole-hearted in his admiration of the republican form of government, though he would certainly have admitted that it was the most adequate that man, in his present state, could devise. Nor could he express much interest in the metaphysical notion that the voice of the people was the voice of God. But he did have an abiding faith in the idea that man, the common man, would be able, when presented with the facts, to make up his mind about what was best for him.

It can be seen that the elements of the reform movement in the Navy fall into a familiar pattern. The zealous spirits of the men who fought from below; the opposition of the men who defended from on high; the flamboyant yet calculated activity of President Roosevelt; the technique of exposure; the faith in public opinion; the doctrine of the limited objective — these are but the elements of the larger reformation which, in the early years of the twentieth century, was directed against the heritage of the nineteenth.

Key and Sims had profited greatly by the assistance of the President, but he had failed to help them accomplish their three greatest purposes. They wished to establish a system of promotion by selection which would ensure the rise of the ablest officers; they wanted to alter the methods by which our warships were designed; and most of all, they hoped to reorganize the administrative system of the Navy Department. Though Mr. Roosevelt had publicly endorsed their aims in messages to Congress, he had failed to take decisive action in their behalf. Sims and Key found the cause for the continued defeat of their plans in the alliance between certain bureau chiefs and members of Congress who had a stake in the *status quo*. The central figure in this opposition was the United States Senator from Maine. Eugene Hale was a commanding influence in the political life of the country in 1907. His small, compact, dignified body, his shrewd, powerful, heavily bearded face, made him look every inch a Senator. In spirit he was a Roman, implacable and skeptically conservative. With such men as Nelson Aldrich and Henry Cabot Lodge he was ranged, in the larger public issues, against the forces of progressivism. The Navy had been for long his special interest. Early in his public career he had hoped that the American Navy would soon become what it ought to be, 'the pet of the American people.' This wish, expressed in 1884, he acted upon in his earnest support of the reconstruction of the new Navy that began in the eighties. Until 1900 he exerted all his intelligence and will to improve the lot of our first line of defense. From that date forward, however, he set his face like flint against the forces of reform within the service. Against those who advocated a change in the administration of the Department and the introduction of dreadnoughts, he was especially vindictive. As Chairman of the Senate Naval Committee he was in a position to make his influence felt. This change of heart his enemies attributed to his own selfish desires. Big ships could not be built or repaired in the small yard in the state of Maine; and any sound military administrative organ would jeopardize his own control over the naval establishment.

These considerations may well have influenced Mr. Hale, but he was impelled to his position by far sounder motives. The garish imperialism that followed the Spanish-American War offended his sensibilities, as it offended those of such men as Senator Hoar. Since he saw in the Navy the primary instrument of this imperialism, he sought to curtail its growth and power. Big ships he believed were a costly, dangerous experiment. With equal dislike he viewed the creation of a General Staff, which might attempt to saddle Congress with its own militaristic conceptions. Near the end of his career he expressed his attitude toward the Navy in unmistakable terms. 'As I look back upon the years, for the last twenty years, I recall that the more we have done for the military the more they have claimed. It is the theory of the Army and the Navy that the Government is run for the benefit of those establishments.' [1]

Whatever motives, selfish or patriotic, determined his course, Senator Hale became and remained an adept and unshakable opponent of the reforms advocated by the insurgent officers. Since by virtue of his knowledge, his ability, and his position he dominated the Naval Committee of the Senate and, to a more limited extent, the same committee in the House, his views were widely accepted and detrimental to the aims of the men who opposed him.

Such was the discouraging situation that confronted Sims and his friends in the summer of 1907: failure in their aims; consolidated, powerful opposition to their plans. To make matters worse, the end of the Roosevelt Administration was in sight. When the President had left the White House, the hopes for change would be dead. In such a pass Sims decided to 'shoot the works.' All the regular means of reform had been tried and they had come to nothing. He would, therefore, place his case before the people. He hoped to arouse so much popular indignation in the process that the entrenched power of the bureaus and the politicians would be blown apart. In that hope lay the genesis of the article 'The Needs of Our Navy,' which appeared, significantly enough, in *McClure's Magazine* for January, 1908.

The article had a curious history. Its author, to begin with, was not Sims, but Henry Reuterdahl. It had been written, not in 1907, but in 1904. Reuterdahl, the American editor of *Jane's Fighting Ships*, was a marine artist who had been commissioned in the latter year to design the target-practice trophy for the North Atlantic Fleet. In this way he met Sims, with whom, as time passed, he formed a fast friendship. Reuterdahl was more than an artist. He had made a good many cruises on our ships and was, for a layman, well acquainted with naval matters. His knowledge had been increased by frequent conversations with the Inspector of Target Practice, who, naturally, had not taken any particular pains to conceal his own views on naval subjects. Reuterdahl, an apt pupil, wrote in the late fall of

[1] *The Dictionary of American Biography*, vol. 8, pp. 102–104.

1904 an article entitled 'A Plea for Naval Efficiency' which was largely a condensation of Sims' analysis of the Navy's faults. When the work was done, Reuterdahl showed it to his mentor, who advised him strenuously not to publish it. At that moment in 1904, Sims, believing that the current had set his way, did not want to do anything that would jeopardize the success of his plans for reform.

But time dimmed Sims' hopes. By 1907 he had decided that it would be foolish to hold his fire. Therefore, when Reuterdahl approached him again in 1907 with the idea of an article, he was more than willing. The artist thus encouraged took the matter up with S. S. McClure, who was, as a friend of Sims', interested in the Navy and an old hand at muckraking. The editor set one of his crack men, George Kibbe Turner, to work with Reuterdahl. These two, with the assistance of Sims, produced the article that was finally published in the January, 1908, issue of *McClure's*, under the title, 'The Needs of Our Navy.' No more opportune time could have been chosen, for the Fleet, when the magazine appeared on the stands, was just setting forth on its historic cruise around the world.

To the reader who has come thus far there will be a tedious familiarity with the contents of 'The Needs of Our Navy.' But the public read in frank amazement that the main armor belt of our ships was under water; that our ships had such low freeboard that it was impossible to fight them in a moderate seaway; that an open shaft led from the turrets to the powder magazines; that our officers were promoted by an inefficient and dangerous system of seniority; that the bureau system of administration was incapable of performing the major military task assigned to it, that of maintaining our Navy in a state of readiness for war. In conclusion, Reuterdahl did not fail to point out that an enlightened group of officers had long worked for reform and for as long had been successfully opposed. The whole article, not entirely free from bombast, was written in a crisp, clear style and illustrated by pictures and sketches that made the nature of the criticisms painfully clear to the reader.

The thing dropped like a well-aimed bomb. Papers all over the country carried résumés of the story and many of them printed editorials expressing great concern and surprise, but also expressing caution against a too hasty acceptance of all the information contained.

No citizen of the United States was more surprised by the appearance of the article, and no member of the service was more irritated by it, than the President of the United States. It came at a particularly unhappy time for him. The Panic of 1907 was scarcely over, his Congress was rebellious, and he had endeavored in his message of December, 1907, to convince the country of the necessity of a greatly expanded building program. His whole naval policy seemed placed in jeopardy by the work of Reuterdahl. The fact that the article contained only those criticisms with which Key, Sims, and others had supplied him for the past four years did not simplify his position. As a result, he was profoundly annoyed, especially with Sims, whose influence it was not hard to discover.

Indeed, many officers had seen the handiwork of the Inspector of Target Practice and his fellows in Reuterdahl's arguments. They had likewise seen in this fact an opportunity to crush revolt before it was fairly started by making use of a Navy Regulation (Number 252) which forbade officers to publish directly or indirectly ... any information ... concerning the acts or measures of any Department of the Government. On February 15, 1908, Sims, with various other men, received a letter from the Secretary, asking him if he had anything to do with the writing of the article. The suspicion of the Department had been aroused 'by a very unusual similarity between statements made by you in various communications to the Secretary of the Navy and some of those contained' in Reuterdahl's article. An immediate, categorical, and specific reply was requested. Sims understood the implications in this letter and did not hesitate to act. He saw the Secretary and then he went to Mr. Roosevelt. 'When I took the letter to the President, he said in a severe tone, "Well, you have been insubordinate, haven't you?" I replied, "There have been others." This referred to the round robin from Cuba during the Spanish War. He laughed heartily, sent for his [private] secretary, and told him to telephone the Secretary to come to see him the next day.' The letters that had been sent to the officers were recalled, and Sims could again thank the special Providence that had put Roosevelt in the White House at the time when his own energies ran at their highest.[2]

Other, more significant repercussions from the article in *McClure's* were soon forthcoming. In the press, among the people, and in Congress doubts had been raised about the Navy and questions were being asked which called for answers. In the face of this rising tide of unrest, some positive action was required. Senator Hale, who never flinched in the face of opposition of any kind, ordered an investigation into the issues raised by Reuterdahl. It is possible that he saw in such an investigation a weapon with which he could club into silence the reformers who had so long plagued him. Certainly his activities, before the investigating committee met on February 25, 1908, would indicate that such was the case. Early in January he obtained from Rear Admiral George A. Converse and Rear Admiral Washington L. Capps refutations of the charges brought by Reuterdahl. These Hale introduced into the *Congressional Record* and they were, by order of the Senate, made public documents.[3] More impressive or able men he could hardly have called to his defense. Converse in his time had been Chief of the Bureau of Equipment, Chief of the Bureau of Ordnance, and Chief of the Bureau of Navigation.[4] In 1908, though he had passed the retirement age, he had been continued in service as President of the Board on Construction. Rear Admiral Capps, a much younger man, was at the time the Chief Constructor of the Navy and Chief of the Bureau of Construction and Repair. In addition, he was probably the best-educated officer in his field in America, for he had studied naval architecture abroad in London and Glasgow and had regularly visited shipyards in England and on the Continent.[5] From these two men Senator Hale received information which convinced him that the case against our battleships could not be made to stand up in the face of the facts.

It was apparent at the outset that the Senator was anxious to

[2] This incident is well told by W. S. S. in 'Roosevelt and the Navy,' *McClure's Magazine*, December, 1922.

[3] 'Report Concerning Certain Alleged Defects in Vessels of the Navy,' Sen. Doc. 297, 60th Congress, 1st Session.

[4] It is interesting to notice here that, in his Report as Chief of the Bureau of Navigation, Converse had criticized the bureau system of administration.

[5] *Ibid., passim.*

confine the investigation to narrow limits. This is borne out by his opening words at the first session of the investigating committee. 'I shall not ask him [Admiral Converse] to go into the lengthy detail which his very full paper of examination covers, but to bring out before the Committee the essential charges in the *McClure's Magazine* article, relating mainly to the position and extent of armor, the height of freeboard, the positions of the guns, the turret and the turret hoists, and such other matters as are important in an investigation.'[6]

At their face value these words seem harmless enough, but it will be noticed that, in effect, they limited the field of investigation to the specific defects of our men-of-war as set forth by Henry Reuterdahl, and they did not permit consideration of the underlying causes of dissatisfaction, our faulty naval administration, of which these defects were but a symptom. Converse and Capps[7] appeared first before the Committee. Their testimony is chiefly a study in comparative values.

It will be recalled that two of the most damaging criticisms made by Reuterdahl concerned the main armor belt, which, he said, was either wholly or partially submerged on most of our battleships, and our open and direct turret hoists, which were, in his opinion, chiefly responsible for the explosions that had occurred. With these criticisms the testimony of the two men chiefly dealt.

In connection with the distribution of the armor belt, Admiral Converse asserted that 'we base all of our figures, all of our location of armor, our gun height, and our freeboard on what we call the "normal displacement line of the vessel."'[8] Taking this normal displacement line as the point from which all measurements should be made, Admirals Converse and Capps proceeded to compare our ships with foreign vessels. By this method it was found that our battleships had as great or greater freeboard than most of their foreign counterparts; that the armor was distributed around the vessels in such a way as to afford the greatest possible

[6] *Hearings Before the Committee of Naval Affairs, United States Senate, on the Bill (S. 335), 1908*, p. 3. Hereafter this will be referred to as *Hearings, 1908*.

[7] Capps, though younger than Sims, was by virtue of his position as Chief of a Bureau entitled to a Rear Admiral's rank. The papers found in this an opportunity for heavy sarcasm and usually set off the title in quotation marks.

[8] *Hearings, 1908*, p. 20.

protection, and that our gun heights compared favorably with those of our possible foreign adversaries. Admiral Capps dealt with especial emphasis upon this point. 'The reason,' he said, 'we speak of the designed displacement and the designed water-line and refer all height data to the designed waterline as a base line of reference is because that is the method of reference used by all designers in all countries and is quite as accurate and jus-tifiable as any other base line. Therefore, when critics compare the deep load displacement and draft of American vessels with the designed load displacement of foreign vessels, they are mak-ing an error which, if made by a well-informed technical man, would seriously impair his creditability in all such matters.' [9] Using this method of reference both men were able to prove con-clusively by figures that our ships were the equal or superior of foreign vessels in the particular characteristics under discussion.

When Admiral Converse came to consider the danger of the open and direct powder hoists, he gave his opinion that 'Not a single accident that has happened has been due to the open tur-rets.' He explained that there was an open shaft from the turret to the handling room. The magazines surrounded the handling room, but were separated from it by watertight doors and a passing scuttle fitted with a metal flap. In the case of the *Missouri* the accident had resulted from an unnecessary accumulation of powder in the handling room, on which a spark from a flare-back had fallen. The reason for this unnecessary powder lay in the fact that the ship was trying to fire too rapidly and the crew had thus brought the charges from the magazine prematurely in the hope of speeding up the shooting. The remedy for such accidents was not so much to change the design of the open turret as it was to keep the powder in the magazine until it was re-quired, and also to fit the turret hoists with shutters that would close when the gun was firing. Such shutters were already in-stalled, but they were frequently left open by crews in a hurry to fire the guns. Furthermore, as Capps pointed out, most navies used an open and direct turret hoist, notably England, with re-sults that were considered wholly satisfactory.[10]

Once, in the course of the cross-examination of Admiral Con-verse, the subject of the bureau system was touched upon, when

[9] *Hearings, 1908*, p. 57.   [10] *Ibid.*, pp. 13 ff. and 16 ff.

Hale asked if seagoing officers had been consulted in questions of design. 'Always,' replied Converse. ' . . . There have been innumerable boards. Take battleships 5 and 6, or at least the battleships that followed, 7, 8, and 9. A board . . . was appointed before any appropriation was made for the construction of these vessels to make suggestions in regard to the type of future battleships. They went out to sea on the *Indiana* to see about the interference of gunfire. They criticized the *Iowa*. They criticized the *Kearsarge* type. They made recommendations on which were built the *Alabama* class of vessels. They were all seagoing officers with the exception of the constructor on board, and their views governed, and the vessels that were built were built on [their] recommendations.' [11]

It is interesting to observe that a board of seagoing officers should have found it possible to criticize two classes of ships which then made up our line of battle. The point was lost on Senator Perkins, who irrelevantly replied, 'I am very glad to hear you refute this statement as to the bureau management, in view of the fact that I think the Chairman and other members of the Committee all agree with you that it is the best system devised, not only by our own Navy, but by any other navy in the world.'

Capps and Converse, the main supports of the case against the critics, were very effective advocates. With a wealth of historical data and technical information they built up a convincing explanation for and defense of our naval designs. In the course of their testimony many smaller matters were taken up, such as the reasons for the large gunports of the *Kentucky* that Sims had originally criticized. In each case well-constructed explanations for the described conditions were presented. When the two left the stand, the position of the critics seemed less tenable than the public had been led to believe by the article in *McClure's*.[12]

Other officers came to their side. They, too, were able and convincing men. Admiral Mason, the Chief of the Bureau of Ordnance, stated that 'The four unfortunate accidents that have

[11] *Hearings, 1908*, p. 40.

[12] The press at this stage of the proceedings was, generally speaking, unwilling to take sides in the matter.

involved loss of life were all caused not by the ammunition hoist, but by the guns, by the powder, by flarebacks.' He, too, pointed out that England had about one hundred and sixty open hoists.[13] Others followed — Captain F. F. Fletcher, Lieutenant Commander Joseph Strauss, who had designed the turrets of the *Kentucky*, Sims' old classmate Professor Philip Alger, Lieutenant Commander Cleland Davis, and others.[14] Each in one way or another and with varying ability substantiated the case as set forth by Admirals Capps and Converse. How much the opinions of these men might have been shaped by their experience alone it is, of course, impossible to say, but it is interesting to discover that each of the officers had been or was at the time of the investigation connected with some bureau within the Department. No clearer indication of the cleavage between the seagoing officers and the bureau men could be obtained than from this fact, which in itself contains sombre implications about the organization of the Navy Department.[15]

On February 29, the first officer to support the contentions of Reuterdahl appeared before the Committee. Lieutenant Commander Frank K. Hill confined himself principally to the single subject of the distribution of the main armor of our battleships. He recalled that Admiral Converse had taken all his measurements from the designed or normal waterline of a ship and that by this method he had proved that our armor was properly distributed, our freeboard adequate, and so forth. With the conclusions presented by Admiral Converse by this method he would not cavil, but he drew the attention of the committee to the fact that the designed line hardly ever coincided with the actual

[13] *Hearings, 1908*, p. 84 ff.

[14] It should be noticed that the order in which these men appeared before the Committee has been violated. In order to present the entire case of the defenders of the existing conditions, the witnesses have been grouped together, though in actual practice 'friend and foe' followed each other indiscriminately.

[15] This point was not lost on contemporary observers. R. D. Walker, in 'The Administrative Organization of the Navy Department,' *Army and Navy Life*, October, 1908, asserted that 'An examination of the testimony and the history of the various witnesses develops a very illuminating and important fact — without a single exception each naval officer called before that committee in refutation of the structural defects charged was either a member of the Board on Construction ... or an officer serving under, or connected with, the Bureaus of Construction, Ordnance, or Equipment. In other words, *not a naval officer could be found who was willing to defend the alleged defects except the defendants — the men who were responsible for the defects.*'

waterline of a vessel in service. He had dug about in ships' logs and from the information there obtained had found that the difference, with normal coal on board, between the designed waterline and the actual one varied from one to two feet on five of our first-line vessels. 'This shows,' he concluded, 'that with about normal coal on board, these vessels draw from one foot to two feet, one inch, more than the so-called normal or trial draft where they were designed to be best protected.' When the vessels were nearly filled with coal the discrepancy was even more apparent. Thus loaded, the armor belt of the same five ships was at the most only two feet above water and on certain ships it was actually submerged. In revealing this information, Commander Hill also brought out the fact that the recommendations of the Walker Board, to which Admiral Converse had referred in discussing the influence of the line officers upon ship design, had never been followed by the constructors. This Board had recommended that the normal line 'in our Navy be fixed in this way: The ship is supposed to have on it at that time two-thirds of the stores, two-thirds of the ammunition, and some coal.' The constructors varied the amount of coal to suit their own desires and thus the designed waterline was purely a fictitious and, worse, a varying thing. Therefore, any measurements made on this basis were wrong and highly misleading.[16]

When Hill had finished his testimony, Lieutenant Commander Vogelgesang took the stand. He confined himself to the question of turrets, on which he was well equipped to speak because he had served on the Turret Board that had been ordered to meet after the accident on the *Georgia*. He recalled that 'The distinctive thing, as I understand it, was that the people had evidently gotten tired of the disasters in the turrets.' Of the report of this Board he said, 'the crux of the whole thing is that it is the sentiment of the service, of the seagoing officers who have to use this material, who have used it and have had experience with it over ten years, that there should be absolutely some structural separation between the turrets proper and the handling rooms, which does not now exist and never has existed in our Navy.' 'The faults of the system,' Vogelgesang continued, 'I should attribute entirely to the open structure of the turret.' The solution of shut-

[16] *Hearings, 1908*, pp. 102–103.

ters, so frequently referred to by Admirals Capps, Converse, and Mason, had not impressed the Turret Board. 'Although the *Georgia* was provided with automatic shutters which were supposed to more or less segregate the handling room from the turret, that did not do it. My opinion of [those shutters], Senator, is the consensus of opinion of all the officers of the fleet, that [they are] cumbersome and thoroughly inefficient, and it is so stated in the Turret Board's report.' Much had been made, Vogelgesang noticed, of the direct hoists of Great Britain, but he pointed out that in England the hoist itself was thoroughly enclosed and provided no opening from the gun to the handling room.[17]

The essence of the problem of the turrets, as revealed in the statements of Mason, Capps, Converse, and Vogelgesang, is this: The defenders of existing conditions said that precautions should be taken at the gun to prevent accidents which might send sparks showering down into the handling rooms and that such accidents were best prevented by slowing the firing. Vogelgesang and the Turret Board, which represented the line-officer opinion, believed that it was far safer to isolate the handling room from the turret in such a way that the sparks resulting from accidents above could not damage the lower part of the ship. The judgment of history has decisively confirmed the critics.

For a brief moment, in the course of the cross-examination of Vogelgesang, the underlying issue of reorganization was opened to view. Senator Perkins asked him how the Government ought to select plans for battleships. Vogelgesang replied that he would like a differently constituted board of design. 'We do not,' he went on, 'think that the Chiefs of Bureaus have enough time beyond their other duties to give the attention that should be given to the particular subject of designs.' At which point Senator Hale struck in with 'So you are against the bureaus?' 'No,' replied the naval officer, 'I am not against the bureaus if they are properly coordinated. Provided there is a line officer who has the power to coordinate the different bureaus and see that their work is done for the good of the whole service, and is the responsible man to the Secretary of the Navy, I am not against the bureaus.' When this note had been struck, the Committee for the first time began to lose its temper. Senator Hale inter-

[17] *Hearings, 1908*, pp. 126–130.

preted a remark of Vogelgesang's about the overworked members of the Board on Construction to mean that the officer believed these men to be 'old fogies.' The witness protested that he had simply said they were overworked, to which Hale replied, 'Rather overworked and comparatively useless?' [18]

It was in this mood that the Committee approached Sims when he began his testimony on March 2, 1908.[19] The damaging evidence of Hill and Vogelgesang had done much to destroy the original case of Capps, Converse, and Mason. Since this had not been the intention of most of the Committee members, they were beginning to get out of sorts. To most of them Sims appeared as the ultimate cause of the whole controversy. They were not, accordingly, disposed to handle him gently. Senator Hale gave some indication of this attitude at the very beginning. Sims opened his remarks with the observation that 'There is only one thing I want to make clear. I do not know whether you understand it. I do not want anybody to think that these criticisms of the Navy have sprung up out of the ground in the last two or three months or in the last two or three years. It is a very serious matter. It goes back a long time. I want you to understand the attitude of the service. I don't think it has been presented at all. I mean the point of view of the men. That is what I propose to put before you and as a preliminary to telling you about the criticism. It will not take so much time.' The Chairman replied sarcastically that 'The error of the Committee has been that instead of examining these other officers we ought to have examined you first and then we would not have needed to examine the other officers.'

Sims had planned to give a prepared statement covering his past struggle to bring about reform. He had hoped to explain how he had been thwarted in his first attempts to improve our gunnery, how opposition had prevented our obtaining good sights, and how he had explained the necessity for new turrets ever since 1901. From this review of the facts he had expected to progress to a general discussion of the organization of the Navy Department. When he explained this to the Committee, he was immediately cut short. 'You may leave out,' said Senator Hale,

[18] *Hearings, 1908*, pp. 132–134.
[19] Sims' testimony appears in the *Hearings*, pp. 155–198.

'from your statement all that part in which you propose to discuss the incomplete organization and the necessity for a central advisory authority with the Secretary.'

This turn of affairs disconcerted Sims considerably. He had left to Hill, Vogelgesang, and the others the task of collecting data to answer the specific questions. It was to have been his job to draw general conclusions from their well-substantiated cases. So he tried another tack. 'One of the points . . . that I should like to go into, and I think it is one the Committee is interested in . . . is the question as to whether it is true that there is resistance to criticism to a certain extent, and resistance to adopting new ideas.'

> *The Chairman:* That you need not spend a word upon. That is a matter of ethics, and it puts you in the position of telling us why it is that criticism is resented. We do not care anything about that.
>
> *Sims:* You do not care to know the fact as to whether it is done or not?
>
> *The Chairman:* Not from you.

With such backing and filling, pointed up by the sarcasm of the Chairman and the occasional protests of Sims, the hearing continued. Confined as he was, Sims could only repeat in large part the earlier remarks of Hill and Vogelgesang and make occasional references to his own reports. Inasmuch as it was his first experience before an investigating committee, he lacked the utter poise he later acquired in the face of sharp questioning. The testimony ended as it had begun:

> *The Chairman:* I think Commander Sims believes that our Navy is just about as bad [as the Spanish Navy].
>
> *Sims:* Oh no; oh no. Excuse me, Mr. Hale. I said it was in a condition of extreme inefficiency back at the time I mentioned.

And again:

> *Tillman:* I suppose Captain Sims has finished?
>
> *The Chairman:* Yes, he has finished. I suppose Captain Sims is through?
>
> *Sims:* I have said hardly anything of what I wanted to say.
>
> *The Chairman:* I know it, but on our basis we have gone over the different subjects.

Disconcerted as he was by what one paper called the 'heckling' of the Committee, Sims could still feel that his appearance had been a success. His presence provided the first splash of color for the reporters, who had not previously displayed much enthusiasm. Some of them, in their anxiety for good copy, wandered occasionally beyond the boundaries of accuracy, but ordinarily Sims' own words could satisfy the most exacting. He had a gift for overstatement which at times amounted to real genius.

Of our shooting during the Spanish-American War he remarked that 'It was as disgraceful an exhibition as ever took place on the globe.' Even when supported by the evidence that only one hundred and twenty hits were scored out of nine thousand shots, this appeared too inclusive an indictment. In any case, it could hardly have been convincing to a country that still clearly remembered Cervera's almost total annihilation.

The observation achieved an impressive circulation. One column of the *New York Sun* was devoted to its author, while a cartoon in the same paper showed a sadly mutilated Spaniard responding to Sims' opinion with a murmured 'Caramba! It is to laugh.' The *Salt Lake City Telegram*, expressing its indignant belief that there was 'a loose pulley in his brain,' suggested packing him off to a sanitarium. Even less charitable was the acidly inaccurate comment of the *Pittsburgh Press* that this 'relative of the President had run amuck.' Vindictiveness had robbed his remarks of all value, and it was surprising that 'the President should retain a man with so much temper and so little tact as his naval aide.'

Other papers defended Sims. The *Baltimore Sun*, for example, thought that he had been unfairly hazed, and the *New York Post* could find no adequate reason why 'Admiral' Capps should be retained by the Committee as a cross-questioner. An examination of the attitude of the press seems to indicate that it was about equally divided between those papers which objected to what Sims said and those who objected to the way he had been treated by the Committee. Most of the journals that at this time were favorable in their reaction made little attempt to defend his more dramatic pronouncements. Yet these pronouncements were an important part of Sims' testimony.

In 1908, Sims employed the technique of the China Station; he sought to blast his audience from its apathy into a startled wakefulness. Actually he seemed to care little whether it listened to him with resentment or sympathy as long as it listened. The overcharged remarks that flew from him were rarely the sparks of an excited moment, for he delivered his shocking statements with calculation.

The technique has defects, several of which he fully realized. Sometimes he was unable to create sufficient sympathy to serve as a solvent for the inevitable resentment. Sometimes the channels of popular interest were diverted from his arguments to himself as a personality. Frequently, too, when he reserved his heaviest charges for the most formidable bulwarks of public belief, he destroyed his credibility as a witness. It was very hard, for example, for people to believe that open and direct powder hoists were dangerous when from the same source they had learned that the world had never before witnessed so humiliating a spectacle as the victory at Santiago.

Yet with all its defects the technique had much to recommend it. Before one could hope to educate an audience it was necessary to capture its interest. A public indignant was, at least, a public interested and aroused. At this time, certainly, in the age of the muckrakers, Sims could justify his methods by their results. The amount of space devoted to his testimony in the newspaper columns is quite surprising. Though it is impossible to say that he was primarily responsible for the attention with which the press followed the investigation, it is equally impossible to deny that his appearance won a wider audience for his friends who followed.

Among those friends were such familiar men as Bradley Fiske, Cameron McCrae Winslow, and George C. Remey. Each testified to the truth of the criticisms in so far as his own knowledge and Senator Hale's restrictions permitted him. On March 11, A. L. Key took the stand, to deliver perhaps the most telling blows against the earlier arguments of the defense. Having studied the questions at hand for a longer time than the others, he could substantiate his case with impressive statistics. On armor he concluded that 'we continue to distribute the waterline belt on the wrong line, a fictitious draft line.' Of the turrets he said: 'All of them [European countries] isolate the turret from the handling room, so if there is an accident it will be confined to the turret. You see, it is six years since this matter was called to the attention of the Department, and we have had four turret accidents, fifteen men killed in the handling room since that time.' [20]

Key's carefully prepared statement delivered the *coup de grâce* to the case of the defense. The Committee recognized that there was more truth in the assertions of the article in *McClure's* than it had been led to expect by Admirals Capps and Converse. With this recognition their attitude toward the investigation changed. The limitation of discussion imposed by Chairman Hale was dispensed with in the course of Key's testimony, while the members of the Committee wandered away from the specific questions of turrets and armor. How greatly the Senators had been impressed by the evidence brought before them by the insurgents is revealed by the following interchange.

> *Senator Tillman:* Very well. Now, with the facts staring us in the face that the ships that have been built even as far back as six or seven years ago had these blunders continued in the face of the recommendation of a board of naval officers and the indorsement of the Secretary of the Navy, and in view of the fact that there is no guaranty that we will not have the policy of continued frequent changes in the Navy Department, and with the acknowledged or alleged defects, what reason has Congress to continue to order battleships? How do we know that they will not be badly constructed and inadequate when they are finished, although they cost us eight or ten million dollars apiece?
>
> *Key:* I think you ought to make some officer under the Secretary of the Navy responsible to the Secretary that his orders are obeyed and the work of the various bureaus properly coordinated and supervised.
>
> *Tillman:* Ah, but he might not be any good himself. Who is going to appoint him?
>
> *Key:* The Secretary of the Navy.
>
> *Tillman:* But you have just said that the Secretary appoints these boards.
>
> *Key:* They are not responsible under the law. They are irresponsible.[21]

[20] *Hearings, 1908,* p. 320.   [21] *Ibid.,* pp. 309–310.

And so the argument went. The Committee was getting dangerously close to the fundamental issue of the investigation which Sims had tried to bring to the attention of the Senators. For the problem of proper organization of the Navy Department, Key was proposing the solution of a General Staff or a Chief of Staff. It was clear to him, as it was to all his colleagues, that the evils of the bureau system were proved by the demonstrated defects of our men-of-war. To the Committee these defects were explained in a convincing fashion by the insurgents, but the Senators were unwilling to accept the suggested remedy. The conclusion which Senator Hale drew he clearly stated when he observed that 'The one thing that the Commander is bringing out, ... is the lack of necessity under present conditions, of any more naval program of big ships, until things are straightened out.' [22]

By the middle of March the Chairman must have recognized that he could not obtain his ends. The evidence supplied by the insurgents had been too convincing and plain to ignore. Even the Committee was reluctantly compelled to admit that some of Reuterdahl's charges had been proved, though they valiantly tried to remember that they must always speak of 'alleged' defects. Moreover, the investigation was meeting with an increasingly hostile press. The *Washington Pathfinder* spoke for a large public when it said that 'It is too plainly evident that Senator Hale, as Chairman of the Committee, and a majority of his Republican colleagues on the Navy Committee have started out to "whitewash" the bureau system of administration.' The *Brooklyn Eagle* objected to the 'attitude of prejudgment,' the assumption of the 'inaccuracy of the criticism and the infallibility of those put forward to controvert it.' 'Men like Sims, Goodrich, and Winslow are not to be dismissed with a mere wave of the hand by bureaucrats like the lordly Capps, backed up by Senators like Hale,' said the *Pittsburgh Sun*. And the same paper later added, 'What the country will hardly stand for is the hushing up of these ugly controversies in an inconclusive finding.'

Unfortunately, that is just what the country had to stand for. In the middle of Key's testimony the Committee suddenly went into executive session and shortly after adjourned without giving Key permission to finish his prepared statement. No report was

[22] *Hearings, 1908,* p. 341

ever issued, no recommendation of any kind; simply the record of the hearings.

It is impossible not to conclude that the investigation was rigged from the beginning.[23] The published statements of Capps and Converse before the hearings opened would indicate as much. The effective but hardly subtle manipulation of witnesses precludes any assumption of impartiality. The fact that Capps was retained to cross-examine the insurgents, who were not permitted a cross-examiner of their own, strengthens the belief. Most of all, of course, the abrupt termination of the hearings argues for the validity of such a conclusion.

Sims always thought that Hale, after the affair had ended, called in Capps and Converse and gave them 'a dreadful going-over' for misleading him into thinking that their case was sound. Whether he actually did so cannot now be positively asserted, but color is lent to the story by the following evidence. Shortly after the hearings, Key wrote to his wife: 'I heard today, through Victor Blue, that Senator Tillman told him last night that every member of the Naval Committee except Perkins considered the main criticisms (defective turret design and distribution of water-line armor) absolutely established. That the Committee is not at all satisfied with the administration of the Navy Department and intends to give it a thorough probe.' [24] Tillman, old Pitchfork Ben, had been the most objective Senator throughout the proceedings, and his occasional altercations with the Chairman had enlivened several of the meetings. Upon several occasions he had held out the prospect of a further investigation into the administration of the Department. For that reason he was probably unduly optimistic about the possibilities of 'a thorough probe.' At any rate, no such 'probe' was made.

Thus ended the Investigation of 1908. For all concerned it

[23] The conclusion of Sims' friend R. D. Walker seems entirely justified. Writing in *Army and Navy Life*, October, 1908, he said: 'An unprejudiced consideration of the above testimony [excerpts quoted from the *Hearings*] must necessarily, in our opinion, convince the reader that the independent, non-coordinated, non-controlled bureaus of the Navy Department, as they now exist . . . "*plod along in ruts, behind the times, non-progressive and self-satisfied. And refuse to acknowledge, or correct, serious defects that are well established, and called to their attention by written official reports and communications.*" And, moreover, the above-quoted record shows *decided resistance on the part of the Senate Naval Committee to criticism, or correction, of the manifest and vital defects in existing legal administrative organization of the Navy Department.*'

[24] Quoted in a letter from A. L. Key to the writer.

had come to a disappointing or frustrating conclusion. The men responsible for the designs of our Battle Fleet found their handiwork convincingly criticized and discredited. The members of the Committee, most of whom had hoped that the hearings would demonstrate the virtues of the bureau system, had been presented with contrary evidence which could not be lightly brushed aside. The insurgents, as they liked to be called, had believed at the beginning that their revelations could result only in a changed method of naval administration and the improvement of our new warships. By the middle of April their revelations had been made and it was obvious that no action of any kind would follow.

They had hoped for too much. It required more than a few weeks of able testimony to sweep away the prejudices, vested interests, and attachments surrounding a system that was almost seventy years old. But since they might reasonably have expected something tangible from their courageous fight, it came as a bitter disillusionment that their time and effort had gone for nothing. To Key and Sims it was, of course, especially disappointing. They had the largest stake in the game that had been played. For almost seven years the two had fought together and individually to improve the Navy. In April, 1908, their rewards seemed as far removed as when Sims first penned his report on the *Kentucky* in February, 1901.

One thing especially troubled the two men; the President himself appeared to be wavering. On April 16, Key wrote that he was discouraged and that 'The President ought to be made to understand that neither a large section of the public nor the great mass of the officers of the Navy will accept a whitewash of the Capps, Converse, Hale combination.' Four days later, he wrote in an even more sombre mood:

> The thing I am disappointed in and practically hopeless about is the attitude of the President. Briefly, we convinced him early in the game that there should be a line officer Chief of Staff in the Navy Department. He considered this, but considered that he must put Converse or Pillsbury in the billet. In my confidential letter to him I utterly demolished as illogical and untenable his proposition to put any line officer more than fifty-nine, or any officer involved in the defense of existing defects, in the billet, and showed him that the practice of retaining old retired officers or

officers about to retire in important positions involving the efficiency of the Fleet, is diametrically opposed to all his contentions in his various annual messages, and to his special message relative to the personnel, in which he emphatically demands that younger men be pushed ahead.

After reading this letter the President found himself confronted with the proposition that there should not only be a Chief of Staff, but that he must stop permitting retired officers to serve as chiefs of bureaus and president of the Board on Construction, and that the Chief of Staff must be a man not more than fifty-nine years old. . . .

He then shifts his position and takes the attitude that all of our troubles are due to the age of our flag officers and captains, and their lack of experience with battleships before they had reached the age of fifty.

The President was indeed wavering. He had excused the publication of Reuterdahl's article, but he never did approve of it. He believed that his aides were sometimes too high-handed and vigorous in their assaults. He was counselled by the older and respected men in the service, such as his brother-in-law, Cowles, and Evans, not to make too drastic changes in the Navy Department. And he could not forget that, with the end of his administration drawing near, it was unwise to irritate so powerful a Senator as Eugene Hale.

These were dark days for the insurgents. They had proved their case, but lost the decision. The man on whom they chiefly relied was proving unreliable. Something, however, they could salvage from the wreckage of their hopes: the people had been aroused. 'I am convinced,' wrote Key, 'that under present conditions, our hope lies in educating public opinion and a fair, thorough, professional investigation and report by men who have no axes to grind.' It was a slender hope, but enough for men of stamina. Early in the summer of 1908, Sims and Key had found a new issue on which to start the fight all over again.

13

Amid the unresolved chords struck off by the Investigation of 1908, no peace was possible. Errors had been left uncorrected while issues had been obscured and not settled. The testimony of the men on both sides had roused animosities that only sharpened the lines of cleavage that ran down through the service. The conservative elements in the Navy had been deeply shocked by the methods of their opponents. They were thus reinforced by personal considerations in their determination to defend their position. On the other hand Key and Sims, denied success in the investigation, measured their strength by the size of the obstacles placed in their way. In such an atmosphere there could be no discharge in the war. Given an opportunity the insurgents would return again to the attack. That opportunity was not long in coming.

After the investigation, Key had gone off to Fore River to get his new command, the *Salem*, ready for sea. In the same yards the new *North Dakota* was building. This battleship together with her sister the *Delaware*, authorized by Congress in 1907, had been accepted by the public as the first real 'American dreadnought.' Twenty different plans had been considered before a special board under Assistant Secretary Newberry had decided upon the final designs for these two vessels. In his moments of leisure Key took the time to inspect the *North Dakota* carefully as she lay in the yards across from his own cruiser. After several weeks of study he reached the conclusion that she was not the powerful dreadnought of popular belief. This opinion he forwarded to the Secretary of the Navy on June 9, 1908.[1]

Five principal criticisms Key made of the *North Dakota*. The guns of the torpedo-defense battery were placed too close to the waterline. They were protected only by five-inch armor that was easily penetrable by eight-inch shells. Since the *North Dakota* would engage ships mounting twelve-inch guns, such protection was inadequate. Furthermore, since it was impossible to protect the secondary battery from the shells of the enemy big guns, it was better, in Key's opinion, to do away with the five-inch armor and use the weight saved for additional protection to turrets for the torpedo-defense batteries. The twelve-inch powder magazine of the Number 3 turret was completely enveloped by steam pipes. High temperatures caused by such pipes would inevitably change the ballistic quality of the powder that was stored in the magazine. The twelve-inch guns on the *North Dakota* were less powerful than similar guns in foreign navies; they were in fact about equal in power to the eleven-inch gun of the German Navy. The Number 5 turret, placed on the same level as the Number 4 turret, interfered with the end-on fire of the latter.

This letter Key wrote to the Secretary in accordance with General Order Number 49, which invited officers to submit suggestions that would 'tend to promote the efficiency of the service.' In each case he followed his critical comments with recommendations that would improve the existing defect.

When the Secretary received the communication he referred it to the Board on Construction. Two weeks passed during which no action on the criticisms was taken. Key, anticipating some such result from his labors, had taken the precaution to send Sims a copy of his letter to the Secretary. Both men knew that, placed in the proper hands, it would produce a more prompt and satisfactory reaction. On June 23, the Inspector of Target Practice sent to President Roosevelt a copy of Key's letter to the Secretary, together with a communication of his own. 'Generally speaking,' he informed the Chief Executive, 'these

[1] A. L. Key to Secretary of the Navy, June 9, 1908. A copy of this letter, together with a great many others bearing on the Newport Conference, is in the Key papers. It has recently been made more accessible in *Hearing Before a Special Subcommittee on H.R. 9266, 1940*, p. 2865. This will be referred to hereafter in the chapter as *Hearing*.

criticisms show that our most recent designs embody many of the defects of our earlier vessels, defects which have long been corrected in advanced foreign navies.' The responsibility for this state of affairs he laid squarely upon the Board on Construction, 'controlled by the Chief Constructor [Capps] and Admiral Converse.' Departing from the impersonal attitude of his confederate, Sims told the President that one officer had been made 'sick at the stomach' by the bureau chiefs' testimony during the investigation. Another had been 'appalled and disgusted' at the concerted effort 'to befog the Committee by misleading terms and phrases.' 'I beg,' he concluded, 'to assure you that I regret exceedingly having again to invite your attention to such discouraging matters; but it seems to me clearly my duty to do so in compliance with your request that in such cases I fully state exactly what I believe to be essential to the best interests of the service.'

A week passed without word from the White House, before Sims returned to prod his chief into action. On June 29, he urged that Key's letter be placed before a conference.[2] The Germans submitted all designs to a board composed of several officers of all grades from Lieutenant through Admiral. Constructors attended board meetings to give technical advice, but they took no part in the discussion of the purely military requirements of the warships. Sims proposed 'that the men on the General Board and on the staff of the War College should meet together to provide the President with: 1. An opinion on the defects of design, if any, of these vessels. 2. An opinion on whether any or all of these defects can be partially or completely remedied in vessels actually building. 3. Particularly the Board should give recommendations as to all the military characteristics which should be required in battleships to be built in the future.'

This second letter produced the results desired. On July 2, the Acting Secretary informed the service that the President had directed the General Board and the officers at the Naval War College to give a joint report on the subjects mentioned in Sims' letter of July 2.[3] The actual phrasing of this communication follows precisely that suggested by Sims.

[2] W. S. S. to William Loeb, June 29, 1908. Loeb was Roosevelt's secretary.
[3] *Hearing*, p. 2869.

Key and his friend had won the first skirmish, but they wanted to assure themselves of final victory. One week later the President heard from his Naval Aide once again.[4] Younger men were needed to leaven the conservatism of the Conference's membership. Lieutenants, Lieutenant Commanders, and Commanders with a knowledge of gunnery, so important in questions of ship design, should be ordered to the Conference that was to meet at Newport. Roosevelt agreed to this new proposal.

On July 22, the officers met at the War College in Newport to begin their consideration of Key's letter. The insurgents had laid their plans for the opening of the Conference with consummate skill. Mr. Roosevelt himself had been prevailed upon to come down from Maine for the occasion. Before the assembled members he gave a speech that put the Conference upon the first pages of the metropolitan dailies. With words that struck 'like blows of the fist,' reported the *New York Herald*, Mr. Roosevelt 'urged the imperative need of a great fighting Navy.' The imperious mood the nation loved so well was on him as he told the officers that 'no fight was ever won yet except by hitting, and the unforgivable offense in any man is to hit soft.'[5] It was, in fact, a speech to the country, for it had little to do with the actual work of the Conference. It dealt in general terms with our need for a big and strong fighting arm to defend our interests. The value of the performance lay chiefly in the publicity it gained for the Conference that was just beginning its labors.

There was other work for the President to do in Newport. When Sims arrived in the city, he had found what he believed to be a 'powerful clique' forming against the insurgents. This group was prepared to ask Mr. Roosevelt to detach all officers attending the Conference save those connected with the War College and the General Board. Should the President accede to their wishes, Sims and Key would be robbed of the support they counted on from the younger men. Accordingly Sims wired to his chief before Roosevelt arrived in Newport. In the telegram he outlined the situation as it was developing and made some suggestions for a speech the President might make to a confidential meeting of the officers. As soon as Roosevelt arrived, his

[4] W. S. S. to Theodore Roosevelt, July 10, 1908.
[5] *New York Herald*, July 23, 1908.

Naval Aide took up a position at his side and thereafter 'never left him for a moment.' Thus insulated from the forces of the opposition, Roosevelt listened while Sims urged him to stand out for the full Conference and for voting by name when a division occurred. The pressure worked successfully. In the secret meeting with a copy of Sims' telegram in his hand the President ordered the officers to follow the procedure devised by the insurgents. After this meeting Sims was jubilant. 'The rout of the enemy,' he wrote, 'was complete.' [6]

Information about the President's action reached the public, though the meeting was supposedly confidential. The description in the *New York Herald* is suspiciously accurate and detailed. Mr. Roosevelt, it reported, 'insisted that existing methods must be revised if the maximum of constructive efficiency is to be obtained in building our warships. . . . A way must be found to avert such results as have provoked recent criticism of certain constructive features of the *North Dakota*. Naval officers who are engaged in actual navigation of war vessels and in first-hand grappling with problems of the seagoing service must have a full hearing. . . . They must not hereafter suffer from pigeonholing in desks of bureau chiefs.' The *Herald* felt it could state authoritatively that 'while the President did not urge the abolition of the Board on Construction, he did suggest that the bureau system should be altered.' [7]

Sims and Key had reason to congratulate themselves as they reviewed the situation after the President departed. A hearing for Key's criticisms before a full Conference had been assured. Furthermore, all the officers had been thoroughly acquainted with the fact that Mr. Roosevelt was supporting the insurgents. Yet there were certain things that caused them uneasiness as they weighed the chances of victory. Most significant was the personnel of the Conference itself. Of the fifty-seven members, thirty-eight had been in one way or another connected with the

[6] W. S. S. to W. B. Whittelsey, July 22, 1908. In this letter Sims explained the situation as outlined in the above paragraph and told his friend that 'It is a fight to the death. . . . Very dirty work. . . . The enemy were beaten in the Committees and were desperate. The O[ld] M[an] [Mr. Roosevelt] asked me whether he had not better ask the Conference to report a plan of reorganization of the Department, but I advised against it, saying that I had a better scheme to propose, and that it would be best not to complicate the present fight.'

[7] *New York Herald*, July 23, 1908.

designs.[8] By every rule of human nature these officers could be expected to disapprove of Key's criticisms. It was because of this that Sims had been so anxious to have the names of the officers recorded in case of a division in the voting.

Against the working majority possessed by the men in some way connected with the ships under discussion, Sims and Key could expect to throw the weight of seventeen or eighteen younger officers whom they classified as 'independents,' since they had no previous interest in the designs. The two could also count upon the support of the President. For the rest it was a question of their own skill.

This skill was made manifest on the second day of the Conference. Key submitted a resolution declaring that 'votes of the Conference upon resolutions based upon separate characteristics of the designs of the *North Dakota* are not to be considered in any way as adverse criticisms of the design of the *North Dakota* as a whole. . . .'[9] The intention of this resolution was obviously to put the members in a good mood before work began. In this Key succeeded, for the passing vote was unanimous.

For two weeks the criticisms set forth in Key's letter were discussed and considered by the Conference. Despite much heated argument on the floor, the existence of many of the defects he had described was ultimately admitted. The forethought of Sims, in insisting that the vote be taken by name, had much to do with this result. By the first week in August the Conference had gone on record that the *North Dakota* was defective in the following particulars:

1. The five-inch upper casemate armor was inadequate to protect the five-inch battery and ammunition uptakes.
2. The position of the five-inch battery, so near the waterline it could not be successfully operated in ordinary trade wind weather, was 'indefensible.'
3. The location of the Number 3 powder magazine between the engine and the fire rooms was 'extremely faulty.' The fact that the magazine was surrounded by steam pipes was undesirable.
4. The location of the Number 4 turret on the same level with the Number 5 turret interfered with gunnery efficiency.

[8] *Hearing*, p. 2844.   [9] *Ibid.*

5. The main battery guns of the vessel were inferior to guns being built in England for ships of like date of completion.

6. Two other criticisms made by Key were accepted with qualifications.[10]

To obtain the admission of the Conference that these specific defects existed in the *North Dakotas* was a distinct triumph for the insurgents. It was, however, a Pyrrhic victory, for attempts to correct the errors in design were met by formidable opposition. It was argued by the majority of the Conference that the *North Dakotas* were so far along in the course of construction that changes would involve too great a waste of time and money. After a good deal of argument it was agreed to increase the armor surrounding the five-inch uptakes and supply ventilators. It was also voted to provide refrigeration for the Number 3 magazine. These were half-measures that did not satisfy the critics. A worse defeat was suffered by them in the final resolution on the *North Dakotas*. The defects were therein described as 'minor' while the general design was defined as 'excellent.' On this resolution Key fought desperately to replace the word 'minor' by a list of the defects upon which the Conference had agreed. He was, however, decisively voted down.[11] Failing here he presented a resolution to strike the word 'minor' from the original resolution embodying all the defects. Here again he was defeated, though by a close vote of 32 to 25.

The strategy of the majority grew more clear during the weeks that were spent in discussing the *North Dakotas*. While it was impossible not to admit the presence of errors in the designs, these errors could be discounted before the public as long as they were considered unimportant or not subject to correction. The essential nature of the struggle between the minority and the majority likewise can be understood after an examination of the proceedings.

On August 11, the following resolution was passed: 'The Conference is of the opinion that the location of Number 4 turret on the same level with Number 5 presents undesirable

[10] *Hearing*, pp. 2844–2845.

[11] A selected list of important resolutions is contained in General Order Number 78, the summary of the Conference issued to the service by the General Board. A fuller mimeographed record of the resolutions is in the Sims papers. General Order 78 appears in *Hearing*, pp. 2861–2877.

features from a military point of view, but that this disposition was adopted to avoid excessive girder stress and that it cannot be remedied in the *North Dakota* and *Delaware*.' The only thing with which the insurgents were concerned was 'the military point of view'; while the constructors were primarily involved in structural problems. The issue raised in this resolution is the same one Sims discovered in his report on the *Kentucky* in 1901: Is the design of a battleship to be determined primarily by military requirements or by matters of structural convenience? The two leaders, Key and Sims, wanted, naturally, to correct the defects in the *North Dakota*, but they were far more anxious to obtain some recommendation from the Conference that would make the building of such ships impossible in the future. They wanted in other words to obtain some reorganization of the Navy Department that would ensure the construction of battleships in accordance with 'the military point of view.' This was the underlying purpose of the men who were most responsible for the Newport Conference. An understanding of this explains much that went on in the heated sessions at the War College.

When consideration of the *North Dakota* was finished, the Conference turned to the problem of the *Utah* and *Delaware*. These were two new ships for which designs similar to the *North Dakota* had been prepared. Guns for these vessels were already in the course of construction, but contracts for the hulls had not yet been assigned. Sims and Key were anxious to correct in the *Utahs* the defects that the Conference had recognized in the *North Dakota*. Especially they were anxious to replace the twelve-inch guns with a more powerful battery of fourteen-inch rifles. The Conference agreed to a few minor changes, but headed off the insurgents in their attempts to obtain a new design. The strategy of the opposition involved the question of time. Philip Alger led a group who maintained that to build new guns of fourteen inches would mean costly delay in construction of the ships. The purpose of this strategy is clear enough. To make sweeping changes in the *Utahs* would mean quite obviously that the defects of the *North Dakotas* were not in fact minor.[12]

[12] Sims expressed the same idea in a letter to Theodore Roosevelt August 8, 1908. 'Their [the conservatives'] game,' he wrote, 'is to make the *North Dakota* seem good by building new ones like her.' In view of the manoeuvres made by the majority this interpretation seems more than probable.

This in turn could be construed to mean that the ordnance and construction men had been derelict in their duty. By the same token this could suggest that some need for reorganization such as Sims and Key had proposed in the Investigation of 1908 was necessary.

The majority of the Conference appeared to be in favor of continuing the *North Dakota* design with only minor alterations. Sims, therefore, took steps calculated to head off the opposition. He asked the Bethlehem Steel Company how long it would take to build new fourteen-inch guns. They replied that delivery could be made in twenty-four months — ten months before the contract time would expire if the contracts for the *Utahs* were let on September 1.[13] This seemed to answer the objection that delay would result from new guns. But with the opposition having a clear majority Sims left no stone unturned. He wrote the President on August 13. 'If you think we are right,' he said, 'in having you decide [about whether new plans should be drawn up for the *Utahs*] it will be necessary for you to have an order issued to the Conference to have both plans, the conservatives' without delay and ours with delay, placed in your hands for a decision.' The President came immediately to the rescue of his Naval Aide. 'I desire,' he wired to Newport on August 15 ' . . . recommendations covering plans to remove all defects found in the *North Dakota* and *Delaware* without regard to delay and without regard to any existing plans or arrangements relative to the *Utah* or *Florida*; also to state how much delay there will be if the recommendations for the changes are adopted; also submit recommendations for these two ships that will involve practically no delay in their plans. I desire to have the whole matter before me for my judgment.' [14]

The order from on high produced immediate action. Two plans were drawn up and submitted to the President. One, based with minor modifications on the *North Dakota*, was supported by the majority with the understanding that it would cause a delay of two months in construction. Key, Sims, and a minority supported a second design that would provide heavier armor and a main battery of eight fourteen-inch guns. In the

[13] W. S. S. to Theodore Roosevelt, August 8 1908.
[14] *Hearing*, p. 2864.

opinion of its advocates adoption of this design would delay construction by only *four* months. Before it went to Mr. Roosevelt, however, the majority succeeded in passing a resolution that estimated the delay at *fifteen* months.[15]

Shortly after these two designs for the *Utahs* were voted upon, the Conference finished its work. On August 28 the President passed down his decision on the new ships. 'I have,' he wrote to the Assistant Secretary, 'reluctantly come to the conclusion that the only course now open is that recommended in your letter of the 26th [to take the majority plan].' With what reluctance he took this course, the President made plain. 'I cannot but feel that if the officials responsible for the plans had been willing, not merely to listen to, but to try to get the opinions of the younger officers of the type represented at the Newport Conference, the *Utah* and *Florida* would be much more powerful vessels than will actually be the case. I do not for one moment accept the view that under the act of Congress it was unnecessary that there should not be improvements upon the two vessels already partially built [the *North Dakotas*]. It would be simple absurdity to suppose that any such wording as you quote would prevent us from making ships the best of their kind. But the officials responsible . . . seem to have limited themselves to the desire not to lag far behind other nations instead of doing what, of course, they ought to have done; that is, try to lead other nations.' [16]

This was not speaking softly, nor was it wielding the big stick. Obviously the President disapproved of the majority plan which perpetuated the design of the *North Dakota* in later vessels. Yet for a variety of reasons he found himself forced to accept it. A President, about to retire from public life with slumbering political ambitions, who has for years appeared as the champion of the Navy, can hardly in his last days admit inefficiencies within the Navy. To have done so, in fact, would have played into the hands of Eugene Hale, who had gone on record as preferring not to vote more money for big ships until he knew it would be well spent. Then, too, the President was a layman sitting in judgment upon highly technical matters. Against the recommendations of Sims and Key he had to weigh the advice of most

[15] W. S. S. to Theodore Roosevelt, August 22, 1908.
[16] Key papers; *Hearing*, p. 2845.

of the senior officers of the service. Able men, such as Rear Admirals Merrell, Couden, and his own brother-in-law Cowles, who had been at Newport, voted against the insurgents. This was evidence that could not be lightly brushed aside. Finally, had the President accepted the minority design, he would have been in the unenviable position of disregarding the majority opinion of a Conference that he had convened especially to recommend designs for the *Utahs*. His was a very difficult decision. Key and Sims were forced, rather wistfully, to admit to Mr. Roosevelt and themselves that he could not have done otherwise than he did.

A veil of silence was drawn across the actual proceedings of the Newport Conference almost as soon as it adjourned. The newspapers were left to speculate upon the results of the deliberations that had taken place at the War College.[17] A few of the resolutions were made public; especially the one which pronounced the *North Dakota*, save for minor defects, excellent.[18] The lack of information can easily be explained. In the first place, the full report of the Conference drawn up by the General Board was never released to the press; it was issued only to the service in Confidential Order Number 78. In the first week of November, 1908, Sims had written to Mr. Roosevelt about this summary in the following terms: 'As the officers of the General Board who have this in hand were, with no exceptions, among those who systematically defended the bureaus and condemned the critics before the Conference, it may reasonably be assumed that their report will be unconsciously colored accordingly.' Because of this Sims suggested that the President review the summary before it was sent to the service. A week later, on November 12, Sims could write again to his Chief that 'several changes had been made' in the Board's report as a result of Mr. Roosevelt's interference. 'At times,' he concluded, 'I become some-

[17] These speculations covered a wide range of opinion. On November 7, 1908, the *New York Times* observed that 'Criticisms of American battleships, which have caused much turmoil both in and out of the service for the last year, were almost wholly rejected by the great naval Conference which met at the Newport War College last summer.' On the other hand, the *New York Sun* announced November 8, 1908, that the 'Naval critics [were] sustained by ninety per cent of the officers of the Fleet.'

[18] On November 7 a few resolutions were published in various newspapers. All of these presented the case for the *North Dakota* in the most favorable light. Next day the *New York Sun* printed all the resolutions sustaining Key's criticisms. Where it obtained what it called these 'suppressed portions' of the Conference proceedings, it 's impossible to state with assurance.

what discouraged over the continuous exhibitions of resistance to and prejudiced misrepresentations of fair and beneficial criticism, and I cannot but hope that you may soon see your way clear to appoint the Commission to go into the whole question of our present organization.'

General Order 78, the report of the General Board, was issued on November 18, 1908. Nine days later Special Order Number 101, forbidding any officer to make public any information about the Newport Conference, was sent throughout the service. Conveniently enough, this order followed by only a few days a banquet that was held in Chicago. On that occasion, said the *New York Sun*, November 26, 1908, ' "Admiral" Capps . . . read aloud certain letters, notably from Dewey, Evans, and Schley, to prove that everything in the Navy is just as it should be and the so-called "critics and insurgents" are persons of no consequence.' The Annual Report of the Secretary of the Navy appeared a few days after Special Order Number 101. Mr. Metcalf devoted a page to the Conference which ended with the conclusion that the *North Dakota* and *Delaware* designs 'are superior to those of any battleship now in course of construction for any other Navy.' [19] In commenting upon the cruise around the world the Secretary paid further attention to the events of the year 1908. 'Whatever may be said in technical criticism of the Navy, the American people, to whom the ships belong and who paid for them, know, as the result of this extended cruise, at least, that the vessels will float; that their officers and men can handle them; and, so far as actual tests in time of peace can show, that the men and the ships are fit in every particular for any duty.' [20]

Chief Constructor Capps in his annual report devoted considerable attention to the Newport Conference. No small part of his energy was spent in an investigation of why Commander Key had failed to send in his criticisms of the ships at an earlier date. For the rest he quoted the resolutions of the Newport Conference dealing with the minor alterations in the *North Dakotas*. He failed, however, to mention the five resolutions supporting Key's criticisms.[21]

[19] *Report of the Secretary of the Navy*, 1908, pp. 15–16.
[20] *Ibid.*, p. 7.   [21] *Ibid.*, pp. 463–473.

This ended all official or unofficial public comment on the Conference for some little time to come. Key in an official letter to the Secretary attempted to get some official action on the criticisms made about him personally in Capps' published report. He hoped a Court of Inquiry would be called which would place the real facts of the Conference on record. This came to nothing. Not until 1939 was anything placed on Key's record to show that he had anything to do with the discussions at Newport.

The Newport Conference is a very complicated tangle of men, methods, and issues. Most of the members who were assigned to it arrived at the War College in no judicial frame of mind. In the thoughts of all lingered the memory of the investigation the preceding February. That investigation had created only division and bitterness within the service, since neither side could claim outright victory. Thus the Newport Conference became only another test of strength. In addition a clear majority of the Conference had been connected with the designs or were serving under men who had been. That this had influence upon the voting must, in the nature of things, be obvious. Sims prepared for Mr. Roosevelt a memorandum which revealed that of the thirty-seven expected to defend the *North Dakota*, thirty regularly had done so. By the same token, of the twenty-three men who had no connection with the ship, eighteen ordinarily voted with the insurgents. An even more interesting division was that between youth and age. Of the twenty-two line officers of the rank of Commander and below, only six voted with the majority group. Five of these were officers on the *Dolphin*, which had been assigned to Assistant Secretary Newberry. Mr. Newberry had been chairman of a special board that had approved the *North Dakotas*. The sixth dissenter was an ordnance expert.

There were at the Conference, therefore, men who were divided against each other by past memories and by the recognition that one group was on the attack against a ship design in which the defending group had an interest. It was not a body of men from whom one could expect dispassionate judgments.

Objectivity was further destroyed by the methods employed by both the majority and the minority. The majority used the weight of numbers to crush all the desires of the minority at critical moments. On the other hand, the members of the minority used the President of the United States as a constant threat against their opponents. Nothing could have been more irritating to the leaders of the conservative group than the speeches and telegrams of Mr. Roosevelt, inspired as they had been by the insurgent leaders.

The issues involved are perhaps less complex than either the factors of personality or method. At least four of the defects described by Key were in fact so serious that they impaired the fighting efficiency of the *North Dakotas*. Though it might have been difficult to correct these defects in the ships that were building, all of them could have been corrected in the *Utahs* — including an increase in the power of the main battery — and such correction was not made. The fact that the imperfect design could be perpetuated despite the opposition of independent line officers who would have to fight the ships, and of the President himself, illuminates the great purpose of the Newport Conference — the reorganization of the Navy Department.

This final purpose the insurgents failed to obtain. As in the investigation of the previous months, they were beaten back by superior forces. As Senator Hale had terminated the hearings before they were over and omitted to publish a report of the Committee's findings, so the authorities failed to present the full story of the Newport Conference to the public. The immediate result was not so much progress in reform as bad blood between the opposing forces.

One great contribution of the Newport Conference has not yet been discussed, since attention has been placed upon the particular ships that were the subject of debate. One of the resolutions put forward by Key and passed by the members recommended that all future designs of warships be passed upon by a board of seagoing officers. Not until 1911 was this resolution put into force. In that year Richard Wainwright, then Aide for Operations, with the support of Secretary George Von L. Meyer and Chief of the Bureau of Construction and Repair R. M. Watt, convened such a board to determine the military qualities of two ships about to be built. In 1914 these two, the *Nevada* and the *Oklahoma*, went into commission. Ever since that time *Jane's Fighting Ships* has observed that they 'marked a new era in naval construction, being the first to

embody the "everything or nothing" idea in the matter of protection.' Every battleship built in America since that time has
been similar in principle and general plan.

Such rewards lay too far in the future for the insurgents. No
sooner was the Newport Conference a matter of history than
Sims was turning once again to the President for a third and final
assault upon the bureau system, that had withstood his attacks
twice in the past year.

14

1909 *'Hope On, Hope Ever'*

IN THE years immediately preceding the Newport Conference
the reform element in the Navy had carried on what is called a
war of limited objectives. They had concentrated their attack
upon specific things: telescope sights, armor belts, systems of
gunnery. Success had attended their efforts in this restricted
theatre of activity. Remedies for most of the defects that had
been exposed to view were gradually provided. But, as time ran
on, it became apparent that these men could not accomplish by
such methods their fundamental purpose. Above all other things,
they wanted to eliminate the cause for such unsatisfactory conditions; they hoped, in other words, to reconstruct the system of
administration within the Navy Department. By 1908 the reformers had discovered that the forces arrayed against them
could yield on many particular salients without in any way
jeopardizing the security of their central position. Ultimate
victory for the insurgents in this long campaign depended upon
their ability to mount a successful offensive against the organization of the Navy Department itself.

This recognition that a change of strategy was necessary was
accompanied by the realization, after the Newport Conference,
that there must be speed in execution. No small part of the
striking force possessed by the insurgents had derived from the
support of the President. In March, 1909, Mr. Roosevelt would
depart from the scene of his triumphs to make an attempt to live
as a private citizen. His retirement would leave Sims and his

friends without visible means of support from on high. Whatever was to be done had to be done quickly.

Sims was well aware of his position. Even while the sessions at Newport were taking place, he began mapping out his plans for the future. To assist him he sought the services of one of the ablest, most experienced, and progressive spirits in the Navy. He called one afternoon at the home of Admiral Luce, who lived in Newport.

Stephen Bleeker Luce had entered the Navy in 1841.[1] For forty-eight years thereafter, until his retirement in 1889, he had served his profession with rare distinction. Possessed of a clear, liberal intelligence and a gentle yet remarkably resolute character, he had continued in retirement to labor and to hope for the Navy he loved so well. Long before Sims went to see him in Newport while the Conference was in session, he had been active in the effort to obtain a new organization for the Navy Department. Only the previous year, in 1907, he had sent to the Secretary two memoranda expressing his views on the question. The suggestions contained in these papers were the result of years of mature reflection.

The solution Luce proposed for the administrative problem was the creation of a body that could harmonize the military and political requirements; 'some board or organ of administration that could reconcile the two influences that are at present in constant conflict with each other.' The Secretary in 1906 had suggested that a commission be appointed to consider the entire question of naval administration. Admiral Luce expressed his hope that such a body would be called together to make recommendations on which could be based some constructive legislation.[2]

No action was taken on these memoranda at the time they were prepared, but their author was not the man lightly to drop the aims of a lifetime. He turned to the composition of a series of articles on Naval Administration for the *North American Review* and awaited a favorable opportunity to bring his ideas once again before the proper authorities. Such an opportunity was pre-

[1] Albert Gleaves' *Life and Letters of Stephen B. Luce,* New York, 1925, is an adequate summary of his career.

[2] Stephen B. Luce to the Secretary of the Navy, March 25 and May 16, 1907. Copies of these two memoranda, in Luce's own hand, are in the Sims papers.

sented during the Newport Conference when Sims went around to see the old man who had been Commander-in-Chief of the North Atlantic Squadron when Sims was an ensign on the *Swatara*. Together they discussed the possibilities of reorganization.

Luce was enthusiastic. He urged his caller to ask the President to appoint a committee such as he, Luce, had previously recommended to the Secretary in his memoranda of the year before. Sims required little prodding. On the tenth of August, he sent a letter to Mr. Roosevelt suggesting a mixed commission to report on the organization of the Navy.

Three days later, August 13, the President replied enthusiastically. 'All right, but are you sure of the personnel of that commission? We cannot afford to slip up. Would it not be well to have Ex-Secretary Herbert on it among the civilians? He is a Democrat and the ones you have named are all Republicans.' A draft of the letter Mr. Roosevelt intended to send 'when I appoint the commission' was enclosed. It followed almost verbatim the suggestions made in Sims' original letter.

On the sixteenth Sims replied thanking his Chief. He had shown the latter's letter to Key and Luce, who were delighted with it. Would not Mahan be a good member, he inquired? And also would not his dear friend Fullam be a good secretary for the Commission? Perhaps, he added, Ex-Secretaries Moody and Morton should be included.

The plans of the reformers seemed to be maturing successfully and as rapidly as possible. After the Newport Conference when Sims returned to Washington, he was in a position to keep his views steadily before the eyes of the President. Yet September passed and also October with no further word from Roosevelt about the proposed commission. In November, when Luce wrote from Newport to inquire into the reason for delay, Sims could only reply that Roosevelt was still with them. Luce in return was 'delighted' to hear that the President 'would take hold and be our standard bearer,' but, after all, he had virtually assured them of his support in the previous August. November passed with no word from the White House, but on the twenty-eighth of that month the *Philadelphia Ledger* heard that 'President Roosevelt [was] going to make a last and strenuous effort to

secure a general reorganization of the Navy Department.'
Elihu Root, who had presented the Army with a General Staff,
was reported as willing to head a voluntary commission that
would be appointed by the President to suggest the basic principles for reform legislation.

About the same time Henry Reuterdahl published an interview with the President.[3] In it Roosevelt was quoted as saying,
'I have from time to time recommended the reorganization of
the Navy Department; it is absolutely necessary and we will
work and work until we get it, and we shall get it.' In the
same article the President gave his opinions on his naval aide.
'You may say that the President has often said that Commander
Sims has done more for target practice than any other man in
the United States and that it is chiefly due to him that we shoot
as well as we do. . . . We do not recognize the value of preparedness. Sims had an uphill fight and would never have won out.
It was partly because his appeal was brought to my attention
that his target practice scheme and his other reforms went
through.' When Reuterdahl asked what could be done to
recognize Sims' services, the President replied, 'Yes, what reward
is there for a man like that in our country?' By the end of November it looked as though the storm signals were flying.

On the first day of December, however, an event occurred
which altered the whole situation. Truman Newberry, Assistant
Secretary of the Navy, was appointed to take the place of the
retiring Secretary, Victor Metcalf. Mr. Newberry, the sixth
man to hold the office in the seven years of the Roosevelt Administration, was looked upon by the press as a very good choice.
He came to his task, after several years' previous experience in
the Navy Department, with the justified reputation of an able
and efficient administrator. He likewise took office with a plan
of reorganization which he was not long in making public.
The General Board was to be enlarged to include representatives
from all the bureaus in the belief that the independent work of
the separate bureaus would thereby be brought into a more
complete coordination. The Board on Construction would include a few line officers. The new Secretary also announced
his intention of placing the Bureau of Steam Engineering under

[3] Henry Reuterdahl in *Pearson's Magazine*, December, 1908.

the Bureau of Construction and Repair in the hope that greater efficiency would result.[4] Much waste and confusion resulted from the fact that each bureau maintained separate shops and jurisdiction at each yard. The new Secretary made it clear to newspapermen that the President was supporting his efforts.

Immediately hostile comment was forthcoming. The *New York Press* on December 3 saw in 'the announcement that President Roosevelt has entrusted the task of reorganization not to Mr. Root but to his new Secretary [who, it admitted, was a very able man], another surrender to Senator Hale and the naval bureaucracy.' 'Coordination of the separate little sovereignties so stubbornly defended by the bureau chiefs is impossible unless compelled by law.' The *Press* found in the proposed reforms only a thin cover for retreat. 'It fails to hide the fact that once more Senator Hale and the special interest in naval appropriations . . . are still strong enough to crush the reorganization program no sooner than it is breathed to the public.'

No less candid was the *New York Sun* on December 4. 'There is nothing serious in the project so far as it has been revealed. To elaborate the superstructure of a blundering and futile system is not to achieve or even approach reform. Nothing can come of enlarging the membership of either of the boards that have been mentioned. They exist by the indulgence of the Secretary of the Navy. They are not creations of the law, and their authority is purely Pickwickian.' It was, they concluded dryly, 'reorganization in ambush.'

The program of education pursued by Sims and Key was apparently bearing fruit. As a whole the newspapers commented unfavorably on the Newberry plans except where they touched the navy yards, which were widely accepted as plums for the politicians. The attack on Senator Hale was especially vindictive, though jesting remarks about 'Admiral' Capps were gratuitously thrown in by many commentators. It was said, for example, that Secretary Newberry had 'Cappsized the Navy.' Many papers believed that the 'bureaucracy' had forced the President to give up his plans for an independent commission that could recommend sound legislation for a new organization of the Department. One even suggested that Root had been

[4] Details of the plan appeared in *The Army and Navy Journal*, December 5, 1908.

thrust out of the picture by the pressure brought by Eugene Hale. Such was not actually the case, since Root told the President he was far too busy to accept the chairmanship, but the story illustrates the temper of public opinion.[5] The newspapers were far more sharp in their comments, far more willing to believe that the critics were right than a year previously on the publication of the Reuterdahl article.

During the month of December it became increasingly obvious that Roosevelt had for the time being at least shelved the idea of a commission in favor of Newberry's plan. He was persuaded to do this for several reasons. In the first place, Newberry was an able and effective man with the confidence of the officers in the Department who were opposed to reorganization. These latter would, therefore, be more willing to accept reform from him than from the insurgents whom they thoroughly disliked. In the second place, the plan itself was an improvement over the existing conditions. Finally, it could be established without appeal to Congress. At this time, just as he was about to hand over power to his chosen successor, Roosevelt was very anxious not to antagonize that body. Past experience had taught him that any proposals of reform in the Navy would provoke a fight at least in the Senate. All these things, especially the last, appear to have influenced the President.

Still, he pursued a most confusing course of action. In his annual message in December, 1908, a few days after Newberry's plans were announced, he said, with old-time fervor and decision: 'There is literally no excuse whatever for continuing the present bureau organization. The Secretary must be supreme, and he should have as his official advisers a body of line officers who should themselves have the power to pass upon and co-ordinate all the work and all the proposals of the separate bureaus.'[6] No words could set forth the President's intentions more clearly, but the speech contrasted oddly with Mr. Roosevelt's acknowledged support for Newberry's enlarged General Board, which had no power over the bureaus.[7]

[5] *The Army and Navy Journal*, January 16, 1909.

[6] *The Scientific American*, December 19, 1908.

[7] The *New York Times*, December 12, 1908, however, believed 'The President's assertion and the Secretary's statement are not so much at war the one with the other as they seem to be.' This conclusion was possible for the *Times* because of its

It was a depressing month for the bewildered insurgents. Luce from Newport wrote to Sims on the twenty-ninth in disillusion, 'The fallacy at present is that we are blinding the public by pretending a reorganization within the present law.' Yet his bright spirit never faltered as he closed with his favorite 'Hope on, hope ever. We'll get there sometime.' A few days later, not far from his eighty-second birthday, he added, 'Never say die.'

From such buoyant letters Sims took heart. On the thirtieth of December, he sent off to the President a delicately phrased piece of advice. Mr. Roosevelt was reminded first of his recommendation in his annual message for a General Staff. 'Counter to all opinion,' Sims told his Chief, no such body was included in the proposed plan of reorganization. In fact, the new scheme did not separate advisory from administrative bodies but associated them more closely. The enlarged General Board, representing all eight bureaus, would only aggravate the evils already present. As for the amalgamation of the Bureau of Steam Engineering and the Bureau of Construction and Repair, it would constitute what was popularly called 'a mutual admiration society.' Where the remedy lay he did not fail to indicate rather pointedly. 'In this connection I beg to remind you again that the great improvement we have made in the last few years was really due to the fact that your powerful influence has largely suspended the evils of the bureau system; but that if you should leave us with an unsound organization, unrestrained by your influence, not only must we relapse into our former condition, but our failure in this respect would be remembered long after our minor improvements were forgotten.'

Three days later, on January 2, 1909, he spoke more clearly to his superior. The time was running out, there were only sixty-four more days of the Roosevelt Administration, and Sims was desperately trying to win the President over to the original plan of a commission. The whole idea of reform, he said, involving the consolidation of Steam Engineering and Construction and

tranquil assumption that Mr. Roosevelt's 'plan [for a General Staff] is not at all out of harmony with the views of the Secretary.' That such a General Staff was needed the *Times* admitted. 'Under such a system the bureaus would no longer do their work, not only independently of each other, but without reference to each other, and we should no longer hear of a ship of the Navy being ordered to sea by one bureau the day after another bureau had ordered her boilers taken out.'

Repair, 'would further mix the administrative and advisory functions.' It would mean a 'practical amalgamation of the General Board, the Board on Construction, and the Board of Inspection with the Bureaus.' 'I believe,' he added, 'that Senator Hale and Chief Constructor Capps are working toward that end. . . . Secretary Newberry is doubtless in favor of reform . . . but he confuses successful (harmonious) administration with successful preparation for war.' 'If we don't act,' Sims concluded, 'Congress (Senator Hale) will doubtless put through a reorganization that will have the effect of strengthening the power of the bureau system.'

In the early weeks of January the insurgents, aware that they were making their last stand, kept hammering away at the President. To this continuous pressure Mr. Roosevelt finally succumbed. A large commission was appointed containing several ex-secretaries, several retired officers, and several active officers. Most of the recommendations made by the men from Newport in the previous August were followed. Mahan was a member; so were Luce, Sims, and Fullam. In answering the President's letter asking him to act as a member of the commission, Mahan said almost everything that could be said about naval administration.[8] What we needed, in his opinion was something that had mastery of diplomatic, naval, and military considerations, home and foreign, that bore on our naval policy. 'The only means by which such consecutive knowledge can be maintained is by a corporate body continuous in existence and gradual in change. That we call a General Staff.' Knowledge should rest in this body but — 'and here, perhaps, is my principal point . . .' — the Chief of Staff should be 'solely responsible for information and advice given the Secretary.' The advice must be single, not corporate. 'Jomini taught me to scorn the sharp distinction between diplomatic and military considerations. The Chief of Staff should know the administration policies at home and abroad.'

The heart of Mahan's argument was contained in a series of those felicitous quotations he knew how to use so well. Corbett had convinced him that for a military establishment 'the distinction between a state of war and a state of peace is one of

[8] A. T. Mahan to Theodore Roosevelt, January 13, 1909.

words, not fact.' This military consideration he told the President should give the General Staff power to lay down all military aspects of design and so forth, using the bureaus only for information. 'The essence of the thing,' he concluded, 'is delightfully phrased in Nelson's last order: "The order of sailing is the order of battle."' Our Department sailed well enough, but it fought badly.

Holding such views as these, Mahan, along with his fellow committee members, must have been sadly disappointed at what took place in Washington upon their arrival. *The Army and Navy Journal* describes the deliberations of the commission of notables as follows:

> It seems that when President Roosevelt summoned to Washington Jan. 16 the Washington Naval Conference, as it was formally named at the White House, the expectation was that it would take some time and thought and paper to perform the task that had been cut out for that body of experts in naval practice and administration. But the unexpected happened. The Conference met with Mr. Newberry present as its president and for perhaps half an hour he explained to his associates of the conference the precise difficulties to correct which they had been asked to advise. He also submitted a plan for accomplishing the work and there was a copy laid in front of each member of the conference. Mr. Newberry withdrew to go to the Cabinet meeting and his ideas were discussed fully. He returned in an hour and resumed his place with the conference. In less than another half hour his plan had been approved and the findings of the conference were signed. This was a more decisive action than had been anticipated. The momentum of the affair carried it straight through the White House, with the President's approval, and the Secretary was so far forth master of the situation and the process of reforming the Department had begun.[9]

The President had hedged his bets. The impressive commission that he had appointed to satisfy the demands of the reformers had been used simply to sanctify Secretary Newberry's program of reorganization. The members had been called to Washington presumably to deliberate upon and to investigate the complex problem of naval administration, but upon their arrival they had been asked only to sign on the dotted line. What may

[9] *The Army and Navy Journal*, January 30, 1909.

have begun as a sincere attempt on the part of the President to get information on the subject of reorganization had ended in what looked suspiciously like shrewd politics. Mr. Roosevelt seemed to have lost his celebrated nerve.

What followed was even more confusing. In the third week of January, 1909, Newberry revealed to reporters the full detailed outline of his scheme.[10] Only two days later, January 27, the President sent out letters to eight men asking them to form a new commission to investigate the Navy Department. It was all very bewildering to observers on the outside, to whom it certainly looked as though Mr. Roosevelt were not informing his left hand of the activities of his right. Rather acidly the *New Orleans Times-Picayune* remarked on January 29 that 'It looks as if the Navy Department is getting a surfeit of reorganization. Only Wednesday Secretary of the Navy Newberry issued an order approved by the President making important changes along lines recommended by a special commission. Hardly was the ink dry when the President himself announced the appointment of a special commission to consider the whole subject.'

Bewildering though these developments may have been, they ended in a triumph for the men who desired a carefully digested scheme of reorganization. The new commission, composed of ex-secretaries Dayton, Moody, and Morton, with Admirals Luce, Mahan, William M. Folger, William S. Cowles, and Robley D. Evans, was asked to consider the questions Sims had first proposed to Mr. Roosevelt on August 10, 1908. Fullam served as the secretary.[11]

For a month the Commission deliberated before presenting its review of the situation to the President. On February 25 Mr. Roosevelt, in a special message to the Senate, placed before that body a preliminary report on the general principles of naval organization. Two days later he sent the specific recommendations of the Commission for the reform of the administrative system of the United States Navy. These two remarkable documents have deserved far wider attention than they have re-

[10] Complete information on the Secretary's plan was published in the *Washington Star*, January 27, 1909.

[11] Roosevelt's letter to the members of the Commission which set forth the specific questions to be discussed can be found in *Hearings Before the Committee on Naval Affairs*, House of Representatives, 64th Congress, 1st Session, 1916, vol. 3, p. 2663.

ceived.[12] In the first report on general principles, the hand of Mahan is everywhere apparent, as is, to a lesser degree, the influence of Stephen B. Luce. No clearer view of the aims of naval administration can be obtained than that provided in the few brief pages.

It was first established that the office of Secretary of the Navy was executive in nature. Nothing could be admitted which would qualify that official's authority or diminish his responsibility. The holder of this office should always be a civilian.

The division between the civil and military duties of the official was recognized and clearly defined. 'The civil duties embrace the provision or preparation of all the material of war. This is the function of the present bureaus.' On the other hand, the military duties concerned the use of that material, and 'For the direction of these military duties, no subordinate provision corresponding to the bureaus on the civil side exists in the present organization established by statute.'

At the outset, the Commission uncovered in these observations the central failure of the existing system of administration. From here it turned to a specific criticism of the bureaus. 'Independent authority, with undivided responsibility [such as the bureaus possessed by law], though in principle proper, suffers historically from intrinsic inability to cooperate, where a number of such independent units are present. The marshals of the first Napoleon — especially in Spain — [it is a favorite example of Mahan] in the absence of the Emperor, offer a familiar illustration. The bureau system as at present constituted by law contains no remedy for this inherent defect.' This, more concisely, is the argument Sims put forward from the China Station in 1901 in his criticisms of the Board on Construction.

The power to coordinate the work of the bureaus lay, as the Commission recognized, in the power of the Secretary. But since his tenure was short and his professional knowledge inevitably limited, 'the organization should provide him with such knowledge and experience, digested formally, so as to facilitate his personal acquirement.' In short, there should exist some

---

[12] These two reports can be found in Senate Documents Nos. 740 and 743, 60th Congress, 2d Session. They were reprinted in the *Hearing, 1916*, cited immediately above, vol. 3, pp. 2662–2669.

advisory body 'equipped not with advice merely, but with reasons.' Such a body should have the continuity which can only exist in a corporate entity; but the principle of undivided responsibility would dictate that only *one* of the advisory body should be responsible for the advice given in common to their superior — the Secretary.

Since the end of a navy is war, and the agents of war are the military naval officers, the advisory body 'should be taken entirely from the class to which belongs the conduct of war, and upon whom will fall, in war, the responsibility for the use of the instruments and for the results of the measures which they recommend.' Such a group of officers could answer the chief need of a Secretary: 'a clear understanding and firm grasp of leading military considerations. Possessed of these he may without great difficulty weigh the recommendations of his technical assistants, decide for himself and depend on them for technical execution of that which he approves.'

This was the argument of the Commission for a General Staff at the head of which there should be a single officer, the individual adviser of the Secretary personally responsible for his advice. Many of the members of the Commission were old hands at the game of reorganization. They knew what the objections to such a plan would be. With care, therefore, they met the argument before it could be stated. 'The provision of a responsible adviser does not compel the Secretary to accept his advice, nor prevent his consulting whomsoever else he will. The provision suggested does not limit the authority of the Secretary; but it does provide him with the weightiest and most instructed counsel, and it lays upon the prospective Commander-in-Chief the solemn charge that in all he recommends he is sowing for a future which he himself may have to reap.'

In conclusion, the Commission laid down what it took to be the cardinal principle of naval organization. No administrative system 'can possibly be effective which does not recognize that the requirement of war is the true standard of efficiency in an administrative military system; that success in war and victory in battle can be assured only by that constant preparedness and that superior fighting efficiency which logically result from placing the control and responsibility in time of peace upon the

227

same individuals and the same agencies that must control in time of war. There should be no shock or change of method in expanding from a state of peace to a state of war. This is not militarism; it is a simple business principle based upon the fact that success in war is the only return the people and the nation can get from the investment of many millions in the building and maintenance of a great navy.'

Two days after this declaration of general principles had been laid before the Senate, it was followed by the Commission's specific plan for reorganization of the Navy Department. At the top of the administrative structure was, of course, the Secretary. The general duties placed under his care were to be divided up among five great divisions. The first division, under an Assistant Secretary who was to be 'a civilian and man of affairs,' had charge of the business of the Bureaus of Yards and Docks, Supplies and Medicine and Surgery. The next division was called Naval Operations, the chief of which was to be a flag officer who was to serve as the principal military adviser of the Secretary. No administrative duties were assigned to him, but he was to serve ex-officio as head of the General Board and the Board on Construction. In his special care were war plans, naval policy, the War College, and the Office of Naval Intelligence. Personnel was the third division, also presided over by a flag officer who was charged with all the business of the Bureau of Navigation, with discipline and the education of naval officers. Another flag officer had charge of the fourth division, called Inspection — concerned with ship trials and the inspection of fleets, navy yards, and sites for naval stations. The Chief of the fifth division, Material, could be a flag officer, a naval constructor, or a civilian with technical training. This man was to superintend the business of the four technical bureaus — Construction, Ordnance, Engineering, and Equipment. Beneath these five grand divisions the bureau system was maintained intact, but strictly subordinate to the superior coordinating power of the chiefs of the main divisions.

To advise and consult with the Secretary two Councils were established. The first, the General Council, made up of all five chiefs of division, was charged with giving the civilian Secretary advice and information upon any matters connected with the

Navy Department. A smaller Council, the Military Council, was composed of the Chief of Naval Operations, the Chief of Personnel, and the Chief of Inspection. But of these, the first was the sole responsible military adviser of the Secretary. No bureau chief while active could serve also as a chief of division.

Through such a system as this, the Commission believed the general principles enumerated in their first report could be successfully realized and applied.

These two reports were placed by the President before the Senate on February 25 and 27. Whatever their defects, they at least contained ideas which were a distinct advance over the notions of naval administration then in force. Unfortunately, the documents were sent to Capitol Hill when the Roosevelt Administration had only one more week of life. Little attention was paid to the recommendations by a Senate diverted by more pressing and less controversial legislative activity. It is doubtful, anyway, if Congress would have taken any favorable action at this time. The politicians were in the customary revolt against a retiring executive, and, as Key sourly pointed out, the Moody Commission was filled with Rooseveltian supporters. So all the fears of the insurgents were realized. On March 4, the seven years of Roosevelt were brought to an end without any fundamental change in the organization of the Navy Department.[13]

The hopes of reform might have died on that day had it not been for the new Secretary of the Navy, George Von L. Meyer. This man had served as Postmaster General in the Cabinet of Mr. Roosevelt, who had recommended Meyer to Mr. Taft for the Navy post. He proved himself to be one of the ablest men ever to hold the position of Secretary. In knowledge, native ability, and interest, he was far superior to most of his predecessors. When he began work in March, 1909, he was thoroughly

[13] Roosevelt himself could have expected no other result from the deliberations of the Commission. He was politically far too astute to believe a hostile Congress in the last week of his administration would grant him what friendly Congresses had failed, for seven years, to provide. *The Army and Navy Journal* on January 30, 1909, made an attempt to explain the President's tortuous course as follows: 'On good authority it is learned that the President does not expect the Commission to make its report ... before the 4th of March. This would imply that there has been some sort of a tentative understanding between the outgoing and the incoming President. It is hardly conceivable that Mr. Roosevelt would demoralize an executive department, and then complacently wave his successor upon the scene of chaos to create and harmonize and bring order again.' Conceivable or not, this is about what the President did.

acquainted with Roosevelt's views on the Navy. Indeed, the retiring President, fully aware of the apathy of Congress to any change in organization, had taken some pains to impress upon both Taft and Meyer the imperative necessity of reform.

It did not take the new Secretary long to discover the obstacles that lay in his way. On May 1, he confided to his diary that 'I can see that sooner or later I shall have a struggle with Senator Hale on this whole subject, who is against the Fleet and the line officers.' [14] Equally quickly he understood that if he waited upon Congress for action on the reports of the Moody Commission, he would wait in vain. Therefore, he resolved to try his hand at reorganization alone. As a first step he appointed a board, under the chairmanship of Rear Admiral William Swift, to review all the suggestions that had been made in the past upon the subject. This board reported in favor of the conclusions of the Moody Commission, recommending to the Secretary that the plan devised in February, 1909, be given a trial.[15]

Throughout these early months of Meyer's administration the insurgents had not been inactive. In reply to a request from Meyer, Sims had written him twice, in July and August, 1909, to emphasize the need for change in administration. The burden of these letters is the familiar one that, though the bureaus were competent to superintend the construction of ships and guns, they needed some coordinating authority superior to them. Other line officers supplemented Sims' views. More than any previous official, Meyer gave his ear and his support to the men who had fought so long to alter the administrative structure of the Navy Department.

By December, 1909, he was ready to act. He recognized that he must move swiftly to establish his system before Congress met in the early weeks of that month. With the advice of the Attorney General as to the legality of his actions, he set up the following organization. The bureau system, of course, remained as created by Congress, but above it he established four grand divisions, Operations, Personnel, Material, and Inspection, with a line officer at the head of each to coordinate the work of the bureaus.

[14] M. A. De Wolfe Howe, *George von Lengerke Meyer*, New York, 1919, p. 433.

[15] The deliberations of the Swift Board are fully explained in Meyer's own words in M. A. De Wolfe Howe, *George von Lengerke Meyer*, pp. 466–467.

The chiefs of these divisions formed his Council, the advisory body, 'equipped not merely with advice but reasons,' as he said to Roosevelt later, quoting the language of the Moody-Mahan Commission.

These four men were, in fact, the long-sought General Staff enabling 'the Secretary to obtain a clear understanding and a firm grasp of leading military considerations' through responsible advisers. The whole system, though it depended for existence not upon the law but the good will of the Secretary, was really that which the Moody-Mahan Commission had previously recommended.[16]

When Congress met, soon after this reorganization had taken place, Meyer found how justified his fears of the politicians had been. '. . . I found opposition and an endeavor to overthrow what I had done,' he wrote to Roosevelt. 'I found that the movement was led by Hale, Foss, Naval Constructor Capps, Paymaster General Rogers, Admiral Goodrich, and supported quietly by Newberry. At one time it looked as though everything would be upset, but I finally won over the Committee to leave everything in operation until Congress convenes again, so that they may be able to judge by actual results.' [17]

The plan never did receive the active approval of Congress. For four years the aid system (the Chiefs of Divisions were called aids) continued to exist through the will of the Secretary alone. When Meyer retired from office, an entirely different organization was substituted and legalized; an organization more in keeping with the desires of Congress than with the needs of the Navy.

Thus ended the strife that had divided the Navy throughout the two administrations of Theodore Roosevelt. Yet to restrict this conflict within the limits of a few years, to describe it in terms of the adroit manoeuvres of both sides, to reduce it to arguments over gunsights and turret hoists, to dramatize it with rich and powerful personalities is to divert attention from its real significance. Sims and Key, Capps and Hale were but temporary figures in a great debate that had been maintained

---

[16] The material for this discussion of Meyer's work is taken largely from Howe's life of the Secretary cited above. Chapter 6 of that work contains a summary of his accomplishments as Secretary of the Navy.

[17] Quoted by Howe, p. 469.

ever since the Civil War first revealed the defects of the Navy Department as organized by the law of 1842. This long struggle revolves around one of the great problems of any representative government: military administration in the democratic state.

In theory it is easy enough to devise the machinery for successful naval administration. A General Staff empowered to direct military preparations and activities, but responsible and subordinate to representatives of the civilian government, would seem to fulfil the necessary requirements. In practice it has been difficult to construct such machinery in America for two reasons. In the first place, it appears to grant the naval authorities an independence that most civilians believe would not always be used to improve the efficiency of the first line of defense. The layman distrusts the conservatism of the military mind, and with some reason. Roman seamen fought to retain oars when sails were introduced; American sailors tried to continue with sails long after steam had proved its possibilities. In 1862, the Army rejected the Gatling gun; in 1902, it rejected the Maxim gun; in 1916, it rejected the Lewis gun.

For another, far more compelling reason, the creation of a General Staff has been consistently opposed in America. It has been believed that such a body, if granted sufficient power to direct the means, would likewise be strong enough to determine ends. Using their superior knowledge to confuse and outwit the representatives of the government, the powerful military, so the arguments run, would usurp control of national policy. In other words, the establishment of a General Staff meant the creation of militarism. The persistence of this fear cannot be overestimated. The members of the Moody-Mahan Commission took particular pains to point out that their plans were based not upon 'militarism' but 'sound business practice.' Several years later Josephus Daniels brought about the emasculation of a bill creating a kind of General Staff and accused the sponsors of the legislation of trying to 'Prussianize' the Navy. In Mr. Daniels' time no less than now, that particular epithet had an ugly sound.

This fear of establishing a militaristic cabal has had far-reaching consequences. Down through the years it has prevented successive Congresses from making any serious effort to investigate methods of sound military administration. An example is found in the fate of the Moody-Mahan report. Excellent though the recommendations of the Commission were, it is possible to criticize them on the ground that the Secretary's Council was heavily weighted with military men. Instead of four officers and one civilian, it might well have been better to provide for four officers and three civilians, thus including a leaven for professional conservatism. Had objections of this sort been made, remedies might well have been supplied. Instead the whole plan was rejected.

Another result of this attitude has been the consistent refusal of the legislators, at least until 1915, to disturb the bureau system in any way. They have assumed that, if no properly constituted General Staff were established, the civilian secretary would be free from untoward military influences. The result of this refusal to act contains a mild irony. The Navy was kept from that state of efficiency it might have obtained, but the Secretary was placed at the mercy of a military bureaucracy. The experience of Mr. Metcalf was typical. 'I had my head full of the great things I was going to accomplish,' said he. 'I know better now. My duties consist of waiting for the Chief of the Bureau of Navigation to come in with a paper, put it down before me with his finger on a dotted line, and say to me, "Sign your name here." It is all any Secretary of the Navy does.' [18]

It may appear that Congress has been too greatly blamed for the opposition to reform. Perhaps it has been. Congress, in the last analysis does, however roughly, express the will of the people. In America the people have ordinarily viewed the Navy with suspicion, apathy, and ignorance. Until the present day we have never lived in that continuous fear of attack which haunts the mind of every European. Armies and navies have, therefore, existed through long periods of peace considered by many as a questionable luxury. Probably the citizens of no other great power are as uneducated in military matters as Americans. This attitude, colored as it is by our hatred of war as an instrument of policy, has prevented us from taking measures that would have ensured our security.

[18] Quoted by Lindsay Rogers, 'Civilian Control of Military Policy,' *Foreign Affairs*, January, 1940. Those who wish to pursue this subject of military administration further are referred to the above article as well as the same author's 'National Defense: Plan or Patchwork,' *Foreign Affairs*, October, 1940.

The insurgents of the Roosevelt era thus faced a more formidable opposition than that provided by a few contemporary bureau chiefs and senators. The spectre of militarism, the consciousness that the Navy had never lost a war, the great national apathy were ranged against them. It is not remarkable that their hopes outran their achievements. Reform in any democracy is, perhaps fortunately, a slow process. Yet they did not labor in vain. The record written by Sims and his colleagues through these years is filled with many triumphs. Not the least of these is that they gave renewed life to the struggle which from that time forth has gone on almost unabated, and which has made the present Navy a far sounder fighting arm than it was on the day the insurgents knew their immediate hopes were all in vain.

15

N ow and then,' wrote Theodore Roosevelt to Sims on July 7, 1906, 'I feel a little cast down and gloomy and in consequence it does me real good to receive a letter like yours. By George, how good it is to read and re-read a letter like yours.'

The communication that rallied the President from his despondency had been written by Sims on July 5. It revealed to Mr. Roosevelt the full extent of the improvement in target practice since the fall of 1902. A few figures will explain the Chief Executive's return to high spirits.[1] In 1902 the *Terrible* had established a world's record by making 3.3 hits per minute with her six-inch guns. Every American vessel had at least equalled that record in the spring practice of 1906. Twelve of them had established the remarkable average of 6.25 hits per gun per minute with their six-inch batteries. Just before 'Dotter' Grounds died of the cholera in Hong Kong, he had set up an individual record of eight hits in one minute. In 1906 eighty American pointers duplicated the feat for which the 'Dotter' had gone down in song and story. One man had almost doubled the Englishman's great performance.

The firing of the great guns had likewise improved startlingly in the four years. In 1901 the British ship *Ocean* had rocked naval circles when her great guns made .75 hits per gun per minute. In

---

[1] These figures are taken from Sims' letter of July 5. Unfortunately, it has been impossible to obtain, save for the year 1905, exact official figures on target-practice records during Sims' duty as Inspector. From his own correspondence, Annual Reports of the Secretary, and newspapers the gradual improvement of fleet gunnery can be clearly seen.

1906 at Guantanamo American rifles of the same calibre had doubled this performance.

It was with pardonable pride that the Inspector of Target Practice sent off this information to the White House. Enclosed in the same letter was an invitation to the President to attend target practice in the fall. The idea appealed to Roosevelt, who, in September, came to watch the six-inch pointers run through a practice in Long Island Sound. It was a day of triumph, for the men, the President, and Sims himself.

Like woman's work, the labors of an Inspector of Target Practice are never done. Four years of constant effort had brought American gunnery back from the doldrums, but ahead lay new challenges that had to be met if the Navy was to remain on equal terms with any possible enemy. Fire control had assured greater accuracy and increased rapidity of fire at the conventional known ranges. Newly developed mechanisms gave the promise of far greater accuracy and rapidity of fire at much longer ranges. Guns, sights, and range-finders had been improved in the years since 1900; methods of communication between the spotters in the fire-control tower and the pointers at the guns had been simplified, range-keeping devices had been introduced enabling vessels to keep their guns on targets even when the range was constantly changing. It was to the problems that were posed by these new technological improvements that Sims now applied himself.[2]

In 1906 the fall target practice revealed several defects in our shooting that required immediate attention. To the Secretary of the Navy Sims wrote on October 22 that 'range clocks, range and deflection transmitters must be procured immediately on all ships.' Such equipment would speed up the shooting immeasurably and increase the accuracy appreciably. 'We are forced to resort to a known rate of change of range — in this case a course of thirty degrees to the plane of the target because we can't figure fast enough.' Despite these difficulties the practice of 1906, the first in Sims' career that was carried out at ranges in excess of four thousand yards under battle conditions, was a great success.

[2] Wilbur R. Van Auken in 'Notes on a Half-Century of United States Naval Ordnance,' Washington, 1939, gives (pp. 13–24) a fuller description of these technological improvements.

Far more exciting, however, was the battle practice of the next year. Newer ships of the line opened fire at the little target, thirty feet by sixty feet, at ranges up to 5.3 miles; the older ones, with less powerful guns, began shooting at around three miles. The exact range was unknown to the spotters before firing began. One gun alone opened to get the range for the spotter, who signalled to the pointers below the proper corrections for elevations and train. Then the big guns went off at these extreme ranges, in 'runs' controlled by the spotter in the tops. The records established under these conditions were impressive. The pointers for the great guns averaged one hit per gun per minute; at closer quarters the secondary batteries surpassed previous accomplishments. Excluding everything below six pounders, the Fleet average for all guns was 77.6 per cent hits. In 1903 it had been forty per cent.[3]

The record was more remarkable because, as Sims wrote to Theodore Roosevelt, no ship was fitted with fire-control instruments equal to the requirements of modern gunfire. The fire of all ships but one was controlled by appliances improvised by the officers.

In 1908, the last full year in which Sims held office as Inspector of Target Practice, proper fire-control equipment was installed on all the big ships.[4] The practice of that year wrote a glorious finis to Sims' tour of duty. Ships began firing at unknown ranges of between seven and nine thousand yards. Two hundred and ten shots were fired from the great guns, of which one hundred and twelve found their distant mark.[5] 'I wish,' wrote an assistant in the Target Practice Office, 'President Roosevelt could have seen the *Connecticut* open fire at ninety-seven hundred yards (5.5 miles) and then make all those hits, thirty-two in five and a half minutes.'

In December of the same year, the Chief of the Bureau of Navigation summed up the history of gunnery since Sims had taken over in the following terms:

> The present system of gunnery training was adopted in 1903, and has been in use ever since. The records of this year show a

---

[3] W. S. S. to Theodore Roosevelt, October 8, 1907.
[4] *Annual Report of the Secretary of the Navy*, 1908, p. 421.
[5] W. S. S. to Theodore Roosevelt, December 28, 1908.

gratifying increase over the records of preceding years, both in rapidity of fire and percentage of hits made, although the conditions governing the practice were more difficult than heretofore, all casualties or interruptions being counted the fault of the personnel. The enthusiastic support of the officers and enlisted men has been obtained and we have every reason to believe that as much improvement will be made in the future as in the past. The system of gunnery training develops the initiative of the commanding, the gunnery, and the division officers, as they are actuated by a spirit of competition between individual ships as well as between individual guns of various calibres and types. . . .

The battle practice for vessels of the Navy for the year 1908 has not yet been held, but will be held this autumn. At this practice the vessels fire under way at ranges varying from five thousand to nine thousand yards on unmarked ranges. The distance of the target, course, and speed of ship being in a sealed envelope which is opened just before going on the range, the conditions being such as to simulate approximately the conditions of firing action.' [6]

This was a far cry from the conditions of 1901, when ships firing alone made 'constructive' hits against a target that was largely imaginary at ranges of eighteen hundred yards.

Target practice became a subject of general concern. The papers followed the annual results with great interest and the magazines were full of dramatic, illuminating, and, at times, highly erroneous descriptions of what took place in the big Fleet during battle practice.[7]

The basis for this improvement was Sims' method of training gun-pointers. This had remained basically unchanged through the years. By constant subcalibre practice the men were trained to follow the target throughout the roll of the ship. At record practices after weeks of preparation the individual skill of the pointers was tested. Battle practices afforded the opportunity

[6] *Annual Report of the Secretary of the Navy*, 1908, p. 335.

[7] As stated in the previous chapter on target practice, *The Scientific American* for these years is the most rewarding single source of information in gunnery matters. Two articles in other periodicals are of particular interest. Stewart Edward White's 'Breaking World's Records at Naval Gunnery' in *World's Work*, April, 1909, is vivid, interesting and informative. The author recaptures especially well the exciting and dramatic atmosphere that prevails at a target practice. Henry W. Lanier's 'Efficiency at Work,' *Review of Reviews*, August, 1914, is less entertaining but more instructive about technicalities. The article is illustrated with magnificent photographs.

for gauging the effectiveness of individual ships and thus of the Fleet as a whole. It should be pointed out again that continuous-aim firing was impossible with the great guns, which were too ponderous to manipulate in rapid fashion; but subcalibre training taught the pointers how to follow the target efficiently.

Sims was aware of the success of his methods, but he did not take the credit to himself. An exceptionally able group of men had assisted him throughout his labors. Ridley McLean was, of course, the most valuable. 'I have repeatedly stated,' his superior wrote to the Secretary of the Navy, 'and I wish here again to emphasize the statement, that Mr. McLean was the brains of my office while he served with me during the all-important fundamental development of the system, and that he has been so ever since.' Others followed McLean in his post of Assistant Inspector of Target Practice when that able man assumed the position of Fleet Gunnery Officer. Harrison, Bradshaw, and, for a little time near the end, Baldridge all performed valuable service for their chief. But Sims did not rely on these men alone. His method of improving upon his past performance is described by one of his assistants as follows:

> Each fall there gathered in the Washington basement office of Sims, in the State, War, and Navy Building, a board of officers from the Atlantic Fleet to meet with him and his assistants; they all discussed the faults of that year's rules for target practice and drew up new rules for the next year. Everything was delightfully informal, everything thoroughly debated, and unanimously decided upon. Sometimes these conferences lasted from ten to fourteen days — Sims would never end the discussions until unanimity had been reached. In this way he received fresh ideas from the Fleet, which worked out the new methods in practice at sea. It had the advantage of enabling the Fleet to feel it shared in the running of things. He was like that. All the youngsters adored him and the Fleet Gunnery Officer under Admiral Evans, Lieutenant Commander Mark Bristol [who had been Sims' best man] would return to the Fleet with us, keyed up with enthusiasm for the new work ahead.[8]

Great as was the importance of Sims' system of gunnery train-

[8] H. A. Baldridge in 'Sims — The Iconoclast,' *N.I.P.*, February, 1937.

ing, it must not be considered the sole factor in the development of our modern shooting. His turret captains, pointers, and spotters had to have the tools to work with before they could make their world's records. For these tools the Bureau of Ordnance was directly responsible. This bureau Sims had looked upon as his first enemy ever since the day he had read Admiral O'Neil's unfavorable endorsement of his report on continuous-aim firing. In the early years of his duty as Inspector of Target Practice, the progress of gunnery reform had been definitely retarded by poor elevating gear, inadequate gun sights, and other faulty material. This increased the antagonism between Sims and the men in Ordnance. He criticized their work frequently, bitterly, and at length. Much of this criticism was definitely deserved. It required the efforts of Theodore Roosevelt to equip the ships with good sights, and the President had stepped in only after Sims had been at work on the defective instruments for four years. On the other hand, the Bureau found itself confronted by a revolution in gunnery, which made much of the existing material obsolete or which required the development of mechanisms never before needed or thought of. It could not have been expected to supply immediately all the new tools required of it by Sims.

This skirmishing between the Target Practice Office and the Bureau continued throughout Sims' tour of duty. As the years passed, however, he had less of which to complain. Admiral Mason, when he became Chief of Ordnance, did a great deal to improve the slothful conservatism of his organization. In the relatively short space of six years, from 1903 to 1909, modern guns, modern sights, modern fire-control equipment, modern shells, modern range-keepers were all produced by the Bureau of Ordnance. The change in tempo can well be seen in the fact that while it took four years to introduce adequate sights, it required only three years for the Bureau to equip every ship in the Fleet with the far more complicated mechanisms of fire control. Sims never did do justice to the men in Ordnance. All that was apparent to him was the fact that they did not produce equipment as rapidly as changing conditions and his progressive mind demanded. By the same token Ordnance men were inclined to discount the work done by Sims, to look upon him as rather a gadfly. In justice to both it should be observed that

Ordnance did, in the course of time, produce required material of a very high type, while it certainly produced it far more rapidly because of the pressure brought to bear by Sims.[9]

By 1909, when Sims left the office, American gunnery was probably the best in the world. Germany, as might be expected, had produced fire-control instruments that were as good if not better than those in other countries. But throughout the first decade of the century, the nation suffered from poor training methods, inefficient officers, and uncertain morale among the enlisted men. The French, better manned than their traditional enemy, were handicapped by improper gunnery training. The British Navy was probably almost the equal of the American Navy. Though still handicapped somewhat by the tradition of 'spit and polish' and by the inherent conservatism of the organization, England did have excellent tools, progressive training methods, and Percy Scott. During much of the time Sims was Inspector of Target Practice in America, his old friend held the same post in England. In this position he was greatly aided by the work of John Jellicoe as Director of Naval Ordnance. Jellicoe possessed an understanding of gunnery problems and a grasp of gunnery possibilities possessed by few ordnance men in any country.

That English and American gunnery were almost equal in effectiveness was not entirely an accident. Sims visited England every year and picked up a great deal of information by personal conversation with his friends. He and Scott swapped secrets and assisted each other in a variety of ways. In 1904 the Englishman confided to his friend: 'I have a scheme which I believe will turn out to be the way of using the guns at long range. I submitted it to our Admiralty and, of course, it was boycotted, so I must wait till I go to sea again before I shall use it. . . . About ten days ago I carried out an experiment to get rid of backfire in big guns and to prevent the smoke coming into the turret when the breech was opened. . . .' A sketch of the device was enclosed. A closing

[9] With this view Van Auken, who was friendly to both sides, is not in entire agreement. He says (*op. cit.*, p. 17): 'As the ranges increased from year to year and the tasks imposed were heavier and heavier, the ordnance was improved accordingly in an attempt to keep ahead of the demands of gunnery. It is a question which was in the lead — ordnance design or gunnery in the Fleet.' He adds what is obviously true, 'Each enabled advancements to be made in the other.'

line must have been balm to the American's soul: 'It is dawning on our authorities that the sights are all wrong and I fancy that we shall re-sight the whole Navy.'

Two years later 'that wonderful man' was enlisting Sims' aid in more occult matters. On August 19, 1906, he wrote, 'When I receive your gun-layers' test results, I shall draw up a comparison with ours so as to keep my people up to the mark; for our own sake, I hope yours will be better than ours; if it is not, I shall try to make it so. At the end of the year I shall send you ours and you can draw up a similar padded bludgeon for your government.' 'You are fortunate,' he said in closing, 'in having the President's interest in shooting. I wish I could get some of our members of Parliament to come and learn one end of a gun from the other.'

Six years later Scott's prayer was answered when Winston Churchill took over as First Lord of the Admiralty. At this time the gunnery expert appealed to Sims once again. 'You can help me,' he wrote on December 30, 1912, 'if you will write me a letter which I can show to Mr. Winston Churchill, our First Lord, if you will embody the following:' Scott then asked his correspondent to emphasize that firing by salvos was the only possible method; that target practice must take place in a rough sea, and that the new German target was excellent. 'Put in something,' he suggested, 'about a young, clever, energetic lord like Winston. I've no doubt he will be pleased.'

Sims' reply of January 13, 1913, was a minor masterpiece for Scott's purposes. 'Long ago we found that effective firing can only be done by salvo.' Rough weather was the only time for target practice. 'I rather like the new German target.... I would like to meet your extraordinary First Lord, Winston Churchill. He has been "written up" so thoroughly in this country we feel we almost know as much about his astonishing capacity as you do in England. A "hustler," a "crackajack," and an all-around efficiency man. I envy you a Big Chief who does things. He is like our Roosevelt....' [10]

---

[10] This intimacy with Scott which permitted English and American naval gunnery to enjoy a parallel development is no less suggestive than Sims' relations with Lord John Fisher at the time the *Dreadnought* was a matter of controversy. It points up the interrelation of naval and foreign policy. Certainly Sims could not have worked in such close harmony with the British if the governments of the two coun-

One year after Sims left the Target Practice Office he wrote a letter on April 24, 1910, to Ridley McLean on the 'very important' subject of director firing. 'If director firing is successful, it will do away with continuous-aim difficulties in turret guns. *We must find out* if two turret guns can be fired together from one key — one going off before the other might throw off the lateral train. If it does not, it is a very important development. Up to the present time we have figured each of the turret guns fires only seventy per cent as fast as a single gun. If we can fire them together, then three guns in one turret are not impossible.'

Director firing was a 'very important' development, but it was not altogether new at the time Sims wrote to his former assistant. Twenty years before, the ingenious mind of Bradley Fiske had explored the possibility of such a method of shooting. In 1890 'during the trials of the *Baltimore*,' he writes, ' . . . the most important idea I had ever had flashed into my mind. Firing had finished with the port battery and begun with the starboard, when a large fleet of schooners got in the way, and practice had to be stopped for a while. I amused myself by looking at the schooners through the telescope of the forward instrument, and noticing how definitely the cross hairs of the telescope moved across their sails with the gentle rolling and pitching of the *Baltimore*. I had watched this in an idle way for a few minutes when the thought came that anybody could fire all the guns in the broadside from that place, and hit the target every time, by setting the telescope at the angle of depression equal to the proper angle of elevation of the guns, leaving the guns parallel to the deck, and firing when the roll of the ship brought the cross hairs on the target.' [11]

At the time Fiske thought of this idea — that is, of firing all the guns in a battery from one place and at one time — it was impossible to put it into practice. The scheme depended for its success upon devices not yet developed and more particularly, as he knew, upon 'an exact parallelism of the platforms on which the guns turned.' Ordnance had not been sufficiently developed to ensure such perfect parallelism, and therefore it was impos-

tries had believed their aims were contradictory. It is not the belief of this writer that the naval friendship between England and America at this period had any influence upon the policies of the two governments, though obviously the friendly relations of England and America facilitated the interchange of naval information.

[11] Bradley Fiske, *From Midshipman to Rear Admiral*, p. 124.

sible to obtain the necessary uniform elevation and aim of each gun. Yet Fiske envisioned the possibility. He hoped that he might combine his range- and position-finders with some electrical apparatus that could direct and fire all guns simultaneously from a single central position.

It was left to Sir Percy Scott to apply the idea which he apparently arrived at independently. The precision gained by continuous-aim firing and the even greater accuracy assured by controlling batteries firing in salvos led him on to the notion of firing the salvos from one elevated position. He and Jellicoe tried to convince the Admiralty of the value of the idea when Scott was Inspector of Target Practice, but without success. In 1909 he improvised the necessary mechanism on the ship *Neptune* and proved the value of director firing in a battle practice. Not until two years later, however, did the Admiralty really accept the new system.[12]

Sims, by 1910, was, as his letter to McLean reveals, thinking in terms of director firing. Since he had left the Target Practice Office, he had little or nothing to do with its introduction into the American Navy. By the time the World War broke out, Fiske's and Scott's theory had become the basic principle of naval gunnery, and it has remained so ever since.

It is beyond the scope of this study to discuss modern gunfire at sea, but a few facts about our present methods may prove interesting to the reader. Ranges have now been extended to thirty thousand yards (seventeen miles) and more. Guns have been increased in calibre to fifteen and sixteen inches. Range-finders, range-keepers, and communications systems have been refined to a degree unimagined in 1909. Much of the computation necessary to arrive at the compensations to keep guns on their targets is done automatically by machinery. Since the enemy is frequently out of sight, spotting officers have been transferred from lofty fire-control towers to airplanes.[13] Under such conditions, of course, continuous-aim firing with big guns is impossible. But the basic principles of fire control and of director firing as worked out in the first decade of this century remain the same. The

---

[12] Percy Scott, *Fifty Years in the Royal Navy*, chapter XV.

[13] A popular and interesting account of present-day gunnery is Herbert Allen's 'Secrets of Our Navy that Japan Fears Most,' *Boston Herald*, November 23, 1941.

changes in our systems of gunnery have been largely in the refine-
ment and improvement of the tools used. To Fiske, Scott, and
Sims must be given most of the credit for our superb modern
gunnery. Fiske and Scott had most of the ideas. Sims lacked the
creative mechanical mind and the technical training of his two
brilliant colleagues, but he followed the direction of their
thought before most other men were willing to do so. Furthermore, he translated their ideas into action far more rapidly and
successfully than either of them. By his training methods, by the
morale he created, by the ceaseless experimentation with new
devices, he laid the permanent foundations of our modern gunnery. The epitaph the papers wrote for him at his death is true.
He taught the Navy how to shoot. He taught it so thoroughly it
has never forgotten the lesson since that time.

For the last year and a half of his duty in Washington, Sims
left much of the active work of the Target Practice Office to his
capable subordinates. On November 21, 1907, when he was appointed the Naval Aide of the President, he assumed obligations
which made complete attention to gunnery problems impossible.
His relation with Mr. Roosevelt was one of the great experiences
of his whole life.

Socially as well as professionally the duty was valuable for
Sims. The two men, not unlike in their attitude toward and
enjoyment of life, came to have both respect and affection for
each other. Sims was naturally much in the White House, both
informally and at the numerous official functions which spotted
the presidential calendar. He was a favorite of Mrs. Roosevelt,
serving her as well as he did her husband. One Christmas Eve a
party was given for various celebrities, who showed no inclination
to depart. The First Lady obviously tired as the hours passed
with no sign from the guests of their intention to leave. Finally,
Sims looked up with a bright smile and observed, 'Well, it's too
bad the party is breaking up.'

On less formal occasions, Sims was sometimes a member of
the group that clustered about the President. His endless stories
were a source of continual amusement to his host and hostess.
Indeed, Archie Butt was moved to the awed conclusion that the
naval officer was the one person who could successfully over-
whelm the presidential powers of conversation.

It is difficult to assess with accuracy the influence upon the development of the United States Navy which Sims and Key as Naval Aides to the President were able to exert. Certainly Mr. Roosevelt relied upon and trusted both these men and acted frequently upon their advice and information. Occasionally, he was more irritated than persuaded by their radical suggestions or actions, but on the whole he stood by them even at moments when to do so tried his fortitude. Sims was more consciously in the President's debt than was Key, and had greater faith in Mr. Roosevelt's ability to alter existing conditions in the Navy. Key, who was closer personally to his Chief, could at times express his flaming independence in terms his fellow officer never used to the President.

If Sims could not use the same words and if he was less capable, in purely official matters, of speaking with the President of the United States as 'man to man,' the spirit behind his actions was the same as Key's. Together they labored constantly to bring the situation of the Navy as they understood it to the attention of the President. He, for his part, seldom failed them. In the closing months of his administration, he came once more to Sims' support.

Three incidents occurred in the first seven months of 1909 which served to emphasize in Sims' mind the price exacted of a man who pursues an independent course. The first began when a strange clerk entered his office one morning in February, 1909, and laid an unsigned paper on his desk. This paper 'described the various disagreeable things [some principal officers in the Department] proposed to do to [Sims] as soon as President Roosevelt went out of office.' [14]

Two days later another clerk entered on a similar errand. The paper he left 'purported to give certain conversations between some of the principal officials of the Department upon the advisability of a court of inquiry into my alleged misconduct.' The second paper stirred its recipient into action. He went immediately to the White House.

[14] W. S. S., 'Roosevelt and the Navy,' *McClure's*, December, 1922. The account which follows is based on this article, which closely follows an undated memorandum on the subject in the Sims papers. Both the article and the memorandum agree in substance with letters written in 1909 to various brother officers.

When he arrived between four and five in the afternoon, Mr. Roosevelt was having his daily shave at the hands of a colored retainer. Sims told the President of his two communications and stated that 'I did not think I should be punished because of the technical irregularity of the methods employed, largely with his approval, in bringing about reforms necessary to the efficiency of the Navy; and I explained that in case I should be called to account by the Department, I could not even present in extenuation of my offenses, any official acknowledgment of my offenses, because my Reports of Fitness . . . contained practically no mention of the results of my activities in the improvement of naval marksmanship, ordnance, naval designs, training, etc., and that the bulk of the reports and recommendations that I had made upon these subjects since 1897 had been destroyed.'

The President assured his guest that he must be mistaken. Sims suggested that Mr. Roosevelt send for the record. Next day the Inspector of Target Practice was summoned from his office to the Executive Mansion. There Mr. Roosevelt admitted his astonishment at finding the record contained no citation for Sims' service.

'What can I do about it?' he asked the naval officer.

'I suggested that he might write a letter to the Navy Department stating in general terms what he knew about the nature and value of my services and directing that my record be completed.'

'Draft it for me,' replied Mr. Roosevelt.

On February 16, the letter was sent to Secretary Newberry.[15] In it the President ran briefly over the main events in Sims' career and stated that he noticed that the officer's record contained 'practically no account of the influence of his work. . . .' Mr. Roosevelt added as his own personal opinion that 'Commander Sims has done more than any other man in the United States' to improve gunnery, 'and that it is chiefly due to him that we shoot as well as we do.'

He directed that the Secretary compile a full statement of Sims' duty, which would be filed, together with the Roosevelt letter, with the officer's record. Secretary Newberry went to work. He wrote the bureau chiefs for a list of Sims' reports on

[15] Copies of this letter and those which follow from the Secretary and various bureau chiefs are in the Sims papers.

file in their offices and asked Sims to draw up a list of his own accomplishments. To this request Sims replied on February 23, 1909, in a letter which he afterward always referred to as 'The Sad Story of My Life.'

The career was insufficiently condensed into thirty-two typewritten pages. Beginning with his work as Intelligence Officer in 1895, all his reports, articles, and contributions to the Navy were reviewed. He explained that the twenty-two letter-press books he had industriously filled while in Paris had all been burned after his departure. He summarized each of the thirteen great reports from the China Station in 1900–1902 and added that some of these had been lost, mislaid, or eaten by cockroaches that had found their way to the pigeonholes of the desk used by the chiefs of the bureaus. One hundred and thirty-two reports written between the years 1903 and 1907 were given by name. Most of these dealt with gunnery problems or ship design. The history of the author's part in the introduction of the all-big-gun battleship was set forth at some length, as was the controversy over the open and direct turret hoists. In conclusion, Sims quoted from letters he had received from various officers, all of whom praised him for the leading part he had played in the life of the Navy from 1900. These commendatory remarks were pointed up by frequent observations about the extent of the opposition directed against many of Sims' suggested improvements.

From the various bureau chiefs, Mr. Newberry received further information on the activities of the Inspector of Target Practice. Admiral Cowles of the Bureau of Equipment reported that 'Regarding fire control, Commander Sims' efforts were influential in having this subject thoroughly studied. . . .' The Bureau of Construction and Repair summarized fifteen reports written by Sims that were found in their files. Much of the critical comment contained in these communications bore upon 'earlier battleships whose designs had been prepared and the vessels themselves practically completed prior to the submission of the criticism thereon.' 'Moreover, many of the features criticized were such as had already received attention' as a result of increasing knowledge and experience on the part of those directly responsible. The Bureau Chief, who was Washington Lee Capps, did, however, give 'unquestioned credit' to the Inspector of Target Practice for the 'marked improvement in rapidity and accuracy of fire of large-calibre guns. . . .'

Admiral Mason, Chief of the Bureau of Ordnance, wrote to the Secretary that the effect of Sims' numerous 'critical essays' upon the practice of gunnery was 'immediately felt and reacted upon ordnance with great benefit to its progressive development and improvement.' Sims was given great credit for his 'enthusiastic and persistent' advocacy of modern methods of gunnery. In conclusion, Admiral Mason wrote that 'The renaissance in gunnery, which came about chiefly through the instrumentality of Commander Sims, has, as would naturally be anticipated, led to great improvements in ordnance. Improvement in the training of the gunner resulted in his better knowledge of the tools of his trade and led to his enthusiastic and impatient efforts to improve them.'

On March 1, 1909, Secretary Newberry wrote to President Roosevelt to assure him that all these letters, together with the President's and Sims' of February 23, had been filed with the naval officer's record.

The second thing to cloud Sims' last days as Inspector of Target Practice occurred very shortly after Roosevelt had interceded in his behalf. It had to do with the selection of his successor. The situation at the time of Sims' detachment was very complicated, but the main elements are clear enough. George Bradshaw in 1908 had been offered the position of Inspector of Target Practice.[16] After he reported for duty, the President persuaded Sims to remain in office, and Bradshaw handsomely agreed to assist him until such time as Sims should go to sea. In the year that followed, Sims was so busy with the Newport Conference, the Investigation, and his duties as Aide to Mr. Roosevelt that Bradshaw and Richard Drace White really ran the office between them. It was, throughout this time, understood that Bradshaw would take over from Sims, and that upon the former's detachment, Ridley McLean would return as Inspector of Target Practice.[17] These three men between them knew more about gunnery than anyone else in the Navy at the time. Nothing had occurred to alter this arrangement when Sims was detached on

[16] W. S. Sims to L. C. Palmer, March 5, 1909.

[17] *Ibid.*, and Captain H. A. Baldridge to the writer, October 23, 1940.

February 23 and ordered to assume command of the *Minnesota* on March 1. When he left, Bradshaw was given written orders as Inspector of Target Practice. Within a very few days, these orders were changed; Bradshaw was sent to sea and Commander L. C. Palmer, who was the gunnery officer of the best ship for 1908, was designated as his relief.[18] Sims did not hear of this change until the day after President Taft had been inaugurated. He immediately wrote to Palmer, for whom he entertained a high regard, asking him to decline the position. He explained that both Bradshaw and McLean knew more about the Target Practice Office and he made it clear that, after a tour of duty as Fleet Gunnery Officer, Palmer would be in line for the inspectorship. 'I think,' he added, 'I need not explain (in fact I am not at liberty to explain) that there is something else besides efficiency behind the apparent desire to sidetrack Brad and Mack. You will easily guess that this is closely connected with the fact that they have always been thoroughly loyal friends of mine. ...' [19] The same day Bradshaw wrote his old chief in the same vein. He believed he was let out because he was one of the insurgent members of the Newport Conference. A word of warning he gave as well, advising Sims 'not to get up on your hind legs and raise any kick or get into the papers, because if they could get the slightest opportunity to get you out of that ship [the *Minnesota*], they would seize upon it.' When it became apparent that Bradshaw could not return to the position he had held so short a time, Sims wrote to the Secretary advocating McLean's appointment. McLean himself wrote to the Chief of the Bureau of Navigation asking for the job. Nothing came of this. Palmer replied to Sims' plea with the perfectly reasonable argument that if the authorities had already failed to appoint either Bradshaw or McLean, his (Palmer's) refusal of the post would hardly alter their opinion. Palmer remained as Inspector of Target Practice.

The third thing which occurred in 1909 affected Sims in a more personal way. Secretary Newberry had, at the time of the Sad Story, written to Robley D. Evans for his opinion on Sims' career. Evans, or 'Fighting Bob,' as he had long been called, had just retired from the service after taking the Fleet as far as San

---

[18] Baldridge to the writer, October 23, 1940.
[19] W. S. S. to L. C. Palmer, March 5, 1909.

Francisco on the voyage around the world. A colorful, forceful personality, as skilled with his pen as he was well known in his profession, he was second only to George Dewey in the public eye. In March, 1902, he had gone out to the China Station to take command of one of the squadrons of the Asiatic Fleet. The *Kentucky* had been his flagship. While on this tour of duty, Evans had taken keen interest in target practice. In July, 1902, the cruisers under his command had carried out a practice using the methods of continuous-aim firing. In his letter to the Secretary in 1909, Evans gave the credit for this practice to his own staff, adding that Sims at the time was a Watch Officer on the *New York*. He went on to say that 'the work of preparing the gun-pointer for straight and rapid shooting was done' by members of his staff, and that while rumors had reached him of valuable papers prepared by Sims, he had never received any of them himself [20]

In July, 1909, Admiral Evans enlarged on this subject in an article printed in *Hampton's Magazine*.[21] He explained how the men on the *Kentucky* had rigged a 'Ping Pong' machine that was superior to the dotter used in the English Navy and how one of them had devised a telescope sight.

> Our success, such as it was, was due to their efforts and the system we had adopted, and was not in any remote degree the result of what had been done in any other Navy.
>
> I had never heard of the wonderful firing done by that excellent officer, Captain, now Admiral, Sir Percy Scott, of the British Navy, and I doubt if anyone of my able assistants ever had. Certainly if they had, they did not follow his methods, but worked out their own and followed them. Yet for all the good work they did, one never hears their names mentioned in connection with naval target practice. Lieutenant William S. Sims, who has since given much advice as Inspector of Target Practice, was, at the time of which I speak, doing duty as a Watch Officer on the *New York*, flagship of the commander-in-chief.
>
> [Later] Lt. Sims, who has since done excellent work, was appointed Inspector of Target Practice, and held that important

[20] A copy of this letter is in the Sims papers.
[21] R. D. Evans, 'Hitting Power of the American Navy,' *Hampton's Magazine*, July, 1909. Evans' account of the origins of the American target practice methods was also printed in his *An Admiral's Log*, New York, 1910, pp. 135–136.

office until the present year. He is now Captain of the *Minnesota.*
Before he received this order the work with the guns in the East
had been done and the credit for the work should go to those who
did it, viz: Chapin, Brittain, McLean, Merritt, Twining, Upham,
Wiley, and Andrews.

The three incidents that fell so strangely close to Sims' retirement from office would seem to suggest the existence of a deliberate effort to rob him of just credit and eliminate his influence.
It is hardly extraordinary that Sims himself thought that such
was the case. Before reaching a similar conclusion, it will be well
to examine the three incidents more closely.

If one assumes that the talk about a Court of Inquiry brought
to Sims by some unknown agent was simply gossip; if one recognizes that there was no reason why the Chiefs of Ordnance and
Construction should enter remarks of any kind on Sims' record;
if one admits that Chiefs of the Bureau of Navigation, who were
Sims' reporting seniors, had paid great tribute to the improvement of target practice in annual reports; still the fact remains
that not one word about his work as Inspector of Target Practice
was entered on Sims' record. Only when the President of the
United States entered the picture were the glowing tributes
forthcoming. Point is given to this by the similar case of Key,
who found in 1939, to his amazement, that no mention of his part
in the Newport Conference had ever been entered on his record.

The selection of Palmer as Sims' relief in the Target Practice
Office can be justified on the grounds that Palmer had been
Gunnery Officer of the best ship in the Fleet in 1908 and that
he was coming to Washington as the President's aide. If Sims
had held the dual position, so, it could be argued, might his successor. These considerations cannot alter the fact that Bradshaw
was detached after holding the office for only a few days and that
McLean's request for the appointment was denied. Both these
men had had long experience in gunnery and both had received
assurances that they would follow Sims in his position.

Rear Admiral Evans' letter to the Secretary and his article in
Hampton's Magazine were apparently written in an attempt to obtain for his staff credit for the introduction of continuous-aim
firing. Certainly he and his men deserve great credit for the
work they did on the China Station. Perhaps too little attention

had been paid to their efforts. But in attempting to redress the balance, Evans permitted his intentions to outweigh the evidence on which his claims were based. He said, for example, that the system of firing developed by his staff was not 'in any remote degree the result of what had been done in any other Navy.' In support of his contention the Admiral asserted that he had never heard of the record established by the *Terrible* two years before he took command in Asia and that he did not think his staff had known of it. Certain members of his staff definitely did know of Scott's work. Sims had been in correspondence with Ridley McLean, a member of Evans' staff, on the subject ever since October, 1901. Nor was Sims, as Evans claimed, simply a Watch Officer at the time Evans instituted his system of gunnery; he was in fact Inspector of Target Practice for the Asiatic Station. For over a year he had been spreading the news of Scott's work throughout the Fleet. The most curious statement in the article had to do with a gun sight developed by Ridley McLean. In commenting on this, Evans said, 'a telescope sight had been invented years before by Lt. Bradley Fiske, but for some reason it had not found favor in the service.' When Fiske first tested his telescope on the *Yorktown* in 1892, Robley D. Evans, the Commanding Officer, had reported that 'In its present shape it is of no value on board ship.' [22] If the intention of Rear Admiral Evans in writing this article was to restore credit he believed due to his staff and himself, the fact remains that he could succeed in doing so only by eliminating Sims from the history of the introduction of continuous-aim firing.

A review of all these three incidents permits the following conclusions. There was probably, though not certainly, no determined effort to punish Sims personally for his record. There appears to have been some attempt to withhold, both officially and unofficially, the credit due to him for his work as Inspector of Target Practice. It seems beyond all reasonable doubt that, upon his detachment, steps were taken to eliminate his influence from his office. [23]

[22] Fiske, *op. cit.*, pp. 171–172.

[23] These conclusions are borne out by the letters received by Sims from officers to whom he told the Sad Story. A typical reaction came from as experienced and wise an officer as Cameron Winslow. 'It is perfectly plain that [the Chief of the Bureau of

That much can be said on the basis of the available evidence alone. Almost without such evidence it would be possible to say as much, unless one misread the meaning of the conflict within the service during the period under review. The reform element had, by every means at its disposal, tried to rid the service of the influence of the men who opposed reform. One of the projects dearest to Sims and Key was the removal of Capps from office. By the same token the conservative element had tried to eliminate the reformers. Each side understood that peace could only be made on terms of the complete subjugation of its rivals. Had no attempt to get rid of the Sims influence been made at the one moment when Sims was left unprotected by Theodore Roosevelt, it would have been quite astonishing. The difference is not, in this case, so much in method as in aim. The conservatives wanted peace and security. The insurgents cared nothing for peace and little for their professional security when such things interfered with progress in the Navy.

These three incidents have been discussed at such length chiefly because of the quite justifiable impression they left upon Sims. If their full impact upon him is to be understood, they should be considered as the culminating events in the long struggle that had gone on within the Navy since 1902. These were 'the fighting years,' and the men who lived through them had the marks to show. In some ways Sims was singularly free from the blemishes left upon personalities by the reforming temperament. Never, for example, was he merely vindictive about the men who opposed him. Save in very rare instances, he kept the issues involved well above the heads of the men who were at war beneath. Far more significant, he never became a doctrinaire. There were no Verduns in his career, no occasions when he threw away his forces in defense of a position he protected for reasons of sentiment or consistency. On his last trip to England as Inspector of Target Practice he learned that director firing would cancel out much of the work he had done in developing continuous aim. Upon his return he told his wife 'joyfully': 'We're all wrong. There's a new kind of firing.' This freedom of motion becomes clearer in the pages that immediately follow. It

Navigation] wants to make a clean sweep of anything tainted with Simsism.' Most officers, however, did not believe that Sims was in danger of severe punishment.

should be noticed in this connection that his change of opinion came less through the arguments of friends or enemies than through the independent working of his mind.

But he could not emerge from the conflicts of these years of achievement totally unscathed. He early came to believe that many attacks were directed against him personally. Dark hints were dropped to his confederates about plots that were being hatched against him. In time, too, he began to exaggerate the lengths to which the opposition would go to defeat him. This colored his recollection of his past and influenced his attitude toward the future. 'I left behind my letter-press books [in Paris] with copies of them all for my successor. I have got a letter from him in which he states that those books were burned by order of the Department. That is the extent to which opposition will go if the criticisms are severe enough.' Thus had his memory in 1925 been conditioned by experience. The letter which his successor sent him had, it is true, explained that his reports had been burned, but for quite different reasons than Sims assumed. His successor, Giles Harber, had asked the Department what to do with all the reports which were overcrowding his small office. In reply the Department instructed him to destroy them since the originals were on file in Washington. Sims' recollection of the past fell into a pattern which supported his attitude toward the future.[24] The achievements of the six years in Washington had been won, indubitably, against opposition; progress had been accomplished only through attack. These years gave him increased assurance that his methods were the only effective ones. They confirmed him, too, in his belief that he would always meet with opposition from above.

The Sad Story, the detachment of Bradshaw, the article by Admiral Evans, coming as they did in such startling conjunction with each other, could only point up the moral of the insurgent's tale. The corollary to 'Hope On, Hope Ever' was 'Fight On, Fight Ever.' From the disillusioning moments no less than from

[24] He exaggerated, too, the significance of the disappearance of so many of his reports. As Mark Bristol, a close friend, told him March 3, 1909, 'A good deal of this [losing papers] is due to the fact that there is no central office in Washington to which all such papers should be referred and left on file; instead, reports and papers of like nature are sent roaming around amongst the several bureaus and the record of their path is lost.'

the exciting victories of his career he took increased devotion to his own cause.

These splendid years of achievement need no recapitulation here. Yet it is interesting to notice that Sims' life had a kind of structural perfection. The great themes of his career were set forth clearly in the opening passage on the China Station. What followed was a set of dramatic variations in which the major themes were fully developed through heightened activity. This period of his life began with his first letter to Theodore Roosevelt and it ended, quite fittingly, with the President's retirement from office. In one of his rotund phrases Mr. Roosevelt had declared that it was 'far better to dare mighty things . . . than to rank with those poor spirits who neither enjoy much nor suffer much, because they live in the gray twilight that knows not victory nor defeat.' It was a wonderful age, with no gray twilights, that passed on March 4, 1909.

Yet where there is victory and defeat, heads must be broken; sometimes the heads of innocent bystanders. One such belonged to Captain John Hubbard, commanding the battleship *Minnesota*. In 1908, while Hubbard was taking his ship around the world with the rest of the Fleet, Sims had been ordered to duty as Commanding Officer of the cruiser *Chester*. Theodore Roosevelt had asked Sims to give up the ship to remain one more year as Naval Aide and Inspector of Target Practice. Should he do so, the President would see that his aide obtained as good a command as the *Chester* when the time for his detachment came. With this understanding Sims complied with the request of his superior. At the very end of 1908 or early in 1909, the matter of the Inspector's future came up once more for discussion. Mr. Roosevelt wanted very much to do something for the man who had served him so long and well. Would Sims like a battleship? If so, he could 'practically have [his] choice.' [25] The Inspector of Target Practice looked over the list before choosing the *Minnesota*. His choice was, in part, determined by the fact that Hubbard's cruise was almost over. The President informed Secretary Newberry of the decision.

There were several complicating factors in the project. The *Minnesota* was still at sea with the Fleet, which was returning from

[25] W. S. S. to John Hubbard, February 20, 1909.

its long cruise. She would not reach this country until about February 20. Captain Hubbard was not due for relief for some months. He 'was entitled to lay his ship up' and he certainly knew more about the repairs that were needed than 'any living man' since he had just been around the world on her. Yet it seemed important to get Sims on the ship by March 4. Roosevelt was anxious to have the matter settled before he went out of office. He was not unaware of the hostile attitude maintained in some quarters of the Department against his Naval Aide. Likewise the whole thing was most irregular. Sims was a Commander, and no Commander in the modern Navy had ever been given a battleship. In fact, until the middle of 1908, when Secretary Metcalf had, for some obscure reason, altered existing regulations, no Commander could have had a battleship. In a service where tradition counts for so much, such an irregularity was bound to arouse opposition. So the necessity to get the thing over and done with before the President retired from office was obvious to all concerned. Sims was no less anxious to assume command than Mr. Roosevelt was to have him do so. The *Minnesota* was to be equipped with new 'basket masts' and ammunition hoists. Its new Commander wanted very much to supervise the work personally.

On February 20, Sims wrote to Captain Hubbard, who was still at sea, explaining why he had chosen the *Minnesota*. This letter could not have been delivered before February 22, when the Fleet arrived in Hampton Roads after its long journey. This was Hubbard's first intimation that he was to be detached before his cruise was over. Shortly he heard the unpleasant news officially. The President and Mrs. Roosevelt, Secretary and Mrs. Newberry, the Assistant Secretary Satterlee with his wife went to Hampton Roads for the great welcome to the Fleet. Sims accompanied his Chief on the *Mayflower*. All the commanding officers came aboard to be welcomed and congratulated by the President.

It was a day of gaiety for all hands save the Assistant Secretary, who had a disagreeable job to perform. To Captain Hubbard he handed written orders requesting him to report the next day in Washington. When Captain Hubbard appeared at the Navy Department, the Assistant Secretary informed him that he was relieved of the command of the *Minnesota* and ordered to report to duty in the Department. Hubbard had naturally expected to remain with his ship and had apparently made arrangements to bring his family to the ship's home port for the period during which repairs on the *Minnesota* were being made. The intelligence conveyed by Mr. Satterlee made him 'very angry,' and he asked to speak unofficially to the Assistant Secretary. Granted such permission, Hubbard stated that such orders 'were tantamount to a reprimand' and that he was entitled to stay with his ship as were all the other Captains. Since this was indubitably true, Mr. Satterlee could only repeat the instructions that had been given him by his superiors and soften the blow by asking Hubbard to serve as his Naval Aide.[26]

There was nothing Hubbard could do, of course, but accept as best he could this distressing turn of events. He came to Washington, and Sims on March 1 became the new Commanding Officer of the *Minnesota*.

In such fashion ended his long service as Inspector of Target Practice. A good many officers who were loyal to him regretted the way in which he had begun his new duty. Several wrote to express their feelings, and for a time he was kept busy answering their letters.

In leaving Washington he did not forget the train of events that had first brought him there in 1902. The day before he left the office, he wrote to an old friend. Poor Will Arnold had not fared so well as his younger protégé in the years that had passed since they parted on the China Station. He had left the Navy only to find the world a crueller place in which to live. To him in his distress Sims wrote: 'I am about to leave, tomorrow, to take over the *Minnesota*. That duty now marks the end of a campaign which has lasted since 1895 and before I give it up — I wish to recall for my own satisfaction the very considerable part that you have taken in helping along the good work. I remember with gratitude the time we had almost no friends and you supported me very valuably not only morally, but actually.'

It was on the *Charleston* in 1895 that Sims had first met this 'most extraordinary man.' In the same year he had been appointed the ship's Intelligence Officer and had written a report

[26] H. L. Satterlee to the writer, February 7, 1941.

on the ordnance of the British cruiser *Crescent*. For fifteen years thereafter, Sims had concerned himself primarily with the gunnery of the United States Navy. By the time Arnold read the letter announcing the close of the long campaign, its author had entered upon new and exciting duties.

PART THREE

The Years of Command

There is no experience in the world
quite so agreeable as commanding a
successful ship.

WILLIAM S. SIMS *to J. K. Robison*
August 8, 1917

16

1909 - 1911 *U.S.S. Minnesota*

COMMANDER SIMS,' observed the *New York Sun*, 'is a specialist in gunnery who has spent the last thirteen years at a desk or in foreign billets, has never commanded even a gunboat in the whole course of his career, and so far as experience goes cannot possibly have the faintest idea of the intricate responsibilities that will confront him when he raises his flag on the battleship *Minnesota*.' That Sims lacked the practical training necessary for his new position was the opinion of many who shared the *Sun's* alarm. There were those, too, who opposed his appointment because of the irregular way in which it had been made, and there were some who did so because they disliked the man himself. William Shepherd Benson, then a Captain, sought to warn Sims of this hostile attitude in an honest and friendly letter of congratulation. Benson did not begrudge the younger man his reward, but as an officer devoted to the service, its traditions and regulations, he personally 'would have rather seen [Sims] promoted to the next higher grade and then given a battleship than to have established the dangerous precedent of giving battleships to Commanders.' Moreover, while Sims had 'shown to all officers what anyone prompted by right motives and high ideals with a thorough knowledge of the subject and the best interests of the service at heart can accomplish against all odds,' still, 'with the great revolution of target practice have come evils as will ever be the case with reforms. Younger officers have come to feel that there is but one God and the Inspector of Target Practice is his prophet.' If Sims failed in his first command, and

263

if there were not lacking men who would be pleased by his failure, he could not say that he had not been warned.

But one officer at least did not share the *Sun's* forebodings nor the uneasiness of some of the older men. To Benson, Sims replied that Pasteur and Jenner had likewise fought against the forces of darkness to triumph only after bitter battles. He cited the testimony of Capps and Converse and suggested that 'it should not be wondered at that the active younger officers should get the idea that there is but one God and one prophet.' A cheering word he had also for the *Sun*: 'I have never commanded a gunboat, but I may say in this connection I have had seventeen years' sea service, have navigated a ship and taught navigation for three years (not to mention writing a book on navigation now in use on this ship), and as I have been most intimately associated as Inspector of Target Practice with the intricacies of battleships and other vessels I have so much more than "the faintest idea" of the responsibilities involved that, I may say, with all respect, that you need not lose any sleep through anxiety concerning the hazards to human life and government property.' Reassuring as these words may have been to the editor of the *Sun*, they still lacked the proof which only a successful cruise could supply.

The *Minnesota*, laid down in 1903, had just returned from the voyage around the world when Sims took her over at Norfolk in March, 1909. She was one of the finest battleships in the Fleet, four hundred and fifty feet long, capable of eighteen knots speed, and displacing sixteen thousand tons. Though not a dreadnought, she was nevertheless powerfully armed with a main battery of four twelve-inch and eight eight-inch guns. In addition to fourteen other guns of smaller calibre, there were also four torpedo tubes to complete her impressive armament. Like other battleships she was a small city equipped to house, feed, and amuse her population of men and officers. Like other ships, too, she was an enormous responsibility in the hands of her Commanding Officer, representing an expenditure of seven and a half million dollars and containing twelve hundred souls within her well-armored walls. The *Minnesota* was a flagship, the leader of a division of the Atlantic Fleet. As such she flew the flag of a Rear Admiral. This officer was responsible for the

movements of the four vessels of the division, but his authority
did not extend to actual command of any of the ships, the
Minnesota included. It is sometimes disturbing to a Commanding
Officer to have an Admiral on board with him, for, in a sense,
it places him in a position of inferiority on his own ship. But
much depends, quite naturally, on the personalities of the two
men involved. When Sims took over the *Minnesota*, Rear Admiral
Hugo Osterhaus was the Flag Officer in charge of the second
division. The latter had been a staunch friend and supporter of
Sims since the days on the China Station, but he was one of those
who disapproved of the way in which the ship had been given
to his young friend. The Admiral, however, accepted graciously
enough the explanation made by Sims, and throughout the
year the two spent together their relations were more than
cordial. One observer, in fact, recalls that they were almost like
a father and a son in their affection and respect, a condition as
unusual as it was fortunate. In 1910, when Osterhaus hauled
down his flag, he was succeeded by Rear Admiral Joseph Ballard
Murdock. He was a man of a different stamp, with whom Sims
could never be friendly. 'Old Navy' by training and temperament, he was devoted to those forms and practices which his
subordinate considered unnecessary. But the two respected each
other and worked in harmony save on rare occasions.

Sims had assured the *Sun* that he was competent to command a
battleship. From a purely nautical point of view, at least, he
soon proved his point. From the pages of Admiral Murdock's
diary it is clear that the Navy had by 1909 learned the lesson
that Luce and Taylor had been at such pains to teach. The
Fleet, or divisions of it, constantly sailed together. Almost every
day manoeuvres of some kind were undertaken. In this difficult
work, operating great ships at high speeds in close formations, a
Commanding Officer is subjected to a testing examination of his
abilities. For the seamanship Sims displayed during these trials
his superior officers had nothing but praise. Only once in the
whole two years can a critical comment be found. Admiral
Murdock once informed him that the steering on the *Minnesota*
had been very erratic over a period of two or three days. Since
she was the division leader, the Admiral was considerably concerned.

Simply on grounds of seamanship it is safe to assume that Sims was well qualified for his task, but he was more than a salt-water sailor handling his vessel with intuitive artistry. Always, in every endeavor, he relied more on his mind than on his instinct. On the *Minnesota*, as elsewhere, he attempted to apply to the problems confronting him the lessons he had learned from study and from books.

In 1909, he was introduced for the first time to the countless difficulties, both nautical and military, which vex a Commanding Officer. He found the problems fascinating and, taking nothing on faith, explored the many facets of his duty with painstaking care. Early in his cruise the Commander-in-Chief prepared a set of new instructions which were sent to all the vessels with the warning that the Fleet would shortly be asked to carry out the new manoeuvres prescribed therein. Sims gathered his staff in the cabin and studied the instructions with the aid of ship models and a game board. In the course of the work it was discovered that 'There was nearly a complete misunderstanding of the new signals' by which the Commander-in-Chief intended to give his orders. Only after a series of experiments on the game board was the meaning of one particular signal made clear. It referred to manoeuvres to be undertaken when the various divisions were drawn up in parallel lines. It was obvious to the men at the cabin table that if the adjacent division misunderstood the signal, as all the officers on the staff had at first misunderstood it, a collision would probably result between ships of the two divisions.

A few days after this conference the Commander-in-Chief gave the confusing signal, which required the *Minnesota* to go ahead full speed on a particular course. Sims, anticipating difficulties, held the ship in her original position and slowed the engines. Admiral Osterhaus, beside him, asked why this was done, and Sims replied that 'There is doubt as to the meaning the other divisions have of the signal, so I am waiting to see what happens.' He did not have to wait long, for the Fleet drifted into confusion and two battleships collided.

There is a pleasant sequel to the story. The Captain of one of the damaged vessels was summoned before a Court of Inquiry. Sims explained to this Captain that his error was the natural result of an ambiguity in the signal book. At first the man was reluctant to believe that the fault was not really his own, but he finally decided to defend himself. Sims, acting as counsel, explained to the court the results of his staff's play at the game board, cleared the Captain, and brought about a change of wording in the confused interpretation of the signal book.[1]

Much later, when Admiral Murdock had the division, another and more dramatic incident occurred which confirmed the value of the theories of 'the paper man.' One foggy night the Fleet was proceeding to sea from Hampton Roads. The first division led the way, followed by the second with the *Minnesota* in the lead. Before the Capes were reached the fog thickened and Sims suggested to the Admiral that the speed be cut to avoid a collision with the last ship of the first division, but the Admiral refused. Suddenly, splashing along in the water, the distance buoy of the ship ahead danced into sight. It was apparent that the Commander-in-Chief had reduced his speed. A collision, since the *Minnesota* had not slowed down, appeared almost inevitable, but Sims decided upon a daring manoeuvre of which he had recently read in an article by Naval Constructor Taylor. This paper dealt with the results of an experiment carried out in the model basin at Washington to determine the action of vessels passing each other close aboard. Taylor had found that the overtaking ship lost her steerageway and that her bow was 'sucked in toward' the other vessel in spite of having her helm hard over. To avoid this difficulty Taylor pointed out that the overtaking ship had necessarily to keep steerageway by proceeding at full speed. But here another obstacle presented itself: the bow of the ship stayed clear, but the stern, the experiment had revealed, sucked in toward the other vessel. To avoid a collision in this way it was necessary, therefore, to reverse the helm while still going at full speed.

In the fog and darkness Sims ordered the *Minnesota's* helm hard over. The quartermaster reported that the ship was not

[1] Memorandum on the *Minnesota* prepared by Sims in August, 1931. Correspondence between him and the Commander-in-Chief, Admiral Seaton Schroeder, in 1909, supports Sims' recollections of twenty-two years later. Information about the events described in this chapter was obtained chiefly from the above memorandum, Sims' correspondence, Murdock's papers, and conversations with various officers, notably Captain E. S. Kellogg, who was the Executive Officer of the *Minnesota*.

obeying. The Admiral at Sims' side said, 'Now be very careful,' but made no other suggestion. Sims ordered the engines full speed and the bow went clear to the starboard. But in a moment the stern sucked toward the other ship. The helm was reversed, the stern cleared, and the *Minnesota* at full speed headed across the bows of the vessel she had just passed. Into the opening between the last ship of the first division and the one immediately preceding it the battleship passed as the manoeuvre was completed successfully. It was, Sims admitted, 'a hair-raising experience.' He had the courage to risk his ship and his reputation upon a daring action and he had the greater courage to believe the printed word.

A Commanding Officer must know more than seamanship to have a successful cruise. He must know how to handle men. Many officers have ruined themselves and their reputations because they lacked such knowledge. The task of maintaining proper human relationships on board ship is somewhat simplified by naval regulations or by hallowed traditions, which govern almost every aspect of personal and professional conduct. Even with these rules and customs it is still possible to err in their application. Sims, when he took command, had more positive ideas on this question of discipline than upon any other aspect of his duties. He had grown up in a navy still bound by ancient prejudices, still confined by systems of discipline which he believed to be too restrictive. He had sailed on vessels that were, in the Navy's phrase, 'madhouses,' and he had witnessed the tyrannical actions of Commanding Officers who were omnipotent. All this offended him — the blind obedience to stupid orders, the assumption of infallibility by men he knew were fallible, the debasing punishments that followed swift upon transgressions.

By 1909 the rigid code of conduct that had come down from the days in sail had been greatly modified, but he set himself to modify it further. The day after he took command he wrote to his wife: 'There is every evidence that both officers and men are pleased to have me in command and that is a valuable thing to start with. I have never had any difficulty in handling men because I feel a real interest in them and have never kept them at a distance. Today my yeoman asked permission to go on shore with his father and mother. . . . I told him I would like to meet them and had quite a chat with them, told them their boy had a very good record and that I intended to promote him right away to chief yeoman. The good people beamed with pleasure. I have given the men to understand that I want to meet their people when they come on board. After a while I am going to inform them that I expect them to learn to handle the ship and the guns without any of the officers, and carry out any of the drills because I would expect them to do it in battle if their officers were killed.'

On March 24 he outlined further plans to Mrs. Sims: 'I have been thinking a lot about the discipline of this ship. The "brig" gets on my nerves and I do not approve of restricting shore leave as a punishment. According to regulation men are divided into first, second, third, and fourth classes in conduct. When a man is in first class he can go ashore every other day. It takes a month to get up one class and three months to get from fourth to first. In the meantime men are not allowed ashore but once in so many days. The consequences are that they jump ship and if they do not desert they have to be court-martialled. It is all wrong and should be abolished.' He planned to get all men into the first class, keep them there, and 'simply give some other punishment and have done with it, for I don't think a man can be any good unless he has proper recreation.'

A man sentenced by court martial he found was reduced as well to the fourth class. Therefore, he had to endure two punishments. To this he put a stop 'at once' and found that it had an 'excellent effect.' 'The unfortunate part of it all,' he realized, was 'that the laws were all wrong. The Commanding Officer can award deprivations of leave, extra duty, and confinement in the brig up to ten days, but he cannot fine the men. My scheme is to abolish confinement and deprivation of leave and award loss of pay and extra duty, with dismissal by court martial for bad eggs.'

As much of this scheme as possible Sims put into effect, and he gave life to his system by his own interest in the men. He was a master of the little things by which human hearts are won. Mrs. Sims was taken into the galley to see how neatly and efficiently the cook filled the icebox. On inspection trips he stopped to congratulate a fireman when the day's coal consumption was low. Recognition was given when some gun-pointer made an unusual record.

With the junior officers he did the same thing, dropping into the steerage for an hour of conversation after dinner, joking with them or drawing upon his inexhaustible supply of stories. One man, then a junior officer on another ship, still marvels at the air of camaraderie that marked the steerage when he visited the *Minnesota* while 'the Old Man' was with the junior officers. But he remarks, 'The man never lost his dignity.' Perhaps he never did, but there were times when his boyishness, that bubbling juvenility he never outgrew, made him less or more than a Commanding Officer. At Guantanamo he would take his staff through the long jungle trails, walking ahead for miles in the blistering heat. At such times he carried a sinister machete with which he slashed branches off the giant cacti that flanked the path. He laughed uproariously to watch his officers leap aside behind him to avoid the sharp barbs.

Relations with men and officers are only half of discipline on a ship; administration, efficient and effective, is the other half. The secret of Sims' efficiency was trust. 'There are more things that a Commanding Officer is responsible for than one man can attend to in twenty-four hours, if he looked into all the details. Some men try to do it and get nerves and are depressed. I am happy to say that I was not built that way. All the heads of the departments are good men and I put it up to them each in his own department to keep all details correct and not to refer to me anything but affairs of a general nature. As for the responsibility — it never touches me. I like my job and will be glad when we are out of the navy yard and in clear water.'

There were times, of course, when men needed punishments as well as rewards. For any plain disobedience and for 'the bad egg' Sims delivered swift and exacting justice, but he preferred even here the soft hand when he could make his point. One day before going ashore he ordered his gig for four o'clock. When it failed to appear at the appointed time, he had to return in the wardroom boat an hour later. As he came aboard he asked the Officer of the Deck why his gig had not been sent. The officer replied that he had forgotten. Sims answered, 'If you do not

feel much worse about this than I do you are a very poor officer.'
When the Admiral, who had overheard the conversation, asked
later what punishment Sims would give the young man, he replied, 'He has already had it.'

Once during the cruise when he gave an ensign a bad fitness
report, he wrote, as required by regulations, to the young man
explaining why this had been done. The Ensign had been careless and sloppy in his attention to duty and in his habits, but Sims
sympathized with him, recalling his own past when for ten years
out of the Academy 'he had been of no use to anybody until he
had waked up.' He suggested that the young man write to the
Roycrofters and obtain a copy of the *Message to Garcia*.[2]

That his system of discipline was successful Sims himself had
no doubts. He wrote to his wife that the *Minnesota* was a 'happy
ship' and 'easily the most popular in the Fleet.' It was true
that some took advantage of his refusal to restrict liberty and
overstayed their time on shore. There were also, of course, the
usual reports of misbehavior, but on the whole he was sure he
had proved his point. There were others who were not as positive. In the report of his final inspection of the *Minnesota* Admiral
Murdock made some interesting observations about the ship.
He found the general condition of the engines, fittings, store-
rooms, fire-control equipment, and so forth excellent. Her
upkeep was likewise excellent, especially since a good many of
the necessary repairs were performed on board. Throughout he
found the *Minnesota* was well organized, particularly in her
gunnery training. For the personnel he had good words — they
were a fine class of men, contented and capable, under the supervision of zealous officers. But he would not call her a 'smart
ship,' only efficient; and he observed that the system of discipline,
designed to secure work by the acquiescence of the crew, did not
provide for 'adequate disciplining of unwilling men.' The report,
approving in very generous terms of almost every detail, closed
with these final remarks: 'If the system of discipline carried out
on the *Minnesota* were in accord with that of other ships in the
Fleet, I should consider her one of the very best in the Navy.'
Here, as Sims would have been the first to point out, spoke the

[2] For years Sims prescribed this little essay by Elbert Hubbard as a sovereign
remedy for slackness and inefficiency.

old Navy; but there may be more truth in the words than Sims was willing to admit.

The essence of his system of discipline can almost be said to be that it was no system; it was a personal relationship depending for its effectiveness almost solely upon the vigor and charm of his own personality. He was the captain of a team, an inspirational leader, sweeping his men along on the waves of his enthusiasm. In 1910, when he heard that an officer might be sent to him as his Executive he wrote the following letter to the man: 'Considering the fact that the relations between a Commanding Officer and an Executive Officer are very close and very personal — it seems a plain duty to inform you that I do not believe that these relations (necessary for the military efficiency of a man-of-war) could be maintained between us. It would of course not be profitable to enter into the grounds for any such condition, but I regret exceedingly to be obliged to state that my personal antipathy toward you is so strong as to be entirely beyond my control.' Mrs. Sims, shocked by the directness of this letter, took her husband to task for his apparent lack of delicacy. His answer revealed his whole point of view on the question of military discipline and administration. 'You say that personal antipathy is not a good ground for objection to serving with an officer, but in this you are mistaken. It is a perfectly well-recognized ground in military life, particularly where the relations are largely personal. It is, in fact, the only ground on which an objection can be based.'

These are the words of one who believes more in men than in institutions; they were written in the spirit of the amateur and not of the professional. For Sims, with his driving desire to lead and with his keen instincts for leadership, the doctrine was sound; but a navy is an institution and sailors are members of a profession. Long-lived institutions are held together only by customs and traditions, while large bodies of men are moved to common action for a common purpose only by allegiance to accepted codes or creeds. Sims being Sims could do no other than he did, and his justification was 'a happy ship,' but men with other gifts could follow along the more familiar paths of duty, in many cases, with equal success.

Before leaving this subject it may be well to notice one other

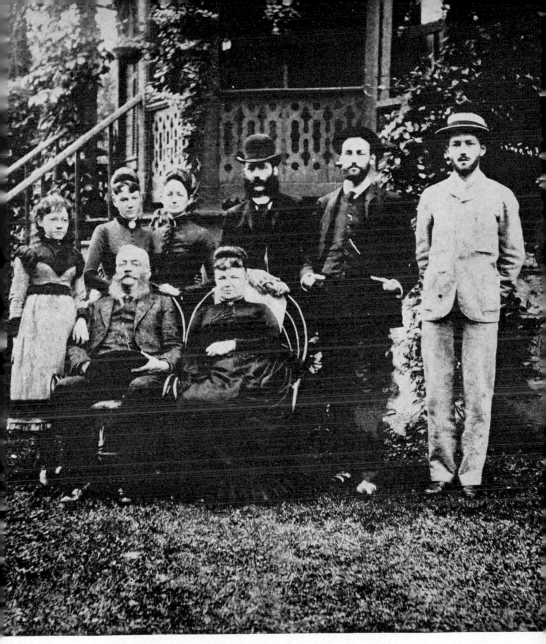

The Family at Rock Hill Furnace. The children, left to right: Adelaide, Mary, Louisa, Harry, William, and Alfred Varley

At Annapolis

About 1885

Commander Sims, 1908

Miss Anne E. Hitchcock and Miss Margaret Hitchcock wearing the dresses in which they were presented to the Russian Czarina in 1897

Ridley McLean

Albert Lenoir Key

Bradley A. Fiske

Hutchinson I. Cone

Sims Flies his Flag at Queenstown. For the first time in history, in May, 1917, an American Admiral commanded part of the British Fleet

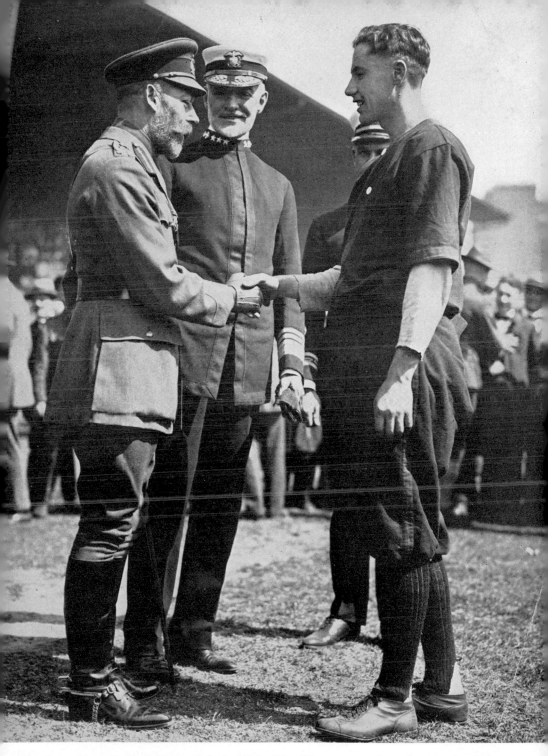

The Army-Navy Baseball Game, July 4, 1918. The King congratulates the captain of the
Army team

Four Stars, December, 1918

thing. It has been said that Sims looked upon his crew as a team, and upon himself as the captain of that team. A team must beat someone else. In Sims the will to win burned high. The *Minnesota* was expected to coal faster, shoot straighter than the others; its boat crews had to win all their races; in every endeavor the ship was expected to prove itself the best. The morale, the spirit, which makes all this possible not infrequently produces a kind of assurance, a kind of cockiness that irritates some observers. It is one thing to have a ship that is 'easily the most popular'; quite another to say so. Sims, with what was at times a disarming and at other times an annoying candor, had no hesitation in saying so. It made him the idol of his men, but it also occasionally complicated his relations with his equals and superiors. On the *Minnesota* this trait was not disturbingly apparent because Sims himself was, for most of the two years, feeling his way toward his ultimate methods of command; but later it was to cause him trouble, and much later it was to diminish his influence within the service.

Poetic justice would seem to demand that the *Minnesota* should have won the target-practice trophy for the years that Sims was in command, but it is necessary to record that the ship, though always appearing high in the final ratings, never was first. Her crews were well trained and performed their work with an enthusiasm that warmed the heart of her Captain. On several occasions she made unusual scores, but her old gun gear prevented her from competing successfully with the newer ships. During the two years, however, Sims was more concerned with the general development of target practice than with the record of his own ship. The battle practice of 1909 took place in smooth water, so that it was impossible for anyone to tell how effective the shooting would be in rough weather or under usual battle conditions. There were other considerations which made Sims believe this practice was 'a total failure.'[3] The next year, 1910,

[3] The Commander-in-Chief was, on the other hand, well satisfied with the results of the practice. '... I was able to carry out schemes of battle target practice which were more advanced than they may seem when viewed with the retrospect of twelve years.' Seaton Schroeder, *A Half Century of Naval Service*, New York, 1922, p. 384. This difference of opinion is easily explained. Sims believed it was necessary to discover more about the accuracy of individual ships firing in a seaway, while Schroeder believed that such accuracy was sufficiently developed to enable three

the percentage of hits to shots necessary for any grade was set before firing instead of after it. In other words, the pointers were rated according to absolute standards instead of relative ones. By this method no consideration was given to the various conditions under which the target practice might be held, and it was possible that no gunner could attain the highest grade. Under Sims' old system all gunners were competing, not against some arbitrary score set before firing, but only against the best record established by any one gunner during firing. As Sims pointed out, this change in regulations could only dampen the enthusiasm of the men.

So greatly disturbed was he by the changes in our gunnery that he wrote October 20, 1910, to the Secretary of the Navy that 'the recent battle firing was practically a complete failure — as a training to increase our rapidity of hitting at long ranges.' This damaging criticism he followed up with the remark that certain of the regulations were received 'with derisive disapproval' by the Fleet. It was a phrase that may have cost him dear, for it irritated even such a staunch supporter as Admiral Wainwright, who, it will be remembered, wished at one time to see Sims promoted over himself. Wainwright could make his irritation count, for at the time he was Aide for Operations. Remarks such as this had been used by Sims so often that they were beginning to lose their force. R. D. White, his former assistant in the Target Practice Office, wrote: 'Patience, I realize, was never your strength. Criticism was — and is. You damn it all in a sweeping fashion in the last paragraph of your letter by saying: "I have not found a single officer who does not condemn..." Of course, you haven't. You haven't given anybody a chance to say anything about it.' [4]

But as always, he had a case. Target-practice records began to slip backward. Two years later they reached such depths that the authorities became alarmed. At this time, in addition to the

ships to concentrate on one target, though in the process scores of individual ships would be difficult to estimate.

[4] White was at the time Flag Lieutenant for the Commander-in-Chief. On October 27 he wrote, 'The C.-in-C. appeared the other morning in a state of rank indignation over your letter, in which you said that the Department's decision in regard to a certain question on target practice was received by the Fleet with "derisive disapproval." '

controversy over the regulations, there was a turmoil in the Department over the proper development of fire control at the new range of ten thousand yards. At such distances a spotter could no longer control the fire accurately even with a telescope, and there was much discussion over adequate methods of keeping the correct range. Sims believed that much of the argument was carried on by men who knew little from experience and were merely defending their prejudices, as had the supporters of the superposed turrets. On his own ship, a range-keeping machine had been constructed by two very able junior officers, Lieutenants Pye and King, which he was anxious to have tried out along with various other instruments. The only way to solve the problem was to equip a ship for various experiments. This was a very sensible suggestion and one that was eventually carried out.

While Sims was on the *Minnesota*, she cruised with the Fleet or the second division through most of the time. There were constant manoeuvres as the ships ran down the long miles to the target-practice ranges in Cuba or returned again to the ranges off the Massachusetts coast. In 1909, the ship went to New York, where Sims led his men in the parade which was a part of the Hudson-Fulton Celebration. With few such diversions the ship made her monotonous round, but after seven years ashore, Sims enjoyed his cruise. Like many naval men he got almost more joy from his family while at sea than on land. Removed from the inevitable frictions, decisions, and problems of family life, he could view his home from that distance which lends enchantment. Mrs. Sims sent long letters daily, enclosing the 'children's diaries' (for there were two when a second daughter, Adelaide, was born in 1909), which she wrote herself. Every word of their activities he read with fascination. His thoughts turned constantly to the 'little mother and the two wee ones,' who were his greatest pleasure in life. Now and again his fancy plunged into the future and he saw the girls' children bouncing on his knees.

Nearly two years after he took command of the *Minnesota* and only a few months before his cruise was up, the Fleet was sent to Europe. The ships were to call at England and France for brief visits before returning home. The whole voyage was in the nature of what we now call a 'good-will tour.' The omission of Germany from the itinerary was considered by some to be rather pointed, since that country was well into the stretch of its naval race with Great Britain, and the rumblings of the war to come could be heard over the horizon. The *Minnesota* and the other ships of the division arrived off Gravesend near the end of November, 1910. For a week there were celebrations, parties, and courtesy calls. It was all very pleasant, though rather tiring, and there were times when Sims looked forward to the long voyage home. On December 2 there was a large dinner at the famous Guildhall in London, where the Lord Mayor played host to all the officers. It proved to be 'one of the most interesting occasions of my experience.' Admiral Murdock made a fine speech, and the Lord Mayor, in his welcome, said that 'if the British Empire were ever seriously menaced from without he believed that there would be an immediate response from the other side.' Sims wrote to his wife that since he himself had always believed this to be true he was pleased to notice the prolonged burst of cheering which followed the Lord Mayor's comments. He wished he could tell her more about the occasion, but he was so busy making arrangements for the next day that he would have to put his description off. The arrangements he was concerned with were for the luncheon which the Lord Mayor was giving for eight hundred enlisted men at the same Guildhall. There were carriages to arrange for, schedules to fix, and 'of course there will be more speeches. I called for volunteers to make reply for the men, and one of our quartermasters will respond.' He added reassuringly that 'of course I will have a look at his speech.'

The next day, December 3, dawned cold and rainy, but the men, with Commander Sims at the head, marched from Charing Cross Station to the Guildhall behind the band of the Cold Stream Guards. It was a brave sight to thrill the crowds that lined the streets. At lunch the Lord Mayor and the officers sat at a high table where they were served with white wine and champagne while the men sat below and drank ale. After the oratory of the day before there were to be no speeches beyond a toast to the King and President. Sims, however, 'felt perfectly sure that the Mayor would make an address of welcome, but it was not intended that there should be replies. I suppose the idea was that they did not wish to risk embarrassing any of us by asking us to reply. I had, however, made our plans.' These plans included speeches by the aforementioned quartermaster and by Sims himself, for he 'wanted to say something.' The Mayor, when informed at lunch of his intention, was 'perfectly delighted.' The names of the two were therefore given to the Toastmaster, a supernumerary at every British banquet 'with a voice like a foghorn' whose greatest responsibility was to call for quiet for the coming speaker.

The King was toasted, the President was toasted, and the Lord Mayor made another address. It was a speech delivered not so much for the men as for its 'political effect' since

the Mayor assured me that the government was directly concerned in what he said. I understood that he had received information as to what they would like to have expressed in reference to the relations between the two countries. You will remember that in my letter of last night I told you that the Mayor strongly intimated that in case of danger they would look with confidence to a response from the other side of the water. We talked of this during the lunch. I ate hardly anything. I was too busy. He said that on account of his official position, he had to be guarded in his speech; that he could not say all that he believed — which is exactly what I believe, namely, that America could never stand seeing a foreign flag flying over the mother country; that in case of grave danger to the Empire we would certainly come to their assistance. I asked him if he thought it would be advisable for me to state the matter thus strongly as a personal opinion. He said he would be glad if I would.

Well, since before we landed in England I had been turning this over in my mind so as to have it ready in case I got an opportunity to say it. I had done this in the same way that you know of the manner in which I form a paper in my head (by 'mulling' over it) without putting anything on paper. I had really arranged every paragraph and most of the phrases. I wanted very much to say it and to shake the old Guildhall with it, with the assistance of the men. And I did it.

Well, when the Lord Mayor had finished his speech, and the sailors had cheered him and in a manner which I think the Guildhall has seldom experienced, the Toastmaster called silence for 'Commander Sims, Commander of the *U.S.S. Minnesota.*' When each speaker gets up he is received with a certain amount of applause. Well, my dear, I wish you could have heard the sailors. They cheered and clapped their hands and stamped their feet for many minutes. Now I do not know where I acquired, all of a sudden, the confidence I felt, but I give you my word that it was complete. I felt not the slightest particle of nervousness or embarrassment. I had the headings of what I wanted to say written on a small piece of paper lying on the table before me, in case I should omit anything, but I did not need to look at it as I had been thinking about it so long. I did not hesitate for a word or get the wrong word at any time. The hall is immense, but I think I made my voice reach every person. I spoke slowly and distinctly and pronounced every word carefully. Well, apparently I said just what they most wanted to hear. It would of course take pages to give you the details of the speech. In fact I do not know that I could write down in cold blood what I managed to say under the inspiration of the moment. I began by thanking the L. M. for the sentiments he had expressed, referred to the courtesies extended to the men, related what the men had told me of the friendliness with which they had been treated by the citizens on the streets, went on to speak of the numerous cases of blood relationship between the two peoples, referred to the facility with which Englishmen married American women who pleased them, and vice versa, gave an account of the numerous applications for leave by our men to see their relatives here or visit the parts of the country their people came from, told them they heard only of the international marriages between people of rank or wealth, that they did not even suspect the number of those they never heard of, stated my own relationship, pointed out that there was no boundary between the U.S. and Canada, and finally stated that the impressions that had been made upon us by the official and semi-official entertainments were as nothing compared to the deeper impression made by the very apparent brotherly feeling of the people of all classes — that the former could be made by any country but that the latter was absolutely impossible without the ties of blood and language — all the above to illustrate the strong peace sentiment of unity; but that beneath all this there was another and stronger sentiment lying dormant ready to spring into life at the first threat to the integrity of our race. I said I would express this sentiment in the form of an opinion, but that I particularly wished to emphasize the fact that it was purely personal opinion. I then stated as my opinion that if ever the integrity of the British Empire should be seriously threatened by an external enemy, they might count upon the assistance of every man, every ship, and every dollar from their kinsmen across the seas. I may say that the little speech was listened to with perfect attention and was received with most generous applause throughout, but the applause at the climax was an uproar. I then turned to the Mayor and asked his permission to propose in my own way three American cheers for three British things. He bowed his permission. I asked all the American officers and men to stand up, and then proposed three cheers for the Sailor King, the British people, and the integrity of their Empire, and at the first cheer sent my cap sailing out into the middle of the hall. Well, my dear, the response not only of our men but of the British was the most enthusiastic that I have ever witnessed anywhere. It continued for a long time. The Lord Mayor was delighted and shook my hand with unmistakable warmth. When the affair was over, many of the Englishmen present came up and shook hands with me and said that they had never seen such an occasion. Our officers and men were exceedingly gratified. Afterwards when we got to Dorchester House, Mrs. Simpson shook me by both hands and expressed her enthusiasm with a strong suspicion of tears in her eyes. If you had been there you would have doubtless been on pins and needles for fear I should have made a bad break, but I am sure you would have been gratified in the end. . . .

But now I must go back and finish telling you about the lunch. After I finished my speech, I asked the Lord Mayor's permission to propose another cheer. He said I could do anything I wanted to do. So, without the assistance of the Toastmaster (he had given up running the job long before this) I got up and raised my hand for silence, and said that the Guildhall was five hundred years old, had witnessed innumerable celebrations and scenes of enthusiasm, but that never up to the present time had any assemblage been able to raise the roof even the fraction of an inch; that I thought we might at least try to do it, and to that end I wished all officers and men to do their best in response to a toast I was about to propose. I then proposed three cheers for 'The Lord Mayor of London,' and I think they did at least shake the old roof a bit. The Mayor was evidently greatly pleased and entered so much into the spirit of it all that he whispered to me that he would be pleased to have me propose three cheers for the Lady Mayoress (who was in the gallery with a number of guests). Of course I did so, and the sailors responded with a will. The Mayor was onto the fact that his toastmaster was out of a job and was much amused by it, and so was the Toastmaster. He told me that he had never enjoyed an occasion so much; that it had really been much more impressive by reason of its enthusiasm than the more formal lunch of the day before. And I am convinced that he meant every word of it. It is safe to say that in all of its five hundred years, the old Guildhall never witnessed such a scene. You know the British take their pleasures sadly. They love solemnity, but I think no people are more pleased by enthusiasm if they can once be stirred up to it — it is such a novelty.

In such vivid terms did Sims describe the incident at the Guildhall to his wife. Many, many years before, when he first set foot in England in 1889, he had found the English 'to say the least very trying' and he had cynically dismissed the talk 'of the brotherly love of England and America when they make speeches.' A great deal of water had flowed beneath the bridge since that far-off time, and even before December 3, 1910, he was thought by some to be a rather boisterous Anglophile. This change of heart had come slowly. They were wrong who assigned it to so simple a cause as his Canadian birth or his English grandparents. Far less sentimental and far more compelling reasons explain his growing respect and admiration. Had not Darwin and Huxley and Herbert Spencer first dazzled him with the power of the human mind; had they not provided him with a whole philosophy of life? Had not Percy Scott first shared with him the secret that placed them both upon the high road of success? Had not John Jellicoe, the most important officer in British gunnery, sought his advice, while the Chief of the Bureau of Ordnance wrote endorsements to prove that Sims was advocating a mathematical impossibility? Had not the great Lord John Fisher bidden him to dinner, congratulated him for his article on the all-big-gun battleship, and permitted him to see the *Dreadnought*, while Mahan had written his reflections on the battle of the Japan Sea, and Senator Hale had crudely shut his mouth at a committee hearing?

Such debts as these could never be repaid, but there were, too, other claims which England laid upon his affections. If Sims was skeptical about the virtue of mere tradition, his symmetrical mind was attracted by formality. Though not unaware and never approving of the inequalities in English life, he liked the

precision and restrained elegance of its society. He was delighted
to find, as it was difficult to find in America, naval officers, civil
servants, and political figures, who displayed a knowledge of art,
literature, and culture. In England, he believed there were a
few of what he thought all men should be — cultivated gentlemen.

Does all this suggest that Sims loved England more than
America? It is not begging the question to reply that probably
he respected the Anglo-Saxon race more than he loved either
country. He liked the British ways and he respected their many
talents; but he was forever fascinated by the phenomena of his
own country — the hot dog, baseball, campaign platforms, and
all the rest of it. America was his country and therefore more to
him than England, but the two together were the English-speaking race and the sum was greater than either of the parts.
That race stood for free men, free minds, and free spirits; it
stood for the highest forms of culture then on earth; it stood especially for the dignity of man. Here was a common heritage so
priceless that it took precedence over a local patriotism. If the
time ever came when the integrity of that heritage was menaced
on whatever front by whatever enemy, he felt the imperative
necessity of a common defense. In 1910, he heard things and
saw things that made him sure that Germany was preparing to
destroy his cherished birthright, and he felt it his duty to warn
that hostile country with a prophecy that would not fail.

That his remarks were calculated and carefully prepared is
apparent from his letter to his wife, but the depth of feeling
behind them was spontaneous and in that sense the speech was
extemporary. He was, it is clear, almost awed by his unusual
and breathless excitement which spurred him at that moment
to an unfamiliar eloquence. The final words of his speech, so
often quoted incorrectly, have a ring and cadence which in
calmer moments he would have scorned as 'Fourth of July stuff.'
'If the time ever comes when the British Empire is seriously
menaced by an external enemy, it is my opinion that you may
count upon every man, every dollar, every drop of blood, of your
kindred across the sea.' [5]

[5] Note that this version differs from the one he sent to Mrs. Sims. It is, however, the version he sent officially to the Navy Department.

For a time after the speech Sims heard nothing but words of high approval. The English papers naturally applauded his sentiments; [6] everywhere he went in London people grasped his hands, one even with 'a suspicion of tears in her eyes,' and Admiral Murdock sent round a complimentary note. Then quite unexpectedly, at least to Sims, criticism began to be heard. By December 6, when the Fleet left Gravesend for Brest, he realized that he had stirred up a hornets' nest. The attack, naturally enough, had German origins, for Germany was disturbed because the Fleet had failed to make a visit to her shores. When coupled with this significant omission the words of Sims appeared like a studied warning to that ambitious, sensitive country. A clamor was likewise raised amid certain elements of the press in America for disciplinary action against the speaker. The agitation became so great that finally the Navy Department was forced to take action. On December 20, Secretary Meyer cabled to Sims in France to ask him exactly what he had said. To this Sims replied that his speech was in no way a formal one, that he had not known that he was to speak until he had sat down at the table, that his remarks had been 'entirely extemporaneous,' and that he had no copy of it. He then quoted as his recollection the words of his most damaging phrase heretofore noticed above.

This was the last he heard from Washington until the Fleet arrived back at Guantanamo in early January. Naturally, during this period of silence, he worried over the outcome of the affair and believed it possible that he might be detached from his command; but he was not unduly concerned for his future, as he

[6] How many reporters were present at the Guildhall is a matter of conjecture. Several London papers, among them the *Times*, on December 5, had very full stories of the whole occasion. This would suggest the presence of at least several reporters. On the other hand, A. E. Hanscomb, writing in the *London Daily Telegraph*, September 18, 1941, leaves the definite impression that he alone was responsible for the publicity Sims' speech received. 'His [Sims'] remarks, cabled to America from my report, caused some sensation there.' During the First World War in London, Hanscomb says, 'I took the opportunity of expressing to the Admiral my regret that I should have been the innocent cause of so much trouble to him. He said, "Oh, was it you who did it?" I again expressed my regret. The great, stalwart, honesthearted sailor put his hand on my shoulder and simply said, "Here we are!"' How accurate Hanscomb's recollection is, is open to some question. He reports for example that Sims spoke to a gathering of East London school-children at the Guildhall.

never was.[7] Whatever the outcome, he wrote his wife, 'I am glad I did it.' The silence in Washington was not due to any lack of activity. Officially, Germany took no notice of the incident, but it was plain from the comments of some of her officers that the country was highly incensed. Likewise, the increasingly hostile remarks of our own aroused press placed Secretary Meyer in an awkward position. At a Cabinet meeting in December the case was fully discussed, but no plan of action was decided upon.

After the Cabinet meeting Charles Nagel, the Secretary of Commerce and Labor, went to Meyer and asked if he could help the situation by his intercession. Nagel, a resident of St. Louis, had been a close personal friend of Mr. Hitchcock's. He knew Sims well and was anxious to assist him. The Secretary of the Navy was delighted by his offer and suggested that Nagel call on the President. This Nagel did at the first opportunity. He presented Mr. Taft with a very convincing case. Sims, he began, was a valuable officer as well as the most indiscreet man in the Navy. Both he and Mr. Taft had heard Sims say things at private dinners which, if repeated publicly, would have terminated Sims' naval career long ago. The President, Nagel noted, appeared 'to share his impression on that subject.' He then went on to say that the speech was unprepared and that Sims might even have 'had one under the collar.' [8] These were all arguments which could weigh with the President when he was in his open-minded and professionally jovial mood. Nagel suggested a punishment but not a humiliation — perhaps a presidential reprimand on his own ship. He wound up with the

[7] The public displayed far greater interest in his future. Mrs. Sims was widely reported, quite erroneously, to have sent her husband a cable urging him to resign. Many papers announced that he was to lose his ship. Others shared the view of Mrs. Murdock, who wrote her husband that 'If Captain Sims can get a good-paying position, I should advise him to resign, for he is smart enough to get along anywhere.' Less support came from the press for her belief that 'Captain Sims has never felt independent of the Department.'

[8] Nagel seems to have believed that Sims had taken too much of the wine and champagne at the Guildhall dinner. On at least one occasion he even quotes Sims as saying to him, 'I may have had one too many.' This explanation is almost certainly more plausible than true. Sims wrote his wife immediately after the affair that he took very little to drink at the time, and it is hard to believe he was not reporting accurately. Even in his earliest years he seldom drank much and never to excess; while after 1895 he almost gave up the practice altogether. It would also be entirely out of character for him to jeopardize the success of his performance by intemperance.

cajoling idea that Sims 'had only been indiscreet enough to say what you think.' [9]

How much Nagel had to do with what followed is hard to say. Meyer had, from the start, opposed drastic punishment. President Taft, after his momentary anger had cooled, agreed with his Secretary that leniency was the better course.[10] Sims himself believed that 'our friend from St. Louis in the Cabinet probably had considerable to do with it.' At all events, on January 13, 1910, Sims, together with every other officer in the service, received General Order 100, which was a public reprimand for Sims from President Taft. The President made it clear that the Navy was an instrument of peace and that no officer should therefore do anything beyond conveying our good-will to foreign countries in times of peace. Nor should he in any way embarrass the government. Even though Sims had expressed only what he emphasized was a personal opinion, though only 'grateful words had crowded to the lips under the enthusiasm of the cordial welcome,' nevertheless, he had been unable to restrain himself within the limits of diplomatic intercourse and for this fault he must be censured publicly.

It was a mild enough reprimand for an officer who had, as he cheerfully said to Charles Nagel, 'made a darn fool of myself.' Actually, he did not believe that he had done so, and if he was proud of his 'indiscretion' he was prouder still of what he had said. A half-dozen years later, when the prophecy was fulfilled, the reprimand of the prophet was forgotten as he set forth to assist in the maintenance of the integrity of the British Empire. Not quite forgotten, for Mr. Taft, who was not unacquainted with Clio's feminine caprice, remarked philosophically: 'The ways of history are strange. When I was President I reprimanded an officer for saying exactly what he is doing now. That officer was Commander, now Vice Admiral, Sims in command of the American Navy in Europe.' [11]

[9] This description of Nagel's intercession is based upon a memorandum sent by Mr. Nagel to the writer, October 26, 1938.

[10] W. K. Harrison, then on duty with the Bureau of Navigation, wrote Sims January 16, 1911, that the President was 'profanely indignant when the matter came up, and has been handling the situation himself, I believe. Stacks of letters from Irishmen and Germans have come in protesting against it.'

[11] In his last letter to Doctor W. F. Arnold on September 3, 1917, Sims wrote:

Yet the dramatic fulfilment of the prophecy should not obscure the fact that the words at the Guildhall should never have been spoken. In making his prediction, qualified though it was as a purely personal opinion, Sims entered upon forbidden territory. He took a position in public upon the future policy of the government under which he served. He had no business to do so. Five years after this speech he wrote that he could not 'understand why there should be so much opposition to giving the Secretary a military adviser charged with full responsibility to that official for preparing us for war.' A large part of that opposition grew from the fears of laymen and politicians alike that naval officers provided with a General Staff would become not efficient agents but irresponsible masters of national policy. Innocent though Sims' intentions may have been, sound though his personal convictions were, at the Guildhall in 1910, he gave strength to an opposition which, for the best years of his life, he sought to defeat.

By the time the excitement over the speech had died down, Sims' cruise on the *Minnesota* was almost over. It had been a very full two years, fuller than these pages can reveal. The eager energies of the perfectionist were constantly at work, striving to achieve a new system of promotion, supporting the drive carried on by Meyer for a better naval organization, relentlessly pressing improved ship design. He sat on a board to consider changes in the methods of fire control; he travelled to Washington to confer, along with Albert Lenoir Key, about a new kind of conning tower with the Board of Construction (and he was elated 'by this tangible recognition which was paid' to such insurgents). From all his other duties he found time to write long letters to the Department about the inadequate complements with which men-of-war were furnished. In this he was supported by Admiral Murdock, who shared his views on the inefficiency caused by the limited size and inexperience of the Navy personnel. He sent in long reports about the badly constructed and expensive targets, about the kind of oars his boat

'Who would ever have thought during the days when the S.R.I.A. was in full working order that I would one day be selected by the P.D.'s to hold down this job? Or that having been reprimanded for my prophecy in the Guildhall speech of 1910, I would be helping to carry it out. Life is certainly a curious thing.'

crew had to use in their races, and when the crews won, he criticized the trophy as 'an object of ridicule because of its evident cheapness and its grotesque attitude and design.' [12] When time permitted, and even when it did not, he wrote to a traction company giving the number of a conductor who had permitted a man to smoke on a streetcar; he had a heated and painfully frank correspondence with a railroad company which had failed to clean out a stateroom after the last occupant had left it. The cheerful crusader rode off in many directions and if he did not always deliver Jerusalem, he killed a gratifyingly large number of infidels on the way.

As always, when a cruise is nearly over, there was the problem of what duty would follow. Sims began in October, 1910, to think of his future when he wrote on the twenty-fourth to his loyal friend, H. I. Cone, who was then Chief of the Bureau of Steam Engineering: 'One thing I wanted to ask you about is the prospect of my getting duty in Washington at the end of my cruise next spring, so that I can be in the game and see the wheels go round. Do you think the Secretary would object to an insurgent being on duty at headquarters? I would like the General Board if possible.' Three days later he wrote again considering his chances at some length. Dewey, he thought, would be for him — 'he was always complimentary about my gunnery work and moreover he is in love with my daughter. She [Margaret, aged four] sent him a photo with her love and he sent her his favorite photo.' More cold-bloodedly he recognized that two more were 'probably' for him and two others against him.

Whatever possibilities there ever had been for such duty were dealt a shattering blow by his report that 'the target regulations of 1910 had been received with "derisive disapproval."' Occasionally at some critical juncture in his career, Sims managed to do something which irritated his superiors or tied their hands in such a way that it was impossible to do for him what he desired. The General Board became an impossibility after this, especially when there was talk of making an official objection to Sims' disrespectful language. Lieutenant Commander W. K. Harrison advised him from the Bureau of Navigation 'to saw

[12] It was, in fact, all he said it was. Through his efforts the rather sad little rooster was replaced by a suitable trophy.

wood and sit tight and write nothing in return,' while Cone asked him to compose a letter 'backing Meyer which I can show around to prove you are not always agin the government.' It would have taken more than a letter to convince many officers of this, particularly after the turmoil surrounding the speech at the Guildhall.

McLean wrote in February that 'The General Board is out, but Reddy [the indefatigable Cone] has fixed it for you to go to the War College to step into the Presidency when Rodgers retires.' He added a hint that Sims must still walk carefully. 'Cone says to do nothing until you come to Washington. Then the very first thing call on him at his office and find out how things are going. Then go down and call on the Secretary, then possibly on Nicholson [the Chief of the Bureau of Navigation] and then skin out of the building and keep clear.' Apparently, this warning startled Sims into an unwonted caution. He wrote to his friend, Philip Andrews, the aide to the Secretary, to find out if the Guildhall speech would affect his future duty — meaning his permanent career, for he had by then given up the General Board as lost. Andrews assured him that the incident would have no influence beyond, he added with unbelievable restraint, 'the slight doubt which may be raised as to your absolute fitness for a diplomatic job.'

McLean had reported matters correctly; Cone had 'fixed it' for the War College. In a letter to Sims, Cone himself explained that this was the best that could be done under the circumstances. He held out the hope that Sims would become President of the College after finishing the long course. 'Much to your credit,' he added, 'there has been running through all this "Sims is one of the ablest men we have etc.," and the War College idea is meant to "tone down his ideas etc.," and make him proper stuff for an able Commander-in-Chief.'

Whatever the idea behind the appointment Sims did not look forward with pleasure to studying at the War College. In April he left the *Minnesota* with many misgivings. During his two years of command he had more than justified the grandiloquent assurance of Theodore Roosevelt, 'Why, my dear fellow, I was so sure you would be a success I never gave it a second thought!' As Sims went overside for the last time the knowledge that he was about to have two full years with his family did not prevent him from having a momentary throb of sorrow at leaving his happy ship. After a short leave, during which he was promoted to captain, he and his wife and children settled down in Newport for his student years.

17

1911 - 1915   *The Band of Brothers*

MUCH of the success of the Atlantic Destroyer Flotilla during the period of Sims' command rested upon the training he received at the War College from 1911 to 1913. Though in later years he never forgot his debt to the institution, he entered it reluctantly after leaving the *Minnesota*. 'It may even be,' he wrote to his wife, 'that things [the aftermath of the Guildhall speech] will blow over to such an extent that I may get some duty I would like better — something in closer touch with practice and less on the theoretical side.'

To Stephen B. Luce, who had founded the College, these words would have sounded discouragingly familiar. For thirty years he had fought, with very few supporters, to keep his War College alive against the opposition of practical people who refused to believe that the naval profession had a 'theoretical side.' Since men who go down to the sea in ships necessarily lead lives of action, the service as a whole found it hard to accept Admiral Luce's idea that 'by reasoning from the facts of naval history to general principles' it would be possible to raise 'naval warfare from the empirical stage to the dignity of a science.' It was, in fact, surprising that the War College survived the early hostility of the apathetic and the ignorant. Once in the nineties a Secretary of the Navy set out from Washington to rid the service of a wasteful extravagance by closing the institution. When he arrived at Newport, he was possessed of a burning conviction that the College must be kept alive at all costs. On his journey he had read *The Influence of Sea Power Upon History* which some thoughtful subordinate had placed in his hands upon his departure from the capital. For the first time the Secretary then realized the importance of an institution where such a book had been written. Upon such slender chances its existence in those first years depended.

That it survived at all is to the lasting credit of Stephen B. Luce and his few disciples. Through all vicissitudes, lack of money, lack of students, lack of sympathetic understanding, he rallied the little group who followed him by the vigor of his tremendous spirit and the constancy of his hopes. Gradually hopes were fulfilled, though Sims could say, not, to be sure, with entire truth, that as late as 1910 'it was the only college that had been maintained at considerable expense for twenty-five years without any students.' The popularity of Mahan's great works, most of them simply his collected lectures, Captain William M. Little's practical work in the development of the game board, Admiral Henry C. Taylor's wise and continuous support when he was Chief of the Bureau of Navigation; these things slowly converted the doubters. Slowly, too, it was recognized that steam and long-range rifles had introduced strategic and tactical problems which could not be solved by practice alone. But it must be remembered that even when Sims entered the College as one of four members of the first 'long course' in 1911, only a relatively small minority understood the real purpose for which it had been established. In that minority Sims, at the time, could not be included.[1]

For two years he remained in Newport. When the work during the first few months convinced him of the value of his study, he entered on the new duty with his usual enthusiasm and intensity of purpose. For the first time he read such masters of the profession as Jomini, Henderson, Derrecagaix, Hoenlohe-Ingelfingen, Mahan, and Corbett. From his work at the game board he obtained a wide knowledge of tactics. Most important of all was the understanding he gained of the principles and meaning of military doctrine. By the end of the long course he was delighted to admit that what he had taken to be a backwater was really the main current of professional thought.

[1] The early history of the War College is well told by W. D. Puleston, *Mahan*, Yale University Press, New Haven, 1939, chapters XII and XIII, and Albert Gleaves, *Luce*, chapter X.

There was more than professional profit in the tour of duty
at Newport. In the large, comfortable, homely frame house on
Rhode Island Avenue, Sims could lead the life of a family man.
Here it was possible to establish the kind of routine so dear to
his heart. In the morning and early afternoon, of course, there
was work to do; but every day an hour was set aside for tennis
or for walks along the shore. There was, there always had been,
a religious quality in his attitude toward exercise. This feeling
was intensified as he grew older, and he was delighted to find
that at fifty-five he could still beat the young lieutenants at their
own games. In the afternoons, too, there was always tea with
the family and occasional guests, where he could relax and tell
his stories and light-heartedly 'pull the legs' of his listeners.
Rarely he and Mrs. Sims would go out for dinner, for they preferred to remain with their books and their children at home.
Those children, whom he had hardly known before, were his
chief joy.

Margaret was five and Adelaide two when they went to
Newport. A year later a boy, William, Junior, was born. Where
children were concerned Sims was the son of his father. If he
did not send out to 'borrow a baby,' it was only because he had
enough of his own. There was enormous pleasure in 'watching
the young minds develop,' but it was primarily, as he once wrote
to his wife, 'their helplessness that appeals to me.'

It is probably impossible to express everything that family
meant to him, though the superlatives he used in writing or thinking of his wife and children reveal the tremendous satisfactions he
took in his position as a husband and father. Until he was forty-
six he had never allowed himself to think of marriage; until he
was forty-eight he did not have a child. Only at fifty-three did he
find himself the head of a young and handsome family. Here
were rich rewards for the years he had gone his way alone, unable
to turn with love to anyone upon whom he could lay the first
claims for affection. Those constant day-dreams of which he
wrote his wife so frequently were slowly being fulfilled; his family
was the substance of those shadows which softened the enforced
austerity of his emotional life. Small wonder he thought of it
with pride and joy and uncritical love.

These were happy and valuable years, but after twelve months at Newport he began to think of sea duty again. He was not, as many of his contemporaries believed him to be, a student like Mahan, who enjoyed the pleasure of using his mind solely as an end in itself. Unless learning could be applied to the pursuits of daily life, it had little value. As early as 1912, he wrote his friends in the Bureau of Navigation to find out what billet he would get when his time at the War College was over. He hoped it would be possible for him to take command of the battleship *Texas* when she was commissioned. For a time his chances for such duty looked very bright, but in January, 1913, he received a letter from his old friend, Philip Andrews, then aide to the Secretary, informing him that he would probably be given the Atlantic Destroyer Flotilla. 'There is much to be done in the Fleet,' wrote Andrews, 'and we all thought that you would be the best man. The Secretary [George von L. Meyer] approved it before he went out, though he and the Department wanted an Admiral.'

Though Sims recognized the importance of this duty, he refused to be stampeded into it. He still preferred the *Texas*, for, as he wrote a friend, 'to command a successful battleship is the best job in the world,' but he was especially reluctant to take the Flotilla because he disapproved of the way in which it was organized. 'Up to that time' (when he took command), he said later, 'the Flotilla had not been taken very seriously. It was not supplied with a sufficient staff for the Commander-in-Chief to handle it properly, and when I took command of it, it was not a military weapon; it could not be used as destroyers must be used in war.'

Finally, upon certain conditions, he decided to accept the command if it were offered to him. These conditions reveal how much he had learned from the War College. 'The torpedo fleet,' he wrote in February, 'could be made an enormous game board — an exceedingly valuable school for trying out all kinds of manoeuvres at small expense. There is a lot to be learned. None of us knows very much about it as yet. But one thing is sure, and that is that it can only be learned by STUDY combined with *actual manoeuvres* with the Fleet.' This ambitious program could be carried out only after the existing administration had been completely reorganized. The Commander had to be given an adequate staff 'that has been trained in a knowledge of war (one old indifferently trained man cannot do it all).' He must also be provided with 'a flagship that will always be available for the numerous exercise manoeuvres that will be necessary in order to develop anything worth while.' Unless these conditions were met he would prefer some other billet.[2]

Sims got his own way and in July, 1913, assumed command. Within the Flotilla, composed of about thirty destroyers, he was permitted to develop the organization he desired. He was supplied with a flagship, the light cruiser *Birmingham*, though this was withheld for a time because of inevitable delays, and he was allowed to choose his own subordinates. This staff, made up principally of young officers he had met at the War College, was his pride and joy. Commander William V. Pratt, in command of the flagship, served as the Chief of Staff. For the success of the Flotilla in these years this able man deserves much credit. Sims and he worked together in the harmony that is built upon professional respect and personal affection. There was also Lieutenant Commander Dudley Knox, who had married a daughter of Sims' early supporter, Admiral McCalla. Knox, perhaps the ablest of all the men, played the largest part in the development of the 'Destroyer Doctrine.'

Sims was always fond of expressing his affection for officers in jocular, unmetrical verse and these two did not escape his rather heavy-handed blows.

> 'There's a frisky young sailor named **Pratt**
> Who is a tactical acrobat.
> He thinks the point of the speed
> The greatest tactical need,
>
> BUT
>
> When he tries to explain you all that
> He doesn't know quite where he's at
> And he talks through the top of his hat.'

> 'There's a certain young chappie named **Knox**
> Who is terribly heterodox.
> There's no tactical rule
> That he don't ridicule —
> He's got something loose in his box.'

[2] These conditions were more revolutionary than they may appear. Sims' predecessor had no staff at all. He ran his command of thirty destroyers with one assistant after the Navy Department refused to send him other officers.

Together with Knox and Pratt there was Lieutenant J. V. Babcock, who was in charge of the work with torpedoes. This young 'torpedo doctor,' as Sims called him, began in the Flotilla the long and loyal service to his chief that ended only when the World War was over. On the *Dixie*, the repair ship for the destroyers, famous in the war as the mother ship based at Queenstown, was Commander J. K. Robison and later Commander Hutchinson I. Cone who needs no introduction here. It was a splendid group of men with whom Sims began work in July, 1913. Of their Commander he had his own opinion which he also expressed in poetry.

> 'By nature shy and gentle
> And in manner meek and mild,
> With the winning ways of happy days
> Of a winsome little child.
> The opinions of his confreres
> He accepts as Nature's laws
> In spite of their jeers and his numerous years
> And the whiskers on his jaws.
> He's a lover of peace and quietness
> And inclines to a placid life
> And would rather give in than suffer the din
> Of argumentative strife.
> Now who is the man who is under the ban
> Of such very singular whims?
> You never could guess, so I'll just confess
> That his name is Willie Sims.'

Shortly after he took command in July, 1913, he called together all the officers in his cabin and 'made them a little speech.' The naval officer could not exist, he suggested, whose judgment upon each aspect of his profession was sounder than that of all others with whom he was associated. Conclusions based upon maximum knowledge and experience could only be reached after a full and frank discussion by all the members of the organization. He proposed, therefore, that the various problems should be solved in frequent conferences attended by all commanding officers. In these discussions he would appear more as a moderator than a dictator. It was an idea he had learned at the War

College where the 'conference system' was used to develop theories of tactics or strategy.[3]

At first there was some opposition to this revolutionary proposal. Some felt they could not spare the time from their own ships while others believed that the scheme would result in much talk and little intelligent action. But Sims proved his point when he asked each man to write out his own conception of the mission of the destroyers. From the answers he received, it was plain that very few had a clear idea of the reasons for which the Flotilla existed. One thought that 'the ships ought to be kept efficient to do all destroyer work'; another asserted that the Flotilla ought to be trained to make successful torpedo attacks; while a third considered his chief duty to be the maintenance of his own vessel. Sims pointed out that no force could be expected to operate effectively unless there was some common agreement among the members upon the ultimate objectives. In the conference this subject was debated for some time before it was decided that 'the mission of the Flotilla shall be to determine the manner in which the Flotilla may best assist the Fleet in accomplishing its main objectives, before, during, and after battle; to train the personnel so that before, during, and after battle they can co-ordinate internal effort and effectively coordinate the effort of the Flotilla as a whole with the operations of the Fleet as a whole.'

The conduct of the Flotilla, it was decided at future conferences, 'was to be governed by a doctrine which was to be subject to constant revision based upon experience as determined by conference conclusions.' This doctrine was more completely described in the Instructions which were printed and distributed to each officer.[4] It was a 'body of information serving as a guide in formulating all actions and decisions in the absence of specific orders, with a minimum recourse to intercommunication between forces or with superiors.'

Reduced to its simplest terms doctrine is really like the whole repertoire of plays used in football. On a well-coached team

[3] W. S. S., 'Naval War College Principles and Methods Applied Afloat,' *N.I.P.*, March–April, 1915. A brief and interesting history of the work of the Flotilla is contained in this article. Much that follows is based upon it.

[4] *Destroyer Flotilla, Atlantic Fleet, General Service Instructions*, 1915. This mimeographed booklet of forty-six pages contains a complete outline of the mission, organization, doctrine, and administration of the Flotilla.

each member can identify a particular formation by the number assigned to it; no long description of each play by the quarterback is necessary. Constant practice has revealed to each player his own and his fellow members' duties on any particular play. Doctrine is simply a series of well-recognized plans guiding the activities of several separate entities toward the achievement of a common goal.[5]

Sims had first been introduced to military doctrine at the War College. It was of German origin, developed as a method of co-ordinating the activities of widely distributed troop units. The German theory of envelopment required first the deployment of large semi-independent army groups over a wide front, but it also demanded the successful cooperation of these separated forces. To ensure this German officers were educated in the same school of thought; they were indoctrinated. By such instruction not only was the necessity for a highly centralized command reduced, but unity of thought and action was assured under all circumstances.

The value of doctrine was soon recognized by other nations. In our own War College the subject was carefully studied, but one of the best-informed students of doctrine in this country felt justified in asserting in 1915 that 'of all great navies, our own is probably alone in completely ignoring this great aid to the waging of decisive war on the sea.' [6] It was Sims, with the assistance of this student Dudley Knox and the other members of his staff, who first introduced this subject to our own Navy. There with various mutations and refinements it has remained ever since.

In his own racy rambling phrases Sims has described how the conference system was used and how the doctrine of the Flotilla was developed.

> When I took command of it [the Flotilla] I made inquiries as to what they had been doing, and I found they had certain operations with the fleet which were absolutely cut and dried. Each captain was furnished with a report or statement of twelve hundred words, with two blue prints, showing what he was to do in a projected attack on the fleet.

[5] This description of doctrine is, for the sake of clarity, oversimplified. An excellent discussion of its origins, developments and uses can be found in Dudley W. Knox, 'The Rôle of Doctrine in Naval Warfare,' *N.I.P.*, March–April, 1915.

[6] *Ibid.*, p. 345.

After taking charge, and after having been through the War College, and after having discussions with the officers in the War College on the war game, and these discussions that we had with each other, what we would like to accomplish, I called these gentlemen, the commanders of these destroyers into my cabin. Now, these men were educated naval officers, graduates of the Naval Academy, and having had from 15 to 20 years' experience in the Navy. And I said to them, this is what I conceive to be the function of the North Atlantic Destroyer Force. Imagine the cruising party of a number of destroyers in the presence of an enemy. Suppose the commander had a second force ahead of him in a line, spread out perhaps 100 miles long, trying to find the enemy. Suppose in that situation you got a signal from the Commander-in-Chief, 'The enemy has been sighted in a certain position, away on the other side of the fleet; a certain known position. Attack at once.' How are you going to do it? The Commander-in-Chief and those under him cannot take time to send a report of 1200 words to each captain and send with it two blue prints. He cannot send signals what to do. They must have learned what to do without any particular orders from him, except the initial one. I said, 'Are any of you the destroyer officers here that understand how this is done?' They said, 'No; we do not.' I said, 'Neither do I.' I said, 'I know what we want to do, because we worked it out on the practical War Board of the War College. I am not a practical man in these affairs. I am not capable of knowing from one station to the other in the night what to do, but you people ought to know that. It is up to us to get busy. Here is the cabin floor, and here are a dozen or so model ships, and we will work out a scheme.' We worked over it for several days and worked out a scheme. 'Now,' I said, 'I am going to take the fleet outside and try it out. But I will make you this bet, when you try it out at sea you will find that half of your dope is wrong, because you have not had the experience.'

We took it out and tried it out at night. The Flotilla did find the fleet and attacked it. But we came back the next day and compared notes, and we did find that half of it turned out to be wrong. I said, 'What do you think of yourselves, and what do I think of myself? But we have got to keep on until we find the scheme.' We corrected the scheme until we found the mistakes in the first operation. We went out and tried it again. And we found some more. And we put it on the board, and we kept that thing up for a solid year before I was willing to go to the Commander-

297

in-Chief, Admiral Badger, and say, 'If you will give your flotilla a reasonable chance, I believe we will be able to find you any night, you representing the enemy, and attack you in a practical way.'

We were at Guantanamo. He said, 'All right. I am going out. You have your fleet in the Guantanamo Bay at sundown and you will hear from me.' We were in Guantanamo Bay at sundown and were waiting, and we heard this signal: Enemy fleet sighted, Navassa Island — which is between Haiti and Cuba — 3 p.m. Attack at once. That was all. This is what we conceived the flotilla ought to be able to do. It was a simple matter for the staff on the flagship to lay down a line on a course which would intercept his ship. So I sent a signal to the destroyer commanders by wireless: 'Deploy latitude so-and-so and longitude so-and-so, 9 p.m., course east by south, speed 20 knots.' to each destroyer, no matter where he was, and I was sure that he could get there on time, regulate his speed to arrive there 9 p.m. Each destroyer had his prescribed position in that line, and each one knew the place of the other. They all arrived 9 p.m., and thence went east by south 20 knots.

Now, we had worked out what we called a doctrine of attack that must be carried out, almost necessarily in war, be carried out by the men themselves. Briefly, it was this: The first destroyer of the line sent out a few ticks, to show where the flotilla was. That destroyer would not attack, but keep in touch. The destroyer on the side was to come in and also keep in touch, and the ship here was to go and take a position ahead of the fleet. The Commander-in-Chief changed his course and speed from time to time to fool us. But here were these three, and each time he changed his course he sent out word, and they were all informed. And so if he changed his course or speed, or anything, it was worked out so-and-so. It was worked out successfully.

The next thing I heard was — now, they all had their positions, — and I sent out a single word, and that word was, 'position,' meaning, I am in position to attack; because it is a military principle if you attack you want to attack with all your force at the same time, and not give them a chance to get your force killed like rats coming out of a hole. I kept them in that position until the Commander-in-Chief, a couple of hours later — until the word went down the line that we had successfully attacked.[7]

[7] *Hearing Before the Select Committee of Inquiry Into Operations of the United States Air Services*, House of Representatives, 68th Congress, 1925, Part 4, p. 2965.

That was the way the conference system and doctrine were used in the Flotilla. Through their use the twelve hundred words and two blueprints necessary to order a night search and attack could be reduced to thirty-one radioed code words. By their constant employment new tactics for the torpedo were developed and improved methods of scouting and screening were devised. Time and again, after the first year, the classic double screen thrown around an enemy battle line by its auxiliaries was pierced so easily that a new protective formation had to be devised. In continual manoeuvres and games new theories were tried out and the Flotilla became, as Sims said, 'a war college afloat.' These were fruitful years for Sims, his staff, and the little ships whose possibilities had never been fully understood before; they were fruitful, too, for a Navy that had never investigated the possibilities of the conference system and the necessity of military doctrine.

The list of accomplishments could be extended at great length, but two more will suffice. The traditional method of turning a column of ships at right angles to its original course was a simultaneous turning action carried out by each ship upon a signal from the Commander-in-Chief. The dangers of this manoeuvre lay chiefly in the fact that ships well down the line could miss the Commander's signal, thus breaking up the formation and blanketing the fire of the other vessels. The Flotilla devised what was called the 'ripple manoeuvre' in which each ship turned separately after the destroyer immediately to stern of it had turned. In this way no confusion could result and experiment showed that little valuable time was lost, since the thirty-five ships of the column could turn in thirty-eight seconds. Historically the manoeuvre is important because it was later used by the Germans with such success at the battle of Jutland. It is still the belief of many, despite the meaning of the order, that Scheer's famous 'Gefechtskehrtwendung nach steuerbord' was the signal for each ship of his line to alter course simultaneously. But in fact, his Fleet performed the 'ripple manoeuvre.' [8]

[8] The manoeuvre performed by the German Fleet at Jutland will probably remain a matter of constant debate between authorities. After the war the German Admiral Behncke spoke at the War College in Newport. He had been in command of Division V at Jutland. With the aid of a blackboard he explained that Scheer's turning movement had been the 'ripple manoeuvre.' Whether the Germans learned this from the Flotilla is impossible to say, though the claim has been made.

299

Of greater permanent value was the rejuvenation of the Reserve Flotilla during these years. For more than a decade the Navy had suffered seriously from a shortage of men, enlisted and commissioned. The situation was in no way improved in 1913 when Secretary Josephus Daniels refused to accept the General Board's recommendation to increase the personnel. Because of this shortage it had been found necessary to lay up a good many older destroyers in navy yards. These ships, manned by skeleton crews, deteriorated over a period of months until they were unfit for sea duty. In fact, in 1914, an officer who inspected them arrived at the conclusion that they could not go from the Charleston Navy Yard to Culebra in ordinary trade-wind weather.

Sims suggested that these vessels, manned by reduced complements, should undertake practice cruises to ensure their proper maintenance. As a corollary to this he advised that the Reserve Flotilla formed from these ships should be included in the Fleet administration of the Commander-in-Chief. Before this time they had been under the control of officers commanding the various navy yards in which they were stationed. At first there were a good many objections to these proposals. Some felt that it would be impossible to form an efficient force of older ships manned by limited crews; others, even on the General Board, believed that the system of administration proposed by Sims was unorthodox and therefore open to question. After a year of consideration, during which Sims was aided by the able arguments of his Commander-in-Chief, Rear Admiral Charles Badger, the scheme was tried.

A reserve was formed under Commander Frank Taylor Evans, the son of Robley D. Evans. There were possibilities of friction and difficulty in this appointment that did not escape either Sims or Evans. The latter had inherited from his father a dislike of Sims, which he had expressed several times to brother officers. Inevitably, of course, the critical remarks had drifted back to Sims, who dismissed them with the observation that, 'This means nothing. It's simply commendable filial piety.' At first, in view of this situation, Evans was reluctant to accept the command, but he was persuaded to do so after talking the matter over with various men who were mutual friends of the two involved. It was a wise decision, for each came to have a respect and affection for the other. Under Evans' careful training the Reserve Flotilla proved its usefulness on numerous occasions. To the younger officer Sims once wrote, 'Your cruise is convincing the principal dignitaries that the Reserve is the real thing.' To this compliment he added a philosophical comment on the length of time it had taken to convince the principal dignitaries. 'My experience with reform has been — first they say it is impossible. Then they say it is impractical. Finally they say, "But that is just what we have been telling you all the time."' [9]

For most of the three years Sims was in command the Destroyer Flotilla was taken up with the peacetime routine. There were endless manoeuvres, alone and with the big ships. There were regular target practices with guns and torpedoes. Unusual records were established with the latter; a tribute to the industry and ability of J. V. Babcock. There were the short cruises from Guantanamo to the coast of Massachusetts. Only once was this schedule varied by the not very stern necessities of armed conflict. In 1914 our troops engaged the guerrilla bands of Mexico and the destroyers went down to lie off the coast near Tampico. It was dreary and unexciting patrol work for the most part and Sims wrote home jeeringly of 'this grapejuice war,' 'this unfermented campaign.' The greatest annoyance of the whole thing was that it prevented him from returning home for the birth of his last daughter, Anne, in February, 1914.

The achievements of the Flotilla were substantial; not a few were of permanent value. But Sims himself would have been the first to deny that he alone was responsible for the success of his command. Knox had much to do with the development of the destroyer doctrine; Babcock was chiefly responsible for building up the new torpedo tactics; Pratt, the Chief of Staff, with his wide knowledge and sound training, was a constant source of inspiration and wise advice. The essence of the conference system was that every man was given the opportunity to contribute to

---

[9] This development of the Reserve Flotilla was another product of Sims' work at Newport. He may well have gotten the idea from his Chief of Staff, Commander W. V. Pratt, who made a study of the subject while attached to the War College Staff. Sims in 1914 delivered a lecture to the officers of the Reserve Fleet. The main outline of this talk had been made by Pratt. Entitled 'What Should be the Relations Between the Battle Fleet and the Reserve Fleet,' it was printed in *N.I.P.*, May–June, 1914.

the common success. So fixed was Sims' belief in the value of this system that he even invited radio operators into the discussions. Upon one occasion he was rewarded for including these enlisted men by a suggestion from one of them which solved a most difficult communications problem. It must therefore be remembered that the remarkable accomplishments of the Flotilla were the work of many hands. But equally it should be borne in mind that the coordination of the separate efforts without which success was impossible was the work of Sims.

During the World War when some spectacular exploit such as the attack on Zeebrugge took place, admiring friends used to write Sims that they could discern in such operations the 'Sims touch.' Touch, as so used, implies the existence of something accidental and involuntary; some flair that permits certain men to cut through the rules and regulations which govern human conduct; some illuminating intuition beside which the mind appears painfully slow and pedestrian. The 'Sims touch' was not specifically naval or professional; it applied more generally to his leadership of men. Upon this leadership rested the success of the conference system and of the Flotilla itself.

In one of his chiselled aphorisms Napoleon suggested that men are led by trifles. It was upon the foundation of a thousand trifles that Sims built the structure of his command. Every afternoon in the cabin of the *Birmingham* he had a pot of tea with his staff. The exercise that was an inevitable part of his day's routine he took in the company of as many officers as he could persuade to join him. When the Fleet lay in Guantanamo or Guacanayabo, the 'Hungry Gulf,' they would walk together; at sea they played shuffleboard together, and always they talked and chaffed together. Whenever there was an occasion it was a great occasion. When J. K. Robison, who commanded the *Dixie*, was detached in 1914 there was a party. A parade of lifeboats decked out in gaudy colors and bearing affectionately insolent signs rowed round the mother ship while officers and men cheered. In the evening there was a dinner and a cake and, of course, poems. When the 'only Jakie' went overside 'there wasn't a dry eye in the house.' By these intimate, simple associations the Flotilla was bound together.

Sometimes the little incidents carried more point. One of the men in command of a destroyer was a very efficient, conscientious officer whose only fault was an inability to accept a refusal as the first and only answer to his requests. Once, after the ships had been kept at sea for an extended period, he tried persistently to get permission to go to Norfolk. His reason was a good one; that the morale of his crew after so long a period of arduous work would be improved by liberty ashore. But permission for such a visit could not be given to one destroyer without giving it to all. This Sims was unwilling to do, since some of the vessels had not finished their work. After some days of discussion the officer, quite legitimately, obtained permission to go part way to his objective, Hampton Roads, to get his gunsights corrected. From Hampton Roads he sent off a wire containing a long list of necessary repairs which could only be made at the navy yard at Norfolk. He closed his message with the question, 'Shall I proceed to Norfolk or remain at present anchorage?' Sims replied, 'Yes,' to the officer, who in mystification sent back his original request. To this Sims replied, 'No.' By nightfall the truant had returned.[10]

Such things were good for the spirit of the individual, but Sims could also bolster the morale of the whole organization. This ability was an important part of his success, for work with destroyers while exciting is likewise frequently arduous and unpleasant. The little ships provide only the most cramped quarters for officers and men; they are so fast and small that in rough weather navigation is sometimes difficult; in high seas they are most uncomfortable. Upon one memorable occasion observers from the battleships were stationed on the destroyers through one rough night during which a search and attack problem was played out. To the delight of the Flotilla almost all the men from the big ships were seasick and unable to give the Commander-in-Chief any information about the activities aboard the destroyers. Men who worked constantly under such conditions must rely greatly upon the encouragement and support of their leader.

One dark and very rough night the destroyers were engaged in a search and attack problem against the Fleet off Guantanamo.

[10] There are so many fine stories about the Flotilla it has been very difficult to select the best. For those included here I am indebted to many officers who served under Sims at this time. In particular, I should like to mention the remarkable letter, really an essay on Sims and leadership, written by J. V. Babcock to T. B. Kittredge, April 17, 1929.

The conditions of wind and weather worked constantly against success. One can guess at the despair of the individual commanders as the hours wore on. Each was alone in the black night 'unable to see because of spray and the occasional rain, unable to stand without clinging for long hours to the bridge for support; dependent for knowledge of the degree to which he was playing his part as a team member upon the few laconic messages which were addressed to him.' Over a wide expanse of stormy water the destroyers were attempting to make contact with the enemy and to collect enough information to allow Sims to describe the enemy formation in preparation for an attack.

On the *Birmingham* there was more comfort, but an equal despair. In Sims' cabin, brightly lighted and warm, shut away from wind and rain, the staff officers lay on the floor studying a chart. They were trying to decide the latest moment at which an order for concentration upon the 'enemy' could be made before the daylight hours set in; but the decision was made difficult by the fact that it depended upon an accurate knowledge of the position of the 'enemy' and the formation of the opposing fleet. This information the staff did not possess because the destroyers had been unable to supply the Flagship with adequate information. In disgust the officers on the *Birmingham* studied the apparent situation as it had been plotted on the chart. Ruefully they looked upon an enemy formation that appeared like nothing so much 'as a sweet potato at a country fair.' It was, in fact, a discouraging moment; and time was running out.

In a corner of the cabin, in a large armchair, Sims sat, as he had sat since the beginning of the problem, reading a book. About two o'clock, when his staff was bewildered by its lack of knowledge, he looked up and suggested to his Flag Lieutenant that he broadcast to the officers, 'Well done, Flotilla, keep it up.' The Lieutenant 'could see no point in the order' in view of the existing circumstances. He was amazed to discover later at the conference which followed the problem that it had produced the encouragement necessary to carry out the manoeuvre successfully. Sims had offered his praise at the psychological moment when men's spirits were burning low.

By such experiences as these the Flotilla was bound together as an organization. The officers learned to operate efficiently as independent units, to set aside their individual desires in the effort to cooperate with all. Above everything they came to understand the necessity of undeviating loyalty to the general mission of the whole. One, perhaps, never did understand the vital necessity of this loyalty. He was a brilliant but unstable officer, apparently the kind of man it is almost impossible to break into double harness. Once, when the Flotilla was engaged in preparing for the annual torpedo practice, each division was assigned general areas in which to prepare on its own initiative for the coming practice. The only specific orders given were that the Flagship should be kept informed of the progress of each ship, while the vicinity of the *Birmingham* was to be the rendezvous of the vessels when they were not engaged in practice. The officer in question took his command up a near-by river and granted liberty to the crew. Returning home the ship struck bottom in leaving the river, damaging her propeller so badly that she had to proceed to dry dock. When Sims heard about the incident, he immediately wired to Washington recommending the detachment of the commanding officer. A tempest of conflicting opinion was stirred up. Officers pleaded with Sims to recall his recommendation; some volunteered to appear for their colleague. He was deaf to their arguments. He even refused to interview the officer of the damaged destroyer, who was eventually detached. Sims made clear the reasons for his conduct — the offender had deceived his superior and had proved himself capable of disloyalty to the plans of the Flotilla. Trust was the basis of the whole organization; any indication of untrustworthiness, no matter how small, could not be condoned.

The detached officer proved his mettle to his Commander and his colleagues. Upon returning to the Flotilla, just before his final departure, he paid a call on the Flagship. In his dress uniform and sword he was piped aboard while the side boys stood at attention. He presented himself to his Commanding Officer, thanked him for the opportunity he had had of serving with him, told him how greatly he appreciated all he had learned in the Flotilla, and departed.

Such an unhappy incident as this occurs in any organization. It was the only disturbing episode in Sims' relationship with his officers. Indeed, in considering the Flotilla one's mind turns inevitably, and not presumptuously, to Nelson and his 'band of brothers.' In the days before the battle of the Nile the great Englishman held his 'school for captains' on the quarterdeck of the *Vanguard*. There, in the bright summer weather of the Mediterranean, through discussion and conference the officers composed their doctrine. Through constant association, talk, and practice the men became familiar with one another's habits and characteristics; they were knit together by affection and understanding into a team. Nelson granted wide initiative to his subordinates and inspired their loyalty to the common mission of his Fleet. So familiar did his officers become with his own plans and so loyal were they to them that communication between the various units of the Fleet was reduced in time of war to a minimum.[11] The famous last signal at Trafalgar, 'the order of sailing is the order for battle,' was made possible only because the men knew each other and their commander so well. This was Nelson's system, long remembered and praised because of the Nile and Trafalgar; but it was likewise in large measure the system used by Sims, who was denied dramatic vindication of his methods in a trial by battle.

This resemblance between the two should not escape notice, but it also cannot obscure the fact that Sims was always and primarily himself. To certain observers this man who was quite without fear was not at times above reproach. One of these was the Commander-in-Chief of the Fleet, Rear Admiral Frank Friday Fletcher, who in 1914 and 1915 wrote two fitness reports of a critical nature about Sims. A fitness report is of tremendous significance on an officer's record, for it contains the judgment which a superior officer has placed upon his work and ability. Whenever the marks or comments indicate dissatisfaction, the

[11] Dudley W. Knox, 'The Great Lesson From Nelson for Today,' *N.I.P.*, March–April, 1914. In this essay Knox sets forth the following elements of Nelson's 'method': Education, Training, Indoctrination, Inspiration of Loyalty, Giving of Initiative, Formulation and Dissemination of Plan, Stimulation of Morale. In discussing the loyalty of Nelson's officers Knox says: 'Now, making all due allowance for a generous, charitable and impulsive nature, it can scarcely be fairly maintained that he was oblivious to the *military* value of stimulating the personal loyalty of his subordinates, nor that to some degree he did not do so studiously and deliberately. ... It is certainly true that the enthusiastic support given to Nelson's plans, even making due allowance for their excellence, was unusually great, and was no doubt colored by loyalty to his person.'

Navy Regulations require the reporting senior to inform his subordinate of the reasons for his criticism.

In September, 1914, and in April, 1915, Admiral Fletcher sent in his comments upon the Commander of the Flotilla. In general he found that Sims was an unusually able officer, but on both reports he added his personal impression that Sims was 'careless as to facts, premises, and conclusions,' and that he was 'less efficient in carrying out the plans of higher authority than upon independent duty.' The Bureau of Navigation allowed the first report to go through unquestioned, but a friend of Sims' caught the second one and suggested to the Chief of the Bureau that it ought to be referred to Sims, since its comments indicated dissatisfaction on the part of Admiral Fletcher. When this was done, his superior's criticisms were, for the first time, brought to Sims' attention. Frankly amazed, he demanded that the Commander-in-Chief must either alter his opinion or send the report to him for comment before filing it officially with the Department. Sims, in making this demand, used the very strong argument that no superior should be allowed to make a criticism of a subordinate without citing specific reasons for his conclusions. The report was returned to Fletcher, who kept it for two weeks before qualifying his previous statements with the words, 'but not to an unsatisfactory degree.' [12]

This satisfied the Bureau of Navigation. The matter was dropped officially, though Sims retorted that it placed him in the position of the unwed mother who defended herself with the observation that her baby was very little, so little that 'it was not a baby to an unsatisfactory degree.' He won his case on the question of the mechanics of the report by forcing Admiral Fletcher to alter his comments to such an extent that the Department could take no cognizance of them officially. Yet the problem of why the Commander-in-Chief made his remarks at all remains to be considered.

Sims believed that his superior had attempted, by unfair means, to discredit him officially. He knew, of course, that Admiral Fletcher had appeared before the Investigating Committee in 1908 in support of Capps and Converse. This in itself branded him as 'an enemy.' He knew, too, that the Commander-

[12] Copies of these reports are in the Sims papers.

in-Chief had refused to mention any specific information to support his claims, and he believed that this was true only because such information could not be obtained. He remained convinced that Fletcher had acted in this case only from the least admirable of motives, while he himself was innocent of any of the charges brought against him.

There can be no doubt that Sims honestly held his point of view, but there can be equally little doubt that he was mistaken. Behind these fitness reports lies a tangle of personal and professional prejudice, difficult, perhaps impossible, entirely to unravel. The two men involved had little in common; in many of the controversies that had taken place in the service they had found themselves on opposing sides. Fletcher was a sound, respected officer, who was less interested in problems of tactics than in those of material, with which he had had most of his previous experience. With this kind of superior, whose virtues he not infrequently mistook for vices simply because they opposed his own, Sims could rarely cooperate. On personal grounds, therefore, some friction could have been expected.

A more fertile source of disagreement can be found in the discussions the two had over professional problems. Whenever Sims disagreed with his Commander-in-Chief, there is reason to believe that he pressed home his point without much consideration for the older man. One officer, a friend of Sims' who was sometimes present at these conferences, recalls that Sims 'would speak and argue loudly and almost contemptuously to the evident disgust and discomfort of the others present.' Admiral Fletcher's Chief of Staff remembers that 'there was a feeling of dissatisfaction on board the fleet flagship with Sims for his lack of loyal cooperation with his Commander-in-Chief.'

Against such a background as this it is easier to understand the critical comments made by Admiral Fletcher. But apparently he had one special incident in mind, a night search and attack made by the destroyers, when he wrote his remarks. At this distance, and in the absence of any official report, it is impossible to give full details of the action. Men on the staffs of both Sims and Fletcher remember enough, however, to reveal the nature of the manoeuvre in fairly clear outline. The result, at least, of the search and attack is unquestioned. The destroyers found

the Fleet with ease and actually hit a good many battleships with
dead torpedoes. Unfortunately, Sims and Fletcher arrived at
opposite conclusions about the meaning of the results. The latter
held that the destroyers had won by the use of tactics that could
not have been employed in actual war. They could not, in his
opinion, drive home their attack in the face of 'an inferno of
gunfire' from the enemy fleet. Sims on the other hand maintained that his destroyers certainly could do so. Here was a
sharp difference of opinion complicated by the fact that the truth
of neither view could then be demonstrated in actual war.
Fletcher, convinced of the justice of his position, apparently decided that his subordinate was 'careless as to facts and conclusions.' Over this matter a discussion between the two took place
in a conference at which the staffs of both were present. Sims,
in striking words, directly contradicted his superior to the delight
of his own men. When Admiral Fletcher sought to close the conference with the remark that the success of the Flotilla 'depended
upon more than could be expected of human nature,' Sims arose
and said that, 'if he thought for a moment that any officer or man
in the Flotilla would hesitate from motives of mental fear to drive
to their decisive conclusion any adopted Flotilla plans to which
they were committed, he would consider himself wholly unjusti-
fied in holding his commission as their Chief.' [13]

It should, in this connection, be clearly understood that Sims
on his feet before a group of men was quite different from Sims
on paper. In a remarkable letter to his Commander-in-Chief he
took issue in measured and respectful terms with some of Fletcher's conclusions after another problem had been played out.[14] In
a memorandum composed at this time he said: 'Doubtless both
the officers of the battleship fleet and of the flotilla were at times
inclined by enthusiasm to claim more efficiency for their particular branch than was their due.... Doubtless each side considered the other as more or less careless in the handling of what
is considered facts, and in the formation of conclusions based
thereon. In this connection, I would specially invite attention
to the fact that in all such cases, without exception, the flotilla's
facts and conclusions were not mine personally, but were the

[13] Babcock to Kittredge, April 17, 1929.
[14] W. S. S. to Commander-in-Chief, U.S. Atlantic Fleet, November 11, 1915.

result of thorough discussions in conference of all members of the flotilla staff. . . . I am informed that this conference method of all commanding officers was not employed, or very frequently employed, in the battleship fleet.'

There is another troubling question in this night search and attack. Some evidence exists to support the idea that the destroyers made such short work of the battleships because Sims deliberately disobeyed the rules of the problem as set down by Fletcher. This view is vouched for by the secretary of the Commander-in-Chief who was with Fletcher throughout this period and who handled all his official correspondence.[15] There is excellent reason to feel that Sims believed the conditions imposed by his Chief were 'arbitrary' and 'artificial.' That he actually disregarded them is far harder to accept, despite the unquestioned integrity of Fletcher's secretary.

None of the officers on Admiral Fletcher's staff remember that Sims violated the prescribed conditions. None of the officers on his own staff and in the Flotilla who have been consulted remember that he did. Many feel strongly that he was absolutely incapable of disobeying the direct orders of his superior in a matter of this sort. In the face of such evidence it is impossible to maintain with much conviction that Sims wilfully disregarded Admiral Fletcher's rules. Moreover, such a thing would have been entirely inconsistent with his past career and his character. Irregular methods he sometimes employed, but he never resorted to disobedience to accomplish his ends.

It is still possible, however, that Admiral Fletcher believed that such was the case. It would have been quite natural for him to assume that the closing action of the destroyers, which he believed impossible in actual battle, was a violation of the conditions. At all events, it seems clear that the Commander-in-Chief was not activated by the hostile motives attributed to him by his subordinate. Rather he seems to have been anxious to express his own dissatisfaction in such a way as not to harm the latter's professional reputation or career. In view of all the circumstances considerable credit must be awarded to him for the part he played.

When all the evidence bearing upon this incident was laid

[15] Memorandum sent to writer by F. F. Fletcher's secretary, November 7, 1940.

before one of Sims' most loyal and discerning friends, he remarked: 'Whether or not the man who wrote the fitness report
knew it, it was a good report. It indicates the source of Sims'
strength. Emphasize it.' The observation referred specifically
to Fletcher's belief that Sims was less efficient as a subordinate
than as an independent commander. With this should be taken
the tribute of Commander Holloway H. Frost, the great authority on the battle of Jutland. 'It might be added,' he says, 'that
night destroyer attacks for many years before 1916 were one of
the favorite operations of the United States Navy. Our destroyers, under the able and inspired leadership of Captain W. S.
Sims, had developed great proficiency in those attacks. As an
Ensign about 1912, this writer distinctly remembers performing
the duties of an assistant torpedo umpire in *U.S.S. Michigan*. It
was my task to determine the torpedo hits made by a destroyer
division on that ship, while steaming as one of a battleship division on a dark night. The attack was conducted in a most im
pressive and effective manner. If the 4th Flotilla [at Jutland]
had been American destroyers on the night of May 31, I am certain that there would have been disaster to either the Germans or
ourselves, probably to both!' [16]

It is by his accomplishments that we should take the measure
of a man. Sims did more with the Flotilla than anyone had ever
done before him. He was a wonderful leader, and leaders can
follow, ordinarily, only themselves. Admiral Fletcher, who later
served on the selection board promoting Sims to flag rank,
apparently understood this and made allowances for it. Sims may
never have completely understood it. It makes no difference. On
the record of the destroyers and his men in peace and in the
Great War he can rest his case.

There was always, as he used to say, more fun this year than
last, but this period of his life must be reckoned as perhaps the

[16] H. H. Frost, *The Battle of Jutland*, Annapolis, 1936, pp. 442–443. The same
thought has occurred to J. V. Babcock *op. cit.*: 'Having had the advantage of that
school [the Flotilla under Sims] I have been fascinated with contemplation of what
might have happened if the "Old Flotilla" could have been in the place of the
British Grand Fleet Destroyers the night of Jutland. We never thought in those
"Old Flotilla" days of taking such simple elements to compose our problems as those
which prevailed at sundown at Jutland, to wit — with every destroyer of the team
within twenty miles of every major enemy ship and in fact having had the centre of
mass of enemy capital ship strength in sight within a few previous hours.'

happiest in a life that was always happy. The theoretical knowledge he had acquired at the War College he put into practice with satisfactory and at times spectacular results. With his command he was doing things that men had said could not be done. Knowledge of this sort is always gratifying, but it is safe to say that his greatest pleasure was in the men with whom he worked. Loyalty to the mission held this group together professionally, but there was an emotional quality in this loyalty that lifted it above allegiance to a plan.

'It was "Sims' Flotilla" — not the officially designated Atlantic Destroyer Flotilla. It was his organization, body and soul — principally in soul. Even down to the enlisted men everyone's constant concern was with the problems and fortunes of the Chief. His problems were their problems. If we had disagreeable duty to perform it was done with sympathy for the "Old Man" — sympathy because he had been confronted with such problems. And is this not true leadership? Can an organization be inspired or fired with enthusiasm and a "will to victory" by abstract motives? and cold orders? In the ultimate analysis the weapons and the forces available to leadership in war are not ships, guns, mines, and torpedoes — but just plain units of human nature. Does not the secret of the success of every great captain lie in the fact that he personified the organization in his own person?' Whatever the nature of that secret, Sims knew all its inner mysteries. Unlike most great captains, he was not called upon at some splendid moment to prove its subtle power by sending men to die, but by its use on the Flotilla he taught a hundred how to live more usefully than they had lived before.

18

1915 - 1917   *The Cheer Up Ship*

Sᴵᴹˢ was detached from the Flotilla on October 25, 1915.
The battleship *Nevada*, his new command, was not commissioned
until the following March. For those five months his days were
filled with the numberless activities which attend the preparation of a big ship for active duty at sea. It will be well to turn
aside from his career during this interval to notice briefly the
changing conditions in the Navy and the world outside. Some of
these changes were a testament to the value of Sims' past activities; some bore directly upon the future of his career.

Three things must be remembered in connection with the
Navy of 1915. There was, first of all, a general spirit of reform
in the air. There was war in Europe. There was a Democratic
Administration in power; more particularly there was Josephus
Daniels as Secretary of the Navy. It would be natural to expect
that the second thing, war in Europe, would condition the nature
of the first; that is, that the lessons of the European war would
be applied to the improvement of our military forces. To a
limited degree this was true, but in the main the administration
of Woodrow Wilson proceeded, until 1916, to act as though the
entire world were at peace. The nature of the reforms within
the Navy was therefore principally determined by the personality
and character of the new Secretary.

Josephus Daniels had been born in North Carolina during the
Civil War. Before 1913 he had devoted a large part of his life
to the rejuvenation of his native section which had been left
prostrate by what the North called Reconstruction. Unlike many

of his neighbors he had not remained content with those memo-ries of a happier and more graceful time handed down by a pre-ceding generation. For thirty years after 1885 he gave expres-sion to his energetic and liberal spirit in the columns of his news-paper at Raleigh. He was one of those who provided the South with the leaven of hope and truth she most needed. At bottom he seems to have shared the humanitarian creed of William Jennings Bryan, for he was firm in his conviction of progress, so-licitous for the fate of the common man, devoted to the tenets of the traditional Christian morality. Something of Bryan's ability with words he had and something, too, of the great commoner's faith in their mass effect. Though he had been little in active political life, he had a politician's resiliency. No man who knew him doubted his natural charm or remained untouched by his graciousness in social intercourse.

In his first report in 1913, Mr. Daniels revealed some of his plans for the United States Navy. He advocated publicly owned oil refineries, powder plants, and armor-plate factories, which would break the strangle-hold of the great private monopolies. He hoped that the Navy might become a 'great university' where men could obtain an academic education. He believed that 'it ought not to be difficult to secure an agreement by which navies will be adequate without being overgrown and without imposing overheavy taxes upon the industry of a nation.' In regard to the building policy he struck a nice balance between those who wanted a small Navy and those who wanted a large one.[1]

It was apparent from this Report that, like so many of his civilian predecessors, Mr. Daniels knew little of the material re-quirements or the spirit of the profession he was directing. This in itself might not have been a bad thing, for the duties of a Secretary are not strictly military. But there was a disturbing absence in this Report of any word to indicate that Mr. Daniels understood the main purpose for which any Navy is established or that he realized the relation of the forces under his command to the nation's foreign policy. A good deal of space was devoted

[1] *Annual Report of the Secretary of the Navy*, 1913. An admirable summary of this Report and of the naval situation at the beginning of the Wilson Administration is given in Sprout, *The Rise of American Naval Power*, pp. 302–311.

to a presentation of the Secretary's enlightened and well-integrated social philosophy which, had it been permitted to operate in the America of 1913, would undoubtedly have produced some admirable results. Mr. Daniels, however, made it clear that he intended to apply it to the United States Navy. It was this intention which revealed a fundamental misconception. A Navy is not, as he apparently thought, a whole society. It is but part of one; a highly organized profession trained to a peculiar end. Since Mr. Daniels' ideas were chiefly social, moral, and economic, they could not easily be applied to an organization essentially military in character. His civilian reforms were sometimes introduced without a proper calculation of their effect on the Navy. He distrusted, quite properly, militarism, so he attempted at certain points to democratize or civilize the Navy, not recognizing that such activity might well endanger the ability of the Navy to defend democracy and civilization.

It was a confusion of ends and means which beset the Secretary and led him into curious situations. On the one hand where the Navy is civil in character he did great good. More than any of his predecessors he recognized the value of the War College, which he supported with energy and courage against its enemies within and beyond the service. More clearly than most he saw the dangers of promotion by seniority and worked, again with vigor and intelligence, to introduce a method of promotion by selection. But where the Navy is military he made mistakes that were sometimes amusing, but more often damaging to the organization. It should be said of Mr. Daniels, however, that he represented the prevailing lay opinion of our military services. If his faults stood out more clearly than in others, it was only because he was in a position to expose his beliefs to public view and because he had the desire and energy, unusual in a Secretary of the Navy, to support his convictions with action.

Early in 1915 a most important piece of legislation came before Congress. The original bill, as introduced by Representative R. P. Hobson, hero of the Spanish-American War, was the culmination of that struggle for a General Staff which had begun around the turn of the century. It will be recalled that after the reports of the Moody-Mahan and Swift Boards, Secretary Meyer established his system of aids patterned upon the recommendations of those two boards. Although this system had been a distinct advance over previous methods of administration, all attempts to give it legal existence had failed. Agitation for a bill creating a General Staff therefore continued. In this movement Sims, almost continually at sea since 1909, played a negligible part, though he followed the efforts of the officers responsible with great interest. Chief among these was Bradley Fiske, the Aid for Operations, who, with several younger officers, was the chief author of Hobson's bill.[2] As first drawn in 1915 this measure provided for a Chief of Naval Operations supplied with fifteen assistants who would be 'responsible for the readiness of the Navy for War and be charged with its general direction.' In effect, this officer with his assistants formed a General Staff empowered to coordinate the work of the bureaus in the great task of military preparation for war.

Opposition immediately developed in Congress. Before the law could be passed, the powers of the Chief of Naval Operations were severely limited. 'Under the direction of the Secretary he was charged with the operations of the Fleet and with the preparation of plans for use in war.' This change of wording cut away much of the value and point of the measure.

The use of the word 'direction' and the specific mention of the Secretary are indications of the fears which beset the opposition. The men in Congress in 1915 as in 1909 were frightened lest they should create a military cabal which would be independent of all civil authority. In Hobson's proposal there lurked, of course, no such danger, for his bill established only a naval officer who was *responsible to the Secretary* for the military preparation of the Fleet for war. Every other large country in the world had some such officer or group of officers to perform this essential duty under the ultimate control of the political authority. But the Congressmen in their ignorance and fear sought to ensure the dominance of the civil authority by making the Chief of Naval Operations powerless over even the independent bureau chiefs. The Secretary himself did nothing to weaken this opposition nor to unravel its confusions which he, in fact, shared. Instead, he took an active part in emasculating the original

[2] A complete summary of Fiske's part in this movement is contained in his *From Midshipman to Rear Admiral*, chapter 36.

legislation and was willing to shoulder the praise for its defeat. In his Report of 1915 he said that the changes were made 'upon my recommendations,' and a year later he added that 'while civilian control, essential in a Republic, has been preserved, responsibility has been placed with the Chief of Naval Operations and the Chiefs of Bureau.' [3]

Fiske and his supporters failed to achieve their full purpose, but they made an important advance in the long journey toward a General Staff. The powers of the Chief of Naval Operations have not, since 1915, been enlarged by law. However, time, custom, and sheer necessity have extended in some measure the coordinating and directing force of the officer holding the position. Though it is impossible to consider the Chief of Naval Operations and the General Board as a General Staff in the sense that the phrase has been used throughout this book, the two acting together have provided the Navy with a better administrative system than existed before 1915.

Sims had played no part in the immediate attempt to obtain a Chief of Naval Operations, but when the revised statute was passed, his name was mentioned to fill the new position. An article in *The Army and Navy Journal* first suggested him. Then from Washington he received a letter from one of his best friends who had assisted in drawing up the original bill. 'I hear your name mentioned nearly every day by naval officers as the logical man to succeed Admiral Fiske in his newly enlarged job. . . . I know you do not want the job. Nevertheless, I hope sincerely that if it is offered you will accept. The Navy needs you very much and are practically united in wanting you here. So much harm could be done should the new chief of N.O. be a reactionary or a weak man that I sincerely hope you will come here and save us from dire extremities. . . . If we are to be saved, we must have somebody who can make the Secretary see daylight.'

It was true that Sims did not want the job. He set forth his reasons to an officer in the Bureau of Navigation who wrote to

[3] Secretary Daniels' views on this subject are set forward at somewhat greater length and in more colorful detail in *Hearings Before the Subcommittee of the Committee on Naval Affairs*, United States Senate, 66th Cong., 2d Session, vol. II, pp. 2279–2287. Among other things he says, '. . . Admiral Fiske and other disciples of the Von Tirpitz school sought to organize the American Navy on the Prussian plan . . .'

him about the new position. The Chief of Naval Operations had no responsibility for the adequacy or condition of the Fleet. He could only 'amuse himself making paper plans for [the Fleet's] use in war. The law as enacted would not justify the Secretary of the Navy even in accepting his advice as to preparing the Navy for war any more than the advice of any other officer.' 'I do not pretend,' he went on, 'to understand why there should be so much opposition to giving the Secretary a military adviser charged with full responsibility to that official for preparing us for war. I picture the new chief seated at a desk, with inadequate assistants, and surrounded by a barbed-wire fence charged with electricity.' With some irony he said that, 'Of course, with the sympathy of a strong Secretary who understood something of military necessities, with the sympathy of all the Department officials, and particularly with the sympathy and understanding of the Committees of Congress something could be accomplished by the unanimous consent of all.' But sympathy is prized by men because it is rare and Sims knew that 'all forces indicated would be against him [the Chief of Naval Operations].'

The Navy had been 'buncoed good and plenty.' Those who said the new law was an entering wedge were wrong. 'It's clearly an axe and the new chief and the Navy will get it in the neck.' 'I hope,' he concluded, 'that everyone refuses the post.' He himself was not at this time given the opportunity. When Bradley Fiske departed after a period of continued friction with the Secretary, Captain William Shepherd Benson was named to the newly created position.

Shortly the new Chief of Naval Operations was to call on his old friend for assistance. In September, 1915, while Sims was still with the Flotilla, Benson wrote to Sims that 'Ever since assuming this duty I have felt that I should be more than glad if I could persuade you to accept the detail of Director of Target Practice. . . . As you know there has been considerable criticism of our target practice of late, and the Department feels that if you would accept this duty it would give a new confidence not only to the service but to the country at large that every possible effort was being made to bring the target practice up to the very highest standard.' To this appeal the Chief of the Bureau of Navigation, Victor Blue, added a word of his own.

There was no doubt that our target practice had fallen off since 1909, as Sims had been at pains to point out frequently while he was at sea with the *Minnesota* and the Flotilla, but he was in no mood to accept the invitation of Benson and Blue. In return he wrote to the former on September 10, in the following modest but forceful terms: 'In the first place you are both under a misapprehension as to the part I really played in developing the new system of gunnery training. I did not initiate any part of it. It was taken bodily from Percy Scott.' New methods were of course developed as long-range firing improved, but 'I did not do it. I was never anything of an expert in this question of the development of the details of gunnery training.'

'If you will look,' he suggested, 'at Ridley McLean's record you will find a letter in which I protested with all the energy of which I was capable against any other man to succeed me. He was the brains of my office. . . . Instead, the Department made a clean sweep of my office and put in a man who was fine in all respects except he not only lacked experience, but was fundamentally unsound on basic principles of training.'

'Though I protested,' Sims continued, 'to the extent of being reprimanded by the Department for the unofficial energy of my language, the short range [essential practice] was abolished and the Gunnery Instructions [written by McLean and Sims in 1903] withdrawn and destroyed.'

This failure on the part of the Department to observe the essential and fundamental training methods had caused all the difficulty. Without preliminary short-range practice it was impossible to train individual gunners and to score their individual hits, with the result that competition was impossible and gun-pointers' morale disintegrated. In a letter to Secretary Daniels on July 9, 1916, Sims explained that this mistake was 'due exclusively to naval officers' and that it 'had nothing to do with the administration of the Navy Department.' He was anxious, as he later said, to make clear that his own colleagues and not 'The Democratic party' should be made to carry the blame for this short-sighted attitude. He did not accept Benson's offer, but recommended one of his old friends, C. P. Plunkett, instead. Plunkett received the appointment and justified Sims' belief in him by his fine work as Inspector of Target Practice.

About the time that Benson first wrote to Sims in September, 1915, the latter's aid was requisitioned for two efforts at reform by his old friend Ridley McLean, then Judge Advocate. Certain officers within the Navy had fought on to increase the authority of the Chief of Naval Operations ever since the office had been created in May, 1915. At the end of August McLean sent to him a list of specific powers that he believed ought to be included in the office. Sims replied that it was a mistake to suggest specific things. 'He should be under the Secretary of the Navy — all his authority flows from the latter. He should be charged with the preparation of the Navy for war and should be the only official responsible to him for the integrity of his military advice. The whole matter is of the utmost simplicity. The Powers that Be (or rather the invisible government in the background) understood it perfectly, but don't want it that way, hence the removal of all backbone from the original bill. . . . The law as it stands means nothing, the enemy attended to that.'

By this time Sims was an old campaigner and there was in these words no clarion call to action as there might have been ten years before. Yet his interest had not waned. It was simply that he had been to the wars too often not to be able to differentiate between the possible and the impossible. He would not waste his strength on the latter, thus jeopardizing his chances of obtaining the former. He knew that the original bill was sound, but he also knew that it could never be passed in the present state of political and civilian feeling. A sage comment was therefore all that he vouchsafed to his former assistant.

In this reply to McLean he discussed also another question raised by the younger officer, who had sent him an elaborate plan for promotion by selection based upon the method the two had worked out years before. The system established in 1899, the 'Plucking Board' which eliminated the least desirable officers, had not been entirely satisfactory. It was obvious that a change was required.

To McLean, Sims wrote as follows: 'About a hundred years ago I began to take an interest in naval personnel bills, but as soon as I realized that the object was: (1) To increase the efficiency of the commissioned personnel and at the same time, (2) To present a bill that would meet the approval of the majority of naval officers, I lost interest. It is years since I have read more of a personnel bill than just enough to see that, as usual, the effort was to improve the Navy and please all hands.' 'History contains no record of the human race ever having devised a softer snap than the system of promotion in our Navy.' Until human nature changed, the Navy would not change. Most men needed a 'fire built under them' or the 'Message to Garcia was an absurdity.' The majority of men do not like to work, do not like responsibility, and dread an uncertain future, and yet 'The Department tries to get them to approve a system that will make their future dependent upon getting a move on and demonstrating their fitness. You might as well,' he concluded sadly, 'get schoolboys to vote for longer and heavier birch rods.'

Promotion should not be determined by a board of high-ranking officers who were necessarily unacquainted with the personality and fitness of the many junior officers; it should be based upon selections made by all the officers of the grade next above. 'Years ago you and I worked this all out.'

To get this adopted, he suggested to McLean that each officer should be asked if he favored promotion by selection and that his reply should be filed with his record. All those who covertly and unofficially opposed the system would thus be forced to express their official favor. With this support filed away, it would then be possible to go ahead and get a desirable bill. But he ended on an unfamiliar note: 'I have written volumes on the subject. . . . I am a little tired of it, for I have little faith that anything will ever be accomplished. I have a feeling the Department has never been seriously interested.'

Perhaps, after all, he was losing his fire. As he said at the end of the letter he was 'getting old.' For twenty years he had set the pace for younger men and now at fifty-eight, with only four more years remaining, his future seemed chiefly behind him.[4] It was about this time that he wrote asking if he might have the War College if the opportunity offered itself. That he was convinced of the value of the War College is perfectly obvious, but that he was also aware that it was removed from the central and immediate sources of power within the Navy is equally appar-

---

[4] Flag officers retired at sixty-two until an act in 1916 extended the age to sixty-four.

ent. The truth seems to be that at this time he was discouraged
at the prospects for further reform and weary of the trafficking
that went on in Washington. He may never have been a typical
member of his own profession, but he was by temperament a salt-
water sailor. He recognized that he could never mix with the
oil of politicians within and beyond the service.

McLean kept after his old friend, but only when Sims heard,
somewhat to his surprise, that Mr. Daniels was interested in the
subject did he take action. In December he wrote to McLean
that his plan was all right except that he ought to get an official
letter from all officers on the question of promotion before
attempting a bill — because 'I still fear underground opposition.' Also he believed that it was better to have the opinion of
the whole service on a particular man than just the opinion of the
officers under whom he had served, as McLean desired. 'A
lieutenant who has danced with the horse-faced daughter of an
admiral for a couple of years at a Navy Yard and then been flag
lieutenant with him for a couple of years would probably be put
number one on the list.'

In October, 1915, he had been to Washington and had
'talked things over with him [Secretary Daniels] with *entire
frankness*. I urged him very strongly to go into Mack's scheme of
promotion by selection, *very thoroughly*. I told him that if he
could put this through it would be remembered long after anything else he might do would be forgotten. He seemed to understand it very well and himself offered some arguments in favor
of it. He was impressed by the letter I wrote Mack on the
subject.' [5]

The Secretary's interest bore good fruit. Franklin D. Roosevelt, the Assistant Secretary of the Navy, was made chairman
of a board to investigate the personnel. At the express wish of
the Secretary a method of promotion by selection was recommended to Congress by the Board. McLean was elated and
wrote to Sims, 'as a result of my paper, combined with your
strong representations to the Secretary when you were down
here, the Secretary made them rewrite their former report and
insert a scheme of selection.' [6] The scheme was not what either

[5] W. S. S. to Mrs. Sims, October 22, 1915.
[6] Ridley McLean to W. S. S., February 28, 1916.

322

McLean or Sims had recommended, for it established a selection board of nine Rear Admirals who made all the promotions. Both Sims and McLean believed that such a Board would have to act on insufficient knowledge. Still it was an advance. McLean, though disappointed, was ready to embrace the plan with open arms while Sims wrote less ecstatically to Reuterdahl, that 'The personnel part of the bill is punk. It is butt end to, but bad as this present scheme is, it is important. The necessity for the principle has been recognized.'

By 1916 it was possible for the men interested in reform to find some tangible rewards for their long labors. Only Reuterdahl refused to believe that progress had been made. He poured out his dissatisfaction in a magazine article that failed to arouse the public's indignation as had 'The Needs of Our Navy' in the great days of 1908. Sims comforted his old friend. 'Of course, you are not satisfied with an article unless the immediate result is that several people are shot, or several cabinet officers commit suicide, etc.' In another letter he sought to soften Reuterdahl's harsh criticism of the condition of affairs within the Department.

'There is,' he began with strange mellowness, 'doubtless some truth on both sides. It is not the same now as it was in the first part of the Administration, when the effort apparently was to make political capital out of "prohibition," the "Navy a great University," the Secretary the "father of the oppressed enlisted men," etc., all combined with the suppression of the general staff principle, a gradual return to the old bureau system to please Congress, and a suppression of the facts concerning the real condition of the Navy, target practice, etc. All this went on up to the time that the firing out of Fiske made the situation clear enough to the public to bring down a regular storm of criticism.' Following this there had been 'a very real effort to get on the Military Efficiency Bandwagon.'

For Reuterdahl's benefit he listed several improvements in the state of the Navy. Benson as Chief of Naval Operations had been given power 'they swore would never be given to any officer.' Fleet training had been put directly under the supervision of the Department with the result that any Commander-in-Chief had to make good. The War College had been assured of continuous large classes and of the cooperation of the Fleet in the study of strategy and tactics. If the method of promotion was still improper, the sound principle of selection had been accepted in the new law. The one disturbing note was the lack of confidence, amounting to 'contempt,' within the service, for the Administration. Despite this Sims believed that 'these are real reforms even though forced from outside. Fiske really should have credit for them.'

On such a note of generosity ended this fair and honest letter. Fiske had had much to do with the changes made in the Navy. He had stuck to his guns at the risk of his career in his altercations with the Secretary. By retiring from his position as Aid for Operations in 1915, he had ensured the maintenance of his principles. Yet it does not detract in any way from the credit due him to place him beside Luce, Taylor, Sims, Key, Fullam, and all the others, who had for years led the long march of reform.

Reform in a democracy is a tedious business. The partial victories Sims described to Reuterdahl were the result of the drawn battles of earlier years. Much had been accomplished when he sent his letter to his old friend in January, 1916. How much there was yet left to do he did not learn until fourteen months later, in April, 1917.

Return can now be made to Sims' own career. On October 25, 1915, he left the Flotilla, but several months intervened before he could take his new ship to sea. Throughout most of this time he was at the Fore River Yard in Quincy, Massachusetts, where the last touches were being put on the *Nevada* before her commissioning. While there, he was called to Washington early in March, 1916, to appear before the House Naval Committee which was holding hearings on an appropriation bill. It was very pleasant compared with his previous experience in 1908, for he was allowed to talk freely about the subjects that interested him.[7] Of the need for a stronger Chief of Naval Operations he said: 'The Chief of Naval Operations, as I understand his position now, is charged with the responsibility of preparing the Navy for war, but I do not know anybody that he can give a

[7] His testimony appears in *Hearings Before the Committee on Naval Affairs,* House of Representatives, 64th Congress, 1st Session, vol. 2, pp. 2601–2769.

legal order to. He can give an order to no one at all. He has to write the order and take it to the Secretary and get the Secretary to actually put his signature on it. He has the Secretary's authority — by Naval Regulations that may be changed at will — but no authority under law. He would correspond to the Chief of Staff of a navy abroad if you simply give him by law the same kind of authority that you have already given to the Chiefs of Bureaus, but the authority, of course, should be inclusive over the Chiefs of Bureaus and everybody else.'

Of the War College he talked at some length, emphasizing its importance and praising the Secretary's interest in it. 'I said, "I want to ask you [Mr. Daniels] some questions," and he said, "Let it go." I asked him what he thought was the relative importance of any particular battleship in the Fleet as compared with the War College. "Well," he said, "I think the War College is more important." I said, "Do you mean that?" and he said, "Yes, I mean it." I said, "Then when you go back to Washington at least put it on the plane of a battleship; establish a complement for the War College, in consultation with the President of the War College, and then write an order to the Chief of the Bureau of Navigation, and tell him to keep the War College filled, even if he has to diminish some unimportant ship's complement," and he went back and did it and the College is booming now. . . .'

His testimony of a hundred and fifty printed pages contained most of his views about the Navy since 1900. If the treatment was extended ('I am like the parrot who talked too much'), most of his listeners were not sorry. His ideas were clear; his statements both modest and balanced; his talk as always was entertaining. From time to time he wandered back into the past, and if he showed his scars from former wars with considerable relish, he also displayed a winning detachment. Something of the flavor of the elder statesman crept into his account of the tense days on the China Station. The things he talked of seemed old, unhappy, and far-off and the battles long ago.

> *Capt. Sims:* . . . I wish to make it clear that these mistakes and the failure to rectify them were the fault exclusively of naval officers.
>
> *Mr. Butler:* And not of the civilians in the department?

Capt. Sims: Absolutely not.

Mr. Callaway: We have been told that naval officers never have any faults.

Capt. Sims: That is all right, but they are made out of the same kind of stuff that Congressmen are; they are just the run of the mine, and they are subject to the same human impulses; but the trouble in our Navy Department has been, if you want to go into it, that all of the human impulses were working against the efficiency of the Navy with the organization we had. It is a great deal better now, and things are going much better; but where we formerly had a number of bureaus and no Chief of Naval Operations, and one of those bureaus designed a gun, and another one designed a ship, and I or any officer as captain of a ship, or as an officer on a ship, wrote a criticism, that criticism went to the Secretary of the Navy, and his clerk looks at it and says, 'That is construction; that goes in chute No. 1,' and down it goes to the construction department. Now, the head of that department, or bureau, is the official adviser of the Secretary of the Navy, by law, as to whether that criticism is just or not, and you simply could not get it. There was no way you could get by it. Criticism after criticism came in, and you can imagine what the man who was responsible for it would say. He had designed the appliance criticised, and naturally he believed in it. As soon as we found out we could not shoot, that criticism was sent in, and I reported the defects of the open turrets, etc., to the department. I was a young officer out in China — a young lieutenant — young in grade though not in years.

Mr. Oliver: About 1904?

Capt. Sims: 1900 and 1901. I had been naval attaché for four years in Paris and St. Petersburg, and was sent to the China Station and from there made those criticisms, but they could not 'get by' in Washington, not because the bureau chiefs were not good men, but because they were human. When you go up against a stone wall like that, up against the man who has designed a thing, it is hard to make that man believe that he is wrong. They almost never got by. That is all there is about it. I do not know whether this is interesting to you, because it is more or less personal.

Mr. Butler: Yes, it is. I want to know how much blame I am to take for this.

Capt. Sims: You are not to blame at all. Any organization that is made up that way, will work that way. In the first place, a man has got to defend himself, and if he is to be the judge, it is difficult to convince him that he is wrong.

Mr. Butler: If the Secretary of the Navy had a big enough club, could he not get by?

Capt. Sims: The Secretary of the Navy seldom knows anything about it.

Mr. Callaway: Explain, Captain, why it could not get by.

Capt. Sims: Because here is the Secretary of the Navy, a civilian— you, for example — and let us take the case of a criticism from a young whipper-snapper of an officer, out in China — a lieutenant — and he says, 'this ship is wrongly designed, in these following respects:' Now, that does not mean anything to you, necessarily. You send for the man who designed that ship; you have no one else to send for, because Congress gave you that man as your official adviser in his specialty, and if you take the advice of anyone else, you do it at your own risk. Therefore you send for the constructor, or the chief of the Bureau of Ordnance, as the case may be, and you say, 'look what this young fellow says. How about that?' Then they will take it, and later they will write you a letter and say, 'there is nothing to it,' and back go the papers into the file.

Mr. Callaway: I understood you to say that they never got to the Secretary of the Navy?

Capt. Sims: No; I said it seldom got by — got by the bureau chiefs.

Mr. Callaway: Do you mean to say that any civilian would not see that the objections that you have made here were potent?

Capt. Sims: It depends upon how clever the other people are in presenting their side of the case. You have seen that done many a time. Let me show you the difficulty about the thing. I was young and innocent at that time, and I supposed, of course, that when such things were brought to the department's attention like that, they would jump at the chance to rectify them, and it was not until some time afterwards that I found not only that there was nothing being done, but that there was nobody in the Navy Department who had heard about those reports, and I wrote a great many of them from China, and I used deliberately rather unofficial language, because I wanted to tear something loose, but I saw later that it was an entire failure. I, therefore, wrote a letter to the President of the United States.

The Chairman: When was that?

Capt. Sims: 1902 — over the head of the Commander-in-Chief of the China Station, and over the head of the Navy Department. Now, that is the rankest possible kind of insubordination.[8]

Mr. Butler: What happened to you?

Capt. Sims: That is what I am going to tell you. That is the rankest kind of insubordination, but, according to my idea, when a situation like that arises, where you know that you are absolutely right, and where there is nothing doing, complete military subordination becomes cowardice. I conceived it to be my duty to take the chance; I did not know the President at all at that time. He went into the matter with the Navy Department, particularly in reference to target practice, and we were extremely inefficient in that respect at that time. The British Navy was then beginning to do some wonderful stunts. After investigating the thing, I was telegraphed to come home from China, and I was placed in charge of the target practice. Now, I do not claim any credit for what resulted, but we immediately bounded into the air with our shooting, because I brought home the ideas that were originated by that wonderful man, Vice Admiral Sir Percy Scott, and since that time we have gone along quite well in target practice, but I will come to that later. I have gotten away off the line I started on, how those defects got into those ships.

When his testimony before the Committee was concluded, he returned to the *Nevada* which was at last ready for sea. The ship was, as Blue had written, the 'newest and finest' in the Fleet. With her length of 575 feet and her displacement of 27,500 tons, she was far larger than the *Minnesota*. Her main battery of ten fourteen-inch guns was one of the most powerful afloat. Six of these rifles were mounted in two triple turrets, the first of their kind in the Navy. Altogether she carried twenty-four guns of all sizes, and was capable of taking up action at upwards of thirty thousand yards. The new oil-burning engines, another innovation, drove her through the water at a speed of over twenty knots on her trials.

In 1883, Sims had gone to sea on the nineteen-hundred-ton third-rate ship-rigged sloop-of-war, *Swatara*. In her mixed batteries there had been six nine-inch muzzle-loading smoothbores, one eight-inch pivot rifle, one 5.3 breech-loading rifle, one three-

---

[8] In justice to Admiral Remey, it should be pointed out that Sims, in the excitement of testifying, neglected to mention the tremendous support which Remey had given to Sims. Remey, in fact, knew of the letter to Roosevelt, and took no action against his subordinate.

inch howitzer, one half-inch **Gatling.** The horizontal back-acting compound engine could push her wooden, unarmored hull through the water at about six knots. Almost a half-century before Trafalgar, the *Victory* had been built, yet the span between the *Swatara* and the *Nevada* was only thirty-three years; so great was the revolution wrought by steel and steam and rifled cannon.

By the time Sims took over the big ship, the last touches had been put upon his art of command. He had worked out a system of administration which was printed up in a little looseleaf book so that any 'necessary changes could be made.' 'I did not,' he wrote to McLean, 'have much to do with details, but specified that the basic principles of operation should be to pass responsibility and initiative down the line and to employ the conference method which worked so well on the Flotilla. Each branch makes a practice of consulting (conferring with) subordinates. This brings out many useful suggestions and makes a team out of the gang.'

It was a fine gang he had; some of them he had taken with him from the Flotilla and some, like his Executive 'Tommy' Tompkins, were friends newly made. Every afternoon he had tea, which he looked upon as a military necessity, with his officers. When he found to his dismay that the junior officers did not have the proper equipment to serve tea, he wrote promptly off to the Paymaster General. 'Our Junior Officers are serving tea in a pitcher or a three-inch cartridge case, cream in a toothbrush mug. This is not proper for a first-class battleship. Assuming, therefore, that you are an advocate of adequate preparedness, can you allow us enough for tea tools? Peary drank tea at every meal on the dash for the Pole and I take it every afternoon. It is the Warrior's beverage.'

But it was not only the ship's officers he was interested in. Like most Captains in our service, he was solicitous for the enlisted men. Shortly after the *Nevada* put to sea, he gathered the crew together and 'made them a little speech.' 'Why are we here?' he began, and answered that their purpose was to make an efficient fighting ship and an efficient unit of the fighting Fleet. Carefully he explained the relationship of the men to their officers and of the officers to the Navy Department, of the Department to the Government and of the Government to the country. 'Loyalty' meant 'doing your best with hands and brains to help along the man above you and to carry out the orders you get.' Loyalty to the petty officers signified a loyalty to all the branches of the hierarchy up to the President of the United States. Without it no ship was efficient. The twin of loyalty was initiative. Every man's assistance was required, and anyone's suggestions were always welcomed.

Into the keeping of every member of the crew was given the reputation of the *Nevada*. 'She is our ship, say "we" and "our," for she belongs to us. When you go ashore on liberty remember that we are all in this together.' There would be as much liberty as possible, but he would call the men's attention to several things about the responsibilities they assumed when they went ashore. There was first of all the possibility of returning late, either deliberately or because one was willing to take the risk of missing the last car or of sleeping through the alarm clock. For the deliberate offender, there was no excuse and punishment was severe. For the man who gambled on the last clear chance and lost, there would be waiting the punishment of all unlucky gamblers.

There were other dangers in liberty and the greatest of these was rum. 'Get in the habit of leaving it alone,' he counselled. Of the havoc he had seen among his friends who had looked upon the wine when it was red, he spoke at length. At least the men could be moderate, but if, through inexperience, they got drunk, they should remember that the *Nevada* was their home. 'We are your friends — we will take care of you.' 'I would rather you came back with too much than stayed ashore and took more. If you come back, turn in and do your work next day, I promise you no trouble.'

Women, of course, there would be, too, but where there were women there was apt to be disease with all its dread results. He asked the crew also to think of the women themselves, of the frightful evil of white slavery which it lay in the power of his men to help stamp out.

Behind these rules and regulations stood the officers who had to carry them out. They were friends. Come, he begged them, to the Old Man and the officers. 'We are all part of the ship's company, our interests are the same. We will do what we can.'

That Sims' discipline was successful is beyond any reasonable doubt, for both his ships, and especially the *Nevada*, were models of conduct. Once after a long stay in Boston there were no reports of drunkenness and disorderliness ashore and no desertions, and records of this sort were rare in the Navy of twenty-five years ago. More positively both the ships were ranked high in the Fleet for efficiency and gunnery, the *Nevada* again especially. Times have now changed and Sims' method may not seem quite as unusual nor his results, perhaps, quite as astonishing. But still his commands are among the brightest accomplishments of a great career. The *Nevada* is still known by the name his own crew gave her — the 'Cheer Up Ship.' Almost every letter he wrote to brother officers ended with the words 'Cheer Up'; the phrase became a kind of signature. Some of the men on the *Nevada* wove a mat for his cabin on which the words appeared. Some others made a box which flashed the phrase in electric lights at officers who came into his cabin with 'a grouse.' In that sunlit personality the sophisticated concepts of many philosophies were reduced to their basic assertions of man's perennial optimism. He talked of hope in uncomplicated language to every man and the impact of his faith was strengthened by the clarity of his expression and character.

Much has been said about Sims' discipline, for it was the clearest outward manifestation of his whole philosophy of life. The major premises of that philosophy, as has been remarked before, were that man is a creature to be respected and that he is perfectible. There was no sentimentality about these fundamental beliefs. In 1911, the Navy had been sorely troubled by desertions, and the Admiral of his division asked all of his commanding officers to make suggestions for improving the situation. In a remarkable letter Sims complied with the request.

In any organization, he began, there are young men who are misfits. Some enter the Navy who have ideas of naval life which can never square with the reality, who do not belong, and who, however long they remain, cannot conform. 'We are well rid of them. We pay good money to scrape a ship's bottom — therefore, why should we not pay a bit to remove human barnacles inside?'

But he was more concerned with the causes of desertion which could be remedied. Once he had a good many applications for transfer to another ship, all of which were withdrawn suddenly when it was learned that a new paymaster was arriving who had a reputation for supplying sweets. 'Why should not more sweets be supplied in regular ration? A quarter of a watermelon puts the whole ship's company in a good humor for days.'

Minor things of this sort were more important than they seemed, but there was a basic matter he wished the Navy to consider. It lay at the root of much of the dissatisfaction the men had for navy life. Absence without leave was a very serious matter from the point of view of discipline. It should be met with severe punishment — instant dismissal with bad conduct charges and loss of all pay save twenty dollars. Under no circumstances, however, should the punishment be restriction of liberty — a common method in those days. This only encouraged the men to desert because such restriction 'merely repressed the uneducated man's normal passions and rendered him an abnormal being.' He was convinced that it was 'an unmitigated evil simply because it actually creates the *strongest possible impulse* in the direction of jumping ship. This, of course, has direct reference to the social evil, the great curse of military establishments. The same kind of prudish public opinion that forced the Bull Durham Tobacco Co. to paint a fence across a certain part of a bull's anatomy prevents its proper sanitary regulation.'

'The majority are men whose enjoyments are mostly physical. ... This being true a man (whose liberty is restricted), while under the impulse of the most compelling of all passions at the period of their greatest force, is no longer amenable to discipline. Therefore, fine him, appeal to his sense of justice and make the punishment one of finality. The young man who can accept a punishment of three months' restriction on board ship without bitter resentment against his officers has got holy water instead of red blood in his veins and is of no use for fighting purposes.'

Long before, on the China Station, a brother officer had brought a widow of uncertain virtue into the wardroom. Sims told the man that the woman should never appear again in the place which was home to him and where he might someday wish to bring his mother and sisters. Still longer before on the *Yantic* he had believed with all his 'heart and intellect' that it was 'the hearts of gold in the breasts of pure women [that] are the vital and moving forces in our civilization.' Like so many men of action Sims talked about his own heart in the words of a sentimentalist. Like some men, too, who find it hard to excuse the frailties of individuals, he understood the basic impulses that determine human conduct. Without any feeling of shame or sorrow or regret he remained cheerful before the awful fact that human nature is human nature.

Sims was perfectly willing, in some cases anxious, to make moral judgments, but they were a purely personal matter. In attempting his reforms he tried always to devise systems that would permit the energies of human nature to work naturally for the accomplishment of our best purposes. 'Most men need a fire built under them or the Message to Garcia means nothing.' Since the Navy was not filled with fellows named Rowan he proposed a method of promotion that would produce a spirit like Rowan's. 'The trouble in our Navy Department, if you want to go into it, has been that all of the human impulses were working against the efficiency of the Navy with the organization we had.' The remedy lay in an organization more in accord with the realities of life. Toward discipline his attitude was the same. Give a man a sense of his own value; give him a feeling of solidarity with the group; give him a mission to fulfil; give him sensible rules to live by; punish his deliberate disobedience; reward him for his contributions, and you will have no trouble.

The months on the *Nevada* were very happy and all too short. Most of the time was filled with cruises along the Atlantic Coast, with landfalls and routines that were familiar, but all of which were made more full of meaning by the thought that his days at sea were almost over. In August when the first Selection Board met, he was one of the five chosen to assume flag rank.[9] With this promotion he became the junior officer in a list of thirty Rear Admirals. Four months later, he was detached from his last command at sea, and as he 'went over the side the crew

[9] Of Sims' selection to flag rank one officer says, 'I believe they [the Selection Board] could not have done otherwise without precipitating a storm that would have wrecked the keeping of selection in naval hands.'

gave him three cheers. It was,' he wrote to his wife, 'a sad business.'

He had been ordered, as was his wish, to the War College. Early in January, 1917, he and his whole family settled down in the President's house overlooking Narragansett Bay. Behind him lay thirty-seven years of service; before him only five more, three of which he would spend at Newport. Behind him, too, lay the China Station, the All-Big-Gun Battleship, the Investigation of 1908, the Newport Conference, the Moody-Mahan Commission, the conference system, the development of doctrine, promotion by selection, The 'Cheer Up' Ship, and the man who taught the Navy how to shoot. It was already, as the Navy goes, a full and distinguished career. Few men in the service could equal his accomplishments. Yet equally few beyond the service were aware of them. Had he died on January 1, 1917, his name would soon have been lost along with the names of thousands of other naval officers who have found anonymity in serving their country.

Three years after January 1, 1917, Sims was again President of the War College when the aide to the Secretary of the Navy wrote to him and asked for a list of the Navy's fifteen most prominent and distinguished officers since John Paul Jones. At that time he sent back twenty names, from which 'you can take your choice.' In longhand he added at the bottom, 'With few exceptions, this list is based upon the assumption that an officer must kill a lot of people in order to gain distinction.'

For twenty-two months of that three years Sims had not been at Newport. During that interval he had been in command of the greatest naval fighting force this country had ever assembled. When he returned to the College, the war was over, victory had been achieved, and he himself had won his 'conflict with oblivion.'

PART FOUR

The Years of Fame

I believe there is no case on record where Allies
have operated together for any considerable length
of time without more or less friction. I am out to
make an exception in this matter.

WILLIAM S. SIMS *to W. V. Pratt*
June 7, 1917

19

The Crisis of the Naval War

ON MARCH 23, 1917, the American Ambassador to the Court of St. James's cabled his government that 'I know personally and informally that they [the British leaders] hope for the establishment of full and frank naval interchange of information and co-operation. Knowing their spirit and their methods, I cannot too strongly recommend that our government send here immediately an Admiral of our own Navy who will bring our Navy's plans and inquiries. The coming of such an officer of high rank would be regarded as a compliment and he would have all doors opened to him and a sort of special staff appointed to give him the results and methods of the whole British naval work since the war began.'[1]

Similar messages had been sent in the preceding months by Mr. Page, but little attention had been paid to them.[2] By the last week in March, 1917, however, official Washington was preparing itself for the possibility of a war with Germany. At long last, therefore, action upon the Ambassador's recommendation was taken. A telephone call was put through to Newport, Rhode Island. William Sims was asked to proceed immediately and in secret to Washington.

Next day in the Navy Department he was told by the Chief of the Bureau of Navigation that he was 'to be sent abroad to confer

---

[1] The whole text of the cable is quoted in Josephus Daniels, *Our Navy at War*, New York, 1922, p. 36.

[2] Burton J. Hendrick, *The Life and Letters of Walter H. Page*, New York, 1923, vol. II, p. 274.

with the Allied Admiralties. . . . I was to go secretly, under an assumed name, and not even to take any uniforms with me.' From the Secretary and the Chief of Naval Operations he received further advice about his mission. On March 28, he obtained written orders 'to carry out the confidential instructions which have been given you.' [3]

These instructions had been given in the conversations Sims had held with the men in the Department. Unfortunately, none of the people involved could later agree upon what had actually been said. Secretary Daniels recalled that Sims had been told to 'keep the Department fully posted on conditions as he found them in London.' He also remembered that the naval officer had been informed that President Wilson was 'decidedly of the opinion that ships should be convoyed.' Sims himself said that in his 'very brief talk' with the Secretary he had been urged to use the cables freely in advising how the United States Navy could best cooperate with the Allied Navies in case of war.[4]

The Chief of Naval Operations remembered that he had impressed upon Sims the seriousness of the situation and the importance of being very careful that his feelings toward the British did not lead him into any 'indiscretion.' Sims recalled that Admiral Benson's warning had been put into the following words: 'Don't let the British pull the wool over your eyes. It is none of our business pulling their chestnuts out of the fire. We would as soon fight the British as the Germans.' An officer who was present at the conversation believed that 'a remark of that character' was made.[5]

As confidential instructions these conversations amounted to little. Mr. Page had asked for an Admiral 'who will bring with him our Navy's plans and inquiries.' Mr. Daniels believed Sims was being sent to England to 'keep the Department posted on conditions as he found them in London.' Sims understood that he had been warned against a partisan attitude and instructed to

---

[3] *Hearings Before the Subcommittee of the Committee on Naval Affairs*, United States Senate, 66th Congress, 2d Session, vol. I, p. 268. Hereafter this will be referred to as *Hearings, 1920.*

[4] *Ibid.*, vol. I, p. 268; vol. II, p. 1993. Daniels recalled that he told Sims at this time that he (Sims) had been selected in spite of and not because of the Guildhall speech. Sims denied that any mention of the speech had been made.

[5] *Ibid.*, vol. II, pp. 1881–1882.

report on how 'America could best cooperate with the Allies in the event of war.' When all allowances are made for the frailty of memory, the divergence in these views is quite startling. Likewise, when all allowances are made for the need for secrecy, it seems impossible not to conclude that some clearer definition of Sims' mission should have been put in writing.

From Washington Sims returned briefly to Newport for hurried packing and the last good-byes. On the evening of March 31, he and his aide, Commander John Vincent Babcock, got aboard the American steamship *New York* bound for Liverpool. It was a solemn errand on which he was setting forth, the thought of which produced in Sims a sudden and intensely personal humility. To his wife he wrote before the steamer departed:

> It would have been a grief to me if you had been selfishly a peace-at-any-price woman and had been willing for me to remain at home in security when I could be of possible service to Uncle Sam and the Allies in the great cause.
>
> I doubt whether I can fully realize how much a tender woman's heart goes out to the father of her children, no matter what his conduct or spiritual defects as a husband; but within the limits of my realization of this, you have been splendidly brave, and I admire you for it and thank you for it with all my heart.
>
> Since I have received this new order I have admired you and loved you more than ever — and that is saying everything — and I regret that my unfortunate reserve prevents me from showing all I feel.

It was, as his wife said, a man's work on which he was beginning. It was, too, an 'honorable mission that I am sent upon, and I hope the results may show that it justifies any reasonable risk, though, as you know, I do not consider the risk on this swift and well-defended steamer even considerable. But if God should so will it that I should not return to you, you may assume that I will meet my fate worthily and with the conviction that you will accept the just sacrifice for the sake of the just cause for which it is made, and that you will bear it bravely for the sake of our precious ones.'

The two men had decided, in the interests of secrecy, to call themselves V. J. Richardson and S. W. Davidson. The cloak of their incognito was first pierced by a member of the armed guard of the *New York* who had served on the *Nevada*. When Sims swore him to silence, the man promised not to tell even his wife. Later in the voyage 'an enterprising steward noticed that the initials on the pajamas of one of these passengers differed from those of the name under which he was sailing.' The steward reported this intelligence to the Captain of the vessel, who calmed his fears of spies. The two officers were not, in fact, very accomplished conspirators. Mr. Granville Barker, a passenger, became interested in 'shall we say the clear-cut opinions of Mr. Davidson' and suspected he was not what he seemed. The suspicions of Mr. Barker were further aroused by the ever-watchful Babcock who anxiously approached him with the request that he would not pass on any of Mr. Davidson's views to those in authority.

During the long days at sea, Sims could reflect on the singular destiny that was sending him to England. Who had chosen him for his present mission he did not know. Yet the choice, while gratifying, was hardly surprising. As he reviewed the past; the years he had spent collecting information in France, his friendships in England, his ability to speak French, the sound logistics that sustained his career from the time he was a Lieutenant, he could only conclude that he was 'the logical man.' [6]

That he was well prepared for the task at hand there could be no doubt, but he could hardly have comprehended the magnitude of the work which lay before him. Like all naval officers he had, after 1914, been intensely interested in the course of the war. It had been his fixed conviction that the United States should have entered actively into the struggle long before he started for England. Indeed, he had several times written his wife that had he been single he would have resigned his commission and placed his abilities at the service of the Allied Powers. From his study of the situation as it appeared in the newspapers and in the few reports available at the Navy Department, he had reached several conclusions. At Jutland, he was convinced, the British had

---

[6] There are four or five different explanations of how Sims received his appointment. It seems most likely that the Assistant Secretary, F. D. Roosevelt, and the Chief of Naval Operations, W. S. Benson, were his chief supporters. It is interesting, in this connection, to notice that the General Board, unaware that Sims was already on his way to England, recommended on April 5, 1917, that he be sent to London as the head of an American Commission of ten officers. It would seem that he was indeed the 'logical man.'

violated 'the most important principle of warfare of any kind, namely to bring to bear upon the enemy a superior force at the point of contact. They did the opposite and got what was coming to them.' He was sure that the British had blundered especially in the use of their battle cruisers and 'were lucky to get off as well as they did.' [7] But save in his judgment of Jutland (which he subsequently changed) he found little fault with the British methods. As the *New York* sailed toward Liverpool, he was reasonably sure that the situation was well in hand and that the Allied Powers were on their way to victory in a short space of time. This conclusion was reinforced on April 7, when word came from the United States that Congress on Good Friday had declared war on Germany.

Two days later the *New York* reached England. As she was entering the harbor of Liverpool, she struck a mine. Damage was slight, but, as a precaution, the passengers were taken off in lifeboats. A little later they transferred to an excursion steamer that was coming in from the Isle of Man. In making the change, Sims left a little tin dispatch box in the lifeboat. Upon realizing this, he called out that it was essential for him to have the little box. No one in the steamer was quite sober, it was just after the Easter Bank Holiday, and a sailor told Sims to 'stow his bloody lip' or go back to the lifeboat. Lip was stowed and the dispatch box was returned later by a thoughtful passenger.

At the dock Sims was met by Rear Admiral Hope, R.N., who presented him with a letter from Admiral John Jellicoe, First Sea Lord of the Admiralty. The communication began with an expression of pleasure that Sims had been selected, but it ended on an unexpected note. 'The situation is far from easy, solely on account of the submarine warfare, but difficulties are there to be overcome, and they will be overcome, I am convinced; although I fully expect our losses to be very heavy before all is over.' This was sombre news for Sims to ponder as he rode on a special train toward London.

On April 10, the day he reached the city, he paid a call on Admiral Jellicoe. The two were old friends. In happier days, when Sims had made his annual gunnery trips to England, they had met and worked together. The acquaintance was more than

[7] W. S. S. to F. L. Pleadwell, July 26, 1916.

professional, for the American had dined occasionally with the Jellicoes and had played with the Admiral's children in the drawing-room after dinner. Of all the foreigners with whom Sims served during the war, Jellicoe was the first in the American's affections. In this first conversation all of Sims' pleasant notions of England's security were destroyed.

After a moment of greeting, Jellicoe, with a calm, almost tranquil face, handed his friend a memorandum. As he read the paper Sims learned for the first time the extent of the ravages of the unrestricted German submarine warfare. In the first quarter of the year 1917, 1,300,000 tons of British and neutral shipping had been sunk. The memorandum indicated that in the month of April alone the losses would mount to about 900,000 tons. After reading these figures, Sims could only voice his consternation.

'Yes,' replied Jellicoe quietly, 'it is impossible for us to go on with the war if losses like this continue.'

'It looks,' said Sims, 'as though the Germans were winning the war.'

'They will win, unless we can stop these losses — and stop them soon,' the Englishman agreed.

'Is there no solution for the problem?'

'Absolutely none that we can see now,' Jellicoe answered.[8]

During the next few days Sims further investigated the appalling situation. At first the Admiralty, reluctant to reveal the true state of affairs, sought to withhold information. Nothing, Sims maintained, could be gained by such a course. All the facts must be laid before him. After a few days of study, supplemented by conversations with officers, Cabinet members, the Prime Minister, and the King, he learned the truth that was concealed from the public behind a mass of confusing figures. The truth was that England's position was desperate.[9]

[8] W. S. S., *The Victory at Sea*, New York, 1920, p. 9.

[9] W. S. S. to Secretary of the Navy, April 19, 1917. The communications between Sims and the authorities in America can be found in several places. Almost a complete file for these years is contained in the Sims papers. A full collection of all his existing communications is in the World War Archives of the Office of Naval Records and Library in the Navy Department. A fairly complete record is in the *Hearings, 1920*. Unfortunately, the letters and cables are scattered through the thirty-five hundred pages of testimony. Since there is no index, research in these volumes is

From the very beginning of the war the fate of the Allied Powers had depended upon the successful maintenance of the lines of communication with the outside world. Along these lines flowed the sea-borne supplies of food, munitions, and raw materials that sustained the warring nations and maintained the fighting armies. For the first twenty-eight months of the war, England had been able to ensure this flow of supplies by virtue of her command of the sea. This command had at all times been threatened by the German High Seas Fleet and the German submarines, but in December, 1916, however uneasily, Britannia was still ruling the waves. Some concern in the last months of 1916 had been expressed in England over the increasing activity of the submarines, but few believed the situation critical.

The first three months of 1917, however, shattered any illusion of security that had been previously held. At the beginning of that year the Allied Powers had at their disposal about 21,500,000 tons of shipping or 6,000,000 tons more than the 15,500,000 needed to carry on the war. One-third of this margin of safety was wiped out in the first quarter of 1917 and, in April, the curve of destruction was sharply rising.[10] If sinkings continued at the rate predicted, the defeat of the Allied Powers could be prophesied with the aid of mathematics alone. By October 1, 1917, available tonnage would be less than the amount required to carry on the war.

The situation in April, 1917, was the more appalling because no relief could be expected. The chief weapon in the destruction of tonnage had been the submarine, which in February had been turned loose upon the shipping of the world in all the horror of unrestricted warfare. The men at the British Admiralty were presented with a new and unexpected problem. Since time out of mind, command of the sea had meant only the command of the surface of the sea. The weapons at England's disposal had been designed with this in mind; none appeared capable of

---

difficult. An excellent digest of important communications on important questions is found in the War Diary prepared by the Historical Section of Sims' staff in London. This is not in print. A copy is in the Sims papers. Unless otherwise specified citations will refer to the Sims papers, though it should be remembered that the same documents can be more easily found ordinarily in the well-indexed files of the Office of Naval Records and Library.

[10] *Hearings, 1920,* vol. I, p. 303.

combating an enemy which attacked merchant shipping in force beneath the surface of the water.

To this lack of offensive weapons was added a complication of nature. From the four corners of the earth ships brought the sinews of war to England. But since England is a tiny place, these widely dispersed carriers were forced to concentrate in slender vestibules of the sea as they neared the island. It was in these narrow approaches, crowded with the shipping of the world, that the submarines struck with deadly effect.

How to protect these ships in the danger zones had become, by April, 1917, the major preoccupation of the British Admiralty. For months it had experimented. The home waters of the submarines had been mined, merchantmen had been armed, smoke screens and decoy vessels had been used; yet the tonnage losses mounted. At the time Sims arrived in London, a patrol system had been established. The lanes along which shipping travelled had been divided into areas, each guarded by small light craft armed with guns and depth charges. Since such craft merely informed the enemy of what lanes were then in use, and since there were not nearly enough ships to carry out an effective patrol, this method proved little better than the others. There seemed to many of the men in the Admiralty nothing to do but wait as calmly as possible for the end.[11]

One frequently suggested method of defeating the submarine the Admiralty had not put into practice. It had been suggested that ships, gathered together in groups, could be protected from raiders on the open sea by a single cruiser or old battleship. When the ships approached the narrow lanes near England, they could then be escorted to port by destroyers or light craft armed with depth charges to be used against submarines. This was the convoy system which, as far back as November, 1916, had been recommended officially to the Admiralty by the government. At that time the naval officers had refused to consider it. In the

[11] The various measures taken against the submarine are well described by J. R. Jellicoe, *The Crisis of the Naval War*, London, 1920, chapter III. Other works of interest on submarine warfare are R. H. Gibson and M. Prendergast, *The German Submarine War, 1914–1918*, London, 1920; J. R. Jellicoe, *The Submarine Peril*, London, 1934; Bernard Brodie, *Sea Power in the Machine Age*, Princeton, 1941, chapter XVI. The German view can most easily be obtained in R. Scheer, *Germany's High Sea Fleet in the World War* (translated), London, 1920.

same month the Admiralty informed Mr. Asquith, the Prime Minister, that 'No conclusive answer has as yet been found to this form of warfare; perhaps no conclusive answer ever will be found. We must for the present be content with palliation.' [12] Nothing at the time of Sims' arrival, in the month when losses were to approach one million tons, indicated that the Admiralty had changed its mind.

The major objections to the convoy maintained throughout the first quarter of 1917 were four in number. It was feared that by reducing the speed of the convoy to that of the slowest ship valuable time would be lost. In the second place, it was believed that the arrival of a whole convoy of ships at one port at one time would inevitably jam the unloading facilities. Moreover, it was asserted, no merchantmen could sail in the close formation required by the convoys. Finally, it was believed that there were not nearly enough small craft available for escort duty through the danger zone. These arguments weighed very heavily with those who opposed the convoy system. They prevented the Admiralty from even considering it as a possibility.

As soon as Sims had informed himself on the situation he sent, on April 14, a cable to the Navy Department. First, he explained the real seriousness of the submarine warfare; that sinkings were rising; that U-boat construction was increasing; that destruction of the underwater ships was greatly exaggerated in the press; that the morale of the submarine crews remained unbroken. Quoting the figures for February and March and the first ten days of April, he concluded that the 'control of the sea [was] actually imperilled.'

America's contribution was clear. 'The issue must inevitably be decided at the focus of all lines of communication in the Eastern Atlantic, therefore, I very urgently recommend the following immediate naval cooperation.' He then urged the dispatch of a 'maximum number of destroyers, accompanied by small antisubmarine craft.' The destroyers could be based at Queenstown, Ireland, and used for patrol; the light craft could be used for inshore work. To serve these forces there must be supply ships and bases established. Further than this, the great need was for merchant tonnage.

[12] Lloyd George, *War Memoirs*, Boston, 1934, vol. III, p. 80.

In conclusion, he said that it was 'very likely' that submarines would approach our coast to 'divert attention and keep our forces from the critical areas in the Eastern Atlantic,' but he added that logistical difficulties would restrict such operations to 'minor importance.' A final paragraph contained information supplied by Herbert Hoover that England had on hand a three weeks' grain supply.

Five days later, April 19, he wrote his first letter to the Department amplifying his earlier views. He told first of the reluctance of officials to acquaint him with the truth about conditions and of his insistence that he be considered 'a part of the Admiralty organization.' In a general estimate on the situation he stated that the submarine campaign had resolved itself into the real issue of the war and that the 'Allied governments have not been able to, and are not now, effectively meeting the situation presented.' Criticism of the Admiralty was frequent. There was an increasing demand for the adoption of the convoy. He stated the four arguments raised against such procedure by the Admiralty and said that a lack of vessels to carry out the work seemed to be the greatest obstacle. He reported that he himself had raised the convoy question in talks with Jellicoe and had assured the Englishman that merchantmen could sail in formation.

Other complicating factors in the problem were set forth in the letter. Until recently it had been impossible to convince some Cabinet members that the submarine war was actually the great enemy. Civilians, in England as at home, were loath to believe in unseen dangers. Even the civilians who understood the situation proposed impossible remedies. Sims told how Lloyd George was anxious to seal the submarines in their own ports, and reported that 'I finally convinced the Prime Minister of the fallacy of such propositions [by saying] — that in order to maintain our obstructions we would have to match the forces the enemy brought against them until finally the majority if not all of our forces would be forced into dangerous areas where they would be subject to continual torpedo and other attacks; in fact in a position most favorable to the enemy.' The most immediate reply to submarine warfare, he pointed out, should be ships and 'more ships.'

This very full review of all that Sims had found in his ten days of research revealed both the dangers of the moment and his full recognition of them. Recognition he admitted had come rather slowly; he had been reluctant to alter his previous conclusions formed on press reports in the United States. But the facts could not be altered.

The reference in his letter to the conversation with Lloyd George was not without some guile. On April 17 a cable signed 'Daniels' had asked if the German coast could not be so effectively blockaded that egress and ingress of submarines would be impossible. To this Sims had replied that such blockade was 'unfeasible,' necessitating as it did a wide dispersion of forces that at any particular point could be broken through by a concentrated enemy attack. He repeated again the need for light craft. Through the month of April these messages were repeated, all similar in tone, all emphasizing the vital necessity of more ships.

From the first moment of his arrival in England, Sims grasped the essential fact that the decision of the great struggle turned upon the outcome of the submarine warfare. He so informed his government repeatedly, and as often, he recommended dispatching ships from America to assist in meeting the challenge of the undersea menace. But he was not satisfied that the British Admiralty would use these ships, when they arrived, in the most effective possible manner against the hidden enemy, and he set himself the task of persuading the responsible authorities to change their methods of attack.

It will be recalled that at this time the Admiralty was using the patrol system to combat the submarine in spite of its obvious inadequacy. Sims, in one of his first talks with Jellicoe, 'suggested that merchant ships would have to be convoyed eventually in fleets,' but the suggestion was not received with approval. The idea of convoying was, of course, not new. Since the beginning of the war it had been recommended by certain people, and after December, 1916, it had won increasing support from many sides. There was a younger group of officers at the Admiralty, led by Commander Reginald Henderson, who favored it.[13] These men

---

[13] J. S. Corbett and H. Newbolt, *History of the Great War, Based on Official Documents: Naval Operations*, London, 1920–31, vol. IV, p. 324. Chapter IX of this volume gives a vivid description of the Admiralty's recognition of the danger from the submarine and its inability to take successful measures against such warfare.

were supported by the government of Lloyd George after he took office in December, 1916.

Sims, after reviewing the entire situation, threw in his lot with those who sought to adopt the convoy system. For three weeks after his arrival he labored to persuade the senior officers at the Admiralty that the convoy was not only possible but practical.

The history of these three weeks is excessively tangled and confused. Since it has been written for the most part by men with axes to grind or reputations to save, the evidence presented by these historians is not infrequently conflicting. The central theme of the narrative is clear enough. Mounting pressure upon the Admiralty finally became so great that, on May 1, the officers capitulated and agreed to experiment with the convoy. But since this pressure was exerted by many hands, it is exceedingly difficult to assign to any group or individual the credit as the determining factor in the conversion of the senior officers at the Admiralty. The part played by Sims during these three weeks has frequently been overlooked.

Upon his arrival in London, he was amazed to learn from Jellicoe that 'no systematic study had been made of the [convoy] problem.' After some discussion he convinced the Englishman that it was imperative that such a study be undertaken.[14] This investigation was begun, apparently, by Commander Henderson in conjunction with Sir Norman Leslie of the Ministry of Shipping. Sims may have taken some part in the study, since he reported to the Navy Department on April 19 that he was 'now consulting with the director of shipping as to the practicability and advisability of attempting some approach to such a plan [the convoy system].' In the first week after his arrival he talked with Lloyd George and several Cabinet ministers. In these conversations he left no doubt of his belief that the convoy system should be adopted.

On April 22, twelve days after Sims reached England, Jellicoe submitted a long memorandum to his government in which he maintained that the only immediate remedy for the tonnage losses was the patrol system. He did not even mention the possibility of the convoy.[15] At the time this memorandum was writ-

[14] W. S. S. to L. C. Palmer, May 1, 1917, and W. S. S. to Mrs. Sims, April 30, 1917.
[15] Lloyd George, op. cit., p. 105.

ten Lloyd George thought it was not unreasonable to conclude that Germany would bring England to her knees by August. He therefore, in the three days following the presentation of these views, held Cabinet meetings at which the convoy system was thoroughly discussed. In these meetings the Prime Minister used the arguments of Sims and Beatty to support his own views that the adoption of the convoy system was imperative.[16] Shortly after, the Admiralty reported that the convoy was 'under consideration.' Lloyd George, aware that this meant only further delay, decided to visit 'the Admiralty and there take peremptory action on the question of convoys.'

This threat to overrule the Sea Lords 'in their own sanctuary,' Lloyd George believed, apparently 'galvanised the Admiralty' into action. Before he arrived, the officers examined some 'plans and figures' prepared by Commander Henderson. In his memoirs Lloyd George leaves the impression that the Admiralty had possessed these plans for some time and had deliberately disregarded them until he threatened to overrule the officers.[17] This is certainly possible. In view of the continuous opposition of the Admiralty to the Cabinet's recommendations, it is not an unnatural assumption for the Prime Minister to make. But it seems far more likely that Henderson's figures were in fact the study of the whole question which Jellicoe had ordered at Sims' insistence. Henderson may privately have begun this investigation before Sims arrived. He knew a great deal about the subject, since he had been in charge of the French coal convoy that was instituted in February, 1917. For the same reason he was the logical person for Jellicoe to assign to the task of making a thorough study of convoys.[18] On April 29, Sims was called to the Admiralty and shown a well-digested, formal study of the convoy which revealed that the system was 'entirely practicable.' [19] On April 30, the Prime Minister went himself to the Admiralty to talk over the question. That same day the Sea Lords gave at last a reluctant consent to an experimental convoy.[20]

[16] Lloyd George, *op. cit.*, p. 106.   [17] *Ibid.*, p. 107.

[18] Until the Admiralty archives for this period are opened, it will be impossible to say beyond all doubt that Henderson prepared the study which Sims recommended. On the basis of all the evidence the writer feels it safe to assume that he did.

[19] W. S. S. to L. C. Palmer, May 1, 1917.   [20] *Ibid.*

From the above chronicle of events certain things stand clear. The 'plans and figures of Commander Henderson' were almost certainly contained in the study undertaken at Sims' insistence. This study had been begun before Lloyd George threatened to overrule the Admiralty in its own sanctuary. The support given the convoy by Sims strengthened Lloyd George and his Cabinet in their determination to bring great pressure to bear upon the senior officers. Sims himself weakened the opposition of these men by his persuasion. The day before Lloyd George went to the Admiralty, the study which showed the convoy to be 'entirely practicable' was completed.

The significance of Henderson's work lay in the fact that it blasted the argument of the Admiralty that there were not enough ships available to convoy the existing shipping. This argument was based, according to Lloyd George, on a singular misconception. The Admiralty had reported sinkings in such a way that the public would not become alarmed. Each week the number of vessels lost was reported together with the total number of arrivals and departures in British ports, usually around twenty-five hundred in number. The latter figure included the entrances and clearances of coastwise shipping and small craft of any dimensions. It was a comforting but wholly deceptive set of statistics that was placed before the people. Actually only about one hundred and twenty to one hundred and forty-five ocean-going ships were coming through the danger zone. These vessels were the only ones which would require convoys, but the Admiralty, the victim of its own deception, believed until April, 1917, that it would have to supply protection for the twenty-five hundred vessels of all sizes. The figures compiled by Henderson revealed this 'grotesque' miscalculation and assured the conversion of the Admiralty.[21] On May 1, Sims could cable his government that the convoy would be tried.

From the above account it is clear that three different forces were at work on the Admiralty — the younger officers under Henderson's leadership; the government under Lloyd George; and Sims himself. Sims' influence because intangible is the hardest to weigh. No man has said that he was the deciding factor in

[21] Lloyd George, *op. cit.*, pp. 93–94 and 107. The Admiralty's miscalculation would seem almost incredible save for Lloyd George's word and their own actions.

the deliberations. Jellicoe, though praising him highly as a friend and a man, makes no mention of him in this connection. But in his books the First Sea Lord is at pains to build up a reasonable case for the Admiralty, and this can only be done by occasional omissions. The Henderson figures likewise receive no consideration. Lloyd George pays high tribute to Sims, acknowledges his support of the convoy, and states that he used this support to convince the Cabinet. But he leaves the impression that the influence of his government was decisive in altering the views of the Admiralty. Newbolt, in his history of the war, gives qualified credit to Sims.[22] Even in September, 1917, the Admiralty was not fully aware of the value of the convoy, he remarks, and 'Admiral Sims must be given credit for being the first naval expert in high position who had the insight to realize the remedy for which the Allies were still seeking had actually been found.' Sims himself throughout his life did not publicly set forth his claims in definite language.

To his wife he wrote on April 30, 1917, describing the dinner he had attended that night at the Waldorf Astors'. He and Lloyd George had discussed the experimental convoy to which the Admiralty had agreed that afternoon. The Prime Minister at dinner had turned to him and said, 'You are responsible for this.' Sims' aide, J. V. Babcock, remembers arriving at the Admiralty one morning to be met 'with congratulations and joy, because the decision had finally been reached to go ahead with the convoy system as the general plan of campaign. The cause of extending congratulations to me was that the influence of my chief, Admiral Sims, who, through his messages to the State Department, had proved the determining factor in finally bolstering up the courage of the Admiralty Board to accept responsibility of adopting the convoy system. Admiral Sims' messages were so vehement and telling in force of argument that the Admiralty officials, who saw them all, did not dare risk post-war analysis of their régime in the face of such documents which would, of course, eventually receive publicity. These statements,' Babcock concluded, 'are not a question of opinion. They are facts.'

Seven years after the war Babcock sent these memories to the

[22] Corbett and Newbolt, *op. cit.*, vol. V, p. 133.

Admiral, suggesting that they might be published. In reply Sims said:

> I am still of the opinion that, in the absence of an authorized statement from the Admiralty, which, of course, will not be made, or a statement someday by an officer who was high up in the council of the Admiralty, which also will doubtless not be made, it would be a mistake for any officer to publish or to authorize the publication of the claim that the influence of our officers was the determining factor in the adoption of the convoy by the Admiralty.
>
> Our influence may have been the determining factor. It is at least probable that our influence accelerated the decision, but there is no single authoritative statement to prove that this is true, much less to prove that but for our insistence the convoy would not have been adopted at all. I think there can be no doubt that in the absence of our advocacy the convoy policy would have been adopted before very long.
>
> Your statements are certainly impressive as showing our probable influence, but I think the essential statements are not evidence of fact so much as they are expressions of opinion. The younger officers of the Admiralty were evidently of the opinion that the arguments in our dispatches were the determining factor, but they did not claim that their seniors were of the same opinion.

In this carefully phrased memorandum the strongest argument Sims could think of against his claims was that no one had as yet asserted them.[23] Since the authors of military memoirs are seldom distinguished for either their impartiality or their modesty, he was well aware that he would wait in vain for confirmation of the part he had played. On the basis of the evidence presented, it seems possible to reward Sims with far greater credit than he asked for himself. The great obstacle to the adoption of the convoy was the attitude of the senior officers at the Admiralty. Against these men Lloyd George's government and the younger officers had struggled so vainly for at least four months that upon Sims' arrival no study of the convoy had even been made. Three weeks after Admiral Sims reached London, weeks during which he threw his whole weight against the opposition of the

[23] W. V. Pratt has, however, paid tribute to his old Commander. In his 'Warfare in the Atlantic,' *Foreign Affairs*, July, 1941, he says, ' ... Admiral Jellicoe ... was loath to resort to the slow method of convoy, and finally yielded only after much persuasion from Admiral Sims.'

Admiralty in ways already discussed, the convoy was accepted. Doubtless, as he said, the convoy system would have been introduced sometime, and, as he so cautiously told Babcock, all the Americans could reasonably claim was that they had accelerated its adoption. But in April, 1917, almost one million tons of Allied and neutral shipping were sunk, and it was believed in England, by those who knew, that the country would be on her knees in August and prostrate before Imperial Germany in October. At such a time the salvation of the Allied Powers may well be said to have rested upon the speed with which the Admiralty experienced a total conversion.

Though Admiral Jellicoe was mistaken in believing that the convoy system was impossible without American assistance, it was yet true that the complete success of the plan rested upon the number of anti-submarine craft our country could send to the dangerous area. The great task posed for Sims during the first three or four months after his arrival was to see that such ships were provided in sufficient quantity. In his first cables, even before the convoy was agreed upon, he had set forth the crucial nature of the submarine warfare and suggested that every possible anti-submarine vessel be sent into European waters. Specifically he asked in those first weeks for tugs, converted yachts, and most of all for destroyers. The greatest enemy of the submarine was the destroyer, as Admiral Goodrich suggested in his delightful quotation from Eliphaz the Temanite, 'A dreadful sound is in his ears; in prosperity the destroyer shall come upon him.'

Twelve days after he reached London, Sims heard by cable that six destroyers would be sent immediately to such place as he should designate.[24] Then for a week he heard no more. Near the end of April, aware that the situation of the Allies was desperate, he appealed to the Ambassador for assistance. To Mr. Page he presented all the evidence he had obtained from the Admiralty, reinforced by his own conclusions as to the seriousness of the situation. On the twenty-seventh of April, the Ambassador cabled to the State Department and the President that 'If the present rate of destruction can be kept up, we shall have soon to contemplate the defeat of Great Britain. Whatever help the

[24] W. S. Benson to W. S. S., April 22, 1917.

United States may render at any time in the future or in any theatre of the war our help is now more seriously needed in this submarine area for the sake of all the Allies than it can ever be needed again or anywhere else.' He recommended 'the immediate sending of every destroyer and all other craft that can be of anti-submarine use. Thirty or more destroyers,' he concluded, if sent immediately 'would very likely be decisive.' [25] With this message Sims sent one to the Navy Department reiterating his belief that 'we can not send too soon or too many.' [26] '[The] breaking of enemy submarine morale [is the] immediate mission.' On May 3, the day before the first division of six destroyers reached their destination at Queenstown, Sims heard for the first time that 'ultimately thirty-six destroyers' with two mother ships would be sent into the critical area around the British Isles.

Ultimately was a long word to Sims who saw the greatest enemy as time. There was, as he said, no mystery in this thing. Before his eyes on a graph the rising line of sinkings rose steadily to meet the falling line of available merchant tonnage. When the two lines met, the issue would be decided. By August it then seemed the Allies would be at the mercy of their enemies. With thoughts such as these he reiterated his belief in the need for haste. Throughout the months of May, June, and July, no less than thirty-two times he called specifically for ships.

There was a rising sense of urgency in his messages home. 'The outstanding fact which cannot be escaped is that we are not succeeding.' 'If sufficient United States Forces cannot be thrown into the balance at the critical time and place there is little doubt that early success [for the Germans] will be assured.' 'If the shipping losses continue as they have been for the last four months, it is submitted that the Allies will be forced to dire straits indeed, if they will not actually be faced with an unsatis-

---

[25] Sims papers and B. J. Hendrick, *op. cit.*, pp. 278–279. Hendrick tells graphically of the despair of both Page and Sims at the inactivity of America. When Sims first appealed to the Ambassador, he gave him a copy of a cablegram he hoped Mr. Page would sign. Page read it and said, 'Admiral, it isn't half strong enough.' The message quoted is the one the Ambassador prepared by himself. It is worth noting that the cable as quoted in Hendrick omits a sentence that appears in the copy in the Sims papers. That sentence is the first one quoted above.

[26] W. S. S. to Secretary of the Navy, April 28, 1917.

factory peace.' 'I trust I have made the critical nature of the military situation clear. I consider it my duty to report that if we cannot offer more immediate actual assistance — we will fail to render the service to the Allied cause which future history will show to have been necessary.' On July 7 there was 'a wholly inadequate number of forces of all descriptions' at the disposal of the Allies, and 'briefly stated I consider that at the present moment we are losing the war.' Ships, he heard on all sides, ships, ships, and more ships.

Ships were coming. On April 6, 1917, the Congress of the United States declared war on Germany. On May 4, the first six destroyers appeared off Queenstown Harbor. In the course of the month, twelve more appeared accompanied by one mother ship, the *Dixie*, which Sims had known so well in the Flotilla. In June, ten more destroyers were sent with one more tender. In July, nine more arrived. On August 1 the United States had been at war with Germany three months and three weeks, and there were at that time in European waters thirty-seven destroyers, two tenders, and eight converted yachts.[27] No ocean-going tugs had been sent for the purpose of salvaging ships crippled by torpedoes, though Sims had asked for them at least thirteen times. No cruisers had been assigned to convoy duty until the first week in July, although he had asked for them at least seven times.

Ships came, but not rapidly or in sufficient number. On the Navy list, when the war started, there were sixty-six destroyers, twenty-four of which were coal-burners, thirteen converted yachts, fourteen ocean-going tugs (fifty-one privately owned ones were on the Atlantic Coast at this time), and twenty-nine cruisers. Not all of these vessels were immediately available, some were in dry dock, some were considered indispensable to the Fleet, some had inadequate personnel. Still it is impossible not to reach the conclusion that many more could have been sent from this nucleus of ships than were actually dispatched into European waters. This conclusion is reinforced when one considers the patrol force of fifty-five vessels (thirteen cruisers, thirty-four destroyers, five coast guard cutters, and three gunboats) that was ordered to guard the Atlantic coastline of the

[27] *Hearings, 1920,* vol. I, pp. 1235–1240.

United States at the beginning of the war.[28] This force never quite reached its full paper strength before it was disbanded, but in the last week of June there were seventeen destroyers still in service on the American side of the Atlantic.[29] There were ships enough in the United States if the Navy Department had felt it wise to send them.

Material aid was not forthcoming in the quantity hoped for and recommended by Sims because the Navy Department was unwilling to accept during these months the view of the situation which he presented to it. On May 1, he cabled twice that the convoy was to be tried. At the same time he explained how the system was organized. Yet, by the end of that month, he had received no word from the Navy Department on the subject. On May 25, he asked if the United States could supply cruisers for the New York convoy. Upon receiving no answer, he again, on May 30 and 31, requested advice on the amount of material cooperation the Department could give in the maintenance of the convoy system. Again, in the first week of June he took the matter up in a long cable, and on the eleventh he asked that an officer be sent to England to cooperate with the Admiralty on the problem of organizing overseas convoys.

In the middle of the month he was informed that a convoy of troops was on the way for which he should arrange an escort of American destroyers through the danger zone. But it was not until June 20 that he received in a cable from the Department the first word from the Navy Department on the convoy as a policy. 'In regard to convoy,' the cable read, 'I consider that American vessels having armed guard are safer when sailing independently.' Four days later, June 24, this was followed by the information that 'The Department is strongly of the opinion — based on previous experiences — that the question of supplying adequate guns and trained gun crews to merchant ships is one which can — in no wise — be treated as a minor issue.' In the same cable the Department explained that it recognized the necessity for 'sending all anti-submarine craft which can be spared from the home waters into active European waters, and when such craft become available will send them.'

[28] *Hearings, 1920*, vol. I, p. 882.
[29] W. S. S. to W. H. Page, June 26, 1917.

The partial rejection of the convoy implied in the cable about vessels with armed guards, coupled as it was with the suggestion that some anti-submarine craft could not be spared from American waters, made it clear to Sims that he had failed to establish his case after two months of exposition. In May, with the introduction of the convoy, sinkings had fallen, but the total for that month was around six hundred thousand tons. Throughout June, with its longer days, the curve was on the rise again. Thus the two communications from Washington shocked him into renewed efforts to convince his government of the need for escort vessels.

First he turned once more to his friend the Ambassador. 'Can you not,' he asked, 'do something to bring to our government an understanding of how very serious the situation is? I cannot understand why our government should hesitate to send the necessary submarine craft to this side. There are at least seventeen more destroyers employed on our coast *where there is no war.*' [30] Mr. Page agreed with the Admiral that the Allies were in fact losing the war. He, therefore, sent off to the Secretary of State and the President an urgent message in support of all Sims' recommendations. From the British government Sims obtained a dispatch to the same effect, a dispatch approved by Mr. Balfour and Sir Edward Carson, the First Lord of the Admiralty. This, too, went to the Secretary and the President.

To the Navy Department Sims sent a cable of his own in this last week of June. Chiefly he expressed his disapproval of the idea of armed merchantmen. British experience, by which America should be guided, had revealed that such vessels merely encouraged submarines to sink without warning. Merchant ships lacked both the speed and proper protection to stand up to undersea fighters. In the six weeks just passed, thirty armed merchantmen had been sunk in the critical area. Supplementing this cable Sims sent two letters and four cables in the last four days of June asking for more ships and stressing the imperative necessity of adequate protection for convoys.

In reply to this barrage of messages let loose upon Washington

[30] W. S. S. to W. H. Page, June 26, 1917. Hendrick (*op. cit.*, vol. II, p. 282) gives the date of this letter as June 25. A copy of the letter in the War Diary of the London Headquarters is dated June 26.

from London, the Department capitulated. On July 2, it accepted by implication the convoy system as it had been outlined by Sims in his first dispatch of May 1. But it suggested a kind of dual administration that would place in America's hands the routing of our convoys and the designation of rendezvous in American waters. To this Sims replied with another plea for more ships and the observation that it would be a 'fundamental military error ... to change present established administration. ...' [31]

This long exchange of cables between America and England reinforced two convictions that had been growing in Sims' mind: first, that the Navy Department had been unable to determine its exact policy of cooperation with the Allied Powers, and second, that until such policy was determined upon, material aid would not be dispatched to European waters in the quantity Sims believed necessary. It had been with such convictions that he had turned to the Ambassador and the British government to gain their assistance in impressing the Navy Department and the President with the gravity of the situation. Mr. Wilson responded on July 4 with a long cable.[32]

It began with an expression of Mr. Wilson's surprise at the 'failure of the British Admiralty to use Great Britain's great naval superiority in an effective way.' In the present emergency the English seemed to Mr. Wilson 'helpless to the point of panic.' They had rejected every plan set forth by the United States government 'for some reason of prudence.' To the President it was not a time for prudence but for boldness 'even at the cost of great losses.' Sims had quite properly informed the United States of the sort of aid and cooperation desired by the British, but 'the trouble is that their plans and methods do not seem to us efficacious.' Therefore, Mr. Wilson would like to have Sims' own views of the situation and his own suggestions for action, 'without regard to the judgments arrived at on that side of the water.' The English, he concluded, had been very slow to adopt the convoy system and did not seem willing to give adequate protection to the convoys through the danger zone.

This cable from the President was actually less a definition

[31] W. S. S. to Secretary of the Navy, July 3, 1917.
[32] Woodrow Wilson to W. S. S., July 4, 1917, through the American Embassy.

of policy than an expression of dissatisfaction with existing British plans. Its significance can only be understood when it is considered alongside a cable from the Secretary of the Navy which arrived five days later on July 10. This cable, transmitting a copy of a letter from Mr. Daniels to the Secretary of State, set forth six basic principles that were to govern the naval efforts of the United States henceforth.

First, there was expressed the desire for the 'most hearty cooperation' with the Allies to meet the submarine situation compatible with an adequate defense of home waters. Second, a similar desire for such cooperation to meet any future situation. Third, it was asserted that the termination of the present war was the first aim, but it was stated that 'the future position of the United States must in no way be jeopardized by any disintegration of our main fighting fleet.' Fourth, it was recognized that the present main military rôle of the Navy lay in safeguarding the lines of communication of the Allies. Fifth, it was suggested that the offensive must be the dominant note, but the primary rôle in the offensive operation must belong with the Allied Powers and so the Navy Department was willing, in general, to fall in with any joint action approved by the Allies. Sixth, the Department announced its willingness to do the following things: First, to send all anti-submarine craft not incompatible with home needs. Second, to send the entire Fleet abroad to act as a united but cooperating unit if the emergency was deemed to warrant it. (It specifically stated, however, its unwillingness to send any *separate division* of the Fleet abroad.) Third, its willingness to discuss more fully any plans for joint operations with the Allies.

These two cables from the highest civilian authorities of the Navy arrived on Sims' desk within five days of each other. In the replies he sent to the Secretary and the President, much the same in principle if not in phraseology, he set forth his ideas of the general strategy of the war.[33] He had assumed since the beginning that 'our mission was to promote the maximum cooperation with the Allies,' and therefore that such questions 'as the possibility of post-war situations, or of all or part of the

[33] W. S. S. to Woodrow Wilson, July 7, 1917; W. S. S. to Secretary of the Navy, July 16, 1917.

Allies being defeated and America being left alone, were not given consideration — in fact I cannot see how we could enter into this war wholeheartedly if such considerations were allowed to diminish in any way the chances of Allied success.'

'Maximum cooperation' with the Allies implied a total effort on the part of America against the submarine. Such effort could not take the form of crushing the hornets in the nests because 'a sea attack alone upon German ports could not succeed against concealed guns and modern fortifications.' Nor could U-boats be sealed in the harbors by mines. Thirty thousand had been laid and still the submarines stole out to sea through neutral waters or slipped through the mined areas. The only weapon to use was the convoy which had proved its worth by the fact that sinkings had gradually diminished ever since it had been introduced. In supporting this system America could not be deterred by thoughts of the safety of her own coastline. Submarines could not operate successfully three thousand miles from home. Anti-submarine forces had to be concentrated in European waters 'where the war not only is but must remain.' To maintain a fraction of such craft at home was to fall into a policy of dispersion which all military experience had proved to be fatal. By the same token thoughts of the disintegration of the American Fleet must not deter the authorities from sending over all the forces at their disposal. The German High Seas Fleet was contained by the British Grand Fleet, and even should the High Seas Fleet escape from the trap they had set themselves, the American light forces in European waters would still stand between the enemy and the American battle line. Strategically they would, therefore, not be separated from our battleships, for they could fall back upon the main body of our Fleet or meet it at any appointed place without let or hindrance from the enemy. No argument of strategy or of policy could persuade Sims from his original view that the submarine was the source of real danger, that the convoy system was the effective weapon against it, and that America was in a position to throw her whole weight into support of this weapon.

To both men, Mr. Daniels and Mr. Wilson, he explained that it was difficult if not impossible to achieve the 'maximum cooperation' necessary with the limited resources of man-power at his command. Since his arrival in London no single officer had been sent from Washington to assist him. Babcock, his aide, had with almost fanatical devotion to himself and the cause worked himself to the verge of a nervous breakdown in those first months. Sims himself had performed duties no one in his position could be expected to have the time or willingness to do. Two men, with the aid of two or three junior untrained officers Sims had managed to obtain temporarily, could hardly be expected to direct adequately the American efforts at maximum cooperation.

There is a unanimity of opinion expressed in these communications between the Secretary of the Navy, the President of the United States, and the Commander of the United States Naval Forces Operating in European Waters in so far as all three men recognized that the United States was at war and that the chief threat to Allied success lay in the submarine. On the equally important question of how the war was to be carried on and the submarine thwarted, the disagreement is startling. The views each took of the situation are important because of the elevated position each man held and also because each represented a considerable body of opinion on how the Navy should be used.

Mr. Wilson in his cable of July 4 had counselled boldness in our war against the submarine. In stating that the plans of the Allies 'did not seem to us efficacious' and in asking for Sims' own suggestions, he by implication denied that the convoy was the best weapon against the submarine.[34] These views he later amplified in a speech he gave in August on the Flagship *Pennsylvania*. At that time he characterized the methods of sea warfare as carried on by the Allied Powers in the following fashion: 'We are hunting hornets all over the farm and letting the nest alone. None of us knows how to go to the nest and crush it, and yet I despair of hunting for hornets all over the sea when I know where the nest is. . . .' In the same speech the President said: 'This is an unprecedented war, and therefore, it is a war in one sense for amateurs. Nobody ever before conducted a war like this and therefore nobody can pretend to be a professional in a war like this.' Mr. Wilson was still clearly dissatisfied with

[34] It should be noticed here that Mr. Wilson in this cable accepted the value of the convoy as one method of warfare against the submarine. He expressed his opinion, however, that England was even in July using too few ships to ensure its success.

the way in which the submarine was being attacked on the seas. He wanted someone to come forward with a method of crushing the hornets in their nests. 'I do not care where it comes from . . . but I want the officers of this Navy to have the distinction of saying how this war is going to be won.' [35]

Mr. Wilson's military thinking during this period was conditioned by two considerations. He believed that the British Admiralty had been inexcusably slow to adopt any kind of adequate defense against the submarine. This gave him a natural and quite justified prejudice against the British Admiralty; it likewise apparently led him to distrust the professional mind. This distrust appeared the more justifiable because, to an amateur, the convoy system seemed like a clumsy and inefficient weapon against the submarine. It was with thoughts such as these that the President counselled increasing boldness in thought and action. Mr. Wilson was quite right in his assumption that British naval authorities had almost fumbled away the war, but he was unfortunately mistaken in his belief that an amateur or professional could find a better weapon against the submarine than the convoy system.

In failing to grasp the drab efficiency of the convoy, the President and those who believed with him committed the very error he described on the Flagship *Pennsylvania*. Energies were dispersed 'all over the farm' in attempts to find solutions for the submarine problem while they should have been concentrated on supporting the convoy. The point is important because several men have claimed for the President the credit for the convoy system. It will be remembered that the Secretary of the Navy recalled that he told Sims just before the latter left for London that the President 'could not understand why the British did not convoy their ships.' Sims was never able to remember that the Secretary had told him this, and there seems to be very little other evidence available to suggest that Mr. Wilson had

[35] *Hearings, 1920*, vol. II, p. 2022. Lindsay Rogers makes some illuminating comments on this speech in 'Civilian Control of Military Policy,' *Foreign Affairs*, January, 1940. As Mr. Rogers suggests, the President was making a strong case for the need for civilian or political influence in the conduct of war. None will deny that such influence is both necessary and valuable. Lloyd George's desire for the convoy system and the Admiralty's rejection of it is a case in point. But the civilian or politician who exerts influence should at least understand the basic principles of the military art and profession.

anything to do with the introduction of the convoy. Even if, however, it is assumed that he did, it is hard to understand why the President thought so little of his creation that four months after the country entered the war he failed to see that proper steps were taken to ensure its success.

If the President counselled boldness, the cable of the Secretary which expressed the views of the Navy Department appears to have been excessively cautious. Thoughts of the present safety of America three thousand miles away from the actual war and of the future security of the country after the war limited the scope of its policy of cooperation. Political considerations probably conditioned the thinking of the responsible men in the Department, for the residents of the eastern coast displayed a vocal hysteria at the thought of invasion. Likewise in these first months the Department apparently was not fully convinced of the critical situation in the war zone. Their information on this subject came chiefly from Sims, and Sims was known to be 'pro-British.' His chief supporter was the American Ambassador, who had the reputation of a hopeless Anglophile. So some of the forebodings of these men were written off as mere emotional unbalance.

Historically, if no other way, the view which Sims took of the situation has been proved correct. Mr. Wilson was closer to his heart's desire than he guessed when in August he told the Fleet he wanted the officers of our Navy 'to have the distinction of saying how this war is going to be won.'

When this exchange of cables was over in the middle of July, 1917, the main policies of the American Navy were decided upon. By implication if not by actual assertion the theories of Sims were finally approved in Washington. From that time on, the flow of ships grew ever greater, the convoy system was continually improved and strengthened, and the curve of sinkings dropped slowly away from the curve of available tonnage. Black days were yet ahead, but the blackest of all were behind.

20

Getting on With the War — I

In 1936 the *New York Herald Tribune* believed that 'Admiral William Sowden Sims bids fair to rank in American history with our other two great naval heroes — Farragut and Dewey. The three make a triumvirate that stands alone.' If time proves these words true, it will be a triumph of popular understanding. Every schoolboy knows the story of the *Hartford*, the damned torpedoes, and the victory at Mobile Bay; every child of ten has heard of the *Olympia*, of Gridley, and the dewy morning at Manila. But from these brief and splendid moments it is a far cry to an Admiral who flew his flag on a little destroyer tender he rarely saw; who slept almost every night of a great war in a suite at the Carlton Hotel in London.

'Fighting,' wrote Sims to his brother Varley in 1917, 'is one of the smallest aspects of military operations.' For him, the Commander of the United States Naval Forces Operating in European Waters, there was, during the twenty months of his command, no active fighting at all. Nor was there, after the first few weeks, much opportunity for him to display whatever strategical or tactical talents he might have possessed. After the introduction of the convoy, Sims firmly believed it was better to accept the methods three years of war had tested rather than to waste his energy in a search for new and untried schemes. The more conventional triumphs of a force commander were, therefore, denied him. His claim to stand with the naval heroes must rest in large part upon his work in the great and treacherous field of naval administration.

It was an unusually complicated administrative task that confronted him. His headquarters were situated in the city of London. From here the American forces, scattered from Murmansk to the Bay of Otranto, were directed. But it was not a direction that Sims could maintain independently. Three thousand miles from the war zone were his superiors at the Navy Department relying upon him for information, advice, and the execution of their military decisions. Yet, since America herself could not act independently, to Sims fell the added burden of cooperating with the Allied Powers. It was his duty to coordinate the forces of his own country with those of countries already engaged in war against Germany; to reconcile the national naval policies of America with the established aims of the Allies.

Sims had in the past refused such positions as Chief of Staff on the grounds that he lacked any administrative ability. His want of tact had been celebrated throughout the Navy. But here at the flood tide of his career he found himself in a position where success depended almost exclusively upon his qualities as an administrator and his gifts as a diplomatist. In his relations with each of the varied elements of his command, he had to rely principally upon what, if he is to be believed, were unexpected virtues.

The central figure in the command was, of course, the Admiral himself. Though he had arrived in England with only the vaguest verbal orders, his position was gradually clarified. On April 28, 1917, after the first six American destroyers had been ordered abroad, he was notified that he was to assume command of all American destroyers operating from British bases. One month later, May 26, he was commissioned a Vice Admiral to his surprise and disapproval. 'It will be curious,' he wrote to Mrs. Sims, 'to be a Vice Admiral after being a captain but a few months ago,' but he did 'not like it.' 'It seems to me inappropriate at this particular time and under these peculiar circumstances. In this war British officers have been promoted only for really valuable service, and it does not seem fitting that while operating with them I should be promoted before anything to speak of has been accomplished.' He even thought of refusing the rank, but was discouraged by the British Admiral Sir Lewis Bayly, who told him that it was a good thing for public opinion and that the position demanded it. Two weeks later he was detached from all previous duty (until this time he was still technically the President of the War College) and given the title he held throughout the war, Commander, United States Naval Forces Operating in European Waters.

The schedule of his life varied little from the day he arrived until the day he returned to America. He took up quarters at the Carlton Hotel, where he remained for the duration of the war despite pressure to move into a private house. His reasons for staying were typical. He was leading a bachelor existence, was rarely at home save to sleep, and was not interested in spending his government's money on the pleasant but wasteful extravagance of a home. Breakfast, taken usually with his aide in his own rooms, was followed by an hour with the morning papers. From the hotel he walked to the Admiralty for a conference with the British officers, after which he walked to his own offices at the American Embassy. These walks gave him the exercise he felt it his duty to himself and his country to take. They supplied him with other pleasures as well, for along the way he could see the friends with whom he struck up an acquaintance. Most of these friends were little children with whom he would stop to talk and play.

After an hour or two at the Embassy, he would go out to lunch, usually with Allied naval or political leaders. Not infrequently in the late afternoon he would arrange for an hour of tennis before going out to dinner with Cabinet members, generals, admirals, and other important figures in the Allied cause. Sometimes these dinners were purely social, but more often they served as committee meetings. From a dinner of this sort he would return either to his office for another hour or two of work — sometimes indeed he remained until the small hours of the morning — or to his hotel for further correspondence and reading. Part of this correspondence was to his own family who 'never left his thoughts' throughout those months of war.

Occasionally trips broke into this routine. Frequently he went to Paris for meetings of the Allied Naval Council. Sometimes he went off to the Grand Fleet for a conference with Beatty or to inspect the American battleships after they arrived, in December, 1917. He went also to Italy, to the bases in France, and most

of all, to Queenstown, where at first most of the American destroyers were based. It was an exacting life of travel and work,
containing few of the conventional diversions. For the theatre
he cared little and it seemed to him inconsistent with the nature
of his task to see a play, especially a comedy. About parties and
week-end visits he felt the same. But if life was arduous and the
responsibilities great, he was well equipped to endure the difficulties of his position. His splendid physical condition was proof
against the wear and tear of twenty months of war, and he took
care that nothing he did himself should jeopardize his health.
He exercised regularly, slept as much as he could, and avoided
elaborate food and any kind of wine or spirit. When he felt
the need of relaxation, he could find it in an hour with the
Jellicoe children, in a discussion with Balfour of Captain Slo-
cum's voyage around the world in the sloop *Spray*, or in his relations with his own men. The men closest to him during this
period were his own staff.

Until August, 1917, this staff consisted chiefly of Sims himself
and that most faithful of aides, Commander John Vincent
Babcock, 'the only Babby.' In their work they were assisted by
the regular Naval Attaché, Captain W. D. MacDougall, and by
such officers as the Admiral could attach temporarily to his
office. Three months after his arrival in England, in spite of
repeated requests for assistance, only three additions to his staff
had been made. One of these officers had to be sent on vital
duty elsewhere; the other two were assistants to the Naval
Attaché, ordered to additional duty with Sims.[1]

It was during this period that he was in constant discussion
with the Allied Powers about the convoy system, that he was
collecting information to assist himself and his government in
reaching major decisions of policy, that he was endeavoring to
answer a flood of specific questions from America about such
matters as the design of destroyers, the construction of mines,
and the manufacture of flat-nosed bullets. During the month of
July alone, his office handled 1430 letters and dispatches.

This lack of proper assistance greatly reduced the efficiency
of the London Headquarters, as the Navy Department was fre-

[1] *Hearings, 1920*, p. 211. For Sims' attempts to get proper assistance, see his testimony, pp. 203–228.

quently informed. On April 30, the Admiral sent his first recommendation for a staff. The names of four men whom he would like to have with him were suggested. Sims asked especially for William V. Pratt, who had been his Chief of Staff on the Flotilla and was then in the Office of Naval Operations. Five times in the first three weeks of May he repeated his requests, but on May 25, he heard only that Captain Pratt was unavailable. Throughout June, at an increasing tempo, cables were sent to Washington, reiterating the need for officers in London. At least thirty times during the first four months of the war he stated his requirements. Not until early in August did six men arrive. Among them was Nathan Crook Twining, who, in the months to come, proved himself of tremendous value as Sims' Chief of Staff. From that time on, the force at London was slowly increased, but as late as October, 1917, when he had a total of twelve men on his staff, Sims felt it necessary to ask for eight more.

Since no single man can adequately control and direct the many factors of modern warfare, he must inevitably be dependent upon the work of the officers assisting him. It can almost be said that a Commander is no better than his staff; and by the same token that a staff is no better than the Commanding Officer. Proper relations between the two are of the utmost importance in war.

The staff with which Sims carried on the war cannot be said to have been entirely of his own selection. Yet, once organized, the London Headquarters worked with remarkable efficiency. Sims, as the Force Commander, was assisted by Twining, the Chief of Staff, Captain W. R. Sexton, the Assistant Chief of Staff, and Babcock, the Admiral's Aide. Together these men formed a kind of executive council. The work of the London Headquarters was divided up among various administrative sections. Operations had charge of all the activities of the forces afloat. Captain Byron A. Long supervised, in cooperation with the Admiralty, the routing of convoys. Commander William Ancrum directed the ships in the coal trade. Two other men had charge of the anti-submarine offensive. Intelligence, under J. V. Babcock, controlled publicity, censorship, and counter-espionage. There were, in addition, sections of Correspondence and Communication, Material, Aviation, Disbursements, and Medical Care. The most remarkable division of this staff was devoted to Planning. Under such officers as Captain Harry E. Yarnell, Captain F. H. Schofield, Captain Dudley W. Knox, and Colonel R. H. Dunlap, United States Marine Corps, plans for future operations were developed; studies of particular military problems were made; criticisms of existing methods and organization were prepared. None of the men attached to the Planning Section had any administrative duties. All were graduates of the War College. They served as both the imagination and the conscience of the London Headquarters. This section, established by Sims, was the first of its kind in any Navy.

One project, dear to the Admiral's heart, was never fully carried out. Early in the war, he suggested that the Department send a professional historian with several trained assistants to set up an Historical Section. Such men were never sent, but later in the war, Sims established his own Historical Division under the direction of Captain Knox and a reserve officer, T. B. Kittredge.[2]

Under Sims, at the height of our naval effort, were three hundred and seventy ships of all classes, about five thousand officers, and seventy thousand men. These were distributed over forty-five bases. Questions, orders, decisions concerning these forces, were contained in the flow of cables that arrived daily at the Headquarters in Grosvenor Gardens. No single man could hope to attend to each detail of this vast responsibility. Detail, Sims knew, was the first enemy of a Commanding Officer. In the administration of his staff, he simply applied the lessons he had learned on the Flotilla. Among the various sections he subdivided authority and responsibility. Each day Captain Twining met with the department heads to discuss and decide questions presented by the rising tide of cables. Only the results and final decisions of these conferences were referred to the Force Commander. Frequently, in matters of lesser importance, the facts

---

[2] W. S. S., *The Victory at Sea*, pp. 249–250. An illuminating description of how the London Headquarters worked is given in a memorandum prepared by Captain N. C. Twining for the English War Office. One of the officers in the Personnel Section was Commander H. R. Stark who had served with Sims in the Flotilla. In 1942, Stark, then an Admiral, was sent to England to take command of all our forces operating in European waters. He took with him, among others, the reserve officer, T. B. Kittredge.

behind a conclusion were unknown to the man who was ultimately responsible. 'I pick,' he used to say, 'the best man I can to do the work and then I trust him.' It is the first if not the last law of the art of command.

To his wife Sims explained that he signed 'routine orders' without looking at them. Upon such technical matters as aircraft, about which he knew next to nothing, he took unhesitatingly the word of his subordinates who had studied the questions. Even in questions of policy, he wrote, 'Our planning section discuss it, study it, and reach a decision before bringing it to me. In any case when a final decision is reached I never write it. . . . In all the time I have been here, I have not composed a half a dozen letters or cables.'

'This will,' he believed, 'make it clear how the organization works, and how small an amount of work it puts on me. And this will be true no matter how large the organization gets. . . . With able and efficient assistants, to do the work, there can be no limit to the amount of business that can be handled. And it can be done without strain *provided one does not worry* and borrow trouble. . . . I trust everybody completely, and thus all do their best work and all are thoroughly loyal, and I have time to give attention to questions of general policy.'

Two problems confronting a Commander, Sims failed to mention in the deceptively simple rules he sent to his wife. A few months before this letter was written, John Jellicoe, exhausted by unnecessary labors, had left the Admiralty. An English Admiral wrote at the time of his departure that 'It depends not only on the head but on the men he [a First Lord] surrounds himself with. Nelson had a ring; Lord Wolseley had a ring; Fisher had a ring. Each one chose his men, and then secure in his choice, trusted them with details. I think that Jellicoe shewed too much friendship and too little judgment in the appointments that followed his arrival at the Admiralty and that caused him to do most of the work himself. Hence his fall.' Unlike the First Sea Lord, Sims was not given a free hand in the choice of his subordinates; in London at first he had no ring. The men he asked for were frequently not considered available by the authorities in Washington. Some of the men ordered to duty with him were not well qualified by training or temperament for staff work. Sims rectified this situation, as far as he could, by exchanging officers on duty at London with others serving elsewhere whom he desired. Yet, this collection of subordinates became in time a ring, an efficient loyal staff. The morale of 'Simsadus' was one of the great achievements of his leadership.[3] The men themselves deserved all the credit he gave to them for their work, but it was their commander who developed their spirit. One officer, not so successful, defended his failure by observing that his subordinates were disloyal. 'He does not,' wrote Sims, 'understand that a commander is wholly responsible for the attitude of his subordinates toward him.'

The second problem of command which Sims failed to mention is implicit in his assertion that he trusted his subordinates completely. That is an act of moral courage, the significance of which can best be understood when taken with Stonewall Jackson's dictum that 'The service cannot afford to keep a man who does not succeed.' Sims recognized that his success rested upon subordinates with whom he would not interfere in the performance of their several duties. Frequently he warned his wife that it might be necessary for him to resign if things went badly, or that the political authorities might find it necessary to sacrifice him to the public interest if an error were made. His removal, after the mistake of a subordinate, could not be considered unjust, since his was the ultimate responsibility. The best he could do was to organize his staff as well as he could and to place his trust in the competence of the individual officers. When a man's future is at stake, this is no easy thing. Sims did it with more success than most, in part because, in his buoyant optimism, he never 'borrowed trouble,' but principally because he had schooled himself, through the years, in the self-discipline of command.

Besides his staff at London, there stretched a wider responsibility: the American forces in the fighting zone. Of the forty-five bases of all types established during the war, the most important were at Brest into which most of the troops were con-

---

[3] 'Simsadus' was the cable address of the London Headquarters. A book by that name, J. L. Leighton, *Simsadus: London*, New York, 1920, written by a reserve officer who served at Headquarters, gives an appreciative description of the work done by the Navy and the Force Commander.

voyed, at Gibraltar where were based the forces convoying the Mediterranean trade, at Inverness and Invergordon where the North Sea Mine Barrage Force had its headquarters, and at Queenstown, focus of the trade from the Americas. In addition there was Battleship Division Nine of five dreadnoughts, operating with the British Grand Fleet (in which it was designated the Sixth Battle Squadron). All these units or forces, with the exception of Queenstown, were under the command of Rear Admirals. In each case, the American men and material were maintained as separate commands under officers subordinate to Sims, but under the general supervision of the Senior Naval Commander in the district. Rear Admiral Henry B. Wilson at Brest, for example, was called Commander of United States Naval Forces in France. He was, as he said, 'under the senior allied commander technically' in the distribution and operation of his forces, yet his general orders came from his Force Commander at London.[4] In such a complicated administrative situation constant friction and misunderstanding might have developed.

For Sims, the situation was doubly complicated, because he had chosen none of the men serving at these bases. Wilson was at Brest, succeeding Captain, later Rear Admiral, W. B. Fletcher at that post in November, 1917. Rear Admiral Albert P. Niblack had command of the important Gibraltar base after November, 1917. He had been Sims' roommate at the Academy. The great affection that existed between the two may never have wholly died. But after Sims took over the Target Practice Office from Niblack in 1902, their friendship ceased. Another classmate, Hugh Rodman, had the battleships with the British Fleet and won by his work the admiration of both the Americans and the British. But he and Sims had little in common and had never, since their graduation, served together. The man in charge of the North Sea Mine Barrage was Rear Admiral Joseph Strauss.

Whatever the merits of these appointments or the wisdom of leaving the selection of subordinates wholly to a Force Commander, Sims felt he deserved more consideration. Some of these men were selected for their positions before he was given even an opportunity to express an opinion. In a communication to the Navy Department, he wrote near the end of the war ex-

[4] *Hearings, 1920,* pp. 903–904.

plaining that 'regrettable difficulties' and 'resulting inefficiency' had been caused 'by the assignment of men to vitally important positions who have in the past been opposed to me in official matters and who are not in sympathy with my methods.' [5]

It is wholly unnecessary to examine here the merits of the professional and personal differences between Sims and his subordinates. That such existed, in the case of at least some of the men mentioned, is beyond all doubt.[6] The significant thing is that, in the face of such obstacles, all these men were able to carry on the war so effectively.

To each officer in charge of a base or force, Sims issued a set of General Instructions. In these the general mission of 'cooperation with the allied forces in destruction of enemy forces' was laid down, together with the immediate mission of 'conservation of allied and neutral shipping and the saving of life.' The instructions from Headquarters were not military orders and should not in any way interfere with the demands of the local military situation. They were intended to 'impart the policies of the Force Commander, to facilitate administration, and to disseminate information.' The fundamental policies set forth were: cooperation with the Allies; the carrying out of operations in accordance with the plans of the Senior Allied Commander in the several areas; the encouragement of individual initiative to a maximum degree. 'Commanders should act in accordance with their best judgment under such general policies of their seniors as have been previously made known to them.' All information of value was to be transmitted to the London Headquarters immediately. To each commander, the value of doctrine was especially com-

[5] W. S. S. to Chief of Naval Operations September 30, 1918. This note is repeated frequently in his correspondence. Typical is his letter of January 5, 1918, to the Chief of the Bureau of Navigation: 'I particularly wish that you could send all officers who served under me in the old Flotilla. This desire is not for sentimental reasons, but is, I believe, in accordance with sound military principles.' On May 12, 1918, he wrote Pratt: 'All I ask is that the responsibility for success should be put up to me, and that my recommendations as to the methods of carrying on the work, and as to the personnel to assist me, should be accepted. Try and fix it so that when officers of considerable rank are to be sent out here that I be consulted.' This attitude seems entirely justified. A counter-view is expressed in Von Tirpitz's dictum that if his plans depended for success upon the work of any particular officers, something was wrong with the plans.

[6] It is interesting to notice that in the Investigation of 1920 every one of the officers mentioned above appeared before the Committee in opposition to Sims' criticism of the conduct of the war.

mended. Until every force developed its own, the Flotilla doctrine was to be used. It was the War College and the Flotilla all over again.[7]

Within these wide latitudes, the various subordinates were left to act alone. In practice, the system worked as Admiral Niblack later explained to a senatorial committee.

> *Chairman:* Under whose operation orders were the forces under your command?
>
> *Niblack:* Admiral Sims'.
>
> *Chairman:* Operation orders I asked?
>
> *Niblack:* Largely my own; and in conference with the Mediterranean officers. The convoys were under the regulations of the senior convoy officer in the Mediterranean, that is, Admiral Calthorp (Eng.).
>
> *Chairman:* Was this situation satisfactory?
>
> *Niblack:* Entirely so.
>
> *Chairman:* Did your forces, the forces that were under your command become, therefore, an integral part of the British Navy?
>
> *Niblack:* Not in the slightest degree.
>
> . . . .
>
> *Chairman:* Were you allowed satisfactory initiative by Admiral Sims?
>
> *Niblack:* Absolutely.
>
> *Chairman:* Did he interfere in any way with the administration of your forces?
>
> *Niblack:* Not except to help me. He interfered oftener to help me and I needed it.
>
> . . . .
>
> *Chairman:* Those are all the instructions (the General Instructions referred to previously) received by you from Admiral Sims?
>
> *Niblack:* I suppose I got about fifteen cablegrams a day of various kinds.
>
> *Senator Pittman:* What was the substance of those?
>
> *Niblack:* Sailings of ships, orders transferring officers, notification of sending me supplies and reserve officers and men, dispatch of materials, and all kinds of information that came through Operations. He had a very large force in London that kept us informed. And then we got daily bulletins from Admiral Sims of all the happenings in our command and in the war zone, which

---

[7] Force Instructions Number 2, September 22, 1917. These are most easily found in *Hearings, 1920*, pp. 1032–1033.

were very nice to have and very illuminating, and we had a free interchange of information, so that we would all know what the other fellow was doing, as far as we could. The thing was beautifully managed; very efficient.

Pittman: He gave you all of the information that he had at his command?

Niblack: And we, in return gave all of ours. The situation of the submarines momentarily was given us by radio and telegram (from W. S. S.) and we had a great operating board in the office of the Commandant, where every convoy was kept in position from hour to hour, relatively, on the chart, and there were dozens of convoys at sea all the time, and as soon as a submarine would be signalled as in a certain spot, it would be placed on the board, and then if necessary a radio signal would be sent to the meeting convoy ship to change course a certain number of degrees, or to a certain definite course, to avoid this submarine.

Pittman: Then when you received this information it was up to you to operate your forces?

Niblack: To operate my forces at need. We never closed.[8]

Thus was the war carried on from Headquarters through the various local units, whether at Brest, or Gibraltar, or Queenstown. The buffer state of system was laid between the individuals, and conflicts of personality were avoided. In his efforts for harmony, Sims was assisted by the traditional naval spirit which instils in subordinates loyalty to the office regardless of the man who holds it. This system of command produced magnificent results. One sad incident serves only to give perspective to its general excellence. In the early months of the war, an officer, whose methods of administration were at variance with those of his Force Commander in London, was in command of one of the bases. He attended to matters of detail himself and sought to keep close supervision of the forces under him. Those forces, at the time he was in command, were entirely inadequate to the demands of escort made upon them. They were few in number and, for the most part, unable to keep the sea in all kinds of wind and weather. The problem confronting this man was discouraging in its complexity. Soon after his arrival, Sims provided him, as he did all other officers in similar position, with a convoy doctrine which set forth the number of escort vessels

[8] *Hearings, 1920*, pp. 1028–1038.

required by convoys of various size. Upon one occasion, a convoy under this officer's supervision put out to sea with a smaller number of escort vessels than prescribed by Sims' doctrine — which was based upon Allied convoy experience. The officer had not deliberately disobeyed orders; a combination of circumstances within his command had resulted in the failure to supply the protection deemed necessary. A submarine attacked the convoy and sank an empty transport returning to America. The officer in charge of the base was immediately detached by Sims and sent home. With a bitter irony the ship on which he was returning home, though protected in accordance with the convoy doctrine, was likewise torpedoed.

Sims defended his action on the grounds that he had long been dissatisfied with the officer's administration, and that the officer had failed to comply with the convoy doctrine which all experience had proved sound. He pointed out that no convoy was ever entirely safe from attack, but that convoys, protected as he prescribed, were as safe as possible. A Court of Inquiry held some years later sustained the position taken by Sims. The Court did indicate that Sims may have relied, from the beginning, too completely upon his own staff for information about the base in question, and it definitely asserted that the force under the officer's command was inadequate for the demands placed upon it.

Sims was not blind to the human factor in this sad affair, though the suddenness and decisiveness of his action may have left such an impression upon those most intimately involved. But, as he said in another connection, in war there is no place for personal feelings. The responsibility upon him was that of winning a war and that responsibility transcended all personal considerations.[9]

One base, above all others, presented problems beyond the reach of rule or regulation. The Irish city of Queenstown was

[9] Sims' position is well described in several letters he wrote to his wife at the time and in a letter he wrote to a friend, February 27, 1924. 'The case was most unfortunate,' he said, 'but the action taken was inevitable. The whole business was investigated by a Court of Inquiry that lasted a month and which completely justified my action. It was a sad and hopeless case.' For permission to read certain correspondence bearing on the incident and the finding of the Court of Inquiry, I am very greatly in the debt of the officer in question.

the headquarters for the forces guarding what were called the western approaches to England. Through these approaches passed almost all of the traffic coming from the Americas with the elements of war upon which England's survival depended. It was to Queenstown that Commander Joseph Taussig brought the Eighth Division of six destroyers, as our country's first contribution to the Allied cause. His words to the English Admiral in command of the base are now legendary. When asked by the latter when the destroyers would be fit for duty, Taussig replied, 'We are ready now, sir.' [10]

It was on Queenstown that a large force, at times the largest force, of American ships was based throughout the war. The Irish Sea surrounds this port, and upon these mad waters, in fair season and foul, our ships and men first proved their stamina and valor. It was at Queenstown, from the tender *Melville*, that Sims flew his flag throughout the war. Of all his varied professional memories, until the end of his days Queenstown remained one of the fondest and fairest. It was his masterpiece. [11]

When Sims first arrived in London, a heterogeneous collection of small ships was operating out of the Irish city, on patrol duty in the western approaches. In command of this force was an English Admiral, Sir Lewis Bayly. For England and the ships of England, this singular man had a passion the more consuming because it was unspoken, the less rewarded than its intensity deserved because of the austerities of his own temperament. [12] Fate, especially during the war, had not been altogether kind to him. At the beginning, he had been in command of the

[10] 'Legendary' is perhaps the most accurate word. There are various versions of what Taussig actually said at this famous interview. An officer present at the time asserts that he used the less dramatic 'I shall be ready when fuelled.' This in itself is startling enough when one considers the voyage the destroyers had just finished. This voyage and the welcome given to the Eighth Division is well described in J. K. Taussig's 'The First Six,' *N.I.P.*, December, 1922. The author gives a clear picture, among other things, of the confusion and delay attendant upon the departure of the ships.

[11] An admirable and exciting narrative of the Queenstown command is given by J. K. Taussig in 'Destroyer Experiences During the Great War,' *N.I.P.*, December, 1922, January, February, and March, 1923. A more detailed account is E. Keble Chatterton's *Danger Zone*, Boston, 1934.

[12] A full account of Admiral Bayly's career is given in his own book *Pull Together!* London, 1939. 'Pull together' was the watchword of the Queenstown command. The American officers at Queenstown presented the Admiral with a silver model of an American destroyer called the 'U.S.S. Pulltogether.'

First Battle Squadron with the Grand Fleet, flying his flag from the new *Marlborough*. But in December, 1914, he was ordered to command the Channel Fleet, which meant to him 'the sacrifice of all the aims of my career.' Suddenly withdrawn from the field of possible decisive action, he held his peace, for 'in war these things happen, and no officer has any right to refuse to accept an appointment in times of national emergency.' His stay with the Channel Fleet was brief. In accordance with Admiralty orders, he took his ships to Portland for firing practice. On the way, every precaution urged by the Admiralty was observed, but off Start Point about two in the morning, the last ship of the line, the *Formidable*, was torpedoed and sunk. Next day he was ordered to haul down his flag, and his request for a court martial was refused. With a Roman stoicism, he accepted what amounted to his disgrace. 'It is well to remember that in a disciplined force, an essential of that discipline is the facing of injustices with a smile. One of my favorite maxims to officers is that success teaches us nothing; failures only teach.' Shortly afterward, he was made the President of Greenwich Naval College. In July, 1915, he was summoned to the Admiralty to take command of the Queenstown Forces, which, at that time of relative quiet on the part of the submarines, must be considered a minor command.

Such experiences could not leave untouched a spirit that was proud and understood its own value. Sir Lewis Bayly was a British officer in the grand tradition; àn admirable seaman, with a deep-seated dislike of shore duty; an exacting disciplinarian; a brave man with that dogged determination that sometimes flashes into inspirational recklessness. He was also intelligent. Seven years before the war began, he had been in command of the destroyers, in which position he became, in Sir Julian Corbett's words, 'the father of destroyer tactics and organization.' He was, moreover, a student of war, having read and thought far more deeply on the subject than most of his colleagues. More clearly than most, he had understood the intentions of a hostile Germany. Small wonder that during the first years of the war, the iron entered into his soul.

Unfortunately for him, there was iron enough in his temperament before 1914. There was much that was grim in the swept surface of the personality he revealed to his colleagues. His temper was uncertain and cantankerous. He had a reputation for not getting on with people he disliked, and he was believed to care for few. Like some Scotch Covenanter, he pursued his duty with an uncompromising tenacity. At times he was startlingly brusque. To an officer, just detached, who wired to him, 'Sorry [my] destroyers were not of much use to you,' he replied, 'Why say much?' Beneath the flintlike austerity there were, however, warmth and gentleness and poetry. With his own hands, he used to brew the coffee for the survivors of sunken merchantmen who arrived at Queenstown, sometimes after days on the ocean wastes. Whatever the time of day or night, he was always there with food and drink and comfort for the exhausted and bewildered men. On the first anniversary of the arrival of the American destroyers, he issued an order which ended, 'to command you is an honor, to work with you is a pleasure, and to know you is to know the best traits of the Anglo-Saxon race.'

Such moments of simple eloquence were rare; he could not speak facilely of 'Comrades of the Mist.' Beneath his words of praise or affection, there lay always a charge of emotion he sought to conceal. Strangely contradictory in his character, devoted yet embittered, loyal yet independent, forbidding yet lovable, proud, stern, almost pathologically shy, he was no ordinary man.

When it was decided that our first destroyers should be based on Queenstown, Jellicoe expressed his concern about the situation to Sims. He feared that cooperation would be difficult. Bayly had 'a reputation of being very difficult' and 'was supposed to have it in for all Americans,' since 'he was practically fired out at the request of our people' when he was the Naval Attaché at Washington. Later Sims learned that, despite the critical nature of the submarine warfare in 1917, the Admiralty itself had been unable to work successfully with their commander on the western approaches. The friction had, in fact, gotten to such a point that 'the anti-submarine people in the Admiralty no longer corresponded with him nor he with them.' Also Bayly would not ask for the men he needed in Queenstown and 'would not ask for the detachment of men who were totally unsuited to the work.'

Such was the condition of affairs when Sims first met the English Admiral at London. 'On that occasion,' wrote the American, 'he was as rude to me as one man can well be to another,' and Sims had had considerable experience with rudeness. Bayly was, in fact, deeply incensed at having been summoned to the Admiralty. Jellicoe, much upset by the incident, offered to remove his subordinate if necessary, but Sims preferred to wait and see. 'I did not know what the cause of the friction was,' he wrote a short time later, 'but I believed I could find it out and indicate how it could be corrected.' Shortly thereafter, during the first week in May, he went in person to Queenstown. None of our destroyers had arrived, but the Eighth Division was on the way.

Admiral Bayly was polite, but not enthusiastic at first. After the two had 'walked around each other' for three days, the Englishman told his niece, 'That man is on the square.' From this niece, Miss Violet Voysey, who kept house for her uncle, Sims learned much. None understood or loved the Englishman better than she. The success of Queenstown rested in no small part upon the wisdom, tact, and insight of this pretty young woman. She and her 'American Admiral,' from this time forth, were in league with one another on behalf of 'Uncle Lewis.'

From this visit Sims returned to London with a complete understanding of the causes of the friction that had been built up between Queenstown and the Admiralty. For two years Bayly had been on exhausting duty with no leave; one of the chief subordinates 'had always been a thorn in Bayly's side,' and he had been left desperately short-handed. Of all the officers in similar position, Bayly alone had not been given the title of Commander-in-Chief. To Jellicoe, Sims suggested that he write a letter to Bayly arranging for a short leave. Sims also said that it was absolutely essential for the Rear Admiral in charge of anti-submarine work in London to write to Bayly, requesting permission to visit him for purposes of benefiting by his long experience. The Rear Admiral objected, but Sims insisted that 'this was war and that personal feelings should have no place in its conduct.' The officer went. To the First Lord of the Admiralty, Sir Edward Carson, Sims explained the necessity of making Bayly a Commander-in-Chief. This was done the same day. After these steps had been taken, the relations between London and Queenstown were greatly improved.

At the bottom of all Sims' efforts lay his respect for Admiral Sir Lewis Bayly. That he had brought about cooperation between the Admiralty and this subordinate whose irascible independence was almost legendary in the English service, was a triumph of which he was not unaware, but he would not have made the effort solely to display his own diplomatic talents. He regarded Bayly 'as one of the ablest Naval officers with whom I am acquainted in any Navy.' Thus he was willing to make any reasonable concessions to his 'peculiar' temperament in order to make use of his brilliant abilities.[13]

Sir Lewis was not slow in recognizing the debt he owed his ally. On May 30, he wrote to Sims: 'I have a suggestion. If I go on leave from June 18th to June 23rd, would you like to run the show from here during my absence? I should like it (and you are the only man of whom I can truthfully say that), your fellows would like it, and it would have a good effect all round.' To this Sims replied on June 1, 1917, that the suggestion was the

> surprise of my life. I will not attempt to express my appreciation of the honor you have done me, or my gratification for the confidence your suggestion implies.
>
> While I have never yet had occasion to hesitate to accept, or unduly feel the weight of, any of the lesser responsibilities of my service, I would hesitate to accept this were it not that I would simply be carrying out your plans, by your methods and with the assistance of a staff trained by you.
>
> Under the circumstances I shall be more than glad to act as your representative, particularly as I assume that in case of an unforeseen problem of a serious nature I can fall back upon your more mature experience. . . .
>
> Please present my best respects to Mademoiselle Voysey, my fellow conspirator in our common cause.

This last sentence was filled with the humor that bubbled up through Sims' most serious thoughts, for the letter from Sir Lewis was probably not the surprise of his life. With Miss Voysey ap-

[13] All the material for this account of the relations between Sims, Bayly, and the Admiralty is based upon a letter written by W. S. S. to W. V. Pratt, August 30, 1917.

parently he had arranged to put the idea of his taking command at Queenstown into Admiral Bayly's head. It was an imaginative gesture designed to publicize American and British cooperation, and to head off any criticism from home that American interests were being subordinated to England's. With the aid of 'the only niece' and Sir Lewis' generosity, the more real because Bayly was unaware of the delicate manoeuvres, Sims gained his end. For five days in the middle of June, his flag flew from Queenstown where, for the first time in history, an American commanded a part of the British Navy.

The Queenstown Command grew to be the second largest of the war. Only Brest, the centre of troop-convoy activity, was greater. At the end of the conflict, there were almost seven thousand men in Ireland and fifty-nine vessels of all types. In the twenty months of active service, the forces there supplied ninety-one per cent of the escort for three hundred and sixty convoys.[14] Many of the commanding officers of the destroyers had worked with Sims in the Flotilla. They had been trained by him, understood his methods, and used the Flotilla Doctrine to govern their activities as far as possible. But beyond this indirect influence, Sims, after he hauled down his flag when Sir Lewis returned from his leave, had little to do with the active command of the base. The organization of the forces was, in fact, very complicated and irregular.

In theory, Sims was the Commander-in-Chief of the destroyers operating out of Queenstown, but since he was, for the most part, in London, the burden of the work fell upon his Chief of Staff in Ireland, Captain Joel R. Poinsett Pringle. The extent of Pringle's success depended in large part upon a happy co-operation with the British, because the forces were under the operational orders of Sir Lewis Bayly. The Americans estab-lished an entirely separate organization for the maintenance of their vessels and their discipline. But the United States ships went out to sea in company with the Allies, and the united forces, while on duty, were under the orders of the senior officer of the group, whether he was English or American. Because of this close relationship, Sims' Chief of Staff was also appointed

[14] *Summary of Activities of U.S. Naval Forces Operating in European Waters*, prepared at London Headquarters, 1919, p. 13.

United States Chief of Staff for Admiral Bayly. As such, he was entered on the British Navy list, the first foreign officer on an Admiral's staff to appear there.[15] The success of this irregular arrangement, which was, at times, severely criticized by Americans, depended greatly upon the man who held these dual positions, Captain Joel R. Poinsett Pringle. No choice to fill this delicate office could have been happier.

Pringle's powerful mind, well trained professionally, moved easily in realms quite beyond the borders of naval interest. He was a balanced, finished, sophisticated personality, well equipped to handle the difficulties of his peculiar position. So rigorous a judge as Sir Lewis Bayly considered him his 'beau idéal' of a naval officer. Throughout the war Pringle handled his ships — and there are no more difficult ships than destroyers — with consummate professional skill. With equal understanding he handled his officers and men, who were occasionally offended by some peremptory order from the English Admiral or irritated by some inexplicable difference between Americans and Englishmen. Most of all he distinguished himself by the intuitive wisdom of his relationship with the Commander-in-Chief, whether Sir Lewis was toying with the idea of refusing a Birthday Honor or of refraining from appearing at the American Men's Club for reasons clear only to himself. No less of an achievement was his relationship with his own superior, Admiral Sims. Had he been less of a man, he might have been offended by the bluntness with which Sims called attention to the occasional defects of his command. Once, the older man, hearing in London that there was some immorality and drunkenness amongst the Queenstown men, wrote to Pringle one of his unblinking letters on the subject: 'You know, of course, as well as I do that if gossip like that gets started, and if it is believed, the person or place gossiped about gets just the same kind of reputation as though the statements made were entirely true. The point about the whole business is that what we would like to have would be such a condition of mind on the part of all hands, and such a loyalty to the whole organization, that there would not be anybody who would make such statements as those in question.' This would appear to be the council of perfection to a man who

[15] Lewis Bayly, *op. cit.*, p. 222.

was engaged in a most delicate task, involving personal relationships where nothing is perfect. Pringle, with good cause, could have replied with some annoyance, especially since Sims subsequently admitted that his reports were probably more gossip than truth. At the same time he told Pringle that 'there was certainly less of that sort of thing in Queenstown than in any military organization I have ever known.' But Pringle made a thorough investigation of the situation before replying in a letter which fully accepted the spirit of the criticism though denying its entire justice. Sims, on his part, accepted the explanation, adding with candor that some of his own men had been drinking, though he had not heard about it until two of them had gotten into the hands of the 'Bobbies.'

This exchange contained the one cause of possible friction between the two men. Trouble was avoided by the fairness and frankness of both. For the rest, Sims left Pringle, as he always left his subordinates, to run his own show save in rare instances where he felt it necessary to act as the Commander-in-Chief. To one officer at Queenstown, he did write a letter which reveals the existence of the kind of minor irritation that can disrupt a command. 'Even I,' he said, 'have heard that you have criticized Admiral Bayly unfavorably; or rather that you have made remarks which indicated criticisms of this kind. I was told that you referred to him as "Old Frozen Face." This is a dangerous business, even when no harm is intended, and remarks are purely facetious or for the purpose of passing the time. However, every man is responsible for the reputation he has because if he puts his mind on it he can acquire any particular kind of reputation.' It was a stitch of this kind that Sims always tried to take in time.

The candor of these letters is significant. Not only was he honest with his own men; he spoke the truth as he saw it to his Allies. The Americans at home, who later charged that he was more than half English in his sympathies, would have felt a thrill of horror had they read the ungrammatical sentences he wrote to Admiral Bayly on July 14, 1917. 'I fully realize the awful muddle that has been made and is being made in dispatching troops from the other side. It would almost seem as though anybody who could collect a regiment on the other side, marched it down to New York and went and boarded a steamer as passengers and then called on me to see it safely convoyed. It is almost incredible but neither any of our military officers here nor the British War Department knew anything about the prospective sailing of these regiments on British Liners!' Rather sadly he concluded that 'my reading of military history leads me to believe that no war will ever be fought without troubles of this kind. Also the business of the military man is to do the best he can with the tools he has in hand.'

Through such letters as these, to Pringle, to the destroyer Captains, and to Admiral Bayly, Sims sought to head off trouble and complaints, before they came. This was especially important in connection with Queenstown, because of the unique nature of the organization. During 1918, there was some agitation at home to put a Rear Admiral in command. Articles expressing dissatisfaction with arrangements at Queenstown appeared in *The Army and Navy Register*, March 16, and in the *New York Tribune*, March 21. It came to Sims' ears that some change in the system of command was contemplated. He wrote off on April 16 to Admiral Benson that it was imperative that he, Sims, be left in command of the destroyers, with Pringle as his Chief of Staff. Benson, as he did so often during the war, came to Sims' support and assured him that no change was contemplated.[16] Yet Sims remained constantly on the alert to close any opening of which the critics could take advantage.

It may appear that too much time has been given to the Irish base at the expense of the others, especially since Queenstown was second in the matter of size and importance to Brest. Yet the city, as the centre of convoying activity for all the trade from the Americas, was vital to the Allied success. In its organization it called forth all the administrative abilities Sims used to a lesser degree at the other bases. In its history, his methods of dealing with the complicated problems of his command are most clearly illustrated. The intent here is not to slight the work of such men as Strauss in Scotland, Niblack in Gibraltar, Wilson at Brest, Rodman with the Grand Fleet, and all the others who contributed to the victory at sea, but to indicate through Queenstown, the most difficult of all commands, how Sims performed his duties at every base. And Queenstown of them all was closest

[16] W. S. Benson to W. S. S., May 8, 1918.

to his heart. Indeed for all the men who worked out of this port during the war, the duty was one of the great experiences of their lives.

Not only professional success but enduring personal ties bound Sims to this base. Admiralty House on the hill overlooking the harbor became a home for him during the war. Every now and then, he would slip away from London for three days with Admiral Bayly and 'the only niece.' Queenstown was the one place where he could intimately see and hear and touch the realities of the war that at times seemed so remote in London.

For the men of both nations who served there, the base has become a precious memory consciously perpetuated by the Queenstown Association. The splendor of its success has hidden many of the difficulties that lay in the way of that success. To a few officers, Admiral Bayly remained 'Old Frozen Face.' At times, in his pride in the men under him, he exceeded his authority and reprimanded American officers to their chagrin and mortification. British officers noticed that they usually paid for more drinks at the officers' club than did the Americans. The enlisted men of both countries, upon occasion, irritated one another. There is even a tale, which may not be true, that the last American destroyer to clear from the harbor had a sprig of mistletoe hanging over her stern. Forgotten though these things are now, they serve, when recalled, but to brighten the achievement. Inevitable difficulties and frictions frequently could not be solved by the ordinary salvation of command, an appeal to rules and regulations. Adjustments had to be made by instinct, tact, and intuition. Upon the leaders, Admiral Bayly, Admiral Sims, and Captain Pringle, fell the heavy burden of the command. To all of them belongs the credit for a great achievement. With this triumvirate quite properly belongs another, Miss Violet Voysey. Each man appealed and not in vain to this young woman. 'Petticoat influence' has seldom been used by woman with such wise restraint.

It is not to be wondered at, that the spirit of Queenstown, like so many of the things in which Sims had a hand, transcended professionalism. After the war, Admiral Bayly came to America to see the members of his old command. While entering New York Harbor, his ship was met by an escort of seaplanes and dirigibles. A lady from Cincinnati, standing on the bridge with Sir Lewis, turned to him and said, 'What a magnificent thing it must be for you to be a British Admiral.' He replied, 'You are making the greatest mistake in your life; that has nothing to do with being a British Admiral at all. It is the greatest proof that has ever been seen of a true friendship between two hundred and fifty or three hundred people.'

21

Getting on With the War — II

QUEENSTOWN illustrates Sims' methods of dealing with the forces under his command; no less it provides an example of his settled determination to cooperate with the Allied Powers. When Napoleon was once asked against whom he would prefer to wage war he replied, 'Allies.' Sims was no less aware of the prejudices, jealousies, and conflicting aims that divide and sometimes rule the military efforts of a coalition. 'I believe,' he wrote to his friend Pratt on June 7, 1917, 'there is no case on record where Allies have cooperated together for any considerable length of time without more or less serious friction. I am out to make an exception in this matter. There has been to date material for any amount of friction, due to peculiar personalities, but I believe they have been successfully overcome.' The dangers of disunity hung always in the back of his mind. He wrote a short time later that 'the greatest obstacle in the way of success up to the present time has been lack of coordination between the Allies.' This obstacle he set himself to eliminate in so far as he and his own country were concerned.

His first step was a declaration of policy. 'The first course open to us which naturally occurs to mind is that we should look upon our service as part of the combined Allied service,' which involved, as Sims understood, putting our men and ships under ultimate Allied control. In this view he had the stated approval of the Navy Department in Washington. The arrangements made at the various bases as heretofore discussed reveal how completely this policy was carried out. This idea can hardly be considered novel, but the fact that Sims early announced it and continuously labored to ensure its achievement gives him a distinction rare among Allied commanders of any age. His efforts ensured, as Jellicoe later pointed out, a unity of command.[1]

It was the easier for Jellicoe to accept this plan of action because the principle of unity of command, undoubtedly sound militarily, placed control of the Allied Naval Forces in the hands of England. Sims was willing to accept the necessity of placing his forces under Allied control and to acquiesce in the logic which placed England as the leader of the Allies, but his views on cooperation did not extend from here to the passive acceptance of English decisions. His struggles over the adoption of the convoy, his insistence that he be shown all material in the Admiralty before making up his mind, indicate the degree of real independence he permitted himself.

Theoretically, and to a certain extent in practice, the broad naval policies were determined by all the Allies in concert. Representatives of the nations met frequently to discuss the problems that daily arose in the prosecution of the war. Until November, 1917, when the Allied Naval Council was created, the meetings were informal, but the procedure before and after the formation of the Council varied little. Admirals from Italy, Japan, France, England, and America met together ordinarily in Paris or London to thrash out differences and settle policies. Sims, in these discussions, had a chance to see the influence of those prejudices and jealousies he feared so much. Italians objected against the use of Allied ships in the eastern Adriatic, maintaining that only Italian ships should serve there and then only when chances of success were assured.[2] Or he heard the French and Italians argue that their ships could not remain on a barrage in the Adriatic in winter weather. This kind of thing 'got on his nerves,' and he would astringently point out that American and British destroyers were daily serving on the North Atlantic.[3] But differences in these meetings were far rarer than agreements. The Allied Naval Council performed valuable work not only in the shadow but in the substance of cooperation. It decided shipping routes, allocated the limited supplies of coal and

---

[1] J. R. Jellicoe, *The Crisis of the Naval War*, p. 161.
[2] W. S. S. to W. S. Benson, February 15, 1918.   [3] *Ibid.*

oil to vital places, distributed forces over dangerous areas. It provided a vehicle for rapid and unanimous decision that was greatly needed.[4]

To these conferences Sims brought the weight of his clear mind, his incisive speech, and his irresistible humor. Of particular value was his ability to speak French. Upon many occasions he played the part of interpreter as well as representative of America. Since personal relationships in councils of this kind are frequently of paramount importance, it was fortunate that with all the varied nationalities he got on well. With Jellicoe and his successor, Vice Admiral Rosslyn Wemyss, he was on terms of intimacy, while for the Frenchmen, Rear Admiral Lacaze and Vice Admiral De Bon, he had both affection and admiration. The latter especially impressed him. De Bon combined a genial humanity with the limpid mind and gift of exposition so generally found among members of his race. As Sims wrote to his wife, Frenchmen were always better in discussion than Englishmen or Americans who had to fumble for words and ideas. For the Italian Vice Admiral di Revel, about whom a London paper remarked that 'unlike Admiral Sims he looked every inch a sailor,' he had a regard he extended to few of that officer's countrymen. Rear Admiral Funakoshi, the Japanese representative, was a source of surprise and pleasure to Sims. The two found constant enjoyment in each other's witticisms. Personally, he may have respected the abilities of the Frenchmen most. But he got on well with all of them, which is half of any committee meeting, because he liked them and because he made up his mind that he would like them.

For Lloyd George, Sims had the respect he had for all men who saw their task clearly and performed it energetically. With the Prime Minister, that outspoken, buoyant, restless Welshman, the American of such similar characteristics had no real or important differences.

To facilitate discussion with the English, it was proposed by them in December, 1917, that Sims be made an honorary member of the Board of Admiralty. Membership on the Board, where Sims would sit without voice or vote, would have been, as he

---

[4] An excellent description of the members of the Allied Council and the work performed by them is given in *The Victory at Sea*, pp. 256–262.

pointed out to the Navy Department, a great advantage. From participation in its deliberations he could learn much of the information that it was not possible to set before the Allied Naval Council and could obtain a clearer insight into the problems and personalities with which he was dealing. At first Washington opposed his membership on the grounds that 'such action might create unfortunate feeling on part of other Allies,'[5] but this objection was swept away when the French and Italians both assured the English that they heartily approved of the idea.[6] The approval of the Allies was forwarded to Washington, but officials there delayed action while Sims became increasingly embarrassed by their obvious reluctance. The King himself asked twice if America had accepted the invitation. Finally permission was, as the Secretary of the Navy later said, 'gently, but firmly declined.' Why the Navy Department felt such a decision necessary in view of the values accruing from acceptance of the invitation is difficult to imagine. Perhaps the advantages were not fully recognized or were obscured by prejudice. Mr. Daniels, who had a gift for expressing his personal interpretation of events in rather conventional eloquence, believed Sims was moved only by his coveting of British honors. 'Privately at the time,' he confided later, 'I regarded it as rather a love of glitter and foreign recognition and honor than anything else.'[7] These private views of the Secretary may have been the determining factor in the refusal; at all events more compelling reasons were not forthcoming.

From the first Sims believed it was as important to win the confidence of the British people as it was to gain the respect of the British government. Methodically he set about accomplishing his task. He appeared in public as often as he could, dined out, and spoke at luncheons and meetings of all kinds. The newspapers were quickly acquainted with all the dramatic incidents of his past, for he was always ready to receive reporters. As he wrote to his wife it was good policy for a commander to share his face and his biography with the people for whom he was fighting. Familiarity was the first step on the road to confidence. With his peculiar attributes of body and mind it was not difficult for

[5] W. S. Benson to W. S. S., January 9, 1918.
[6] W. S. S. to W. S. Benson, January 31, 1918.   [7] *Hearings, 1920*, p. 1984.

him to accomplish his purpose. Sir Arthur Pollen, the great English naval scholar, reported in Washington that 'Sims has taken the country by storm, he is so preposterously good-looking.' England, in fact, gave him a kind of public recognition and affection that he had never received in America. Such wide popularity strengthened, as he had foreseen, his position both at home and abroad.

The problems which Sims encountered in dealing with the forces under his command and with the various representatives of the Allied Powers were great. For solving them Sims is entitled to the praises accorded him by his subordinates and Allies. In his relations with the Navy Department he was confronted by even more imposing obstacles. Any commander can look forward to friction between himself and the administrative forces at home. Distant from the scene of conflict, the men in the capital inevitably take a different view of the battle from those engaged in it. Communication between the two is frequently difficult and information exchanged must inevitably be incomplete. Of greatest significance is the fact that the commander on the spot is concerned primarily, if not wholly, with the military aspects of the situation, while the directing forces at home find their decisions complicated by political considerations, and, not infrequently, by military ignorance as well. Both the commander in the field and the members of the military establishment at home can justly claim a voice in the decisions affecting the course of war, but the zones of authority belonging to each are never clearly defined. Hence, there is always friction, sometimes so much friction that the wheels of war stop turning. One of the great duties of a commander is to avoid such a possibility. The student of war who was the biographer of Stonewall Jackson believed that the Confederate made his greatest contribution to his cause when he attempted to resign after the Secretary of War had exceeded his authority in issuing an order that was purely military in nature.

These are some of the ordinary obstacles Sims could expect to meet in his dealings with the Navy Department. There were some extraordinary ones as well. In the first place, his position as Commander of the United States Naval Forces Operating in European Waters was never clearly defined. Apparently even his superiors never quite understood his exact place in the chain of command. By law the Chief of Naval Operations was the highest responsible official in the Navy. Directly beneath him was the Commander-in-Chief of the Fleet, who was, in 1917, Rear Admiral H. T. Mayo.

It was only after the war that his superiors attempted to define his position in relation to these men. Such efforts then resulted only in explanations that his title meant the opposite of what it appeared to mean. Secretary Daniels observed that 'The title . . . is wholly misleading. His real function was that he was in substance an assistant abroad to the Chief of Naval Operations and was also Naval Attaché in London.' [8] This definition the Secretary later amplified as follows: 'He was not given such power because he was never Commander-in-Chief, but, though called "force commander," really exercised no important duties except such as inhered in a liaison officer and representative of the Department for such duties as were specifically given him by the Secretary of the Navy and the Chief of Naval Operations.' [9]

The intricacies of naval rank and authority might well be expected to escape a civilian secretary so ignorant of the naval profession as Josephus Daniels, but the confusion in the minds of high ranking officers is more difficult to explain. Admiral Benson believed that 'there is an exaggerated idea as to Admiral Sims' position that he occupied.' This he amplified in the following fashion: ' . . . I will say this, that in the strict sense the title of commanding officer of the naval forces in Europe in this particular case was almost a misnomer.' Benson explained further that Sims was subordinate to Admiral Mayo, 'but the situation was such that as a rule the orders were given directly from Washington to Admiral Sims by me. . . .' After such explanations it is not difficult to understand why Benson could ' . . . feel that Admiral Sims' interpretation of his mission was not in accord with the mission that the Department intended him to perform or fulfill.' [10]

[8] *Hearings, 1920*, p. 1995.   [9] *Ibid.*, p. 2003.

[10] Benson's full exposition of this matter of Sims' rank is given in *Hearings, 1920*, pp. 1917–1919. Throughout his testimony he emphasized Sims' rôle as a transmitter of information. The attempt, at this time, was made by various officers to show that Sims was only in fact 'a relay office for all communication between Washington and the forces in the field' — a kind of liaison officer.

At the time that these opinions were given, the men quoted were for one reason or another anxious to score a few points against Sims. Probably that is the reason for the arresting unanimity in their assertion that his title meant almost the reverse of what it appeared to mean. But for whatever reason the testimony was offered, it does indicate a spectacular carelessness on the part of authorities in failing to clarify the duties of our chief naval officer abroad. The situation was the more complicated because Sims took his title at its face value as did the Allied Powers with whom he worked. In so doing, Sims redeemed a situation that might have caused his failure. Had he not accepted the authority and responsibility implied in his position, though left unstated in his orders, he would have retarded our war effort and greatly reduced his sphere of decisive action. As Nelson at Copenhagen put the telescope to his blind eye, so Sims in London disregarded doubts about the nature of his authority. Both officers took, in the phrase of a student of war, 'the strong line' when failure to do so would have placed success in jeopardy. Such an act of moral courage is the hallmark of a great commander. In the opinion of one of Sims' most discerning subordinates this action is the greatest lesson of his career for those officers of the future who will command.

A second handicap in his relations with Washington lay in the fact that he was under suspicion as an Anglophile. An officer in Washington reported that 'Admiral Benson seemed to think that Admiral Sims and our officers abroad were in danger of becoming obsessed with all things British to the detriment of clear judgement.' Few Americans who have gone to England on official business have escaped this charge and the accusation was natural in Sims' case. His past offered ample evidence of his respect for that country. Yet as reliable a witness as John V. Babcock reports that Sims would occasionally return from a banquet in London with the observation that 'It makes me damn mad. All through their attitude one can see "He's a damn good fellow and an American into the bargain."'

Sims himself did not attempt a denial of his pro-British feeling, though he did qualify it as follows in a letter to his friend Pratt: 'In all this you must give me credit for being reasonably honest. You must not assume that because I am pro-British and pro-French and pro-all the rest of the Allies I am necessarily anti-American. I have lived a long time in the United States (forty-six years). I have shown some interest in the efficiency of our Navy. I am fifty-nine years old and have a modest reputation for reasonable independence of thought. So do not assume in the pride of intellect that I am owned by the British or any other Admiralty. If you do not think a pro-ally is the right kind of man for this job, they should have sent a pro-Prussian with a trunk full of bombs.'

Whatever the truth of the matter the important thing is that some of his superiors believed that Sims' affections had been captured by the British. This was especially unfortunate, since naval officers share with most Americans that strange blend of respect and antagonism which has ever complicated our relations with the older country.

In addition to the uncertainty about Sims' exact position and his suspected British sympathies, the condition of the Navy Department itself complicated Sims' relations with his superiors in Washington. For two reasons the Navy Department was not equipped to carry on the kind of war America was waging in 1917. The first was a matter of personalities. The civilian head, Josephus Daniels, despite his set of firm convictions on naval questions, hardly possessed sufficient professional and administrative equipment to run a large Navy at war. He apparently tried to keep control over most of the activities of the Department, in any case an impossible task, but especially dangerous because, as one officer put it, the Secretary was a 'slow decider.' Sims heard that 'he (Daniels) is personally handling the allotting of floor space to the different bureaus as they expand out of the main building and he won't decide how he will do it. Half the bureau chiefs are semi-paralyzed and on the fence on account of this little item alone.' [11]

The Assistant Secretary was the energetic Franklin Delano Roosevelt. His contribution, however important, did not meet with universal approval. Sims was informed that 'the Secretary

[11] The name of the writer of this letter is withheld. There is, however, no reason to doubt the information. The same source reported that the feeling in Washington was that 'Admiral Sims is all mugged up with British ideas.'

and the Assistant Secretary do not agree, and the Assistant Secretary and the Chief of Naval Operations do not agree.' [12]

The Chief of Naval Operations was William Shepherd Benson. The virtues of this man, and they were great, were his undeviating honesty, his complete reliability, and his unfaltering loyalty to the office of the Secretary. Unfortunately these were offset by defects that were grave when found in the highest responsible officer in the Navy. With no War College training and little imagination he failed to grasp completely the true nature of the war he was fighting. Ungrudgingly he worked himself to the point of exhaustion and, apparently, permitted himself to be overburdened by the weight of administrative detail. It was said that he held his job 'largely because he won't cross the Secretary.' This harsh judgment does not do justice to the solid qualities of Benson as a man or a naval officer, but it does suggest the nature of his inadequacy in the position he held.

Beneath him for most of the war as Assistant Chief of Naval Operations was William Veazie Pratt who succeeded the industrious Volney O. Chase upon the latter's death in June, 1917. Pratt, it will be recalled, had been Chief of Staff in the old Flotilla days. Strategically he was placed between Sims and Benson and served as a means of communication for the two. During the war he worked himself almost to the breaking point on more than one occasion. It was well for the country that he did so, since he had a clearer conception of what was going on both in Washington and London than any other man in the Department. After a trip to Washington in 1918, J. V. Babcock wrote to Sims that 'I now realize how much we are all dependent upon that one man — that is, the Department as well as ourselves. He has a grasp upon the entire situation; his point of view is surprisingly similar to yours, and I can assure you that you would be surprised to find how closely he is in agreement with you in everything. Wherever the Department has failed to support you it was not due to Pratt, and, further, that he did everything he could to have your wishes carried out.' [13]

[12] As in the case of the preceding letter, the name of the writer, a different man, is withheld. Both letters simply repeated information or opinions Sims obtained from several sources.

[13] J. V. Babcock to W. S. S., January 31, 1918.

Of these four men, who were the controlling members of the Department, the two ablest were in subordinate positions. Pratt alone, by training, temperament, and professional knowledge, was really equipped for the task at hand and he was possessed of the least authority. But no single man, however capable, could have made the Department equal to the demands placed upon it in the first months.

Before America entered the war, relatively little attempt had been made to prepare the Navy for possible conflict. Existing ships were not placed on a war footing, the personnel was deliberately limited to less than peace-time needs. 'Especially serious,' says one commentator, 'was the Department's failure to envisage the problems that lay ahead, and to formulate plans with reference to actual conditions in the war area. While there was no pressing need for more battleships, the Department kept on with its regular building program, ignoring the imminent demand for large numbers of destroyers and other craft especially suited to the exigencies of anti-submarine warfare. While certain officers gave thought individually to ways and means for combating submarines, the Department undertook no systematic official study of this problem which now overshadowed every other phase of the war on the sea. And when Congress declared war, April 6, 1917, the only official plan for war with Germany envisaged a campaign, not against submarines in European Waters, but against a battle fleet in the Western Atlantic, with the probable focus of operations in the Caribbean.' [14]

The fact that the United States started to fight a war without sufficient man-power, suitable ships, or an adequate battle plan is attributable in part to the peculiar interpretation of neutrality employed by the Wilson Administration in the years after 1914. In part, too, this disgraceful situation can be explained by the inadequacy of the Navy's administrative system. This lack of proper organization limited the American effort in early months of the war.

All the criticisms that had been levelled against the organization since 1842 came home to roost in 1917. The Office of Naval Operations, created in 1915, did not have the legal authority necessary to impose its will. This weakness was the more appar-

[14] Sprout, *op. cit.*, p. 354.

ent because the Office had not been in existence long enough to acquire by time and custom the prestige and power necessary to coordinate the varied activities of the Department in time of war. One officer wrote that, 'Operations is supposed to coordinate all bureaus and don't coordinate their own office.' Pratt, who knew the situation better than anyone else, felt that 'Navigation has not entirely cooperated. Say what you please, there is a lack of get together between Navigation and Operations which should not exist. . . . There are strong influences at work I think to discredit the work of this office. . . . The Fleet cusses us out — everybody does it . . . but I am learning something of the game and I AM SURE that the only thing for a CHIEF of Operations to do is to lay the LAW down. . . .' [15]

In January, 1918, J. V. Babcock returned to Washington for a time and sent back to Sims his jaundiced view of the situation. Perhaps he rather overstated his case, since he was by temperament pessimistic and was attached to his Chief in London with a deep loyalty. Yet, when due allowance is made for these things, the story Babcock had to tell is dark enough. Most of the Department, he reported, were loyally supporting Sims and admitted he was doing a good job, but the errors of the Department were due chiefly to faulty organization, which was so loosely knit that it gave plenty of opportunity for the play of individual idiosyncrasies, jealousies, etc.

'The sum and substance of the situation is simply that no one has sufficient information on which to reach decisions. They have not time to look up all the information on any one subject. . . . It would be a long story to tell you of the difficulties under which Navigation has worked. The Secretary keeps a close hold on all personnel matters and some of his actions and policies are beyond understanding. Palmer has done a tremendous piece of work. . . . Captain Pratt's situation is nothing but pitiful. He is the brains of the Department and how he stands up under it I am unable to understand. Practically every dispatch that comes in has to go through his hands and this is simply due to the faulty organization around him and a wholly inadequate number of officers.'

For most of the men involved Babcock had nothing but praise;

[15] W. V. Pratt to W. S. S., May 27, 1917.

his criticism was reserved primarily, as he said for 'the wretched organization [which] is the principal stumbling block.' The general air of confusion appalled him. He suggested tartly that 'offhand the destroyer escorts are needed in the corridors of the Navy Department more than in the war zone — messengers, officers galore bumped into me at every turn.' [16]

The difficulties in the way of perfect harmony between Sims and the Navy Department were obviously great. Yet there was a possibility that all of them could be overcome. In many ways Sims sought to eliminate the imposing obstacle of distance which prevented adequate communication. His cables were long and detailed. Whenever he made a request, he tried to justify it with reasons; when he made a decision, he tried to give all the important factors that had determined it. To supplement this necessarily limited information he wrote long letters to the men in Washington. To the Secretary he sent chatty, rather colorful descriptions of the general situation as it unfolded. Benson received communications that Sims composed in spare moments throughout his day. These were more professional in character though lightened by humorous incidents or anecdotes. He would review the military situation; 'at this date it would seem almost that the Germans have been definitely checked.' There would be the gist of a conversation with some statesman; 'Lloyd George said, "No, that kind of thing [unified command] is not possible among allies until they are sufficiently alarmed."' Usually he would add some interesting personal note: 'Our battleships have had a very remarkable effect on the spirits and morale of the British Fleet — I am told by an officer in the fleet. This same man expressed the general astonishment of the British Navy at what they considered the taming of Admiral Bayly. There was a common saying in the British Navy that what they ought to do with Bayly was put him in an iron cage and feed him raw meat until war broke out, and then turn him loose on the enemy. They cannot quite understand not only the respect but the positive affection they [our people] have for him and he has for them.' [17]

With the chiefs of the various bureaus, who were responsible

[16] J. V. Babcock to W. S. S., January 30, and February 5, 1918.
[17] W. S. S. to W. S. Benson, April 2, 1918.

for supplying him with men and material, he kept up a constant correspondence. To the Chief of the Bureau of Navigation he once wrote: 'From time to time we hear through correspondence or people coming over here that so and so has said — "Why in the devil don't those chaps on the other side do so and so." When this happens several times it creates irritation. What I should like would be for everybody concerned, instead of blowing off a growl like that, to call a stenographer and put it on paper and send it over to us. Paste us good and hard when you think we're wrong. We cannot improve our methods unless we know where they are wrong. Don't hesitate to fire criticism at us.' [18]

One man in the Department was piped a different tune. With Pratt, that old and trusted friend, Sims did not feel it necessary to hold his fire.

I have learned accidentally and incidentally today that eight destroyers have left for the Azores. . . . I am sure that you can readily imagine that it is somewhat embarrassing for me to be asked questions about the orders under which these are operating and thus to learn for the first time that the vessels have left the United States. [19]

Or on another occasion,

Please remember while you are reading this, and remember it all through, that I am writing to you from the point of view of a man who is handling a very big and very responsible job, with the assistance of one military aide. Just keep this fact in your mind about this one military aide. . . . It is a matter of the utmost astonishment to the people over here that I am left without a staff. . . . It goes without saying that no other official of any other Army and Navy is in such a position. . . . I am obliged to go from one Department of the Admiralty to another, consulting officers of all ranks to dig out information. . . . You tell me that everybody is trying to send me help *as fast as it can be spared*. Then you recite to me why it cannot be spared. It is because you need so many officers for so many different things — trawlers, motor boats, converted yachts, and so forth and so forth. Did it ever occur to you that this must necessarily sound to me as though you were trying to make fun of me? Is there any billet in the Navy today, barring a few, that is more important or more

[18] W. S. S. to L. C. Palmer, February 26, 1918.
[19] W. S. S. to W. V. Pratt, August 18, 1917.

responsible? Is not the success of the work that I am trying to do more important than the *existence* or the *efficiency* of one or two converted yachts? [20]

Sims used these letters to Pratt as a safety valve, but he apparently did not know that the steam that thus escaped from him was very hot. Pratt had, with Sims' knowledge and approval, shown the Chief of Naval Operations all the letters that had been arriving from the London Headquarters. 'I requested him not to let me read any more of them,' wrote Benson to Sims, 'as I was afraid that the constant spirit of criticism and complaint that pervaded them at all times, showing unmistakable inference that most of the good that was being accomplished in this office was due to Pratt and possibly Schofield, would gradually produce a state of mind on my part that was undesirable to say the least.' [21]

Benson in fact disliked the assurance of the younger man, but he did respect the professional ability of his subordinate. He was convinced that Sims was the best officer for the post in England; and he relied implicitly upon his given word. Sims, for his part, believed that Benson lacked the knowledge and training necessary for the discharge of his responsibilities. Never once throughout these years, however, did he question his motives or doubt his integrity. Across the chasm of professional and personal differences the two built an arch with a keystone of personal trust. During the war this arch was strong enough to bridge the Atlantic. Afterward the keystone fell and with it tumbled the whole structure of their mutual regard.

Several months after Benson wrote this letter, he came to England to see the situation for himself. He went everywhere and saw everything. Upon his return to Washington, he wrote Sims that he had been very pleased with what he had found in Europe. Certainly, too, his understanding of the condition of affairs abroad had been improved by this first-hand inspection. From that time forth the relations between London and Washington were better, though never without some feeling of dissatisfaction on both sides.

The tempered approval of Sims on this aspect of his command is best illustrated by an exchange of cables that took place late in

[20] W. S. S. to W. V. Pratt, July 28, 1917.
[21] W. S. Benson to W. S. S., September 24, 1917.

December, 1917. The Department wired on the twenty-second as follows:

> At House Committee hearing of conduct of Navy representative Britten said Quote, I would like to have copy of complaints which have come from Admiral Sims on the other side Unquote. If you desire to make statement of action of Department in reference to sending and supplying force under your command since war began please send in code.

To this Benson added:

> Effort being made to create impression you have been hampered by failure of Navy Department to meet your request for various things particularly personnel. I feel that a strong positive statement on this subject from you is highly desirable.

On the next day, December 23, Sims replied:

> I strongly deprecate any effort to create an impression that our naval forces in European waters have been avoidably hampered by failure of the Navy Department to comply with my recommendations for various things particularly personnel. It is, of course, well known that the anti-submarine campaign and the protection of allied shipping have been, and still are, hampered to a certain extent by insufficient numbers of certain types of vessels, especially destroyers, and by certain classes of personnel, and I have repeatedly made recommendations in accordance with the requirements of this situation. To these recommendations the Department has always responded with the assurance that reinforcements of both vessels and personnel were being sent to the maximum extent consistent with the many other requirements of the Department in these respects. The decisions as to the relative importance of the employment of our naval vessels and personnel in the theatre of actual war operations in European waters and at home must necessarily rest with the Department, and I consider it the first duty of those at the front loyally to accept such decisions and to make the best of conditions which are at present admittedly unsatisfactory and must so remain until the energetic measures now being taken to increase our anti-submarine forces produce the necessary reinforcements.

To his wife Sims explained this answer in the following terms:

> This is just a note to enclose a copy of a cablegram I received and a copy of my reply.
>
> You will recognize that the cablegram was an appeal for help in refuting criticisms in the House Naval Committee of the de-

partment for not supporting me, particularly in my requests for adequate personnel. You know, of course, that for several months I was not supported in this respect... was in fact, shamefully neglected, and that my official letters and private letters and cablegrams clearly showed this.

Of course I could not make the 'strong positive statement' that was considered 'highly desirable.'

You will see the kind of statement I did make. It was in effect, a refusal to make the desired 'strong' statement. I fancy they did not derive much comfort from it. I have heard nothing more from it, but do not consider the incident closed. There is talk of a congressional investigation, and if this is forced, it may bring out the whole business. If so, it will be a fine, large-sized row. If I am called upon for a statement, I will simply refer to my cables and letters on the subject by date and number. And if these are produced there will be no misunderstanding possible — for they are 'complaints' of the most energetic character.

I have never known where the block was, but it was perfectly successful in keeping me from getting any assistance from the time of my arrival until about the first of August.

It must be assumed that all these communications of December, 1917, were written in good faith. Thus composed, they serve only to illuminate the differences that divided Washington from London. The men in the Department assumed that their request for a 'strong statement' from their representative in the field was justified. They had worked tirelessly to overcome the obstacles set in their path by an unprepared and clumsy organization. They had sent all the assistance compatible with what they believed to be the home needs. In doing something, they assumed they had done enough. Sims, on the other hand, could judge their work only by its results as revealed in Europe. He had not been given the men or material he needed to fight a war in the danger zone. This was the rift between the two; it was fundamentally a difference of policy. Until this difference was reconciled, as it was by the end of 1917, friction between London and Washington was inevitable. The position of the Navy Department is not improved, in this matter, by the fact that it was Sims' views on the nature of the war that were proved correct by the time the Allies won the war in November, 1918.

A proper ordering of human relations is a large part of military administration. But it is not the whole. Sims and his staff, Sims and the Admiralty, Sims and his subordinate commanders were able to work together because fundamentally they agreed upon their mission and the methods of obtaining it. No such unanimity of opinion existed for the first months between Sims and the Navy Department. No skill in human relationship could bridge this rift of policy. Without in any way minimizing the contribution made by the men in Washington, it can be said that Sims did all he could to establish harmony between his Headquarters and the Navy Department, and that success attended his efforts when his views were finally accepted.

From the moment Sims arrived in England, he knew that the effectiveness of his forces rested primarily upon his ability to co-operate with the Allies. He determined, at all costs, to work in harmony with the other navies at war against Germany. By subordinating every personal or irrelevant consideration to this central necessity, he accomplished his purpose. With what complete absorption he devoted himself to his task is made clear in a letter he wrote to his wife in August, 1917. In it he describes the impression made upon him by a dinner conversation with Winston Churchill. 'He is of the most aggressive, cocksure type. He has had a brilliant career for such a young man (in the early forties). It seems wholly impossible for him to believe himself wrong in anything. His hobby at the present moment is that the Allied armies and navies are without intelligent direction — just bungling along from day to day without any plan. His criticisms are not exclusively destructive. He has so much confidence in his own opinions that he does not hesitate to tell them what should be done and denounces them because they do not get busy at once.' A good many of Sims' acquaintances would have had little difficulty in recognizing a familiar type in this description.

Churchill at the dinner belabored 'with excited gestures' both the military and naval commands. When he had finished Sims asked him: '1. Was the Allied Council too ignorant to understand what should be done? 2. Was the Council too cowardly to carry out what they knew should be done? 3. Was the failure to carry out obvious plans due to political consideration, international suspicion, jealousies, etc.?' The questioner was quick to notice that 'Winston Churchill floundered considerably and there was a twinkle in Lord Cecil's eyes.' Sims then gave it as his opinion that 'neither the British or Allied Navies were too ignorant to know what to do, nor too cowardly to do it; that in military matters the only logical and safe way was to rely upon the decision of military men.' 'All hands,' he reported, 'agreed with me.'

It was a strange position in which William Sims found himself that night at dinner. He was, for the moment, a Principal Dignitary meeting the arguments of a young insurgent. It would seem that much is explained by this momentary transformation, the more interesting because both before and after this event he expressed his great respect for Winston Churchill. Better than Churchill, perhaps, he knew the strange paralysis that had affected the Admiralty during the first months of 1917. Yet not a word escaped him.

This letter must explain why Sims would pardon in Jellicoe what he could not find it in himself to excuse in Benson. It explains the days he spent in organizing the Queenstown Command around Sir Lewis Bayly while he objected strenuously to some of his own subordinates. It explains, too, why he never claimed or permitted his men to claim that he had been primarily responsible for introducing the convoy system. In dealing with his own he would remain the insurgent, but in working with the Admiralty he would become one of them: not to the extent of losing his own convictions, but to the extent of submerging his own tremendous personality.

If in so doing he sometimes took over a few of the less tenable opinions of his Allies, he, at the same time, assisted in establishing that unity of action and purpose without which the winning of the war would have been difficult if not impossible. It is testament to what a man can do with himself if he only will.

Sims now can never hold the same exalted rank as Farragut, Porter, and Dewey. He may not even, as the *Herald Tribune* hoped he would, go down in the history books as their equal. Whatever the meaning of the rank he took with him to his grave, whatever his place in the hearts of his countrymen, his record in the First World War remains. Though he fought it out in a room overlooking Grosvenor Gardens, he helped to win a war as surely as did any Admiral in his conning tower.

22

The Victory at Sea

B IOGRAPHY,' James Boswell maintained, 'occasions a degree of trouble far beyond that of any other species of literary composition.' One need not seek far for reasons justifying this opinion handed down by the man who best solved the problems of his craft. If it is difficult for a biographer to tell the truth, it is impossible for him to tell the whole truth. Though history may be the essence of innumerable biographies, not even a small part of the past can be written as the projection of a single life. Yet no biographer can quite escape the dangers of creating history in the image of his subject.

One chapter of this brief study of the World War has been devoted to the part Sims played in the formation of military policy during the time of crisis in 1917. Two other chapters have been devoted to analysis of his administrative methods. Some part of this fourth chapter should properly include a description of the efforts of the United States Navy to implement the Allied strategy.[1] From the labors of innumerable men came the victory at sea.

[1] There are several easily accessible and competent histories of America's part in the war. W. S. S., *The Victory at Sea*; T. G. Frothingham, *The Naval History of the World War*, Cambridge, 1924–1926, vol. III, are the most informative single volumes. An excellent shorter account is contained in Dudley W. Knox, *A History of the United States Navy*, New York, 1936, chapters XXXV, XXXVI, XXXVII. The *Reports* of the Secretary of the Navy for 1918 and 1919 are chiefly devoted to the United States' part in the war. Josephus Daniels, *Our Navy at War*, New York, 1922, is a flamboyant account of certain aspects of our naval contribution. The summary of our general naval effort which is contained in this chapter is simply a condensation of the above secondary works.

By the first of August, 1917, the idea that the convoy system was the most effective known method of dealing with the submarine had gained general acceptance. Men could be found on both sides of the Atlantic who would not agree that it was the only way, or even the best possible way, to meet the menace of undersea warfare, but all the responsible officers of the Allied Powers were ready to admit, at that time, that the convoy system should be continued. Throughout the early summer of 1917, however, there had been disagreement over the method of controlling convoys.

The greatest difference of opinion existed between authorities in the United States, the country which was the most important producer of goods to be shipped, and the officers in England, the nation which was the principal port of deposit for the goods. Some indication of this divergence of opinion was given while the idea of the convoy was still being debated. Commodore Gaunt, the British Naval Attaché in Washington, cabled his government on July 1, that the 'United States are urging that routing and control of all merchant shipping should come under one party. They seem rather inclined to want control. I have pointed out that we already have an organization which works well, to which they agree, but say it is necessary to have the offices in the American customs and have arranged for that with sole exception of Portland.' [2] On the following day Sims received from the Navy Department their proposal. The Admiralty was asked to predict a week ahead the days on which ships would be escorted through the danger zone. At the same time, the position of the rendezvous between the merchant ships from America and the escorting vessels would be selected. This information would be forwarded to British agents in America who would communicate with the United States authorities. Then, it was suggested, these authorities would direct all shipping from American points to the rendezvous.[3]

To such a plan Sims presented a host of objections. It had proved impossible, he said, for isolated ships to assemble on time at any ocean rendezvous. Such a procedure involved a

[2] Naval Attaché, Washington to Admiralty, July 1, 1917.
[3] Secretary of the Navy to Alusna (cable address of London Headquarters), July 2, 1917.

great deal of radio communication by which the destination of the ships could easily be detected by the enemy. Finally, it robbed convoys of the necessary formation drill and training, upon which in large part the safety of the convoys in the danger zone depended. A week later, the Department proposed a lane of shipping that could be constantly patrolled by anti-submarine vessels. To this idea Sims replied that there were not enough ships to patrol the lane adequately. Furthermore, such a lane would make an excellent target for submarines, no matter how often its position was shifted.[4]

The arguments presented by Sims were not all of his own devising. British experience had revealed the inefficiencies and dangers in the proposals of the Navy Department. In all of his cables on this subject, Sims supplemented his objections to the proposed plans with the recommendation that all convoying methods be placed in the hands of the British. On July 14, he stated in a letter to the Department, the position from which he never departed. 'I have not intended to convey in my dispatches the idea that I consider the British methods of handling shipping as the best. Improvements are doubtless possible, but we should not attempt to improve at the cost of lack of cooperation and hence at the cost of losses which cannot be afforded. My only aim has been to attempt to point out the entire necessity for thorough cooperation.' On the same day, he said that 'in any case we should always utilize the central control here in London where all information is available, and from where the orders should be issued to the escorting forces. The British Admiralty will be only too glad to accept a representative from our Navy Department with his proportionate share of responsibility in the Admiralty. This fact has been cabled in the past.'[5]

Eight days later, he heard from Washington that 'Your letter No. 17. Rules for convoy therein accepted and will govern ends.'[6] Thus was established between the two great naval forces of the Allied Powers agreement on the control of the convoy system. In a short time, an American officer, Captain Byron A. Long, was sent to the Admiralty to cooperate with the English and to

[4] W. S. S. to Secretary of the Navy, July 3, 1917.
[5] W. S. S. to Secretary of the Navy, July 14, 1917.
[6] Commodore Gaunt to W. S. S., July 22, 1917.

assist in the direction of the convoys. Though improvements and refinements were, from time to time, added as the war went on, the basic system remained unchanged from August, 1917, until the Armistice.

What Admiral Sims called 'the central nervous system' of the convoy was located in London. In a room at the Admiralty worked the men who gave some pattern to the movements of the 'swift shuttles of an Empire's loom.' One side of this room was covered by an immense chart on which appeared the east coast of North and South America, the Atlantic Ocean, the British Isles, and the west coast of Europe and Africa. The terminal ports used by the convoy, Sydney, Halifax, New York, Hampton Roads, Gibraltar, Sierra Leone, and Dakar, were boldly marked out on the chart. From these ports ran threads 'to certain positions just outside the British Isles.' On each thread were little paper boats representing convoys. Every day these boats were moved along the threads to give the position of the advancing ships. When the ends of the threads were reached, the convoys had arrived at the rendezvous where the escort vessels would pick them up. On the chart, too, around the British Isles, little circles were marked off. These represented submarines. Every day the position of these circles — there were rarely more than eight at one time — was changed. Their exact course was determined by the radio direction-finders that picked up radio messages from the undersea boats, and by information obtained from merchantmen which had sighted or had been attacked by the Germans.

Day by day, at the Admiralty, the progress of the huge game played out upon the seas was revealed. As a submarine approached dangerously close to a rendezvous or to a convoy, this information was relayed to the officers at sea, and the position of the rendezvous or the course of the convoy was altered. So accurate was the information obtained about the activities of submarines that the men in the Admiralty could make their moves with complete knowledge and assurance.

The pieces — the merchant vessels — used by the officers in London for their vast chessboard were scattered all over the seven seas. By following the course of one ship from the time it left America until the time it docked in England, the convoy procedure for all ships can best be understood. A merchantman cleared from Boston in cargo and proceeded to New York — the nearest station. In New York, the master went to the English Consulate, where he was told to take his ship to a particular assembling point. When the ship reached the assembling point, other ships were waiting there, all under the supervision of a convoy commander. The commander, a naval officer, received instructions from the Admiralty in London. After a few days of waiting, the convoy was filled. There were twenty or thirty, perhaps forty ships in all. Before the departure, all the masters were called together, given a book of instructions and a talk by the naval officer in charge. As the convoy left the assembling point, it was joined by a cruiser or an old battleship, which would protect it from any surface raider that might be encountered. The convoy, spread out over perhaps ten square miles of ocean, jogged along at the speed of the slowest ship, usually eight knots. The first days at sea were spent in constant manoeuvres designed to thwart the menace of the submarines. No such menace existed at the beginning of the trip, but the masters were taught to zigzag, to read the signal code, and to steam in formation, against the day when the danger zone was entered.

Far at sea, the commander opened his orders and learned, for the first time, the exact position and time of his rendezvous off the British Isles. At the rendezvous, the destroyers that escorted the convoy through the danger zone were met. The American cruiser or battleship that had come thus far returned to the United States, usually with an empty convoy that was on the way home. A British warship would hasten ahead to England protected by a destroyer or two. Through the danger zone the convoy proceeded, its course and formation changed at varying intervals. The destroyer Captains and the Commander of the convoy heard frequently from London of the positions of the submarines that were known to be operating. Sometimes the direction of the convoy was altered and the submarines were left far away; sometimes a submarine unexpectedly appeared and was blown apart by the depth bombs of the escorting ships; sometimes the enemy sunk a ship or two. Once port was made, the merchantmen were unloaded as quickly as possible. The ships did not return home unguarded, however, for every bottom was more important than any particular cargo it carried. Through the danger zone the empty vessels were again escorted until the wide, safe wastes of the Atlantic were reached.[7]

When the system was firmly established, no railroad ran more efficiently. Every sixteen days a convoy left New York for the west coast of England, and every sixteen days one departed from the east coast. Hampton Roads sent them out every eight days. For all the American shipping, Captain Byron A. Long in London was primarily responsible.

Once the convoy system had been firmly established, the rate of losses began to drop. By the end of December, 1917, roughly 350,000 tons of all kinds of Allied shipping were going to the bottom. By June of the following year, the figure was around 250,000 tons a month; 112,427 tons was the best the submarines could achieve in October, 1918. Sims viewed these steadily dropping figures with increasing approval, but hardly with satisfaction. Throughout the last of the war, he reiterated in his letters to Admiral Benson his belief that 'the submarine situation is not encouraging yet.' Always he supplemented this conclusion with a plea for more destroyers. When in May, 1918, it seemed likely that the Germans would send a few submarines of the *Deutschland* class to harry the Atlantic Coast, he saw the psychological dangers for America in such a move. Pressure would be brought upon the authorities to keep anti-submarine vessels on the eastern coast of the country. 'Of course I understand something,' he wrote, 'about the effect of public opinion, but this public opinion must necessarily be an ignorant opinion viewed from a military standpoint. It would therefore seem that it was up to us to instruct this opinion so as to prevent the effect the enemy wishes to produce.' With disarming sanguinity he added, 'This should not be difficult, as the question [explaining the purpose of the cruising submarines to the public] is one of marked simplicity.'[8] To Niblack at Gibraltar, he wrote in more irritated tones in the same month. Niblack

[7] W. S. S., *The Victory at Sea*, pp. 122–141. This description of the convoy system is simply a condensation of the one given by Sims. Of the many brief descriptions of the convoy, his is as informative and clear as any.

[8] W. S. S. to W. S. Benson, May 17, 1918.

had called for, and badly needed, more anti-submarine craft. Such could not be supplied, since production of destroyers was 'dreadfully behind hand.' 'You need, I know, faster destroyers. They are not available. . . . The number of destroyers escorting merchant convoys have been cut away below the safety mark, so much so, that the submarines no longer fear to attack them. When the convoys were less numerous, we could supply enough destroyers to make it so dangerous for submarines that they practically abandoned the attacks on the convoys and went inland to get stragglers, split up convoys, etc. It is since we have been obliged to reduce these escorts that the submarines have now moved out and are attacking convoys. Of three that came in the other day all were successfully attacked. On top of this I am informed that the Department expects me to further reduce the escorts supplied merchant vessels in order to make the safety of the troops absolute. This is what I call a paper alibi. We all know it is impossible to make any convoy absolutely safe.' [9]

Though Sims could reasonably view the slowly diminishing losses with only tempered satisfaction, the figures on the convoy service are impressive. When the Armistice was signed, there were, at the three great escort bases of Brest, Queenstown, and Gibraltar, 190 United States naval vessels. From May, 1917, until November 11, 1918, 1124 Atlantic convoys with a total of 16,530 vessels, had been organized by the British, while 350 convoys, with 2123 vessels, had been organized by the Americans. For all these convoys Great Britain supplied about 70 per cent of the escorting ships; America, about 27 per cent. France contributed the remaining 3 per cent. More attractive from the American standpoint are the following figures: 'From Brest the forces supplied 90 per cent of the escort for 350 convoys,' while at 'Queenstown the forces supplied 91 per cent of the escort for 360 convoys. Of the deep-sea escorts, for these same convoys, Great Britain provided 61 per cent, America, 45 per cent, and France, 4 per cent.' [10]

The convoy system was the great weapon against the submarine, but constant efforts were made on both sides of the

[9] W. S. S. to A. P. Niblack, May 23, 1918.

[10] All these figures were taken from *Summary of Activities of United States Naval Forces,* in World War Archives, Office of Naval Records and Library.

Atlantic to supplement it by more decisive methods of warfare. Of all instruments devised, the most dramatic was the Q or Mystery Ship. These vessels, of which there were in all a hundred and eighty, travelled the seas disguised as merchantmen. Lured by this mask of peace, submarines would approach to sink innocent commerce carriers, only to find themselves opposed by guns that had been concealed. Since the crews of mystery ships deliberately exposed their vessels and themselves to destruction in order to destroy, the work was dangerous as well as exciting. The commanders were celebrated, and a chance to serve with them was eagerly sought. Sims, who met at Queenstown the most successful and famous of them, Captain Gordon Campbell, R.N., was much impressed by the valor of the men who did this work. He gave active encouragement to the construction of the American Q–ship *Santee*, Captain David Hanrahan, which was sunk within twenty-four hours of its departure from port.[11]

The vivid splendor of the work has concealed, it seems safe to say, the comparative inefficiency of the Q–ship as an anti-submarine weapon. Campbell, who accounted for more enemy U–boats than any other, can claim with certainty only three. All the one hundred and eighty Q–ships together accounted certainly for only eleven submarines. Much juggling of the figures has been done to prove that this contribution was important, but there is still a decided difference of opinion on the question.

Less dramatic than the activity of the Q–ships was the construction of the North Sea Mine Barrage, which stretched across the two hundred and forty miles from Scotland to Norway.[12] At the beginning of the war, England had considered laying such a mine field as an effective barrier against submarines operating out of the Baltic. The great distance, the extreme depth of the water, and the lack of suitable mines caused the British to give up the project as impossible. As soon as America entered the

[11] A dramatic and exciting account of the work of these ships is given by Gordon Campbell, *My Mystery Ships*, London, 1928.

[12] For an account of the Mine Barrage see Office of Naval Records, Publication No. 2, *The Northern Barrage and Other Mining Activities*, 1920; also R. R. Belknap, 'The Yankee Mining Squadron,' *N.I.P.*, October, November, December, 1919.

struggle, the idea was again put forward by the Navy Department. In late June, 1917, Rear Admiral Ralph Earle, the Chief of the Bureau of Ordnance, wrote Sims, 'The only offensive proposition against the submarines that at present seems practicable has been that of making barriers, either of mines or nets or both combined, between Norway and Scotland and from just below Zeebrugge to the coast of England.' With this contention, Sims did not agree, if it depended, as it seemed to, on a patrol of two hundred and forty miles length. A concentrated enemy force, he pointed out, could do great damage at any single point. Besides, he hoped that Earle would recognize that 'the people over here are fighting for their very existence and that they know that this depends upon their success or failure in putting down the submarine. . . .' They have thought of everything, of course, 'and it would therefore seem that anyone would hesitate to be dogmatic in their opinions as to what could and should be done. Every scheme,' he assured the Chief of the Bureau, 'had been examined' and the real solution to the problem lay with the convoy, which was the most practical answer. Therefore, America could best help the Allied cause by sending every possible anti-submarine craft over to the battle front.[13]

The Navy Department remained unconvinced by such arguments and continued to put the question before Sims, whose opposition was greatly influenced by the English arguments. One of the most compelling of these derived from the fact that the English had been unable to develop a mine suitable for such a barrage. The deep water in the strait between Norway and Scotland appeared to require a mine field of such great depth that adequate production of mines seemed impossible. This objection was eliminated as early as April, 1917, however, when the Navy Department was able to offer an electric antennae mine that solved the numerical problem. Still the British were skeptical. As Sims wrote to Earle:

> The gist of the whole matter is that the British Admiralty has had a very serious and very bitter experience with every new mine that they have designed and developed subsequently by actual experience.
> After having designed the mine that bore the stamp of approval

[13] W. S. S. to Ralph Earle, July 11, 1917.

of the Admiralty and all its experts, they have blown up people with it and blown up ships or parts of ships with it, and have moreover found that when they came to lay the mine in actual practice, four hundred at a time, it was not successful and various parts of the gear had to be modified.

In the same letter, Sims rehearsed all the other objections to a mine barrage which the British had discovered through experience. The strong tides of the area in question carried mines out of position. This meant that laying would have to be continuous. Such a procedure involved the use of more ships than the Allies had. He went on to criticize the new mine, developed in America, without, as he said, knowing much about it.[14]

The Navy Department went ahead with its plans to lay a mine field despite the objections of its representative abroad and the well-controlled enthusiasm of the British. Months of preparation produced the following impressive results: 'not only the manufacture of 100,000 mines each carrying 300 lbs. of T. N. T. but also (1) a great loading depot at St. Julien's Creek, Va., under Commander Pryor, (2) a special fleet of 24 cargo steamers [of 'lake' type] manned by Naval Reserves, (3) two landing points located on the west coast of Scotland to minimize the danger from submarines, (4) a transportation system across Scotland and the establishment of two large assembly plants under Captain Murfin on the east coast (at Inverness and Invergordon), and (5) the preparation of a squadron of ten large vessels as mine-layers under Captain Belknap.'[15] After such elaborate preparation, work on the Mine Barrage was at last started in June, 1918. By October 24, 1918, when the last trip of the mine-layers began, the field was virtually completed. Of the 70,117 mines planted, the Americans put down 56,571. The total cost for the whole project was over $40,000,000. Probably the barrage accounted for eight submarines in the short span of its existence.

The return on the time, money, and energy spent in constructing the curtain of explosive across this strip of water may seem small. It was, nevertheless, in its fulfilment a tribute to American enterprise, technical skill, and organizing ability. Sims never

[14] W. S. S. to Ralph Earle, September 25, 1917.
[15] Knox, *op. cit.*, pp. 416–417.

quite brought himself to believe in the military value of the idea. Though he spoke of it in his book on the war as a magnificent technical accomplishment, he wrote to Benson on October 19, 1918, that he was 'sorry to say that I am afraid the northern barrage is not going to prove effective.'

Undoubtedly, the unhappy experiences of the British strongly influenced Sims' thought on the subject; certainly he used some rather poor arguments, in the light of the successful laying of the barrage, against the whole endeavor. But his basic military assumption was correct. From the first he opposed the scheme on the grounds that, 'the convoy is the one sure naval plan . . .' which in April and May held forth the certainty 'of checking the submarines' and that 'no time or material or effort should be diverted from the successful organization and implementation of this plan.'

Two men that Sims had long known were directly responsible for the laying of the mine barrage. Rear Admiral Joseph Strauss was in command of the Mine Force and Captain R. R. Belknap, a friend from the days on the China Station, was the very able Commander of Mine Squadron One. On December 12, 1918, Sims spoke to the men of Mine Squadron One on Belknap's flagship, the *San Francisco*.

> This mining force [he told them] has done a stunt the like of which has not been done in the world before. . . . As to the efficiency of the mine barrier, that is something that has not concerned you so particularly as those who designed it; but the stunt of fitting out the vessels, learning to handle the mines, planting them, and going through the strenuous work has been really one of the finest stunts the Navy has accomplished on this side.
>
> Another thing particularly gratifying is that the conduct of the men of the Mine Force at their bases and at sea has been exemplary. . . . They were inclined to regard us when we first came over here, as men out of the wilds of America. I think they rather wanted to strengthen their police force when we came around. They found out it was not necessary. . . . I saw your show, the second part of it, in London the other day. It has anything of its kind I have ever seen skinned to death. There isn't another one that holds a candle to it. It is particularly gratifying that the show included a number of the young girls of Inverness. The show was clean and refined and splendid in every way. It was a pleasure to

go behind the curtain and thank them and kiss that wee bit of a girl who used to do the dance. You know the one I mean.

. . . It makes good feeling on both sides of the ocean, and to keep the peace of the world, we are going to need that feeling among all Anglo-Saxons. . . . When you get back [home], you can tell them all about it. You need not feel that you have to tell them you did the whole thing. Just tell them a straight story and you may be more than satisfied with that.

The convoy, mystery ships, and the mine barrage were supplemented by other agents of destruction. Chief of these was perhaps the airplane. By the time of the Armistice, there were 16,200 men and 500 planes based on 27 different places in Europe. This force was used to gather information on the location of submarines, to destroy the sub-surface ships, to escort shipping, and to attack submarine bases.

Sub-chasers, little 110-foot craft, were active in many dangerous areas. One hundred and twenty were sent to Europe by way of Bermuda and the Azores.[16] The crews of these tiny ships were made up in large part of college boys. They were based at Plymouth, Brest, Queenstown, Gibraltar, Portsmouth, and Corfu. On October 21, 1918, eleven chasers, under Captain C. P. Nelson, participated in the most dramatic action performed by these ships. This force carried out a screening operation for the British and Italian cruisers that bombarded Durazzo.

Three other forces of the United States Navy deserve mention. At Berehaven, four battleships were stationed, to deal with any surface raiders that might escape the blockade. At the Azores, a few destroyers were based in case any cruising submarine began to operate that far at sea. With the Grand Fleet were Rodman's five battleships to supplement the battle line of the British Fleet. A small force was sent to Murmansk to prevent the Germans from establishing a submarine base there.

All these ships, planes, and men combined in America's naval effort against the Imperial German Government. To the convoy, all the rest were subsidiary, but all performed service valuable in varying degree. Had the war continued for another year, the size of these forces would have increased and the service

[16] A racy account of the work of these sub-chasers is given by Ray Millholland, *The Splinter Fleet*, New York, 1936.

rendered would have appeared more impressive. Many of the projects were begun of necessity some months after our entry into the war, and all were reaching their full effectiveness only with the signing of the Armistice.

Because peace usually waits upon the decisive triumph of armies in the field, the influence of seapower upon history long went unrecognized. Only after Ludendorff's last great drive had been hurled back was the Armistice signed in November, 1918. The close and obvious relation of these two events at least partially concealed the fact that victory on the western front depended upon the victory at sea.

Naval victory was attained in terms of the defeat of the submarine. When this had been accomplished, the Allies regained command of the sea and established free lines of communication among themselves. Along these lines flowed the goods which kept the warring nations alive and supported the military effort of the men in the field. Along them, too, passed, in ever-increasing number, soldiers to fight the armies of Germany. One of the greatest achievements of the United States Navy was the transport of these soldiers upon the sea lanes of the Atlantic.[17]

When General John J. Pershing arrived in France in June, 1917, he found the situation of the Allies critical. The offensive of General Nivelle in the west had failed. Morally and physically, the forces were too exhausted to begin a new drive in the near future. Russia, it was obvious, was approaching the collapse that would leave the Germans free to turn unhindered against the western front. Surveying this discouraging scene, Pershing could only conclude that the issue of the war depended upon the arrival of fresh American troops. The first months of his duty in France saw little improvement, and he was forced to cable in December, 1917, that 'The Allies are very weak, and we must come to their relief this year, 1918. The year after may be too late. It is very doubtful if they can hold out until 1919 unless we give them a lot of help this year.' [18] How much help could be sent depended upon the naval forces of the Allied Powers.

Sims had been in London almost two months before he re-

[17] The best and fullest account of this phase of the Navy's activity is Albert Gleaves, *A History of the Transport Service*, New York, 1921.

[18] Quoted in Knox, *op. cit.*, p. 400.

ceived any word from Washington about the transport of troops. During May the Navy Department had held discussions on the subject with the English and French missions in the United States, but, for some reason, no information about these meetings had reached Sims. Early in June, however, he did receive a confidential cable from the Secretary of the Navy announcing that 'a convoy of American troops to France will sail about the 9th of this month [June]. It is now contemplated to dispatch four convoy groups of three or four transports under separate escort in each group.' These convoys would sail for a meeting place of which Sims would subsequently be informed. He was instructed to 'furnish escorts to consist of one division of destroyers for each convoy group from the point of meeting to the port of debarkation.' [19]

In the course of the following week, Sims sent to Washington a series of cables and letters setting forth the nature of the problem of troop transport. On June 14, he got at the heart of the difficulty. 'There are not now sufficient vessels available for escort duty to ensure safety of all vital supplies and also prospective movements of our troops and their supplies. As our troops and their supplies will approach European coast outside of zones used by shipping and shipping convoys, it is mandatory that information be given immediately as to the probable numbers and times of sailing of all army shipping in next three months as on this depends the program of merchant ship convoys which must be arranged some time ahead. The approach of our first army convoys will seriously embarrass the shipping situation as it will require all destroyers based on Queenstown, thus necessitating entire suspension of patrol and escort duty in that area.'

The nature of the problem outlined above is simple. Goods coming from America were brought along the sea lanes into England. Troops from the same country were sent to France upon sea lanes farther south. With a limited number of escort vessels, it was difficult to give proper protection to vessels on both lanes, especially if they were approaching Europe simultaneously. Next day, June 15, Sims elaborated his explanation in a letter. 'As our army and naval forces and our mercantile shipping

[19] Secretary of the Navy to W. S. S., June 1, 1917.

abroad increases, the demands on the anti-submarine forces for convoy duty on this side will be greatly increased at the sacrifice of the offensive campaign against the submarine. As previously reported, the majority of our troops and supply ships for armies in France will approach the European coast well outside of the dangerous parts of the submarine zone — that is, outside of the area in which submarine activity has been the most intense and in which it must continue if it is to be primarily directed against merchant shipping. This fact will, of course, not remove the necessity for meeting and escorting the troop and supply ships, and hence the strictly offensive campaign against the submarine will suffer severely.'

After thus stating the problem, Sims made his recommendations. Escort duty within the danger zones was directed by the Admiralty on the basis of the latest information concerning the location of submarine activity and the disposition of the Allied forces. Such information Washington could not possibly have in its possession. Therefore, the control of troop convoys should rest with the Admiralty alone: the 'number and nationality of ships to be detailed for escort duty [should] not be specifically ordered by the Department but [should] be determined here [London] upon disposition of Allied forces and circumstances of arrival at appointed rendezvous.' To facilitate such central control, America should send at once a 'capable and tactful' officer to work in the convoy section of the Admiralty. The strain on escort vessels should be relieved by the immediate dispatch of all possible anti-submarine craft. Because a large part of the success of the troop transportation system rested on secrecy; the American code, easily deciphered by the Germans, should be abandoned and the Admiralty code adopted.

The history of the first few troop convoys sent from the United States at the time and arriving at the rendezvous appointed by the Navy Department, bore out the wisdom of Sims' recommendations. The initial convoy reached St. Nazaire on June 26. Sims had complied with the Department's request to have American destroyers, taken from Ireland, escort the big ships. During the absence of these destroyers on this duty, the forces in Queenstown were reduced to ten destroyers and ten sloops. Thus the safety of cargoes in the western approaches was, during this time, endangered to a great extent.[20] Furthermore, the destroyers were held, contrary to Sims' orders, at St. Nazaire to escort the empty transports out to sea, though the French had already agreed to give this protection with their own fleet of anti-submarine vessels based on this port.[21] It should be noticed too that the Navy Department had wired its recommendations about these transports in its own code, despite Sims' warnings that the Admiralty code was the only safe one. Some color was given to his contentions by the fact that the first group of transports reported submarine attacks, leading Sims to suspect that the Germans had obtained information about the convoy from the American code.[22]

It was some little time before agreement on methods of troop convoy could be reached. As late as July 14, he could write to Washington complaining that 'Very serious embarrassment has been experienced in the last few days owing to the unexpected announcements from the United States of the sailing of an Army transport convoy and of troops or hospital units on the *Mongolia* and the *Adriatic* and *Baltic* and other British liners. It happened that the prospective arrivals of these various ships coincided with the arrivals of merchant convoys from Russia, from the Mediterranean, from Hampton Roads and from New York.'[23] In the case of the *Mongolia*, no rendezvous was given. Commenting on this situation afterward, Sims observed that, 'All I can say about that is that God was good to us, that we did not have some very serious losses, with all that confusion.'[24]

Confusion was probably, at the beginning of the war, inevitable. The Department was anxious to control as much of the procedure of troop transport as possible. Not only was this a matter of natural professional pride, but of political considerations as well. In ordering the escort for the first troop convoy of June, 1917, Washington required American destroyers in view of what it called 'sensitive public opinion.'[25] What is less under-

[20] W. S. S. to Secretary of the Navy, June 20, 1917.
[21] W. S. S. to Navy Department, July 7, 1917.
[22] W. S. S. to Secretary of the Navy, June 30, 1917.
[23] W. S. S. to Navy Department, July 14, 1917.
[24] *Hearings, 1920*, p. 101.
[25] Secretary of the Navy to W. S. S., June 10, 1917.

standable is the Department's delay in accepting Sims' recommendations once it had approved of them as sound.

It was July 22 before the Department cabled its approval of a plan outlined by Sims in a letter of July 6. On the eighth of August, Byron A. Long arrived in London to work with the Admiralty on the problem of routing convoys.[26] From this time forth the procedure was never altered in its fundamentals. The system, first proposed by Sims on June 8, restated in his letter of July 6, and accepted July 22 by the Navy Department, was in fact the same as that which governed the operations of merchant shipping.

In London the schedules, rendezvous, and escorts for troop ships were decided upon. Long, as an American, assumed most of the work in connection with these arrangements. His was, as his Chief said, 'the master mind,' who performed his task so efficiently that 'once the convoy system was in successful operation, I [Sims] eliminated the whole subject from my anxieties and requested Captain Long not to inform me when troop convoys sailed from the United States or when they were due to arrive in France or England. There seemed to be no reason why both of us should lose sleep over the same cause.'

It will be recalled that one of the difficulties of troop transport in the early days before there were sufficient escort vessels lay in the fact that the troop ships came in over a different lane to France from that used by the merchant vessels on their trip to England. When the system was in full swing, these separate lanes served as an advantage. The seven or eight submarines operating in the danger zone had to concentrate for full effectiveness upon one of these lanes alone. Invariably the route used by the merchantmen was chosen. This was not from purely humanitarian considerations. Each day on the western front five thousand men were being killed. Against these staggering casualties, the sinking of a troop ship or two, simply in terms of man-power, appeared a small contribution to the German cause. Furthermore, the merchant lanes were more crowded than the troop-ship lanes, and the chances of the kill, therefore, far higher. But the most compelling reason for keeping the submarines in the danger zone around England was the fact that Allied victory

[26] *Hearings, 1920*, p. 101.

rested upon the continuous flow of food and supplies from America to Europe. To win the war, Germany had to interrupt this flow of goods. Had a transport of five thousand men been sunk, Americans would have thrilled with horror, yet the catastrophe would have equalled the butcher's bill of but one day on the western front. On the other hand, each cargo that was lost, each merchant bottom that was sunk, brought the Allied Powers nearer to starvation and a shortage of war materials. It should be noticed, too, that every American soldier that was safely landed simply increased the demands upon the supply line. For these reasons the submarines ordinarily operated exclusively against the merchant convoys.[27]

Until the end of 1917, the number of American troops that landed in Europe was comparatively small. In December, there were about 175,000 in all. Beginning in January of the next year, the forces rapidly increased. Troops at home were ending their preliminary training. Escort vessels were arriving in Europe in ever-mounting numbers. The transformation of the German liners held in America into transports had been completed. The American organization for maintaining and administering the troop convoys had been established under the able direction of Rear Admiral Albert Gleaves. The monthly figures after January astounded the Germans, and they are still astounding. In round numbers, 40,000 soldiers arrived in January; 104,000 in April; 317,000, the highest month, in July. By November almost 2,000,000 men had been safely brought to the shores of France. Of this vast number, American ships carried 44 per cent, and escorted 62 per cent. Not a man under American protection was lost.[28] Looking back upon this achievement two years later, Sims remarked, 'Only four or five convoys were attacked, no torpedo ever touched a loaded transport, and not a single soldier was lost under the protection I gave them.' Of the significance of this safe transport of the troops, another has written, 'The triumph of the American naval transport service was that, within a very brief interval of time and in the face of all but insuperable ob-

[27] W. S. S., *The Victory at Sea*. Chapter XIII gives an excellent description of troop transportation.

[28] *Summary of Activities*, p. 14.

stacles, it furnished the margin of military power that was able to prevent imminent defeat in March and April and to bring decisive victory in November.' [29]

The signs of that great victory multiplied as the months of 1918 passed. After the early force of Ludendorff's last drive in the west had spent itself in vain, there were increasing indications that the German armies in the field were nearing exhaustion. On the seas, the gathering might of those forces marshalled against the submarine revealed itself. The convoy system, the mystery ships, the mine barrages, the airplanes, and the sub-chasers worked in combination toward the defeat of the deadly enemy. The downward curve of monthly tonnage losses but measured the sinking hopes of the German Empire. In January, 1918, about 300,000 tons of shipping were lost; in June, about 250,000; in October, 112,000. What were at first but distant portents of the end became in time the promises of peace.

For Sims, those months of 1918 were the greatest of his whole career. That secret journey of April, 1917, brought him into the pages on which history is written. At a time when armies and navies decided the fate of nations, he was in command. The skill with which he performed his difficult mission is a tribute to his professional knowledge and ability. Yet his success rested in no small part upon the greatness of his own personality.

His influence, simply as a man, began in the London Head-quarters. One day, for example, he called a thoroughly con-scientious, hard-working officer in to him to explain that he was unsatisfied with the officer's work. The man blushed and stammered until Sims pointed out that, 'In all the time you have been here you have never once disagreed with me.'

Others failed to arrive at such complete cooperation. J. V. Babcock, his aide, felt almost a blood relationship with his Commander, but this did not prevent him from expressing occa-sional and at times violent disapproval of his superior's actions. Upon one occasion, Babcock delivered a furious attack on one of Sims' views. He became so enraged that he announced he could no longer serve under Sims; with the two at such cross-purposes, he said, efficiency was obviously impaired. The older man listened attentively throughout the exposition of Babcock's

[29] Knox, *op. cit.*, p. 402.

case. At the conclusion, he tossed the Navy Register across the table and said, 'If you can find anyone you would rather work with in this list, go ahead.'

With his English secretary, Miss Lillian Thompson, who was with him throughout the war, Sims had a close relationship. She took most of his letters to his family, for he had little time to write longhand, and thus came to know his household through his own words. She sometimes bought the dresses, dolls, and keepsakes he sent back to his children. This service was invaluable to a man who could never interpret colors, materials, or patterns, as recommended by his wife.

One action of their Admiral, the men at London Headquarters never forgot. During the war there was some agitation to change the service uniform from the blouse to the double-breasted jacket. When Sims was asked for an opinion in the matter, he referred it, as he did all things, to his staff. The staff reported almost unanimously in favor of the change. Some weeks later, Captain Twining approached Babcock with the copy of a cablegram to Washington, expressing Sims' disapproval of the new uniform. It developed that the Admiral had waited until the staff had gone home, before personally sending off his own opinion. It was perhaps the only time that the conference system broke down. Sims' objections were based on good grounds. The existing uniform was distinctive; to change it in time of war seemed unnecessary trouble, and to change it to a 'cheap imitation of the British uniform' inexcusable.

On July 4, 1918, the United States Army played the United States Navy in a baseball game, to which the King and Queen were invited. Protocol failed to cover the procedure when royalty attended such an event. No one knew who ought to meet the royal couple and escort them to their box. Wires flew to Washington, and there was a conference between someone at the London Headquarters and the Under-Secretary. Washington announced that in the absence of the Ambassador, Sims was to represent the country. The Admiral met the Queen at the gate and escorted her across the field on his arm, explaining the while to the King that he would be expected to throw out the first ball.

Most of all, Sims had fun with the English sense of humor. He never tired of revealing its inflexibility. His favorite test, applied upon countless occasions, was the 'apple pie story.' To the American Society in London, he explained the whole problem one night.

'Now, the oldest chestnut that I have got, but one that has given me the most amusement, is the hoary old apple pie story. When I first came over here, I told it at the Savage Club. I am going there again in a couple of days and I shall tell it again to give them another chance to understand it.' He then listed off a series of distinguished Englishmen who had heard the anecdote, but had failed to get at the point.

'It is,' he went on, 'a very simple story. The difficulty of understanding it was first brought to my attention out in the Far East. I was serving on a vessel that happened to be in Hong Kong for quite a long time in company with a British man-of-war. We got to know the officers very well. One evening some of them were dining with us in the wardroom when somebody made the remark that occasionally the Britisher was a little hard on the trigger as regards the so-called American joke. One of the British lieutenants, by the name of Shackles, rather warmly resented this, so I said "Shackles, Old Top, that may or may not be so, but with your permission I would like to try you with an easy one." . . . A commercial traveller came down to breakfast one morning in a small hotel in the pie belt, that is to say, one of the New England States. The little waiter maid came up behind his chair and said, "Beans, fish, hash, and sausage; cranberry, mince and apple pie." The traveller said, "I'll take some beans and fish, some hash and some sausage; some cranberry and mince pie." Whereupon the little waiter maid cocked her nose up and said, "What's the matter with the apple pie?" Lieutenant Shackles' face took on the expression of a concrete image. I pointed at him and said, "Shackles, you don't know now what was the matter with that apple pie," and he said, "No, I'm damned if I do." ' Hundreds of Shackles' countrymen never did.

One man reported that Sims always told it and few ever laughed. It became, in time, a kind of *cause célèbre*. A member of the Athenaeum Club wrote off to the *Times* with the announcement that Admiral Sims was not as smart as he thought he was. He was trying, in fact, to fob off as American a story that was as old as the hills and English in origin. Babcock showed the letter to the Admiral, who replied to the *Times* that he never had claimed the story was American; that his only intent was to show that the English did not have a very ready sense of humor. The correspondent would seem to bear this contention out. Here was a story that he said was as old as the hills, and yet, to Sims' 'certain knowledge, no Englishman had seen the point yet.'

He loved these speeches he had to make so constantly. Sometimes his wit was less premeditated than on the occasions when he sought to defeat the British sense of humor. One July 4 he travelled around from place to place listening to 'all sorts of people who blew off speeches telling what a wonderful thing the Declaration of Independence was and how noble was the struggle of our patriot fathers.' At the end of the day he went to a large dinner at which Lord Asquith spoke. When Sims' turn came, he said, 'I've been attending a number of these functions, and the conclusion I've drawn from all I've heard is that the most glorious day in the history of the British Empire was the day we licked you.' 'Old Asquith,' he reflected afterward, 'I'm not so sure he knew quite what to make of it.'

With Balfour, who could 'charm a bird out of a tree,' he had more luck. At dinner he would talk of the war and his past to the aging statesman, who listened spellbound to the flow of talk. To Sims he would murmur, 'I never knew that. You fascinate me.' This irrepressible American must have fascinated many of them. When the Allied Naval Council met in Paris, the French government would send a special train to meet the Channel boat. It was a very gorgeous affair, all done up in satin. Speeding along toward Paris in this typically French conveyance, Sims poked his head into the compartment of the English General Robertson, the Chief of Staff, and remarked, 'War is hell, isn't it?'

With his own people he had an equally good time. Some members of the Naval House Committee came over to inspect the naval bases in Europe. A few of them, as Sims wrote to Bayly, 'came from a considerable distance back in the woods,' but he knew that their intentions were of the best. For the chairman, Lemuel Pagett, he had a real affection. 'He is earnest, honest and square and has the kindliest manner. He puts his arm around my shoulder and thanks me very often for everything and anything.' But he revealed the suspicions that every military man has always had of the politician. To Benson he wrote, 'Inevitably they [the Congressmen] will talk with many; confuse opinions, reinforce their own ideas. It is, of course, a foregone conclusion that they will either collectively or individually (probably the latter) form many opinions. I have no intention whatever of suggesting any measures or actions. If perchance it should be stated that any such opinions or recommendations are based upon opinions of mine, you may assume them to be mistaken.'

Not all the attention he turned to the British was humorous. In the early spring of 1918, he went down to St. George's School outside of London. He talked to the pupils about his own boyhood in Canada, about the dreadful school at Bletcher's Corner. He told them how he just 'scraped through' into Annapolis. And then he counselled them to take advantage of the opportunities he had never had, opportunities their country was giving them, even in wartime. When he returned to London, he arranged to have the Navy's coach go down to teach the children how to play baseball. He saw that they were supplied with the necessary bats and balls. To Mrs. Sims he wrote for some of the Montessori equipment that could not be obtained in England. This in due time was sent, along with an American flag, to the school. Finally, he wrote to the headmaster of St. George's School in America, suggesting some mutual correspondence and assistance between the two institutions. 'I know so little,' he admitted, 'about the practical side of education that I hesitate to make any suggestions, but I should think that an actual personal contact would be essential for the attainment of the maximum results in the way of good understanding.' Wouldn't, he asked, an exchange of masters and boys between the two institutions be possible?

Children were never far from his thoughts. One of the longest letters he wrote during this period was to a little boy he never knew. After the child had seen the Admiral's picture in the newsreels, he had written to put himself at the service of the Allied cause in any way possible. 'There are many ways,' the Admiral told him, 'to help besides fighting. You and your mother and father are doing excellent war service in cultivating your garden, raising a fine pig and canning five hundred cans. You say you hope that someday your turn will come to do your share of the fighting. Let us hope that this war will be settled in such a way that it will not be necessary for hundreds and thousands of fine young men to be killed in order to preserve the liberties of all nations. I hope I can see you and talk this over when I return.'

Of all children he thought most, of course, of his own. 'I enjoyed so much all the accounts of the dear babies . . . particularly their dear voices from the record I got a few days ago. . . . I was pleased with your remarks about the dear, homely, everyday things of life. It is the search for something else that makes so many people unhappy. They never learn that the greatest of pleasures are the simple ones. A walk with you and the wee ones, afternoon tea with perhaps a real friend or two and the babies, a game of cards and a romp, tucking the small ones in bed, a game of cards and supper with our big girls, a fit of the giggles, reading our books and a quiet talk in the evening. How my heart aches for all this.'

They were, in fact, always in his mind. When he played tennis, he thought of how he would teach the game to his children; when he received letters from the older ones, he reflected that there was no 'excuse for anyone acquiring an illegible handwriting. I think that it is important while they are young that they be encouraged with everything they write.' Get them ruled paper, he advised.

They were his constant referent in all things outside his profession. One day during the war he saw that a novel by Harold Bell Wright had sold seven million copies. He bought books by the author because he was 'curious to know why they appealed so strongly to the public.' The characters were fine, just the kind his wife would admire. One reviewer had called Mr. Wright the apostle of the wholesome. This was the kind of book 'we will want our children to read when they are about to take their places in the world.' 'They are, too,' he concluded, 'the kind of book you would write if you were a writer.'

Thus he swung through his life in London; always healthy, alive and buoyant, always on top of his job. He revealed himself in many ways, and to many people. With mutual delight he and Lady Astor listened to the social indiscretions of each other, and with equal pleasure, he and the cabmen discussed the progress of the war. Yet always he remained the same man, enjoying himself, his work, and his audience hugely.

As the end of the war drew near, however, a strange mood descended upon him. Not that he doubted that good would come. 'This will not be the same world after the war,' he wrote, 'the last great war, I am sure. We are learning many valuable lessons. The war is making a real nation of America as nothing else could have done. And we will come out of it so strong both morally and materially that we need never fear the enmity of any nation or combination of nations. We will never again neglect the Navy or the military training of our young men.' It was not so much the world that troubled him as his own position in it. 'I have never liked it [the Navy]. I would rather have been in a productive occupation. There has never been a time when I have not been uncomfortable in a uniform. It is always embarrassing for me to walk through the streets here in a uniform.' This mood was reflected in a conversation he had with the First Sea Lord, Admiral Wemyss. 'What,' asked Wemyss, 'are we going to do after the war?' It seemed impossible to consider going back to the old routine. Sims agreed and replied that he would rather retire. He wrote his wife: 'I might be offered Chief of Naval Operations, but I would not like that under any circumstances. I would rather have the fleet, but I feel that I would not care to take up again the routine of training. I feel that I have worked enough, and had better make room for the young men. I would like to devote all my time to you and our precious babies and to anything you wanted me to do.' Frequently in the past, he had given voice to his dissatisfaction with the service, to his desire to leave it for the domestic comforts of home. Now there was a real, special sadness in his words as the long lane neared its turning.

These momentary intimations of mortality gave way before the portents of approaching victory. By October, it was clear that the endless war was almost over; swiftly it drew to its close. On the night of November 11, Sims went to the balcony window of his office that looked out over Grosvenor Gardens and made a speech to the cheering crowds below.

In the months that followed, there was anticlimax. The motions of war went on as the bases were demobilized, but the tension of the past eighteen months gave way to the relaxed atmosphere of peace. In December, Sims was made a full Admiral. That, too, was anticlimactic, though the congratulations poured in. To the First Lord, Sir Eric Geddes, he wrote as he wrote to many friends, that he appreciated the kind remarks, but 'I cannot help but regret that I could not have had the use of the grade while the war was in progress. Personally, it is a bit sad that I received this promotion just in time to give it up, which I must do on being detached from this position. You doubtless know, we have no permanent grade in our Navy higher than Rear Admiral. However, the festive Hun is now down and out for all time, so that nothing else really matters very much.'

In July, 1918, there had been some articles in the newspapers suggesting that Sims be made an Admiral. Benson had cabled to him, pointing out that such discussions were 'detrimental,' to which Sims replied that he entirely agreed and that he deprecated such 'unnecessary and undesirable discussion.' Still he could not but feel that December, 1918, was a curious time to promote him.

For some months, Sims waited in London, not quite sure of what would follow. Early in the new year it became apparent that he would not be asked to go to Versailles as a naval expert. When this was clear, his only thought was to get home as soon as possible. Especially, he wished to leave Europe before the Secretary came over on what Sims was sure would be 'a political junket.' Late in March, after a series of farewell celebrations, he got aboard the *Mauretania* and sailed for home and his family.

The good wishes of his colleagues were yet ringing in his ears. Pershing had written that, 'There has been such good cooperation and such lack of friction between the land and sea forces [which] I am well aware is due in the largest measure to your helpful attitude and big way of looking at things.' Benson, the cares of the past months gone, felt himself unable to express in adequate language his 'sincere congratulations for the most efficient and excellent manner in which you have performed your duties abroad.' The Board of Admiralty hoped that 'now that you are leaving, they may also allude to the part that your own individuality has played in the achievements of the last two years. They cannot but recognize that in you was the source whence the United States drew that spirit of unity which since 1917 has welded the two British speaking Naval Forces into one service.' Praise, gifts, and honors were showered upon him. From the London Headquarters, Miss Thompson, his secretary, wrote, 'Oh, we do miss you most dreadfully. It was very deadly at Headquarters after you left, Admiral.' And his Paymaster Tobey gave the perfect tribute, 'The light went out for us old fellows when you left London.'

All this was left behind as the *Mauretania* made Ambrose Light on a brisk April day in 1919. On the North River and along the docks there were flags flying, whistles blowing, and people shouting. Mrs. Sims and some of the children had come down to meet him. He had returned to America, but until they were all together in Newport, he had not really come home. Newport welcomed him with a spontaneous joy. All the paraphernalia of an American celebration was there — bands, flags, speeches, and noise. In the afternoon a vast parade, which he reviewed from a wooden stand set out on the lawn, filed by the house. He stood there before the cheering people in the old uniform blouse, two stars on either side of the high collar. The war was over, the festive Hun had been defeated. Nothing else mattered very much.

23

I USUALLY know what I want to say and I usually succeed in saying it. . . . Of course, it is more comfortable not to send in . . . criticisms. You subject yourself to unjust criticism, your motives are impugned, your object mistaken and misused. If you have ever been before a Congressional Committee you know what I mean.

'It is not only the privilege but the duty of Army and Navy officers to direct letters of constructive criticism to their superior officers, and the officer who chooses to accept personal comfort in place of responsibility for such criticism is not only not worth his pay, but he is not worth the powder to blow himself to hell.'

Thus, on the night of January 21, 1920, Sims explained to four hundred military men and their guests in the ballroom of the Waldorf Astoria why he had broken the silence surrounding him since his return from Europe. It was an appreciative audience. As he finished, the 'entire crowd rose to its feet. The men shouted and threw up their napkins, and the shrill cry of excited women could be heard over the tumult.'

The demonstration was called forth by Sims' inflammatory words of the moment, but it was likewise a tribute to the testimony he had just concluded before a Senate Committee. The purpose of the Senate investigation was to discover whether the medals given to naval men for their services during the World War had been improperly awarded. Sims, believing that such was the case, had considered it his privilege and duty to say so.

When the United States went to war, no decoration beyond

the Congressional Medal of Honor existed. European countries, all with histories that had been written chiefly upon battlefields, had medals for every conceivable kind of service and heroism. These awards were given promptly throughout the conflict to soldiers and sailors who distinguished themselves, but Americans could not by law receive decorations from either the Allied Powers or their own government. Sims, on December 30, 1917, had recommended in the interests of morale that his men be permitted to accept foreign decorations. Such permission had been refused. It was not until July, 1918, that Congress, over the opposition of Secretary Daniels, made it possible for our men to accept foreign awards.[1] Nothing was done about American decorations until February 4, 1919, when Congress made provision for decorations on the following terms:

1. No award could be authorized without a specific statement from a naval superior, setting forth the act or service of a subordinate.
2. The Distinguished Service Medal was to be given for exceptionally meritorious service in duty of great responsibility.
3. The Medal of Honor was to be given only for acts of heroism in action involving actual conflict with the enemy.
4. The Navy Cross was given for two very different types of service:
   a. For extraordinary heroism in less degree than that which would warrant a medal of honor.
   b. For distinguished service involving less responsibility than that which would warrant a distinguished service medal.[2]

After this law was enacted, commanding officers were instructed to send in their recommendations for awards for men serving under them. The Secretary of the Navy appointed a board to review these recommendations. Rear Admiral Austin M. Knight was the Chairman of this board which was composed

---

[1] T. B. Kittredge, *Naval Lessons of the Great War*, Garden City, 1921, pp. 44–45. This book contains an admirable, though not entirely unprejudiced, condensation of the two investigations treated in this chapter. Kittredge had been a member of Sims' staff in London and assisted greatly in the preparation of Sims' testimony for the investigation into the conduct of the war.

[2] *Hearing Before a Subcommittee on Naval Affairs*, 66th Congress, 2d Session, on S. Res. 285, 1920, p. 458. Hereafter this will be referred to as *Hearings on Medals* and *Hearings, 1920*. It should be noticed that the law was loosely drawn, especially in defining services for which the Navy Cross was awarded.

of eight retired officers, only two of whom had served in the line of the Navy.

Throughout the spring and summer of 1919, these men reviewed the list of medal awards sent in to them by the commanding officers. In October, before the work was completely finished, Mr. Daniels dissolved the Board after receiving three reports of its work.[3] Two months later, in December, 1919, the Secretary issued his own Annual Report. In the appendix there was included a list of 'Medals of Honor, Distinguished Service Medals, and Navy Crosses Awarded.'

A few weeks after this list had been made public, Mr. Daniels received letters from Rear Admiral Henry T. Mayo and from Sims. Both men expressed their disapproval of the medals awarded by the Secretary. Sims, in view of his dissatisfaction with the list as published, declined in his letter to accept the Distinguished Service Medal that had been awarded him. A short time later, two more officers, Admiral Hilary P. Jones and Captain R. D. Hasbrouck, announced their refusal of the decorations the Secretary had given to them. When news of these communications reached *The Army and Navy Journal*, the matter came to the public attention. A subcommittee of the Senate Naval Committee was appointed to investigate the whole question.[4]

On January 16, 1920, the Committee began to hold hearings under the chairmanship of Frederick Hale, the son of Eugene Hale who had conducted the Investigation of 1908. Sims appeared as the first witness. His testimony was principally an elaboration of the objections he had raised in his letter of December 17, 1919, to Mr. Daniels against the list of awards published in the Secretary's Report.[5] The particular points he made were four in number. The Knight Board and the Secretary had both changed the 'estimate of relative merit of the services of officers — made by their immediate and active superior in command.' In Sims' opinion, and Admiral Mayo supported him in this contention later, a commanding officer was the only person who

---

[3] Kittredge, *op. cit.*, pp. 47–48, and *Hearings on Medals*, p. 454.

[4] Kittredge, *op. cit.*, p. 55.

[5] Sims' testimony appears in *Hearings on Medals*, pp. 245–361. All quotations are taken from these pages.

could form a just idea of the relative value of officers beneath him. In the second place, the Secretary's published list had been compiled on the assumption that services at sea were more important than certain vitally significant positions ashore. This assumption Sims believed to be false. 'The most important duty in time of war is that of planning and directing the military operations of the whole force.' Such duty in the war just passed had been chiefly performed ashore. In the third place, Distinguished Service Medals had been given to 'many, if not all, of the officers who were defeated in action or whose ships were sunk or seriously damaged by enemy submarines.' Such decorations were contrary to all naval traditions, and thus in Sims' opinion destructive of service morale. Finally, neither the commanding officers nor the reviewing Board had been provided with a settled policy upon which to make their recommendations. In the absence of such policy, the officers, the Board, and the Secretary himself had acted upon individual interpretations, both of the law providing for the awards and of the actions for which awards were given.

These four points contained in Sims' letter of December 17, 1919, and in his testimony before the Investigating Committee were the issues around which debate revolved in the hearings. The most important witnesses to appear besides Sims were Admirals Mayo and Knight and the Secretary of the Navy himself.[6]

By the time all the evidence was in, three weeks after Sims first testified, the following things were clearly established by the testimony offered. No general principles had been provided to ensure unanimity among the three authorities charged with selecting officers for awards. Admiral Knight's testimony on this point was especially conclusive.[7] In the absence of such princi-

[6] The position taken by Admiral Mayo throws some interesting light on the technique of reform. He made points similar to those of Sims on the question of medals, but he received little attention. Sims' argument was dramatized by his refusal to accept his D.S.M. It was a gesture of this sort, as sincere as it was effective, that always put him in the forefront of the struggle. Then, too, of course, his testimony always had more verbal fireworks than that of his supporters. After Sims refused to accept his D.S.M. he never wore any of the decorations bestowed upon him by England, France, Japan, Belgium, and Italy.

[7] *Hearings on Medals*, p. 453.
The Chairman: That is, you were to determine the policy on which you were to act in making the awards yourselves?
Admiral Knight: In so far as it was possible to fix a policy, yes, sir.

ples, both the Knight Board and the Secretary had revised the recommendations of the commanding officers. Such revision had frequently violated the estimate of relative merit of subordinates arrived at by commanding officers. The Secretary had been especially active in making changes. Only 41.5 per cent of his published list was in accord with the recommendations of commanding officers and the Board of Awards. Sometimes Mr. Daniels revised these recommendations upward, sometimes downward, and sometimes he added names of his own.[8]

In making these changes, the Secretary, as he freely admitted, had acted frequently upon his belief that 'individual duties ashore are always and necessarily of secondary importance to duties afloat. There are a few exceptions as in the instance of service of the highest character.'[9] Finally, he stated that he had given Distinguished Service Medals to men who had conducted themselves well when their ships had been sunk by submarine action.

'The principle,' he said, 'enunciated by the Secretary of the Navy is that the Distinguished Service Medal should not be denied to the Captain who, when his ship is struck by an enemy torpedo or mine, is thereby placed in a position of great responsibility and distinguishes himself by his conduct in the crisis, evidencing fearlessness in direction, disregard of death, and resourceful leadership with the utilization of all those attributes that show a man a hero when the hour strikes for his supreme trial. In the stiletto attack of submarine warfare, it is not the fact that a man strikes or is struck that tests true mettle and true naval leadership. The question is: Does he play the part of the man, with chivalry and thought only of others and of his country?'[10]

Stripped of its excess baggage this statement means that if officers who lost their ships through no fault of their own conducted themselves in accordance with the ordinary traditions and regulations of the Navy, they deserved a medal which was granted for 'exceptionally meritorious service in a duty of great responsibility.'

[8] A statistical analysis of the Secretary's action appears in Kittredge, *op. cit.*, pp. 59–63.

[9] *Hearings on Medals*, p. 504.

[10] *Ibid.*, p. 505.

These points were established by the witnesses. Though it may be a matter of personal opinion, two of the policies pursued by the Secretary appear to be mistaken. Certain duties ashore or on the staff of commanding officers can, in the larger view of the war, be considered far more important than any single command afloat. There seems, too, to be no reasonable explanation for awarding Distinguished Service Medals to men who did no more than to handle themselves well when their vessels were lost.

It seems impossible to make the other objections that were raised to Mr. Daniels' actions mere differences of personal opinion. Sims and his colleagues were absolutely right in maintaining that only a superior officer can correctly estimate the relative values of the services of his subordinates. Such officers may err, naturally, but far less rarely than outside authorities. In addition, the Secretary handled the whole business of awarding medals with incredible ineptitude. He should, at the very beginning, have laid down some policy that would have governed the procedure to be used by commanding officers, the reviewing Board, and himself. He should not have dissolved the reviewing Board before its work was finished. His reconvening of it just before the Investigating Committee met indicates his own understanding of this fact. Finally, he should never have published the list of medals awarded until he had ascertained the opinion of the commanding officers and reviewing Board upon the changes he had made. At the investigation he maintained that this published list was not final — a difficult assertion to substantiate, inasmuch as he had headed the list 'Medals of Honor, Distinguished Service Medals, and Navy Crosses Awarded.' Even if one accepts the Secretary's statement, it is impossible to approve of his action. Publishing a list in which changes were to be made could hardly be good for the spirits of men whose awards might well be altered or eliminated.

The issues before the Senate Committee were clear enough, but unfortunately they became of secondary importance to the more diverting questions of politics and men. At the outset, Key Pittman, a member of the Committee, observed that, 'Say what you want to about the matter here, it is in the nature of a trial of the acts of the Secretary of the Navy.' If such were the case, it was hardly to be expected that the judges, three Republicans and two Democrats, would weigh the evidence dispassionately. Nor did they. The majority report issued after the investigation condemned most of the actions of Mr. Daniels. It was signed by the three Republicans. Two minority reports upholding Mr. Daniels were written by the Democrats. This division of opinion, conforming so closely to political allegiances, did much to vitiate the findings of both majority and minority members. Personalities likewise beclouded the hearings. Men rather than merits of the case were more fully displayed to public view. As time ran on, Sims and the Secretary emerged as the great antagonists. The investigation became a political and personal controversy which failed to arouse the people to the justice of Sims' position.

He was disappointed, too, in the reaction of the service. With considerable optimism, he apparently expected that his brother officers would follow his lead in renouncing the awards. To an old friend he wrote, 'My protest created a unique opportunity for the Navy to express an opinion in a very dignified way, and thereby to definitely turn down Mr. Daniels and his exploitation of the Navy for political purposes.' He even thought that Mr. Daniels might have been forced out of office. This was a spectacular miscalculation.

Sims in this matter was motivated by no considerations of selfishness or exhibitionism. But, it is clear, he anticipated a response he never obtained. Only two officers wrote him to ask if they should refuse their medals. To them he replied that the whole value of renunciation was in its spontaneity.

The protest failed.[11] Mr. Daniels was left to distribute his awards on Armistice Day, 1920, two years after the fighting was over. This, wrote Sims, was one of the great disappointments of his life. Shortly, there awaited him a yet profounder disillusion.

Admiral Sims had first appeared before the Committee investigating the medal awards on January 17, 1920. On the afternoon of that day, the Chairman, Frederick Hale, had suddenly said to him, 'I think in connection with this matter, if you have had any further correspondence with the Secretary of the Navy about the question of awards and their effect on the morale of the service, it

---

[11] It should be noticed, however, that in the present war, medals are being awarded promptly for heroic action.

would be well for you to give that correspondence to us at the present time.'

Sims replied that such correspondence as he had recently had with the Secretary bore upon 'the question of the morale of the service.' 'Then,' concluded the Chairman, 'I think it is decidedly germane to the issue.' [12] Forthwith Sims produced a long letter he had written to Mr. Daniels on January 7, 1920. It was entitled 'Certain Naval Lessons of the Great War.' Before examining its contents, it will be well to consider why it was written and how the Chairman came to know about it.

In May, 1918, Sims had written to his wife that 'The history of our part in this war will be such a sad one that our children will see to it that we are never again placed in such a defenseless and humiliating position.' A few months later he had explained to Pratt, 'When the history of this war comes to be written, there will be a number of features that will not be very creditable to the United States Navy. If hearings are held on the conduct of the war, a number of rather disagreeable facts must inevitably be brought out.' That was the attitude he brought back with him from London.

For almost a year he held his peace on the subject which interested him most. Then, two weeks after his letter to the Secretary about the medals, and ten days before he was to appear before the Investigating Committee, he sat down to write the letter on 'Certain Naval Lessons of the Great War.' One week after the letter was mailed from Newport, the *Washington Post*, on January 14, carried a story written by Albert W. Fox. It was headlined 'Sims Attacks Daniels' Policies.' One sentence will indicate the tone and content of Mr. Fox's article. 'It [Sims' letter of January 7] is a frank and fearless exposé of the hopeless story of maladministration, mistakes, and blunders into which the American Navy has fallen as a result of Mr. Daniels' policies. . . .' The next day the *Post* in a follow-up story hinted that the Committee investigating medal awards might strike out into the more fertile field of the Navy Department's conduct of the war. In this way the matter became public. Frederick Hale followed the suggestion of the *Post* and asked Admiral Sims to read his letter to the Committee.

[12] *Hearings on Medals*, p. 304.

It was a very long and detailed analysis of conduct of the naval war. The first paragraph explained that 'Upon the conclusion of a war in which large naval forces have been engaged, and after a sufficient time has elapsed to permit of a careful estimate of the manner in which the war was conducted, it is of the first importance that the many lessons to be derived from this experience be recorded in order that they may serve as a guide in future wars.' [13] There followed a list of what Sims believed the most serious errors of policy, tactics, strategy, and administration that had been committed by the Navy in time of war.

When this letter had been read into the record, it was apparent that it covered matters which the Committee was not then empowered to investigate. Therefore, Senator Hale sought and obtained permission for his subcommittee to conduct an investigation into all questions raised by Sims' letter to the Secretary of the Navy. This investigation was deferred until the hearings on the medal awards were completed. On March 9, 1920, a subcommittee composed of Frederick Hale (Maine), L. Heisler Ball (Dela.), Henry W. Keyes, (N.H.), Key Pittman (Nev.), and Park Trammel (Fla.), began its investigation into the conduct of the war.

The ultimate purpose behind the letter of January 7, 1917, was the reorganization of the Navy Department. Since the days, long past, of the Moody-Mahan Commission, this had been for Sims a cherished dream. He was not so naïf as to believe that his single letter to the highest official responsible for the conduct of the Navy during the war would bring about this desirable result, but he was likewise not so innocent as to believe that the letter would never go beyond the Secretary's desk. In the early stages of the investigation, which began in March, attempts were made to suggest that Sims himself was responsible for the publicity which his communication received. Nothing of this sort could be proved. In fact, Albert W. Fox subsequently denied that he had gotten wind of the existence of such a letter from Sims or anyone connected with him.[14] Nevertheless, it is impossible not to conclude that Sims knew when he composed his indictment that it would reach a wider audience than the Secretary.[15] His early

[13] *Hearings on Medals*, p. 309.   [14] Kittredge, *op. cit.*, p. 77.
[15] Sims explained to the Committee how easy it was for news to leak out of the

letters to his wife and Captain Pratt reveal that even during the war his mind was on the possibility of an investigation afterward. He timed his communication to the Secretary so that it would arrive just as public opinion was aroused over the medal awards. He did nothing to prevent his criticisms from reaching the public; in fact, he had the letter containing them in his pocket when the Chairman asked him to produce it at the hearings on the Medal Awards. It was a fight that he sought; his last campaign in a struggle that had gone on for twenty years. Later it appeared to him as the great fight of his life.

His purpose, then, was at bottom the reorganization of the Navy Department. To prove that this was necessary, he had to prove first, that the Navy had been unprepared for the war, and second, that it had been slow to act in the first five or six months after our entry into the war. The proof of these general indictments depended upon his substantiation of a series of specific criticisms, as set forth in his letter of January 7, 1920. He set himself the task of showing that the material of the Navy was in general unfit for immediate military service; that the number of officers and men was too small to maintain the ships on a war footing; that the Navy Department possessed no adequate battle plans for the war which was fought in 1917–18; and that it failed to grasp the nature of that warfare until some months of fighting had passed. Finally, he set out to prove that because of these various factors the Navy Department had failed to supply him with the forces, information, and men necessary for him to carry on the war as he believed it should be fought. These were the principal specific criticisms he had to substantiate in order to establish the major premise that the military administration of the Navy must be altered.

In his path there were many imposing obstacles. Success depended wholly upon arousing public opinion to his cause. But the people were, not unnaturally, tired of the war in 1920. They were satisfied, too, that America had won the war. No explanation of the errors that had retarded the process could divert at-

Navy Department. *Hearings, 1920,* pp. 281–282. He added, 'Now, the game was played perfectly fairly and squarely. I am no spring chicken in this business, and I am not putting my head in a noose unnecessarily. I saw that the letter was confidential, of course, and I took particular pains to see that it did not get out to any of our own people, and I even carried the only copy in my own pocket. . . .'

tention from the fact that the final result was victory. Likewise the citizens of this country were not, in 1920, and never have been, sufficiently interested or well educated in military matters to follow, with understanding, the technical arguments of soldiers and sailors. Finally, Sims did not have that hold over the public which enables a leader to find support among men who will follow him when they cannot follow his arguments.

There were other obstacles no less impressive. Much as he may have wished to avoid personalities, it was impossible for Sims to establish certain of his specific criticisms without offending the sensibilities of naval officers in high place. Men like Benson and Pratt had been denied the greater glory of service abroad. They had worked as hard as men could work to ensure our naval success in the war. Psychologically, therefore, they were naturally unprepared to agree with Sims' indictment of the Navy Department. It was inevitable that they should oppose him, and in their opposition lay some of the seeds of ultimate failure. Sims, if he was to succeed, had to avoid anything that looked like a squabble between naval officers; he had to be able to present to the country the united support of the service for the reforms he advocated. By the same token he had to make the Navy Department as an impersonal organization the main target of attack. Yet this was extremely difficult. The Secretary was a Democrat, the majority of the Investigating Committee were Republicans, and Republicans who had not enjoyed the benefits of a Republican administration in eight long years. With a Presidential election taking place eight months after the investigation got under way, neither Senators nor reporters were likely to miss the political aspects of an attack on the conduct of the war. Nor was the Secretary himself a person who could be kept in the background. He was an articulate, rather dramatic, extremely human, being, who, with his provincial mind, took a very personal view of both criticism and praise. A public, rather bored by the issues and bewildered by the arguments, could find some pleasure in reducing the relative merits of the debate to the relative merits of the two most persistent debaters.

Finally Sims had to avoid creating the impression that he was motivated purely by personal pique. Since much of his case rested on the fact that his recommendations had not, in the early months of the war, been followed, and upon the point that he had for the same period been inadequately supplied with men for his staff, this was extraordinarily difficult. The vindictive blasts of old warriors against the politicians and against their brother officers was an old familiar story in men's ears. Sims had perforce to handle his case with extreme delicacy, to keep himself well in the background.

That some of these obstacles were apparent to Sims, and that more of them were clear to a few of his followers, is abundantly clear. Babcock remembers that several of the younger officers pleaded with Sims to avoid the investigation on the grounds that it would become a matter of politics. To them Sims replied: 'I know that it will be simply a politicians' field day, but I plan to go through with it. Someday when there are flowers sprouting on my grave, there will be another war, and perhaps these records of the investigation will be taken down and dusted off and several lessons learned from them. Then you can all put some more flowers on my grave.' Thus he stated his minimum hopes. In reality he apparently expected far more. His surging optimism, his great faith in public opinion, his absolute assurance that his case was sound permitted him to have far greater expectations. He swung off to his last encounter in 1920 with all the jubilance and every trusted weapon he had possessed in 1908.

Sims' letter of January 7, 1920, fills ten pages of small print. Each one of his general criticisms was supported by detailed explanations and descriptions. The seventh of his seventy-eight points stated that he had received no formal instructions from the Department upon leaving for London beyond the admonition: 'Don't let the British pull the wool over your eyes. It is none of our business pulling their chestnuts out of the fire. We would as soon fight the British as the Germans.'

This letter Sims read to the Committee investigating medal awards on January 17. Next day, Sunday, the *New York Times* carried a headline across the whole front page reading as follows: 'Sims Arraigns Navy Department, saying that he was warned, we would as leave fight the British as Germans.' The subheads of the column one story reported, 'Sims Startles Senators,' 'Was told not to let the British Pull Wool Over His Eyes, he says.' 'Reads Letter to Daniels.' 'Declines to name "Person in Authority" who gave the Instruction Quoted.' 'Asserts He Was Hampered.' 'Members of Congress Deplore Development in the Dispute as Unfortunate.'

He had his audience. He did not know, and he did not care, as he went off to Newport to prepare his case for the investigation that was to open March 9, that he did not have them where he wanted them.

For six weeks before the hearings opened, Sims was at Newport working upon his opening statement for the Committee. Several of his stalwart friends, like H. I. Cone and many of the officers on his staff in London, assisted him in his task. Of these Knox, Babcock, and Tracy B. Kittredge, a reserve officer, were the most tireless in his behalf. A few went to Washington with him when the hearings began.

Early on March 9, Sims began his long statement before the Committee. Almost three months later on May 28, the hearing ended. In the interval, twenty-two witnesses had passed before the Senators. To Sims' side rallied many of the older familiar faces, Rear Admiral C. P. Plunkett, Rear Admiral W. F. Fullam, Rear Admiral Bradley Fiske. Younger men like Captain Harris Laning, Captain L. C. Palmer, and Captain J. K. Taussig joined these older officers. Against Sims were ranged some men whose names are likewise familiar — Rear Admirals F. F. Fletcher, Joseph Strauss, W. S. Benson, Henry B. Wilson, Hugh Rodman, A. P. Niblack, and Captain William V. Pratt. In the course of the three months a great deal of evidence bearing upon Sims' criticisms was introduced, a good many flat assertions were made, a large number of charges and counter-charges were filed, over two and a half million words were spoken, and a considerable amount of extraneous material was presented. No adequate digest of the thirty-five hundred pages can be made in the short space permitted here. Too great attention cannot be given to any one witness. Only the major points that were established can be discussed.

Sims had three central points he wished to make. First: that the Navy was unprepared, 'in spite of the fact that war had been a probability for at least two years and was, in fact, imminent for many months before its declaration.' On the basis of the evidence produced, this charge was fully substantiated. It was first established that the Navy went into the war with a shortage of trained personnel. Admiral Benson, when the Chairman asked if the personnel at the beginning of the war was adequate, replied, 'No.' [16] To the same question Captain Pratt answered, 'Not the way I would like to see it.' [17] Admiral Badger of the General Board explained that 'To the General Board it was plain that it would be the part of prudence, and perhaps necessity, to have more personnel for the Fleet, yes. There is no doubt about that.'[18] The Commander-in-Chief, Admiral Mayo, testified that throughout his tour of duty before the war the Fleet had been handicapped by a lack of men. He stated that six days before war was declared 'the personnel was, however, on a peace basis and the transfer of trained personnel for armed guard and other duty was already being felt in a decrease of efficiency.' [19]

Captain Harris Laning, who during the war had been in the Bureau of Navigation in charge of the Officer Personnel Division, devoted a great deal of his testimony to the shortage of men. He quoted from a letter sent by the Bureau to the Secretary in October, 1918. This letter contained information the Secretary had requested in preparing his Annual Report. 'At the time the United States entered the war,' the communication stated, 'the personnel of the Navy, while of a high standard, was entirely inadequate to meet the needs of war as it is waged today. Neither of enlisted men nor of officers were there enough to man the ships of the Navy that were then ready. . . . The newer battleships and destroyers were manned and ready when war was declared, but the older ships, including battleships, armored cruisers, destroyers, etc., had only half crews and a few were not even in commission.' [20] The Chief of the Bureau of Navigation, L. C. Palmer, revealed that in 1916 'we were short at that time approximately 28,000 regulars and 23,000 reserves. . . .' [21]

No reasonable doubt could exist that the Navy went into the war lacking trained personnel or that for several years before the war this shortage was apparent to most of the officers who had anything to do with the question.

One very interesting fact concerning the personnel problem was developed in the course of the investigation. In its Annual

[16] *Hearings, 1920*, p. 1831.   [17] *Ibid.*, p. 1591.   [18] *Ibid.*, p. 1170.
[19] *Ibid.*, p. 585.   [20] *Ibid.*, p. 384.   [21] *Ibid.*, p. 443.

Report for 1914 the General Board pointed out the necessity for enlarging the enlisted force. It strongly urged 'upon the Department the necessity of using its best endeavors to carry out the repeated recommendations of the General Board, made from year to year, to provide the Fleet with a personnel, active list, and trained reserve, equal to the manning of the Fleet for war.' At first, the General Board specifically recommended increasing the personnel by 19,600 men. The Secretary did not accept this recommendation and asked that any mention of a numerical increase be removed from the Report before it was published. This request was complied with by the General Board.[22]

In his Report for the same year, 1914, the Secretary stated that 'By wisely utilizing the present personnel, all ships of the classes named can be maintained in full commission without addition to the present enlistment, and, therefore, no legislation is needed to carry out their [the General Board's] recommendations.' In support of this statement, the Secretary cited the Report of the Bureau of Navigation which indicated that adequate complements for ships could be assigned without an increase in the enlisted force. Both the Secretary and the Chief of the Bureau of Navigation arrived at their figures by reducing the complements below that believed necessary by the General Board. The 'wise utilization of present personnel' meant simply furnishing each ship with an inadequate force.[23] That this is true was established by the condition of the Fleet when war was declared and by the testimony of every officer intimately connected with personnel matters.

The blame for this condition would seem to rest primarily upon the shoulders of the Secretary of the Navy. But this should not obscure from view the presence of a larger issue in this whole matter. The Secretary took the opinion of a Chief of a Bureau while he rejected the opinion and suppressed the numerical recommendation of the General Board. In this he was acting wholly within his legal rights. Had the General Board been a legally constituted General Staff, it could not have forced the Secretary to accept its views, but it could have forced those views, supported by figures, into the light of day. Then the Congress of the United States would have been able to reach

[22] *Hearings, 1920*, pp. 1138–1139.   [23] *Ibid.*, pp. 476–478.

a decision on the question of personnel by judging the relative merits of the arguments presented on the one hand by the General Board and on the other by the Secretary and Chief of the Bureau of Navigation. No clearer demonstration of the fundamental weakness of the General Board as an advisory body could be given. It deferred to a Secretary of the Navy who, with the best will in the world, was profoundly in error. The General Board should not have the right to impose its views upon a Secretary; but a Secretary should, by the same token, not have the right to impose his will upon the General Board without permitting that Board a hearing before a Congress and a people before whom both are subordinate.

Much testimony was given about the material condition of the Navy upon our entrance into the war. Here, too, Sims was correct in believing that the Navy was unprepared for battle. The Chairman of the Investigating Committee asked Admiral Grant how many submarines were ready in 1917. He replied, 'We had none.' [24] On August 20, 1917, Admiral Grant assumed command of Battleship Force One — older battleships that had been in reserve. 'To summarize,' he said, 'the material condition of vessels forming battleship force in August, 1917, was not good.'

Commander Taussig testified at some length about the condition of destroyers. He quoted the Department as announcing that 'The gunnery trophy will not be awarded for the gunnery year 1916, because of the small number of vessels completing the year's work, and because the scores obtained by these vessels do not warrant the award of the trophy.' 'Even the Department,' he concluded, 'recognized that the destroyer force was not as efficient as it should be.' He explained that the first six destroyers which he took abroad to Queenstown had been selected because they were in the best state of preparedness. These six were 'in fairly good condition,' but they needed a thorough overhauling which they could not receive before leaving for Europe. Much of the reduced efficiency of the destroyers he laid to the shortage of men previously noticed. The large building programs had taken sailors from destroyers to serve on battleships. [25]

Admiral Mayo testified that the material readiness of the

[24] *Hearings, 1920*, p. 541.   [25] *Ibid.*, pp. 506–507.

active Fleet which he commanded was 'from good to very good.'
He added, however, that 'this Fleet was lacking in types of vessels essential to efficiency, such as battle cruisers, scout cruisers,
light cruisers, and fleet submarines. . . .' The Fleet was, in other
words, unbalanced.[26] The testimony of Admiral Fullam, Commander of the forces in the Pacific, was devoted in large part to
the unsatisfactory condition of the ships under his command.
Admiral Benson, in response to questions by the Chairman of the
Committee, gave the following answers bearing upon our
material preparedness for the war:

> *The Chairman:* If you had been ordered and permitted to begin
> preparations for war after May, 1915, would not the Navy have
> been better prepared than it was in April, 1917?
> *Benson:* Yes, sir.
>
> . . . .
>
> *The Chairman:* Was its personnel adequate?
> *Benson:* No.
> *The Chairman:* Were all the ships ready?
> *Benson:* They were ready as far as — no, they were not all ready.
> *The Chairman:* Were they fully manned?
> *Benson:* They were not fully manned.
> *The Chairman:* Was the Navy mobilized?
> *Benson:* It was not.[27]

This particular exchange was closed by Admiral Benson's
statement that because of our concept of neutrality, which we
were compelled to guard carefully, 'our vessels were scattered
throughout the world.' For this reason, scouting and screening
vessels essential to the safety of the Fleet were not with the Fleet
when war broke out.

In his Annual Report for 1918, Mr. Daniels had announced
that the Navy in April, 1917, had been ready 'from stem to stern'
for any eventuality. It was an unfortunate generalization. The
modern battleships of the Fleet were, on the whole, ready for
any tasks that might have been assigned to them. With this
qualification it is beyond all reasonable doubt that the United
States Navy was unprepared materially and physically for the
war which it entered in 1917.

The cause of this unhappy situation is not far to seek. Two

[26] *Hearings, 1920*, p. 585.   [27] *Ibid.*, p. 1831.

careful students of the period have expressed it as follows: 'But specific preparation for early hostilities with Germany, such as systematically putting the existing ships on a war footing or laying down a great flotilla of destroyers and other anti-submarine craft, was flatly rejected. In defense of this policy of inaction, it was contended that such warlike measures would constitute "overt acts," likely to precipitate war, and certainly contrary to the spirit if not the letter of neutrality.' [28]

As these students go on to point out, 'this novel interpretation of neutrality' probably was developed in part to meet exigencies of domestic politics. Whatever the origin of the policy of inaction, they continue, the Secretary of the Navy 'apparently enforced it as strictly as he could from the outbreak of the war in 1914 right down to our entry in 1917. He studiedly avoided even discussing the possibility that we might be drawn into the conflict. He persistently ignored the recommendations of his professional advisers and obstructed their individual efforts to put the Navy in readiness for war.'

It is unnecessary here to assess the wisdom of the Wilson Administration's foreign policy. But it is important to notice that the Secretary felt justified in maintaining that highly individual conception of neutrality to the detriment of the military establishment which had been placed in his safekeeping. More significantly still, the highest officer in the Navy, the Chief of Naval Operations, felt it necessary to support this action of the Secretary. The following passage illustrates his feelings on this matter:

> *The Chairman:* Did you not then feel that we were justified immediately after the World War started in preparing our Navy for war?
>
> *Admiral Benson:* From the professional standpoint, I should say yes; but from the attitude of mind of the people of the United States, I should say no.
>
> *The Chairman:* When did you first feel that we were justified in preparing for war?
>
> *Admiral Benson:* As I have just said, from my professional standpoint I would have been prepared for it all the time.

[28] Harold and Margaret Sprout, *The Rise of American Naval Power*, Princeton, 1939, pp. 351–352.

The Chairman: But from the standpoint of the people of America, when did you first feel that you were justified in preparing for war?

Admiral Benson: I think about the time that Congress decided to declare war.

The Chairman: April 6, 1917?

Admiral Benson: Yes.

The Chairman: And not before?

Admiral Benson: Not from the attitude of the people of the country, no. But I want it distinctly understood that that is not my professional opinion.[29]

Later in his testimony, Admiral Benson elaborated on this theme as follows:

I say this. If I had urged the Secretary more strongly to mobilize the Fleet and to bring these ships in and get them all ready, it is possible that he might have done it; so you see it may have been that I did not urge him strongly enough. But I did not think, under the circumstances, that it was necessary to go further than we did, taking into consideration all the conditions of neutrality, and all conditions; because I took this view of it — I will put it this way — that while I had my strong professional views — strictly professional — as to what was the best thing to do, I also appreciated, as I felt it, the general attitude of the country and of the Administration, and that it was the proper thing to try to meet that situation as far as possible.[30]

This is a curious declaration to come from the highest officer in the Navy. The words can only imply, in the first place, that the Chief of Naval Operations admitted Sims' charge that the Navy was unprepared. But a far more significant point is suggested in these strange words. It is one thing to insist that the military arm of a country should be informed of the nature of the foreign policy it is to maintain. It is quite another to suggest that a novel concept of neutrality should be permitted to weaken the strength of a Navy upon which the defense of the country rests. Within the traditional and accepted limits of international law it has always been possible to prepare fighting forces for the business of war. The primary duty of a naval officer is to ensure that such preparation is successfully carried out.

The point here made should have little to do with Josephus

[29] *Hearings, 1920,* p. 1820.   [30] *Ibid.,* pp. 1837–1838.

Daniels or with William Shepherd Benson, who did his work honestly and earnestly. At the risk of tedious repetition a familiar but vital point will again be stated. By law, Benson was charged 'under the DIRECTION of the Secretary of the Navy ... with the OPERATIONS of the Fleet, and with preparation and readiness of PLANS for its use in war.' Thus in effect a lay Secretary was invested with large military powers, while the Chief of Naval Operations was shorn of most of his military independence. The original bill, before it was thus emasculated by Congress in 1915, had recommended a Chief of Naval Operations who was, under the Secretary, 'responsible for readiness of the Navy for war and charged with its general direction.' Here, as was noticed previously, is a vital distinction. The purely military responsibilities of the Navy were clearly defined and relegated to their proper place. Should Secretary and Chief of Naval Operations differ irreconcilably on professional matters, the former could remove the latter or the latter could remove himself. In any case the difference would become public. In no event could the layman silently impose his will in purely professional matters upon the professional. Nowhere was the wisdom of all those men who since 1900 had fought for a General Staff more clearly revealed than in the maladministration of the United States Navy from 1914 to 1917.

The second central criticism Sims made was as follows: 'That we entered the war with no well-considered policy or plans.' The testimony of the witnesses revealed that there was in fact a base plan. It provided, 'in detail for the organization of the fleets, for the establishment of bases, communications, supply services, etc.' [31] It was further revealed that this plan had been based upon the assumption that the United States Navy would encounter alone, probably in the Atlantic, the naval forces of some European power. As such, it was useless for the war which the Navy actually fought and was not indeed referred to in the course of the conflict. Another war plan attracted a good deal of attention in the course of the investigation. In February, 1917, the General Board received a request from the Secretary for advice upon 'operations necessary to conduct the war, taking up the question of submarine warfare among the others.' [32] Unfortunately,

[31] *Hearings, 1920*, p. 3214.   [32] *Ibid.*, p. 1193.

the reply of the General Board was lost. Admiral Badger, the Chairman of that body, testified that 'I have searched for that letter, and it has disappeared from the records.'

The Chairman and Republican members of the Committee had a good deal of fun over this vanished plan. Actually, it was probably not very significant save as a commentary on the Navy's filing system. The plan, according to Admiral Badger, was similar to others made by the General Board in early February.[33] One of these was a survey of the merchant marine, and another was a recommendation of 'Steps to be taken to meet a possible condition of war with the Central European Powers.' The title of this latter is reassuring, but it was demonstrated that the Navy Department took no action in regard to the recommendations of the General Board.[34] In fact, the suggestions of this body fared badly at the hands of the Department from 1914 to 1917. During that period forty-five different papers bearing on the war went forward to the Department. Only six of these were officially approved and acted upon. A total of twenty-four were 'officially ignored.' [35]

The question of plans was discussed at great length. Captain Pratt devoted much time in his testimony to this matter and submitted a great number of memoranda which he himself had drawn up, some of which were put into effect during the war. None of these, as was established, were definitely approved Department plans for war against Germany. In fact, there were no such plans. The Chief of Naval Operations, who was in a better position than anyone else to testify on this question, reported as follows:

> *The Chairman:* But there was no definite war plan drawn up?
> *Admiral Benson:* No definite war plan drawn up on paper; no, Mr. Chairman, there was not.[36]

In elaboration of this point, Admiral Benson further said,

> I appreciate the emphasis that has been laid upon the question of plans, and I think that possibly it has played a part that really is not altogether just to the situation. For instance, we did not know

[33] *Hearings, 1920*, p. 1194.   [34] *Ibid.*, p. 1092.

[35] A statistical analysis of the fate of plans drawn up by the General Board is given in Kittredge, *op. cit.*, p. 301.

[36] *Hearings, 1920*, p. 1887.

that we would be drawn into this war with the Allies, but if we were drawn into the war with the Allies we would have to enter it in the way in which they wanted us to enter it; that is to say, that our forces would have to be combined with their forces in the way that would carry out the plans and policies that they had set out and had been following for the past three years in carrying on the war. It would be utterly impossible for the United States to have sent a naval force into the European waters without carrying out a policy or plan of that kind, because we would have had no place to base our vessels or to exercise an absolutely independent command, and we would simply have complicated the situation by attempting any such line of action, so that the only thing to do was to get, as we did, what we had in the best condition possible, and be prepared to enter the war in such a way as would develop when the time came.[37]

As Admiral Benson said, 'in a way that is a plan in itself.' The argument loses much of its force, however, when one recognizes that the Department made little effort from 1914 to 1917 to acquaint itself with the real conditions of submarine warfare or the Allied naval methods. The policy here set forth was used principally to justify a period of inaction on the part of the highest naval officials.

The third central criticism made by Sims was that, 'Owing to [our lack of preparation] and to the lack of proper organization of our Navy Department, and perhaps to other causes with which I am not familiar, we failed, for at least six months, to throw our full weight against the enemy; that during this period we pursued a policy of vacillation, or, in simpler words, a hand to mouth policy, attempting to formulate our plans from day to day, based upon an incorrect appreciation of the situation.' This was by all odds his most difficult point to establish. It is hard to know when a policy vacillates and equally difficult to define an 'incorrect appreciation' of a situation. Personal opinion complicates the reading of dates, figures, and statistics. Much of Sims' case had to rest upon arguments to the effect that his recommendations had not been followed, that his staff was too small, that his authority had not been great enough. It could thus be made to appear that his criticism sprung from no greater thing than personal prejudice.

[37] *Hearings, 1920*, pp. 1824–1825.

Inevitably, too, in making his points Sims had to blame not only an impersonal organization, but a group of men who, throughout the war, had driven themselves to exhaustion to operate a cumbrous and inefficient administrative machinery. Officers like Benson and Pratt, overworked and denied the glory of service abroad, were not prepared to have their efforts disparaged or their judgment questioned by the man who had skimmed off the cream from the naval war. Finally, all of Sims' case depended upon a distinction too fine for most laymen to understand, between the failure in Washington of the first six months and the glorious achievements in the war zone of the last seventeen.

All these things conspired to make Sims' task a hazardous one. To his difficulties he wilfully added by stating that the initial lethargy of the United States Navy cost the Allied cause 2,500,-000 tons of shipping, 500,000 lives, and $15,000,000,000. These arresting figures he arrived at by an incredible oversimplification. The number of days he estimated that the war had been prolonged by our failure to enter upon it wholeheartedly he multiplied by the lives lost, tonnage sunk, dollars spent each day throughout the critical period of the war. By this concrete, colorful accusation unsusceptible of any kind of proof, he succeeded only in rousing men's pride and passions. Never did he discover the difference between rapping for attention and knocking his audience cold. Old campaigners like Key Pittman and Park Trammel could use the statement for their own purposes with damaging effect against Sims' cause.

Two major contentions were the foundation stones of Sims' statement that we did not throw our weight into the war for six months after we entered it. He maintained that the Navy Department failed to realize 'that the critical sea area was in the eastern Atlantic in the so-called submarine zone' and that it likewise did not understand that 'it was impossible intelligently to direct the operations of our forces from Washington.' In his letter to the Secretary of January 7, he had marshalled a mass of evidence by which he hoped to support these two general conclusions. Only the four principal charges need detain us here.

There was first the matter of Sims' staff in London. He explained that for the first four months of the war, Babcock alone

assisted him and that for the first year the staff was wholly inadequate. That these things were true was proved beyond all
doubt at the investigation. Pratt admitted that it was 'an error
in judgment' to keep Sims so shorthanded. Benson with some
qualifications agreed.[38] Two other bits of evidence lead inevitably
to this conclusion. Pershing arrived in France with a staff of
fifty-three commissioned officers in May, 1917. On April 5, 1917,
the General Board recommended that Sims go to England
with a staff of nine officers. This recommendation was made by
the General Board before it learned that Sims had already gone
abroad, before war had been declared, and before it was anticipated that Sims would have command of any forces operating in
European waters.

Next Sims maintained that in the first six months of the war,
material aid from America did not arrive in Europe with the
rapidity demanded by the situation in the critical area. That all
existing forces were not sent was clearly demonstrated at the investigation. Both Pratt and Benson testified to this effect.[39]

A third proof of his major conclusions Sims found in the fact
that there had been a delay of at least two months in adopting
the convoy system which eventually proved itself the most successful weapon against the submarine. This, too, was proved
beyond all doubt. Simply to cite the dates of cables established
the fact of delay, and Admiral Benson, among others, testified to
it.[40]

Finally, Sims pointed out that he had received no declaration
of policy from the Navy Department until July 10. This, too, was
susceptible of proof simply by reference to the cables.

From facts like these, multiplied in the testimony a hundred-
fold, Sims sought to establish the truth of his major conclusions that the Department failed to realize the location of the
critical area and did not understand that the war could not be
run from Washington. Those opposed to him admitted the facts
in the case, but drew quite different conclusions from them.

Sims' staff it was explained was inadequate, not because the
Department suffered from misconceptions about the importance
of his duty, but simply because the men were not available.

[38] *Hearings, 1920*, pp. 1260 and 1901.
[39] *Ibid.*, pp. 1227–1228 and 1907.   [40] *Ibid.*, p. 1908.

Admiral Benson revealed that had he sent the officers Sims asked for, his own office of Operations would have been even more lamentably shorthanded than it was.

Though more material could have been sent to Europe in the early months of the war, it was withheld for two reasons. First, it was not all in condition to leave immediately [41] and second, some of it was retained to protect the American coastline.[42]

The adoption of the convoy system was delayed, not because the Department failed to recognize the dangers of the submarine warfare, but because there was some doubt about the effectiveness of the convoy as a weapon against the submarine.[43] The Chief of Naval Operations explained that England had been at war three years before beginning large-scale convoying activities; that there was some difference of opinion within the Department on the subject; and that it seemed wise to wait two or three months while the English experimented with the convoy before America accepted it.

Finally, on the question of policy it was maintained, by Pratt, that the Navy Department did in fact recognize where the critical area was and that our Navy's chief mission was cooperation with the Allies. He further testified that although Sims received no written declaration of policy until July 10, the Navy Department acted from the beginning of the war in accordance with the policy then sent to the representative in London.

Thus, those opposed to Sims could present reasonable explanations for many of the actions and decisions Sims criticized. They could thus go on to question the truth of the two major conclusions he drew from all these assembled facts. It was argued frequently in the investigation that the Department did understand from the beginning where the greatest dangers lay, but while Sims in London was exclusively concerned with this dangerous area, the Department at home had to think in terms of the whole war. Thus the position of Sims, naturally of singular significance to him, was to the Department at Washington but the most important consideration in a whole complex of factors.

The other major conclusion, that the Department failed to understand that 'it was impossible intelligently to direct the

[41] *Hearings, 1920*, pp. 1227, 1579.
[42] *Ibid.*, p. 1907.   [43] *Ibid.*, p. 1908.

operation of our forces from Washington,' was met by a frontal attack. In this the duties of Sims were investigated at enormous length. It was made clear that the Department, in the person of the Chief of Naval Operations, did believe that it was possible to run the war from Washington. Benson said as much. 'I think, as I said just now, there is an exaggerated idea as to Admiral Sims' position that he occupied. I think that the Allies understood that the operations in Europe were being directed from Washington.' [44]

This is the way that the arguments ran throughout thirty-five hundred pages. The hearings became not so much an investigation into the conditions as an elaborate exercise in dialectic. The points at issue became obscured through varying interpretations, through personal prejudices, and through sheer talk.[45] Did Sims, notwithstanding these difficulties, establish the truth of his criticisms? It seems clear from the evidence produced that he succeeded in doing so beyond question. It will be recalled that Sims believed he could demonstrate the necessity for a reorgani-

[44] *Hearings, 1920*, p. 1924.

[45] Throughout this chapter only the most important points at issue in the investigation have been considered. The evidence bearing upon these points has been reduced to its simplest terms. Personalities have been avoided as they were not in the testimony; what appeared to the writer as minor criticisms of Sims which were substantiated have not been discussed; much that was admirable in the conduct of the war by the Navy, especially after August, 1917, has been omitted. Though a consideration of all these matters would have ensured a better balanced and more complete description of the investigation, it would have in no way vitiated what seems to the writer the essential justice of Sims' position. Because of the importance of the issues involved, no attention has been paid to the variety of ways in which certain men attempted to discredit Sims or to complicate his task by other means than argument or the production of evidence. A few examples will suffice. One witness said that Sims' testimony in one instance was of a kind to be expected of an insane patient at St. Elizabeth's. The Secretary of the Navy in the Investigation of the Medal Awards spread on the record the unfavorable fitness reports written by Sims about an officer who was at the moment the Commander-in-Chief of the Fleet. Sims' correspondence disapproving of this officer's appointment to his high position was not only introduced but broadcast by the Navy Radio Press to every ship and naval station in the service. Another event of these months does not seem the result of pure coincidence. The officer whom Sims detached after a convoy had been sunk during the war had twice asked for a Court of Inquiry. It had been twice refused. In March, 1920, while the investigation was going on, a Court of Inquiry was suddenly ordered, though the officer in question had not at the time asked for one. Sims was, of course, one of the principal witnesses. In fact, it is hard to believe he was not in a sense on trial. Such things as this — in which it is unthinkable that Pratt or Benson had a part — suggest the less attractive methods used against Sims. They also would seem the methods of an antagonist who was uncertain of the justice of his case.

zation of the Navy Department by proving the truth of his charges. There can be little doubt that the investigation, taken as a whole, did reveal the need for a strengthened system of military administration. That such was the case was admitted by almost every officer who appeared on either side. On the other hand, there can be equally little doubt that the need for reorganization was not made entirely clear to the public. For this there were several reasons. Though his case was sound, there was one weakness in Sims' line of argument. All the evidence which he produced to show that his recommendations had not been followed, that he had not been given sufficient freedom of action, that he had not been sent adequate assistance did not prove necessarily that the Navy Department should be reorganized. It did suggest that differences of opinion had existed between the men in Washington and the men in London, but such differences might have existed whatever the administrative system of the Navy Department.

The tactical weakness of his position became clearer as the investigation progressed. Sims had hoped and expected to win the public to his cause, indeed in no other way could he succeed. But in maintaining that the Department had failed to understand the nature of the war and had therefore failed to support him, he could not avoid for the onlookers the appearance of a commander with a grievance. An astute person like Josephus Daniels could take quick advantage of the difficulty of his position. In his testimony the Secretary spoke of the officer's love of 'glitter,' of how he 'aspired' to become a member of the Board of Admiralty. He called Sims a man of cliques, pointed out that he had opposed the Mine Barrage and that he had seemed to care more for the safety of merchant shipping than for American lives. He talked at length of 'a great job greatly done,' and reviewed the excellent work of the Navy in the course of the whole war. In the stump-speech heroics there was much that was sleazy, as there was much that was merely vindictive in the personal assault upon Sims, but such shrewd tactics dealt damaging blows. Ever and again the Secretary embarked upon notable diversions. A long article from a religious paper, the *Sunday School Times*, commending the Secretary's abolition of the wine mess was introduced into the record. This was to prove that Mr. Daniels had been nimble in the preparation of the Navy for war as early as 1914.

In time, therefore, the investigation became for the public what Sims' friends had predicted it would; a matter of personalities, a difference between officers, a fight, as one paper said, between an Admiral and a Secretary. Interest lagged as testimony mounted. The news stories moved back through the pages of the papers. Little notice was taken when the hearings ended on May 28, 1920. A year later, when the subject was almost forgotten, the Senate Committee issued its findings. A majority report confirmed most of Sims' contentions. It was signed by three Republicans. Two minority reports rejected his arguments. They were written by two Democrats. Included in the published account of the investigation were various letters and plans of reorganization proposed by various men. No action on these recommendations was ever taken.[46]

Thus, on the familiar note, ended the Investigation of 1920. Twelve years before, Senator Eugene Hale had closed out an investigation before the last witness had finished his testimony. His Committee had then failed to issue a report on its findings. In that same year of 1908, the full account of the Newport Conference was suppressed. In 1909, the recommendations of the Moody-Mahan Commission, appointed by the President, had been totally disregarded by the United States Senate. In 1920, the pattern was repeated. There were the high hopes, the aroused press, the dramatic testimony, the clinched case, and the rest was silence.

The Investigation of 1920 was the badly timed last stand of the insurgency that has been the main concern of this book. It rounded out the two decades during which a handful of officers had struggled to obtain for the Navy some adequate system of responsible military direction.[47] In all those years the men in-

---

[46] A remarkably clear and comprehensive plan of organization was presented by Rear Admiral Henry T. Mayo. *Hearings, 1920*, pp. 3396–3407. It deserves the attention of all students of the subject. This officer has suffered ill-deserved neglect. Though as Commander-in-Chief during the war he was the second highest officer in the Navy, he played, because of the strategy which relegated the Fleet to a secondary position, a minor part in the fighting. In his anomalous position he comported himself with dignity and tact. His testimony reveals him as a balanced, fair-minded man.

[47] By 1920, the ranks of this 'handful of officers' had been decimated by death or

volved were far more anxious to establish the principle than to decide the exact form of the administrative machinery. As Sims once said, such machinery could be determined by 'a commission of officers and others whose opinions would be of so much greater value than that of any individual that it would be perfectly absurd for any officer to insist upon his opinion.'

In every specific effort that was made, the reformers failed to obtain their purpose. Politicians, bureau chiefs, an indifferent public frequently combined to defeat the attempts to reorganize the Navy Department. But, taken as a whole, the twenty years of struggle accomplished much. The constant pressure maintained against the Department by the insurgents brought gradual change. In 1915, the semblance of a responsible military adviser to the Secretary was created. After the last war, more changes were forthcoming. In 1941, the Chief of Naval Operations had by law no more power than he possessed in 1915, but time, custom, and necessity had increased his strength as a coordinating factor within the complicated machinery of the Navy Department. He and the General Board, which still lacks legal existence, are, in the opinion of some, a kind of informal General Staff. The work of constructors, engineers, and ordnance men has been better harmonized in the new Bureau of Ships presided over by a line officer. These are advances. They might have taken place without the Investigation of 1920, but they could not have been achieved without the historical background of reform of which the Investigation is an important part.

These are advances, but they represent changes of detail and

retirement. Luce died in 1917, Fullam retired in 1919, Key voluntarily retired in 1912, Fiske retired in 1916, Sims, in 1920, had only two more years to serve. Younger men have made some effort to continue the work, though by less dramatic methods. Two years ago Rear Admiral J. K. Taussig attempted to revive interest in sound reorganization. His able article 'An Organization for the Navy Department,' *N.I.P.*, January, 1940, begins as follows:

'The reorganization of the Navy Department has been a subject for discussion ever since the World War demonstrated that the Department, as it then existed, was not adequately or properly organized to administer efficiently the enormous, complex, and intricate affairs of the Navy. This lack of proper organization at the beginning of the period when we became a belligerent resulted in much confusion, lost motion, and other deficiencies. . . .

'Since the war a number of attempts have been made towards a reorganization, but although there have been some changes brought about by the creation of new offices, or by the shifting of cognizances from one office or bureau to another, nothing fundamental has been accomplished.'

461

not of principle. It was the conviction of Sims and his friends that our Navy Department could not operate effectively under all conditions until it was provided with some legally established, permanent, responsible organ of military administration. Evidence drawn from the history of the operations of the Navy Department in the Civil War and the Spanish-American War supported this conviction. To such evidence Sims added the testimony included in the two stout volumes of the Investigation of 1920. While he was preparing his case for that Investigation, he warned his friends that 'someday there will be another war, and perhaps these records will be taken down and dusted off and several lessons learned from them.'

In the early days of 1942, the high command of the Navy was reorganized. Admiral Ernest J. King, an unusually able officer who had served under Sims in the Flotilla, was placed in a specially created post at the head of all our forces. In March, the Office of Naval Operations was absorbed into his jurisdiction. He has assumed, in effect, the powers of a General Staff. From such evidence as this one can only conclude once again that the traditional system of administration had proved unequal to the strains placed upon it by modern war.

But these are emergency powers that were assumed by Admiral King, and they were granted by Presidential fiat. If history repeats itself, they will be withdrawn in the relaxed atmosphere of peace. Sound principles of military administration will be maintained permanently within the Navy Department only if an aroused and enlightened Congress and public insist upon them when this war is over.

Then, perhaps, there will be 'some more flowers' on the grave across the river in Arlington.

24

Arms and the Man

A<small>ND</small> I,' William Schwenk Gilbert's Lord Chancellor assured the Peers, 'embody the law.' It was an arrogant and incorrect assumption shared by many of his predecessors. No man can embody any profession. Though it may be possible, as Oliver Wendell Holmes asserted, to live greatly in the law as elsewhere, still it is only possible to live there as a lawyer. Personalities, however great, however free, must, in a profession, find themselves bound to the accepted standards, restricted within the limits of special knowledge. What religion was to the schoolman a profession is to its practitioner. Both give direction to the mind, both provide controls for the emotions, both minister to the spirit, and both hold the searching energies of the devotee within the iron grasp of doctrine. In its highest manifestations the professional spirit makes the good man better than he is and holds the best men in heroic bondage.

The Navy is, with one reservation, a profession. That reservation is, however, of great significance. Members of the service must act as well as think, and they must act together. To obtain the necessary coordinate effort, it is imperative to have some authority in which resides the power to direct and control. There is, therefore, in the Navy a hierarchy of command which is the frame of the whole structure. In this hierarchy the seven stages of man are nicely ordered by law. From birth by appointment to death by an act of Congress the naval officer mounts rising levels of authority that are predetermined. Necessary as this system is for the efficiency of the whole profession, it nevertheless may create an artificial existence for any particular member. More than ambition, more than ability, it is rules that limit the contributions of an officer in his grade; and rules are the lowest common denominator of human behavior. Maturity itself becomes a question of rank. Ordinarily, not until he is forty-eight is a man old enough to be a captain and not until he is a captain is he wise enough to command a battleship. This rigid codification of human values provides for common action within the Navy; it ensures the authority and efficiency of the good men, but only at the hazard of thwarting the energies of the best.

William Sowden Sims was one of the best. Throughout his life his personality was never wholly contained within the legal limits of his grade. The Ensign, bored with long watches and concerned with himself, read nineteenth-century philosophy and wrote long letters to his mother. The Lieutenant, caught at last in the net of his profession, produced a new system of gunnery and sent long letters to the President of the United States. The Commander, secure in his own professional knowledge, inspired articles, precipitated investigations, engineered conferences to accelerate the process of change. The Captain experimented with methods of discipline and encouraged the development of naval doctrine.

Such activity might satisfy the personal requirements of the man, but it placed him in a curious position within his profession. Since his point of departure was usually a criticism, he had to move constantly on the attack; and since he was, until he reached flag rank, a subordinate in the hierarchy of command, he had to attack from below. Thus he was not only a reformer in a conservative profession, but an independent in a service where obedience and conformity were the first laws of survival. Thus, too, he frequently rose above the arbitrary levels of rank, and hammered against the well-built barriers that confined the hierarchy of command.

The limitations of his position became apparent only with the passage of time. An independent, deprived of the tremendous momentum of an organization or institution, must move forward under his own power. The fuel consumed by his fires is strength of will and the hope of success. Along his chosen course Sims went very far, but the demands upon his purpose and his optimism became yearly greater as hopes were long deferred. By 1916 there were signs that he was slowing down. In that year he talked of his past before a Senate investigating committee in the mellow tones of one whose work is almost done. When Ridley McLean tried to interest him in schemes to improve the system of promotion and to increase the authority of the Chief of Naval Operations, he rose sluggishly to the familiar bait. He was, he confessed, 'tired of the subject'; perhaps even he was 'getting old.' Professionally he certainly was old; in a little more than four years from the time he wrote his reply to McLean he would retire.[1] Four years is too short to bring changes for which sixteen have not sufficed. When the chance of success was slight, the will failed to dictate with the old urgency.

A year later, in 1917, Sims asked to be ordered to the War College as President for his last tour of duty. This choice supplied a logical conclusion to his long career. Ever since he had gone to Newport as a student, he had labored to bring the value of the College to the attention of the service. Yet he could not have failed to realize that upon reaching flag rank and power, he was asking for a position off the main stream of naval life. Such a place would give him, it was true, a greater independence than he could find elsewhere in the high command; but it would be, for the first time, a tranquil independence.

The World War shattered tranquillity. The normal limitations of grade were ripped away when Sims assumed his position as Commander of the United States Naval Forces Operating in European Waters. For the first time the dimensions of his duty were measured solely by his own capacity. It was a big show. Success was his, and for a brief moment it was success on the great stage of the world. During those fabulous years in London in which he drank delight of battle with his peers, he saw much of men and manners, climates, councils, governments; himself not least but honored of them all. The vintage of 1918 was a heady wine.

The year 1919 was hardly less distinguished. Events occurred which took the Admiral far beyond flag rank. No sooner had he

[1] Not until a few months after his letter to McLean was the retirement age advanced to sixty-four, thus giving Sims two more years of service.

returned to his own country than he set off on a tour of the Middle West to encourage the sale of Victory Bonds. It was an arduous trip during which he lost his voice. But it brought him before the people. From city to city he moved, welcomed by reporters, cheered by the crowds, thanked at departure by officials. By the time his private car slid to its last stop in the Boston yards he had learned the peculiar exhilaration of public acclaim. There was even talk, though he scoffed at the suggestion, of setting him up as a candidate for the Presidency.

More serious was the effort to make him a full Admiral. In June, Congress took up the idea and lingered over it for almost six months. Political ignorance and pettifogging prolonged the debate until all semblance of spontaneous generosity was worn away, but the subject held the interest of the newspapers which continued to put Sims before the public in pictures and in stories.

In August his clear vivid narrative of the war, *The Victory at Sea*, began appearing in the *World's Work*. For twelve months it commanded the attention of a large group of readers, though its author found it harder to write about a war than to fight one.

By the middle of 1919 it was possible to speak of Sims as a famous man. He had revealed himself to a large public as a speaker of power and to an even larger one as a writer of authority. The death of George Dewey had left Sims as the closest approach to a naval hero that the country possessed. Within the service as well, he had assumed a commanding position. The foundations of his eminence, mixed as they were from materials of recognition and respect, appeared solid. Here and there, especially in the Navy, fissures of old antagonisms remained; around the country the elements of respect and recognition were not perhaps sufficiently mixed with the binder of public affection. But on the whole the foundations were sound. A little careful shoring up would do the rest.

The unstated problem was what Sims could do in this position. In 1919 he stood at one of those crossroads so obvious to the cartographers who write biographies. In the opinion of some observers, he could then have turned into the path of the elder statesman. The high offices of Commander-in-Chief, Chief of Naval Operations, Chairman of the General Board, may well have lain open to him. 'He was,' says one, 'upon a pinnacle.'

From such elevations he could have thrown the full weight of his intelligence, wisdom, and reputation into the improvement of the Navy. At the heart of the governing hierarchy he could have led the march of progress. It is an alluring prospect.

But careers that run in straight lines reach no partings of the way. Long before 1920 Sims had written his own ticket into the future. While he was still in London, he had asked if he could return to the War College. On the last day of December, 1918, he heard from Washington that his request had been granted. At the bottom of the cablegram containing this information he wrote in longhand, 'Note how pleased all hands are to give me the College. It relieves them from the embarrassment of knowing what to do with me.' To his old friend, Rear Admiral Dunn in the Azores, he expressed similar sentiments.

To all the blandishments of Washington he remained deaf. Hardly had he returned home when someone in the Department asked him if he would care to become the Chief of Naval Operations. 'Don't think,' he replied, 'of speaking to the Secretary about anything else [but the War College]. As the law is rigged, the Chief of Naval Operations is no good.' Yet his decision to remain in Newport was not immediately accepted as final. In June a high officer in the Department asked him if he would take either the position of Commander-in-Chief or Chief of Naval Operations. He replied with a definite negative, but he took the trouble to leave behind him a memorandum on the subject. It looked to him like some game of the Secretary. Should Sims definitely commit himself to refusal beforehand, he thought that Mr. Daniels might offer the positions to him. One month later, the *Washington Post* gave prominence to the rumor that had been floating around Washington that Sims would be the next Chief of Naval Operations. Captain Foote in the Department sent him the clipping in an attempt to obtain some further statement. Sims put him off with the remark that, 'In view of what has already been done in this line [of appointments], I may say that I would not be surprised at anything that might happen even including the appointment of Rear Admiral Grayson [Wilson's naval physician] as Chief of Naval Operations.'

Perhaps Sims was moved to his decision to remain at the War College by the desire to avoid an anticlimax. As he and Admiral

Wemyss had agreed in London, a return to the Fleet would seem pointless after the war to end all wars was over. In addition he was completely out of sympathy, even in 1918, with the way in which the Democratic Administration had handled the Navy. He may have found it hard to consider favors from men whom he believed had 'wrecked' his profession. Then, too, he could not bring himself to sit at the council fires with men he had learned to call the enemy. But the decision to remain aloof was probably not made upon any such specific grounds. The thing was in his character. To play the attractive rôle of elder states-man was quite beyond him. He never did grow old and he never had possessed the qualities of statesmanship. He lived and died an independent.

The investigations of 1920 proved as much. With success, reputation, and fame the ancient desires and optimisms revived. The war gave him strength to begin again his independent travels. Unhappily, once the investigations were begun, there was no turning back for Sims. During the first six months of 1920 he committed himself to the course of the insurgent for his remain-ing sixteen years. During that time he labored under burdens far greater than those which had hampered him in the days of his youth.

America in the twenties was rather less interested in reformers than it had been in the first decade of the century. It was like-wise extraordinarily bored with the war save as an explanation for its own vagaries. Inevitably, interest in the military arms of the country almost vanished. It was Sims' further misfortune that a man who has obtained the conventional kind of fame and official position that was his in 1919 can seldom lead a success-ful rebellion. The public expects a hero to behave like a hero and not like Smedley Butler. In taking up the familiar rôle of insurgent, Sims therefore put too great a load on his reputation and flag rank. People would not follow him beyond his colorful phrases, and his brother officers, to his chagrin, failed ordinarily to respond even to them.

Success did not attend him very faithfully in his endeavors after 1920. When from his rather lonely eminence he hurled his thunderbolts, it was only the sound that startled people. Other satisfactions he did have. Unlike so many naval officers in retirement, he never knew how dull it was to pause and rust unburnished. And if for some people he became the stormy petrel, to himself, following his fixed and luminous star, he remained true.

PART FIVE

The Last Years

I do not know what it will be like on the
retired list, as I do not remember ever
having had any particular leisure. Perhaps I will not have much after I retire.
You may be sure that I will do what I
can to help along the poor old Navy.

WILLIAM S. SIMS *to Capt. J. R. Defrees*
October 9, 1922

25

IN THE YEAR 1892, Alfred Thayer Mahan was stopped at the door of a Washington club by two brother officers. 'Do you,' asked one, 'expect a session of the War College this year?' Mahan replied that he did. 'Well,' returned his friend, 'are you going to do anything practical?' 'What do you mean by practical?' the historian asked. 'Well,' was the rejoinder, 'torpedo boats and launches and that sort of thing.'

It was against such an attitude that Luce and Mahan struggled for years to put the War College, where officers were trained for high command, on a sound footing.   In 1912, while he was still a student at the institution, Sims joined his illustrious superiors in their long campaign. He wrote at that time an essay entitled 'The Practical Naval Officer' which was designed to prove the real value to be derived from a study of naval strategy and tactics. At his own expense he had the essay printed and distributed throughout the service. The response was not encouraging, but, of course, Sims was not discouraged. In 1914, when Josephus Daniels appeared in Newport, Sims and other naval officers talked long and earnestly to him about the necessity of a War College education for the higher officers of the service. The results of these conversations were gratifying. Shortly thereafter, Mr. Daniels directed that 'the staff of the College should consist of nine officers and that the student body should be fifteen officers appointed at periods of six months.' Thus for the first time the size and permanence of the student body was placed beyond the whim of a Chief of the Bureau of Navigation. It was a great step forward.

473

Still the institution was viewed with suspicion from within the service. This skepticism was given expression in a critical article appearing in the *Naval Institute Proceedings* in January, 1916. Sims took up the cudgels in an essay breezily entitled, 'Cheer Up, There is no Naval War College.' In words that would have horrified conventional educators he assured his brother officers that there was no college as the term is ordinarily used — there were no President and professors 'whose duty it is to impose conclusions upon pupils.' Instead there was a faculty made up of officers from the Fleet who taught principles taken from military classics; principles upon which rules of modern warfare were 'formulated from the practical experience of practical officers of the Fleet.' The burden of his message was the value of theoretical knowledge when applied to the practice of his profession. Criticism of the College was 'an exhibition of wholly discreditable ignorance' similar to the remarks about 'them college dudes by cracker box worthies who spit tobacco juice on red hot stoves.'

As a reward for this persistent advocacy, Sims, at his own request, was ordered to Newport as President of the College after he left the *Nevada*. Within two months the war interrupted his work there. But this interruption served only to heighten his interest in the study of naval warfare. When he was informed in December, 1918, that he would return to his post in Newport he wrote a remarkable letter to Mr. Daniels on January 15, 1919. In this he outlined his plans for the future of the institution.

In the methods of instruction — that is, the applicatory system involving the use of the game board — he proposed no real changes. What especially interested him was the establishment of the College on a permanent foundation. He suggested first a substantial increase in the number of students and faculty members ordered to Newport. He requested that officers of high rank — that is, flag rank — be placed in charge of the important departments. Most significant was his explanation of 'the necessity for certain officials to ensure the continuity of work and policy at the College, and to bring into the College certain educational features from civil life.'

The recommendations in this letter were approved by the Secretary. In May, 1919, he made provision for a teaching staff of thirteen officers and student body of sixty every year. Shortly after Sims' return, a librarian and an archivist, both civilians, were attached to the staff as permanent members. These men, professionally trained, proved invaluable in fulfilling 'their primary function of maintaining a continuity of policy.' To Sims for insisting on these improvements and to Mr. Daniels for heeding his advice, great credit is due. It is possible to say that in 1919, for the first time, the Naval War College was placed upon a permanent and reasonably satisfactory basis from which it could perform its necessary function for the service at large.

Much of Sims' time as President was taken up with the ordinary administrative activity that is the lot of any head of a college. Frequently, during his tour of duty, the provisions for adequate personnel were not complied with by the Department. In many letters to the Assistant Secretary and the Chief of the Bureau of Navigation he called attention to this failure to supply the required number of students. Finally, he gained his ends.

With the actual course of study he interfered but little. The applicatory system of Captain Little, built upon the use of the game board to illuminate problems of strategy and tactics, continued as the basic method of instruction. His influence upon the intellectual life of the institution was confined chiefly to the speeches he delivered at the opening and closing of each school year. These speeches lacked the well-rounded philosophical approach, the wealth of allusion, the depth of professional learning of Mahan, but they were models of clarity and simplicity in their exposition of particular points. Where Mahan turned to the pages of history for his analogies, Sims looked back into his own exciting past. To one class that graduated shortly after the Armistice, he talked of his days on the *Tennessee* and *Swatara* after the Civil War. He warned that the Navy of the twenties would inevitably suffer reductions of material and men. 'But we must not lie down because of this,' he counselled. 'We must do the best we can with our tools and wait for the reaction to blow over. Then we will be spiritually equipped to handle our new Navy.'

In 1921, he discussed the question of military conservatism. All men by temperament, he believed, were conservative, but conservatism in the military profession was a source of danger to the safety of the nation. Our country 'was distinctly in the lead in originating many important features of naval design and in the invention of weapons,' but 'our Navy has lagged behind in the adoption of our country's inventions.' For this he believed there were two reasons. In the past we had been untroubled by foreign turmoil and thus free from the pressure to improve. Then, too, the basis of improvement was always laid by criticism of existing conditions, and criticism from junior officers fell with severity upon seniors. These seniors, like everyone else, had personal ambition, and thus felt the necessity for defending their established reputations by defending their work. This created an atmosphere unfavorable to the reception of new ideas. From his own past it was easy to draw illustrations to prove these points.

Into the future he peered with some misgiving. 'Are we approaching the consideration of the influence of the airplane in a judicial frame of mind? I am afraid not. So great was the unwillingness to admit anything at all to the disadvantage of the battleship that many of our senior officers solved the difficulty for themselves by simply denying all the claims made by the airmen.' Many men have suffered from the pain of a new idea. He remembered himself ridiculing the notion that ships might destroy each other at a range of twelve thousand yards. In prescient words he informed the class that 'we are now entering a period that may become still more dangerous if we fail correctly to interpret the significance of the rapid development of enormous destructive power and of relative immunity to effective resistance by any means except a decisive superiority of similar weapons.'

The War College was a big gun in the fight against conservatism. 'The important question now is as to whether the training we are actually giving our officers in systematic and logical thinking will enable our Navy, not simply to adopt improvements after their value has been proved by foreign navies, but so to utilize our undoubted inventive ability and so promptly to recognize demonstrated facts that we may keep safely in the van of progress.'

In all these speeches his endeavor was to point up the importance of the War College, the practical value of intellectual training. For one class he reviewed the work of the old Flotilla. With great affection he spoke of his old associates, Robison, Cone, Pratt, Knox, Babcock. He told the young officers how doctrine had been made. He explained how the system of night search and attack had been used by the Queenstown destroyers; how 'upon no occasion did the destroyer escorts fail to meet and assemble upon the designated convoys at the appointed rendezvous, though there were not a few instances of failure in other forces. If I have convinced you of the value of doctrine, you will recognize that you can implant in the minds of your subordinates the conviction that doctrine is not a highbrow term, and that college training is really of a practical kind.'

Like every college president, he had the pleasures as well as the tribulations of his office. Visiting lecturers stayed at his home when they came to Newport. With some, such as Abbé Dimnet or Professor George Wilson of Harvard, he struck up real friendships. There were various social functions including a weekly reception for the men attached to the College. Though he knew few of the students intimately, he followed the fortunes of all of them with interest, affection, and sympathy. One young officer died under peculiarly harrowing circumstances. To his wife Sims wrote, 'While, of course, I have never experienced anything like the trial that you are now going through, still I have experienced something of a similar nature, and if you are disposed to believe a man of sixty years' experience, you will know that in the course of time your grief will be changed to a loving memory, and you will again find life not only possible, but entirely bearable in the direction it is most likely to take, and that is sympathetic service for and with others.' To all the demands placed upon him in his position, he proved adequate.

Many other interests beyond his professional duties absorbed his time and energy during the period. Immediately upon his return from London, Sims was besieged with offers to write something about the war. For some time he resisted what he called 'the blandishments of publishers.' His speaking tour through the Middle West, however, convinced him that 'the average American knew almost nothing about what the Navy did, and that

477

they were very curious to know.' He was, therefore, in 1919 persuaded to write an account of the naval war for Doubleday, Page and Company. His choice of a publisher was determined in part by his friendship for Ambassador Page and in part by the very favorable financial terms offered by the firm.

Before he could start work he had to apply to the Navy Department for permission to write. Article 1534 of the Navy Regulations, which Sims believed was copied from the Spanish Inquisition, forbade public discussion by naval officers of any questions of politics or criticisms of an administration or the Navy Department. After his application had been made, Sims understood that the President had expressed some anxiety about the discretion of the prospective author. He was called to Washington, where he assured Assistant Secretary F. D. Roosevelt that he would abide by the regulations as set forth in Article 1534. 'From this,' he reported to Fullam, 'you will see that although I may call a spade a "spade," still I am under practically a gentleman's agreement not to mention unfavorable spades.' But he added, 'You may be sure that, at the proper time, I will tell the truth as I understand it.'

Doubleday, Page and Company sent Burton J. Hendrick to Newport to assist in the preparation of the work. He proved of great value to his collaborator. 'His method of procedure,' Sims explained to a friend, 'is to take all documentary information that we can give him on a certain subject and read it over. There is, of course, much that he does not understand. He then comes and asks me questions about it, and asks for supplementary explanations. This I give him in the presence of a stenographer, and with the material he draws up the first draft of a chapter. This, of course, is subject to very considerable correction, and in this way the final chapter is written.'

The book, which was called *The Victory at Sea*, began appearing serially in the *World's Work* in July, 1919. The first installment was a brief biography of the author by Hendrick; the following eleven sections were an unabridged version of the volume that appeared in 1920. The work reached a wider audience through syndication in the newspapers. The narrative covers every phase of the naval war from the time America entered in 1917. Especially good was the discussion of the submarine warfare and the methods developed to oppose the undersea menace. The whole straightforward history is enlivened with humorous or dramatic anecdotes and with character sketches, done with considerable perception, of the principal Allied naval and political figures. No hint of Sims' attitude toward the Navy Department appears. His own personality is kept scrupulously in the background. It is not too much to say that the *Victory at Sea* is the most honest and dispassionate military history written by anyone who participated in the war. It is the best single volume on the United States Navy's part in the great conflict.

The reviews of the work were generally very favorable. In 1921, the attitude of the critics was substantiated by the award to Sims and Hendrick of the Pulitzer Prize in history. Some unfavorable comment the book did receive. It was directed chiefly against a section in which Sims described the activities of the Sinn Fein in Queenstown. He explained that, 'at the moment when these lines are being written, a delegation claiming to represent the "Irish Republic" is touring the United States asking Americans to extend their sympathy and contribute money toward the realization of their project.' In view of this, he thought it necessary to inform Americans of the kind of treatment 'their brave sailors met with at the hands of the Sinn Fein in Ireland.' He then told how American sailors had been beaten up by Sinn Feiners in Queenstown and how the organization had done everything in their power to help Germany in the belief that 'a German victory signified an Irish Republic.' [1] Among certain elements in this country these remarks stirred up a good deal of irritation. A few men even wrote to the Secretary of the Navy complaining about them.

In England, the *Victory at Sea*, published by John Murray, met with other objections. The British were especially upset by the author's revelation of his first conversation with Jellicoe. In this account it was made clear to the English people, for the first time, how narrow was the margin that had separated them from disaster in April, 1917. The Admiralty, Sims heard, was much distressed by the publication of this information. A friend in England informed him that the publicity officer at the Admiralty had justified official silence on the question of submarine war-

[1] W. S. S., *The Victory at Sea*, pp. 83–87.

fare in the following fashion: he had explained 'as if in extenuation that it took a hundred years to write the history of Trafalgar, and they had investigations generations after it happened, and that showed what a difficult subject histories were.'

The general attitude of the English was summed up by Admiral Bayly in a letter to Sims in which he expressed the opinion that the publication of the interview with Jellicoe could do little good and might well do harm. Sims was not unnaturally annoyed by this. To one friend he wrote: 'All that I did was to simply make plain the conditions of affairs when we came into the war. It appears that the British Navy does not even now want to acknowledge that they were really up against it. However, I propose to keep on telling the truth about this matter, though, of course, I am debarred from criticizing the action of our Navy Department and of the various people on the other side. This may come later in a different connection.' [2] To another American in England he expressed himself as follows: 'I thought I had stated with all due modesty the question of the initiation of the convoy system. I had to resist the gang here who wanted me definitely to claim that we had booted the Admiralty into accepting the convoy. It may be true that our insistence had more influence than I have stated, but I concluded that it would not be wise either to say so or to too strongly indicate it. You see I am getting quite diplomatic in my old days!' [3]

He was, in fact, more than diplomatic; he was remarkably self-controlled. Englishmen shortly took up their pens to explain how England had adopted the convoy at the first possible moment. Though credit for introducing the policy was assigned to almost as many individuals as there were men with pens in their hands, all the recipients enjoyed the distinction of being Englishmen. Sims continued for the rest of his life to maintain a public silence on this question.

Every June while Sims was at the War College he was busy acquiring honorary degrees. In 1919, he was made a Doctor of Laws by Yale, Harvard, Tufts, and Juniata; in 1920, the University of Pennsylvania, Columbia, and Williams similarly honored him. That same year Cambridge in England offered a

[2] W. S. S. to E. C. Tobey, November 12, 1919.
[3] W. S. S. to G. L. Schuyler, December 12, 1919.

Naval Aide to President Theodore Roosevelt, 1908

Rear Admiral Sims with Assistant Secretary of the Navy, Franklin D. Roosevelt, 1918

Admiral Sims with Members of his Staff Waiting off Brest for the Arrival of President Wilson on the *George Washington*

King George V, Ambassador Page, Queen Mary, and Admiral Sims

NOT DANIEL,—DANIELS

Two Views of the Investigation of 1920

SOMETHING THE ENEMY NEVER DID

Admiral Bayly's Visit to America. Miss Voysey, Admiral Sims, Mrs. Sims, and Admiral Bayly (extreme right)

Cambridge, 1921. The Prince of Wales and Admiral Sims receive honorary degrees

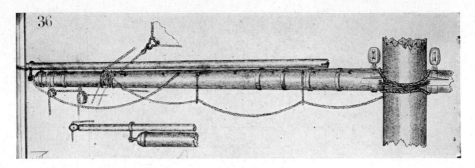

Drawing Taken from Sims' Annapolis Notebook

Doodles Drawn by Sims at Court of Inquiry, 1920

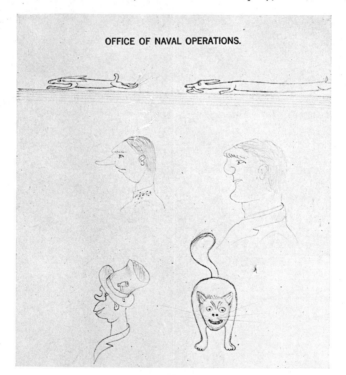

OFFICE OF NAVAL OPERATIONS.

The Sims Family, 1921. Adelaide, Mrs. Sims, Anne, Ethan, William, Admiral Sims, Margaret

Admiral Sims at Seventy-Five

degree, but he could not get away from the War College to receive it. In 1921, the proposal was repeated, and this time the Navy Department granted him leave to go to England. About the middle of May, he and his wife left on the *Cedric*. On the twenty-second the ship made Liverpool where she was met by a destroyer escort at the entrance to the harbor.

Then began a round of festivities of a peculiarly British character. There was a visit to a flower show, a trip to Hurlingham for a polo trial match, an inspection of the Boy Scouts, and a seat in the Royal Box for the Naval and Military Tournament. In between there was a lunch with Their Majesties, a dinner with Lloyd George and the Cabinet, a tea at the House of Commons, a dinner with Lord Bryce, and a lunch with the Prince of Wales before the unveiling of a bronze statue of George Washington. Sir Lewis Bayly had the Admiral and his wife at his home in Devon for two of the pleasantest days of the whole trip.

On May 31, Sims went to Cambridge to receive his degree. The citation was more remarkable for its length and the perfection of its Latin grammar than for the felicitousness of its sentiment, but the occasion was nevertheless a success. An undergraduate reported to a young American girl that on Tuesday

> he [Sims] and the Prince of Wales, both dolled out in uniforms, paraded to the Senate House, accompanied by the Chancellor, Mr. B. in all manner of finery, six beadles with silver maces, a battalion of troops as guard, and 125 doctors in the scarlet robes. It was a splendid sight. The contrast between the two was very great; the Prince, a very young-looking, attractive, embarrassed fellow; the Admiral, tall, trim, quite self-possessed, and very impressive with his white beard, wonderful carriage, dignity — the jam was horrible, like Armistice Day.
>
> In the evening — the Admiral spoke for about half an hour, cracking his jokes, slangy amusing comments, rare frankness, and once more the staid old cantabs nearly fell out of their seats laughing and quite lost all their dignity. It was bully. No one has made such an impression here since Roosevelt.

A week later, Sims was back in London after a brief rest in the country with Lewis Bayly and Miss Voysey. He and his wife were given the same room at the Carlton he had lived in throughout the war. Everything had gone beautifully for two weeks, and the visit was almost over. Monday, June 6, Lady Astor gave a dinner for the two at Saint James's Square. Next day Sims appeared at a luncheon given by the English-Speaking Union. In response to a toast, the Admiral rose to suggest that 'if only the cooperation between the United States and Great Britain which had marked the war period had been continued in time of peace, there would not be as much trouble as there is today.' It was the old familiar theme and the speaker warmed to his subject in the old familiar way.

America was trying to promote the spirit of a mutual alliance. Many Americans were at work trying to counteract the dangerous work of propaganda of 'your enemies and ours.' The enemy to which he referred was the organization of the Sinn Fein. He was not going to speak about the Irish question, but he had written certain articles in which he had told the truth about the 'action of the Sinn Fein faction with reference to our naval men during the war. There are many in our country who technically are Americans, some of them naturalized and some born there, but none of them Americans at all. They are Americans when they want money, but Sinn Feiners when on the platform. They are making war on America today. The simple truth of it is that they have the blood of English and American boys on their hands for the obstructions they placed in the way of the most effective operation of the Allied Naval forces during the war. They are like the zebras, either black horses with white stripes or white horses with black stripes. But we know they are not horses — they are asses; but each of these asses has a vote and there are lots of them.' In conclusion the Admiral explained that he believed that the people who spoke English in the world 'would come together in the bonds of comradeship, and that they would run this round globe.'[4]

As he sat down, laughter and cheers shook the dining-room of the Hyde Park Hotel. Shortly the wires to America were hum-

[4] Almost any metropolitan daily of June 8, 9, 10 contains a paraphrase of the speech. *The Literary Digest*, June 25, 1921, has an excellent summary with a choice selection of editorial reaction.

ming. In Washington, Secretary Denby, reading reports of the speech 'with amazement,' sent a wire off to London to know if the Admiral had been correctly quoted. In reply Sims explained, as he had twelve years before to another Secretary, that he had spoken from a few notes, quite extemporaneously, and that it was impossible to construct the exact phraseology of the speech. He added that reports had been 'garbled.' This was true to the extent that several different versions had been sent across the Atlantic, but the substance of each was the same. Sims had repeated the charge, first made in the *Victory at Sea*, against the Sinn Feiners for their conduct at Queenstown during the war. To this indictment he had added the refreshing analogy of the jackass vote. Of that there could be no doubt, nor did Sims attempt to deny it. His case rested primarily upon the distinction he had drawn between a small group of Sinn Feiners and the whole mass of the Irish people against whom he had never said anything. The distinction was too fine for most of the reading public to master. Secretary Denby cabled to Sims to report immediately in person to the Navy Department. He left England on June 15 with the comforting knowledge that the English press and public highly approved of his sentiments. Three days after the event, the alert *Times* had reported favorably on the speech under a small leader reading, 'Admiral Sims on the Mischief Makers.'

American reaction was more exuberant. Secretary Denby was presumably smoldering away in his office awaiting the return of the Admiral. More eloquent was Representative Gallivan of Massachusetts who introduced a resolution declaring that 'the Admiral was born under the British Flag and has shown himself to be an undesirable alien.' With greater restraint, Senator Pat Harrison of Mississippi moved for an investigation of the Admiral's alleged remarks. The Irish papers were out in full cry as Sims took ship for America. The *New York Gaelic American* characterized him as an 'Anglo-Simian at large,' and spoke darkly of the Admiral's monkey tricks. The *Irish World* of the same city asserted that Sims had already felt the asses' heels and that shortly the mangy cat known as the 'British Lion' would feel their force. Arthur Brisbane, in departing from the question at issue, strained his fertile imagination with the observation that

'The Admiral's face reminds you of a baby flying squirrel that you may catch in the hollow of an old apple tree.' In the Senate a few days later, Sims and Ambassador Harvey, who had recently informed a London audience that America had entered the war 'to save our skins,' were linked together in the quite unaccountable unity of 'The Gold Dust Twins.'

The attacks upon the author of the speech were more remarkable for their ferocity and imaginativeness than for their number. Most of the papers that noticed the affair during the first few days ploughed the safe furrow of simple reporting without editorial comment. A considerable number, however, came to the Admiral's defense. To the *Grand Rapids News* he seemed to have the courage possessed by few men in public life. The *New York Times* and the *New York Herald* definitely ranged themselves alongside the outspoken naval officer.

While the Admiral was on the high seas, a strange turn of events occurred. As the days passed after the first report of his speech in the press, the tide of public opinion turned more and more in his favor. Partly this may have resulted from Denby's hasty action in ordering him home; partly from the industrious way in which the politicians had gotten busy on the issue; partly because Americans in 1920 had little sympathy with the Sinn Fein movement. Whatever the cause, the public rather unaccountably rose to Sims' defense. He was told that five hundred letters a day applauding his stand poured into the Navy Department. Though this figure is probably rather high, it is certain that Mr. Denby received a great many communications, most of them approving of Sims as an officer and an orator.[5] Sims himself received more mail upon his return — considerably over a thousand letters, cables, and telegrams — than he had had upon any other occasion. For the first time, too, the general tone was overwhelmingly in favor of his remarks. There were far fewer threats, far fewer anonymous messages, than he had ever before received. The papers, not unaware of this growing public opinion, more and more shifted their position, if not to approval, at least to the idea that nothing should be done to the speaker.

[5] There are a great many letters about the incident in the Secretary's Files, National Archives. Roughly ten to one seem to be in favor of Sims' position.

It thus fell out that Sims' audience with the Secretary on June 24 became something of an anticlimax. He appeared at ten o'clock in the morning to find Mr. Denby standing behind his desk. The Assistant Secretary and the Chief of Naval Operations were also in the room. Sims remarked that he was sorry if he had caused the Secretary any embarrassment. Mr. Denby made no direct reply, but handed Sims an envelope, saying at the same time that he would like some message from Sims at the latter's earliest convenience. 'Is that all, Mr. Secretary?' asked Sims. 'Yes,' answered Mr. Denby, and Sims withdrew. The envelope contained a message from which all reference to the Irish was eliminated. The reprimand Sims received was to the effect that it was wrong for a naval officer to express an opinion on international topics in a foreign country.[6]

From the Navy Department, Sims went to pay a call upon President Harding. When he appeared on the steps of the White House after his visit with the Chief Executive, the reporters crowded around him with questions. To them he replied, with a sparkling smile, 'I guess I spilled the beans again. I didn't know it was loaded.' Thus ended all official action in connection with the 'jackass speech.' It soon dropped from public notice and was forgotten.

Sims never forgot it; it was one of his more amusing indiscretions. What impression the whole incident left upon him he described to Sir Lewis Bayly. The row had proved a boomerang, he explained.

> Long before I arrived in Washington, the Principal Dignitaries were convinced that it would be dangerous to push their original intentions. The tone of Denby's letter and his unnecessary order cancelling my leave, seemed to convince the public I was to be dismissed from the service, and they simply wouldn't stand for it. Telegrams and letters poured in on all concerned.... This convinced everyone that the practical business was to attack the Sinn Fein. This they did. The reprimand I received was only to the effect that it was wrong for a naval officer to express his opinion on international topics in a foreign country.... The Secretary was badly shaken by the incident. Those who understand such things tell me that his political career is finished.... I got

[6] W. S. S. to E. S. Land, August 11, 1921.

not less than 1198 letters and telegrams from every state expressing approval.

A badly shaken secretary and 1198 letters might vindicate the sentiment expressed; they could hardly vindicate the expression of it by a naval officer. The speech before the English-Speaking Union in London was amusing, but it was wholly unnecessary and wholly wrong. As at the Guildhall, so at Hyde Park Hotel, Sims entered upon territory from which he was by every consideration of law and tradition excluded. After such a pronouncement, it was far easier for the public to believe the fears of civilian secretaries and politicians that military men will seize opportunities to take into their own hands matters of national policy.

Twice Sims escaped unharmed from his excursions into forbidden realms. Personally, he was perhaps more fortunate than he guessed. It seems possible to conclude from the tone of the communications that the men and women who wrote their letters were moved less by horror that he might be removed from the service than they were by annoyance with the Sinn Fein. Professionally he did his cause more harm than he ever divined. Behind the veil of authority that cloaked a General Staff, men could see the spectre of officers who wanted to rule 'this whole round globe.'

Once more before he retired Sims hit the front pages in dramatic fashion: this time with the assistance of no less a journalist than William Randolph Hearst. Behind the story that broke on February 24, 1922, there was a long history. In the middle of the year 1919, a bill to give the rank of full admiral to William Shepherd Benson and William Sowden Sims was placed before Congress. Handsome citations of the work of these officers by the Secretary of the Navy accompanied the proposed legislation. Without much discussion the House of Representatives passed the bill by a vote of 244 to 7 on September 8, 1919. It was believed that the Senate would ratify the work of the lower house without debate. Wide popular support was apparent. The *New York Herald* called the tune for the other papers with the comment that 'They deserve a place with Jones, Farragut, Porter, and Dewey.' In the eyes of the people, then, the deed was already done by the middle of September.

When the bill reached the Senate, however, it encountered unexpected opposition. Pershing had on September 4 been created General of the Armies of the United States, but no unusual provision had been made for General March, who had served in 1918 as Chief of Staff, a position comparable to that held by Admiral Benson. Supporters of March were, therefore, annoyed by the appearance of a bill honoring two Navy men. Even more aggrieved, and more active, were the friends of Admiral Mayo, who had been Commander-in-Chief. Led by Senators Lodge of Massachusetts and Hale of Maine, strong opposition to the bill as drawn developed. Throughout October and early November the measure lay in committee. An alternative was proposed by which Benson, Mayo, and Sims would each receive a vice-admiralship. It was the kind of compromise dear to the hearts of politicians. Like so many legislative straddles, it was less a solution than a screen to cover a problem. When the session of Congress ended, the bill died in committee. By the time Congress had met again in January, 1920, Sims' letters to the Secretary on medal awards and the lessons of the naval war were common knowledge, and no one was in a mood to consider honoring any officer of the Navy.

No layman can understand the meaning of the rank of Admiral. Only those officers who wear them and, more particularly, those flag officers who do not, can know the significance of the four stars. In the Navy, where rank is everything, an Admiral outranks all others. Four stars are the visible, tangible, incontrovertible mark of success. In our Navy of 1920 there was no permanent grade of Admiral. Thus the men chiefly responsible for the success of the American Navy were subordinate in time of peace to those foreign officers with whom they had been equals in time of war.

In England the thing is better done. Though the Admiralty will on occasion, as in the case of Sir Percy Scott, devote most of its energies to thwarting the abilities of its officers; still, when those abilities have made themselves manifest, a grateful government is the first to recognize them. After the war David Beatty, who first won notoriety for his handling of the battle cruisers at Jutland, and then fame for his work as Commander-in-Chief, was created an earl and granted one hundred thousand pounds. Jellicoe after the war was given an earldom and fifty thousand pounds. In a profession where rank is the first consideration the gap between an Admiral and a Rear Admiral cannot be bridged by the ecstatic citations accompanying a bill that does not pass.

William Sims was not in any sense a vain man, but he never fully recovered from the shock of what was, to him, demotion. He left England on the *Mauretania* in March, 1919, with the four stars of an Admiral. A week later, as he stepped into the swinging launch that took him off the big ship near Father Point, there were only two stars on his collar. Publicly he never indicated his belief that he would be restored to full rank. To a friend he wrote, while the bill was still before the House of Representatives:

> I, of course, hope that this business of promotion will go through, but I do not feel very sanguine about it in view of the interesting political conditions in the United States. Everybody down in Washington appears to be too busy fighting [about] the League of Nations to bother with such small things as Generals and Admirals.
>
> Also, I fancy there will be considerable opposition to the President's recommendations as they now stand. There are some other candidates on both sides. There are also some in the recommendation who are not popular on Capitol Hill. . . .

Though he could anticipate the death of the measure, he could not reconcile himself to the actual event. In November, 1919, when it was apparent that the Senate would never take action, he wrote to Jellicoe:

> I am keeping out of all that [speaking, etc.] now as my position has become a rather embarrassing one. The President recommended to Congress that Admiral Benson and I be made Admirals, but the Senatorial friends of Admiral Mayo and some others succeeded in blocking this unless their candidates were similarly promoted. . . . I am now declining all invitations to appear at banquets, clubs, chambers of commerce and so forth and so forth.

To Fullam a week later he spoke more bitterly:

> It [my position] is that of an officer who has been specifically discredited by his government, by the Congress in refusing to grant promotion recommended by the President of the United States. There is no theory about this. It may have been political, but the bald fact is I was refused promotion. No foreigner could understand this.

Undoubtedly, and naturally, he felt the thing too keenly. It was the first time in his career that he had failed to obtain the normal rewards for his service. There is a certain irony in the fact. By his unconventional activity in the past, he had gone up the ladder faster than most men of his age. In Europe he had come as close as he ever could to the conventional triumphs of a naval officer in time of war, and the reward for this service was withheld. It was a problem in adjustment this proud man could not quite solve.

As time passed, he tied up the idea of his reduced rank with the failure of the United States to pay proper recognition to the part the Navy had played during the war. To Philip Andrews he expressed the belief that the Administration was 'trying to discredit all who fought on the other side.' Even after the investigations of 1920 had eliminated all hope of advancement, the thought still rankled and hope still remained. During his visit to England in 1921, surrounded on all sides as he was by Admirals, the bitter thought lay heavy in his heart.

Shortly after his return from this trip, a strange thing happened. Quite without Sims' knowledge three men, unaware of each other's existence, began simultaneously to think of ways of rewarding the officer for his service abroad. Two were newspaper men and one was a reserve officer who had served at the London Headquarters. Within the space of two months in the fall of 1921, all of these men informed the Admiral that they were interested in 'justice for Sims.' Beyond bringing the three together so that their resources could be pooled, Sims did nothing to encourage the project. In fact he told his supporters that the chance of success was remote.

By the first week of January, the three had joined forces and were ready to act. Whether they were anxious to obtain 'justice for Sims' or 'recognition for the Navy' for its part during the war was never clearly stated after the first of the year, but it is clear enough from the correspondence that all hoped to achieve both aims by getting Sims the rank of Admiral.

Late in January, the reserve officer, John Leighton, began a tour of the country at his own expense to sound out opinion. He made the rounds of the newspaper offices and talked with editors in every part of the nation. He reported gratifying responses everywhere; in Oregon he even dug up an editor favorable to Josephus Daniels who supported the scheme. It was all very encouraging.

Out of a seemingly clear and placid sky, the storm broke on February 24, 1922. The Hearst papers splashed all over their pages various letters that Leighton had had in his possession. One, which was published in facsimile, was from the Admiral himself, expressing gratification at the good results of Leighton's trip. The implications of the letters were clear enough and the news stories told the rest. 'Inasmuch as the only two occasions upon which Rear Admiral Sims came conspicuously before the American people were occasions on which he was reprimanded for public addresses in London which displayed humiliating subservience to Great Britain, the people of the United States will probably not sympathize with the plan of Mr. Sims and his propagandists to secure him the rank that would place him next to our three great American Admirals — Farragut, Porter, and Dewey — who did come into contact with an enemy and who did not humiliate the American people by snobbish speeches abroad.' [7]

The rest of the press was shortly out in full cry. 'Sims plots promotion,' 'Admiral Sims wants to be in class with Farragut and Dewey,' ran the headlines. All the past was raked over to find exciting material on the Admiral; the Guildhall and the jackass speeches were especially emphasized. It was the worst reception Sims ever received from the press.

Leighton gave out a statement explaining that he believed the papers had been stolen from him, since his briefcase showed signs of having been tampered with.[8] He sought to put the whole matter in its best light by saying he was primarily interested in ascertaining 'the attitude of the country toward the Navy.' Sims from Newport gave a statement of his own. He said that he had been 'informed by the latter [Leighton] that they proposed to ascertain the attitude of the people toward the treatment accorded the Navy since the war, and I was glad to know this, because I considered what they proposed to do would

[7] *Boston American*, February 24, 1922. The Chicago *Herald Examiner* headed the same story on the same day, 'Worshiper of England Craves Rank.'

[8] *New York Evening World*, February 24, 1922.

be a valuable service not only to the Navy, but to the people, and this because there can be no doubt that the American people are sadly misinformed as to certain facts of importance to the Navy.'

Not for a moment did he wish to convey the impression that he was not human and had no ambition for himself and children. Nevertheless, it was not a question of the personal interests of any one man, 'but it is very much a question of the influence upon the morale of the failure of the Navy to receive adequate recognition for the services rendered by it in the war zone.'

At some length he then reviewed the hearings of the investigations of 1920. Had he not written the letter which precipitated it, 'there would probably be no necessity for discussing the question of my promotion at the present time.' Yet he submitted that to withhold the letter would have been 'rank cowardice.' [9]

He pitched his case upon as high ground as was possible, but the statement was not a success. The papers and the public were quick to see the essential weakness of his position. It was his word that he was interested in the morale of the Navy against the written evidence that some men were trying to make him an Admiral. Whatever connection Sims could see between the two, those outside could see little. 'Sims Urges Grounds for His Promotion,' was the caption one daily gave his statement. 'Denied Honors for Criticism of Chief, Says Sims,' boomed another. Others were not quite so forthright, though most of the papers took the trouble to point out that Sims implied in his statement that he would have been an Admiral if he had not written the letter on lessons of the naval war to Daniels.

The *Washington Times* had the most fun out of the affair. 'Sly Tar,' they said, 'In Meshes of Article 95. Sea Dog who Had Bombproof Duty can be Disciplined by Brother Officers.' Article 95 forbade officers to seek legislation of any kind without the consent of the Secretary of the Navy. Off went the reporters to the Navy Department to find out if Secretary Denby would take action. He was said to have replied, 'with an ill-concealed smile,' that 'We have too many serious things to consider to bother about such trifling matters as this.' The trifling matter dropped from the news.

[9] *New York Herald*, March 1, 1922.

Sims remained cheerful. 'I cannot help,' he wrote to F. W. Wile, 'being amused at the complete scoop that the Hearst gang made of Leighton's correspondence. It seemed to me that it was up to me to issue a statement. . . . It brought out some facts which the American people do not know.'

How much Sims may have wished to be an Admiral is beside the point. He would have been an extraordinary human being had he not felt keenly the failure of Congress to give him the rank. Two other aspects of the incident may deserve more attention. One of his motives was to obtain recognition for the Navy's part in the war. He chose a very poor time for doing so. The investigations of 1920 should have convinced him that the public was sick to death of the Navy's part in the war and the state of the Navy's morale as described by Sims. Even though he failed to recognize this, he should have understood how fatal to his cause it would be to couple recognition of the Navy with a full admiralship for Sims. Few neutral observers could avoid the conclusion that his interest in his profession was motivated by personal ambition. Finally, purely from a practical point of view, he never should have allowed his name to be associated with this haphazard scheme proposed by a few newspaper men and naval reserve officers. It is a safe guess that Leighton had talked to only two or three newspaper publishers before the Hearst men were on his trail. Failure of the whole project was in the cards before a hand was played.

In the two years since January, 1920, Sims had produced a good deal of public excitement. The medal awards controversy, the investigation by the Senate Committee, the jackass speech, and the affair of an Admiral's rank — it was quite a record. There were times when he felt a momentary contrition. To Hutch Cone, he confessed that 'I seem to have a faculty of antagonizing people to a rather astonishing degree'; while Lady Astor received the following comment from him upon her maiden speech: 'I knew perfectly well the kind of success it would be; that it would scatter conservative ideas like chaff before a real gale; that it would shake up a lot of dry bones; and it would do so wittily and amusingly and with straight-from-the-shoulder thrusts delivered so good-temperedly as not only to leave no sting, but actually to win your hearers. I wish I could do the same in my controversies. I always want to cut my opponents' hearts out — which is all right if one can convey the impression of doing so, not in anger, but in sorrow — for the opponents' own good as it were.'

These moments passed. To Mrs. J. K. Robison he wrote, thanking her for a 'little magic gimcrack,' she had sent to him. 'It fulfilled its purpose of amusing us, and we are duly thankful during this time of normalcy when we have no row on.' One can hardly blame the newspaper reporter who concluded that the Admiral's natural element was hot water.

But in the most sombre moments, cheerfulness kept breaking in. Only a few weeks after the Hearst press had characterized him as 'a sublimated clerk in the British Naval Staff Headquarters,' and 'a hero created by British propaganda,' an employee of the publisher wrote to Sims. Since so many young people held up in their own minds his work and achievements as an ideal, would the Admiral dictate 'a word of advice, of suggestion, of inspiration' that could be published? In reply Sims suggested an incongruity that had possibly eluded the editor. It was hoped, in return, that the Admiral could rise above the past. That, the Admiral gave assurance, he could do; it was the future that worried him.

Of cheerfulness, there was more than enough during the years at the War College. One of the pleasantest interludes was the visit paid to America in 1921 by Admiral Sir Lewis Bayly and Miss Voysey. The two were wined and dined and escorted throughout the country. In New York the Queenstown Association gave a big dinner where both Sims and Bayly spoke to men whose hearts were full of old and splendid memories. For a time the English couple visited at Newport, as had Jellicoe and DeBon before them.

More permanently rewarding was the presence of the growing Sims family in the President's frame house overlooking Narragansett Bay. The older children were off during the day at school, but Ethan and Anne walked with their father to his office and remained to dictate chaotic notes to his stenographer. He loved just having them near him while he worked at his desk. On Sunday the whole troop marched off to church with the proud father at the head of the parade, the children spread out behind them sometimes on both sides of the street. His, and the children's, greatest pleasure occurred on the way home, when they all stopped at the fire station to slide solemnly down the pole.

This active household was presided over in the gracious fashion he had learned to expect from his wife, but she was ably assisted by the two servants he liked the most since the days of Woo Sing on the *Charleston*. These two men, Spriggs and Collier, assisted by the cook Vera, served their Admiral with a devotion that was quite complete, and which was returned in kind. One of Sims' greatest pleasures was the luncheon he gave to the graduating class to which all the officers' children were invited. In his last year, the class was so large that it seemed impossible to go through with the project. Sims was terribly disappointed, and his chagrin came to the notice of Collier and Spriggs. They arranged a buffet from which everyone could be served and the Admiral and the children all rejoiced.

There came at length the inevitable hour. On October 14, 1922, one day before he reached the age of sixty-four, Sims left the Navy forever. There was a ceremony at Newport arranged with affectionate care by Taylor Evans, the son of Robley D. Evans. It is a comforting ritual the Navy puts between a man and his own emotions at such a time. In the slanting autumn sunlight the Admiral read his orders to the officers attached to the War College. Then he shook hands with each of them. As he walked down between two long lines of enlisted men to his barge, he could see his flag flying from an old ship that lay at the wharf. Overhead a Navy plane circled the bay. When the Admiral was piped aboard his barge, there was a thirteen-gun salute. On the old ship his flag came down for the last time. Forty-two years before he had first gone to sea on that same ship, the *Constellation*. As his barge moved slowly up the harbor toward the Government landing at Newport, the career had come full circle.

26

Rɪcʜᴀʀᴅ Roe, a creation of the lively mind of Christopher Morley, kept in his office a little, brown-paper parcel which he called his 'Iron Ration.' The name he had taken from the emergency store of food carried by soldiers in the last war. In the parcel were a shirt, socks, a little money — 'just enough stuff to last me overnight — if I couldn't stand it any longer.' This package was a strange solace to Richard Roe; he knew he could use it if things got too bad. In a reflective moment Roe's biographer realized that there were more people 'than we ever dreamed... relying on some sort of Iron Ration.... Sometimes it's the pretense of an escape they don't even desire.'

From first to last there is no more lonely calling than the sea. When daily routines have been worked out upon the enormous waters, mariners can find nourishment in iron rations. The classic staple is the little farm, the winding stream, the good brown earth. But there are others. Admiral Murdock filled his cabin for twenty years with plans and sketches for the alteration of a house he seldom saw. Time and again Sims thought of leaving the service to return to the hearthside with his books, his wife, his children, to bear him company. It was only the simplest pleasures he desired; walks with Mrs. Sims, card games with Margaret and Adelaide, bouncing young Ethan on his knee. In the fastest going these thoughts crowded closest to his heart. Throughout the exciting months of the war he dwelt continually in his letters upon the old refrain.

The day came when the law and not the Admiral's inclination determined the end of service. On October 15, 1922, he returned to the tranquillity of the family. Not for long. Throughout the summer preceding, he had investigated methods for filling in the time. There was the possibility of a lecture tour, but he submitted gracefully enough to the decision of his family and friends that such procedure was undignified. Still, he found, the 'simplest pleasures' needed spice. Not for him a little bungalow in California; the garden patch behind, the well-kept lawn in front, the endless hours in the little study surrounded by pictures of his old commands. As Huxley had been one of his first teachers, so he was one of the last. The great end of life was indeed action. Though much had been taken, much remained, and for his last fourteen years he 'did with his might whatsoever his hand found to do.'

Nine days after he had hauled down his flag, he was busy writing a trustee of a boys' school who had asked for his picture to hang in the school library. 'I should be very honored — were it not for the fact that you express your intention of trying to secure a picture of ex-President Wilson for the same purpose. You designate him as one of the great leaders of the World War. As I was one of those who had the experience and anguish of seeing the lives of men uselessly sacrificed on account of what I believe to have been the actions of this man, I do not feel disposed to have my picture in the same gallery.' A similar bill of particulars was forwarded to other startled men who had invited the Admiral to send a picture of himself for a memorial gallery.

Meanwhile, Sims was busy paying off another old debt to a different President. Loyalty and faith in the Bull Moose were never shaken; in the first disappointing years after the World War, he wished frequently 'that Roosevelt were here.' S. S. McClure gave him the opportunity to express his gratitude publicly when he suggested a series of articles on 'Roosevelt and the Navy.' The editor was making a last desperate attempt to rejuvenate the magazine that had so proudly borne his name, and when the naval officer responded to his call, old acquaintance was brought to mind as the names of Roosevelt, McClure, and Sims were joined in the November, 1922, issue of the magazine. For three installments Sims traced the rise of the modern Navy under the late President. He told of the China Station days, the development of continuous-aim firing, the All Big Gun Battleship, the Newport Conference, and the 'Sad Story.' It was a clear, convincing, graceful tribute to the achievements of Mr. Roosevelt. Other familiar names received their due — Key, Fiske, McLean, and the colleagues of times past.

January found the Admiral's name bobbing up into prominence again. He had been invited to deliver a speech in Boston before the Loyal Coalition on February 1. The Mayor of Boston, James M. Curley, had likewise been invited to sit on the speaker's platform. The Mayor explained in a letter to the Secretary of the Coalition that he had 'no desire to sit on any platform with Admiral Sims, retired, whose best service to the American Navy was his retirement from it.' In amplification of this idea, the Mayor 'would suggest that when he is done shooting off the only weapon he is expert at — his mouth — he be escorted to the Cunard or White Star dock and given an opportunity to follow the trail and example of his ante type, Benedict Arnold.' [1]

The latter-day traitor went his way placidly enough and delivered his speech in Symphony Hall on February 1. Shortly, he departed for the West to make more news. He had been asked to deliver the Charter Day Address at the University of California. While on the coast, he made two speeches of even greater interest to the public. In Los Angeles, in the first week of April, 1923, he announced, so the papers reported, that 'during the war there was no brutality on the part of the commanders of German submarines and the official records of the Navy would not disclose even one instance where a German submarine fired on an open boat.' Sims denied that he had used these words. He had intended only to convey the thought that German officers were not habitually guilty of acts of savagery and brutality. It was, again, one of those fine distinctions that a generation brought up on the notion that the Kaiser had little children for breakfast was unprepared to understand. A controversy with the *Nation* began during which the press and the Admiral enjoyed themselves thoroughly. In San Francisco, a day or two after his speech in Los Angeles, Sims gave it as his opinion that the history of our military preparedness was 'disgraceful' and 'appalling.' The

[1] *New York Times*, January 24, 1923.

thought was dutifully brought to the public attention by the papers.

Sims returned at the end of April to Newport, but not to peace and quiet. It was announced early in May that R. E. Coontz was to become Commander-in-Chief of the United States Fleet and that Edward W. Eberle was to assume the position of Chief of Naval Operations. Both of these men were well known in the service, both were acquaintances of Sims, and both had his respect. Neither of the two, however, had been to the War College for a complete tour of duty. This defect in their education was soon made public, when on May 8, 1923, the *Boston Transcript* printed an interview with Admiral Sims. 'In my opinion,' Sims was quoted as saying, 'the attitude of the Navy Department toward the Naval War College has long been a crime. The appointment of an officer who is not a graduate of the War College to be Commander-in-Chief of the great United States Fleet is a crime against the people of this country and so is the appointment of a non-graduate to the most important position in the Navy, that of Chief of Naval Operations.'

The Admiral went on to say that the fact that no War College graduate had ever been head of Annapolis was a scandal. 'More than half of the officers given preference in the transfers recently announced and to take effect this summer are not graduates of the War College,' the interview continued. 'The service is disgusted with the situation, disgusted that the same old game of service politics is being played. It believes that the best place is a seat next the dealer in Washington. Personal influence brings greater rewards than War College training.' [2]

---

[2] *New York Times*, May 9, 1923. Writing in 1939, Rear Admiral Yates Stirling said: 'While in Washington (1929–30), I did have an opportunity to observe the operations of the Navy Department, the thing I had been taught to fear, yet not to respect, for over thirty-seven years. I became quite aware of the several cliques forming around officers calculated to have promise and a certain amount of political finesse.' Stirling was advised by a high-ranking officer to 'go after the Bureau of Navigation; from that you can get anything you want.' This officer further told Stirling: 'I tied up with two other high-ranking officers and you'd be surprised how effective that was. Each of us got just what we wanted, and all of us got all the plums there were. Remember by yourself you can get nowhere.... Cultivate the women in Washington. Go out and be seen.... But don't play favorites, for that will arouse jealousies among the rest.' Stirling believed in 1939 that 'High commands in the past and at present usually go to men who work for them by organization and publicity of the right sort.' He says: 'I am looking back now dispassionately

The familiar cycle began. 'Sims, the Nuisance,' 'Sims in a Familiar Rôle,' 'The Unsilenceable Sims,' ran the editorial headings. 'Just because he had gone on the retired list, it was not to be expected that Rear Admiral Sims would become inarticulate or subordinate, and he has not.' Two newspapers discovered the phrase, 'A common scold.' The long suffering Denby found it 'hard to believe that Admiral Sims made the statements attributed to him.' A few, a very few, papers spoke up in defense of the Admiral. The *New York Times* suggested that 'the principle enunciated by Sims was sound, but the character of the men he attacked was such that the Navy would not suffer by their appointment.' The able Theodore Joslin, Washington reporter for the *Boston Transcript*, described with some relish the consternation wrought in the Department by Sims' interview and stated that 'it is a certainty that many of the officers with the Fleet will commend him.' 'They [some officers with whom Joslin had talked] said that apparently there was an inner circle in the naval establishment and that the time had come when it should be broken.' [3]

To Bradley Fiske, who deeply regretted the whole tone of the interview, Sims fully explained the cause behind it. 'Some of the officers concerned have explicitly stated that they saw no reason for going to the War College and cited their own cases to show that without it one could achieve success — personal success, and to Hell with the interests of the Navy and the country. Do not imagine that my interview in the *Transcript* was anything in the nature of slopping over. It was not only deliberately done, but I overhauled it carefully after it was written up. . . . Of course, I

---

and thinking most of all of how the Navy is going to fight the next war, well or badly. I am sure that many officers who obtain high commands are not the best that can be selected from those available.' His remedy for this situation is, 'a General Staff and a board of Admirals from the Fleet to select for high commands without favor.' *Sea Duty*, pp. 225–226.

[3] *Boston Transcript*, May 10, 1923. This whole question of 'an inner circle,' politics, and promotion is a very interesting one. (See Stirling's remarks in 1939 as quoted in footnote 2 above.) In 1923, at the time Sims gave his interview, the following changes in command were ordered: The Chief of Naval Operations became the Commander-in-Chief; the Commander of the battle fleet became Chief of Naval Operations; the Commander of the Asiatic Fleet became Chief of the Bureau of Navigation; a member of the General Board was given the battle fleet; the Chief of the Bureau of Navigation became Commander of the Asiatic Fleet. None of the officers in question were War College graduates.

have had experience enough in this line to understand that nothing will be accomplished in the immediate future by my blast; but here's betting you it will prevent anything like the present crime in the future.'[4]

Fiske remained unconvinced that the Admiral had done his cause any good. 'I do not object in the least your pointing out the great desirability of having a graduate of the War College as Ch. Nav. Op. [sic]. I object merely to the language you use. I have just looked up the definition of the word "*crime*" in the Standard Dictionary. "Go and do thou likewise." I wish it had occurred to you to say, "It was worse than a crime; it was a blunder." By the way, was it Talleyrand or Napoleon who said it?'

The memory of twenty years flooded over Fiske as he wrote, 'In all our fights with the Department, you and I have pursued the same end, but by different methods.' A few days later, his memory recalled a more significant fact. 'It is a little odd that I did not recognize your "Sims invention" in using the word "crime." It was the one you first used, so I remember, in the Sims-O'Neil bout, after which bout you explained the seemingly undue violence of your language by pointing out that "there are some men so constituted that you cannot attract their attention except by insulting them."'

The exchange of letters went on between the old comrades at arms. Sims had looked up the word 'crime' in the dictionary before he gave the interview. 'I found: "Crime — any aggravated offense against morality or the public welfare."' He took great pleasure in poking fun at Fiske's delightful habit of quoting Scripture or lesser authorities to prove his points. Seneca was introduced to brighten up the narrative. '*Deprendi miserum est*' (It is grievous to be caught), 'Horace,' concluded one paragraph.

'I would,' admitted Sims, 'almost as soon have said, had it occurred to me, "*C'est plus qu'un crime, c'est une faute*" (It is worse than a crime, it is a blunder), except that it was not a blunder. They knew it was a betrayal of confidence, but they did it all the same — "they" being the gang that had no difficulty in persuading the civil P.D.'s that "four years as Chief of Naval Operations

[4] The Selection Board of 1924, on which there were only three War College men, selected only non-War College captains to be Admirals.

is better *training* for the command of our fleet than a course at the War College."

'Incidentally, it was neither Napoleon nor Talleyrand who made the remark; it was Joseph Fouché, Napoleon's Chief of the Secret Service as quoted by himself in his *mémoires*, in reference to the murder of the Duc Enghien.'

Perhaps the whole record never would have gotten straight if Admiral Fiske had not come to Newport shortly after and talked the whole matter over.

After a summer of relative quiet with his family at Marion, Massachusetts, Sims set off on his travels again. A trip to Florida began the busy fall of 1923. Upon his return, he made a tour of the eastern colleges, speaking to the students upon a subject near to his heart. Prohibition seemed to him to offer a solution to the drinking problem. He had grown up in the old Navy where drinking was heavy; he had seen several of his classmates and friends ruin themselves by looking on the wine when it was red. These experiences had made a profound impression upon him; he would therefore do anything to protect the younger generation from the evils of drink.

Off he went to the campuses of New England to urge the support of the Eighteenth Amendment. To large audiences he explained that he could pose neither as a teetotaller nor a reformed drunkard. But he could describe how alcohol makes young men drunkards and causes them to fall. Furthermore, 'if you create the demand for liquor, that makes the bootlegger bring it in, you are violating the law — you are in reality a bootlegger.' It was his faith in youth and the perfectibility of man that made him speak to them on this subject. 'The influence of our young men on the future of the United States will be very great. In a few years you will control this nation. You young men are coming up today under better conditions than yesterday. The only thing you have got to steer clear of is the bootlegger. Our future and perhaps the world's future will be determined by your mental equipment, your moral principles, your clean body, and your ideals of private and national life.'

The response to this kind of talk was gratifying. The Chairman of the *Yale News*, torn between understandable caution and beguiling optimism, wrote that 'It is of course still difficult to pick out definite results from your forceful address, but I can say most assuredly that the general attitude of the undergraduates has undergone a marked improvement. I believe that the situation in regard to the Eighteenth Amendment has taken a well-defined trend upward.'

By Christmas the speaking trip was over, and the Admiral had come back to Newport for the holidays with his family. Something always turned up to keep his days full of interest. On New Year's Day he woke with unaccountable indigestion. When the thing persisted, he went to Boston to have the matter, so unusual, investigated. Shortly afterwards his friends were informed that 'a large stone the size of an English walnut' had been removed from his insides. Details of the operation were supplied for his audience at some length. 'Everyone was surprised at the rapidity of my recovery.'

Rapid though the recovery was, Sims remained comparatively quiet throughout the year 1924. In the summer his family again went to Marion to stay with Mrs. Sims' sister, Mrs. John Shepley and her husband. There 'I lived out of doors practically all the time. I did a lot of work fixing up a clay court, calking a boat and played tennis, baseball and went in swimming.' McClure wrote in the fall to ask the Admiral if he would write some articles about the Navy, but Sims declined to do so, 'at least until after the election.'

Shortly afterwards he embarked upon a more exciting business than mere authorship. He was thrust into the debate that was raging around the airplane. During the war aircraft had performed well on errands of reconnaissance and had demonstrated its value as a weapon against the submarine. But with its small bombs, short cruising radius, and inaccurate sighting arrangements, the plane had failed to prove its effectiveness against surface ships. In the years following the Armistice, however, the airplane was improved so rapidly that a good many observers believed it necessary to reconsider its rôle in warfare. In view of this startling development, it was asked by some whether the plane might not supersede the capital ship as a major weapon of offense. Men like Fullam and Fiske, who invented the torpedo plane, in the Navy, and Brigadier General William Mitchell in the Army made the most spectacular claims for the new military instrument.

'Aircraft,' said Mitchell, 'now [1921] in existence or in development, acting from shore bases, can find and destroy all classes of seacraft under war conditions with a negligible loss to the aircraft.' [5] Those in authority in the Navy Department, inevitably, took a more cautious view of the situation. The General Board scarcely recognized the existence of the plane in 1919, and in 1920 it admitted only that the plane was the adjunct of the capital ship, which was the backbone of the Fleet.[6]

The difficulty in the debate was that no one involved in it really knew much about the potentialities of the weapon under discussion. To provide some concrete evidence, experiments were held in the summer of 1921. Three ships, among them the old German dreadnought *Ostfriesland*, were placed off the Virginia Capes as targets for bombing planes. All three were sunk. Unfortunately, the results of the experiment merely added fuel to the fires of both sides.

The defenders of the plane could argue that the ships had been indubitably sunk. On the other hand, the more conservative authorities could respond that the ships had been destroyed under circumstances that vitiated the arguments of the defenders: the targets had been stationary; the weather conditions excellent; the approaching planes had not been harassed by anti-aircraft fire since no crews had been on the ships; the *Ostfriesland*, an obsolete vessel, had suffered sixteen hits before she had gone to the bottom. The results were, therefore, inconclusive.[7] Three years later, the new *Washington*, scrapped under the Limitation Treaty of 1922, was subjected to severe bombing attacks which failed to sink the vessel. She was finally sent to the bottom by the guns of the *Texas*.

Thus, in the years after 1920 each side maintained a lively interest in the debate; each side scored occasional points of a dialectical nature; each side failed to convince the other of the

[5] Quoted by Harold and Margaret Sprout, *Toward a New Order of Sea Power*, Princeton, 1940, p. 218.

[6] *Ibid.*, pp. 214, 216.

[7] These arguments and others about the results of the test are contained in a review of the experiment in Bernard Brodie, *Sea Power in the Machine Age*, Princeton, 1941, pp. 401–403. Part V of this book ('Aircraft in Modern War') is devoted to an excellent summary of the rise of the airplane as a naval weapon. In view of recent developments the conclusions reached by the author about the place of the airplane in modern naval war may seem too cautious.

justice of its position. In 1925, the question of the rôle of aircraft in the future was as far from an answer as it had been in 1920. In the fall of 1924, a select committee of the House of Representatives was set to work to investigate the whole subject. For a time its hearings were carried on in quiet obscurity. The appearance of General Mitchell as a witness transformed the nature of the investigation, especially when his views were opposed by General Hugh Drum. In his usual dramatic fashion the great champion of air power presented his claims before the politicians. As Sims later wrote to Philip Andrews, 'Mitchell had the time of his life.' The hearings were reported on the front pages of the papers and a full-dress investigation was presented to an aroused public. In February, 1925, Sims was asked to appear before the committee.

For many years before he went to Washington in February, Sims had been interested in the subject of aviation. During this time his views had undergone profound changes. On June 19, 1909, he had written to a friend: 'I am afraid that you are up against it good and hard in writing an airship article, provided that you expect to show that such craft can ever be particularly dangerous to men-of-war. According to the papers, one of the Wright brothers has stated that it would be impracticable to hit anything by dropping a projectile from his flying [machine]. This Wright man is right, all right.'

Ten years later, in 1919, his ideas had not been changed by anything he had seen during the war. Fullam sent him a clipping of a newspaper which quoted Sir Percy Scott as saying 'that the battleship was dead; that the great fighting machine of the future is the airship.' 'I should think,' replied Sims to Fullam, 'that he [Scott] would keep reasonably quiet. All the aeroplane carrying ships in the world could not make an attack upon a foreign country unless they were supported by a battleship force that was superior to that of the enemy.'

In the first months of 1921, Sims repudiated all his previous views. During 1920, after reviewing the whole problem in his own mind, his faith in the invulnerability of surface craft had been shaken. It was a problem played out on the game board at the War College that convinced him of the superior strength of the air-borne weapon. To Fiske, who earlier than almost any other understood the potentialities of the airplane, he wrote on

January 6, 1921, that he was going to have a 'money game.' 'That is, give each side at the War College a certain amount of money; one side to build sixteen battleships, six airplane carriers, and six battle cruisers; the other, to build twenty-two aircraft carriers.' Each side was to have the same supporting vessels. 'This afternoon,' he wrote to his friend, 'we had a discussion with the entire staff over the whole matter, and it was easy to see that the question of the passing of the battleship was not an agreeable one to various members.'

Three weeks later, he had apparently become convinced, as a result of the play on the game board, that the days of battleships were numbered. 'Now I assume,' he told Fiske, 'that you are sufficiently acquainted with the history of the introduction of new weapons of warfare to know that the first decision in the case, as in practically all previous cases, will be wrong, because the great majority of opinion will be of the unreasoned, and therefore conservative, kind. Therefore, when this subject comes up for serious discussion, I have no doubt that the overwhelming *amount* of opinion will be on the conservative side, that is, in favor of the capital ship.'

He himself was at this time prepared to scrap the machinery of the past. 'If I had my way, I would arrest the building of great battleships and put money into the development of the new devices and not wait to see what other countries are doing.' Two months later, March, 1921, he was repeating the familiar lesson to the man who already knew it by heart. 'It is a singular thing, however, that you can present irrefutable arguments to officers on this subject and they will still defend the old methods and the old surface ships. I know, of course, something of the psychology of opinion, but this seems to go beyond the theories of psychological experts. Can it be that the Navy is reluctant to give up the big ships to live in?'

The bombing experiments off the Virginia Capes in 1921 confirmed Sims' belief in the power of the aircraft. 'Command of the air' ensured 'command of the surface, whether it be sea or land,' he announced after the tests were over. The essence of Sims' position is this: Testimony by experts and the *Ostfriesland* experiments had confirmed his previous conviction, expressed to Fiske in January, 1921, that battleships were vulnerable to bombs dropped by planes. Therefore, a fleet which had command of the air had an enormous superiority over a fleet which did not. A fleet of aircraft carriers, which would inevitably have more planes than a mixed fleet of battleships and airplane carriers, could easily establish command of the air over its weaker opponent. 'Therefore,' as he wrote to Fullam in March, 1922, 'the battleship is dead.'

From this time forward, he took the position from which he never receded — that the aircraft carrier was the capital ship of the future. In 1923 he said as much in the *New York Times*. When he appeared before the Senate Investigating Committee in February, 1925, he restated his case. Drawing upon his article in the *Times*, he set forth at the beginning of his testimony the following arguments: 1. Numerous experiments reveal that air pilots can bomb accurately. 2. Actual bombing experiments against the *Ostfriesland* demonstrate that vessels can be sunk by bombs. 3. Torpedoes fired from planes are more dangerous than bombs. 4. A fleet without auxiliaries cannot operate effectively and auxiliaries 'are practically defenseless against the attack of even relatively small bombs.' 5. Anti-aircraft fire is the only defense individual ships have against aircraft. 'Moreover, mathematicians have stated that the effect of gunfire against planes by guns installed on ships will always of necessity be negligible.'

From the above-stated evidence Sims concluded that 'no surface vessels can long escape disablement or destruction if they remain within reach of airplanes that are in control of the air. This is not disputed,' he said, 'even by those who claim that the battleship is still "the backbone of the fleet." . . . Manifestly this is a matter of the greatest military importance because it means that a fleet, however powerful in surface vessels, cannot successfully operate against any country or any position that is defended by more planes than can be brought to bear against it by that fleet; . . . It follows from the above that an airplane carrier of thirty-five knots and carrying one hundred planes . . . is in reality a capital ship of much greater offensive power than any battleship.' [8]

[8] Sims' testimony is contained in *Hearing Before the Select Committee of Inquiry into Operations of the United States Air Services*, House of Representatives, 68th Congress (1925), Part 4, pp. 2959–3015.

His position established, Sims roved at will over his favorite subjects in his testimony before the committee. 'Now, as I said before, it is an astounding thing, the conservatism of the military mind. It is absolutely historical that they never give in. You have got to shed their blood before they do it. . . . Lots of the people that differ with me on these points are old friends of mine that I have known for forty years. They are men of absolute integrity of character. They believe absolutely what they say. But, by God, you cannot get it out of their heads at all. It is a very curious thing, but it is something to be recognized.'

A Representative asked him if it would be wise to have an aviation expert on the General Board. Sims conceded that it might be useful, but that the General Board's views were colored by the members' attachment to familiar and traditional concepts. 'With a gang like that, I have my doubts. . . . It [an aviation expert] would be useful; I said useful; yes, it would be useful, but it would not determine the question.'

The old days on the Flotilla were recalled; the details of his eventful career set forth. 'Well, my career in the Navy has been largely getting into trouble with the principal dignitaries, you know that. . . . Really this is only chit-chat, but it may be more or less interesting. . . . When I went over on the other side [1897], I got acquainted with the French Navy and the British Navy and, God help our souls, the Russian Navy, too. I found that we were not in it all, either in design or in marksmanship, and I made report after report.'

A kind word he had for Mr. Daniels in his usual plug for the War College. 'Secretary Daniels, who was a man that I personally liked — officially not quite so much. . . .'

Nor did he fail to get in his little dig against the politician. 'To give an example of what I mean in that respect: When I first came to Washington along in 1901 or 1902 as inspector of target practice, the Chief of Naval Operations asked me, "Where do you want the fleet to go this winter for target practice?" I said, "In the present state of the situation, I think it should go to Pensacola." He said, "In the present state of the situation, I think it has to go to Guantanamo." I said, "Admiral, I am very much disappointed. Would you mind telling me why it has to go to Guantanamo?" He said, "No; we want to start building a supply base at Guantanamo, and we dare not ask Congress to give us any money for that purpose, because Congress does not know where Guantanamo is." And he said, "If we start to ask for money for a supply base at Guantanamo, and some Congressman from the West gets up and says, 'Where in hell is Guantanamo?' there will be nothing doing for ten years.'" It was all very much like old times.

Of course, he said one or two things that made excellent copy. 'Let me state in conclusion that... our vital positions will be rendered safe from attack from the sea if we are able readily to concentrate at the threatened point many more military planes than an enemy fleet can bring across the sea — always provided, of course, that the defense is not messed up by the presence of our battleships within a couple of hundred miles of the scene of action, thus diminishing our defensive air power by the number of airplanes required to protect them. In case of such an attack, the best position for the battleships would be as far up the Mississippi as they can go.' The last sentence of this paragraph in various forms is still making the rounds of publications and books on air power.

Perhaps his most prescient remark was made about the war of the future: 'But the point I make now is this, no matter how strong the combination, or how strong the battleships and battle cruisers, they could not do that thing [bottle up our Navy or destroy it in action] if we have a reasonable number of submarines, and if we have more airplanes... than they could bring against us.... Any nation adequately defended by submarines and airplanes, is, in my opinion, immune from attack from overseas.'

When asked about the advisability of a separate air force, Sims entered strenuous dissent from General Mitchell's views. His experience in the Flotilla had taught him the imperative necessity of proper coordination between isolated fighting units. 'I do not say it [the Navy] shall not be assisted, in cases of certain emergency, by the air forces on shore that belong to some other agency, but if the Fleet is to operate successfully and protect our coast against the attacks of hostile shipping, then the air forces, one of the most important things, the command of the aircraft, must be with the Navy, the same as it was on the other side.'

The Admiral made an excellent impression upon the House Committee and the public at large. Wrote one editor, 'He is a fighter before he is a sailor, he is a captain before he is an admiral, and before everything else he is a patriot deeply concerned in the future of his country.' It was clear to most observers that the man was engaged in no grandstand play; that he was speaking from deep inner conviction.

But his views were not accepted. A few, of course, believed him; a few dogmatically contradicted him; but the vast majority assumed the middle ground that aircraft was a necessary auxiliary in a well-balanced fleet. Several apparently valid arguments were raised against his position. He had greatly underestimated the potential effectiveness of anti-aircraft guns. He had accepted too readily and too uncritically the results of the *Ostfriesland* experiments. He had forgotten that new weapons breed new methods of defense. All these things at least were true and the future of the country in 1925 lay with the men of the middle ground.

One editor in 1925 was ahead of his time. He wrote, '"No army or navy can exist if the enemy controls the air," says Sims. And now that he has said it everybody realizes that everybody has known it for a long time.' Other names than Sims' had to be written into history before 'everybody realized it'; names such as *Bismarck*, Taranto, *Repulse*, *Haruna*, and Pearl Harbor.

A few months after he appeared before the investigating committee, Sims was again to find himself by the side of General Mitchell. That impetuous army officer shocked the nation with a statement appearing in the papers on September 6. Just before, the airship *Shenandoah* had met with disaster and the plane PN-9 No. 1 had been lost on a flight to Honolulu. 'These accidents,' said Mitchell, 'are the direct result of incompetency, criminal negligence, and almost treasonable administration of the national defense by the War and Navy Departments.' [9] There was more, much more, in the same vein, but this was enough. The man had been a trouble-maker for the Army long enough. This interview was but the culmination of a long series of outspoken at-

[9] *New York Times*, September 6, 1925. Sims himself, when he appeared before the Morrow Board, said that the '*Shenandoah* business' was the result of 'unreasonable, unscientific, and unmilitary administration' in the Navy Department.

tacks against the administration of the military aviation of the country. Mitchell was brought before a court martial and tried.

Sims appeared for the defense, though he knew the officer was doomed from the beginning. He was more interested in defending Mitchell's views than his methods. For his pains Sims was rewarded with the most impressive description of himself ever given. Major Gullion, assistant trial Judge Advocate, characterized him as 'opinionated, narrow-minded, hobby-riding, egomaniacal.' The Major had a flair for this sort of thing, though he confessed that another witness for Mitchell, Fiorello La Guardia, was 'beyond my powers of description. Thank Heaven, he is *sui generis*.'

It is hardly strange that Sims felt a close affinity with such men as Lincoln Steffens, Percy Scott, and Billy Mitchell. It is more curious that he never got caught in one of those whirlpools that trap men who swim against the main current of public prejudice and opinion. For a reformer his temperament and mentality were in singular balance. Though he and Admiral Mayo both wrote letters to the Secretary disapproving of the medal awards, Mayo got lost in the shuffle, while Sims went on to become a commanding figure in the investigation by virtue of his refusal to accept a Distinguished Service Medal and, also, by virtue of his startling testimony. Sims never allowed himself to get into a position where the axe could fall. 'I am no spring chicken in this business and I am not putting my head into a noose unnecessarily.'

That able and discerning officer, Clarence Williams, once made the penetrating remark that 'We agree with what Sims means, but he doesn't say it.' On the other hand, even when Sims really forgot himself, as at the Guildhall, as in the jackass speech, as in the conference with the Commander-in-Chief during the Flotilla days, even then he never quite spoke the unforgivable word; he never quite took the indefensible action. Thus, though there were frequent threats of court martial, there never was one. Credit should be given to officers like Williams and all the others who understood the man with whom they were dealing; but the greatest credit must go to Sims himself, who never did the simply violent, causeless, irrational thing. For a reformer who goes his way without the benefit of the conventional rules, that is an accomplishment.

Though there was work in these years, there was also play. Sims settled more easily into the life of retirement, partly because he kept so busy and partly because he loved his family life. All five children and their mother were gathered round him, first in the rented house on Rhode Island Avenue and later in the home he bought at 73 Catherine Street. It was a big, rambling old house with plenty of room for all of them. He had a big study where he would work, and a shop full of tools to which he repaired almost daily. There was, of course, a routine. The mornings were given over to reading the papers, writing articles, answering letters; all the things a man does at his own desk. In the afternoon there was usually a rest after lunch before exercise began. In the summer he played tennis regularly, despite his advancing age. With some of the money he had made from the *Victory at Sea*, he built a court beside the house which became a centre of neighborhood activity. The children to his great joy were now old enough to play doubles. His game was not designed in conformity with the modern practices, and his strokes were masterful rather than graceful. But he was as efficient on the court as he was everywhere; the children thoroughly enjoyed playing with him. In the winter he walked instead of playing tennis, taking long tramps along the seashore.

Sundays were days apart. Then the family dinner table was enlarged by many guests, ordinarily boys from near-by Saint George's School where William and later Ethan were educated. On good days the guests were treated to a hospitality the like of which they never could find elsewhere. When the mood was on him, as it was frequently at that time, and when he had a young, receptive audience, Sims was a superb raconteur. He would sit in his favorite chair, an impressive and immaculate figure in his blue suit. If the day were rainy, he lightened the gloom with a red tie. Sitting comfortably but erectly, occasionally rolling his own cigarettes from a package of Bull Durham, he spun his tales to an eager audience. He had a flair for anecdote which cannot be set down on paper. At the bottom of it, his was a humor of incongruity. There was a story about a parrot that got into a tar barrel on one ship and another about a monkey trying to climb

511

some greased lines that rocked every listener who ever heard them. His gift of description was that of vivid simile. He described a man as 'having a face that looked as though it had been carved out of soft mud with a broadaxe in a drizzling rain.'

In more serious ways he served the boys at Saint George's when in 1924 he became a trustee of the institution. To the meetings he brought his sound, practical common sense. When a new chapel was given to the school, he entered serious objection to it on the grounds that it was 'too magnificent' and 'more valuable than the whole existing plant.' Maintenance of such a structure, he believed, might well raise the tuition rates. At another time he opposed the adoption of a new school crest. 'I have read La-Rose's statement [a complicated heraldic explanation of the design], but do not find anything in it bearing upon my objection to the adoption of the flag, banner, and the shield in question which is that they are singularly ugly, having a snake-like appearance.' In such forthright fashion he attacked the other more formidable problems which confront trustees of educational institutions.

One of his delights in the school was the success his sons found there. Many of his friends were informed meticulously of their progress up the academic ladder. 'His average for all studies for the last month at Saint George's was 94.94 and he got 100 per cent on all arithmetic examinations' ran a report of one of his son's accomplishments.

These letters to his old naval friends were another recreation. The retired officers discussed professional problems, gave each other excellent advice which was rarely followed, and swapped the service gossip. 'I am thinking very strongly of taking a whack at you on the battleship question,' Philip Andrews informed Sims. Or again, 'Try and remember that parents don't always hit it in trying to shunt their children in any given direction. Remember the initiative of the subordinate.'

In reply Sims remained cheerful and argued pleasantly with his friends. Only one thing caused him to lose his equanimity. 'It [lecturing] is not right,' wrote Philip Andrews, 'for your age, or playing tennis either, or any of the really strenuous things. Old Grumbler W—— should have lived twenty years longer than he did and would have except for his vanity about playing excellent tennis.' Tennis had always bulked large in Sims' letters to his friends and the thrust could not be ignored. Andrews was told 'he had the story on W—— all wrong,' and, besides, Sims' blood pressure was 122/62. It was Andrews, too, who wrote in despair: 'In fact, there is no hope for us. With always, or almost — an ignorant President, ignorant Secretary of State and the Navy, etc., etc., there is no hope except that the Chief of Staff and the Chief of Naval Operations may be dominating persons.' Philip Andrews was a worthy friend. 'One reason I am fond of you,' he wrote, 'is that we have the same enemies of whom I am very proud. I am grateful for them.'

27

1928 - 1936   *Waiting Orders*

GLORY, thought La Pucelle, the divine, is like a circle in the water, broadening into naught. It was an Episcopal divine who confirmed the idea for Sims. 'And what,' asked the genial Bishop, 'did you do during the war?' 'Oh,' replied the naval officer, 'I was on the other side.' The joke was on the cleric, for Sims told the story everywhere; yet the Bishop spoke as one having a majority. Jones, Porter, Farragut, Dewey; these found fame behind the drifting smoke of battle. But Sims was never closer to the pounding guns than when he swung his little Gatling across the Isthmus of Panama.

It was a less obvious, less spectacular line of battle that he commanded. Some men, says Thoreau, serve the state with their bodies. They are the standing army. Others serve with their heads. They are the office-holders. 'A very few, as heroes, patriots, martyrs, reformers in the great sense, and *men* serve the state with their consciences also, and so necessarily resist it for the most part. . . .'

Glory might broaden into naught, but the spirit of resistance lived on. Sims, as he admitted, was only human. That he had been denied the highest honors his country could bestow remained a tiny shard of irritation; that the nation had failed to understand his case or act upon his recommendations as presented in the Investigation of 1920 was a bitter disappointment, rolling like a groundswell against tranquillity. But the conscience remained bright and unimpaired. Retirement withheld

514

the old opportunities for reform in the great sense, but in retirement Sims maintained the spirit of the great reformer.

Yet the man was only human, and in 1928 he reached the allotted threescore years and ten. Though the erect carriage, the proud, sculptured face, the massive figure belied his age, still he was learning that time, unlike the state, could not be served by resistance. In the same year it was rather astonishingly borne in upon him that his family too were getting on. Margaret graduated in 1928 from Vassar. She had fulfilled the promise of her youth and of her inheritance with a college record of which her father was and could be proud. Adelaide had followed her sister to Vassar. The third daughter, Anne, was sent off to Dobbs Ferry in 1928. Her attendance there was a source of pleasure to her classmates, for it brought her father to speak to the school upon occasion. Feminine pulchritude spurred him to a pitch of poetic accomplishment never achieved in the duller surroundings of the wardroom:

> 'My little task, my little speech,
> May lack artistic glow;
> May not amuse, and may not teach
> Just what you want to know
> About your national defense
> On sea and on the land;
> But I can say with confidence:
> "For your bright eyes defense is planned."'

The two boys were in Saint George's. William was now in his last year there, while Ethan was in the lower school. With all the children safely on their way to an education, it seemed wise to move for the winter into a larger city than Newport. Boston was chosen. It was near both Newport and Marion, the two places in which the family spent the summer. The sons, after graduation from school, intended to go to Harvard. Both the Admiral and Mrs. Sims had friends in the city. In October, 1928, the move was made.

Sims knew little of Boston when he first arrived, but this defect was speedily repaired. One year the family lived on Beacon Street, the next in Mark A. DeWolfe Howe's house on Brimmer Street. In 1930, they settled at 104 Marlborough Street. All three were the large, handsome unwieldy brick dwellings that have sheltered prosperous Bostonians these many years. Externally Sims differed little from previous occupants. He took long walks along the Esplanade. Less moved, perhaps, than some by the surpassing beauty of the Charles River Basin at twilight, he was more conscious than most of the joys of exercise in the clean, crisp air. On other afternoons he wandered through the Common watching the children playing with their nurses or the squirrels playing with each other. Walking into town for a haircut, a shoe-shine, or tobacco was an adventure in itself. He could thus talk with the barber or the bootblack about politics, their private lives, or the passing show. These little conversations were not the casual chit-chat of a great man to his subordinates. On both sides a deep impression was made. When the Admiral died, his wife received a telegram from a little jeweller who was 'deeply grieved at the loss of a dear friend.'

Occasionally Sims moved in more rarefied atmospheres. He and his wife went out to dinner with the Brahmins and two or three times a year they dutifully paid off their debts. The Tavern Club enlarged his acquaintanceship considerably, although he rarely went to it since he was not, somewhat to his chagrin, 'a clubby man.' Yet he moved easily and gracefully among the circles presided over by President Lowell of Harvard, Bliss Perry and Mark A. DeWolfe Howe. It was through his acquaintance with Mr. Lowell that he was asked to deliver the Lowell Lectures in 1930. His six talks on the subject of 'Capabilities and Limitations of Modern Navies' were a great success.

Though he went cheerfully through all these motions, he did not become Bostonian. Never more than in these later years did he preserve his essential quality of catlike self-sufficiency. The second-floor living-room of the Marlborough Street house was the inner sanctum of his life. There at teatime the family gathered. In 1929, his daughter Margaret had married a young lawyer, Robert H. Hopkins, and the young couple set up housekeeping on Beacon Hill. Shortly, to his delight, there was a grandchild for him to hold, like his father before him, upon his knee. The other children, when they came to college in Cambridge in the thirties, formed the habit of dropping in on their father at the sacred hour. He listened to their tales of undergraduate life, met their friends, and repaid their interest with treasures from the storehouse of his memory. In certain things he could not follow his children. The humor of the *New Yorker*, which they introduced to him, was never fully understood, nor were the late hours that children seemed to feel it necessary to keep. But if he was not modern, he was tolerant and young in spirit and the gap was bridged.

During the thirties his sons prevailed upon him frequently to make the rounds of the Harvard undergraduate organizations. One such occasion was fully reported by the *Harvard Crimson* of which his son William, to his father's great delight, became President. 'The United States has no single harbor equipped to maintain the Atlantic Fleet in case of war,' Admiral Sims stated, in 'the course of a discussion which broke up with the centre table covered with matches illustrating the "ripple movement" at the battle of Jutland.' Many dinner parties he attended broke up in the same fashion. 'Force of public opinion will alone bring about reorganization of the Navy Department now operated on principles long demonstrated as unsound....' He called 'the situation at Annapolis another situation requiring the application of public opinion.... The most our Fleet or the British could do towards attacking the respective countries would be to steam across, place the ball of the thumb on the nose, make a disrespectful gesture and steam back for more fuel. Each would wreak such havoc on the convoyed commerce of the other, however, that the publics would raise so much hell that the war would be stopped.'

The core of this busy, comfortable, private life was Mrs. Sims. By day she was busy with much serving in and around the city, but at night the two would sit down in the living-room for hours of reading. The papers were carefully investigated. The *New York Herald Tribune*, the editorials of Uncle Dudley in the *Boston Globe* and, of course, the *Boston Transcript*, were combed for information on public issues or little items of human interest. Magazines were also critically examined. The new-fangled style of *Time* proved an insurmountable obstacle, but the *Literary Digest*, a friend of many years, supplied all the necessary material on current events. *Harper's*, *Foreign Affairs*, and *Current History* were fully explored. Books poured across the living-room table in a torrent. The printed word established a perfect union between the Admiral and his wife. To her, as his eyes lost their early sharpness, fell the pleasant task of reading. Occasionally, when the adventures of the day had proved too exciting, she would drift off for a cat-nap in the middle of a paragraph. The Admiral would patiently wait until consciousness returned and would then accept with perfect gravity the explanation that 'I must have lost my place.' She would begin again while he rested easily in a favorite armchair, clad in a red velvet dinner jacket, a snowy white shirt, and black trousers and pumps. It was a comfortable, tranquil, satisfying private life the two led in these declining years.

There was much to remind him, however, that he was still a public figure. In 1930, a bill was passed by Congress elevating all officers in retirement to their World War rank. Sims then became, by this blanket measure, an Admiral on the retired list. To those who wrote to congratulate him he explained the situation. 'Unfortunately it is neither a personal distinction, a recognition of special war service, nor a material benefit, since the blanket bill giving the officers the rank they held "during the war" promotes officers who served at home, were not engaged in any war operations, and bore no responsibility. . . . In Haiti, when the revolutionary governments had no money to pay the troops, they used to advance them in rank and play the bugle for them. The action of the Congress is no more dignified.' A condensed version of this letter he gave to a lady in a box at the Newport tennis tournament who had offered her congratulations. 'Admiral, hell!' he responded.

Two years later, his name was in the news in connection with an issue of more universal importance. In a speech in 1932 in Boston, given under the auspices of the National Economy League, he opposed the soldiers' bonus. He believed, of course, in proper compensation for those injured in our wars, but he opposed the widespread distribution of bonuses to able-bodied veterans and described the Spanish War pensions as 'a steal of the nastiest kind and an outrage to American taxpayers.' Next day he wrote to the national commander:

> When the national organization of the American Legion gave me the honor of making me one of its honorary members I was assured that its governing body would maintain the patriotic

ideals expressed in the preamble of the constitution and that it
would continue to 'inculcate a sense of the individual obligation
to the community, the state, and the national government.'

As it now appears that the action on the bonus taken by the
Legion at its recent national convention at a time of national
distress is in direct repudiation of these ideals, I feel that I can
no longer retain my membership.

As soon as his views on the subject reached the public, the
flood gates were released. He was 'a gangster at heart,' a representative of 'Wall Street.' He was advised to hide his face and
keep quiet. A man with a highly inaccurate knowledge of history had told one correspondent that Sims was 'fifty miles away
when Schley fought the battle of Manila, yet you want credit
for it.' Hutch Cone dropped a line to say it 'made me homesick
to read the press notices about your attitude, for it took me back
some years to the good old "golden era." '

During the last six years of his life, Sims made several lecture
tours. On each he undertook to fulfill a schedule that would
have taxed the strength of a vaudeville team. Up and down the
Middle West he moved talking, talking, talking. If his audience
put in a special request for reminiscences of a naval life, he would
acquiesce in their demands, but he preferred to talk about
methods of keeping the peace. This became for him a crusade.
He had read carefully a good many books about the origins of the
war, among them Admiral Consett's *The Triumph of Unarmed
Forces*. These had tarnished his belief in both the good faith
and the competence of the statesmen who had precipitated the
conflict. He came to accept the idea that it was the business interests that had shoved us into war. The aftermath of the peace
had troubled him even more. All this reinforced his horror of
war as an instrument of decision among disagreeing nations.

He took the road, therefore, to help America keep at peace.
As always, his solution was an eminently practical one. 'This
course is for our Congress to declare that all trade in contraband,
which nowadays means nearly everything, must be at the risk
of the traders; and that no compensation for loss by action
of belligerents would be demanded by our government. . . . The
individual trader out for huge profits would have to bear the
risk himself.'

That there were difficulties in the way of such a program he was aware. 'But to resist the political pressure for protection in such trade would be a difficult job for any President. Yet it would not, I think, be impossible. And it would be much easier for the President if every American citizen understood the grave choice that would face us — and did his part. And the time to decide is now, while we can think calmly and clearly before war propaganda gets in its deadly work. Much may be done by preparing in advance a wise foreign policy that aims at a realistic understanding of the vital issues. To this end as a people, we must come to understand that peace is priceless; that it is worth any reasonable sacrifice; that it is certainly worth any sacrifice of war profits; that a decent regard for humanity must be placed ahead of gold.'

This was the antique wisdom of the thirties. It was likewise the intellectual and practical solution of the problem. Sims had not read *The Road to War* and *The Triumph of Unarmed Forces* for nothing. He arrived at his position by hard and painful and uninhibited thought. He approved, too, of other economic measures to keep the peace. Nothing in these later years discouraged him more than the failure of the democratic nations to apply a rigorous system of sanctions against Japan when she entered Manchuria and Italy when she took Ethiopia. Only by resolute, immediate action against the rising aggressor powers, he believed, could the democratic nations avoid once again the dreadful catastrophe of war.

It was all very well to talk to college boys, dine out in Boston, and enlighten the citizens of the Middle West, but Sims was after all a Navy man. There was yet work to do in the 'poor old Navy.'

In 1933, when he was seventy-four, he was appointed a member of the Board of Visitors to the Naval Academy. For long he had disapproved of the educational methods pursued at the institution. In 1927, he had startled newspaper readers with the observation that it was 'the worst school in the world.' When Philip Andrews chided him upon the remark, Sims replied with his familiar formula. The words had been greatly exaggerated; all he had said was that the school was too technical. Anyway, he had not known that reporters were present when he talked.

Andrews, in response, said that he knew Sims had not made the remarks attributed to him, but only something else that was equally bad.

Sims was not alone in his critical attitude. The report of every visiting committee, with one exception, from 1921 to 1926 had expressed only qualified approval of the kind of education provided on the banks of the Severn. Sims gave wider circulation to these reports than they would ordinarily have received — one indeed, that of 1923, was not even made public — in an article he wrote for the *World's Work* in April, 1927. It was called 'Annapolis — Our Amateur War College' and consisted of a summary of the adverse comments of the visiting committees. From 1926 to 1930 the reports contained no criticisms. It is interesting to notice that no civilian educator was a member of the committee during these years, while from 1921 until 1926, at least one educator had a hand in each report.

James Rowland Angell, the President of Yale, made searching criticisms of the curriculum at Annapolis. In 1923 and again in 1931, the committees of which he was a member pointed out at some length the educational limitations of the institution. The chief defects of the curriculum as defined by all these dissenting reports were as follows: the Naval Academy failed to provide for sound training in courses beyond the naval profession. In 1931, the course was 'devoid of any economics, of any substantial course in government, of any biology, geography, ethics or social science, or of any of the literature of foreign languages, or of any of the fine arts which play so large a part in the cultural life of all peoples.' [1] Disturbing as was this defect in the Academy education, an equally serious one marred the professional training. Because, since 1900, such enormous technological and scientific advances had been made, it was 'utterly impossible in the present four years' course to give the training in fundamental physical science which is absolutely essential if a midshipman is to have more than a rule-of-thumb knowledge of the apparatus that he is obliged to use in his daily work aboard ship and in the Navy Yards.'

What all the criticism of the curriculum boiled down to was

[1] *Report of the Board of Visitors to the United States Naval Academy*, Annapolis, Md., 1931.

this: there was not at Annapolis the opportunity for young men to obtain any general knowledge outside the field of their profession, and there was not time to learn all the specialized knowledge of the profession itself. The various boards recognized that it was not possible to supply any immediate or easy solution to 'the problem thus disclosed.' Many of them recommended that a small commission be appointed to investigate the whole situation. This wise recommendation had been repeatedly rejected by the authorities. The only action on the adverse comments was taken in 1932 when the schedule of classes was revised to include more time for cultural subjects.

The problem confronting Annapolis is exceedingly complex. It is defined in the mission of the Academy as the molding of the material provided into educated gentlemen. Unfortunately, the 'educated gentleman' in the traditional sense has gone to lie with the Piltdown man. Even such institutions as that of which Mr. Angell was President have found that goal beyond their reach. Our knowledge of our past, of ourselves, and of our world has grown so large that no individual has either the time or the capacity to absorb it. As a result the educated gentleman has given way to the specialist. Ideally, naval officers should have at least a rudimentary knowledge of geology, ethics, economics, government, and fine arts; so, ideally, should the lawyers, the doctors, the real-estate agents who pour out of Yale, Harvard, Princeton, and their sister institutions. In practice it has been found impossible to achieve this noble aim.

Annapolis is confronted by a further difficulty, unknown to civilian colleges. It must give young men not only a professional training, but likewise a professional spirit. After four years on the banks of the Severn, students must have acquired a knowledge of the traditions, customs, and spiritual necessities of their way of life. Not the least of these necessities is that of implicit obedience and conformity. Here is the great complication in military education. Annapolis must develop within its students the sense of solidarity, the consciousness of the necessity of common action; while it must also nourish the restless, inquiring, and independent minds without which no profession can advance.

Undoubtedly the critics of the Academy were correct in their belief that the curriculum under survey was, by all civilian standards, arid and unrewarding. Undoubtedly, too, the purely professional instruction was spread over so vast a field that it was in danger of covering only the superficial aspects of technical knowledge. The problems described by the critics were of tremendous significance; the more disturbing because those in authority showed little inclination to try to solve them.

It was this apathy that Sims set out to blast in 1933. With the same care with which he had prepared his reports from the China Station, he set about drawing up a memorandum for the other members of the Visiting Committee. His views proved to be too strong meat for his fellows to stomach, though their report shows the influence of his arguments. Unwilling to accept the majority's general approval of the Academy, Sims incorporated his memorandum into a minority report. It is a remarkable document.[2]

He first described the nature of an Annapolis education. Boys came to the school at ages from sixteen to twenty. For four years thereafter, while their character was forming, they were 'practically isolated from civilian life.' The activity of every hour was prescribed, almost every decision was made for the student. So much time was spent on drills and technical studies that little remained for any other reading. After four years the product of such a régime emerged 'cut and dried.' Character had been little influenced; defects and weaknesses had been hidden beneath the shield of prescribed routine.

Over against this Sims laid the civilian education. In the college the boy was on his own for four years. He was subject to every temptation; thus he developed a reliable character or went to pieces. 'The college graduate is relatively a young man of the world. The graduate of the Academy is still a boy.'

The greatest difference between the two young men was intellectual. The college man had a supple, searching mind; the Academy man had not. The emphasis on the practical, on things rather than principles, had frozen the mental processes of Annapolis students. How true this was, said Sims, could be seen from the fact that every single reform introduced into the Navy

---

[2] This minority report appears in *Report of the Board of Visitors, 1933*, pp. 8–20.

had come from without, and most of them against the opposition of men within the service.

Partly this mental attitude was the fault of the system, partly of the untrained instructors. 'One can readily predict the result if a civilian college advertised that neither the President nor the members of the faculty had any professional knowledge or training as educators, and that all would be replaced every two or three years. Few people would be willing to entrust their sons' education to such an institution.'

For the state of affairs he described, he had a remedy. Boys should enter Annapolis only after they had graduated from college, after they had acquired a liberal education and stable characters. 'It would seem, therefore, that the Academy should be solely a professional school, a Post-Graduate School, taught by professional instructors — naval officers.'

One need not seek far for proof of Sims' abiding faith in the educational process. His interest in his children's marks, his visit to Saint George's School in England during the war, his service as trustee for Saint George's in America attest to his belief in the value of a training he never had. Perhaps because he had not had an education, it seemed to him the rock upon which man might lay the fulcrum of his abilities when he sought to move the world. This splendid faith lay at the bottom of the minority report.

Whether his recommendations were as sound as the faith is another matter. Certainly a graduate of a civilian college who had spent two years in a naval post-graduate school would be a broader individual, possessed of greater professional knowledge, than the average graduate of Annapolis. The question remains whether he would be a better naval officer. The mind is not the only weapon of the profession. More than other callings, because of its dependence upon common action, the Navy relies upon the professional spirit. Of this spirit, morale, bred of common memories, common traditions, common standards, is a part. For most boys life begins at sixteen or seventeen; for naval officers it is important that life begin in the Navy.

Morale is a part of the professional spirit, but the essence of it is discipline; obedience to superior officers, obedience to regulations, obedience to duty. This is not an intellectual matter learned at a post-graduate school; it is a spiritual one absorbed in the days of uncritical, unquestioning youth through constant reiteration. Civilians may not feel that the military spirit is very valuable; they may in fact feel that it is a positive evil — as it can be in civil life; but as long as nations need armies and navies, that spirit will be a vital necessity. Civilians can save their armies in the field only by fostering it, and save themselves at home only by learning how to control and direct it.

A practical difficulty in his plan seems to have eluded Sims. Not many young men who have gone through college have, to put it mildly, much interest in the military profession. Filling a naval post-graduate school with students fresh from the freedoms of the campus and ready to get on with the work of the world would prove to be a not inconsiderable task.

Though it is impossible to accept Sims' suggested remedy, there is much of importance in his views. Annapolis is more restricted, more concerned with things than with principles, more rigid intellectually and spiritually than it needs to be. Sims laid bare the fundamental problem; the necessity for reconciling the spiritual discipline and self-denial of the group with the intellectual discipline and independence of the individual. That problem remains still unsolved. He made an effort to offer a solution and in that solution he was willing, at seventy-four, to be radical. He would not stop with half-measures, with tinkering with the existing machinery; he would sweep away all the traditional forms to get the results that he desired. To him with his own discipline and his own regulations his plan seemed sound. All he needed to make himself a better officer was a better education. The same, he thought, should have been true for everyone.

And now his career was making haste to its close. Yet still there was work to do, and he buckled on his armor for one more fight for 'the poor old Navy.' In 1935, he made a last attempt to change the system of promotion. Ever since he and Ridley McLean had investigated the subject when Sims was Inspector of Target Practice, he had maintained an interest in the problem. Almost every Secretary had received at least one letter explaining his theory. That theory changed in its superficial aspects during the years, but in principle it remained the same. Intelligent

525

selection could only be made if the opinion of qualified superiors was obtained on all the men eligible for promotion.

Shortly after he had returned from London after the World War, Sims had been ordered, unexpectedly, to duty on the selection board. It was his first actual experience with the system of promotion and it confirmed all his previous objections to our methods of selection. 'After it had been in session a couple of days, I went to the Secretary [Mr. Daniels] and registered a kick.' [3] The nature of his criticism was as follows: The fundamental defect of the existing method of promotion lay in the fact that it was impossible for a Board of Admirals to obtain adequate information on the relative merits of candidates for promotion. The information was faulty for the following reasons: Reports on individuals were made by relatively few of the officers in the grade above and consequently did not express general service opinion. Since these reports extended from the beginning of an officer's career up to date, only a small portion of the information bore upon a candidate's present fitness. Since all fitness reports 'were of practically uniform merit,' they gave 'no impression of the relative value of the candidates.' [4]

The solution to the problem Sims gave in concrete terms: If forty lieutenant commanders are to be promoted, each commander in the service should be asked to draw up a list of the forty best lieutenant commanders in the order of relative merit. 'It can readily be determined from these lists which officer has the highest average standing and which has the second highest, and so on up to the fortieth. It is a question of simple arithmetic. . . . This final list of forty would, therefore, be based upon the *combined* opinions of the 414 commanders, and their opinions are based upon both their personal knowledge of these men and upon the reputations of the men for ability to perform the duties of the next higher grade — qualities that are under continuous discussion in the grade above.' By this method, Sims believed the great obstacle to intelligent selection, the lack of adequate knowledge of each candidate for promotion on the part of a board of nine officers, could be obviated.

Mr. Daniels was impressed. He drew up a General Order to

[3] W. S. S. to Ridley McLean, August 16, 1919.
[4] W. S. S. to Secretary of the Navy, July 3, 1919.

the effect that Sims' system should be tried when the selection board met in October, 1919. To Sims' great chagrin, however, the selection board failed to make much use of the lists turned in by the officers. From that time forward the system was never tried again.

He did not despair, however. He wrote an article on the subject which appeared in the *Naval Institute Proceedings* for June, 1934. In it he set forth his scheme of promotion, the same one he had recommended to Mr. Daniels fifteen years earlier. One year later in 1935 he sent the article at his own expense to one thousand officers in the Navy, asking them for their comments on it. When the replies were all in, he printed them in a book which he distributed to the service. The replies — 368, or about 26 per cent of those circularized — were interesting. Of the officers 75.3 per cent could be listed as in agreement with Sims' recommendation, while 24.7 per cent were in disagreement with his idea.

The unfavorable comments were of all kinds. One man advised the author to 'Cheer up, stop fussing about how the service is run and let the active birds do without our help.' More thoughtful was the comment that the grade above would frequently have insufficient personal knowledge of the candidates and would have to rely on service hearsay. Sims met this by saying that the men in the grade above, taken as a whole, would certainly know more about the candidates than any board of nine officers. Furthermore, service hearsay was in general a reasonably accurate barometer of ability. The most frequent argument used against his scheme was that it would encourage 'the bootlicker,' 'the greaser.' This did not impress Sims. It rested upon the assumption that 'I am, of course, always able to recognize the greasing type and would not for a moment be influenced by their activities, but I think the great majority of officers are not sufficiently astute to avoid being taken in by them.'

Those in agreement with Sims were in a gratifying majority. Their support was frequently qualified by suggestions of minor alterations and attacks on the prevailing system of promotion. As one reads through the pages of the book, one is more impressed by the dissatisfaction with the existing state of affairs than by the expressions of outright approval for Sims' proposed alterations. Phrases like 'it would certainly be an improvement,' 'anything would be better,' are frequent.

The fact of the matter is that no system of promotion would satisfy all the elements in the service. Officers labor under a tremendous psychological handicap in considering the question of advancement. In civil life a shipping clerk can remain a shipping clerk all his days. In the Navy, a Captain is a Captain for seven years; then, if he is not promoted, he is removed from his lifework. This puts unusual pressure upon Navy men, especially since they are educated in a profession which is so different from the civilian way of life.

But one must weigh the merits of a method not so much by the dissatisfaction it generates as by its results. Sims correctly believed that the method of promotion in use did not always ensure the rise of the best men to the top. It is not possible to demonstrate that his own plan would have been much better in this respect. True, the selection board would have obtained more information on each candidate than it now possesses. But in a service as large as ours, where many officers are almost unknown to men in the grade above, it is certain that the disparity in views presented would be great. Furthermore, other factors than a large vote of immediate superiors in support of the qualifications of a subordinate enter the problem of promotion. Picking the ablest man in any profession is not a matter of 'simple arithmetic.'

No scheme is foolproof. Good men will be overlooked and bad ones selected upon occasion no matter what precautions are taken. What is needed ideally is an unprejudiced board with powers of selection and *placement*, possessed of adequate information on each officer. Sims proposed no change in the nature of the selection boards and severely limited the nature of the information presented.[5] He did not, however, claim that his system was a 'cure all,' but suggested it be used until some 'definite solution' could be proposed by qualified authorities.

It is not possible to agree with all of Sims' solutions for the

[5] Sims did not fully realize how large the Navy had become since he first thought of his system of promotion in 1904. Nor did he understand completely how varied were the occupations in a highly mechanized modern navy. A very interesting article on promotion and placement methods is Captain Charles M. Cooke's 'The Line Officer Problem,' *N.I.P.*, November, 1939.

problems he dealt with in his last years. Such difference of opinion, however, can hardly rob his work of its significance. The problems were real enough. In keeping the attention of men directed to them he performed a great service. In proposing his own methods for correcting defects he remained true to his life-long conviction that criticism should have a constructive purpose. The activities of his retired years comprise a remarkable personal achievement. To name them is enough. He strove to gain recognition for the War College, to keep the record straight on submarine warfare, to explain the significance of air power, to prevent the veterans' raid on the Treasury, to improve education at Annapolis, to ensure a better system of promotion, to keep peace on earth.

His study of the promotion problem had once again turned his mind to the whole naval situation. The results of his reflections were published in an article in 1935 in the *Atlantic Monthly*. 'Naval morale is continually declining, high-ranking officers in the Navy Department are notoriously inefficient and under existing methods of promotion injustice is inevitable,' so ran the indictment. It was the last, for with the publication of this article he wrote no more.

In the thirty-five years that had passed since he first stepped upon the deck of the *Kentucky* at Gibraltar, Sims had constructed a singular career. 'William Sowden Sims,' said the *Boston Transcript* in 1936, 'was what all men should be and what few dare or should even try to be. The United States Navy could not exist if every officer displayed such courage in criticism as he employed from his junior days onward.' 'It is not too much to say,' added the *New York Herald Tribune*, 'that he influenced our naval course more than any other man who ever wore the uniform.'

Yet it will be remembered that Sims disliked to wear his uniform. The fact is somehow symbolic. He was never only a naval officer. But, as one paper observed in well-chosen words, 'he was passionately devoted to the Navy.'

Luce likewise loved the Navy, as did Taylor and Fullam and Fiske and Key. In a profession that is by temperament static, they fought the cause of change. It was a single-minded devotion that possessed each of these men, not the less worthy because each, at times, perforce worked single-handed. No military establishment should reform itself, a student of these matters has asserted; the assertion is interesting and probably true. In the course of internal reform feelings are hurt, morale suffers, hatreds develop, the spiritual fabric of the profession is torn to shreds. More important, since the military reformer thinks, inevitably, purely in military terms, his actions may result in a dislocation of the civil influence. But in America there are no wellsprings of reform beyond the service. Secretaries of the Navy have been with almost no exceptions men improperly equipped with knowledge and understanding for their great task. Congress has been, save in its moments of political indignation, apathetic and selfish. The public has been uninterested, ignorant, and at times hostile.

Progress has thus been largely entrusted to the few, the very few, within the Navy who have possessed the brains and the courage to search behind the screen of things as they are. The fortitude of such men cannot be overestimated. They have upon occasion endured the opposition of politicians, the apathy of the public and the antagonism of brother officers. They have not infrequently risked position and reputation to gain their ends. They have at all times sustained themselves on hopes deferred.

William Sowden Sims was one of these; less a naval officer than a member of the great naval profession. Eager, independent, individual; in Josephus Daniels' phrase, 'one of the most brilliant,' he pitted himself against the inevitable confusions of a Navy in transition. For thirty-five years he struggled with every weapon at his command. When in 1935 he laid down the last weapon left to him, his flowing pen, there was a modern Navy. This Navy was not his alone. It was the work of many heads and hands, but within the vast machinery his enduring influence reveals itself in many ways.

The strength of Sims as a reformer lay, as the *Herald Tribune* understood, 'in the fact that he usually managed to be right.' This was a far greater source of his success than the dramatic methods which he employed to gain his case a hearing. Men were irritated, or shocked, or delighted by his words and gestures, but they were convinced by his arguments alone. That he escaped, in large part, the penalties of some of his actions is the final tribute to the correctness of his views.

But Sims was more than a reformer. He was likewise a man. Whence came his personal hold over his followers? Whence came the strength that sustained him in his active years and buoyed him up in retirement? What kept him on the trail of error until the time ran out?

'It is,' said Mahan, 'not permitted to man so to search the heart of his fellow as to give a conclusive reply to such a question; ... Our quest has been the strength of Nelson. I find it in the inborn power to trust; to trust himself and others; to confide, to use his own word. Whether it is the assurance within, which we call conviction, or the assurance without, which we call confidence, in others' or in one's own action, this is the basic principle and motive force of his career, as Duty was its guiding light and controlling standard.'

Conviction, Confidence, and Duty were the bedrock of Sims' character. If the outward assurance that is confidence was sometimes too apparent, it was never the measure of the breadth of his vanity, but rather of the depth of the inner assurance that is conviction. If occasionally he failed to extend his trust unhesitatingly to those above him, this failure was compensated by the unfaltering trust he placed in his subordinates. If at times he was unsatisfied with the mere performance of his naval duties, it was because he recognized the necessity of a greater duty to himself.

His professional accounts cast up, it was time to turn to his personal affairs. They had prospered during all this period when his attention had been given to the Navy. By 1935, all his daughters had been happily married. His two sons had nearly completed their education at Harvard over the river. Mrs. Sims was yet by his side. All the family, in fact, had settled in and around Boston. They dropped in by twos and threes for tea or dinner during the week and appeared in force on Sundays, birthdays, Christmases, and Thanksgivings. These parties were great occasions which the Admiral loved. Though he took less part in the busy chatter that ran round the table than in the old days, his pleasure was as great. The habit of the wardroom remained with him until the end. Each occasion had its poem, though the quality fell off after the laureate had been exposed to the influence of Ogden Nash. Sentences were extended to incredible lengths and rhymes were manufactured in fantastic fashion. More substantial contribution to the meals was made by the Admiral's artistic carving of the great birds placed on the table by Irish maids who worshipped him, for the Sinn Fein had been forgotten.

Other family matters were put in order. In the late summer of 1935, all of his sisters and brothers came down to visit for a weekend at Marion. Not since the days at Rockhill Furnace had they all been together. Old times were revived once more. Sims' older brother, Harry, whom he had not seen in many years, recalled long dead memories of the farm, and Varley brought along with him a mechanical bug that roused the amused curiosity of the Admiral. The sisters, Adelaide, Mary, and Louisa, laughed and joked with their host and reminded him that though he was an Admiral, he also was simply a brother.

In the fall of 1935, Sims returned to Boston to the new apartment on Arlington Street which he and Mrs. Sims had taken for the winter. William in his first year at the law school lived with them. Fall and winter passed quickly in the familiar routine. There were some speeches, but fewer than usual; some dining out, but less than in the past; some correspondence with his friends, but the friends themselves were disappearing. The long, slow twilight of retirement was giving way to the approaching night.

Yet, as one paper said, he was always news. In June, 1936, his name was in the papers once again. He had been operated upon at the Deaconess Hospital in Boston and was reported to be resting comfortably. It was an operation from which the Admiral expected his customary surprisingly rapid recovery. Through the hot Boston summer he lay in the hospital, diverted at times by the steady sound of his wife's voice as she read to him. Unaccountably, however, his strength failed to return. With the coming of cooler weather he was removed to his home on Arlington Street, but still he did not gain back the ground he had lost.

The thing that was so inexplicable to him was clear enough to the doctors. He had been brought down by something from which no man could recover. It was only a matter of time. The days dragged on in discomfort until his heart, as it had so often in the past, came to his rescue.

In the twilight of a day late in September he suddenly failed rapidly. The children were summoned from their homes. Early in the evening with his family around him, he died of a merciful heart attack.

It was a rainy day in Washington on October 1, 1936. All morning the Admiral lay in state before the altar of Saint John's Church. On his coffin lay the flag of his country and the cocked hat, epaulets, and sword of his calling. Thirty-one years earlier in the coming month of November, he had been married before that same altar.

About noon Navy planes, in the form of a cross, flew over the city.

Two hours later there was a brief service at the church before the coffin was taken out to the gates of Arlington. There it was transferred to a caisson drawn by six white horses and guarded by a Marine regiment and a company of enlisted men. The procession started along the winding roads of the cemetery now lined on either side by the people.

A sailor carrying a flag with four stars led the way. Behind the caisson walked the honorary pallbearers, men who had served with him on the China Station, in the Flotilla, at Queenstown, and in the London Headquarters. A band threw drumbeats and the sad music of fifes up against a wild grey sky. Over at Fort Myer a saluting gun was firing. Slowly the procession filed along until it stopped by a little hill overlooking the broad Potomac. Slowly the six enlisted men bore their burden up the hill to the newmade grave. The gun at Fort Myer fired its seventeenth shot.

The strangely comforting words were spoken as the sun leaped briefly through some chink in the dark, wet sky. For a moment there was silence. Then three shocking volleys and the bugle notes.

The long, the happy, the supremely useful life was over.

THE END

BIBLIOGRAPHY

Cᴵᵀᴬᵀᴵᴼᴺˢ in the text indicate the principal sources of information consulted. What follows, therefore, is in no sense a complete and formal bibliography. Manuscript collections and official documents are described in the hope that such description may prove of use to students. The list of secondary works is restricted to those books which, it is believed, will be of most value to the reader whose interest in the Navy has been aroused by the events of the past three years.

MANUSCRIPT COLLECTIONS

This book has been based principally upon manuscript sources. Of these the most important is the *Sims Collection*. It contains copies of most of Admiral Sims' private and professional letters and official reports written after 1900; almost every letter written to him by anyone after that time, offsets of all his articles, notes of his speeches, official orders, manuals, reference books, and newspaper clippings. The Collection is extraordinarily complete and well catalogued. The *Key Papers* are the most important source of information on the Newport Conference. The *Murdock Papers*, composed of Rear Admiral Joseph B. Murdock's diaries, letters to his family, and a few from brother officers, are less concerned with professional matters than one could wish, but are important for the years he was Commander-in-Chief in Asia in 1911 and 1912 during the Chinese Revolution. The *Letters of Rear Admiral George C. Remey*, edited and arranged by his son, Charles M. Remey, are filled with matters of naval interest, especially for the final twenty years of the last century. Some letters of Commander Homer Poundstone, now in the Museum at Annapolis, contain important material on the development of the All Big Gun battleship.

The most valuable single source of naval information is the *Office of Naval Records and Library*, under the direction of Captain Dudley W.

Knox. This Collection contains files of official correspondence, muster rolls, logbooks, appointments, orders, official letters, and so forth. The records of the Bureau of Navigation are now being catalogued and indexed by the Office. The World War archives are voluminous. In the *National Archives* are the proceedings of Courts of Inquiry, officers' letter books, copies of the *Monthly Bulletin of Information* published by the Office of Naval Intelligence for certain years, and the files of the Secretary of the Navy. The records of the Bureau of Ordnance for the years under review are likewise in the National Archives, but unfortunately for purposes of research, the Bureau retains the index. Correspondence about appointments of students to Annapolis and students' academic records are found in the *Office of the Superintendent of the Naval Academy*. It should be added that investigation among the papers in any of these collections is facilitated greatly by the courtesy and intelligence of the curators and their assistants.

OFFICIAL DOCUMENTS

There is a vast quantity of official published documents. Most important are the *Hearings Before the Committee on Naval Affairs* of both the House of Representatives and the Senate. Such hearings as have been used have been identified in the footnotes. The documents issued by these two committees are equally valuable for the student of naval history. A convenient summary of legislation affecting the Navy up to 1921 is contained in *Laws Relating to the Navy, Annotated*, compiled by George Melling (Washington, 1922). The *Navy Year Book*, a summary of annual naval appropriation laws, 1883–1921, is a mine of information. Unfortunately, it has not been published since 1921. The *Annual Reports of the Secretary of the Navy* are likewise invaluable. It is regrettable that since 1932 the length, and likewise the usefulness, of these reports have been greatly diminished.

SECONDARY WORKS

Histories: No full-dress history of the Navy has been published since E. S. Maclay and J. R. Spears brought out their separate works at the end of the last century. Several excellent single-volume histories have, however, appeared. Dudley W. Knox's *A History of the United States Navy* (New York, 1936) is clear, concise, and accurate. Less reliable, though more racy, is Fletcher Pratt's *The Navy* (New York, 1938). These deal almost exclusively with the Navy in action, which until very recently was the only aspect of the Navy historians thought worth investigating. Within the past few years, however, several books have been published about the development of our naval establishment. First in the field were Harold and Margaret Sprout with *The Rise of American Naval Power* (Princeton, 1939). This volume serves as an excellent introduction to the expansion of our modern Navy. It was followed shortly by the same authors' *Toward a New Order of Sea Power* (Princeton, 1940), which carried their study from 1918 through 1922 and the Washington Conference. Shortly after the appearance of the Sprouts' first book, George T. Davis' *A Navy Second to None* (New York, 1940) was published. It covered much the same ground, though it devoted far more time to our naval course after Mahan.

In the field of naval construction F. M. Bennett's *The Steam Navy of the United States* (Pittsburgh, 1896) is the only, but sufficient, authoritative survey work on American naval design before 1900. William Hovgaard's *The Modern History of Warships* (New York, 1920) is an excellent and comprehensive study of the changes in naval construction wrought by steam and steel. In his *Sea Power in the Machine Age* (Princeton, 1941) Bernard Brodie sets forth the profound changes wrought in ship design by the new technology.

In the field of naval administration there is a lamentable lack of new material. Alfred Thayer Mahan's two essays in his *Naval Administration and Warfare* (Boston, 1908) are a valuable introduction to the subject. The only considerable historical study of the problem in America was done by C. O. Paullin in Volumes XXXII–XL (1906–1914) of the *Proceedings of the United States Naval Institute*. Unfortunately these separate articles have never been brought together in book form.

WORLD WAR

The principal works on the last war are cited in footnotes in the text. The part played by our forces is described clearly and adequately in W. S. Sims' *The Victory at Sea* (New York, 1920) and in Volume 3 of T. G. Frothingham's *The Naval History of the World War*, 3 volumes (Cambridge, 1924–1926). More lyrical in treatment and less informative in content is Josephus Daniels' *Our Navy at War* (New York, 1922), while the seamy side of the administration of the war from Washington is analyzed in T. B. Kittredge's *Naval Lessons of the Great War* (New York, 1921). This book is a brilliant condensation of the Investigation of 1920 which suffers from the author's understandable prejudice against the Secretary of the Navy.

MEMOIRS AND BIOGRAPHIES

Unlike English naval officers the men of our own service rarely commemorate their long careers in print. When they do, they turn their hands, as a rule, to books of harmless recollection. There are, fortunately, some exceptions. George Dewey's *Autobiography* (New York, 1913), Robley D. Evans' *An Admiral's Log* (New York, 1910), Seaton Schroeder's *A Half Century of Naval Service* (New York, 1922), A. T. Mahan's *From Sail to Steam* (New York, 1907), and Yates Stirling's *Sea Duty* (New York, 1939) all contain useful information as well as fondly recalled anecdote. Most important is Bradley A. Fiske's *From Midshipman to Rear Admiral* (New York, 1919). As Fiske led one of the most valuable lives in the United States Navy, so his book is one of the most significant in naval bibliography.

If few Admirals have written about themselves, fewer writers have produced books about them. For the period under review there are only two biographies of naval officers that command attention. W. D. Puleston's *Mahan* (New Haven, 1939) has superseded Carlisle Taylor's life of our greatest naval historian. While carefully written and informative, it rarely departs from the strict limits of narration. In his *Life and Letters of Stephen B. Luce* (New York, 1925), Albert Gleaves rescues that great officer from ill-deserved obscurity, but one could wish for a more exhaustive study of the man for whom there can be 'no successor.' Mark A. DeWolfe Howe's *George von Lengerke Meyer* (New York, 1919) has an illuminating chapter on Mr. Meyer's service as Secretary of the Navy.

MAGAZINES AND NEWSPAPERS

Investigation of newspaper opinion was greatly facilitated by the vast number of clippings preserved in the *Sims Papers*. Most informative are the New York newspapers, the *New York Times*, the *New York Herald Tribune*, and the *New York Sun*. Among the magazines *The North American Review*, the *Scientific American*, *McClure's*, and the *Army and Navy Journal* are the most fruitful sources of information. It is surprising how much attention these periodicals devoted to military and naval matters during the first fifteen years of this century. *The United States Naval Institute Proceedings* stands alone. It sets a standard in format, style, and content that the house organs of those professions which like to call themselves learned would do well to emulate.

A READING LIST FOR TODAY

It is assumed that civilians with an interest in the war may wish to pursue their reading in the subject further. As a background for the events of today the following books are suggested. Alfred Vagts' *The History of Militarism* (New York, 1937) is the best possible introduction to the rôle of armies and navies in our civilization. It is a brilliant and exhaustive study. The slow-moving style detracts only slightly from the fascination of the material and the adroitness with which the author illuminates it. Style also may deter the reader from a full appreciation of the poetic and penetrating *Delilah* (New York, 1941). This novel by Marcus Goodrich, himself a sailor, gives extraordinary insight into the nature of the naval profession and the spirit of naval men. L. P. Lovette's *Naval Customs, Traditions, and Usage* (Annapolis, 1934) is a useful guide to and explanation of the matters suggested in the title. J. M. Kenworthy's *New Wars, New Weapons* (London, 1930) is a brief and telling discussion of military conservatism coupled with predictions about air power that are no longer prophecy. In *The Navy: Defense or Portent* (New York, 1932) Charles A. Beard analyzes the forces that produced our haphazard naval development. The book, filled with arresting evidence and provocative ideas, is perhaps too caustic in its treatment of naval officers who, in this country, have received too little attention from the people they serve. Two books by Bradley A. Fiske, *The Navy as a Fighting Machine* (New York, 1916) and *The Art of Fighting* (New York, 1920), provide a readable introduction to matters of strategy, tactics, and military organization.

Three books will assist the reader to follow the naval war of today. Hanson Baldwin's *What the Citizen Should Know About the Navy* (New York, 1941) answers most of the questions civilians want answered about the life, training, and organization of our Navy. Fletcher Pratt's *Sea Power and Today's War* (New York, 1939) contains information about the navies of every great power and outlines the uses to which each may be put. Paul Schubert's *Sea Power in Conflict* (New York, 1942) reviews the actual history of the past two and a half years of naval warfare.

ACKNOWLEDGMENTS

The kind permission of the following publishers to use quotations from the books listed below is gratefully acknowledged:

D. Appleton-Century Company: *From Midshipman to Rear Admiral*, by Rear Admiral Bradley A. Fiske (1919).

The Army and Navy Journal.

Curtis Brown, Ltd.: *Fifty Years in the Royal Navy*, by Admiral Sir Percy Scott (1919).

Dodd, Mead and Company: *George von Lengerke Meyer*, by M. A. DeWolfe Howe (1919).

From *Naval Lessons of the Great War*, by Tracy Barrett Kittredge, copyright, 1921, by Doubleday, Doran and Company, Inc.

From *The Victory at Sea*, by William S. Sims, in collaboration with Burton J. Hendrick, copyright, 1920, by Doubleday, Doran and Company, Inc.

Harcourt, Brace and Company: *A Navy Second to None*, by George T. Davis (1940).

Houghton Mifflin Company: *Life and Letters of Walter H. Page*, by Burton J. Hendrick, 2 vols. (1923).

J. B. Lippincott Company: *Human Being*, by Christopher Morley (1934).

Little, Brown and Company: *Naval Administration and Warfare*, by A. T. Mahan (1908); *War Memoirs of David Lloyd George*, 6 vols. (1933–1936).

Princeton University Press: *The Rise of American Naval Power*, by Harold and Margaret Sprout (1939); *Sea Power in the Machine Age*, by Bernard Brodie (1941); *Toward a New Order of Sea Power*, by Harold and Margaret Sprout (1940).

G. P. Putnam's Sons: *A History of the United States Navy*, by Dudley W. Knox (1936); *Sea Duty*, by Yates Stirling (1939).

United States Naval Institute: *The Battle of Jutland*, by Holloway H. Frost (1936); *The United States Naval Institute Proceedings*.

INDEX

541